Routledge Handbook of Sport Fans and Fandom

This is the first book to explore the full significance of sport fans and fandom from an international and interdisciplinary perspective, across different sports, communities and levels of engagement. It gives a comprehensive overview of the undeniable economic and cultural influence of sport industries for which fans are the driving force.

The book examines different theoretical and methodological approaches to the study of fans, including typologies of fandom, and presents cutting-edge discussion across broad thematic areas such as performance and identity, the business of fandom, and fandom and media. It considers the experiences of diverse and marginalized fan groups, with an emphasis on intersectional analysis, and shines new light on key contemporary themes such as fan activism, violence and deviance, mobility and migration, and the transformative effects of digital and social media. This volume includes chapters by many of the leading scholars responsible for having laid the foundation for sport fan research as well as early-career scholars who examine the newest developments in media technologies, legalized betting, gaming, and fantasy sports.

Including perspectives from disciplines such as philosophy, sociology, psychology, management, economics, and media studies, this book is essential reading for anybody interested in the study of sport and wider society or fans and subcultures more broadly.

Danielle Sarver Coombs is Professor in the School of Media and Journalism at Kent State University, USA. She has published extensively around politics, sports, and the politics of sport.

Anne C. Osborne is Professor in the S.I. Newhouse School of Public Communications at Syracuse University, USA. Her research and teaching focus on gender, media, and sport.

Routledge Handbook of Sport Fans and Fandom

Edited by Danielle Sarver Coombs and Anne C. Osborne

LONDON AND NEW YORK

Cover image: © Getty Images

First published 2022
by Routledge
4 Park Square, Milton Park, Abingdon, Oxon OX14 4RN

and by Routledge
605 Third Avenue, New York, NY 10158

Routledge is an imprint of the Taylor & Francis Group, an informa business

© 2022 selection and editorial matter, Danielle Sarver Coombs and Anne C. Osborne; individual chapters, the contributors

The right of Danielle Sarver Coombs and Anne C. Osborne to be identified as the authors of the editorial material, and of the authors for their individual chapters, has been asserted in accordance with sections 77 and 78 of the Copyright, Designs and Patents Act 1988.

All rights reserved. No part of this book may be reprinted or reproduced or utilised in any form or by any electronic, mechanical, or other means, now known or hereafter invented, including photocopying and recording, or in any information storage or retrieval system, without permission in writing from the publishers.

Trademark notice: Product or corporate names may be trademarks or registered trademarks, and are used only for identification and explanation without intent to infringe.

British Library Cataloguing-in-Publication Data
A catalogue record for this book is available from the British Library

Library of Congress Cataloging-in-Publication Data
Names: Coombs, Danielle Sarver, editor. | Osborne, Anne C. (Anne Cunningham) editor.
Title: Routledge handbook of sport fans and fandom /
edited by Danielle Sarver Coombs and Anne C. Osborne.
Other titles: Handbook of sport fans and fandom
Description: Abingdon, Oxon ; New York, N.Y. : Routledge, 2022. |
Series: Routledge international handbooks |
Includes bibliographical references and index.
Identifiers: LCCN 2021047569 | ISBN 9780367358310 (hardback) |
ISBN 9781032224350 (paperback) | ISBN 9780429342189 (ebook)
Subjects: LCSH: Sports spectators. | Sports–Social aspects. | Mass media and sports.
Classification: LCC GV715 .R47 2022 | DDC 306.4/83–dc23/eng/20211026
LC record available at https://lccn.loc.gov/2021047569

ISBN: 978-0-367-35831-0 (hbk)
ISBN: 978-1-032-22435-0 (pbk)
ISBN: 978-0-429-34218-9 (ebk)

DOI: 10.4324/9780429342189

Typeset in Bembo
by Newgen Publishing UK

This book is dedicated to all of the outstanding scholars who stuck with us through seemingly endless COVID delays. We are grateful for your work and patience.

Contents

List of Figures *xi*
List of Tables *xii*
List of Contributors *xiii*
Acknowledgements *xvii*

1 Editors' Introduction 1
  Danielle Sarver Coombs and Anne C. Osborne

PART I
What Is a Fan and How Do We Know? **7**

2 Imagining the Citizen-Fan: Sport Metaphor in American Politics and Implications for Democratic Culture 9
  Michael Butterworth

3 Using Sport Fandom to Fulfill Personal and Societal Needs 21
  Daniel L. Wann

4 Experiences of Female Fans in a Female-Defined Sport: Central, Valued and Visible 32
  Toni Bruce and Margaret Henley

5 Understanding Demand for Women's Sports Begins with Understanding Men's Sports History 44
  David Berri

6 Comparing the Cost of Fandom in European Football 61
  Selçuk Özaydın and Cem Tınaz

7 Building Civic Identity Around a Suburban Ballpark District 73
  Timothy Kellison and Beth A. Cianfrone

Contents

8 Studying Sports Fans Through Ethnographic Methods: Walk a Mile in Their Shoes 84
Jessica Richards, Keith D. Parry and Daniela Spanjaard

9 Media Coverage of Sports Fans: A Framing Analysis 95
Mark Turner

10 Rebounding as Praxis: Interrogating Positionality and Proximity in Sporting Fieldwork 107
Courtney M. Cox

11 Should We Admire Athletes? 116
Ben Bradley

12 Centering Race in Sport Fan Research: A Call to Action 125
Anne C. Osborne and Danielle Sarver Coombs

PART II
Who Fans Are **131**

13 Sport Fandom: The Complexity of Performative Role Identities 133
Shannon Kerwin and Larena Hoeber

14 Women Sports Fans 145
Katharine Jones, Stacey Pope and Kim Toffoletti

15 The Sports Fanship Lifecycle 154
Irene I. van Driel, Walter Gantz and Lawrence A. Wenner

16 The Olympics Sports Fan: A Distinctive Demographic 168
Andrew C. Billings, Samuel Hakim and Qingru Xu

17 Para Sport Fandom: Fans and Followers of Paralympians 180
Linda K. Fuller

18 English Football, Sexuality, and Homophobia: Gay Fans' Perspectives on Governance and Visibility 192
David Letts and Rory Magrath

19 Photography, Autoethnography and Mapping Sporting Transformations: A Discussion of Stuart Roy Clarke's Work on British Football 204
John Williams

Contents

20	The Ecosystem of Football Supporter Groups in Brazil: Traditions, Innovation and Hybridity *Ana Carolina Vimieiro*	225
21	Disabled Athletes' Use of Social Media to Cultivate Fandom *Joshua R. Pate and Robin Hardin*	238
22	Engaging the Non-Local Sport Fan *Dorothy Collins*	249

PART III
What Fans Do   259

23	Digital Sport Fandom *Heather Kennedy, Josh Gonzales and Ann Pegoraro*	261
24	Online Performances of Fandom: Selective Self-Presentation, Perceived Affordances, and Parasocial Interactions on Social Media *Kathryn Coduto*	273
25	The Construction of Sports Fandom by Sports Betting Companies *Jason Kido Lopez*	285
26	Fandom in the Realm of Fantasy Sport *Brody J. Ruihley and Robin Hardin*	295
27	Understanding Sport Videogames: The Extensions of Fan *Steven Conway*	305
28	Sports Fans Hunt for Women's Games: Beyond News Media Coverage *Anji L. Phillips and Dunja Antunovic*	316
29	Twitter Discourse in the Southeaster Conference: The Nick Saban Effect *Vincent L. Benigni and Lance V. Porter*	328
30	Football Fan Reactions to Video Assistant Referee: No More Hand of God *Yuya Kiuchi*	342
31	Reconfiguring Transnational Fan Experience Through Digital Media: European Football in China *Yuan Gong*	354

ix

Contents

32 The Commodification and Mediatization of Fandom: Creating
    Executive Fandom   365
    Brett Hutchins, David Rowe and Andy Ruddock

33 Football Fans and Food: Feeding the Desire   377
    Keith D. Parry and Jessica Richards

34 Fan Reactions to Athlete Activism: "Stick to Sports"   388
    Stephen Warren

Index   *401*

Figures

6.1	Absolute Cost of Being a Football Fan in Europe	66
6.2	Cost of Being a Football Fan in Europe as a Percentage of GPD per Capita	67
6.3	Cost of Being a Football Fan in Europe as a Percentage of Minimum Wage	68
13.1	Sagas and Wendling (2019) Multi-Layer Identity Development System Model	134
15.1	Experience of Watching Sports	162
15.2	Extent of Fanship Then and Now	162
15.3	Importance of Sports in Life Then and Now	163
15.4	Extent of Fanship Then and Now Across Fanship Level	164
15.5	Importance of Sports in Life Then and Now Across Fanship Level	164
19.1	Last Days on the Standing Liverpool Kop, 1992	208
19.2	Rebuilding English Football in the Early 1990s: St James Park, Newcastle	209
19.3	Dr. Fun and the Back Balcony on the Standing Kop at Liverpool, 1992	210
19.4	Liverpool, the Day After the Club Won the European Cup in 2005	212
19.5	Red Wall, Barnsley FC, 1995	213
19.6	Yellow Brick Road: Bradford City FC, 1992	214
19.7	The New Huddersfield Town Stadium Grows Wings when Viewed from the Old Leeds Road Ground, 1993	215
19.8	Ticket Office, Hull City, 1990	216
19.9	Newcastle United Fans at Ipswich Town, 1990	217
19.10	The Neon Coffee Women: Tranmere Rovers FC, 1992	218
19.11	Dogged Support: FC United of Manchester Fans at Buxton, 2005	218
19.12	Three Wishes: Wolverhampton Wanderers, 2002	219
19.13	The Juggler, Regent's Park, 2015	220
19.14	The Local Game: The Lake District, 1995	221
19.15	Bradford City Fans in Prayer, 2015	222
19.16	England's Football Women, 2014	222
29.1	Commodification Tweet Categories	334
29.2	Commodification Tweet Categories Over Time (January 1, 2010–June 9, 2020)	335
29.3	Word Cloud: Coaching Tree Category	336
29.4	Top 10 Saban Retweets from January 1, 2010–June 9, 2020	337
29.5	Network Visualization of Influence by Eigenvector Centrality	338

Tables

5.1	NBA Revenue from 1991–92 to 2018–19	47
5.2	Revenues in the Major Men's Sports Leagues in the 1950s	50
5.3	Average Game Attendance in 1956 vs. Today	51
5.4	Stadium and Arena Spending in Men's Sports from 1990 to 2021	53
5.5	Recent Sale Prices of NBA Teams vs. Forbes Valuations	54
5.6	Change in NBA Franchise Values: 2011 vs. 2020	55
6.1	2018/2019 Leagues' Revenues Breakdown	64
6.2	Elements of Cost for the 2018/2019 Season	65
6.3	Indicators of Income for the Selected Countries	67
6.4	Cost of Fandom as a Percentage of Income	69
6.5	Most Revenue Generating Top 20 Teams in the 18/19 Season	70
13.1	Academic Literature Linking Social Identity and Role Identity	136
15.1	Demographics Across Age Groups	158
15.2	Percentage of Fans and Non-Fans Across Age Groups	160
15.3	Extent of Fanship Across Age Groups	160
15.4	Frequency of Watching Live TV Sports	160
15.5	Enjoyment, Passion, Meaning, and Social Importance of Viewing Live Sports	161
15.6	Importance of Sports in Life Across Age Groups	161
17.1	Summer and Winter Paralympics	181
17.2	Overall IPC website visitor numbers 2013–2018	184
17.3	Rankings by Number of Fans/Followers	185

Contributors

Dunja Antunovic is Assistant Professor of Sport Sociology and affiliated scholar with the Tucker Center for Research on Girls & Women in Sport in the School of Kinesiology at the University of Minnesota, USA.

Vincent L. Benigni is Professor in the Department of Communication at the College of Charleston, USA.

David Berri is Professor of Economics at Southern Utah University, USA who teaches and conducts research on economic, sports, and gender issues.

Andrew C. Billings is Ronald Reagan Chair of Broadcasting in the Department of Journalism & Creative Media at the University of Alabama, USA.

Ben Bradley is Allan and Anita Sutton Professor of Philosophy at Syracuse University, USA.

Toni Bruce is Professor of Sport Sociology and Sports Media, University of Auckland, New Zealand.

Michael Butterworth is Director of the Center for Sports Communication & Media, Governor Ann W. Richards Chair for the Texas Program in Sports and Media, and Professor in the Department of Communication Studies at the University of Texas at Austin, USA.

Beth A. Cianfrone is Professor and Co-Director of the Center for Sport and Urban Policy at Georgia State University, USA.

Kathryn Coduto is Assistant Professor of Media Science in the College of Communication at Boston University, USA.

Dorothy Collins is Assistant Professor of Sport Management at Lake Erie College, USA.

Steven Conway is Course Director of the Games & Interactivity degrees at Swinburne University of Technology, Australia. He has published widely on games, play, sport, technology, philosophy, and phenomenology.

Courtney M. Cox is Assistant Professor in the Department of Indigenous, Race, and Ethnic Studies at the University of Oregon, USA and Co-Director of The Sound of Victory, a multi-platform project located at the intersection of music and sport.

Contributors

Linda K. Fuller is Professor Emerita of Communications at Worcester State University, USA, and has written extensively on the Olympics and Paralympics; see her website www.LKFullerSport.com.

Walter Gantz is Interim Dean and Professor at The Media School at Indiana University, USA.

Yuan Gong is Lecturer in the School of Humanities, Media, and Creative Communication at Massey University, New Zealand.

Josh Gonzales is a PhD student and Lang Scholar at the Gordon S. Lang School of Business, University of Guelph, Canada.

Samuel Hakim is Lecturer in the Department of Communication at Clemson University, USA.

Robin Hardin is Professor at the University of Tennessee, Knoxville, USA.

Margaret Henley specialises in media and netball archival research at the University of Auckland, New Zealand.

Larena Hoeber is Professor and Associate Dean in the Faculty of Kinesiology and Health Studies at the University of Regina, Canada.

Brett Hutchins is Professor of Media and Communications and Head of the School of Media, Film, and Journalism at Monash University, Australia.

Katharine Jones is Associate Professor of Sociology and Gender Studies in the College of Humanities and Sciences at Thomas Jefferson University, USA. She has previously published on identity negotiation and women sport fans.

Timothy Kellison is Associate Professor and Director of the Center for Sport and Urban Policy at Georgia State University, USA.

Heather Kennedy is Assistant Professor of Sport Business in the College of Management at the University of Massachusetts Boston, USA.

Shannon Kerwin is Associate Professor in the Department of Sport Management at Brock University, Canada.

Yuya Kiuchi is Assistant Professor in the Department of Human Development and Family Studies at Michigan State University, USA.

David Letts is a PhD Researcher at the University of Winchester, UK, whose research focuses on masculinity in British horse racing.

Jason Kido Lopez is Assistant Professor in the Department of Communication Arts at the University of Wisconsin-Madison, USA.

Rory Magrath is Associate Professor of Sociology at Solent University, Southampton, UK. His research focuses on masculinity and homophobia in the context of elite sport.

Contributors

Selçuk Özaydın is Assistant Professor of Economics in the Faculty of Arts and Sciences at İstanbul Kültür University, Turkey.

Keith D. Parry is Deputy Head of the Department of Sport and Event Management at Bournemouth University, UK and an Adjunct Fellow of Western Sydney University, Australia.

Joshua R. Pate is Associate Professor at James Madison University, USA.

Ann Pegoraro is the Lang Chair in Sport Management at the Gordon S. Lang School of Business, University of Guelph, Canada and Co-Director of E-Alliance, the National Network for Gender Equity in Sport.

Anji L. Phillips is Associate Analyst, Business-Agronomy Portfolio for IT at GROWMARK, Inc., USA.

Stacey Pope is Associate Professor in the Department of Sport and Exercise Sciences at Durham University, UK.

Lance V. Porter is Digital Media Professor and Founding Director of the Social Media Analysis and Creation Lab at Louisiana State University, USA.

Jessica Richards is Lecturer in Sport Management at Western Sydney University, Australia.

David Rowe is Emeritus Professor of Cultural Research in the Institute for Culture and Society at Western Sydney University, Australia.

Andy Ruddock is Senior Lecturer in Communications & Media Studies at Monash University, Australia.

Brody J. Ruihley is Associate Professor and Assistant Department Chair in the Department of Sport Leadership & Management at Miami University (OH), USA.

Daniela Spanjaard is Senior Lecturer in Marketing and the current Director of Academic Program for Sport, Marketing, Hospitality and International Business at Western Sydney University, Australia.

Cem Tınaz is Director of the School of Sport Sciences and Technology at Istanbul Bilgi University, Turkey and has been a board member of the Turkish Tennis Federation since 2009.

Kim Toffoletti is Associate Professor of Sociology at Deakin University, Australia.

Mark Turner is a Scripps Howard Visiting Professional at Ohio University, USA and the former Executive News Editor for the Akron Beacon Journal in Akron, Ohio, USA.

Irene I. van Driel is Postdoctoral Researcher at the Amsterdam School of Communication Research (ASCoR), University of Amsterdam, Netherlands.

Ana Carolina Vimieiro is Assistant Professor in Media and Communication at the Federal University of Minas Gerais (UFMG), Brazil.

Contributors

Daniel L. Wann is Distinguished Professor in the Department of Psychology at Murray State University, USA.

Stephen Warren is Lecturer of Sports Media in the College of Media at the University of Illinois Urbana-Champaign, USA.

Lawrence A. Wenner is Von der Ahe Professor of Communication and Ethics in the College of Communication and Fine Arts and the School of Film and Television at Loyola Marymount University, USA.

John Williams is Associate Professor in Sociology in the School of Media, Communication and Sociology at the University of Leicester, UK.

Qingru Xu is Assistant Professor in the Department of Communication Studies at Eastern Washington University, USA.

Acknowledgements

We are so grateful to the outstanding scholars who contributed their work to this handbook. Thank you for your time, thoughtfulness, and intellectual energy. And this extends to the Routledge team who worked with us through this process, particularly Rebecca Connor and Simon Whitmore.

Both Danielle and Anne are lucky enough to work at fantastic universities with exceptional colleagues. Huge thanks to our deans, directors, fellow faculty, and excellent students for your support and encouragement.

Finally, we could not do this without our families. To Avie, Gennie, Lindsey, and Chip: You are just the best. And to our pets. They're pretty awesome too.

1
Editors' Introduction

Danielle Sarver Coombs and Anne C. Osborne

The importance of sport fans and fandom is evident around the world. Professional sports are multi-billion-dollar industries, and fans are an essential market for owners looking to maximize their profits. Our definition of sports is constantly evolving, as evidenced by discussions about whether or not e-sports should be part of the Olympics, how aesthetically oriented sports such as ice skating are judged, and the long-standing debate over whether or not professional wrestling (notably the WWE) is *really* a sport. Likewise, the ways fans can experience their sports and their teams continue to develop. A 2018 Supreme Court decision allowing sports betting is a landmark moment in the United States, and the continued growth of fantasy sports—both for money and for glory—reimagines how fans can and do align with players and teams, changing our perceptions of what it means to be a loyal fan. These topics and others are essential to understanding sport fans and fandom, and this handbook provides an excellent overview of the various ways scholars are studying fans and related phenomena.

While sports research often is treated as "less serious" than other areas of academic scholarship, we argue that the immense economic and cultural impact of sports cannot—and should not—be ignored by scholars, particularly in terms of exploring and examining the power and influence of fans. The extraordinary work in this handbook is a testament to how very central sports fan and fandom studies are to understanding the global impact of this area. This collection is centered on the fan perspective and thus is intrinsically tied to the cultural and political issues so prevalent around sports (e.g., trans/intersex athletes, fair pay and gender equity, team finances, etc.). The fan perspective often is lost in these discussions until an explosion occurs, often in response to decisions that make clear the power of money within elite sporting organizations. A prominent example of this occurred in April 2021 when football/soccer clubs tried to create a breakaway league for the top teams in La Liga (Spain), the Premier League (England), and Serie A (Italy). This "Super League" quickly exploded in the wake of vocal and passionate fan outrage, providing circumstantial evidence that the promise of international fanbase expansion fans likely outweighed the perspectives of local fans.

Developing this Handbook

Editing a handbook provides a unique opportunity to identify gaps in the field and start offering potential solutions. While that often entails looking at subject areas that have been foregrounded (or ignored) in literature, we also recognized the extraordinary opportunity we had to offer a platform for scholars who represent a range of perspectives. As such, when developing the plan for this book, we explicitly worked toward the goal of providing as comprehensive and widespread representation of sports fan and fandom studies as possible. To that end, our chapters were crafted by 51 authors from across the world, including some of the most prominent scholars in sports fan studies. As is the case in our field overall, the majority come from scholars in North America, Europe, and Australia/New Zealand, a widely recognized limitation which is discussed as a challenge for our discipline in Chapter 12. We also sought to ensure a gender balance among our chapter contributors, including some of the most influential women in this field. Finally, we deliberately leveraged this opportunity to give younger scholars—students, recent graduates, and budding faculty still building their research portfolios—an opportunity to contribute to this work and metaphorically stand alongside some of the most prominent names in our field.

A particular challenge faced by sports researchers as a whole, but sports fandom researchers specifically, is the frequent "silo-ing" of our work within our major disciplines; because most universities around the world do not have sports-centered programs that focus on issues other than the physical act of sports playing and the physical exercise of human bodies, scholars in this area find themselves working within a massive range of home disciplines. The natural outcome of this is our work rarely intersects incidentally; we are at different conferences and often publishing in different journals, so our traditional professional modes of knowledge sharing cannot sufficiently support true interdisciplinary scholarship. Unfortunately, this causes inherent limitations for the questions we ask, the ways we approach those questions, and how we understand or interpret what we learn. In an effort to begin building connections and fostering conversations across subject areas, this book includes chapters written by expert scholars from across relevant disciplines, including sociology, gender studies, kinesiology and health studies, economics, sport and urban policy, cultural studies, psychology, marketing, business, communication, media, gaming, and sport management. This provides a unique opportunity to explore some of the ways scholars are examining sports fans and fandom in a more catholic or universal way. In order to make this as accessible as possible for readers across disciplines, chapters include a mix of high-level syntheses of extant literature as well as new research that shows these areas "in action" to give examples of the kinds of work being done.

Ultimately, this range of contributor disciplines demonstrates the tremendous importance of sports fan and fandom research. As so many of our authors ably note, the experience of sport fandom is one that creates shared meaning and opportunities for engagement across an increasingly segmented world. Global mega-events like the Olympics or the World Cup or even massive one-game events like the National Football League's Super Bowl offers rare opportunities to come together for shared viewing and engagement. Whether in person or through mediated channels, sports viewership brings fans together. There are very few—if any—other areas that cast as wide a net as sports fandom; while pop culture-centered fan communities around such areas as comics and K-Pop are notable for their passion, they often are identified explicitly by their uniformity and exclusivity. Sports fandom, however, cuts across ages, genders, nationalities, socio-economic status, education levels, and all other demographic categories. *Anyone* can be a sports fan, and as we broaden our definition of "sport"—such as the inclusion of break dancing, surfing, and skateboarding in the Summer Olympics—we likewise expand what we think of as a "sports fan." Sport often is at the core of culture and community. It merits serious scholarship, and we are proud that this volume foregrounds the importance of studying sports fans and fandom.

While our chapters do represent a broad range of disciplinary approaches, we were delighted to discover common themes that emerged. As will be the case with any examples of scholarship centered on sports fans, the use of media—both traditional and social media platforms—is an essential component of examining how fans perform and experience their fandom. We also note the connections and contradictions of both the global and local in fandom, including fan experiences within stadia and in countries thousands of miles away. Several of our chapters explore business practices that are employed to engage with fans as consumers, exploring the ways teams and leagues think about and address their fan bases. Finally, this handbook offers a collection of chapters that explore gender, sexuality, and fandom in quite important ways.

As is always the case in collected works like this, we could not cover all of the topics and perspectives that an ideal handbook would include. In some cases, the limited number of scholars with sufficient expertise were not available to write the necessary chapters; in others, so little work has been done that we could not even extend an invitation. We particularly hope that future editions of this handbook (or books like this) will be better able to represent the Global South and include voices from Africa, Southeast Asia, and South America. We also encourage scholarship in key areas of popular discussion around sports that have not yet made their way into mainstream scholarship, including youth sports, expanding the operationalization of "sports" to include more traditionally feminine-defined activities such as dance and cheerleading, and exploring the impact of sports (especially mega-events) on the environment and sustainability. We also anticipate the aforementioned "Super League" debacle will spark scholarship on fan activism and engagement in shaping their clubs, teams, and leagues and we welcome increasing scholarship on this extremely important area. Finally, we hope to see more connections being drawn across the various disciplines represented in this handbook and general fan/fandom studies that often center on pop culture. While we are extremely proud of the collected works in this handbook, the opportunities for growth are endless.

Previewing the Handbook

This text has been organized into three parts. In the first, **What Is a Fan and How Do We Know?**, our contributors offer an exceptional overview of approaches to and perspectives on understanding fans and fandom. In Chapter 2, Michael Butterworth explores sport metaphor in American politics and what this means for democratic culture, using the example of Brett Kavanaugh's nomination and appointment to the United States Supreme Court. In Chapter 3, Daniel Wann examines the individual and societal needs that are met through sports fandom, including such aspects as the need to belong and the search for meaning in life (individual needs) and aiding in socializing as well as fostering integration among society's members (societal needs). Toni Bruce and Margaret Henley take a fascinating look at women fans of an almost exclusively female sport in Chapter 4, presenting some of their own research on netball in New Zealand to add new understanding to the ways we think about women fans. Continuing the theme of women fans and sports fandom, in Chapter 5, economist David Berri provides a historical perspective on the growth of men's sports to demonstrate that women's sports are following the same trajectories and that time will allow for these leagues to flourish. Continuing the economic implications of sports, in Chapter 6 Turkish scholars Selçuk Özaydın and Cem Tınaz turn their attention to the effects of capitalism and industrialization on European football leagues, which ultimately leads to increased costs for fans as customers. In Chapter 7, Timothy Kellison and Beth A. Cianfrone take a more local look at how fans engage with their teams, using the Atlanta Braves' (Major League Baseball) move to a new suburban ballpark to explore how stadia can strengthen local identity and establish a community's political, economic, and cultural distinctiveness.

In the second part of this section we shift attention to "how do we know," centering on the ways we build knowledge of sports fans and fandom, beginning with Jessica Richards, Keith D. Parry, and Daniela Spanjaard (Chapter 8) advocating the use of ethnographic methods to offer a more holistic perspective that allows for deeper insights to emerge. In Chapter 9, Mark Turner explores the use of framing studies as an approach to understanding sports fans, situating this scholarship in the broader use of framing studies in media and journalism. Finally, Courtney M. Cox (Chapter 10) explores issues of power and possibility in this research, using her own ethnographic work on women's basketball to construct a methodological framework for fans and the structures around fandom.

The last two chapters in this section broaden the discussion to ask questions we should be considering as sports scholars and spark discussion among those of us doing this work. In Chapter 11, philosopher Ben Bradley explores and then argues against Tännsjö's argument that we should not admire athletes, instead making the case for when that is appropriate. Finally, the editors of this handbook write a call to action in Chapter 12, noting the dearth of research centering on race and fandom and encouraging more work to be done to continue expanding our perceptions and assumptions about fandom in the future.

Part II, **Who Fans Are**, helps contextualize the calls made in that chapter by offering a range of perspectives on sports fans as they have been explored in extant literature. We begin with Shannon Kerwin and Larena Hoeber's excellent analysis of fan identity and performance in Chapter 13. In Chapter 14, Katharine Jones, Stacey Pope, and Kim Toffoletti focus on women fans specifically, summarizing current debates and emergent issues in this research and including a preliminary model of two female fan types ("hot" and "cool"). In Chapter 15, focus shifts to the sports fanship lifecycle by Irene I. van Driel, Walter Gantz, and Lawrence A. Wenner. This chapter uses Carstensen's Socioemotional Selectivity Theory (SST) to explore the lifecycle of sports fanship, finding that changes over time depend on fanship avidity. We then shift from fan groups to an event focus, with Andrew C. Billings, Samuel Hakim, and Qingru Xu (Chapter 16) analyzing the demographics of Olympics sports fans and Linda K. Fuller's (Chapter 17) examination of Paralympics fandom and sports organizations.

The next two chapters in this section present original research to help address gaps in scholarship on sports fans. In Chapter 18, David Letts and Rory Magrath present results from the first-ever academic research centered on the experiences of LGBT+ fans. John Williams takes an autoethnographic approach in Chapter 19, using Stuart Roy Clarke's legendary photographs of British football clubs to explore his own experiences with sporting transformations. Chapter 20 moves us to Brazil, with Ana Carolina Vimieiro's cultural and historical analysis of the ecosystem of football supporter cultures in Brazil.

The last two chapters in this section shift to understanding how media inform the ways sports fans are understood and defined. In Chapter 21, Joshua R. Pate and Robin Hardin focus on athletes with disabilities' self-presentation use of social media, exploring how these athletes can leverage social media to better connect with fans and promote their sports and own personal brands. Wrapping up this section, in Chapter 22 Dorothy Collins examines the ways media can be used to expand fanbases beyond geographic limits, thus also expanding how we can and should think of "sports fans" in our research.

As the last section of the handbook, **Part III** shifts toward what we know about **What Fans Do**. The section starts with Heather Kennedy, Josh Gonzales, and Ann Pegoraro's (Chapter 23) examination of digital sports fandom, including an examination of how fans, teams, and athletes interact and engage and a discussion of why sports fans use digital media. Kathryn Coduto expands this further in Chapter 24, focusing specifically on how sports fandom is presented and enacted through social media channels and examining the parasocial relationships that develop between fans and players.

Broadening the ways we think about sports fan activity and engagement, Jason Kido Lopez (Chapter 25) writes about the construction of sports fandom by sports betting companies, positing a framework to organize fan and gaming possibilities in sports betting. Brody J. Ruihley and Robin Hardin further the examination of fandom and fantasy sport in Chapter 26, including motives of competition, sport socialization, self-esteem, and surveillance. In Chapter 27, Steven Conway shifts attention to how sport videogames extend the ways we think about fandom by exploring this as a way fandom is available and performed. Anji L. Phillips and Dunja Antunovic return to more traditional mediated fan engagement in Chapter 28, exploring the implications of structural barriers for women's sports fans to access live broadcasts of their sports. Finally, in Chapter 29, Vincent L. Benigni and Lance V. Porter explore the impact of Twitter on fan conversations through research grounded in Bourdieu's field theory to analyze ten years of tweets about the hiring and firing of coaches in the American college football powerhouse Southeastern Conference (SEC).

The next three chapters in this section explore the ways technology and media change or inform sports fan experiences. In Chapter 30, Yuya Kiuchi examines football fans' reactions to the Video Assistant Referee technology, a controversial addition to the FIFA World Cup in 2018. In Chapter 31, Yuan Gong discusses the impact of digital media through a case study of Chinese fans' engagement with European football, particularly in terms of sports consumption as part of everyday life. "Executive fandom" is the focus of Chapter 32, with Brett Hutchins, David Rowe, and Andy Ruddock, examining the ways digital, mobile, gaming, and video streaming technologies facilitate fandom and presenting results of their case study of American football's Fan Controlled Football League.

The final two chapters shift gears away from the impact of technology and instead explore the ways sports fandom connect to social issues (albeit in very different ways!). In Chapter 33, Keith D. Parry and Jessica Richards explore the role of food and drink, including alcohol, within the sports fan experience. They note that sports stadia are linked to unhealthy eating and drinking practices and contextualize this within hegemonic masculinity and social inequities, ending their examination by highlighting a push for healthier options within stadia. Finally, in Chapter 34, Stephen Warren explores how fans react to athletes and activism, arguing that sports and politics have a long been linked and that social media has amplified this relationship.

Conclusion

We are incredibly proud of the caliber of scholarship contained in this handbook, and we believe this provides an essential overview of sports fans and fandom for both established and burgeoning scholars. As noted earlier, we have the express hope that this handbook helps spark discussions among and between scholars in different "home" disciplines and helps foster truly interdisciplinary scholarship that will expand the ways we think about and understand sports fans and fandom. The economic and cultural impact of sports fandom is undeniable, and this research offers an exceptional opportunity to better understand global and local communities.

Part I
What Is a Fan and How Do We Know?

2

Imagining the Citizen-Fan

Sport Metaphor in American Politics and Implications for Democratic Culture

Michael Butterworth

On October 6, 2018, Brett Kavanaugh was confirmed to the Supreme Court of the United States. His confirmation hearings had been embroiled in controversy, primarily as a result of sexual assault accusations made by a former high school classmate, Christine Blasey-Ford. For a group of College Republicans at the University of Washington, Kavanaugh's confirmation was a cause to celebrate, so they made plans to gather that evening at a nearby bar in Seattle. The event, "Beers 4 Brett," was held at Shultzy's, described on the establishment's Facebook page as "a sports-themed bar & grill" (Sun, 2018, ¶ 7). For the Republican supporters, the venue seemed an ideal place to toast the newest Supreme Court justice, especially since they could do so over the judge's well-publicized favorite beverage.

It may not be commonplace to celebrate political outcomes at a sports bar but, considering the nature of political language, it probably should not be seen as unusual. Indeed, researchers and journalists have long recognized the shared logic and rhetorical practices of politics and sport (Butterworth, 2014; Hruby, 2012; Segrave, 2000). From Tannenbaum and Noah's (1959) "sportugese" to Lipsyte's (1975) "sportspeak," we have seen sport's influence on political speech. More recently, however, these metaphorical associations have begun to transform political attitudes and even behaviors. In her book, *Uncivil Agreement*, political scientist Lilliana Mason worries that Americans increasingly define their political affiliations in sporting terms. In other words, Democrats and Republicans do not merely identify with a political party, they are loyal fans of a team. Mason does not see this as a healthy rivalry, instead lamenting,

> Partisan battles have helped organize Americans' distrust for "the other" in politically powerful ways. In this political environment, a candidate who picks up the banner of "us versus them" and "winning versus losing" is almost guaranteed to tap into a current of resentment and anger across racial, religious, and cultural lines, which have recently divided neatly by party.
>
> *Mason, 2018, p. 3*

She adds, "Group victory is a powerful prize, and American partisans have increasingly seen that goal as more important than the practical matters of governing a nation" (Mason, 2018, p. 3).

DOI: 10.4324/9780429342189-3

Mason's book addresses commonly held assumptions that politics in the United States is more bitterly partisan than it has ever been. There appears to be supporting evidence for this assumption, especially as Americans have increasingly "sorted" themselves into highly polarized social alignments (Ellis & Stimson, 2012; Mason, 2018). As Mason puts it, "We have gone from two parties that are a little bit different in a lot of ways to two parties that are very different in a few powerful ways. These underlying social shifts have put the American population into a partisan team-based mindset, through which the country has split itself into us and them" (Mason, 2018, p. 43).

If "team" can be seen as an instructive metaphor for understanding political parties in the United States, then so too can "fan" help us make sense of political behavior. The scholarship on sports fan identity is plentiful in communication and media studies, but it typically directs scholars to issues such as motivation (Gantz, Wilson, Lee, & Fingerhut, 2008; Wann, 2006), consumption (Earnhardt & Haridakis, 2008), and cognitive and social impacts (Cummins, 2009). In this chapter, I invoke the concept of the "fan" metaphorically, using it as an interpretive lens for seeing political partisanship and polarization. To that effort, I draw from existing studies of sports fan identity and, in turn, suggest that conceiving of citizens as fans has implications for democratic culture. Writing from the perspective of rhetorical studies, I am less interested in identifying the characteristics of any given fan category and more interested in the ways fan identity provides a useful vocabulary for understanding politics in a time of increasing antagonism.

For rhetorical and political theorists interested in the idea of *agonism*, it is important to point out that we have always had an "us" and "them." U.S. history is marked by a series of identifiable "thems" against whom we can constitute an "us." Ivie (2005) explains that the enemies of American democracy are found both outside of and within the nation's borders. While the threats to democratic culture may have different points of origin, the nation's responses to those threats are consistent. In short, American politics features a persistent tendency to treat any opposition as a "disease" to be eradicated, even when opposing voices are found among fellow citizens. Ivie contends that the problem can only be met through a more genuine rhetorical attitude that accepts difference and conflict. Consistent with political theorists of agonism, this requires citizens to view conflict as both unavoidable and potentially productive. In Mouffe's terms,

> the aim of democratic politics is to construct the "them" in such a way that it is no longer an enemy to be destroyed, but as an "adversary" that is, somebody whose ideas we combat but whose right to defend those ideas we do not put into question.
>
> *Mouffe, 2000, p. 101–102*

Rather than reducing democracy to its institutions—that is, national citizenship or voting—Ivie (2005, p. 195) suggests redefining it in rhetorical terms:

> [Improving democratic practice] requires revising the very conception of democracy from one grounded in the frightful trope of disease to a healthier notion of democratic persuasion as an exercise in contested and contingent pluralism, an ongoing drama of adversaries who may bridge the divide sufficiently to achieve a relationship of consubstantial rivalry or fall short and into the abyss of sheer enemies.

From this point of view, the language of "rivalry" becomes especially important, for it invites us to consider meaningful parallels between politics and sport.

As a rhetorical critic invested in democratic practices, I believe it is imperative to seek healthier modes of political engagement, and sport is among the sites where we might enact such practices. To an extent, then, I share an orientation with the "Beers 4 Brett" boys. Yet, I find the commonplace use of sport as a simple metaphor for political combat to be limited. Thus, this chapter investigates the rhetorical dynamics of the Brett Kavanaugh confirmation as a means to assess both the limitations and possibilities for thinking of political partisanship in terms of sport. More specifically, I follow the tradition of agonistic democracy in order to think more productively about rivalry as a feature of democratic culture. The Kavanaugh hearing provides a compelling context for inclusion in a book about sports fan identity, and not simply because some college students had some beers in a sports bar. First, the nomination and confirmation processes were both strongly and visibly partisan in ways that mimic the powerful allegiances of sports fans. Indeed, aligning oneself with Kavanaugh or Blasey-Ford might be akin to aligning with Ohio State or Michigan, or the Yankees or Red Sox. Second, because the hearings ended in a vote, there was a clear outcome and narrative closure, much like a sporting event that features a definitive winner and loser.[1] The outcome, therefore, invited "fans" to choose a side, mindful that identifying with a "loser" would be called out as such. Third, and perhaps most importantly, the language of sports was central to the hearings, especially through the testimony of Kavanaugh himself. In this way, the logic of sport was a mechanism for the nominee to bolster his character and build identification with his "fans." For these reasons, I turn to the Kavanaugh hearings as a "representative anecdote" (Burke, 1945), a narrative that brings together a number of features that characterize contemporary politics. In particular, I am interested in the extent to which political partisanship functions similarly to sports fandom. To explore this idea, I turn first to political communication scholarship on the game frame and polarization. I then examine research on fan identity in sports and the metaphorical equations made between sport and politics. Finally, I evaluate the ways contemporary partisanship mirrors sports fan loyalties before concluding with some ideas about a more productive understanding of sport as a metaphor for political identity.

The Game is the Frame

Political communication researchers have long been concerned with the over-emphasis on the game metaphor, especially in the context of elections and campaigns. Operating within the framework of media framing, these scholars note that news coverage of campaigns is highly dependent on strategic frames. This is most obvious with respect to the "game frame." In short, "the framing of politics as a strategic game is characterized by a focus on questions related to who is winning and losing, the performances of politicians and parties, and on campaign strategies and tactics. This framing is often contrasted with a focus on political substance and issues" (Aalberg, Strömbäck, & de Vreese, 2011, p. 163). Multiple rhetorical choices might constitute the game frame—moving the "political football" in a policy proposal, landing a "knock-out blow" in a debate or, most commonly, monitoring candidates' progress through the "drama inherent in the horse race" (Jarvis, 2005, p. 9). Since 1952, the year in which television advertising began to shape presidential campaigns in the United States, the "horse race" has occupied 40 percent of news coverage, far more than any other frame used to cover elections (Benoit, Stein, & Hansen, 2005, p. 359). Although some scholars contend the game frame makes politics more exciting for voters and enhances their participation, the majority fear that characterizing elections as sporting events positions voters as mere spectators, therefore relegating them to passive roles as viewers (Jamieson, 1992).

Most of the work on the game frame is focused on news media and political campaigns. If we move outside of framing, specifically, which is tethered to its interest in media, we can consider how the language of sport influences citizen attitudes beyond elections. This is the underlying question of Mason's book, which uses social identity theory (Tajfel & Turner, 1986) to make sense of the rooting interests of political partisans in the United States. She makes an important distinction between three terms:

> In the social-scientific study of politics the term *polarization* traditionally describes an expansion of the distance between the issue positions of Democrats and Republicans . . . *sorting* is usually defined as an increasing alignment between party and ideology, where *ideology* indicates a set of issue positions or values.
>
> *Mason, 2018, p. 7*

Sorting is what is at stake in her analysis, and her conclusion is that the collapse of the distinction between party affiliation and ideology is driving Americans further and further apart. In short, "Democrats and especially Republicans are feeling closer to liberals and conservatives, considering them to be groups of people that are most like them 'in their ideas and interests and feelings about things'" (Mason, 2018, p. 28).

If political partisanship can be equated to sports fan loyalty, it becomes useful to consider what scholars tell us about the nature of fan identity in sports. The scholarship in this area is robust, with much of the work in Europe focused on negative fan behaviors such as hooliganism and much of the work in the United States focused on fan identifications and motivations. As Wann and Branscombe conclude, much like political partisans, "Highly identified sports fans, in particular, take pride in their loyalty to their team. Such loyalty, developed in early adolescence, seems to be a stabilizing force in the spectators' lives" (1992, p. 59). Loyalty in sports fan identity cultivates in-group status, which once again calls to mind Tajfel and Turner's (1986) work on social identity. For Crisp and colleagues, "The sporting world provides many sources for strong and enduring social identification. In spectator sport, the personal psychological lives of individuals can be tied to the fates of their chosen teams" (Crisp, Heuston, Farr, & Turner, 2007, p. 10). As they add, "Cialdini and colleagues' (1976) classic study of 'basking in reflected glory' demonstrated the simple power of winning and losing upon collective self-esteem, a vivid illustration of the grip that meaningful social memberships can exert over self-perception" (Crisp, Heuston, Farr, & Turner, 2007, p. 10). Given the overlap between political partisans and sports fans with respect to identification and self-esteem, one might conclude that Mason's work on polarization and sorting is really about BIRGing and CORFing.

Metaphors may clarify ideas and enhance interest. More importantly, they function as a "device for seeing something *in terms of* something else" (Burke, 1945, p. 503) that can shape attitudes and influence behaviors. A substantial body of scholarship in rhetorical studies makes clear that metaphor is far more than a colorful figure of speech, as it can have significant constitutive effects on culture and politics (Cisneros, 2008; Ivie, 1987; Osborn, 1967). Given the conflictual nature of politics, it may be that using sport as a metaphor may assist in characterizing the particulars of any political debate (Aikin, 2011). However, there also are inherent risks when we reduce politics to sport, or citizenship to fan identification. In an early study on this topic, Lipsky (1979, p. 28) expresses concern that, "Politicians and political commentators increasingly were using sports metaphors and, by analogical extension, seeing politics in athletic images." The consequence, he contends, is that such language "promotes an interest in 'winning' or 'losing' while obfuscating the reasons that should underlie an interest in winning political power" (Lipsky, 1979, p. 36).

Framing Kavanaugh in Sporting Terms

It is not entirely clear if political partisans lost sight of the reasons the Brett Kavanaugh hearings were important. Nevertheless, in an era defined by polarization and "owning" your opponent on social media, it is clear that much of the reaction to the confirmation process demonstrated the tendencies of sports fans. First, it was obvious that public opinion was divided sharply along partisan lines. Based on substantial polling data, observers concluded that Republicans overwhelmingly supported Kavanaugh while Democrats overwhelmingly opposed him (Dann, 2018; Velencia & Mehta, 2018). The many reports of these polls in the news media reinforced the language of partisanship and polarization. *The Washington Post* called it a "party-line fight" (Barnes & Guskin, 2018), *Politico* referred to it as "sharply partisan" (Shepard, 2018), *Fox News* framed it as "historic rancor" (Re, 2018), and *Vanity Fair* concluded Kavanaugh's appointment "seems to have deepened partisan entrenchment" (Nguyen, 2018, ¶ 5).

These characterizations in news media are representative of the coverage of other political events, including elections, investigations, and congressional hearings. We can easily observe similar language choices in both the marketing and broadcast of presidential debates, for example (Blakenship & Kang, 1991). Or, consider the tendency to cover the 2019 testimony of Special Prosecutor Robert Mueller as anything other than a mediated drama inviting loyalists on each side to embrace the spectacle of it all at the expense of evaluating the substance. More than simply enhancing partisan allegiances, coverage of the Mueller hearings also served to reinforce already established public opinion on the matter of Russian interference in the 2016 presidential election and the prospect of impeachment proceedings against President Donald Trump (Karson, 2019).

In the case of Kavanaugh, the pervasive focus on partisanship certainly gave the impression of two bitter rivals fighting for an on-field victory. The connection to sports was made all the more profound, however, by the degree to which Kavanaugh's actual testimony was grounded in athletic activity and its purported virtues. Writing in *The New Yorker*, Lauren Collins observes,

> By my count, Brett Kavanaugh, speaking before the Senate Judiciary Committee on Thursday, mentioned sports nearly fifty times. . . . Borrowing glory from the playing field, Kavanaugh was exhibiting and exploiting the American patriarchal fallacy that competitiveness is tantamount to character.
>
> *Collins, 2018, ¶ 1*

More than simply talking about coaching his daughter's basketball team or being willing to spend a lot of money to go to baseball games, Kavanaugh invoked his high school memories of bonding with friends over sports and working out. The latter reference inspired much of Matt Damon's parodic performance as Kavanaugh on *Saturday Night Live*, premised on the nominee's old calendar reminders about "lifting weights."

Given that Kavanaugh's confirmation was imperiled by an allegation of sexual assault, his testimony required that he (re)establish his character and credibility. As many observers noted, this recovery effort was rooted in the privilege of being an affluent, white, male. This identity was cultivated and legitimized through sporting fraternity. Collins (2018, ¶ 3) remarked,

The privilege, more specifically, pertains to white men, whose accomplishments we are to take as earned, the result of grit rather than natural gifts. The white-boy amateur, the vaunted "scholar-athlete," incarnates a set of genteel virtues from a homosocial and homogeneous world that many American conservatives would like to rediscover.

Noreen Malone (2018, ¶ 5) wrote in *The Cut*,

They (and here I am thinking also of our president, though he's older and certainly less of a self-professed choirboy) have all the superficial trappings of masculinity—the swaggering aggression, the bombast, the interest in sports and the right women—without paying much more than lip service to what their grandfathers might have called manly virtues.

For *New York Magazine*, Will Leitch (2018, ¶ 4) observed,

Kavanaugh's teenage world was divided into a few simple activities, the way every athlete desires: Working out. Hanging with friends (teammates, really). Drinking beers. All with the idea of close bonding with other men, and mainly other men, all nicknamed in the peevishly belittling but-hey-we're-just-joshing-here way athletes are always nicknaming each other, as the only universe with any judgment or value . . . the only one that matters.

And Diana Moskovitz (2018, ¶ 3) concluded in *Jezebel*,

It's no surprise at all that Kavanaugh ignored all this well-documented history and reached for the comfortable cliché of the moral and masculine athlete. It's an image and ideal that's grown up right along with the idea of America as a world power.

Most direct in a critique of the sporting metaphor was Dahlia Lithwick, writing for *Slate*. Noting the masculine privilege expressed by so much emphasis on sports, she laments (2018, ¶ 1):

Ah, sports. No confirmation hearing can be complete without a little small talk about which teams the senator supports, and which sports the nominee plays, and which sporting events the nominee likens his job to, and also which sports the senator likens the confirmation process to. It's a kind of shorthand way of everyone having a beer in the Senate chamber. We're all just sports fans here, talking about, you know, sports.

Lithwick's critique brings to mind Lipsky's concern about the "athleticization of politics." In other words, with so much focus on athletic virtue and male camaraderie, the merits of Kavanaugh's nomination and the truth about his behavior were subsumed by the metaphor. As Lithwick (2018, ¶ 8) put it succinctly, "It's not a game when the spectators are also the victims."

Beyond the metaphorical associations between politics and sports, the many references linking Kavanaugh's character to his socialization through white masculinity and sport reflect a similar logic within sport itself. Although athletes of color, especially African Americans, have achieved tremendous success through sports in the United States, they nevertheless face any number of barriers based on assumptions about race and character. This has manifested in various ways, perhaps most obviously through historical practices of "stacking," which refers to slotting particular athletes into particular positions based on racial identity. Most visibly, "quarterbacks in football and catchers in baseball have traditionally been White, whereas Black players are more often found playing in the outfield in baseball and as running backs or wide receivers in football"

(Woodward, 2004, p. 357). These characterizations have a long legacy of cementing stereotypical attitudes about African American athletes, which has translated to limits on opportunities for players at specific positions and strict regulations against behaviors—such as wearing flamboyant attire (Griffin & Calafell, 2011) or "excessive celebrations" (Cunningham, 2009, p. 45)—that are deemed "unprofessional."

What is at stake here is found in traditional political attitudes that identify particular bodies as more credible than others. Sport scholars are surely familiar with the notion of "hegemonic masculinity," what Connell (1990, p. 83) describes as "the culturally idealized form of masculine character." Although this masculine character can occasionally accommodate racial diversity, it is commonly associated with White masculinity (Butterworth, 2013; Trujillo, 1991). Grano (2010, p. 256) explains the consequences of this characterization:

> For whites, character and the body are unified so that the white athletic body signifies proof of character (a triumph of inborn, interior will over bodily limits) while for African American athletes, a body wired with primal drives is essentially conditioned against characterological controls and becomes redeemed for civic life not by force of an independent interior will, but through a contingent relationship to external disciplinary structures.

In other words, race provides a cultural shorthand for determining the virtues of individual bodies, thus reinforcing default positions about White men as inherently virtuous and Black men as inherently criminal (Cunningham, 2009).

The emphasis on characterological assumptions in sport is not a theoretical detour, for this history provides a persuasive warrant for arguments validating the character of other men. Consider news coverage of young athletes accused of sexual harassment and assault, for example, many of whom are described as "good" kids from "good families," with "bright" futures. A useful example can be found in the case of Stanford University swimmer Brock Turner, a White male from an affluent family who received a shockingly lenient sentence after being convicted of sexually assaulting a woman who was unconscious. Turner's connection to sport worked alongside his race and socio-economic status to remind the public that the potential future of a young, White male is inherently more valuable than the past, present, or future of women or people of color (O'Neil, 2016; Stack, 2016). Indeed, if one wanted to forecast a possible future for Brock Turner, Brett Kavanaugh makes for a suitable example.

Very little of the discourse about Kavanaugh's confirmation, of course, overtly spoke about masculinity or race. This is why, then, the rhetorical work being done by references to sport are so important. Rather than needing to express outright preferences for whiteness or masculinity, Kavanaugh supporters could point instead to his affiliations with institutions believed to build and reflect character. In the years since the election of President Barack Obama in 2008, political discourses on the far right have increasingly relied on carefully coded rhetoric to exploit racial stereotypes and divisions. By casting Obama and other people of color as "Other" or "un-American," right-wing partisans have capitalized on racist legacies to negate the symbolism of the Obama presidency (Enck-Wanzer, 2011). During the 2016 presidential campaign and the Trump administration, these discourses have intensified, often by relying on demonizing those who would threaten the nation's greatness—namely, women and people of color. Indeed, the muscular, misogynistic, and racist rhetoric of the "alt-right," "incels," and White nationalists (Bergengruen & Hennigan, 2019; Osnos, 2015; Williams, 2018) provides the foundation on which much contemporary polarization has been built.[2]

The extreme polarization exemplified by the Kavanaugh appointment may reveal strong partisan identifications, but it also represents a weak democratic culture. In the words of Levitsky and Ziblatt (2018, p. 9), "if one thing is clear from studying breakdowns throughout history, it's that extreme polarization can kill democracies." Part of the problem is that polarization leads citizens to direct their participatory energy to spectatorship, thereby abdicating their responsibilities to play an active role in democratic practices. Instead of thinking of "citizenship as a mode of public engagement" (Asen, 2004, p. 191), too often Americans are content to reduce their democratic activity to voting and to defer to elected officials for leadership (Barber, 1984).

Given these conditions, it may appear that American democracy is indeed at risk, with polarization a leading cause. Based on a particular view of sports fans, intense political identification promotes increasingly poor behavior. Following the metaphor, intense partisanship is equated with intense fan identity. When we consider that, at least in some cases, "the expression of hostility in sports rivalries is culturally acceptable" (Lehr, Ferreira, & Banaji, 2019, p. 29), we should be concerned that sporting language may have effects on political attitudes. However, there is another aspect to sport that we should seek to cultivate, one in which rhetoric and sport are brought back into conversation with one another. Earlier in this essay, I drew on agonistic political theory and its emphasis on the unavoidability of conflict. From an agonistic point of view, conflict must be addressed under conditions of sustained contest. It is the emphasis on contestation to which I now turn.

Sport as Agonistic Contest

Rhetoric and sport, and democracy for that matter, share a common point of origin: ancient Greece. In both, the *agōn* is a central construct. As Hawhee (2005) explains, agonistic conflict is not an end in and of itself. Rather, agonism privileges the sense of community cultivated by the contest. As she notes,

> The Olympic Games ... depended on the gathering of athletes, judges, and spectators alike. *Agora*, the marketplace, shares the same derivative and a strikingly similar force of meaning as *agōn*, and, as is commonly known, functioned as the ancient gathering place par excellence.
> *Hawhee, 2005, p. 15*

In other words, there is something to be *shared* among and between competitors. Shields & Bredemeier (2011) take up a similar theme in their argument seeking to shift the emphasis in competition from war to partnership. As they point out, the "etymology of the word 'competition' means 'to strive' or 'to seek' with" (Shields & Bredemeier, 2011, p. 33).

This cooperative spirit is something missing from many of the sports metaphors applied to contemporary politics. Although it is common for fans to be hostile toward their rivals and occasionally get carried away (especially when coupled with alcohol consumption), many of the dynamics of sports rivalries are benign or even healthy. In fact, the very best rivalries in sports—Duke vs. North Carolina in college basketball, Roger Federer vs. Rafael Nadal in tennis, FC Barcelona vs. Real Madrid in association football—depend on being able to play again another day. Complete destruction is not desirable because it ends the rivalry. This notion finds its parallel in agonism through Mouffe's focus on "adversaries." Although conflict cannot be eliminated from politics, she argues that it can be minimized and managed through recurring contestation. Adversaries are central to this, for they are "persons who are friends because they share a common symbolic space but also enemies because they want to organize this common symbolic space in a different way" (Mouffe, 2000, p. 13).

An important part of re-thinking politics as sport is to question the dependence on hegemonic notions of masculinity and enemyship (Engels, 2010). In both politics and sport, strength and assertiveness are valued, often at the expense of nuance and compromise. Thus, political leadership is articulated as inherently masculine (Sheeler & Anderson, 2013) and sport valorizes figures such as quarterbacks and head coaches (Butterworth & Schuck, 2016). Instead of celebrating athletic conquest and masculine authority as emblematic of political value, Americans would do well to consider politics as a shared enterprise rooted in consubstantial rivalry.

Given the state of contemporary politics, is it possible to translate the abstractions of political theory and reshape our democratic practices? Mason speaks to this through her appeal to "superordinate goals," mutual aims that transcend political partisanship. As an example of this, she turns to the immediate aftermath of the September 11, 2001 terrorist attacks. She notes, "For a short time afterward, Democrats and Republicans came together, at least in their approval of the president, George W. Bush. However, the activation of a superordinate American identity did not heal the rift between the parties" (Mason, 2018, p. 134). Here, Mason equates approval of the president with American identity—which may or may not be reasonable—but there is value in her sentiment. What is problematic for Mason's point of view, however, is that uncritical obedience to a presidential administration may present an image of "unity," but it is accompanied by the citizenry's collective failure to hold its government accountable for decisions and policies enacted on behalf of the nation. A more effective model requires that we "think of unity as contingent and provisional," and that we shift our use of "sport as a metaphor for political spectatorship and toward a robust engagement with discussion and debate" (Butterworth, 2020, p. 15).

What does such a shift mean for our understanding of sports fan identity? Primarily, it directs our attention to the productive expression of agonistic conflict that could be channeled into political practices. Although some sports fans do exceed the proper boundaries of rivalry, the *accepted norms of sports fan behavior* demand that both rival teams and their fans must be tolerated and even respected within the rules of sport. At a moment when the accepted norms of political behavior seem to treat such boundaries as meaningless, the vocabulary of sports fan identity may well provide a useful intervention for democratic culture. Thus, while the site of analysis in this chapter exists within the arena of politics, the principle insights for communication and media scholars reside within the arena of sport.

If symbolic unity ultimately enables material divisions, what is instead required is a willingness for citizens to see their colleagues, neighbors, and community members as others who share a common symbolic space, even if they want to organize that space in a different way. Levitsky and Ziblatt call this "mutual toleration," which suggests

> that as long as our rivals play by constitutional rules, we accept that they have an equal right to exist, compete for power, and govern. We may disagree with, and even strongly dislike, our rivals, but we nevertheless accept them as legitimate. This means recognizing that our political rivals are decent, patriotic, law-abiding citizens—that they love our country and respect the Constitution just as we do.
>
> *Levitsky & Ziblatt, 2018, p. 102*

It does not mean giving up our loyalties or affiliations, but it does mean that politics cannot be reduced only to "wins" and "losses." Brett Kavanaugh's confirmation may well have felt like a "win" for Republicans and a "loss" for Democrats. Over time, the particular details of his confirmation hearing will become artifacts of the past. It seems clear, though, that we will continue to struggle with partisanship and political hostility. We need not agree with each other on major issues or strive for some transcendental form of "unity." Viewing one another as adversaries instead of enemies, however, would go a long way toward helping us translate the attitudes of sport into the behaviors of a true citizen-fan.

Notes

1 U.S. citizens tend to react with discomfort when a clear winner and loser cannot be determined in sports. Indeed, a sport such as soccer is often denigrated because draws are commonplace, which may explain why some, such as former U.S. Senator Jack Kemp, think of it as "a European socialist [sport]]." Quoted in Foer (2004, p. 241).
2 One might be tempted to note here that "both sides" are guilty of partisanship and polarization. This is true, to an extent, but I think it is important to reject the false equivalency that sees these as two, equally matched sides. Although those on the radical left can be guilty of damaging rhetoric, there is an important documented history that demonstrates conservative and Republican Party efforts to exploit race and masculine authority. Space prevents an extended discussion of this, but helpful sources include Lakoff (2002) and Lee (2014).

References

Aalberg, T., Strömbäck, J., & de Vreese, C. H. (2011). The framing of politics as strategy and game: A review of concepts, operationalizations and key findings. *Journalism, 13*, 162–178.
Aikin, S. (2011). A defense of war and sport metaphors in argument. *Philosophy and Rhetoric, 44*, 250–272.
Asen, R. (2004). A discourse theory of citizenship. *Quarterly Journal of Speech, 90*, 189–211.
Barber, B. (1984). *Strong democracy: Participatory politics for a new age*. Berkeley, CA: University of California Press.
Barnes, R., & Guskin, E. (2018, October 12). More Americans disapprove of Kavanaugh's confirmation than support it, new poll shows. *Washington Post*. Retrieved from www.washingtonpost.com/politics/more-americans-disapprove-of-kavanaughs-confirmation-than-support-it-new-poll-shows/2018/10/12/18dbf872-cd93-11e8-a3e6-44daa3d35ede_story.html?utm_term=.cc90eaa13b7d.
Benoit, W. L, Stein, K. A., & Hansen, G. J. (2005). *New York Times* coverage of presidential campaigns. *Journalism & Mass Communication Quarterly, 82*, 356–376.
Bergengruen, V., & Hennigan, W. J. (2019, August 8). "We are being eaten from within": Why America is losing the battle against White nationalist terrorism. *Time*. Retrieved from https://time.com/5647304/white-nationalist-terrorism-united-states/.
Blakenship, J., & Kang, J. G. (1991). The 1984 presidential and vice presidential debates: The printed press and "construction" by metaphor. *Presidential Studies Quarterly, 21*, 307–318.
Burke, K. (1945). *A grammar of motives*. Berkeley, CA: University of California Press.
Butterworth, M. L. (2013). The passion of the Tebow: Sports media and heroic language in the tragic frame. *Critical Studies in Media Communication, 30*, 17–33.
Butterworth, M. L. (2014). Nate Silver and campaign 2012: Sport, the statistical frame, and the rhetoric of electoral forecasting. *Journal of Communication, 64*, 895–914.
Butterworth, M. L. (2020). Sport and the quest for unity: How the logic of consensus undermines democratic culture. *Communication & Sport*, online first, doi: 10.1177/2167479519900160.
Butterworth, M. L., & Schuck, R. I. (2016). American mythology and ambivalent rhetoric in Friday Night Lights. *Southern Communication Journal, 81*, 92–106.
Cialdini, R. B., Borden, R. J., Thorne, A., Walker, M. R., Freeman, S., & Sloan, L. R. (1976). Basking in reflected glory: Three (football) field studies. *Journal of Personality and Social Psychology, 34*, 366–375.
Cisneros, J. D. (2008). Contaminated communities: The metaphor of "immigrant as pollutant" in media representations of immigration. *Rhetoric & Public Affairs, 11*, 569–602.
Collins, L. (2018, September 28). Brett Kavanaugh and the innocence of White jocks. *New York Times*. Retrieved from www.newyorker.com/news/our-columnists/brett-kavanaugh-and-the-innocence-of-white-jocks-christine-blasey-ford.
Connell, R. W. (1990). An iron man: The body and some contradictions of hegemonic masculinity. In M. A. Messner & D. F. Sabo (Eds.), *Sport, men, and the gender order: Critical feminist perspectives* (pp. 83–95). Champaign, IL: Human Kinetics.
Crisp, R. J., Heuston, S., Farr, M. J., & Turner, R. N. (2007). Seeing red or feeling blue: Differentiated intergroup emotions and ingroup identification in soccer fans. *Group Processes & Intergroup Relations, 10*, 9–26.

Cummins, R. G. (2009). The effects of subjective camera and fanship on viewers' experience of presence and perception of play in sports telecasts. *Journal of Applied Communication Research, 37*, 374–396.

Cunningham, P. L. (2009). "Please don't fine me again!!!!!" Black athletic defiance in the NBA and NFL. *Journal of Sport & Social Issues, 33*, 39–58.

Dann, C. (2018, October 22). Poll: Kavanaugh fallout continues to polarize voters ahead of midterms. *NBC News*. Retrieved from www.nbcnews.com/politics/first-read/poll-kavanaugh-fallout-continues-polarize-voters-ahead-midterms-n922241.

Earnheardt, A. C., & Haridakis, P. M. (2008). Exploring fandom and motives for viewing televised sports. In L. W. Hugenberg, P. M. Haridakis, & A. C. Earnheardt (Eds.), *Sports mania: Essays on fandom and the media in the 21st century* (pp. 158–171). Jefferson, NC: McFarland.

Ellis, C., & Stimson, J. A. (2012). *Ideology in America*. New York: Cambridge University Press.

Enck-Wanzer, D. (2011). Barack Obama, the Tea Party, and the threat of race: On racial neoliberalism and born again racism. *Communication, Culture & Critique, 4*, 23–30.

Engels, J. *Enemyship: Democracy and counter-revolution in the early republic*. East Lansing, MI: Michigan State University Press.

Foer, F. (2004). *How soccer explains the world: An unlikely theory of globalization*. New York: HarperCollins.

Gantz, W., Wilson, B., Lee, H., & Fingerhut, D. (2008). Exploring the roots of sports fanship. In L. W. Hugenberg, P. M. Haridakis, & A. C. Earnheardt (Eds.), *Sports mania: Essays on fandom and the media in the 21st century* (pp. 68–77). Jefferson, NC: McFarland.

Grano, D. A. (2010). Risky dispositions: Thick moral description and character-talk in sports culture. *Southern Communication Journal, 75*, 255–276.

Griffin, R. A., & Calafell, B. M. (2011). Control, discipline, and punish: Black masculinity and (in)visible Whiteness in the NBA. In M. G. Lacy & K. A. Ono (Eds.), *Critical rhetorics of race* (pp. 117–136). New York: New York University Press.

Hawhee, D. (2005). *Bodily arts: Rhetoric and athletics in ancient Greece*. Austin, TX: University of Texas Press.

Hruby, P. (2012, January 4). The SportsCenter-ization of political journalism. *The Atlantic*. Retrieved from www.theatlantic.com/politics/archive/2012/01/the-sportscenter-ization-of-political-journalism/250882/.

Ivie, R. L. (1987). Metaphor and the rhetorical invention of Cold War "idealists." *Communication Monographs, 54*, 165–182.

Ivie, R. L. (2005). *Democracy and America's war on terror*. Tuscaloosa, AL: University of Alabama Press.

Jamieson, K. H. (1992). *Dirty politics: Deception, distraction, and democracy*. New York: Oxford University Press.

Jarvis, S. E. (2005). *The talk of the party: Political labels, symbolic capital & American life*. Lanham, MD: Rowman & Littlefield.

Karson, K. (2019, July 28). Partisan differences on impeachment remain after Mueller testimony, as nearly half of Americans show little movement: Poll. *ABC News*. Retrieved from https://abcnews.go.com/Politics/partisan-differences-impeachment-remain-mueller-testimony-half-americans/story?id=64587293.

Lakoff, G. (2002). *Moral politics: How liberals and conservatives think*. Chicago: University of Chicago Press.

Lee, Michael. J. (2014). *Creating conservatism: Postwar words that made an American movement*. East Lansing, MI: Michigan State University Press.

Lehr, S. A., Ferreira, M. L., & Banaji, M. R. (2019). When outgroup negativity trumps ingroup positivity: Fans of the Boston Red Sox and New York Yankees place greater value on rival losses than own-team gains. *Group Processes & Intergroup Relations, 22*, 26–42.

Leitch, W. (2018, October 2). Along with everything else, Brett Kavanaugh is an obnoxious jock. *New York Magazine*. Retrieved from http://nymag.com/intelligencer/2018/10/brett-kavanaugh-is-an-obnoxious-jock.html.

Levitsky, S., & Ziblatt, D. (2018). *How democracies die*. New York: Broadway Books.

Lipsky, R. (1979). The athleticization of politics: The political implications of sports symbolism. *Journal of Sport & Social Issues, 3*, 28–37.

Lipsyte, R. (1975). *SportsWorld: An American dreamland*. New York: Quadrangle.

Lithwick, D. (2018, September 6). Brett Kavanaugh's confirmation isn't a sporting event. *Slate.com*. Retrieved from https://slate.com/news-and-politics/2018/09/kavanaugh-confirmation-hearing-protesters-roe-v-wade.html.

Malone, N. (2018, September 28). Kavanaugh: Such a Brett. *The Cut*. Retrieved from www.thecut.com/2018/09/brett-kavanaugh-prep-school.html#_ga=2.10965171.625430380.1553701735-440691931.1553701735.

Mason, L. (2018). *Uncivil agreement: How politics became our identity*. Chicago: University of Chicago Press.

Moskovitz, D. (2018, September 28). Brett Kavanaugh and the myth that sports build better men. *Jezebel.com*. Retrieved from https://theslot.jezebel.com/brett-kavanaugh-and-the-myth-that-sports-build-better-m-1829381019.

Mouffe, C. (2000). *The democratic paradox*. London: Verso.

Nguyen, T. (2018, October 10). Will Kavanaugh fever kill the blue wave? *Vanity Fair*. Retrieved from www.vanityfair.com/news/2018/10/brett-kavanaugh-midterms-republican-democrat-turnout.

O'Neil, L. (2016, June 11). Status and race in the Stanford rape case: Why Brock Turner's mug shot matters. *CBC News*. Retrieved from www.cbc.ca/news/trending/brock-turner-mugshot-stanford-rape-case-images-sex-assault-1.3629147.

Osborn, M. (1967). Archetypal metaphor in rhetoric: The light-dark family. *Quarterly Journal of Speech, 53*, 115–126.

Osnos, E. (2015, August 14). The fearful and the frustrated: Donald Trump's nationalist coalition takes shape—for now. *The New Yorker*. Retrieved from www.newyorker.com/magazine/2015/08/31/the-fearful-and-the-frustrated.

Re, G. (2018, October 14). Kavanaugh slugfest could boost GOP in midterms, as polls show voter interest rising. *Fox News*. Retrieved from www.foxnews.com/politics/kavanaugh-slugfest-could-boost-gop-in-midterms-as-polls-show-voter-interest-rising.

Segrave, J. O. (2000). The sports metaphor in American cultural discourse. *Culture, Sport, Society, 3*, 48–60.

Sheeler, K. H., & Anderson, K. V. (2013). *Woman president: Confronting postfeminist political culture*. College Station, TX: Texas A&M University Press.

Shepard, S. (2018, October 1). Poll: Kavanaugh opinion hardens along partisan lines. *Politico.com*. Retrieved from www.politico.com/story/2018/10/01/poll-kavanaugh-ford-opinion-854860.

Shields, D., & Bredemeier, B. (2011). Contest, competition, and metaphor. *Journal of the Philosophy of Sport, 38*, 27–38.

Stack, L. (2016, June 6). Light sentence for Brock Turner in Stanford rape case draws outrage. *New York Times*. Retrieved from www.nytimes.com/2016/06/07/us/outrage-in-stanford-rape-case-over-dueling-statements-of-victim-and-attackers-father.html.

Sun, D. (2018, October 7). Lawsuit threatened over UW College Republicans' Kavanaugh celebration at local bar. *KIRO-7*. Retrieved from www.kiro7.com/news/local/lawsuit-threatened-over-uw-college-republicans-kavanaugh-celebration-at-local-bar/848428093.

Tafjel, H., & Turner, J. C. (1986). The social identity theory of intergroup behavior. In S. Worchel & W. G. Austin (Eds.), *Psychology of intergroup relations* (2nd ed., pp. 7–24). Chicago: Nelson-Hall Publishers.

Tannenbaum, P. H., & Noah, J. E. (1959). Sportugese: A study of sports page communication. *Journalism Quarterly, 36*, 163–170.

Trujillo, N. (1991). Hegemonic masculinity on the mound: Media representations of Nolan Ryan and American sports culture. *Critical Studies in Mass Communication, 8*, 290–308.

Velencia, J., & Mehta, D. (2018, October 5). A final look at where voters stand on Kavanaugh before the Senate votes. *FiveThirtyEight.com*. Retrieved from https://fivethirtyeight.com/features/a-final-look-at-where-voters-stand-on-kavanaugh-before-the-senate-votes/.

Wann, D. L. (2006). The causes and consequences of sport team identification. In A. A. Raney & J. Bryant (Eds.), *Handbook of sports and media* (pp. 331–352). Mahwah, NJ: Erlbaum.

Wann, D. L., & Branscombe, N. R. (1992). Emotional responses to the sports page. *Journal of Sport and Social Issues, 6*, 49–64.

Williams, Z. (2018, April 25). "Raw hatred": Why the "incel" movement targets and terrorizes women. *The Guardian*. Retrieved from www.theguardian.com/world/2018/apr/25/raw-hatred-why-incel-movement-targets-terrorises-women.

Woodward, J. R. (2004). Professional football scouts: An investigation of racial stacking. *Sociology of Sport Journal, 21*, 356–375.

3

Using Sport Fandom to Fulfill Personal and Societal Needs

Daniel L. Wann

There are few pastimes that rival the popularity of sport fandom. Indeed, one simply has to consider the pervasiveness of this activity to understand its seemingly universal appeal (Wann & James, 2019). For example, sport is prominently featured in various forms of mass media, including radio broadcasts, television programing, and Internet sites. Additionally, sport and the fans who follow it are often the focus of movies and songs. And certainly, the multitude of fans attending sporting events suggests that this activity is a driving force in the lives of many people. Researchers (e.g., Thomas et al., 2017) have noted that participation in an athletic event can help individuals meet important needs. Furthermore, given that humans have been interested in observing sporting spectacles for thousands of years (Guttmann, 1986), and followers of sport can be found in almost all cultures (Serazio, 2019), it stands to reason that sport fandom can also play an important role in fulfilling both individual and societal needs. Indeed, a key question within the psychological and sociological study of sport fandom has been how, and to what extent, involvement in the pastime provides personal and societal benefits. In this chapter, we will examine this question by reviewing multiple streams of research and theory to uncover several individual and societal needs that can be – at least partially – be met via sport fandom.

However, before proceeding to a discussion of the specific individual and societal needs impacted by sport fandom, it warrants mention that the current examination is not meant to be an exhaustive list of needs to be met via sport fandom. Rather, the goal of the current chapter is to give the reader a general impression of how fandom matters both to the individual fans and the societies in which they live. There are likely other needs that can be partially fulfilled via this pastime in addition to those targeted in the current chapter.

Individual Needs Met Through Sport Fandom

In this section, we will examine four important individual needs that can be at least partially met through sport fandom. First, we will target the need to belong, that is, the desire to establish and maintain memberships in valued social groups. Next, the discussion will center on the need for distinctiveness, which concerns our desire to feel unique and special. The third personal need we will inspect is our need for uncertainty reduction, that is, the desire to decrease the randomness of life events. And finally, we will review how sport fandom can partially satisfy our search for meaning in life.

Sport Fandom and the Need to Belong

One of the most powerful influences on human affect, behavior, and cognition is our innate desire to "form and maintain strong, stable interpersonal relationships" (Baumeister & Leary, 1995, p. 497). Often referred to as the need to belong, this drive is reflected in our yearning to socialize and spend meaningful time with others. Given that sport is a social activity and the vast majority of fans consume sport as part of a group (Schurr, Wittig, Ruble, & Ellen, 1988; Wann, Friedman, McHale, & Jaffe, 2003), it seems plausible that individuals could partially fulfill their desire to affiliate through sport fandom (Serazio, 2019). Consistent with this logic, researchers have indeed found that individuals use sport fandom to establish and maintain connections with others and, thus, assist in their quest to satisfy their need to belong (Kim & James, 2019; Kim, Kim, & Kim, 2017; Lock & Funk, 2016; Theodorakis, Wann, Nassis, & Luellen, 2012; Wann, Waddill, Brasher, & Ladd, 2015; Wann, Waddill, Polk, & Weaver, 2011).

There appear to be two primary methods through which sport fandom can assist in our need to belong: sport fandom itself and team identification. First, simply being a sport fan (that is, someone with an interest in following a particular aspect of sport – see Hackfort, Schinke, & Strauss, 2019; Wann & James, 2019) could lead to connections by finding like-minded individuals. People are aware that sport fandom is a pervasive activity and that most people are in fact sport fans. Thus, individuals who are interested in increasing their social connections may realize that they can accomplish this goal by becoming or maintaining their involvement in sport as a fan. Second, individuals can increase their social networks by developing a fandom for a specific team. By becoming psychologically connected to a team (commonly referred to as team identification – see Hackfort et al., 2019; Wann & James, 2019), individuals can gain a sense of belonging with other supporters of that team. For example, individuals who live in Boston can become interested in the Red Sox and, as a consequence, add many people to their social network through their membership in "Red Sox Nation." One might want to argue that, because the majority of these associations would be superficial, they would be of limited value. However, research suggests that connections and interactions with others do not have to be intimate to be beneficial (Sandstrom & Dunn, 2014a, 2014b). Thus, even casual acquaintances made via one's general sport fandom or identification with a specific team are valuable and can aid in meeting our need to belong.

Sport Fandom and the Need for Distinctiveness

As predicted by Brewer's (1991) Optimal Distinctiveness Theory, individuals strive for two sometimes opposing social goals: inclusion and differentiation. That is, although people want to feel a sense of belonging with others, they also have a desire to feel unique and different. By selectively choosing to follow non-mainstream sports and teams (or by supporting distant teams), individuals can use sport fandom to help fulfill their need for distinction (Andrijiw & Hyatt, 2009; Asada & Ko, in press; Dimmock & Gucciardi, 2008; Goldman, Chadwick, Funk, & Wocke, 2016). For example, an individual living in New York City could use sport fandom to aid in his or her need for distinctiveness by actively supporting the Boston Red Sox or by becoming interested in less popular sports such as curling or cricket.

In a series of studies, DeRossett and Wann (2018) empirically documented the relationships among sport fandom, the need to belong, and the need for distinctiveness. The goal of this work was to determine if levels of belongingness and distinctiveness would be related to choices of favorite teams and sports. The authors hypothesized that people with higher levels of the need to belong would be more likely to follow mainstream sports and teams, while those with higher levels of the need for distinctiveness would be partial to those that are more unique. Interestingly, in their first study, neither pattern of effects was found. That is, they failed to find a relationship between levels of need to belong and uniqueness and levels of identification with a mainstream and less-mainstream sport team. Similarly, a second study found no relationship between belonging and uniqueness and having a mainstream (e.g., football) or non-mainstream sport (e.g., archery) as a favorite. The authors reasoned that, given that there are many factors that drive one's initial interest in sports and teams (Funk & James, 2001; Wann & James, 2019; Wann, Tucker, & Schrader, 1996), the impact of need for distinctiveness and belonging may be most apparent at the initial stages of one's connection with sports and teams.

Thus, in a third study, participants read a scenario detailing two fictional Australian cricket teams. The descriptions were generally identical (e.g., both teams were said to be equally successful), but one team was described as having a large following (i.e., the mainstream team), while the other was described as being less popular. Participants were asked to choose which team they would most likely support, should they move to Australia. An examination of levels of need for belongingness and need for distinctiveness confirmed expectations. Specifically, those who believed they would follow the more unique team had higher levels of need for distinctiveness than those selecting the more popular team. Furthermore, participants higher in the need for belongingness reported a greater expectation of supporting the mainstream team. As a real-life example, consider NBA fans who move to Los Angeles and have a choice of supporting the Lakers and their large following, or the more niche team, the Clippers. Given the results described above, one could expect those with higher need for belonging to choose the Lakers, while those with higher need for distinction would prefer to support the Clippers.

Sport Fandom and Uncertainty Reduction

A third individual need that can be at least partially fulfilled through sport fandom concerns our desire to reduce uncertainty. Subjective Uncertainty Reduction Theory (Hogg & Abrams, 1993) argues that people strive to reduce uncertainty because decreased randomness (e.g., increased structure) results in better predictably and understanding of acceptable forms of behavior. Given that one common method of gaining certainty is via shared group memberships (Grieve & Hogg, 1999), it stands to reason that individuals may use their associations with fans of specific sports and teams to reduce uncertainty (Asada & Ko, in press). Such was the pattern of effects predicted by Dimmock and Grove (2006). These authors asked adolescents to complete a measure assessing the desire for certainty, and then used these scores to place the participants into groups of individuals low, moderate, and high in the need for structure. Subjects also completed a measure assessing their affective/cognitive identification with their favorite team. Consistent with expectations, the researchers found that the highest levels of identification were reported by those in the high need for structure group, while the lowest identification scores were found among those with a low need for structure.

Hofstede (2001, 2011) identified a number of dimensions on which cultures differ, including the extent to which a culture is individualistic or collectivistic (i.e., the extent to which members of a society are integrated into group) and the culture's degree of power distance, that is, whether or not individuals believe and accept that power is unequally distributed in their culture. Another critical dimension, and one related to our discussion here, is termed uncertainty avoidance. According to Hofstede, this dimension involves "society's tolerance for ambiguity" and involves the extent to which "a culture programs its members to feel either uncomfortable or comfortable in unstructured situations" (Hofstede & McCrae, 2004, p. 62). Some cultures, labeled uncertainty-avoiding cultures, tend to have high number of laws and societal norms to assist in reducing uncertainty. Other cultures are more accepting of uncertainty; these societies tend to have fewer rules and regulations. Given that individuals can potentially use their involvement in sport fandom to reduce uncertainty (Dimmock & Grove, 2006), it would be interesting to examine whether those living in uncertainty-avoiding cultures are particularly likely to utilize sport fandom for this purpose. Future researchers, perhaps those with an interest in sport fandom from a sociological perspective, may be able to test this possibility by examining the correlation between the degree to which members of societies are uncomfortable with uncertainty and the levels of fandom (or at least the importance of fandom) within those societies.

Sport Fandom and Meaning in Life

A final personal need that may be partially met via sport fandom is the search for meaning in life (Frankl, 1963; Lambert et al., 2013; Seligman, 2011). Meaning has been defined as "the sense of purpose individuals derive from feeling a part of something larger than their self" (Doyle, Filo, Lock, Funk, & McDonald, 2016, p. 4). Meaning in life is a critical psychological variable as it correlates positively with both mental and physical health (Czekierda, Banik, Park, & Luszczynska, 2017; Heintzelman & King, 2014).

When asked to indicate factors that provide meaning in life, two commonly mentioned sources are social connections (e.g., friends and family) and leisure pursuits such as hobbies and pastimes (Steger, Frazier, Oishi, & Kaler, 2006; Where Americans find meaning in life, 2018). Given that sport fandom is a highly social leisure pursuit, it stands to reason that fandom could be a factor in promoting beliefs that one's life has meaning and purpose. Furthermore, because sport fandom can add structure and reduce uncertainty in people's lives (see above), and research indicates that life structure and routines predict meaning in life (Heintzelman & King, 2019), sport fandom may be a particularly useful avenue for promoting feelings that one's life has purpose. Consistent with this logic, writers have argued that sport fandom can assist in an individual's search for meaning (e.g., Keaton & Gearhart, 2014; Mandelbaum, 2004; Serazio, 2019) and research has substantiated this claim. For example, Doyle and his colleagues (2016) conducted a qualitative study investigating the extent to which fans believed that following teams assisted in maintaining and enhancing their psychological well-being. One frequently mentioned positive outcome was meaning in life. Experiences such as meeting with players, visiting the team's stadium/arena, and special events were described by fans as ways in which "supporting the team helped them feel like something larger than themselves" (Doyle et al., p. 8).

In another empirical investigation of sport fandom and purpose in life, Wann and Fast (2020) asked individuals to indicate the extent to which they believed that following sport as a fan provided meaning in their lives. The results revealed several interesting findings. First, it was apparent that many individuals believe that sport fandom provides them with a sense of purpose and meaning. However, some individuals were more likely than others to report such a belief. Specifically, perceptions of sport fandom facilitating life meaning were positively correlated with both general sport fandom and levels of identification with one's favorite team. Thus, as one might expect, fandom as a route to meaning in life is more available to those who actually engage in the activity.

A final study worthy of mention was conducted by Wann, Hackathorn, and Sherman (2017). These authors examined the interrelationships among sport fandom, team identification, sense of belonging, and meaning in life. Wann and his associates framed their project within the tenets of the Team Identification – Social Psychological Health Model (Wann, 2006). This perspective argues that, similar to identification in other organizational settings (Steffens, Haslam, Schuh, Jetten, & van Dick, 2017), sport team identification (and perhaps sport fandom – see Wann & James, 2019) leads to improved well-being. Wann et al. (2017) found that belonging mediated the relationship between fandom (both general sport fandom and team identification) and meaning in life. Thus, their data suggest that as one's fandom increases, so too does their sense of belonging. Then, in turn, these increased feelings of belonging result in greater perceptions that life has meaning.

Societal Needs Met Through Sport Fandom

Turning our attention to society at large, research and theory suggests that, similar to individual needs, sport fandom has the capacity to aid in the satisfaction of several societal needs. The Structural-Functionalist Perspective argues that for a societal institution to exist, it must contribute to the maintenance (i.e., survival) of a society. There are several imperatives that societies must address to remain viable (Aberle, Cohen, Davis, Levy, & Sutton, 1950; Parsons, 1951; Stevenson, 1974) and research suggests that sport fandom assists in meeting several of these necessities (Delaney, 2015; Lewis, 2007; Shin, 2007). In the paragraphs that follow, we will examine the impact of sport fandom on four societal needs, that is, methods through which fandom assists in meeting societal imperatives (there are other imperatives impacted by fandom – see Wann & James, 2019 and Wann, Melnick, Russell, & Pease, 2001, for reviews). First, we will discuss how sport fandom gives members of societies an appropriate avenue for affective expression. Next, we will examine the argument that sport fandom aids in enhancing communication among various members of societies. Third, we focus on the manner in which sport fandom aids in the socialization process. And finally, we will discuss the variety of ways that sport fandom can facilitate integration among society's members.

Sport Fandom and Affective Expression

From a societal perspective, the powerful and frequent emotions felt by sport fans would be considered a critically beneficial aspect of the pastime. That is, one of the more important imperatives is that societies provide members with safe and accepted opportunities for emotional expression (Wann et al., 2001). Sport fandom frequently offers such an opportunity (Bain-Selbo, 2012; Cottingham, 2012). This includes positive emotions such as enjoyment, pride, and happiness (Jang, Ko, Wann, & Kim, 2017; Koenigstorfer, Groeppel-Klein, & Schmitt, 2010; Tobar, 2006) and negative reactions such as shame, anger, and disappointment (Jones, Coffee, Sheffield, Yanguez, & Barker, 2012; Partridge, Wann, & Elison, 2010; Rainey, Larsen, & Yost, 2009). Given that Wann and James (2019) highlight research examining over two dozen different fan affective reactions, it seems sport fandom allows for the acceptable and appropriate expression of all facets and forms of the human emotional experience.

Sport Fandom and Enhanced Communication

A second societal imperative that is partially met by sport fandom involves communication among society's members. To function successfully, societies must provide occasions for communication and, preferably, offer individuals different topics of conversation (Aberle et al., 1950). Sport appears to have the ability to assist in each of these endeavors. First, it is clear that sport is a topic of conversation for many individuals. For sport fans, discussions about their favorite teams, sports, and players are commonplace. The saturation of sport coverage on television, radio, and the Internet provides additional topics for conversation and fuels the discussion (in fact, a large portion of sport programing is now based on conversations and debates among members of the sport media – see Serazio, 2019).

However, sport fandom does not simply provide society's members with a topic of conversation. Rather, it also informs on how people are to converse and what they actually say (Serazio, 2019). That is, a second method through which fandom assists in the communication imperative is by providing words and phrases that have moved beyond the realm of sport and are now part of everyday language. Referred to as "Sportugese" by Tannenbaum and Noah (1959), there are literally hundreds of words and phrases that originated in sport, but are now accepted and understood outside the realm of athletic competition (Palmatier & Ray, 1989). Phrases such as "hit it out of the park" and "scored a touchdown" not only describe successful outcomes in baseball and football, but are now also used to describe non-sport endeavors in which one has succeeded.

Sport Fandom and the Socialization Process

Yet another societal imperative aided through sport fandom involves the socialization process. A number of authors have written about the process through which individuals are socialized into sport fandom (e.g., Funk & James, 2001; McPherson, 1976), discussing how family members, peers, and other socialization agents encourage one to become a sport fan, and teach the accepted norms, behaviors, and values in this pastime (Thompson & Forsyth, 2012; Wann et al., 2001; Yoh, Pai, & Pedersen, 2009). However, in addition to being socialized *into* sport fandom, members of a society can be socialized *through* sport fandom (Delaney, 2015; Edwards, 1973; Lewis, 2007; Serazio, 2019). That is, sport fandom has the ability to teach individuals about society at large, and provide strategies for successful living. Consistent with this thinking, research has found that sport fandom can influence the values and attitudes of sport fans (both positively and negatively – see Brown, Basil, & Bocarea, 2003; Wann & James, 2019).

Research on socialization into sport fandom has frequently found cultural differences in the relative impact of various socialization agents (Wann & James, 2019). This seems reasonable given that cultures highlight and emphasize different aspects of the sporting experience and, as a result, different aspects of cultures should play a greater or lesser role in sport fan socialization. For example, consider work by Melnick and Wann (2004) on the impact of different agents on the socialization of Norwegian sport fans. In many cultures, such as the United States and the United Kingdom, one's community is ranked very low in its influence on the sport fan socialization process (Parry, Jones, & Wann, 2014; Wann et al., 2001). However, Norwegian participants ranked their community as having the largest influence on their development as sport fans. Melnick and Wann noted that, because Norway operates via a club youth sports model (i.e., the top youth players play for club teams) rather than a varsity youth sports model (in which the top players play for school teams), it made sense for the community (and the sport clubs in them) to have such a large impact on sport fan socialization. Relating this work back to how members of society are socialized by sport fandom, it seems likely that fandom affects culture at the same time as culture affects fandom. That is to say, if socialization into fandom differs by culture, then it seems likely that there will also be cultural differences in socialization via fandom. Researchers may want to investigate this to determine if such differences do exist, and if so, how cultures are the same or dissimilar in this process.

Sport Fandom and Integration

A final societal imperative impacted by sport fandom concerns integration. Most societies are comprised of people from multiple ethnic, racial, religious, and political backgrounds. Additionally, societies contain people from rural and urban backgrounds, individuals with wide differences in educational experiences, and people from diverse socioeconomic groups. Given this, a key imperative for societies is to find and develop methods to integrate these vastly different persons, that is, provide opportunities and experiences that have the capacity to bring these otherwise different people together. Sport fandom is one such opportunity, and a powerful one at that, as involvement in this pastime can foster integration at multiple levels (Groeneman, 2017; Kim & Walker, 2012; Markovits & Albertson, 2012; Serazio, 2019). First, sport fandom can increase integration at the interpersonal level. As noted above, sport fandom is a highly social activity that has the ability to increase feelings of belonging and connections with others (Koenig-Lewis, Asaad, & Palmer, 2017; Theodorakis et al., 2012; Wann, Waddill, et al., 2015). Even brief encounters with fellow sport fans and supporters of favorite teams can allow for critical interpersonal interactions that will often facilitate integration (Melnick, 1993). These interpersonal encounters and increased integration can have important benefits. For instance, sport fans report high levels of trust in people (Wann & Polk, 2007) and fandom can be positively associated with increased helping of others (particularly others fans, see Levine, Prossner, Evans, & Reicher, 2005; Platow et al., 1999).

However, integration via sport fandom is not limited to the interpersonal level. Rather, it also facilitates connections among larger groups of people. For example, integration at the community and metropolitan (i.e., city) levels are also nurtured via sport fandom (Oja, Wear, & Clopton, 2018; Wilkerson & Dodder, 1987). As a clear example of such integration, consider that the official celebration of the 2016 Chicago Cubs (long-awaited) World Series Championship was attended by approximately 5 million people, ranking it as one of the largest human gatherings on record (Flosi, 2016). Similarly, sport fandom can promote integration at the state level. For example, the University of Nebraska football team is a cultural phenomenon that has a statewide following, promoting interactions from people all across the region (Aden, 2008). At the national level, sport has the ability to integrate an entire country (Hoye & Nicholson, 2008), such as when the 1980 United States men's ice hockey team captivated the county with the "Miracle on Ice" Olympic gold medal. And finally, sport may have the ability to aid in integration at the international level through events such as the Olympics and the World Cup soccer championships (Allison & Monnington, 2002; Serazio, 2019).

Conclusion

A key question for sport scholars has been if and how involvement in sport as a fan can provide personal and societal benefits. As discussed above, research and theory reveal that sport fandom does indeed have the ability to help individuals meet several basic personal and societal needs. In this way, sport fandom seems to reflect the Gestalt psychology adage that "the whole is greater than the sum of the parts" (Galotti, 2018). That is, the value of sport fandom, for both people and societies, is far greater than what it appears to be on the surface. As the preceding pages highlight, these benefits are numerous and far reaching. However, in truth sport scholars have only recently begun to examine and unpack the benefits of fandom and, as a result, there is still much to learn. For example, because the vast majority of published work on sport fandom has targeted English speaking countries (Wann & James, 2019), more research from a cross-cultural perspective is needed. Additionally, investigators need to continue to expand their methodologies and incorporate mixed method and longitudinal designs into their work. By using a wider variety of research tools to examine the potential benefits of fandom, researchers can advance our understanding of the value and importance of sport fandom in the lives of individual fans and the societies in which they live.

References

Aberle, D. F., Cohen, A. K., Davis, A. K., Levy, M. J., & Sutton, F. S. (1950). The functional prerequisites of a society. *Ethics, 60,* 100–111.

Aden, R. C. (2008). *Huskerville: A story of Nebraska football, fans, and the power of place.* Jefferson, NC: McFarland.

Allison, L., & Monnington, T. (2002). Sport, prestige, and international relations. *Government and Opposition, 37,* 106–134.

Andrijiw, A. M., & Hyatt, C. G. (2009). Using optimal distinctiveness theory to understand identification with a nonlocal professional hockey team. *Journal of Sport Management, 23,* 156–181.

Asada, A., & Ko, Y. J. (in press). Conceptualizing relative size and entitativity of sports fan community and their roles in sport socialization. *Journal of Sport Management.*

Bain-Selbo, E. (2012). *Game day and God: Football, faith, and politics in the American South.* Macon, GA: Mercer University Press.

Baumeister, R. F., & Leary, M. R. (1995). The need to belong: Desire for interpersonal attachments as a fundamental human motivation. *Psychological Bulletin, 117,* 497–529.

Brewer, M. B. (1991). The social self: On being the same and being different at the same time. *Personality and Social Psychology Bulletin, 17,* 475–482.

Brown, W. J., Basil, M. D., & Bocarea, M. C. (2003). The influence of famous athletes on health beliefs and practices: Mark McGwire, child abuse prevention, and Androstenedione. *Journal of Health Communication, 8,* 41–57.

Cottingham, M. D. (2012). Interaction ritual theory and sports fans: Emotion, symbols, and solidarity. *Sociology of Sport Journal, 29,* 168–185.

Czekierda, K., Banik, A., Park, C. L., & Luszczynska, A. (2017). Meaning in life and physical health: Systematic review and meta-analysis. *Health Psychology Review, 11,* 387–413.

Delaney, T. (2015). The functionalist perspective on sport. In R. Giulianotti (Ed.) *Routledge handbook of the sociology of sport* (pp. 18–28). New York: Routledge.

DeRossett, T., & Wann, D. L. (2018, April). *The few, the proud, the distinct: The relationship between belonging and distinctiveness on sport team choice.* Poster presented at the annual meeting of the Midwestern Psychological Association, Chicago, IL.

Dimmock, J. A., & Grove, J. R. (2006). Identification with sport teams as a function of the search for certainly. *Journal of Sport Sciences, 24,* 1203–1211.

Dimmock, J. A., & Gucciari, D. F. (2008). The utility of modern theories of intergroup bias for research on antecedents to team identification. *Psychology of Sport and Exercise, 9,* 284–300.

Doyle, J. P., Filo, K., Lock, D., Funk, D. C., & McDonald, H. (2016). Exploring PERMA in spectator sport: Applying positive psychology to examine the individual-level benefits of sport consumption. *Sport Management Review, 19,* 506–519.

Edwards, H. (1973). *Sociology of sport.* Homewood, IL: The Dorsey Press.

Flosi, N. (2016, November 16). Cubs World Series celebration ranks as 7th largest gathering in human history. Fox 32. Retrieved from: www.fox32chicago.com/news/local/cubs-world-series-celebration-ranks-as-7th-largest-gathering-in-human-history.

Frankl, V. E. (1963). *Man's search for meaning: An introduction to logotherapy.* New York: Washington Square Press.

Funk, D. C., & James, J. (2001). The psychological continuum model: A conceptual framework for understanding an individual's psychological connection to sport. *Sport Management Review, 4,* 119–150.

Galotti, K. M. (2018). *Cognitive psychology: In and out of the laboratory* (6th ed.). Los Angeles, CA: Sage.

Goldman, M. M., Chadwick, S., Funk, D. C., & Wocke, A. (2016). I am distinctive when I belong: Meeting the need for optimal distinctiveness through team identification. *International Journal of Sport Management and Marketing, 16,* 198–220.

Grieve, P. G., & Hogg, M. A. (1999). Subjective uncertainty and intergroup discrimination in the minimal group situation. *Personality and Social Psychology Bulletin, 25,* 926–940.

Groeneman, S. (2017). *American's sports fans and their teams: Who roots for whom and why*. Lexington, KY: Seabird Press.
Guttmann, A. (1986). *Sports spectators*. New York: Columbia University Press.
Hackfort, D., Schinke, R. J., & Strauss, B. (Eds.) (2019). *Dictionary of sport psychology: Sport, exercise, and performing arts*. London: Academic Press.
Heintzelman, S. J., & King, L. A. (2014). Life is pretty meaningful. *The American Psychologist, 69*, 561–574.
Heintzelman, S. J., & King, L. A. (2019). Routines and meaning in life. *Personality and Social Psychology Bulletin, 45*, 688–699.
Hofstede, G. (2001). *Cultures consequences: Comparing values, behaviors, institutions, and organizations across nations* (2nd ed.). Thousand Oaks, CA: Sage.
Hofstede, G. (2011). Dimensionalizing cultures: The Hofstede model in context. *Online Readings in Psychology and Culture, 2*(1), 2307–0919.
Hofstede, G., & McCrae, R. R. (2004). Personality and culture revisited: Linking traits and dimensions of culture. *Cross-Cultural Research, 33*, 52–88.
Hogg, M. A., & Abrams, D. (1993). Towards a single-process uncertainty-reduction model of social motivation in groups. In M. A. Hogg & D. Abrams (Eds.), *Group motivation: Social psychological perspectives* (pp. 173–190). Birmingham: Harvester Wheatsheaf.
Hoye, R., & Nicholson, M. (2008). Locating social capital in sport policy. In M. Nicholson & R. Hoye (Eds.). *Sport and social capital* (pp. 69–91). New York: Elsevier.
Jang, W., Ko, Y. J., Wann, D. L., & Kim, D. (2017). Does spectatorship increase happiness? The energy perspective. *Journal of Sport Management, 31*, 333–344.
Jones, M. V., Coffee, P., Sheffield, D., Yanguez, M., & Barker, J. B. (2012). Just a game? Changes in English and Spanish soccer fans' emotions in the 2010 World Cup. *Psychology of Sport and Exercise, 13*, 162–169.
Keaton, S. A., & Gearhart, C. C. (2014). Identity formation, identify strength, and self-categorization as predictors of affective and psychological outcomes: A model reflecting sport team fans' responses to highlights and lowlights of a college football season. *Communication & Sport, 2*, 363–385.
Kim, J., & James, J. D. (2019). Sport and happiness: Understanding the relations among sport consumption activities, long- and short-term subjective well-being, and psychological need fulfillment. *Journal of Sport Management, 33*, 119–132.
Kim, J., Kim, Y., & Kim, D. (2017). Improving well-being through hedonic, eudaimonic, and social needs fulfillment in sport media consumption. *Sport Management Review, 20*, 309–321.
Kim, W., & Walker, M. (2012). Measuring the social impacts associated with Super Bowl XLIII: Preliminary development of a psych income scale. *Sport Management Review, 15*, 91–108.
Koenig-Lewis, N., Asaad, Y., & Palmer, A. (2017). Sport events and interaction among spectators: Examining antecedents of spectators value creation. *European Sport Management Quarterly, 18*, 193–215.
Koenigstorfer, J., Groeppel-Klein, A., & Schmitt, M. (2010). "You'll never walk alone"—How loyal are soccer fans to the clubs when they are struggling against relegation? *Journal of Sport Management, 24*, 649–675.
Lambert, N. M., Stillman, T. F., Hicks, J. A., Kamble, S., Baumeister, R. F., & Fincham, F. D. (2013). To belong is to matter: Sense of belonging enhances meaning in life. *Personality and Social Psychology Bulletin, 39*, 1418–1427.
Levine, M., Prosser, A., Evans, D., & Reicher, S. (2005). Identity and emergency intervention: How social group membership and inclusiveness of group boundaries shape helping behavior. *Personality and Social Psychology Bulletin, 31*, 443–453.
Lewis, J. M. (2007). *Sports fan violence in North America*. New York: Rowman & Littlefield.
Lock, D. J., & Funk, D. C. (2016). The multiple in-group identity framework. *Sport Management Review, 19*, 85–96.
Mandelbaum, M. (2004). *The meaning of sports*. New York. Public Affairs.
Markovits, A. S., & Albertson, E. K. (2012). *Sportista: Female fandom in the United States*. Philadelphia: Temple University Press.
McPherson, B. (1976). Socialization into the role of sport consumer: A theory and causal model. *Canadian Review of Sociology and Anthropology, 13*, 165–177.
Melnick, M. J. (1993). Searching for sociability in the stands: A theory of sports spectating. *Journal of Sport Management, 7*, 44–60.
Melnick, M. J., & Wann, D. L. (2004). Sport fandom influences, interests, and behaviors among Norwegian university students. *International Sports Journal, 8*(1), 1–13.

Oja, B. D., Wear, H. T., & Clopton, A. W. (2018). Major sport events and psychic income: The social anchor effect. *Journal of Sport Management, 32*, 257–271.

Palmatier, R. A., & Ray, H. L. (1989). *Sports talk: A dictionary of sports metaphors.* Westport, CT: Greenwood Press.

Parry, K. D., Jones, I., & Wann, D. L. (2014). An examination of sport fandom in the United Kingdom: A comparative analysis of fan behaviors, socialization processes, and team identification. *Journal of Sport Behavior, 37*, 251–267.

Parsons, T. (1951). *The social system.* New York: The Free Press.

Partridge, J. A., Wann, D. L., & Elison, J. (2010). Understanding college sport fans' experiences of and attempts to cope with shame. *Journal of Sport Behavior, 33*, 160–175.

Platow, M. J., Durante, M., Williams, N., Garrett, M., Walshe, J., Cincotta, S., Lianos, G., & Barutchu, A. (1999). The contribution of sport fan social identity to the production of prosocial behavior. *Group Dynamics: Theory, Research and Practice, 3*, 161–169.

Rainey, D. W., Larsen, J., & Yost, J. H. (2009). Disappointment theory and disappointment among baseball fans. *Journal of Sport Behavior, 32*, 339–356.

Sandstrom, G. M., & Dunn, E. W. (2014a). Is efficiency overrated? Minimal social interactions lead to belonging and positive affect. *Social Psychology and Personality Science, 5*, 437–442.

Sandstrom, G. M., & Dunn, E. W. (2014b). Social interactions and well-being: The surprising power of weak ties. *Personality and Social Psychology Bulletin, 40*, 910–922.

Schurr, K. T., Wittig, A. F., Ruble, V. E., & Ellen, A. S. (1988). Demographic and personality characteristics associated with persistent, occasional, and nonattendance of university male basketball games by college students. *Journal of Sport Behavior, 11*, 3–17.

Seligman, M. E. P. (2011). *Flourish: A visionary new understanding of happiness and well-being.* New York: Atria.

Serazio, M. (2019). *The power of sports: Media and spectacle in American culture.* New York: New York University Press.

Shin, E. H. (2007). State, society, and economic development in sports life cycles: The case of boxing in Korea. *East Asia, 24*, 1–22.

Steffens, N. K., Haslam, S. A., Schuh, S. C., Jetten, J., & van Dick, R. (2017). A meta-analytic review of social identification and health in organizational contexts. *Personality and Psychology Review, 21*, 303–325.

Steger, M. F., Frazier, P., Oishi, S., & Kaler, M. (2006). The Meaning in Life Questionnaire: Assessing the presence of and search for meaning in life. *Journal of Counseling Psychology, 53*, 80–93.

Stevenson, C. L. (1974). Sport as a contemporary social phenomenon: A functional explanation. *International Journal of Physical Education, 11*, 8–13.

Tannenbaum, P. H., & Noah, J. E. (1959). Sportugese: A study of sports page communication. *Journalism Quarterly, 36*, 163–170.

Theodorakis, N. D., Wann, D. L., Nassis, P., & Luellen, T. B. (2012). The relationship between sport team identification and the need to belong. *International Journal of Sport Management and Marketing, 12*, 25–38.

Thomas, W. E., Brown, R., Easterbrook, M. J., Vignoes, V. L., Manzi, C., D'Angelo, C., & Holt, J. J. (2017). Social identification in sports teams: The role of personal, social, and collective identity motives. *Personality and Social Psychology Bulletin, 43*, 508–523.

Thompson, C. Y., & Forsyth, C. J. (2012). Women fans of the rodeo. In K. Toffoletti & P. Mewett (Eds.) *Sport and its female fans* (pp. 61–80). New York: Routledge.

Tobar, D. A. (2006). Affect and purchase intentions of Super Bowl XL television spectators: Examining the influence of sport fandom, age, and gender. *Sport Marketing Quarterly, 15*, 243–252.

Wann, D. L. (2006). Understanding the positive social psychological benefits of sport team identification: The Team Identification – Social Psychological Health Model. *Group Dynamics: Theory, Research, and Practice, 10*, 272–296.

Wann, D. L., & Fast, N. H. (2020). *Using sport fandom to aid in the search for meaning.* Unpublished manuscript.

Wann, D. L., Friedman, K, McHale, M., & Jaffe, A. (2003). The Norelco Sport Fanatics Survey: Understanding the behaviors of avid sport fans. *Psychological Reports, 92*, 930–936.

Wann, D. L., Hackathorn, J., & Sherman, M. R. (2017). Testing the team identification – social psychological health model: Mediational relationships among team identification, sport fandom, sense of belonging and meaning in life. *Group Dynamics: Theory, Research, and Practice, 21*, 94–107.

Wann, D. L., & James, J. D. (2019). *Sport fans: The psychology and social impact of fandom.* New York: Routledge.

Wann, D. L., Melnick, M. J., Russell, G. W., & Pease, D. G. (2001). *Sport fans: The psychology and social impact of spectators.* New York: Routledge Press.

Wann, D. L., & Polk, J. (2007). The positive relationship between sport team identification and belief in the trustworthiness of others. *North American Journal of Psychology, 9*, 251–256.

Wann, D. L., Tucker, K. B., & Schrader, M. P. (1996). An exploratory examination of the factors influencing the origination, continuation, and cessation of identification with sports teams. *Perceptual and Motor Skills, 82,* 995–1001.

Wann, D. L., Waddill, P. J., Brasher, M., & Ladd, S. (2015). Examining sport team identification, social connections, and social well-being among high school students. *Journal of Amateur Sport, 1*(2), 27–50.

Wann, D. L., Waddill, P. J., Polk, J., & Weaver, S. (2011). The Team Identification – Social Psychological Health Model: Sport fans gaining connections to others via sport team identification. *Group Dynamics: Theory, Research, and Practice, 15,* 75–89.

Where Americans find meaning in life. (2018, November 16). Americans most likely to mention family when describing what provides them with a sense of meaning. *Pew Research Center: Religion and Public Life.* Downloaded from: www.pewforum.org/2018/11/20/where-americans-find-meaning-in-life/pf_11-20-18_sources_of_meaning-00-02/.

Wilkerson, M., & Dodder, R. A. (1987). Collective conscience and sport in modern society: An empirical test of a model. *Journal of Leisure Research, 19,* 35–40.

Yoh, T., Pai, H.-T., & Pedersen, P. M. (2009). The influence of socialization agents on the fan loyalty of Korean teens. *International Journal of Sport Management and Marketing, 6,* 404–416.

4
Experiences of Female Fans in a Female-Defined Sport
Central, Valued and Visible

Toni Bruce and Margaret Henley

In this chapter, we respond to calls for further research into women's experiences as sports fans. These include the need for more comprehensive explorations of how women experience sports fandom (Jones, 2008)—based on the reality that females "have rarely been asked for their meanings" (Sveinson & Hoeber, 2015, p. 416)—and a "glaring need" for research in more countries and into sports beyond the dominant focus on male professional team sports (Toffoletti & Mewett, 2012, p. 5).

Our three-year ethnographic study goes further than existing studies of team sport fandom by investigating the most invisible group of sports fans—*female fans* of a *female-defined* sport. Our focus is netball, an international sport played in 80 countries, which is organised, run, and predominantly played by women. We agree with Toffoletti and Mewett (2012, p. 2) that it is time "to reclaim sport spectating as a site and practice of pleasure, empowerment, agency, identity formation and social connection for women". An analysis of fans of a sport that is culturally defined and experienced as feminine is a powerful place to begin that reclamation. The results challenge much of the existing research by exploring a context that is not defined by the articulation of sport and masculinity, and that produces a form of fandom deeply underpinned by women's ways of seeing the world (Andrew, 1997; Henley & Bruce, 2019; Marfell, 2016, 2019) and over which women see themselves as having agency and control.

The absence of female fans in sports fandom research is now widely recognised, and several recent books or edited collections have attempted to address this significant gap (e.g., Dunn, 2016; Osborne & Coombs, 2013; Pfister & Pope, 2018; Pope, 2017; Toffoletti & Mewett, 2012). Indeed, Toffoletti (2017) pointed out that, until recently, women sport fans had "remained largely invisible in both mainstream and academic accounts of sport fandom" (p. 1). The emerging research—which focuses primarily on female fans of *major men's sports*—has identified multiple challenges for female fans wanting to experience pleasure in their fandom, especially their marginality in sport spaces defined by men who are reluctant to acknowledge female sporting knowledge or fandom as authentic (Crawford & Gosling, 2004; Farrell, Fink & Fields, 2011; Osborne & Coombs, 2013). In such spaces, women have to negotiate, navigate and nuance their sport and gender identities to be accepted as knowledgeable or "real" fans (Curtin, 2015;

Esmonde, Cooky & Andrews, 2015; Gieseler, 2017; Osborne & Coombs, 2016; Pfister & Pope, 2018; Pope, 2013; Toffoletti, 2017).

Female fans have identified the need to balance the competing demands of domestic and family responsibilities in order to attend live games (Lenneis & Pfister, 2018), and some resolve this balance by engaging with sports that allow them to spend time with significant others, usually males (Farrell et al., 2011; Mintert & Pfister, 2015). Particularly in male football codes, the influence of familial males was "a lifelong phenomenon spanning generations" that included grandfathers, fathers, brothers, husbands and sons (Farrell et al., 2011, p. 190; Mewett & Toffoletti, 2011; Pope & Kirk, 2014). Women's fandom behaviours in these male-defined spaces are complex—particularly in relation to misogyny and homophobia—and run the gamut from downplaying abuse to reinforcing gender stereotypes to embracing dominant behaviours such as shouting, drinking, swearing, and abusing referees and opposing team players (Chiweshe, 2014; Jones, 2008; Klugman, 2012; Pfister, Lenneis & Mintert, 2013; Radmann & Hedenborg, 2018). Some studies have found that female fans enact a positive and communal fandom that has been overlooked in previous research on male fans, such as rejecting violence (Llopsis, Goig & Flores, 2018), and focusing on positivity, such as cheering rather than booing, having fun, and moderating their language and drinking (Sveinson & Hoeber, 2015). Women have formed women-only fan groups, travelled to games and socialised in female-only groups, and chosen sports and seats they perceived as safe, and where there is little swearing (Crawford & Gosling, 2004; Llopsis et al., 2018). The identified benefits of sports fandom for women include affirming personal and group identities, and feelings of community, pleasure and enjoyment (Obel, 2012; Dunn, 2016; Toffoletti, 2017). Overall, it is clear that female fans enact their *men's sport* fandom in multiple ways. As Toffoletti and Mewett (2012) summarise: "some female fans disturb, disrupt and challenge men's claiming of sport as their domain, a number 'masculinize' themselves, while yet others perform gender in ways that simultaneously conform to and subvert masculine hegemony" (p. 5).

In relation to an even less understood group—female fans of *women's sport*—there is very little research, the majority of which focuses on sports originally developed *by* and *for* men, whether they are played by men or women. Toffoletti (2017) attributes this absence to "the lesser value placed on women's sporting endeavours and the subsequent lack of attention given to female athleticism by a sport media and marketing industry that packages both male and female sport coverage for a presumed male viewer" (p. 20). In these sports, women's playing performances were contrasted with men's, and the female version presented as inferior, secondary, less exciting or less newsworthy (Bruce, 1998; Dunn, 2016, 2018). Female fans of women's basketball in the early 1990s were frustrated and scathing about low production values, arguing that "it's like they *have* to put them on. They don't [do] close-ups, they don't try to get the public really involved, to catch the eye of the viewers or anything" (Bruce, 1998, p. 381). Over a decade later, Meân (2012) identified the failure of WNBA.com to provide for sophisticated and knowledgeable fans, with the result that it "does not build a sense of excitement around female sport or collaborate in the discursive construction of serious female sport fandom" (p. 188). Although women's sport and the WNBA can provide places of belonging and connection, especially for lesbian and bisexual women (Dolance, 2005; Muller, 2007), researchers argue that this significant audience is sidelined by the WNBA's overt focus on young girls and family-friendly spaces (Muller Myrdahl, 2011). More recent research reveals how female fans have created inclusive social media and online communities in which women actively make their own meanings about sport and challenge male standards of fandom (Antunovic & Hardin, 2012; Olive, 2013).

Theoretical Approach

There are strong indications that female fans' motivations, preferences and experiences do not map neatly onto categories of fandom developed from research on male fans. Our ongoing ethnographic study of netball fans integrated a strengths-based indigenous approach that focuses on what "is already going well" and "shout[s] the reality of the lived experience of people" (Paraschak & Thompson, 2014, p. 1047), alongside third-wave and feminist cultural studies perspectives (Adams, Helstein, Kyoung-Kim et al., 2016; Bruce, 2016; Thorpe & Marfell, 2019). Bringing these theories together allowed us to acknowledge how women's experiences of fandom are shaped by a multiplicity of identities, including gender, race/ethnicity, sexuality, age, social class and national context, that must be continually negotiated (Antunovic and Whiteside, 2018; Toffoletti & Palmer, 2017), and simultaneously to question dominant ways of understanding sports fandom. It enabled us to ask third wave feminist questions like what if "our standard of measurement doesn't start with a White-male heterosexual nucleus?" (Baumgardner & Richards, 2000, p. 134; see also Markula, 2005). While numerous studies have identified being female "as one of the dividing lines between the 'real' fan [of men's sport] and the poser" (Osborne & Coombs, 2016, p. 14), the control of netball by women, its overwhelmingly female player, coach and umpire base, and the sport's fundamental association with, and celebration of, dominant forms of heterosexual femininity (Marfell, 2019), is more likely to position females as real fans. These intersecting lenses attuned us to the importance of investigating how sports such as netball are "organized, disciplined, represented, embodied and experienced" (Silk, Andrews & Thorpe, 2017, p. 5) over time and in different contexts. They led to methods that recognised the agency of women (and male fans), and focused on research *with* participants to identify how they understood and enacted their fandom.

Contextualising Netball

With over 20 million players in 80 countries, netball is a rare international team sport primarily run *by* and *for* women, and fundamentally underpinned by women's experiences, knowledge and beliefs. It is a court-based team sport (with some similarities to basketball), played at the elite level in four 15-minute quarters.

In New Zealand, netball is the premiere women's sport, with high participation rates, a strong financial base, an appealing television rights package, significant corporate support, and national recognition (Henley & Bruce, 2019). The elite competition, the ANZ Premiership, includes six teams, representing five regions. As a sporting practice, netball has been central to New Zealand women's lives and social wellbeing for over 120 years. Historically situated on the margins of sport, netball enabled women to physically liberate themselves from constricting social norms, carve out their own unique sporting spaces, and publicly demonstrate physical and organisational competence (Andrew, 1997; Henley, 2016; Marfell, 2019). Its success reflects netball administrators' awareness of, and decision to develop the game "to conform to social expectations" and "adapt to prevailing social conditions" (Andrew, 1997, p. 14).

The game's contemporary importance is evident in netball's sustained position as the most-played high-school sport despite its gender imbalance—98 per cent of players are female (New Zealand Secondary Schools Sports Council, 2019, 2020). In a country whose population only recently reached five million (Stats NZ, 2020), more than 300,000 girls and women participate annually in organised competitions, supported by thousands of volunteers (Netball New Zealand, 2011; Sport NZ, 2014). Netball's style and culture is influenced by the high numbers of players and growing numbers of elite coaches who are of Māori and Pasifika heritage (Andrew,

1997; Tunnicliffe, 2020b). The current national team reflects this ethnic diversity, with a Māori coach and 41 per cent of the players being of indigenous Māori and/or Pasifika heritage, the others being of Pākehā/white ethnicity.

The level of live broadcast coverage on national television since 1990 is globally unparalleled and the envy of many netball-playing nations (Henley, 2012; Henley & Bruce, 2019). Netball has enhanced national pride (Dougherty, 2004), with elite players and teams attracting a passionate and loyal fan base: in 2019, 3.23 million watched televised games, 2.2 million followed social media (Henley & Bruce, 2019; Needs, 2017; Netball New Zealand 2019). Even during the 2020 COVID-19-affected season, the elite ANZ Premiership games attracted a national television audience of 1.45 million and the Premiership social media engagement grew significantly to almost 389,000 (Netball New Zealand, 2020). Then, as New Zealand became the first nation to return to elite-level netball, "starved netball fans" from 96 countries tuned in, with almost 430,000 international streams of Premiership games (Netball New Zealand, 2020; Tunnicliffe, 2020a, para. 5). The national team, the Silver Ferns, are the most followed on social media, reflecting the strong connection of the team to national identity (Henley, 2004). The three most followed current and former Silver Ferns' players on social media are of Māori or Samoan heritage. In 2019, as part of the Silver Ferns preparation for the 2019 Netball World Cup, the national men's team played the Silver Ferns in the first-ever live broadcast in front of spectators. For men's team captain, Kruze Tangira it was a "dream come true" to play against his idols on television (Egan, 2020, para. 7; Silver Ferns TV, 2021). For teammate Junior Levi, such opportunities offer "credibility to men being included into the space that women currently occupy" (O'Keeffe, 2020, para. 11).

Methodology

Our three-year ethnographic immersion in netball fan culture involved multiple methods. We observed, took photographs, audio-recorded soundscapes, and conducted 220 informal "roving chats" of under 10 minutes with 370 spectators at over 20 live netball events between late 2018 and mid-2021. We also chatted with netball journalists, broadcasters and administrators about the realities of writing about, broadcasting or producing social media content. Finally, to understand fan culture beyond the live event, we joined two *private* Facebook netball discussion sites. The research was supported by Netball New Zealand, which provided us with media accreditation and full access to all games in New Zealand. We regularly attended games of the two Auckland-based teams, with data-gathering in four other cities. The "roving chats" were designed as a non-threatening form of collaborative ethnography, in which researchers and participants meet on more-or-less equal terms in natural settings (see also Hoeber & Kerwin, 2013). Reflecting the dominance of female fans at live events, the majority of our chats were with women but we also spoke to male fans—most of whom attended with female partners or daughters. Being invited to chat about netball enabled conversations with a wide range of fans who might not participate in a more formal interview. The nature of chat reflects women-centric and Māori and Pasifika forms of communication that value reciprocal sharing of knowledge and respect the cultural capital of netball fans. Similar to the Māori principle of *kanohi kitea* (the seen face), we regularly attended live games, sat alongside fans, and openly shared our netball passion and knowledge to build connections, which significantly assisted our ability to talk with fans of all ages and ethnicities. We used devices and practices that are common today and "minimise conspicuousness" (Selleck, 2017, p. 156) to record the conversations on our phones, using the Voice Record app. We recorded verbal permission to take photographs either for our records or research publications.

Findings

Our results demonstrate the importance of predominantly female sporting spaces in women's lives, thus providing a further antidote to assumptions that sports fandom is not an important part of women's identities (Antunovic & Whiteside, 2018). We focus here on three findings: 1) the deeply meaningful webs of belonging that exist between netball fandom and familial and social relationships; 2) the ways that gendered values are embraced and enacted in the feminine space of netball's fan community; and 3) the growing integration of Māori and Pasifika cultures.

Meaningful Webs of Belonging

One of the most consistent findings was the profound connections that exist between netball fandom, women's daily lives, familial, social and cultural relationships. Our fieldwork identified the power of netball to forge lifelong friendships and weave together families and *whānau* [kinship groups] across generations.

Lifelong and Multidimensional Involvement. Our chats revealed that most women, and some men, had direct connections to the sport, whether through years of playing, umpiring and/or coaching, or because they were supporting a family member or someone they knew. For many, netball involvement was much more than spectating: We talked to many older women who played as schoolgirls, continued playing into their 40s or even 70s and also held roles as umpires, coaches, bench officials or administrators. Barbara (71) and Christine (72)—who had been umpires and bench officials—began playing as children and ended their playing careers in Golden Oldies netball. Christine finished playing aged 50 and Barbara at 70, although Barbara claimed "I'd still be playing if we had a team". Netball was such a part of their lives that Barbara had not missed a Silver Ferns international game for over 30 years. In our roving chats, most of the significant fan demographic of women aged 60+ had been involved with netball all their lives, and their lifelong friendships were created and sustained through their love of the sport. For example, Peggy (85) could not play due to polio so became a supporter—first for her friends and later her two daughters and four granddaughters—and a fervent fan, following and attending elite games. "I've got friends, and quite a lot of the players just call me Nana because I am always at the matches." Peggy follows multiple netball social media groups and felt netball fandom "adds a terrific lot" to her life. Joydie (43) and Maraea's (43) friendship began when their young daughters—now playing in the ANZ Premiership—played in age-group representative netball teams. Many also had direct personal connections to players and/or coaches as *whānau*, friends and/or former teammates. For example, as the New Zealand men played their first televised games against the Silver Ferns in 2019, Liz (30) and Pauline (30) came to the live game to support friends in the men's team.

Perhaps not surprisingly, but in stark contrast to existing sports fan research, socialisation into netball was matriarchal, including for men, such as netball coach, umpire and board member Matt (32), who attributed his love of the game to his mother: "Because Mum is so heavily involved, so I guess it goes without saying that where she went I would sort of follow along too. … I grew up on the side of the court and I have found a real love for the game." The passing down of knowledge and netball passion was evident. At every match there were women who were watching their granddaughters or younger *whānau* in one of the teams, or had brought their granddaughters because they play netball at school. Daniel (20) attended a game to support his sister who was playing. Netball was clearly an intergenerational playing and spectating practice in his family: "My mum played netball and my nan played netball as well… [we] follow it all the time. When we are down in Wellington we usually pack the house. All the family come over… a lot of yelling!" Leeza (30) described her mother Robyn (60) as "very vocal" on the sidelines when Leeza was playing. Now they attend live games together: "I really like that we can share something together, so it's a really good mother/daughter day out."

Although less common, groups of women used Premiership and Silver Ferns games as girls' weekends or girls' nights out. For example, a group of seven sisters and friends in their late 40s to early 50s, travelled to Auckland to follow their team, explaining "it was a good excuse for a weekend away!" without their partners. These groups were usually linked by a closed social media app such as WhatsApp, where they shared intense netball chat and analysis. They might never post on a public-facing social media site but would check Facebook and Instagram pages and comment on these in their closed groups. Some older women found live netball matches a way to further cement their lifelong netball friendships. For example, Debbie (62), Raewyn (54) and Jan (68) had played, umpired and trained umpires. As Debbie described it, "We like to meet up with each other every so often. We live in varied parts of Auckland miles away from each other so to come to a game like this and do something social like have lunch beforehand is great fun".

Intergenerational Webs. The finding that netball fandom is clearly intergenerational and familial supports the existing sport fandom research. As one fan explained, "it's in the blood" (see also Mewett & Toffoletti, 2011). At games, the most common groupings were pairs of mothers (or occasionally fathers) and daughters. The mothers ranged from their 70s to young mothers with daughters just starting to play. For example, Jill (57) attended the game with her mother Rae (80) and described the love of the game as "our bond, our shared interest… so you can have a chat about it, and I can understand the game better as Mum knows the rules better than I do". Rae was there because "I just love netball. I have coached, umpired and I just love it". We also regularly encountered fan groups comprising three generations: grandmothers, mothers and daughters. For Ann (60s), who attended the game with her daughter (40s) and granddaughter (9), netball "gives us something that we all love. It binds us together as a group of women, and my husband even watches it—he hasn't got a choice!" Many older women had been given a season or individual game ticket as a Mother's Day, birthday or Christmas gift, often by a daughter who accompanied her mother or grandmother to the games. For example, Trudy (50) had just bought tickets for "for my mum and my two girls"—who ranged in age from 17 to 72—and explained "we all grew up with it".

Knowledge and Passion. One effect of this intergenerational and multidimensional involvement is the high level of spectator knowledge of the game. Some fans told us that they love the netball crowd because they "know" the game. Sky NZ netball producer/director Matt Barrett was very aware of fans' in-depth fan knowledge, explaining that "If you want to see purists of a game then you go to a netball match more than you would to go to a rugby match". In stark contrast to WNBA research (Meân, 2012), he told us that his crew needs to provide a complex game narrative to meet the high level of viewer knowledge. He believes that his "passionate" netball production crew "go above and beyond [because] they enjoy the game, they enjoy the contest, they love the pace of the game".

Our observations and recorded soundscapes demonstrated that netball fans focus on the action. There is little talking or use of social media or mobile phones during on-court play. Instead, fans are intensely attentive and reactive to on-court action. They clap, cheer and yell support to players. They react to the almost continuous on-court action with oohs, aahs and roars of pleasure at skilled play on and off the ball. Their reactions demonstrate deep knowledge of the rules and what constitutes skilled play. For example, contentious umpire calls created ripples of intense rulebook discussion as the game continued.

A surprising number have attended quadrennial World Cups or Commonwealth Games, often with other women friends or family members. The widely shared netball community knowledge, of putting aside $20 every week for four years to pay for the trip, reflects the reality that following a national team overseas is an expensive proposition and must be planned for within an individual's or family's existing budget. Cath (69) has travelled to three World Cups with her "lifelong friends" developed as mothers on the netball sidelines. Her description of the 2019 Final in England, won narrowly by the Silver Ferns over arch-rivals Australia, shows the pleasures of the live game and its implicit connection to national identity:

> It was absolutely amazing. Just the atmosphere, you can't explain it. The place was absolutely buzzing. It was electrified. It was amazing… all the crowd around us were shouting for the New Zealanders… The whole 13 days of the netball was fantastic, absolutely fantastic. We loved every minute of it. Everyone was so friendly.

This hard-fought, nail-biting win attracted 1.2 million New Zealand viewers and retains its powerful emotional impact on fans. Many remember where they were, who they were with, the emotions they experienced and what they screamed at the TV or shared on social media. A high number reported crying when the Silver Ferns won, and experiencing the same emotions watching replays when COVID-19 disrupted the Premiership. One admitted that she watched the 2019 final at least once a week.

Netball as a Feminine Sport Space: Feminine Fandom

In thinking about netball as a gendered—feminine—space, we took seriously the idea that we could think differently if "our standard of measurement doesn't start with a White-male heterosexual nucleus" (Baumgardner & Richards, 2000, p. 134). We wanted to investigate netball fan culture *on its own gendered terms*, while remaining sensitive to other dimensions of identity. It was clear that the atmosphere at netball games reflects dimensions of female fandom identified in previous research. For example, there was very little drinking at games, even though wine and beer were available for purchase. In fact we only observed two instances of alcohol-affected behaviour, both involving young men who drank steadily throughout the game and offered increasingly vocal and negative reactions that reflect findings from studies of men's team sports. This behaviour was so startlingly out of place that we could "feel" the discomfort of fans around us, although no-one said anything to them.

Many fans valued what they saw as a family-friendly and safe atmosphere at top-level games. Our chats with broadcasting personnel reinforced this perception. They work across sports and thus are well positioned to understand how the atmosphere at live netball is different from other major (primarily men's) sports. SKY NZ camera operator James Staunton preferred netball to other major male codes, explaining that it is "really friendly at the netball. Everyone's like mums, daughters, family, big family atmosphere". Experienced netball play-by-play commentator Jenny Woods had a similar view, stating that "the vibe has been positive, very supportive, and the interesting thing is that a lot of the crew members—like the camera people, the soundies—who do all sorts of sports, they've always said they love working on the netball". Netball fans particularly valued the spirit in which the game is played. Fans from all demographics told us they enjoyed the chance to watch the positive interactions between players, including between opponents. We saw this during the 2019 World Cup when opposing teams often joined together in a huddle after the game. Fans looked for and strongly appreciated the tiny moments that showed how the players care for and respect each other. This was particularly evident in the

Silver Ferns' 2019 World Cup preparation against the New Zealand men's team. There was broad approval for that tournament, which was the first time the men's team had been televised. They also appreciated the accessibility of the players and how they interact with fans after matches, especially the young girls and some boys who line up several rows deep to talk to their favourite players. Thus, rather than resistance to the incursion of men into the space of female sport, we observed an openness to male fans and men's netball, shown in an excitement about watching the men play, and high fan approval of the 2021 appointment of men's team captain Kruze Tangira to a live commentary role for Premiership games. None of the men we spoke to discussed feeling marginalised, although some who attended with their partners or daughters admitted they knew little about the rules or the players.

Parents saw netballers and coaches as excellent role models for their children and for New Zealanders as a whole: One attended a test match because the "track record" of the national coach and team captain "inspires the team and inspires people… leadership, drive and positivity". In 2020, many positively remarked on the unique involvement of head coach Noeline Taurua in mentoring and supporting coaches of all Premiership teams. Her openness, frank assessments and accessibility were seen as ground-breaking, and all generations of fans noted her welcome influence on how the game is played and the relationships between players and teams. It was not only females who looked to elite players as role models. Two young male netballers said they looked more to Silver Ferns players for inspiration than to male players. Josh (19) said, "I think the girls have got more brains". In a chat Kruze Tangira said, "it's really hard to find idols in this world at the moment that are really positive, really influential, and you can't go past the girls we have on the netball court".

Netball as a Cultural Sport Space: The Influence of Māori and Pasifika Cultures

Fandom research has been critiqued for focusing on white, Western perspectives (Toffoletti & Palmer, 2017). Our study challenged this narrow focus by paying attention to the integration and growing influence of Māori and Pasifika cultures within netball (Tunnicliffe, 2020b). The Premiership teams role model a sense of inclusivity and strongly reinforce the importance of family/*whānau* relationships. Drawing on his immersion in men's netball and recent experience commentating Premiership games, Kruze Tangira believed that Māori and Pasifika fans bring "the sense of *whānau* or family environment" which makes players "feel like they are more than just the game. They are part of a family, they are part of the community that will have their backs, that will be there for them on court". He continued, "probably the biggest aspect that the Māori and Pacific community bring is that sense of love, not just for the sport but for the people that are playing the sport as well".

Some teams have actively embraced learning about Māori culture and recognising the cultures of all players within their squads. In 2019, the Wellington-based Pulse team developed its own *haka* (posture dance with chanting) and learned *te reo* Māori (language) and *waiata* (songs), and have led the way in embracing the importance of culture within a team environment. The South Auckland-based Northern Stars, who represent a highly diverse community that includes 38 per cent of Māori or Pasifika heritage (Counties Manukau Health, 2018)—are on a similar journey. In 2019, all the players learned and performed a siva (Samoan dance) to recognise a Samoan teammate's 100th match (Tunnicliffe, 2020). In 2021, they developed and performed their own *haka* to a rousing response from the crowd. Fans entering the stadium are now greeted by posters of each player, that include their name and *pepeha*—an introduction in Māori language that recognises who they are, their people, where they are from, and where they belong—alongside a large action photograph and smaller photographs of their first netball team and with their family.

The *pepeha* recognises the importance of family present and past, and identification with place. This "welcome" invites fans to be part of the Stars' game space that celebrates the importance of place, belonging, family and friendship, and to behave accordingly.

The sense of family was evident in our observations that fans often turn up in large groups, especially to support Māori and Pasifika players. For example, 30 people—parents, aunts and uncles, cousins, and her partner's *whānau*—turned up to celebrate Māori player Maia Wilson's 50th game in 2019. In 2021 we observed two 15-strong multigenerational groups of *whānau* supporting Elle Temu (Cook Island heritage) and Elisapeta Toeava (Samoan). Finally, for some families, the success of a family member reaching the Premiership was a source of significant cultural pride. For Maraea (43), having a daughter play at the top level was especially important for her Samoan husband in "making a name for the family. … because they are old names. That's the name that came from the Islands, so it's here and it's recognised. It's big. The name on the dress. It's big".

Conclusions

Through studying the unique context of female fans in a female-defined sport, our research significantly expands current understandings of women's sports fandom, and demonstrates that fandom models based on men and men's sports do not accurately predict women's experiences and behaviours (Sveinson & Hoeber, 2015). For example, there is little evidence in existing research of the deep involvement shown by many fans in netball—not only as fans, but as current or former players, administrators, officials, umpires and coaches. This multidimensional involvement was an important factor in the high level of knowledge about the sport expressed by fans, and acknowledged by netball sports journalists and broadcast production crews. A second difference that emerged was the recognition, embrace and influence of cultural diversity, particularly at Northern Stars home games. We observed fans responding positively to performances of team *haka* or *waiata*, half-time cultural performances and the visibility of the players' *pepeha* at the Northern Stars stadium. Fans identified and valued the way that Māori and Pasifika concepts and ways of being contributed to a crowd atmosphere in which fans felt part of a welcoming and safe netball *whānau* that extended beyond direct kinship ties.

An important similarity was the positivity and feeling of community that has been identified as a strong characteristic of female fandom (Llopsis et al., 2018; Sveinson & Hoeber, 2015). Netball fans emphasised the importance of positivity and the spirit in which the game was played. Except for the two groups of intoxicated males discussed earlier, we did not observe any fans yelling abuse or criticism at coaches or players. Nor did we hear abuse based on ethnicity or sexuality. Thus, in contrast to existing studies of female fans of men's sports, there was no evidence of marginalisation, abuse or refusal to accept the non-dominant gender (in netball's case, males) as authentic fans. The netball fan community is undoubtedly underpinned by a heterosexual feminine ethos (Marfell, 2019), but there appeared to be no need to police gender borders or "protect" netball from the invasion of male fans or players.

We identified two important *gender reversals* of existing knowledge. The first *gender reversal* relates to the generational nature of fandom which is passed down through female lines in our study rather than through male lines (e.g., Farrell et al., 2011; Mewett & Toffoletti, 2011; Pope & Kirk, 2014). Male netball fans were in the minority—from counting sections in the stands, we estimated that women comprised at least three-quarters of spectators—and most have become fans through female significant others, such as mothers, sisters, wives or partners, and daughters. While the generational connections are visually evident in the stands, these *whānau* interconnections are also connected to the players on the court, reinforcing an intergenerational sense of belonging and respect for the game. The second *gender reversal* relates to the broader structural marginalisation of players (rather than fans) from the non-dominant gender or sexual orientation. After 120 years of female control of netball, the potency of its connection to heterosexual femininity is so strong that organised men's netball did not emerge until the 1980s, and media coverage of men's and mixed netball is almost non-existent. As a result, it is male players that have faced broader social stigmatisation and suffering, including "heartache … pain … sorrow … struggle [and] being picked on and being made ashamed of for playing the sport" (Silver Ferns, 2021, 5:46–6:10).

Our discussion here is limited to findings related to gender and ethnicity, and fan experiences at live games. It has barely touched on sexuality or social class, and much remains to be discussed in relation to how social media supports female netball fandom, especially since much activity takes place on closed or private sites, safe from the gendered harassment prevalent on public sites (Nadim & Fladmoe, 2021), and where frank discussions will not hurt players or coaches. However, by analysing fandom in a sport that is not defined by the articulation of sport and masculinity, we have identified forms of pleasure and fandom that are grounded in, and value, women's ways of seeing the world. These findings complicate and challenge existing understandings of sports fandom and demonstrate the importance of extending our sites of investigation beyond dominant male team sports.

References

Adams, M. L., Helstein, M. T., Kyoung-Yim, K. et al. (2016). Feminist cultural studies: Uncertainties and possibilities. *Sociology of Sport Journal*, *33*(1), 75–91.

Andrew, G. (1997). *"A girl's game—and a good one too": A critical analysis of New Zealand netball*. Masters thesis. University of Canterbury.

Antunovic, D., & Hardin, M. (2012). Activism in women's sports blogs: Fandom and feminist potential. *International Journal of Sport Communication*, *5*, 305–322.

Antunovic, F., & Whiteside, E. (2018). Feminist sports media studies: State of the field. In D. Harp, J. Loke & I. Bachmann (Eds.), *Feminist approaches to media theory and research* (pp. 111–130). Palgrave Macmillan.

Baumgardner, J., & Richards, A. (2000). *Manifesta: Young women, feminism, and the future*. Farrar, Straus and Giroux.

Bruce, T. (2016). New rules for new times: Sportswomen and media representation in the third wave. *Sex Roles*, *74*, 361–376.

Bruce, T. (1998). Audience resistance: Women fans confront televised women's basketball. *Journal of Sport and Social Issues*, *22*(4), 373–397.

Chiweshe, M. (2014). One of the boys: Female fans' responses to the masculine and phallocentric nature of football stadiums in Zimbabwe, *Critical African Studies*, *6*(2–3), 211–222.

Crawford, G., & Gosling, V. K. (2004). The myth of the "puck bunny": Female fans and men's ice hockey. *Sociology*, *38*(3), 477–493.

Counties Manukau Health. (2018). *Demographic profile: 2018 Census, population of Counties Manukau*. Counties Manukau Health.

Curtin, J. (2015). More than male-gazing: Reflections on female fans of rugby union in New Zealand, 1870–1920. *The International Journal of the History of Sport*, *32*(18), 2123–2134.

Dolance, S. (2005). "A whole stadium full": Lesbian community at women's national basketball association games. *The Journal of Sex Research*, *42*(1), 74–83.

Dougherty, I. (2004). *Southern Sting: The team that inspired a region*. Exisle Publishing.

Dunn, C. (2018). Canada 2015: Perceptions and experiences of the organisation and governance of the Women's World Cup, *Sport in Society*, *21*(5), 788–799.

Dunn, C. (2016). *Football and the women's world cup: Organisation, media and fandom*. Palgrave Pivot.

Egan, B. (2020, Oct 17). Matching up against Silver Ferns paves the way for men's netball. *Stuff*. www.stuff.co.nz/sport/netball/123074764/matching-up-against-silver-ferns-paves-the-way-for-mens-netball

Esmonde, K., Cooky, C., & Andrews, D. (2015). It's supposed to be about the love of the game, not the love of Aaron Rodgers "eyes": Challenging the exclusions of women sports fans. *Sociology of Sport Journal, 32*(1), 22–48.

Farrell, A., Fink, J. S., & Fields, S. (2011). Women's sport spectatorship: An exploration of men's influence. *Journal of Sport Management, 25*, 190–201.

Gieseler, C. M. (2017). "Raise Her Right": (Mis)representing authentic women sports fans in US advertising, *Sport in Society, 20*(11), 1765–1779.

Henley, M. A. (2016). Netball's contestation for physical and mediated space in Aotearoa/New Zealand. In C. Howley & S. Dun (Eds.), *The playing field: Making sense of places and spaces in sporting culture* (pp. 141–157). Inter-disciplinary Press.

Henley, M. A. (2012). A whole new ball game: the symbiotic relationship between broadcast media and netball in New Zealand from cinema newsreels to high definition pay television (Doctoral dissertation, ResearchSpace@ Auckland).

Henley, M. (2004). Going mainstream: Women's televised sport through a case study of the 1999 Netball World Championships. In R. Horrocks & N. Perry (Eds.), *Television in New Zealand: Programming the nation* (pp. 167–183). Oxford University Press.

Henley, M., & Bruce, T. (2019). Netball: Carving out media and corporate success in the game for all girls. In N. Lough & A. N. Guerin (Eds.), *Handbook of the business of women's sport* (pp. 492–503). Routledge.

Hoeber, L., & Kerwin, S. (2013). Exploring the experiences of female sport fans: A collaborative self-ethnography. *Sport Management Review, 16*(3), 326–336.

Jones, K. (2008). Female fandom: identity, sexism and men's professional football in England. *Sociology of Sport Journal, 25*(4), 516–537.

Klugman, M. (2012). Gendered pleasures, power, limits, and suspicions: Exploring the subjectivities of female supporters of Australian Rules Football. *Journal of Sport History, 39*(3), 415–429.

Lenneis, V., & Pfister, G. (2018). Is there a life beyond football? How female fans integrate football into their everyday lives. In G. Pfister & S. Pope (Eds.), *Female football players and fans* (pp. 185–210). Palgrave Macmillan.

Llopis-Goig, R., & Flores, H. (2018). Challenging or accommodating the football system? A case study of female football supporter communities in Spain. In G. Pfister & S. Pope (Eds.), *Female football players and fans* (pp. 259–278). Palgrave Macmillan.

Marfell, A. (2019). "We wear dresses, we look pretty": The feminization and heterosexualization of netball spaces and bodies. *International Review for the Sociology of Sport, 54*(5), 577–602.

Marfell, A. E. (2016). Understanding "the national sport for New Zealand women": A socio-spatial analysis of netball. PhD thesis. University of Waikato.

Markula, P. (Ed.) (2005). *Feminist sport studies: Sharing experiences of joy and pain*. SUNY Press.

Meân, L. (2012). Empowerment through sport? Female fans, women's sport, and the construction of gendered fandom. In G. Pfister & S. Pope (Eds.), *Sport and its female fans* (pp. 184–207). Routledge.

Mewett, P., & Toffoletti, K. (2011). Finding footy: Female fan socialization and Australian rules football, *Sport in Society, 14*(5), 670–684.

Mintert, S-M., & Pfister, G. (2015). The FREE project and the feminization of football: The role of women in the European fan community. *Soccer & Society, 16*(2–3), 405–421.

Muller, T. (2007). "Lesbian community" in Women's National Basketball Association (WNBA) spaces. *Social & Cultural Geography, 8*(1), 9–28.

Muller Myrdahl, T. (2011). Lesbian visibility and the politics of covering in women's basketball game spaces. *Leisure Studies, 30*(2), 139–156.

Nadim, M., & Fladmoe, A. (2021). Silencing women? Gender and online harassment. *Social Science Computer Review, 39*(2), 245–258.

Needs, B. A. (2017). *#welivethisgame: Social media, online communities and the ANZ Netball Championship 2016*. Masters thesis. University of Auckland.

Netball New Zealand (2011). *Netball New Zealand facilities strategy*. https://sportnz.org.nz/assets/Uploads/Netball-NZ-National-Facilities-Strategy.pdf

Netball New Zealand (2019). *Ninety-fifth Annual Report 2019*. Netball New Zealand. www.netballnz.co.nz/useful-info/resource-library

Netball New Zealand (2020). *Ninety-sixth Annual Report 2020*. Netball New Zealand. https://issuu.com/netballnz/docs/2020_nnz_annual_report_-_digital_pages

New Zealand Secondary Schools Sports Council (2020). *School Sport NZ census data—By sport (National Analysis)*. Oakura, New Zealand.

New Zealand Secondary Schools Sports Council (2019). *NZSSSC census—Participation trends by sport (2000-2018)*. Oakura, New Zealand.

Obel, C. (2012). Fantasy, fun and identity construction among female fans of rugby. In G. Pfister & S. Pope (Eds.), *Sport and its female fans* (pp. 130–149). Routledge.

O'Keeffe, M. (2020, Nov 9). Netball: NZ men's team consider bid for ANZ Premiership inclusion. *Newshub*. www.newshub.co.nz/home/sport/2020/11/netball-nz-men-s-team-consider-bid-for-anz-premiership-inclusion.html

Olive, R. (2013). "Making friends with the neighbours": Blogging as a research method. *International Journal of Cultural Studies*, *16*(1), 71–84.

Osborne, A. C., & Coombs, D. (2013). Performative sport fandom: An approach to retheorizing sport fans. *Sport in Society*, *16*(5), 672–681.

Osborne, A. C., & Coombs, D. C. (2016). *Female fans of the NFL: Taking their place in the stands*. Routledge.

Paraschak, V., & Thompson, K. (2014). Finding strength(s): Insights on Aboriginal physical cultural practices. *Sport in Society*, *17*(8), 1046–1060.

Pfister, G., Lenneis, V., & Mintert, S. (2013). Female fans of men's football–A case study in Denmark. *Soccer & Society*, *14*(6), 850–871.

Pfister, G., & Pope, S. (Eds.) (2018). *Female football players and fans: Intruding into a man's world*. Springer.

Pope, S. (2013). "The love of my life": The meaning and importance of sport for female fans. *Journal of Sport and Social Issues*, *37*(2), 175–195.

Pope, S. (2017). *The feminization of sports fandom: A sociological study*. Routledge.

Pope, S., & Kirk, D. (2014). The role of physical education and other formative experiences of three generations of female football fans. *Sport, Education and Society*, *19*(2), 223–240.

Radmann, A., & Hedenborg, S. (2018). Women's football supporter culture in Sweden. In G. Pfister & S. Pope (Eds.), *Female football players and fans* (pp. 241–258). Palgrave Macmillan.

Selleck, C. L. (2017). Ethnographic chats: A best of both method for ethnography. *Sky Journal of Linguistics*, *30*, 151–162.

Silk, M. L., Andrews, D. L., & Thorpe, H. (Eds.). (2017). *Routledge handbook of physical cultural studies*. Routledge.

Silver Ferns TV (2021, April 6.) Pure As: Kruze Tangira [Interview]. *Silver Ferns TV*. www.youtube.com/watch?v=WDe7t5OwiXo

Sport New Zealand (2014). *Sport and active recreation in the lives of New Zealand adults: 2013/2014 Active New Zealand survey results*. Sport New Zealand.

Stats NZ (2020, May 18). *New Zealand's population passes 5 million*. Statistics New Zealand. www.stats.govt.nz/news/new-zealands-population-passes-5-million

Sveinson, K., & Hoeber, L. (2015). Overlooking the obvious: An exploration of what it means to be a sport fan from a female perspective. *Leisure Studies*, *34*(4), 405–419.

Thorpe, H., & Marfell, A. (2019). Feminism and the physical cultural studies assemblage: Revisiting debates and imagining new directions. *Leisure Sciences*, *41*(1–2), 17–35.

Toffoletti, K. (2017). *Women sport fans: Identification, participation, representation*. Routledge.

Toffoletti, K., & Mewett, P. (Eds.). (2012). *Sport and its female fans*. Routledge.

Toffoletti, K., & Palmer, C. (2017). New approaches for studies of Muslim women and sport. *International Review for the Sociology of Sport*, *52*(2), 146–163.

Tunnicliffe, B. (2020a, July 8). Big surge in netball fans outside NZ streaming ANZ games. *Radio New Zealand*. www.rnz.co.nz/news/sport/420777/big-surge-in-netball-fans-outside-nz-streaming-anz-games

Tunnicliffe, B. (2020b, August 11). Māori and Pasifika cultures influencing ANZ teams – netball study. *Radio New Zealand*. www.rnz.co.nz/news/sport/423225/maori-and-pasifika-cultures-influencing-anz-teams-netball-study

5
Understanding Demand for Women's Sports Begins with Understanding Men's Sports History

David Berri

January 20, 2021 was the sesquicentennial of an important event in baseball history. As noted at MLB.com (n.d.):

> On January 20, 1871, the Boston Red Stockings were incorporated by Ivers Whitney Adams with $15,000 and the help of Harry Wright, the "Father of Professional Baseball," who had founded and managed America's first truly professional baseball team, the Cincinnati Red Stockings. Two months later, the Red Stockings became one of nine charter members of the National Association of Professional Baseball Players and the forerunner of the National League.

Back in 1871, $15,000 was a huge sum of money. Average income in the United States in 1871 was less than $200 (Johnston and Williamson, n.d.). That being said, $15,000 is worth a bit less than $300,000 today (Johnston and Williamson, n.d.). And today, the franchise originally incorporated by Ivers Whitney Adams is estimated to be worth $1.8 billion (Bell, 2020).

Which franchise are we talking about? The Boston Red Stockings eventually became (Baseball Reference.com, n.d.):

- the Boston Beaneaters in 1883;
- the Boston Doves in 1907;
- the Boston Rustlers in 1911;
- the Boston Braves in 1912 (briefly the Boston Bees from 1936 to 1940);
- the Milwaukee Braves in 1953;
- and finally the Atlanta Braves in 1966.

Yes, Adams founded the Atlanta Braves. At least, the franchise Adams began in 1871 became the Atlanta Braves 95 years later. And this means the Atlanta Braves of the National League today are the "oldest continuously operating professional sports franchise in America" (MLB.com, n.d.).

For much of that history this franchise played in the National League. This league was founded in 1876. Other major men's sports leagues followed. These include:

- The English Football League in 1888 (Ward, 2008).
- The American League in 1901 (Bendix, 2008).
- The National Football League (NFL) in 1920 (Klein, 2014).
- The National Basketball Association in 1946 (NBA.com).

As the above dates indicate, all of these leagues will reach their sesquicentennial by the end of the twenty-first century. In sum, men's professional sports teams and leagues have been around for quite some time.

A similar story cannot be told about the leading women's professional sports leagues. As Berri (2021) notes, at the time men were first forming professional sports leagues in the latter nineteenth century, men were also actively banning women from playing sports at all.

Consider the following quotes (Mansky & Wei-Haas, 2016) from Baron Pierre De Coubertin (the founder of the Olympic movement in the nineteenth century):

> *It is indecent that spectators should be exposed to the risk of seeing the body of a women being smashed before their eyes. Besides, no matter how toughened a sportswoman may be, her organism is not cut out to sustain certain shocks. Her nerves rule her muscles, nature wanted it that way.*

Coubertin was not alone in banning women from sports. As Berri (2021) details, in the latter nineteenth and early twentieth century bans were created in various places with respect to sports like basketball, baseball, and soccer. For many men at this time, sports were entirely a domain occupied by men, and women were simply not welcome to participate.

Despite the efforts to stop women from playing, some women persisted in playing sports. Opportunities, though, were very much limited. In the United States, high school and college sports were predominantly provided to boys and men.

This all began to change in 1972. More than a century after the Boston Red Stockings started playing professional baseball, opportunities in sports for girls and women began to dramatically increase. That year, President Richard Nixon signed into law the following amendment to the 1964 Civil Rights Act.

> *No person in the United States shall, on the basis of sex, be excluded from participation in, be denied the benefits of, or be subjected to discrimination under any educational program or activity receiving federal financial assistance.*[1]

This clause is known as Title IX. Yes, it doesn't mention sports. But it became clear it very much applied to sports. High schools and colleges definitely received federal funding and the sports these institutions sponsored were considered "educational programs." Therefore, if sports were provided to boys and men then Title IX meant they had to be provided to girls and women. And very quickly that became the case.

Andrew Zimbalist (2001) reports the numbers. In 1971, only 294,015 girls played high school sports in the United States. By 1973, that number was 817,073. And by 1978, 2.08 million girls were playing high school sports. In just seven years, girls participating in high school sports increased by more than 700 percent! A similar story is seen in college sports. As Zimbalist (2001) notes, only 31,852 women played college sports in 1971. But by 1977, that number had more than doubled to 64,375 women.

It was possible for women to participate in a professional sports league before Title IX. The classic movie *A League of Their Own* illustrates that point. Nevertheless, it is somewhat difficult for a league to grow and thrive without a large underlying population of talent. And prior to Title IX, the population of girls and women playing sports was too small for a professional league in women's sports to make much progress.

Given this point, it is not surprising that the most successful women's professional sports league – the Women's National Basketball Association (WNBA) – didn't begin playing until 25 years after the passage of Title IX. And given this starting point, the WNBA won't reach its sesquicentennial until 2147!

Yes, that is quite far in the future. But this anniversary for the WNBA will happen sooner than similar anniversaries for the other major women's professional sports teams that exist today. For example, National Pro Fastpitch (NPF) was founded in 2004 and therefore will reach its sesquicentennial in 2154.[2] And the National Women's Soccer League (NWSL) – founded in 2012 – will reach this anniversary eight years later.[3]

The history of men and women's professional sports tells us much about the observed differences we see today. As we will note, men's sports have higher levels of revenue, attendance, franchise values, and both private and public investment. For many, these differences suggest that men's sports are simply better than women's sports. The real story, though, is that the differences we observe are better understood when we consider the issues of time and gender discrimination.

Billions for Men's Sports!

In 2021 the NFL signed a new broadcasting deal that could pay the league over $100 billion across 11 seasons (Sherman & Young, 2021). This works out to more than $9 billion per season; or more than $280 million per season for each of the 32 NFL teams. The NFL salary cap (i.e. the limit on what each team can spend on players each season) might climb to $230 million by 2023 (Johnson, 2021). This means that each NFL team is capable of paying all of its players (and then some!) before they sell a single ticket.

Of course, the NFL will be selling tickets. In 2019 – before the COVID pandemic hit – 16.9 million people attended NFL games (ESPN.com, n.d.) This number is 95 percent of stadium capacity in the league. The pandemic illustrated clearly how much gate revenue means to the league. In 2020, the NFL only had 1.1 million fans attend games with 14 teams admitting no one (Pro Football Reference.com). It is estimated that this dramatic decline in attendance cost the league $4 billion in revenue (Florio, 2021).

Four billion dollars sounds impressive. The NFL, though, earns less than 25 percent of its total revenue from the gate. As Barbari (2020) notes, in 2018 the teams of the NFL earned more than $16 billion in revenue. Major League Baseball – the second largest league in the world in terms of revenue – brought in $10.7 billion in 2019 (Brown, 2019). This means that before the NFL sold a single ticket, it still generated more revenue than any other professional sports league in the world.

The NFL is not the only league who has seen actual attendance of a game become less and less important to the league's finances. As Table 5.1 makes clear, in the past 30 years the NBA has grown from a league that didn't quite bring in a billion dollars in revenue in a season to a league that brought in nearly $9 billion in revenue in 2018–19. This revenue mark today makes the NBA the third biggest league in the world.

Understanding Demand for Women's Sports

Table 5.1 NBA Revenue from 1991–92 to 2018–19

Year	Revenue per Team	Per Game	Average Ticket Price	Gate Revenue per Team[a]	Gate Revenue as Percentage of Total Revenue
1991–92	$37,033,333	15,683	$22.52	$14,693,275	39.68%
1992–93	$38,155,556	16,047	$25.23	$16,760,728	43.93%
1993–94	$46,633,333	16,226	$27.13	$18,245,990	39.13%
1994–95	$51,959,259	16,727	$30.03	$20,737,384	39.91%
1995–96	$57,386,207	17,254	$31.77	$22,678,720	39.52%
1997–98	$64,631,034	17,135	$36.88	$26,369,547	40.80%
1998–99	$42,062,069	16,752	$42.94	$18,276,605	43.45%
1999–00	$79,862,069	16,865	$48.72	$33,977,866	42.55%
2000–01	$86,068,966	16,784	$51.27	$36,260,145	42.13%
2001–02	$91,862,069	16,974	$50.10	$35,136,615	38.25%
2002–03	$93,827,586	16,883	$43.65	$30,448,808	32.45%
2003–04	$101,103,448	16,805	$44.68	$30,960,581	30.62%
2004–05	$106,166,667	17,319	$45.28	$32,409,069	30.53%
2005–06	$112,233,333	17,497	$45.72	$33,385,356	29.75%
2006–07	$119,100,000	17,734	$46.99	$34,983,094	29.37%
2007–08	$125,500,000	17,394	$48.83	$35,480,162	28.27%
2008–09	$126,200,000	17,390	$49.47	$35,900,325	28.45%
2009–10	$126,833,333	17,150	$48.87	$35,095,588	27.67%
2010–11	$132,000,000	17,319	$47.66	$34,695,547	26.28%
2011–12	$122,700,000	17,274	$48.54	$28,423,524	23.17%
2012–13	$151,866,667	17,334	$50.99	$37,141,800	24.46%
2013–14	$159,600,000	17,408	$52.50	$38,485,139	24.11%
2014–15	$172,666,667	17,809	$53.97	$40,148,756	23.25%
2015–16	$195,533,333	17,849	$55.88	$41,731,804	21.34%
2017–18	$266,900,000	17,830	$66.53	$51,370,899	19.25%
2018–19	$291,966,667	17,832	$71.83	$53,698,176	18.39%

[a] Gate revenue is the team's average ticket price multiplied by attendance (see Fort, n.d. for data). 1997–96 data is missing because league revenue is not available that year. Data from 2016–17 is missing because average ticket prices are not available for that year.

Data Source: Fort (n.d.)
Table created by author

Like the NFL, much of the revenue the NBA earns today is not from attendance at its games. In the past, though, it was a different story. In 1991–92, average attendance in the league was shy of 16,000 per game. Given an average ticket price of $22.52 (and attendance), gate revenue per team was $14.7 million. This works out to nearly 40 percent of overall revenue.

During the 1990s, attendance eventually eclipsed 17,000 per game and gate revenue continued to hover around 40 percent of overall revenues. In the twenty-first century, average attendance hasn't changed very much. Like the NFL, this is primarily due to capacity constraints. Due to a significant increase in ticket prices, though, gate revenue increased from $36.3 million in 2000–01 to $53.7 million in 2018–19. In other words, despite little change in average attendance (average attendance has only grown by 6 percent since 2000–01), gate revenue increased by nearly 50 percent.

Overall revenue, though, for the NBA increased by 239 percent. Like the NFL, this revenue increase is primarily about broadcasting fees. Currently, the NBA has a broadcasting deal that is scheduled to pay the league $24 billion across nine seasons. It is thought that when this deal expires in 2025 the NBA can increase its broadcasting fees to more than $70 billion across nine seasons; or around $8 billion per year (Young, 2021). In sum, with respect to revenue the NBA will be much bigger in the future. And that increase will not be because of dramatic changes to gate revenue.

The NFL, MLB, and the NBA are not the only professional sports leagues earning billions. Although the National Hockey League (NHL) is not nearly as large, it is reported the NHL earned $5 billion in 2018–19 (Jones, n.d.). And in Europe, it is reported that in 2017–18, the five largest European soccer leagues (in England, Germany, France, Italy, and Spain) generated a combined £13.8 billion (Reed, 2019). This is about $19.6 billion in revenue,[4] or about as much as MLB and the NBA combined. Altogether, the top nine professional sports leagues in terms of revenue generated more than $60 billion. All nine are also men's leagues.

Millions for Women Sports!

When we turn to the women's leagues we see a very different story. Whereas publications like Forbes report league revenue for the major men's professional sports leagues, no one seems to make that effort for any women's professional team sports. Nevertheless, we have some clues as to what their revenues might be.

To begin with, we do know league attendance. In 2019 the WNBA played its 23rd season, and it was reported that on average 6,528 fans showed up to watch each game that year (Across the Timeline, n.d.) The average minimum ticket price in the WNBA is about $17 (Bailum, 2021). So, we know the league earned at least $23 million from its gate revenue. In addition, the league also has a $25 million dollar per year broadcasting deal with ESPN (Ourand, 2016). That means, WNBA revenue is – at a minimum – close to $50 million per year.

It is likely a bit more than that. As noted by Berri (2020), there are other sources of revenue for the league. The league has another television deal with the CBS sports cable channel and also earns money from the broadcast of its games on WNBA League Pass. Then there are deals with Fan Duel, Twitter, and Tidal. In addition, teams also earn money from local broadcasting deals, merchandise sales, and sponsorship deals. It is not clear what all these deals are worth. But as Berri (2021) reports, a league source indicated that a conservative estimate places league revenue at about $70 million.

Relative to the WNBA, the NWSL and NPF both appear to be much smaller. In 2019, the NWSL averaged 7,337 fans per match.[5] Despite having more fans per game than the WNBA, though, we suspect NWSL revenue is quite a bit lower. Keh and Das (2020) report that the entire league only has a few hundred employees and the vast majority of those are the players. As Lisa Baird – the league commissioner – stated: "Over 85 percent of our total monthly expenses is player compensation" (Keh & Das, 2020).

That statement allows us to estimate total expenses for the league. As Negley (2019) reports, the salary cap in 2019 was close to $525,000 per team. If teams spent the entire salary cap, then total player compensation for the nine-team league would be $4.7 million. If that is 85 percent of total expenses, then the league is spending $5.6 million. One should note (as a league source indicated) that the league does pay for player housing. Nevertheless, even with this added expense the league source didn't think league expenses were more than $10 million. It is unlikely a league as young as the NWSL is immensely profitable. In other words, NWSL revenue are likely quite a bit less than the $70 million reported for the WNBA.

The NPF is likely even smaller than the NWSL or WNBA. In 2018, Cheri Kempf (league commissioner of the NPF) reported that it only costs $1 million per year to operate each team (Berri, 2018c). With just six teams, this means the league's expenses are much less than $10 million. And that means revenues are again nowhere near what we see for the WNBA.

The WNBA, NWSL, and NPF are the three biggest women's professional leagues in North America. But unlike the top men's sports leagues, the revenues of these three teams are likely less than $100 million.

All these numbers seem to tell a clear story. Men's sports generate billions in revenues while women's sports can only generate millions. And that must mean men's sports are simply more entertaining than women's sports. At least, that is the story one might tell if all one knew about sports was what was happening today.

Once Upon a Time in Men's Sports

Once upon a time, though, the story in men's sports was quite different. In 1957, the Committee on the Judiciary of the House of Representatives held hearings on organized professional team sports. The purpose of these hearings was to review how antitrust law had been – and should be – applied to professional team sports. As part of these hearings, the four major men's professional sports leagues (i.e. MLB, NFL, NBA, and the NHL) submitted financial statements to Congress. These financial records give us a very clear picture of revenues and expenses of these leagues in the 1950s.[6]

Table 5.2 summarizes the story these statements tell. Once again, today the revenues of these four leagues surpass $40 billion per year. More than 60 years ago, though, it was a very different story. To begin with, whereas today the NFL leads all leagues in revenue, in the 1950s baseball was clearly the national pastime. According to the report made by Major League Baseball, league revenues in baseball grew from $31 million in 1952 to $45 million in 1956 and that mark led all North American professional sports leagues.

For sports economists, the 45 percent growth rate in baseball revenues at this time is a very important story. Early writings in sports economics – for example, Neale (1964) – emphasized that competitive balance is crucial to demand in sports. We see this argument when we look at attendance data from 1952 to 1956. Across these years, the New York Yankees won the American League pennant four times.[7] And across these years, American League attendance declined. These two data points led economists to tell a story about how the dominance of one team in a league clearly makes a league worse off. That story, though, would have been very different had these economists looked at the revenue numbers reported to Congress in 1957. While the Yankees dominated the American League, revenue in that league actually grew from $17.2 million to $22.1 million. And that means, a story repeated in the early literature on sports economics appears to be quite incorrect.

For the purpose of this chapter, though, there is an even more important story to be told from Table 5.2. If we convert dollars from the 1950s into 2020 dollars, we see that baseball's total revenues in the 1950s was less than half a billion dollars.[8] In other words, baseball's revenues were less than 5 percent of what we see today.

NFL revenues at this time were even lower. Today the NFL earns $16 billion in revenue each year. Back in the 1950s, league revenues were less than 1 percent of what we see today. In other words, the NFL is more than 100 times larger today than it was 65 years ago.

The NHL and NBA were even smaller. We said that the WNBA earns at least $70 million in revenue today. The NHL and NBA combined earned barely half that amount in 1952. Once again, that $70 million is a conservative estimate. So it is possible the WNBA today is as big as the NFL in 1952.

Whether or not the WNBA is as big as the NFL 70 years ago is not perfectly clear. It most certainly is bigger than the NBA at that time. This should not be surprising. The NBA had only

Table 5.2 Revenues in the Major Men's Sports Leagues in the 1950s

MLB	Season	1952	1953	1954	1955	1956
	Total Revenue	$31,076,342	$32,889,525	$38,974,975	$39,757,340	$45,046,418
	Revenue in Real Terms	$302,351,779	$317,604,816	$374,971,135	$383,925,358	$428,603,418
	Gate %[a]	67.1%	65.2%	70.3%	70.4%	67.3%
NFL	Season	1952	1953	1954	1955	1956
	Total Revenue	$8,327,021	$9,510,603	$10,756,957	$11,455,341	$12,370,101
	Revenue in Real Terms	$81,016,280	$91,841,196	$103,490,724	$110,620,980	$117,697,873
	Gate %[b]	85.9%	77.8%	80.4%	84.8%	82.9%
NHL[c]	Season	1951–52	1952–53	1953–54	1954–55	1955–56
	Total Revenue	$2,157,886	$2,218,727	$2,212,600	$2,307,836	$2,677,042
	Revenue in Real Terms	$20,994,771	$21,425,617	$21,287,022	$22,286,118	$25,471,267
	Gate %	84.3%	86.9%	87.4%	83.7%	86.2%
NBA[d]	Season	1952–53	1953–54	1954–55	1955–56	1956–57
	Total Revenue	$1,648,544	$1,559,567	$1,578,064	$1,798,884	$1,776,181
	Revenue in Real Terms	$16,039,218	$15,060,296	$15,182,266	$17,371,313	$16,899,840
	Gate %	78.0%	73.4%	65.1%	65.9%	74.7%

[a] The Detroit Tigers reported total revenue but not any other revenue details. So the calculation of gate revenue percentage is made with just the 15 Major League Baseball teams that reported both gate revenue and total revenue.
[b] The NFL earned substantial revenue from exhibition games. So, unlike the other sports leagues, gate revenue for the NFL included revenue earned from holding exhibition games.
[c] The NHL only consisted of six franchises at this time. The Toronto franchise did not report its total revenue data to Congress.
[d] Only eight NBA teams reported data to Congress. Two teams – the Indianapolis Olympians and Baltimore Bullets – existed in 1951–52 but went out of business before the hearings in 1957. Although all of the eight surviving teams reported total revenue, the franchises in New York, Philadelphia, and Minneapolis did not report gate revenue. So revenue from these teams is omitted from the gate revenue calculation.

Data Source: Fort (n.d.)
Table created by author

Table 5.3 Average Game Attendance in 1956 vs. Today

League	First Year League Existed	1956 Average Game Attendance	2019 Average Game Attendance	Percentage 1956 vs. Today
MLB	1901	13,428	28,181	47.6%
NHL	1918	12,482	17,456	71.5%
NFL	1920	37,611	66,515	56.5%
NBA	1946	4,498	17,857	25.2%

Data Source: Fort (n.d.)
Table created by author

been established in 1946. Seven years later, NBA revenues were – in real terms – less than 25 percent of what the WNBA is earning today.

In addition to the tale of much lower revenues, the data from the 1950s also tells us how much the composition of revenues has changed. Remember, the NFL today only gets about 25 percent of its revenue from the gate and the NBA today gets an even lower percentage. Back in the 1950s, though, the NFL was getting more than 75 percent of its revenue from paid attendance. A similar story was told in the other leagues. Alternative sources of revenue generally didn't have much impact at this time.

Given the importance of the gate, one might expect attendance to be quite large at this time. But as Table 5.3 indicates,[9] attendance in 1956 in all four of these leagues was substantially smaller than what we see today.

The attendance in the NBA in 1956 is especially noteworthy. The NBA's 10th season was in 1955–56. That year the league averaged less than 4,500 fans per game. Given how important gate revenue was to the league's revenue totals and how few fans actually bothered to attend games, it is not surprising the NBA was such a small operation in the 1950s.

There is an obvious explanation for the relatively low numbers we see with respect to revenue and attendance in these leagues. These leagues were generally quite young in the 1950s. Major League Baseball only came into existence in 1901 (when the American League joined forces with the National League) The NHL didn't first drop the puck until 1918 and the NFL didn't take the field until two years later. And the NBA, once again, had just been founded in the 1940s.

Given the age of these leagues, it is not surprising their fan bases were – relative to today – much smaller. It generally takes time for a fan base to develop in professional sports. For example, college football was already attracting crowds of 40,000 fans to games in the late 1880s (Zimbalist, 2001, p. 7). But 40 years later, professional teams in the NFL couldn't survive. From 1920 to 1935, 52 NFL franchises were created. Only eight of these survived.[10] In other words, the failure rate of NFL teams was initially 85 percent!

Why would college football thrive while a league of the best players from college football generally struggle? The key issue appears to be emotional attachment. In the early history of college football, it was easy for fans of a football team from Princeton or Yale to know who they were rooting for. Yale students, staff, faculty, and alumni came to each game with a clear rooting interest.

But what if we take those very same college players and put them on teams that are called the Bears or Packers? Now fans have a problem. What exactly is the person's rooting interest? How is a person supposed to form an attachment to something called a "Packer"?

Furthermore, what if you invest your time and energy into "the Packers" and no one follows your lead? Unlike a college or university that is most likely going to continue to survive for decades whether or not the football team draws this year or not, a professional team most definitely fails if the fans don't appear. Without knowing if those fans are going to show up, other fans are not willing to invest the time and money to make an emotional attachment today. In sum, until other fans know a team is going to continue, they are not willing to invest emotionally in the team to make sure it will continue.

Consequently, when leagues begin, both fans and revenue are scarce. But as time goes by, customers do appear in greater and greater numbers. And it is important to emphasize what we call these customers. As we have done throughout this story, we call sports customers "fans." This is short for "fanatic" and that word does much to highlight the emotional attachment sports customers make to the teams they follow.

Once again, though, it takes time for that to happen. When it comes to women's professional sports, it doesn't appear enough time has elapsed. The WNBA has only entered its 25th season in 2021. None of the major North American men's professional leagues were that successful after just 25 years.

Major League Baseball's 25th season was in 1925. That season the average team only attracted 7,744 fans per game.[11] The New York Yankees – with both Babe Ruth and Lou Gehrig on the roster – only averaged 8,826 fans per game. This was the same franchise that had just won the American League pennant from 1921 to 1923.

It is a similar story for the NBA. The NBA's 25th season was 1970–71 and average attendance that year was only average 7,812 fans per contest (Fort, n.d.). The Boston Celtics – with All-Star John Havlicek and Rookie-of-the-Year Dave Cowens (and just two years from a streak where the franchise won 11 titles in 13 years) – attracted only 7,565 fans per game that season (Fort, n.d.). Yes, that isn't impressive. But at that point, it was the fourth highest average attendance in franchise history and not far removed from the franchise record of 8,067 fans the team attracted per game in 1966–67 (Fort, n.d.).

How could iconic teams like the Yankees and Celtics fail to attract fans despite fielding successful teams that employed major stars? Again, in the early history of a league many people haven't formed an emotional attachment yet to a team. Hence, there simply aren't many "fanatics."

The story of the early history of men's sports tells us much about the relative struggles of women's sports today. We look at the billions earned by men's sports today and imagine that these sports leagues were always popular. But the data we have seen on revenue and attendance make it clear that once upon a time men's sports looked very much like women's sports today.

So is this our story? Do women's sports just need time to develop? Certainly that is part of the tale one would tell. But women's sports don't just suffer from a lack of a time relative to men's sports. Men have also bestowed huge advantages on men's sports that simply are not available to women's sports. And we can't understand the struggles faced by women sports today without noting the headwinds – created by men – that women face.

Men Have More than Time On Their Side

We have already noted that men literally banned women from playing sports. And we noted that even after women were not explicitly banned, boys and men were historically given far more opportunities than women. The advantages bestowed on males, though, didn't end when Title IX dramatically expanded the opportunities for girls and women in 1972.

As Table 5.4 details, Matheson (2021) – building on the work of Baade and Matheson (2012) – noted that men's sports leagues have received nearly $30 billion in public subsidies. Such subsidies, though, are not bestowed on women's sports leagues. In other words, whereas politicians are quite happy to invest large sums of money to build stadiums and arenas for teams in MLB, MLS, the NBA, NFL, and NHL, there isn't much evidence that politicians are willing to make similar investment in women's sports.

Table 5.4 Stadium and Arena Spending in Men's Sports from 1990 to 2021

League	Total Spending in Real Terms (in millions of dollars)	Public Subsidy in Real Terms (in millions of dollars)	% (real)
MLS	$4,687	$1,853	39.5%
NFL	$23,151	$11,193	48.3%
MLB	$14,444	$8,405	58.2%
NBA	$13,754	$5,528	40.2%
NHL	$8,519	$2,866	33.6%
Total	**$64,554**	**$29,846**	**46.2%**

Data source: Matheson (2021)
Source: Matheson (2021)

As Berri (2018a) notes, politicians tend to be overwhelmingly male and this is likely why politicians tend to favor men's sports. A similar story can be told about the media. As Berri (2018b) notes, sports writers also tend to be overwhelmingly male. This is likely why – as Cooky, Messner, and Musto (2015) report – more than 90 percent of the sports media's coverage goes to men's sports.

Though the advantages bestowed on men's sports by politicians and the media has been noted previously by others,[12] there is another advantage men's sports enjoy that has been less discussed previously. This advantage can be described as a "gender enthusiasm gap."

Consider the story of the Clippers franchise in the NBA. In 1981, Donald Sterling purchased the San Diego Clippers for $13.5 million (or about $38 million in 2020 dollars).[13] In a league where at least half the teams make the playoffs, Sterling's Clippers were shut out of the playoffs in 26 of the next 33 seasons. And once in the playoffs, the Clippers only advanced out of the first round three times (and never went past the second round). In sum, Sterling's Clippers were awful.

In 2014, the NBA forced Sterling to sell.[14] In 2013, Forbes valued the Clippers at $430 million (Fort, n.d.). Had that been the sale price of the Clippers, then Sterling would have clearly done quite well with his $13.5 million investment from 33 years before. But Sterling ended up doing a bit better than "quite well." In the end, Steve Ballmer purchased the Clippers – again, arguably the worst team in NBA history – for $2 billion (Schwartz, 2014).

Table 5.5 reports the last ten reported sale prices of NBA teams as well as the value Forbes placed on the franchise the year before the sale took place.[15] As one can see, the Clippers sale was an extreme event. But it was also part of a clear trend. For each of these ten sales, the final sales prices exceeded Forbes' estimation from just a year before. And on average, the sales price was more than 50 percent higher![16]

The valuations reported by Forbes has been tracking this rapid increase in sale prices. Table 5.6 reports what Forbes reported these franchises were worth in 2011 and what they report in 2020. Across these ten years, the franchise value reported by Forbes has increased on average by 457 percent!

As we have noted, the NBA is an established league that has seen revenues grow substantially overtime. Yes, revenues are not growing as fast as franchise values. But still, there is growth.

It is a different story for Major League Soccer. The MLS began play in 1996; or one year before the WNBA. In 2019, Chris Smith reported at Forbes that most MLS teams were not profitable:

Table 5.5 Recent Sale Prices of NBA Teams vs. Forbes Valuations

NBA Franchise	Reported Sale Price (in millions of dollars)	Sale Year	Forbes Value (in millions of dollars)	Forbes Year	Percentage Increase
Minnesota	1,500	2021	1,375	2020	9.1%
Utah	1,660	2020	1,425	2019	16.5%
Brooklyn	2,350	2019	1,800	2017	30.6%
Houston	2,200	2017	1,500	2016	46.7%
Atlanta	850	2015	425	2014	100.0%
LA Clippers	2,000	2014	430	2013	365.1%
Milwaukee	550	2014	312	2013	76.3%
Sacramento	534	2013	300	2012	78.0%
Memphis	350	2012	266	2011	31.6%
New Orleans	338	2012	280	2011	20.7%
TOTAL	**12,332**		**8,113**		**52.0%**

Data Source: Fort (n.d.)
Table created by author

> In fact, we estimate that, of the 23 teams that played in 2018, just seven turned a profit (and half of those were just barely in the black). Altogether, the league's teams lost more than $100 million last year. And MLS is losing even more money at the league level—as a single-entity operation, player salaries are paid through the league office—which means team owners are on the hook for a sizable capital call in addition to the red ink in their local markets.

Despite a lack of profits, MLS expansion fees keep rising. According to Barrabi (2019), in 2013 the New York FC paid $100 million to enter MLS. Six years later, Barrabi (2019) reported that a franchise in St. Louis paid $200 million. And then just a few months later, the expansion fee for a franchise in Charlotte was $325 million (Newton, 2019).

Smith (2019) doubted these expansion fees were about financial performance:

> Put simply, Major League Soccer's surging expansion fees and sales prices are not being driven by financial performance. In fact, although revenues are broadly on the rise, the league and most of its teams continue to operate at a significant loss.

So what explains these rising values? According to Steven Ryan (former commissioner of the Major Indoor Soccer League), rising franchise costs simply reflect supply and demand (Barrabi, 2019):

> I think it will continue to go up, and the reason for it is that there's really a small number of teams around North America. In order to get into the "club," the demand is outstripping the supply now, and that's going to force the prices to continue to go up, as it has in all of sports. The valuations on teams have, over the last four of five years, incredibly accelerated. One of the beneficiaries has been Major League Soccer.

This story might make some sense. As David Turney notes:[17]

> Professional sports franchises comprise a distinct market where teams typically sell at prices in excess of what would be expected based on traditional valuation methodologies. A significant reason for this is the limited number of teams available (123 total professional sports teams in the US) and the growing

Table 5.6 Change in NBA Franchise Values: 2011 vs. 2020

Team Change in NBA Franchise Values: 2011 vs. 2020	Forbes Value in 2011 in millions of dollars	Forbes Value in 2020 in millions of dollars	Percentage Increase
Atlanta Hawks	295	1,520	415.3%
Boston Celtics	452	3,100	585.8%
Brooklyn Nets	312	2,500	701.3%
Charlotte Hornets	281	1,500	433.8%
Chicago Bulls	511	3,200	526.2%
Cleveland Cavaliers	355	1,510	325.4%
Dallas Mavericks	438	2,400	447.9%
Denver Nuggets	316	1,600	406.3%
Detroit Pistons	360	1,450	302.8%
Golden State Warriors	363	4,300	1084.6%
Houston Rockets	443	2,475	458.7%
Indiana Pacers	269	1,525	466.9%
Los Angeles Clippers	305	2,600	752.5%
Los Angeles Lakers	643	4,400	584.3%
Memphis Grizzlies	266	1,300	388.7%
Miami Heat	425	1,950	358.8%
Milwaukee Bucks	258	1,580	512.4%
Minnesota Timberwolves	264	1,375	420.8%
New Orleans Pelicans	280	1,350	382.1%
New York Knicks	655	4,600	602.3%
Oklahoma City Thunder	329	1,575	378.7%
Orlando Magic	385	1,430	271.4%
Philadelphia 76ers	330	2,000	506.1%
Phoenix Suns	411	1,625	295.4%
Portland Trail Blazers	356	1,850	419.7%
Sacramento Kings	293	1,775	505.8%
San Antonio Spurs	404	1,800	345.5%
Toronto Raptors	399	2,100	426.3%
Utah Jazz	343	1,550	351.9%
Washington Wizards	322	1,750	443.5%
AVERAGE	**368.8**	**2,123.0**	**475.7%**

Data Source: Fort (n.d.)
Table created by author

number of billionaires (increased by 13% to 2,043 in 2017). Given the limited number of available assets and growing number of potential buyers, when a team becomes available for sale, the competition among potential buyers typically results in purchase prices in excess of what might seem rational based on the underlying economics of the business. Buyers of sports franchises are typically wealthy individuals for whom the attraction of ownership is based on its perceived "ego" or "trophy" value, as other individuals might purchase a new sports car.

This story hinges on the idea that the population of sports teams is limited. The population Turney notes (i.e. 123 teams in the U.S.) includes the teams in the NFL, MLB, NBA, and NHL. Of course, there are more teams than this. Clearly billionaire investors (who – like politicians – are predominantly men) see the MLS as worth investing in. But even if we add MLS teams to our total, it seems we are still underestimating the population of sports teams an investor might buy.

Yes, we are obviously omitting women's sports. It very much appears men love spending money on men's sports.[18] As a result, the franchise value of men's sports are often divorced from rational financial analysis. It is a very different story, though, in women's sports.

The NPF is the premier league in women's softball. But the Commissioner Cheri Kempf told Forbes in 2018 that one could purchase an expansion team in the NPF for $250,000 (Berri, 2018c). The price of a NWSL team is reportedly a bit higher. According to Kassouf (2019), the Seattle Reign sold for $3.5 million in 2019. The Reign employ Megan Rapinoe, one of the most famous players in women's soccer history. Despite employing Rapinoe, though, the Reign's price was less than 2 percent of the price of an MLS expansion team in Charlotte.

Prices for WNBA teams are not often reported. But a league source indicated the current expansion price for a WNBA team is between $10 million and $20 million. In 1970 – when the NBA was roughly the same age as the WNBA today – three expansion teams were added. These teams – the Portland Trail Blazers, Cleveland Cavaliers, and Buffalo Braves – paid $3.7 million to join the NBA. Adjusted for 2020 dollars, that expansion fee was $24.7 million.

Back in 1970 it wasn't obvious that a sports franchise could someday be worth much more. Despite this, NBA teams were still priced higher than WNBA teams. It is important to note what happened if you bought those Braves and kept them. Those Braves became the San Diego Clippers in 1978. And once again, in 2014 those Clippers sold for $2 billion.

One suspects that if you went back in time and told people in 1970 that 50 years later these NBA expansion teams would be worth billions, maybe someone would have paid a bit more than $3.7 million to purchase these teams. In fact, the fact MLS expansion teams sell for $325 million today appears to confirm that point.

Nevertheless, teams in women's sports simply don't see this sort of price inflation. For the price of one MLS expansion team, one could buy every single team in the NPF, NWSL, and WNBA.[19] But rich men aren't lining up to buy women's sports teams. Instead they are investing hundreds of millions of dollars in minor league soccer.[20] In sum, there clearly is an "gender enthusiasm gap" in sports!

The Future Was Female!

If these investors were interested in making money in the future, perhaps they would be more anxious to invest in women's sports. At least, that is the argument made by Lee, Westcott, Wray, and Raviprakash (2021). These authors argue that the value of women's sports is likely to increase dramatically in the next few years. Their argument rests on the fact that television audiences for women's sports are growing, in-person audiences for women's sports in recent years have often been quite impressive, and multi-country surveys indicate that 66 percent of people are interested in at least one women's sports (Lee, Westcott, Wray, & Raviprakash, 2021, p. 51).

The television audience numbers are especially compelling. As Ruthven (2020) notes, the MLS is Back Tournament final in 2020 only attracted 394,000 fans on ESPN while the average game in the tournament only attracted 226,000 viewers. In contrast, Gao (2020) reports the opening game to the NWSL Challenge Cup drew 572,000 viewers while the final attracted 653,000 viewers.

The argument advanced here is that women's sports are very much where the major men's sports were decades ago. In the case of the NWSL and MLS, though, it appears the women have already caught up with the men. At least, that's what the television audiences appear to be saying.

The investors, though, are telling a different story. The men investing in sports are saying that a MLS franchise is worth about 80 times more than a NWSL team. Of course, the value of men's teams does not seem connected to financial reality. What they appear to reflect is that when it comes to sports, men really love investing in men.

In the future, though, those who have invested in women's sports are likely to be the real winners. Women's sports very much look like men's sports were decades ago. Despite the headwinds women face, it is very likely revenue, attendance, and franchise values will continue to grow in women's professional sports. And when that future happens, those who own women's sports teams will be saying: "The Future Was Female!"

Notes

1 The discussion of the Civil Rights Act of 1964 and the specifics of Title IX can be found in Averett and Estelle (2013).
2 The Akron Racers of the NPF were part of the Women's Pro Softball League, which was founded in 1998.
3 Since four of its teams came from the Women's Professional Soccer league, one can argue the NWSL really began in 2007.
4 The dollar value of European soccer revenue was calculated with the Pound-to-Dollar exchange rate reported by PoundSterling Live (n.d.) on February 1, 2018.
5 Attendance numbers need to be considered relative to the size of the playing surface. For example, a basketball and hockey team has to limit attendance because the playing surface – relative to soccer and American football – is relatively small. Consequently, we should be cautious about comparing attendance numbers across sports. Given the size of the playing surface, soccer and American football can accommodate far more fans and will therefore likely always have larger audiences than games played on relatively small surfaces.
6 These statements can be found at Fort (n.d.). This site also reports the attendance and revenue data reported here.
7 This was part of a stretch from 1949 to 1958 where the Yankees won the American League pennant in nine out of ten years. And that is part of a longer stretch from 1921 to 1964 where the Yankees won the pennant 29 times in 44 years. Attendance across this longer time period definitely went up. Hence, the story economists once told wasn't valid if one simply looked at a longer time period.
8 Converting 1950s dollars into 2020 dollars was done via the Consumer Price Index reported by the Federal Reserve Bank of Minneapolis (n.d.).
9 Fort (n.d.) reports NHL attendance back to 1963. Prior to this year, Ford (n.d.) reports a sample of data created by Brian Mills. This data is incomplete. Therefore, the NHL number reported in Table 5.3 should be thought of as an estimate.
10 Pro Football Reference reports the years each NFL team was in operation. See www.pro-football-reference.com/teams/.
11 Baseball Reference reports data on average game attendance for each team in 1925. See www.baseball-reference.com/leagues/MLB/1925-misc.shtml.
12 See Berri (2018b) and Agha and Berri (2021).
13 The sales price of the Clippers in 1981 is reported by Fort (n.d.). Data on the CPI from the Federal Reserve Bank of Minneapolis (n.d.) was used to calculate the 2020 value.
14 This was in response to Sterling making racially insensitive remarks (Berger, 2014). It was not because he was a very bad owner (although, his record makes it clear he wasn't very good!).
15 There is a lag in the Forbes valuations. So the reported price could be thought of as the value of the team 12 to 24 months before the actual sale.
16 Without the Clippers sale, there is still a 35 percent average difference between final sales price and the Forbes valuation from a year earlier.
17 www.toptal.com/finance/mergers-and-acquisitions/sports-franchise-valuation.
18 The spending on men's sports league goes beyond what people are paying to buy these teams. For decades, men's sports leagues in North America have invented ways to limit how much owners can spend on playing talent. The list of restrictions includes reverse order drafts, payroll caps, individual salary caps, and luxury taxes. All of these institutions definitely lower the pay of players and certainly one can believe leagues are motivated to put these restrictions in place to reduce their payrolls. But leagues also insist these institutions exist to prevent rich owners from spending so much on talent that the teams'

19 If each WNBA team is worth $20 million (the high-end expansion price estimate), then one could buy the entire league of 12 teams for $240 million. If each NWSL team is worth $4 million (similar to the price of the Rapinoe's Reign), then that ten team league would cost $40 million. And the six NPF teams – given an expansion price of $250,000 – are worth less than $2 million. Hence, all three leagues cost less than $300 million!
20 Men also love investing in minor football leagues. Unfortunately, as Sherman (2019) notes, there is a very long list of football leagues that have failed: *"They're running out of space in the Graveyard of Failed Football Leagues. There are already tombstones for the World Football League, the United States Football League, the original XFL, the United Football League, the Fall Experimental Football League, the Continental Football League, the All-American Football League, the Stars Football League, and a bevy of arena football leagues. Now, they are joined by the Alliance of American Football, whose majority owner has made the strange decision to bury the still-breathing league alive in the midst of its first season."*

References

2020 NFL Attendance Data. Pro Football-Reference.com (n.d.). www.pro-football-reference.com/years/2020/attendance.htm.

2019 NWSL Attendance. Soccer Stadium Digest (n.d.). https://soccerstadiumdigest.com/2019-nwsl-attendance/.

Across the Timeline. (n.d.). Yearly WNBA Attendance. https://acrossthetimeline.com/wnba/attendance.html.

Agha, N. & Berri, D. (2021). "Gender differences in the pay of professional basketball players" in Ali Bowes & Alex Culvin (Eds.) *The Professionalisation of Women's Sport: Issues and Debates.* Emerald Studies in Sports and Gender Series. idrottsforum.org.

Atlanta Braves Team History & Encyclopedia. Baseball-Reference.com (n.d.). www.baseball-reference.com/teams/ATL/.

Averett, S. L. & Estelle, S. M. (2013). The Economics of Title IX Compliance in Intercollegiate Athletics. In *Handbook on the Economics of Women in Sports.* Edited by Eva Marikova Leeds & Michael Leeds. Edward Elgar Press, pp. 175–212.

Baade, R. & Matheson, V. (2012). Financing Professional Sports Facilities. In *Financing Economic Development in the 21st Century. 2nd edition.* Editors Sammis White & Zenia Kotval. Routledge Press. pp. 323–342.

Bailum, A. (2021, January 9). WNBA Ticket Prices: Everything You Need to Know. *Queen Ballers Club.* https://queenballers.club/basketball/wnba-ticket-prices.

Barrabi, T. (2020, February 3). What is the NFL worth? Revenue, team values and other financial facts. *Fox Business.* www.foxbusiness.com/sports/nfl-worth-revenue-team-values.

Barrabi, T. (2019, August 20). MLS expands to St. Louis: Why $200M startup fee may soon seem like a bargain. *Fox Sports Business.* www.foxbusiness.com/features/mls-st-louis-team-expansion-fee-cost.

Baseball Reference. (n.d.). Major League Teams and Baseball Encyclopedia. www.baseball-reference.com/teams/.

Bell, D. (2020, April 9). Atlanta Braves are 12th-most valuable MLB team, worth $1.8 billion according to Forbes. *Talking Chop.* www.talkingchop.com/2020/4/9/21215483/forbes-mlb-baseball-valuations-atlanta-braves-billion-dollars-truist-park-tv-revenue.

Bendix, P. (2008, November 18). The History of the American and National League, Part I. *SB Nation: Beyond the Boxscore.* www.beyondtheboxscore.com/2008/11/18/664028/the-history-of-the-america.

Berger, K. (2014, August 12). Sale of Clippers to Steve Ballmer closes; Donald Sterling out. *CBSsports.com.* www.cbssports.com/nba/news/sale-of-clippers-to-steve-ballmer-closes-donald-sterling-out/.

Berri, D. (2021). Making Sports Economics Inclusive: Why You Aren't Teaching Sports Economics Well if Women are not Part of your Story. Working paper.

Berri, D. (2020, February 22). Basketball's Gender Wage Gap Narrows (but doesn't vanish!). *Winsidr.* https://winsidr.com/2020/02/12/basketballs-gender-wage-gap-narrows-but-doesnt-vanish/.

Berri, D. (2018c, August 6). Now Might Be The Time To Buy A Women's Professional Sports Team. *Forbes.com.* www.forbes.com/sites/davidberri/2018/08/06/now-might-be-the-time-to-buy-a-womens-professional-sports-team/#2637fec57be9.

Berri, D. (2018b) *Sports Economics*. Worth Publishers/Macmillan Education.
Berri, D. (2018a, March 25). In the sports marketplace, politicians are helping men's sports leagues win the race. *Forbes*. Retrieved from www.forbes.com/sites/davidberri/2018/03/25/in-the-sports-marketplace-politicians-are-helping-mens-sports-leagues-win-the-race/#333f3daf78b5.
Brown, M. (2019, December 21). MLB Sees Record $10.7 Billion In Revenues For 2019. *Forbes.com*. www.forbes.com/sites/maurybrown/2019/12/21/mlb-sees-record-107-billion-in-revenues-for-2019/?sh=1655aa405d78.
Consumer Price Index 1913– (n.d.) Federal Reserve Bank of Minneapolis. www.minneapolisfed.org/about-us/monetary-policy/inflation-calculator/consumer-price-index-1913-.
Cooky, C., Messner, M.A., & Musto, M. (2015). "It's Dude Time!" A quarter century of excluding women's sports in televised news and highlight shows. *Communication & Sport*, 3(3), 261–287.
Florio, M. (2021, March 11). NFL revenue drops from $16 billion in 2019 to $12 billion in 2020. *NBC Sports*. https://profootballtalk.nbcsports.com/2021/03/11/nfl-revenue-drops-from-16-billion-to-12-billion-in-2020/.
Fort, R. (n.d.). *Rodney Fort's Sports Business Data*. https://sites.google.com/site/rodswebpages/codes.
Gao, Michelle. (2020, December 13). "Women's soccer set viewership records in 2020 — now it needs to keep them watching." CNBC.com. www.cnbc.com/2020/12/13/womens-soccer-viewership-records-paving-expansion.html.
Historical Rates for the GBP/USD currency conversion on 01 February 2018 (01/02/2018). *PoundSterling Live*. www.poundsterlinglive.com/best-exchange-rates/british-pound-to-us-dollar-exchange-rate-on-2018-02-01.
The History of the Cincinnati Reds Baseball Team. Baseball Almanac. (n.d.) www.baseball-almanac.com/teams/reds.shtml.
Johnson, M. (2021, March 20). NFL Salary Cap Could Climb Past $200 Million for 2022 Season? *Yardbarker.com*. www.yardbarker.com/nfl/articles/nfl_salary_cap_could_climb_past_200_million_for_2022_season/s1_12680_34412705#.
Johnston, L. and Williamson, S.H. (n.d.), What Was the U.S. GDP Then? *MeasuringWorth*, 2022 www.measuringworth.com/datasets/usgdp/.
Jones, W. (n.d.). What is the yearly revenue of the NHL? (plus, where it comes from). *Hockey Answered*. https://hockeyanswered.com/what-is-the-yearly-revenue-of-the-nhl/.
Kassouf, J. (2019, December 19). OL Groupe agrees to take over Reign FC at valuation of $3.51 million. *The Equalizer*. https://equalizersoccer.com/2019/12/19/ol-groupe-acquires-reign-fc-nearly-4-million-dollar-valuation-nwsl/.
Keh, A. & Das, A. (2020, July 2). Federal Loan Saved a Soccer Season Nearly Lost to the Pandemic. *New York Times*. www.nytimes.com/2020/07/02/sports/soccer/nwsl-ppp-loan.html.
Klein, C. (2014, September 4). The Birth of the National Football League. *History.com*. www.history.com/news/the-birth-of-the-national-football-league.
Lee, P., Westcott, K., Wray, I., & Raviprakash, S. (2021). "Women's Sports Gets Down to Business." *Deloitte Insights: Technology, Media, and Telecommunications Predictions for 2021* (pp. 51–65). www2.deloitte.com/cn/en/pages/technology-media-and-telecommunications/articles/tmt-predictions-2021-womens-sports-revenue.html.
Mansky, J. & M. Wei-Haas. (2016, August 18). The Rise of the Modern Sportswoman: Women have long fought against the assumption that they are weaker than men, and the battle isn't over yet. *Smithsonian Magazine*. www.smithsonianmag.com/science-nature/rise-modern-sportswoman-180960174/.
Matheson, V. (2021). "Trends in public financing for professional sports stadiums in the US and Canada." Working paper.
Neale, W. (1964). "The Peculiar Economics of Professional Sports." *The Quarterly Journal of Economics*, 78, n1: 1–14.
Negley, C. (2019, November 1). NWSL raises salaries for 2020, introduces allocation money for world's top talent. *Yahoo! Sports*. https://sports.yahoo.com/nwsl-raises-salaries-for-2020-introduces-allocation-money-for-worlds-top-talent-compensation-203930099.html.
Newton, D. (2019, December 17). Charlotte gets MLS' 30th franchise for record $325 million. *ESPN.com*. www.espn.com/soccer/major-league-soccer/story/4015203/charlotte-gets-mls-30th-franchise-for-record-$325-million.
NFL Attendance – 2019. *ESPN.com*. (n.d.) www.espn.com/nfl/attendance/_/year/2019.
Ourand, J. (2016, May 9). ESPN's new deal double rights fee. *Sports Business Journal*. www.sportsbusinessdaily.com/Journal/Issues/2016/05/09/Media/ESPN-WNBA.aspx.

Reed, A. (2019, May 30). European soccer posts record revenues with the English Premier League leading the way. *CNBC.com*. www.cnbc.com/2019/05/30/european-soccer-posts-record-revenues-as-epl-dominates-deloitte.html.

Ruthven, G. (2020). "MLS is pulling fans into stadiums, but TV audiences remain underwhelming." *The Guardian*. (August 25). www.theguardian.com/football/2020/aug/25/mls-tv-audiences-viewing-figures.

Schwartz, N. (2014, August 12). Steve Ballmer Explains Why He Paid $2 Billion for the Clippers. *USA Today*. https://ftw.usatoday.com/2014/08/steve-ballmer-2-billion-clippers.

Season Review: 1946–47. (2017, August 23). *NBA.com* (n.d.). www.nba.com/history/season-recap/1946-47.

Sherman, A. & J. Young. (2021, March 18). NFL finalizes new 11-year media rights deal, Amazon gets exclusive Thursday Night rights. *CNBC.com*. www.cnbc.com/2021/03/18/nfl-media-rights-deal-2023-2033-amazon-gets-exclusive-thursday-night.html.

Sherman, R. (2019). "The AAF Failed Because All Minor League Football Does." *The Ringer*. (April 4). www.theringer.com/nfl/2019/4/4/18294528/american-alliance-football-aaf-collapse-suspend-xfl.

Smith, C. (2019, November 4). Major League Soccer's Most Valuable Teams 2019: Atlanta Stays On Top As Expansion Fees, Sale Prices Surge. *Forbes.com* www.forbes.com/sites/chrissmith/2019/11/04/major-league-soccers-most-valuable-teams-2019-atlanta-stays-on-top-as-expansion-fees-sale-prices-surge/?sh=74bf9ff551b5.

Story of the Braves. MLB.com. (n.d.). www.mlb.com/braves/history/story-of-the-braves.

Ward, J. (2008, December 29). The Founding Clubs of the English Football League: Where Are They Now?. *Bleacher Report*. https://bleacherreport.com/articles/98145-the-founding-clubs-of-the-english-football-league-where-are-they-now.

What Was the U.S. GDP Then?. MeasuringWorth.com. (n.d.). www.measuringworth.com/datasets/usgdp/.

WNBA League Attendance (n.d.) *Across the Timeline* https://acrossthetimeline.com/wnba/attendance.html.

Young, J. (2021, March 22). NBA is next up for a big rights increase, and $75 billion is the price. *CNBC.com*. www.cnbc.com/2021/03/22/nba-is-next-up-for-a-big-rights-increase-and-75-billion-is-the-price.html.

Zimbalist, A. (2001). *Unpaid Professionals*. Princeton University Press.

6
Comparing the Cost of Fandom in European Football

Selçuk Özaydın and Cem Tınaz

Introduction

The "modern" form of football was born in England in the mid-nineteenth century. Although football has always received the attention of the masses, it lacked clarified rules for a long time and has been subject to prohibitions many times in countries such as England, Scotland, and France from the Middle Ages through to the modern day (Stemmler, 2008). However, with the birth of capitalism, it started to evolve as a "game." The deepening and widening capitalism of the industrialization process turned football inevitably into a "show." Today, modern football has gone beyond being just a game and has begun to function as a social life model, creating roles in and transferring values to social life. Hewer et al. (2017, p. 601) define football as "a global industry where lifestyle, image and brand governance converge and do battle with affective emotion and the tribal language of participation and politics." It contributes to the preservation of the existing status quo and acts as an effective agent in conveying and adopting the economic values of the new era to large masses. One can argue that excessive commercialization and professionalization are two important indicators of today's transformation of industrial football. Global media plays a critical role in this transformation as it reconfigures global sports tastes, attitudes, and values according to their own interests. As the liberal wave experienced worldwide during the late 1970s and early 1980s affected football and accelerated its commodification process, football became massified and commercialized, and football clubs' structures began to change; associations gave way to commercial organizations and, more recently, to professional companies. Football clubs can no longer act simply as sports organizations: they have transformed into business enterprises.

The industrialization process of football reorganized football fans too. In modern times, clubs actively seek out an audience that can pay more. Williams (2007) argued that late-modern football evolved into a product to be sold to eager consumers. The football industry's survival and development depend on new fans. When the power of football to influence large masses is combined with the consumption ideology, it ensures an indispensable sector for the free-market economy. Traditionally, football clubs' main sources of income have been the matchday revenue. However, as with any commodity, the growing costs and increasing quality in football have caused its prices to similarly increase. Matchday revenue's inadequacy in meeting the increasing expenses

DOI: 10.4324/9780429342189-7

of the clubs has paved the way for the emergence of a wide variety of income streams: advertising and sponsorship revenues, broadcasting rights revenues, seasonal ticket and lodge sales revenues, merchandise sales revenues, etc. When the clubs' income streams are examined in detail, it is easily seen that the broadcasting revenues are the main source of income for most of the clubs; however, it is often disregarded that clubs are able to generate millions of euros through broadcasting agreements thanks to their fans. For fans, consuming football has become much costlier than before. The billion-euro broadcasting rights deals cause media subscription fees to increase, which the fans pay. The kit sponsorships generate millions of euros for the clubs but at the cost of increasing prices of club merchandise bought by the fans. In addition, as clubs are always seeking ways to increase their revenues like any other producers, and since they have full control over ticket prices, they are able to increase ticket prices. From TV subscriptions to club merchandise and match tickets, football consumers face increasing costs from all directions. Luckily, some clubs are aware of the increasing burden on fans' shoulders, but some are not.

The cost of being a fan varies greatly both in absolute terms and relative terms. In particular, fans who live in metropolitan areas where life is already costly, such as London, Paris, Madrid or Istanbul, might be struggling to support their teams. This chapter aims to compare the absolute cost of football fandom in seven European countries. First, however, the theoretical background of football fandom and the essential elements of the cost of being a fan will be introduced. Later, the absolute cost of being a fan will be presented for a selection of teams from the Big 5, Turkish Super League and Portuguese Primeira Liga. The teams with the highest game attendance from each league are selected for the comparison. Since the second half of the 2019/2020 season was played behind closed doors due to the COVID-19 pandemic, all the figures regarding attendance and cost belong to the 2018/2019 season. Following the absolute cost, the relative cost of being a fan is analyzed using minimum wage and GDP per capita. The income statistics are gathered from Eurostat's database. The statistics regarding attendance, ticket prices, the cost of TV subscriptions and merchandise prices are collected from newspapers', magazines' and broadcasting companies' websites, all of which can be found in the References section.

Sports Fandom

In the sports industry, the concepts of spectatorship and fandom are differentiated (Keaton et al., 2015). Sports spectators do not have fan affiliations with any specific team – they watch sports competitions because they enjoy the competition between rivals and the aesthetic value of sports. Sloan (1989) defined spectators as simply people who are watching and following sport, and the fans as people who voluntarily take sides in a particular competition and show devotion. Many sports fans are considered spectators: they watch sports events simply due to the excitement and entertainment of sports. The time, energy, and money that these individuals devote to sports can all be regarded as a kind of consumption behavior. What differentiates them from more serious fans is that they can stop watching activities that do not meet their expectations and turn to activities that will satisfy them. On the other hand, the interest of fans who strongly identify with their teams is beyond the cycle of expectation and satisfaction. In addition to meeting individuals' needs for social prestige and reputation, fandom can also respond to their needs for sincerity, unity, and solidarity (Zillmann et al., 1979).

As a component of sports consumption, fandom has different characteristics from the usual consumption definitions (Wakefield, 2007). The difference of fandom arises from the identification that expresses the loyalty of fans to their teams. It is rare for a fan who strongly identifies himself/herself with any sports team to turn into a different team supporter for any reason. The bond between fans and teams occurs at deeper psychological and emotional levels than the bond between customers and brands. In many sectors, when competition between actors (brands) increases, consumer loyalty to brands may decrease. However, in a sports league, when competition increases, fans' ties with their teams tend to strengthen. Fandom can be considered to be a socio-psychological phenomenon in which all fans live interactively with each other as social actors, in addition to being a form of consumption consisting of relations between teams and their supporters.

Abercrombie & Longhurst (1998), as well as Jones (2000), indicate sports fandom is a serious leisure activity. They have validated their claim using Stebbins' (1992) six defining characteristics of serious leisure: perseverance throughout the activity, a long-term career, significant personal effort, achievement of self-benefits, unique ethos and, finally, strong identification. Jones (2000) added a seventh characteristic to this validation: the importance of group membership, which provides a link between social identity and leisure. Fan identity often develops at a young age through socializing agents such as family, immediate surroundings, and the influence of the geographic area (Keaton & Gearhart, 2014; Melnick & Wann, 2011). Fans acknowledge the identity of their teams as a part of their social identity and see this identity as a decisive phenomenon when developing psychological ties not only with their teams, but also with other people (Wann & Branscombe, 1993). Fillis and Mackay (2014) suggested that fandom can allow individuals the opportunity to feel a sense of togetherness and cohesion with fellow supporters. The sense of togetherness and cohesion creates a network of relationships consisting of a collective memory, language, and attitudes. Fandom can also be a way for people to "reinvent" or to "re-imagine" a sense of locality through their sporting ties. In his work on production, consumption and fan identities in European club football, King (2003) concluded that urban or regional sporting affiliations and solidarities are becoming more prominent. He asserted that the fans of major European football teams develop new European identities based around their fellow fans and their international travel to attend games. Furthermore, they connect to the symbolic role of their soccer clubs and raise the international profile of the cities they represent. In this way, in addition to their links to places and communities, globalized sport teams have managed to reach out to masses outside their hometowns and even their home countries.

Due to this developing fan identity, despite the growing costs, the interest in European football is not decreasing. Football is transforming into a luxury good, and, as in the boiling frog metaphor, fans have adapted. The costs increased steadily over the past several decades, and, despite outpacing inflation, many fans have been accepting of the increasing costs because deep down they believe they are helping their beloved clubs by attending games and buying club merchandise. On the other side of the coin, there is a group of fans who are no longer able to afford football. Even though the interest in football is not decreasing, this does not mean that football is accessible to everyone. Some fans are left out because the cost of fandom is increasing rapidly. As Feehan and his colleagues (2003) illustrate, the growing costs exclude poorer fans; therefore, the transformation of football is also resulting in the transformation of the fanbase. For the low-income groups, football is becoming less and less affordable each season.

Elements of Cost of Fandom

Undoubtedly, when talking about being a football fan, the first thing that comes to mind is watching games. It does not matter whether a fan decides to attend games or watch them on TV – either way it is going to cost him/her serious amounts of money. In the last couple of decades, new stadiums have been built all around Europe, and such gigantic infrastructural investments require significant funding. A club undertakes such a project aiming to increase their future revenues. The new stadium is bigger and better than the previous, and obviously, the improvement in quality commands higher prices. Clubs build new stadiums in the hope of increasing future revenues and most of the time, they do. Stadiums are no longer just places where a game is played once every two weeks but are a center of entertainment which operate continuously throughout the year. As a result of transformation in European football, as crowds and stadiums grew and as player wages continued to rise, ticket prices began increasing in the 1990s. However, watching the game from home to avoid high ticket prices isn't much less expensive. Fans can choose to watch games on TV or stream them online. Of the two, streaming has become more common in recent years. Although the billion-euro broadcasting deals generate large revenues for clubs, the broadcasting revenues are passed along to the fans in the form of subscription fees, thereby increasing the cost for fans.

Table 6.1 provides a breakdown of clubs' revenue for 2018/2019. Today, broadcasting revenues account for the highest share of total revenue in all the major leagues of European football. Through satellite broadcasting, millions around the world are able to watch top football games live. Especially during the COVID-19 pandemic when most league games are played with no or a limited number of fans, the importance of live broadcasts has increased for the devoted fans who want to see their teams playing. From 2012/2013 to 2018/2019 the share of broadcasting in total revenue has increased from 47 to 59 percent, whereas the share of matchday revenues decreased from 21 to 13 percent in the Premier League (Deloitte, 2013; 2020). Although matchday revenue has been increasing, its revenue share has decreased due to the faster increase in broadcasting and commercial revenues.

Club merchandise is another important element of cost for the fans. Often fans dress up in the colors of their beloved club, not only while attending games but also while watching the games on TV at home or outside with fellow fans. Today, clubs produce hundreds of different club-branded products from clothes to keychains and from glassware to towels. Among the huge range of alternatives, the most purchased club merchandise is the team kit. Unlike in the past, the team jerseys today are stylish and chic and made of high-quality fabric. A jersey is not something to wear only while watching or playing sports – it is a piece of clothing which is often worn in daily lives.

Table 6.2 presents the various elements of costs for the selected 22 teams from the seven major leagues of Europe. Teams with the highest average attendance in the 2018/2019 season were selected for the investigation, with the exception of Chelsea FC from the English Premier League. Due to Chelsea FC's relatively low stadium capacity, it has the eighth highest average attendance in the Premier League. Even though Chelsea is not among the teams with the highest

Table 6.1 2018/2019 Leagues' Revenues Breakdown

League	Broadcasting	Matchday	Commercial	Total Revenue (million euros)
England	59%	13%	28%	5851
France	47%	11%	42%	1902
Germany	44%	16%	40%	3345
Italy	59%	11%	30%	2495
Portugal	53%	15%	32%	440
Spain	54%	16%	30%	3375
Turkey	51%	12%	37%	748

Source: Deloitte, 2020

Table 6.2 Elements of Cost for the 2018/2019 Season

League	Team	Season Ticket Min	Jersey Price	TV Subscription	Total Cost €
Premier League	Arsenal	1006.47	62.13	1072.35	2140.95
Premier League	Chelsea	847.20	73.37	1072.35	1992.92
Premier League	Liverpool	773.78	62.13	1072.35	1908.26
Premier League	Manchester City	350.18	73.37	1072.35	1495.90
Premier League	Manchester United	600.95	73.37	1072.35	1746.67
Ligue 1	Olympique Lyon	252.00	69.90	233.10	555.00
Ligue 1	Olympique Marseille	170.00	69.90	233.10	473.00
Ligue 1	Paris Saint-Germain	430.00	100.00	233.10	763.10
Bundesliga	Bayern Munich	140.00	89.95	278.91	508.86
Bundesliga	Borussia Dortmund	215.00	84.99	278.91	578.90
Bundesliga	Schalke 04	190.50	82.90	278.91	552.31
Serie A	AC Milan	205.00	90.00	494.10	789.10
Serie A	Inter Milan	235.00	119.00	494.10	848.10
Serie A	Juventus FC	595.00	129.95	494.10	1219.05
Primeira Liga	FC Porto	70.00	80.00	269.91	419.91
Primeira Liga	SL Benfica	90.00	89.95	359.01	538.96
La Liga	Atlético Madrid	290.00	84.95	720.00	1094.95
La Liga	FC Barcelona	150.00	85.00	720.00	955.00
La Liga	Real Madrid	394.00	90.00	720.00	1204.00
Süper Lig	Beşiktaş JK	250.46	35.06	181.98	467.51
Süper Lig	Fenerbahçe SK	222.63	35.06	181.98	439.68
Süper Lig	Galatasaray SK	222.63	35.23	181.98	439.85

[a] The cost figures have been gathered from various websites and industry reports.

Source: Compiled by authors[a]

attendance, it is one of the most successful teams in the Premier League in recent history and it is one of the "big 6[1]" in the Premier League therefore it was included in the investigation. Season ticket prices are used for comparison since for most of the teams, the majority of the fans attending games are season ticket holders. In the Premier League, the percentage of season ticket holders in attendance vary between 50 and 80 percent (Kendrick, 2020). The prices that were not in euros were converted to euros using the exchange rates on July 2, 2018.[2] The television subscription fees are for nine months since seasons in European football last about nine months, and fans can cancel their subscriptions during the summer when the league games are not played.

Each team sells several types of season tickets, and the prices vary greatly depending on where the sold seat is. All presented results are based on minimum season ticket prices. The most affordable season tickets among the Big 5 are in Germany, thanks to the "50 + 1 Rule." In order for a club to be able to compete in the Bundesliga, the majority of the club's shares must be held by the fans. This rule enables the fans to have a say in the club operations and prevents German clubs from being taken over by foreign investors (Bundesliga, 2017). The fans' active participation in club operations causes the ticket prices to be more affordable in comparison to the other Big 5 leagues. The "fan friendly" ticket prices enable German Bundesliga to have the second highest capacity utilization rates[3] in European football with 89.5 percent in the 2018/2019 season (Transfermarkt, 2019). Among the selected seven leagues, Portuguese Primeira Division teams have the lowest season ticket prices, and the most expensive season tickets are in the Premier League.

The lowest jersey prices are in Turkey as a result of the Turkish lira's low value against the euro. Although subscription and ticket prices are very high in England, surprisingly the English clubs have the second cheapest jerseys among the selected leagues. The most expensive jerseys are in Italy and Juventus leads the way with almost 130 euros for a single jersey. It is important to mention that Cristiano Ronaldo's move to Juventus was in the beginning of the 2018/2019 season and Juventus increased their jersey prices by about 10 euros from 2017/2018 to 2018/2019 – which can perhaps be called the "Ronaldo effect."

Watching football on TV or streaming online costs the most in England by far. It costs more than 1000 euro per season, almost 50 percent more than Spain in second place. The main reason for the inflated prices in England is that there are three different broadcasters. If a fan wants to watch all the games of their team, they have to subscribe to Sky Sports, BT Sport, and Amazon. These three broadcasters broadcast different games in different weeks. It should be mentioned that in Germany and Italy there are also more than one broadcaster,[4] but the prices are not as high as in England. The cheapest subscription is in Turkey as in the case of jersey pricing since the subscription fees are paid in lira and are therefore lower compared to the other major leagues in Europe. Turkish lira is much less valuable than euro and sterling, therefore when the prices of subscription and jersey are adjusted they are the cheapest among the investigated teams. Although there is a centralized broadcasting system in the Portuguese Primeria League, SL Benfica is not part of the deal. Benfica's home games are broadcast on Benfica TV (Dixon, 2020). A Benfica fan who wants to watch all Benfica's league games has to subscribe to two different broadcasters, resulting in TV subscription costs higher than FC Porto's.

The top five costliest teams among the selected 22 teams are the English teams. Juventus, Real Madrid, and Atletico Madrid follow the English teams with all their costs totaling over 1000 euros. It is important to mention that the English Premier League also generates the highest broadcasting, merchandise, and matchday revenues. Therefore, it is not surprising to see that the Premier League is the costliest league since these high revenues are generated in part by fans' generous spending.

The total cost's standard deviation is highest among the English teams, indicating the highest variation in the cost of fandom. Arsenal fans' burden is about 650 euros more per season when compared to Manchester City fans. The lowest variation is in Turkey, where the costs of being a Beşiktaş, Fenerbahçe, and Galatasaray fan are very close to each other, although among the three, being a Beşiktaş fan is the costliest.

Figure 6.1 visualizes the total cost of being a fan across Europe. For each country the average of the chosen teams is plotted on the map.

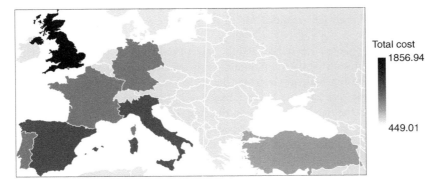

Figure 6.1 Absolute Cost of Being a Football Fan in Europe
Source: Authors' own contribution

The Cost of Fandom in European Football

Figure 6.2 Cost of Being a Football Fan in Europe as a Percentage of GPD per Capita
Source: Authors' own contribution

Table 6.3 Indicators of Income for the Selected Countries

Country	GDP per Capita €	Minimum Wage € (Yearly)
Germany	35,840	19,008
France	33,270	18,468
Italy	26,920	14,560[a]
Portugal	18,590	8,892
Spain	25,200	13,296
Turkey	11,500	4,596
United Kingdom	32,850	18,996

[a] There is no general minimum wage in Italy, wages are set with collective bargaining agreements for each sector. The minimum wage figure for Italy is computed using minimum hourly wage and maximum weekly working hours (De Matteis et al., n.d.).

Among the chosen teams, the fans in England have the highest fandom cost, whereas the Turkish fans cover the lowest costs. But, as mentioned earlier the low cost in Turkey is due to the Turkish lira's low value against the euro. Therefore, the aggregate cost is not a good measure to compare the cost of football fandom in Turkey with other European countries. Following Turkey, the lowest costs are in Portugal with 480 euros per year. After the total costs for the English, the total costs are highest for Spanish football fans (1084 euros), followed by the Italians (952 euros). German (546 euros) and French (597 euros) fans yearly burdens are close to each other.

Table 6.3 presents the GDP per capita and minimum wage figures for the selected countries. The lowest GDP per capita and minimum wage are in Turkey as expected due to the Turkish lira's low value against the euro and sterling. Turkey has the poorest fans among the seven countries. Germany is leading in both measures, followed by the United Kingdom and France. However, these three countries' GDP per capita and minimum wage are very close to each other. Fans in Germany, the UK, and France are the richest. Italy, Spain, and Portugal follow these three, but there is a significant difference between the fans of these two groups of countries. Among the second group, Italy and Spain are close to each other, while Portugal is further behind the two.

Figures 6.2 and 6.3 illustrate the cost of fandom as a percentage of minimum wage and as a percentage of GDP per capita, instead of the total cost. Using these two parameters instead of the total cost enables a better comparison for two main reasons: firstly, these are better measures of

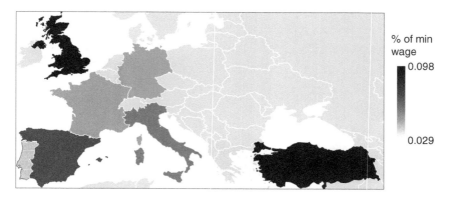

Figure 6.3 Cost of Being a Football Fan in Europe as a Percentage of Minimum Wage
Source: Authors' own contribution

true cost since they take income differences between countries, and secondly, there are leagues in the data set which are not in the Eurozone, thereby negating the differences between domestic currencies.

The cost of fandom is the highest in the English Premier League in both measures. Although the UK has the highest minimum wage and third highest GDP per capita among the selected countries, the high cost of tickets and broadcasting subscriptions cause the Premier League to be the costliest league. The Turkish Super League comes after the Premier League in terms of cost as a percentage of minimum wage. Although the Turkish teams have the lowest total cost, along with the Portuguese teams, due to the Turkish lira's low value, it is relatively costly for the fans. In terms of percentage of GDP per capita, the Spanish teams in the data set are the costliest after the English clubs. The Turkish and Italian teams follow the Spanish teams.

The Turkish Super League and Portuguese Primeira League are the lowest revenue-generating two leagues in the data set. In addition to their lower popularity compared to the Big 5, these two countries also have the lowest income among the selected countries. As mentioned earlier, despite the million-euro sponsorship and broadcasting deals, the real financiers of the clubs are the fans, and, since the fans in Turkey and Portugal do not have as much income as the fans in Big 5 leagues, these two leagues have a lower revenue-generating potential.

Table 6.4 presents the cost of fandom for each of the 22 teams as a percentage of income.

In general, being a fan in France or Germany is relatively more budget-friendly, due to the fact that these two countries have high income and low absolute costs, with the exception of Paris Saint-Germain, whose total cost is 50 percent more than the other German and French teams. Consuming football is relatively more affordable in these countries. Even the low-income groups are able to consume football since it only costs about 3 percent of minimum wage. However, in England and Turkey, consuming football is very costly. Fans that are earning minimum wage would need to devote around 10 percent of their yearly income to be able to support their team. Although some teams like Juventus, Atlético Madrid, and Real Madrid are also very costly for low-income groups, in general football is much more affordable in the rest of Europe.

Despite having relatively lower income compared to the Big 5 countries, consuming football in Portugal is quite affordable. In this sense, Portuguese clubs are very fan friendly. Portuguese clubs have the lowest season ticket prices by far, which enables fans from all income groups to attend games and support their teams.

Table 6.4 Cost of Fandom as a Percentage of Income

Team	% of Min Wage	% of GDP per Capita
Arsenal	0.113	0.065
Chelsea	0.105	0.061
Liverpool	0.100	0.058
Manchester City	0.079	0.046
Manchester United	0.092	0.053
Olympique Lyon	0.030	0.017
Olympique Marseille	0.027	0.014
Paris Saint-Germain	0.041	0.023
Bayern Munich	0.027	0.014
Borussia Dortmund	0.030	0.016
FC Schalke 04	0.029	0.015
AC Milan	0.054	0.029
Inter Milan	0.058	0.032
Juventus FC	0.084	0.045
FC Porto	0.047	0.023
SL Benfica	0.061	0.029
Atlético Madrid	0.082	0.043
Barcelona	0.072	0.038
Real Madrid	0.091	0.048
Beşiktaş JK	0.102	0.041
Fenerbahçe SK	0.096	0.038
Galatasaray SK	0.096	0.038

Source: Authors' own contribution

According to the Deloitte Money League 2020, Bayern Munich was the fourth highest revenue-generating team in European football in the 2018/2019 season (Deloitte, 2020). However, Bayern Munich has the lowest cost as a percentage of income in both measures, whereas the costliest three teams, Arsenal, Chelsea, and Liverpool are not among the top five highest revenue-generating teams. Barcelona was the highest revenue-generating team in the 2018/2019 season, followed by Real Madrid and Manchester United.

The 20 highest revenue-generating teams in Europe were all from the Big 5 in the 2018/2019 season. The last time a Turkish or Portuguese club was in the top 20 in terms of revenue was in the 2013/2014 season when Galatasaray was the eighteenth highest revenue-generating team in Europe. Since then, only one other team from outside the Big 5, Zenit St. Petersburg in 2015/2016, managed to get into the top 20.

Conclusion

The financial gap between the Big 5 and the others in terms of revenue generation has been growing rapidly in the past few decades. The Big 5 outperform the rest of the leagues in terms of sportive performance and popularity, but it should be noted that the differences in countries' populations and incomes are fundamental factors that also contribute to the gap. In rich countries, fans have more disposable income for consuming football. The fans in the Big 5 leagues are relatively wealthier compared to the fans in the other important football leagues in Europe, such as Turkey and Portugal. However, a countries' wealth does not necessarily predict revenues. Sports cultures and traditions also influence sports participation and popularity and therefore the

Table 6.5 Most Revenue Generating Top 20 Teams in the 18/19 Season

Team	Revenue (€)
Barcelona	840.8m
Real Madrid	757.3m
Manchester United	711.5m
Bayern Munich	660.1m
Paris Saint-Germain	635.9m
Manchester City	610.6m
Liverpool	604.7m
Tottenham Hotspur	521.1m
Chelsea	513.1m
Juventus	459.7m
Arsenal	445.6m
Borussia Dortmund	377.1m
Atlético Madrid	367.6m
Inter Milan	364.6m
FC Schalke 04	324.8m
AS Roma	231.0m
Olympique Lyon	220.8m
West Ham United	216.4m
Everton	213.0m
SSC Napoli	207.4m

Source: Deloitte Money League 2020
Data source: Deloitte Money League 2020

ability to generate revenue (Breuer et al., 2011). For example, the leagues of rich countries such as Switzerland and Belgium fail to generate as much revenue as Turkey and Portugal, despite the fans' high income.

Clubs are always seeking ways to maximize their revenues, and fans are an important source of revenue for clubs. How much revenue a club generates through fans of course depends on the number of fans, as well as their income. Among the seven leagues examined, the Turkish and Portuguese clubs are behind in this sense, but they are the most affordable leagues for the fans. Although in absolute terms, the cost of fandom is low in Turkey compared to the other major European leagues due to Turkey's low income, football in Turkey is still not affordable for the poor. Similarly, despite having much more income than the Turkish fans, low-income English fans are also struggling to afford football due to the extremely high costs which results in the transformation of fans in England. The new football fans in England, which are more like customers than fans, no longer have strict ties to social classes or physical places. This new group of football consumers are more inclusive in terms of gender, race, and social class (Williams, 2007).

Although clubs are generally trying to make the most money from the fans, German clubs operate differently because of the 50 + 1 rule as mentioned earlier. This is why German football is much more affordable compared to the other major leagues of Europe, both in absolute terms and as a percentage of income. The cost of fandom for the clubs of the same league are generally close to each other, with a couple of exceptions. Juventus in Italy and Paris Saint-Germain in France are almost 50 percent more costly than the other selected teams from the Italian and French leagues. Both teams have dominated their domestic leagues in recent years. At least fans of these teams are getting something in return for their financial investment, unlike Arsenal which has the highest cost of fandom by far in European football but has failed to achieve any success in recent years.

Even though fans are an important source of revenue for clubs, there are clubs that manage to generate high revenues without treating fans as customers. Among the Spanish teams analyzed, Barcelona is the most affordable one, yet it generated the highest revenue in the 2018/2019 season in European football. Other relatively affordable teams such as Olympique Lyon, Bayern Munich, and Borussia Dortmund are also among the highest revenue-generating teams in Europe (Eurostat, 2020 and 2021).

Fans want to see their team win whether it is on a chilly evening in London or on a sunny afternoon at Madrid. Fans believe that they contribute to their team while they are in the stands, chanting or booing while the players are competing on the pitch. However, from the team's perspective, it doesn't really matter if fans are in the stands or at home on sofas as long as they buy season tickets, subscribe to the league's broadcast and buy merchandise every season. Fans' real contribution to their team is how much money they spend for the team. Sadly, the commercialization of football has turned fans into customers, and, for most of the teams, the best customer is always the one who pays the most.

Notes

1 Big 6 in the Premier League are Arsenal, Chelsea, Liverpool, Manchester City, Manchester United, and Tottenham.
2 Prices in England and Turkey are in pounds and lira. The month July is selected since most of the season tickets are renewed in July. July 1 was a Sunday therefore the exchange rates on July 2 were used.
3 Capacity utilization rates defines how full a team's stadium is on average for a given season.
4 Sky Sports and Eurosport in Germany. Sky Sports and DZN in Italy.

References

Abercrombie, N., & Longhurst, B. J. (1998). *Audiences: A sociological theory of performance and imagination*. London: SAGE.
Breuer, C., Hallmann, K., & Wicker, P. (2011). Determinants of sport participation in different sports. *Managing Leisure*, 16(4), 269–286.
Bundesliga. (2017). *German soccer rules: 50 + 1 explained*. Retrieved September 2020, from Bundesliga: www.bundesliga.com/en/news/Bundesliga/german-soccer-rules-50-1-fifty-plus-one-explained-466583.jsp
De Matteis, A., Accardo, P., & Mammone, G. (n.d.). *International Labour Organization*. Retrieved October 2020, from National Labour Law Profile: Italy: www.ilo.org/ifpdial/information-resources/national-labour-law-profiles/WCMS_158903/lang--en/index.htm
Deloitte. (2013, June). *Annual Review of Football Finance 2013*. Retrieved March 2020, from Deloitte – Sports Business Group: www2.deloitte.com/content/dam/Deloitte/uk/Documents/sports-business-group/deloitte-uk-sbg-arff-2013-highlights-download.pdf
Deloitte. (2020, January). *Money League 2020*. Retrieved September 2020, from Deloitte – Sports Business Group: www2.deloitte.com/bg/en/pages/finance/articles/football-money-league-2020.html
Deloitte. (2020, June). *Annual Review of Football Finance 2020*. Retrieved August 2020, from Deloitte – Sports Business Group: www2.deloitte.com/uk/en/pages/sports-business-group/articles/annual-review-of-football-finance.html
Dixon, E. (2020, March 13). *Inside Benfica's off-field strategy: Record profits, embracing digital and partnering with the 49ers*. Retrieved August 2020, from SportsPro Media: www.sportspromedia.com/analysis/benfica-profit-tv-rights-ott-transfers-49ers-giants-soares-de-oliveira
Feehan, P., Forrest, D., & Simmons, R. (2003). Premier league soccer: normal or inferior good? *European Sport Management Quarterly*, 3(1), 31–45.
Eurostat. (2020, November 26). *Minimum wage statistics*. Retrieved September 2020, from Eurostat: https://ec.europa.eu/eurostat/statistics-explained/index.php/Minimum_wage_statistics#General_overview

Eurostat. (2021, January 22). *Real GDP per capita*. Retrieved September 2020, from Eurostat: https://ec.europa.eu/eurostat/databrowser/view/sdg_08_10/default/table?lang=en

Fillis, I., & Mackay, C. (2014). Moving beyond fan typologies: The impact of social integration on team loyalty in football. *Journal of Marketing Management, 30*(3–4), 334–363.

Hewer, P., Gannon, M., & Cordina, R. (2017). Discordant fandom and global football brands: "Let the people sing." *Journal of Consumer Culture, 17*(3), 600–619.

Jones, I. (2000). A model of serious leisure identification: The case of football fandom. *Leisure Studies, 19*(4), 283–298.

Keaton, S. A., & Gearhart, C. C. (2014). Identity formation, identity strength, and self-categorization as predictors of affective and psychological outcomes: A model reflecting sport team fans' responses to highlights and lowlights of a college football season. *Communication & Sport, 2*(4), 363–385.

Keaton, S. A., Watanabe, N. M., & Ruihley, B. J. (2015). What types of #sportfans use social media? The role of team identity formation and spectatorship motivation on self-disclosure during a live sport broadcast, 89–108. In Brojakowski, et al. (Eds.) *Television, Social Media, and Fan Culture*, Lexington Books.

Kendrick, Mat. (2020, April). Aston Villa have more season ticket holders than Liverpool – but less than these clubs. Retrieved June 2021, from Birmingham Mail: www.birminghammail.co.uk/sport/football/football-news/aston-villa-more-season-ticket-18086765

King, A. (2003) *The European Ritual*. (Aldershot: Ashgate).

Melnick, M. J., & Wann, D. L. (2011). An examination of sport fandom in Australia: Socialization, team identification, and fan behavior. *International Review for the Sociology of Sport, 46*(4), 456–470.

Sloan, L. R. (1989). The motives of sports fans. *Sports, Games, and Play: Social and Psychological Viewpoints, 2*, 175–240.

Stebbins, R. A. (1992). *Amateurs, professionals, and serious leisure*. McGill-Queen's Press-MQUP.

Stebbins, R. A. (2006). Serious leisure and well-being. In *Work, Leisure and Well-being* (edited by J. Haworth) (pp. 129–142). London: Routledge.

Stemmler, T. (2008). *Kleine Geschichte des Fußballspiels*. Frankfurt: Insel Verlag.

Transfermarkt. (2019, June). *Bundesliga Attendances 18/19*. Retrieved October 2020, from Transfermarkt: www.transfermarkt.com/bundesliga/besucherzahlen/wettbewerb/L1/plus/1?saison_id=2018

Wakefield, K. L., (2007). *Team Sports Marketing*. Burlington, MA: Butterworth-Heinemann.

Wann, D. L., & Branscombe, N. R. (1993). Sports fans: Measuring degree of identification with their team. *International Journal of Sport Psychology*.

Wann, D., Melnick, M., Russell, G., & Pease, D. (2001) *Sports Fans*. New York and London: Routledge.

Williams, J. (2007). Rethinking sports fandom: The case of European soccer. *Leisure Studies, 26*(2), 127–146.

Zillmann, D., Bryant, J., & Sapolsky, B. S. (1979). The enjoyment of watching sports contests. *Sports, Games, and Play: Social and Psychological Viewpoints, 1*, 297–335.

7
Building Civic Identity Around a Suburban Ballpark District

Timothy Kellison and Beth A. Cianfrone

When the Atlanta Braves relocated from their downtown ballpark to a new venue on the edge of the central city in 2017, the team's move contrasted sharply with almost 30 years of suburb-to-metropolitan stadium migration across North American cities. Like other projects that have leveraged stadiums as catalysts for growth in large downtown commercial and residential hubs, Truist Park (originally SunTrust Park) was the centerpiece of a new mixed-use development called The Battery Atlanta. However, this project differed from other stadium districts because it was built on nearly 60 acres of undeveloped land in Cobb County, well beyond Atlanta's "intown" boundaries. For Cobb residents (and intown Atlantans), the Braves' relocation to Cobb evoked a significant emotional response and symbolized a broader strategy by Cobb to demonstrate its separateness from Atlanta by underscoring its commercial, residential, and entertainment attributes (Lutz & Brasch, 2017). Furthermore, despite the Braves' ties to Atlanta, the Truist Park–Battery Atlanta development provided Cobb residents an opportunity to strengthen their connection not to the city of Atlanta, but rather to their more proximate suburban community. These enhanced ties are at the center of this chapter.

Sports venues and the events that take place within them are engines of social capital because they provide "societies and/or fan nations… opportunities for interaction to members of that group and reinforce and introduce support for their collective identity" (Seifried & Clopton, 2013, p. 54). Even before a sports venue opens, the mere prospect of a new stadium development offers residents a chance to participate in community affairs through the expression of their support of or opposition to the proposed project (Kellison, 2016; Kellison & Mondello, 2014). For venues planned for or located in the urban core, this collective identity may be largely concentrated inside the central city. Conversely, in rare projects sited outside a major metropolitan center like Truist Park–Battery Atlanta, that civic identity may be anchored elsewhere. In light of this distinction, the purpose of this chapter is to illustrate how a suburban stadium development (prospective or built) can foster a localized civic identity among residents, further developing the suburban community's political, economic, and social distinctiveness from the broader metropolitan region.

As we contend in this chapter, the promotion of civic identity through sports teams and venues is achieved in several ways, and much of this promotion relies upon highly identified fans. As detailed below, a stadium-construction project subsidized by taxpayers may prompt residents to participate in public dialogue, a cornerstone of an active citizenry. Additionally, the team's physical location—in this case, a ballpark and surrounding district—could serve as

DOI: 10.4324/9780429342189-8

a hub for capital, commerce, and culture in the local community. Furthermore, just as local sports fans would likely be drawn to a new team in their city, the relocation of an existing team to a suburban community could cause individuals living there to exhibit new feelings of pride in that community. As we discuss below, the formation of this community pride could be accelerated if the team was relocating to a community already buzzing with highly identified fans.

To address these arguments, we organize this chapter in the following manner. First, we consider how geographic factors (i.e., place) may influence an individual's level of fandom. Next, we contextualize the Truist Park–Battery Atlanta project through the lens of urban and regional planning in the United States. Then, we introduce the concept of an entrepreneurial ecosystem and explain how the Braves' suburban ballpark development may signal to both residents and visitors Cobb's status as a diverse, bourgeoning community distinct from the city proper. We conclude with a discussion of civic identity and the utility of Truist Park–Battery Atlanta in contributing to the broader community.

Place and Fandom

Fandom is often measured by an individual's identity with some aspect of sport, and social identity theory, identity theory, and fan identification are frameworks that most frequently guide discussions of fandom. Those individuals who are highly identified with a team or aspect of the team behave differently than those less identified, including through greater consumption (e.g., spending, attendance, media viewership). Team management can maximize revenues with a strongly identified fanbase and contribute to civic identity and other community-based sports decisions (e.g., voting to subsidize a new stadium). Thus, a sports franchise and its venue are entwined with the surrounding community in many ways (Heere & James, 2007).

Sport marketers have long recognized *place* as an essential aspect of the marketing mix and a key feature for selling and promoting their core product. Furthermore, geography, place, and venues can each influence an individual's level of fandom. The location of a sports team's home facility and its associated live sporting events is the most fundamental aspect of place (Delia & James, 2018). It may include the physical location of a team in a city (e.g., downtown or suburb), region, or state; surrounding neighborhoods and outside amenities (e.g., restaurants, bars); nearby parking and proximity to transit systems; and features of the venue itself (e.g., aesthetics, design, layout, landscape, in-stadium amenities; Mullin et al., 2014). These elements can influence an individual's affiliation or fandom with the team, their game experience, and their subsequent satisfaction (or dissatisfaction) and loyalty. When done well, sport marketers can optimize the facility and its location to help create a sense of community or feeling of home for spectators, as well as establish and develop fan identification with the team. Because identification levels impact consumer behavior, the place-related characteristics of a stadium and its related impact on the community are critical for sports owners to consider.

The geographic location of a stadium can be a strong point of attachment for fans. An individual's geographic identity may be based on their psychological connection to a city, region, state, or nation, and it may be used to predict an individual's level of fandom (Collins et al., 2016; Heere & James, 2007). This geographic identity can be displayed by the fans who identify with their hometowns and thus are fans of the teams within that community (Lee et al., 2012; Lock et al., 2011; Reifurth et al., 2019; Uhlman & Trail, 2012). Fans are socialized to that team through their community, feel they are supporting their community, or see it as a point of pride.

Conversely, in the case of a franchise's relocation to another city, fans left behind in the former city may experience a psychological loss. Researchers found many loyal fans do not continue to be fans of the relocated team; instead, they may adopt other local professional or collegiate teams or turn away from the professional sport altogether (Hyatt, 2007).

In some instances, an individual's attachment to place (such as a city or state) can also be related to their attachment to the local sports venue. The pride in a place can be related to pride in a facility. For instance, in a study by Ballouli et al. (2016), an individual's attachment to the venue yielded the highest explanation of attendance intentions (32 percent). Further, the aesthetics and amenities of sports facilities are often predicted to impact motives to attend. Marketers can focus on the venue itself to develop fandom. As spectators attend, their satisfaction with the experience can influence their loyalty to and re-patronage of the team. The physical aspects around the stadium, perceived safety of the community, ease of ingress and egress, and public transportation availability all play a role in the consumer experience.

Place can also be a driving factor for non-local fans. Some people become fans of teams with a broader geographic reach, such as the New England Patriots (NFL) or Carolina Hurricanes (NHL). In Major League Baseball, the Atlanta Braves are the closest team for four of Georgia's bordering states, so many Alabamians, Tennesseans, and North and South Carolinians identify with the Braves as being "theirs" because of the wider geographic borders of "Braves Country."

Other place-specific aspects of a team, such as team name (e.g., city vs. state), stadium ownership, funding sources, and location within a city, can also impact fandom and community (Heere & James, 2007). These factors are often related, and each can be a tool to create community among fans or as a result of taxpayers' impact on stadiums. It is worth noting the amount of money (e.g., taxes) being spent by citizens in a community on a sports facility may influence their identity with place or facility (Ballouli et al., 2016). For example, the Florida Marlins were established in 1991 as the first MLB team in the state. Through the use of "Florida," their marketers could capture fans throughout the state. In 2011, Marlins ownership changed the team name to the Miami Marlins to coincide with a move from Miami Gardens to a new stadium in Miami's Little Havana neighborhood. Because most of the stadium's cost was financed through the City of Miami and Miami-Dade County, the revision from *Florida* to *Miami* was required. This change may have created a sense of community and ownership for those in Miami while possibly alienating fans in other parts of the state.

The Los Angeles Angels present a contentious and long-running community battle for a team, as they bounced names from the Los Angeles Angels (1961–1965), to California Angels (1965–1996), to Anaheim Angels (1997–2004), to Los Angeles Angels of Anaheim (2005–2015), and back to Los Angeles Angels (since 2016), although now, they are typically just called the Angels by media. These variations resulted from changes to either ownership or city stadium leases, as the Angels have been in the same Anaheim-based stadium since 1965. Typically, the argument to change the name is based on the related implications for residents, whether to help the city gain awareness of perceived economic benefits or provide residents a sense of ownership when paying taxes on a city-owned sports venue. The proximity to the Los Angeles Dodgers has created a divide between fans based on location, and the Angels' back-and-forth name changes have added to the affiliation issue.

According to Lewis (2001), fans sometimes identify more closely with a team's geographic location than the team itself. Therefore, a stadium's location within a city may play an essential role in one's level of fandom, and consequently, that fandom may influence the individual's ties to the local community. In the next section, we consider the function of place in the recent and unusual case of the Atlanta Braves' suburban ballpark district.

The Role of Fandom in Stadium Politics and Local Planning

After moving from Milwaukee in 1966, the Atlanta Braves played in Atlanta Stadium (later Atlanta–Fulton County Stadium) in downtown Atlanta. In 1997, they moved a short distance to Turner Field, which had just been reconfigured following its use for the Centennial Olympic Games a year earlier. Then, in November 2013, the Braves announced they were again moving, this time to a new ballpark in Cobb, a suburban county about 15 miles northwest of downtown Atlanta (McGehee et al., 2020). The Braves provided several justifications for the surprising move, including the high cost of improvements needed at Turner Field, the team's lack of control of the area around Turner Field, and the high concentration of Braves' fans living on the upper edge of the city (and further north). This third claim was especially important, as it suggested that the Braves would benefit by relocating to the suburbs, thereby closing the distance between themselves and the majority of their fans.

The solution to these problems, the Braves argued, was a new, 41,000-seat ballpark that would anchor a mixed-use development that would include retail, dining, and office space, a concert venue, and apartments and hotels (Kellison & Mills, 2020). Truist Park (then SunTrust Park) and the surrounding district, The Battery Atlanta, opened in 2017 at an estimated cost of $1.3 billion (Center for Sport and Urban Policy, 2020). The cost of Truist Park was approximately $722 million, the public portion of which was $392 million. The Battery Atlanta was estimated to be $558 million; it was privately financed, with the Braves accounting for nearly 85 percent of the cost.

In the past 20 years, numerous public–private partnerships have established downtown sports and entertainment districts. In Columbus, the 75-acre Arena District is anchored by Nationwide Arena, home of the NHL's Blue Jackets, and includes a diverse mix of commercial and residential space (Kellison, Kim, et al., 2020). Kansas City's Power & Light District is an $850-million development constructed immediately to the west of the 17,000-plus-seat Sprint Center (L'Heureux, 2015). The Ballpark District in San Diego has been praised for the 26-block neighborhood that emerged (Newman, 2006); Cantor and Rosentraub (2012) argued the neighborhood seemed "on several different dimensions to be stable and a vital part of life in urban center of San Diego" (p. 226). As evidence of these developments' appeal, several have attracted the attention of officials from other cities, teams, and leagues. For example, the Columbus Arena District was visited by representatives from Pittsburgh, Milwaukee, Sacramento, and Edmonton, all of whom eventually proposed or built their own sports and entertainment districts (Williams, 2005). More recently, the *Atlanta Journal-Constitution* reported "a hundred teams" representing the "NFL, NBA, Major League Baseball, soccer, college, Australia, Germany, Spain… [and] Japan" had visited The Battery Atlanta to tour the mixed-use development (Tucker, 2018, paras. 4–5).

Truist Park–Battery Atlanta shares many of the characteristics of the modern stadium district. However, because of its atypical location, it may also serve the function of a suburban downtown. Suburban downtowns serve as walkable and mixed-use social spaces. According to Dixon (2015), these suburban centers "evidence a strong civic mission that reflects growing suburban aspirations for community-rich environments. They are generally sponsored by local government, have an unmistakably public character, and are denser and more socially diverse" (p. 123). While usually existing in the urban core, a stadium district situated outside the city center may have additional value by providing a suburban community with the opportunity to form a civic identity. This possibility is explored further in the discussion below.

Sprawl, Regionalism, and Growth Politics

The story of the American city cannot be told without discussing the issues of sprawl and suburbanization, both of which have played significant roles in the evolution of modern urban spaces. Sprawl, or "low-density, scattered, urban development without systematic large-scale or regional public land-use planning" (Bruegmann, 2005, p. 8), is often characterized by the decentralization of employment and population and the growth of "edge cities" (Glaeser & Kahn, 2004). The causes of sprawl are manifold, but historically, they have centered on population growth; the development of transportation infrastructure; and falling costs associated with homebuying, conducting business, and commuting (Jackson, 1985).

Sprawl is often considered a consequence of poor urban planning, and coinciding suburbanization is viewed as problematic to both the central city and those communities that have developed on the periphery. As Brueckner (2000) argued, the expansion of cities to the suburbs and the resulting diminished demand for central-city properties have created disincentives to upgrade or redevelop urban infrastructure. Furthermore, depopulation can limit a city's capacity to complete such upgrades, as a reduced tax base can result in depleted public coffers. According to Calthorpe (1993), sprawl can similarly degrade suburban life:

> The suburb was the driving force of the post-WWII era, the physical expression of the privatization of life and specialization of place which marks our time. The result of this era is that both the city and suburb are now locked in a mutually negating evolution toward loss of community, human scale, and nature. In practical terms, these patterns of growth have created on one side congestion, pollution, and isolation, and on the other urban disinvestment and economic hardship.
>
> *p. 9*

Moreover, individuals residing in so-called "middle-zone communities" may be disengaged from the sociocultural features of urban centers and the natural ecology enjoyed by those in the outskirts, purposely isolating themselves from the greater metropolitan area (Salenger, 2015).

The lack of connection described above may motivate a suburban community (e.g., those in Cobb) to pursue an identity separate from the central city (e.g., metro Atlanta). In addition to the factors mentioned above contributing to the suburbanization process in U.S. cities, Brueckner (2000) argued another economic condition was "the desire of high-income consumers to form separate jurisdictions for the provision of public goods such as education, public safety, and parks" (p. 168). This desire, coupled with efforts to "fix" sprawl, has led to the creation of suburban downtowns, walkable and mixed-use areas that have the potential to be transformed into desirable urban nodes because they contain employment concentrations and carry the prospect of economic growth (Koschinsky & Talen, 2015). Often championed by local growth coalitions (Phelps, 2012), suburban centers have the capacity for community building by providing residents with a place to engage in activities that support the community's commercial and social advancement. As discussed next, these spaces may be exploited by civic leaders determined to strengthen a city's, suburb's, or region's potential for growth.

Entrepreneurial Ecosystems in Suburban and Small Cities

In contrast to early suburbia that provided residents with single-family homes in quiet neighborhoods away from the urban, industrial centers of employment, the emergence of edge nodes and modern suburban cities offered their own hubs of capital, commerce, and culture (Hayden, 2003). Suburban economic activity sometimes complemented that of the larger cities with which they were connected, like in cities that constructed suburban stadiums during the 1950s–1970s (Kellison, 2021). Other times, they represented competition. This competition reflects a tension between cities and suburbs, which was born out of the "struggle to adjust to diverse restructuring processes that are unsettling inherited patterns of territorial and scalar organization within major US city–regions" (Brenner, 2002, p. 3). In many cases, policymakers in suburban cities have endeavored to promote growth, regulate growth, or adopt a combined approach (Kerstein, 1993).

A growth strategy may be delivered through the cultivation of an entrepreneurial ecosystem, "the combination of social, political, economic, and cultural elements within a region that support the development and growth" of entrepreneurial activity, often measured by the rise of startups and other high-risk business ventures (Spigel, 2017, p. 50). According to Isenberg (2011), entrepreneurial ecosystems are supported by several broad elements, including markets, policy, finance, culture, institutional supports, policy, and human capital. In addition to human capital and culture—key elements of entrepreneurial ecosystems—sports venues and the events that occur within them may serve as economic hubs, particularly when team owners have territorial control over adjacent commercial and residential development. As argued by Mason et al. (2017), "in attaining 'master developer' status, the owner is able to leverage the key asset—the team—which is the anchor tenant of the centerpiece of the development (the sports facility) in order to gain control over the… surrounding district" (p. 369).

A development like Truist Park–Battery Atlanta concentrates multiple elements of the entrepreneurial ecosystem to one area, and the Braves are an inescapable part of the site's identity. Even when Cobb residents visit the area for reasons other than attending a ballgame (e.g., shopping, dining, attending a concert or movie), Braves' iconography is front and center, whether via the easily recognizable ballpark or on signage visible throughout the district. In the same vein, visitors of either the stadium or Battery Atlanta would almost certainly recognize they were somewhere other than the city of Atlanta—an essential experience if Cobb was to become a source of one's civic identity.

Research on entrepreneurial ecosystems has been relatively focused on major metropolitan areas, and less attention has been placed on suburban and small cities (Roundy, 2017). Furthermore, researchers of entrepreneurial ecosystems "have devoted almost no attention to the role of customers" because "traditional small-to-medium-sized ventures are more likely to populate [small city entrepreneurial ecosystems] and be dependent on local customers for their existence" (Roundy, 2018, p. 327). This point underscores an essential function of suburban policymakers: to deliver an environment to residents that supports innovation and entrepreneurship, two characteristics of a thriving, self-sustaining community. A stadium development like Truist Park–Battery Atlanta may serve as one such strategy to encourage the growth of finance, culture, and human capital crucial to an entrepreneurial ecosystem. Additionally, the new ballpark's placement in an area already brimming with Braves fans (according to the Braves' internal ticket-sales data) could enhance local ties to the Cobb community.

The construction of an entrepreneurial ecosystem may be especially important in suburban communities struggling to maintain cooperative–competitive balance with the metropolitan center (and other suburban cities). Similarly, the desire to attract a professional sports team to a city, suburb, or region may be fueled by competition between neighboring communities (Xue & Mason, 2019). In addition to a planning strategy that emphasizes the special characteristics of a community via an entrepreneurial ecosystem, a ballpark district like Truist Park–Battery Atlanta may also serve as a space for building and expressing a collective civic identity that is politically, economically, and socially distinct from the wider metropolitan region. The formation of this community through its individual members is discussed further in the next section.

Civic Identity and Citizenship

For any society to function effectively, it must have the active engagement and participation of its citizens. Inherent in the public's involvement in the community is a foundation of civic identity, "a set of beliefs and emotions about oneself as a participant in civic life" (Hart et al., 2011, p. 773). Individuals may demonstrate the strength of their civic identity by participating in a wide range of community activities, including volunteering for a neighborhood beautification project, participating in a local blood drive, serving on a jury, attending a town-hall meeting, running for elected office, and voting on local issues (Sullivan & Transue, 1999). As Atkins and Hart (2003) noted, civic identity requires individuals to possess a sense of connection to and responsibility for a geographical community, and it develops from citizens' participation in community affairs, their knowledge about the history and culture of that community, and their commitment to democratic ideals.

Civic identity is grounded in the concept of citizenship, or "membership of a political community where all citizens can determine the terms of social cooperation on an equal basis" (Bellamy, 2008, p. 17). Citizenship—and by extension, civic identity—are generally defined by three essential qualities: membership, rights, and participation (Bellamy, 2008; Hart et al., 2011). Membership refers to an individual's sense of belongingness to the community in which she or he is a citizen (Hart et al., 2011). As noted by Bellamy (2008), membership implies an absolute exclusivity in which those who possess membership enjoy certain privileges that are not available to non-members; as seen in both historical and contemporary debates about citizenship, the criteria for membership may be contested (e.g., race, sex, immigrant status). In the same way a highly identified sports fan might celebrate their favorite team's success, an individual holding membership in a community is likely to have a vested interest in that community's prosperity.

Perceived membership in a community serves as the basis for the remaining aspects of citizenship, rights, and participation. One's membership in a society entitles an individual to certain rights. Of course, the influence of these rights (e.g., legal rights, human and civil rights) and the extent to which they are extended to individual citizens range across nation–states and regime types. In fully democratic societies, a citizen exercises her or his rights through participation, which plays a critical role in the construction of civic identity: "A civic identity motivates, is maintained, and is structured by participation in civic life" (Hart et al., 2011, p. 775). Participation occurs in many forms, but as it relates to stadium-centered developments, it can include voting (either directly via referendum or initiative, or indirectly by electing policymakers); canvassing and petition-signing; donating time, money, or other resources to political campaigns; writing letters or telephoning elected representatives; speaking at public meetings; submitting editorials to local media outlets; and taking part in rallies or staging protests (Kellison, Sam, et al., 2020).

A citizenry with a strong civic identity is vital for a thriving community, as an active and engaged public can support initiatives that support economic and social progress while safeguarding against retrogressive laws and policies. In the context of civic identity, Youniss et al. (1997) contended that "identity is not given but must be constructed" (p. 630). In the case of Truist Park–Battery Atlanta, the production of civic identity can occur not only through social engineering but also through the built environment. Specifically, a master-planned stadium district represents a civic space with the potential for the development of human capital, as it can prompt serious public debate during the planning stages, and afterward, evoke a sense of community pride from the teams that play and events that occur within it.

When it was first proposed in November 2013, the Braves' ballpark development and the key officials who championed it faced immediate scrutiny (Kellison et al., 2017). Two weeks after the relocation plan was made public, the Cobb County Board of Commissioners approved it by a 4–1 vote (Leslie & Tucker, 2013). Critics contended the plan was being fast-tracked unnecessarily and that Cobb residents were entitled to vote on the matter directly (e.g., via referendum; Klepal & Schrade, 2014). The chief architect of the public-financing plan was county commission chairperson Tim Lee, who lost his reelection bid in 2016 to challenger Mike Boyce. Boyce primarily campaigned on a message that the ballpark issue should have been put before a public vote (Lutz, 2016). Some media reports suggested that although the stadium plan was likely supported by Braves fans in particular and a majority in Cobb more generally (Tierney, 2014), voters may have "objected to the way the deal was negotiated in secret and committed some $400 million in public money to build and maintain a new stadium without a popular referendum" (Wickert & Lutz, 2016, p. A1). Interestingly, in 2020, Boyce was defeated in his own reelection bid by Lisa Cupid, the commissioner who cast the lone dissenting vote when the original ballpark plan was proposed in 2013 (Lutz, 2020).

Concluding Remarks

The relocation of a professional sports team from the central city to a suburban site can be used to express the suburb's economic growth strategy (by mimicking an entrepreneurial city; Mason et al., 2015). In the latter case, this identity serves to strengthen citizens' ties to the community, resulting in a more active citizenry that participates in civic activities (e.g., volunteering or fundraising for the community), engages in electoral activities (e.g., voting, campaigning), and provides political voice (e.g., contacting officials, protesting, petitioning; Pancer, 2015). Furthermore, a community united by a strong civic identity may prove a more considerate tax base for supporting city services and tax proposals.

The Truist Park–Battery Atlanta development is noteworthy for several reasons, including its distant location from the central city. As detailed in this chapter, despite the ongoing trend of relocating stadiums back to downtown locations, some decision-makers may nevertheless be persuaded to construct new facilities outside the central city. This case illustrates that the community-building capacity of stadium developments like Truist Park–Battery Atlanta is not limited to the teams and events that play in them; they may also engage citizens (comprising both fans and non-fans) in the planning process. We provide this illustration by focusing on the relatively extraordinary case of the suburban stadium district. Drawing from previous work on urban planning and political science, the interdisciplinary approach used in this inquiry delivers a unique perspective on the factors contributing to a suburban community's pursuit of a major sports development. Like its downtown counterparts in cities across North America, Truist Park–Battery Atlanta may not only serve the fans in the ballpark itself but also support a spirit of homegrown entrepreneurship, strengthen local identity, and further establish the community's political, economic, and cultural distinctiveness.

References

Atkins, R., & Hart, D. (2003). Neighborhoods, adults, and the development of civic identity in urban youth. *Applied Development Science*, 7(3), 156–164. https://doi.org/10.1207/S1532480XADS0703_6

Ballouli, K., Trail, G. T., Koesters, T. C., & Bernthal, M. J. (2016). Differential effects of motives and points of attachment on conative loyalty of Formula 1 US Grand Prix attendees. *Sport Marketing Quarterly*, 25(3), 166–181. https://fitpublishing.com/articles/differential-effects-motives-and-points-attachment-conative-loyalty-formula-1-us-grand-prix

Bellamy, R. (2008). *Citizenship: A very short introduction*. Oxford University Press.
Brenner, N. (2002). Decoding the newest "metropolitan regionalism" in the USA: A critical overview. *Cities, 19*(1), 3–21.
Brueckner, J. K. (2000). Urban sprawl: Diagnosis and remedies. *International Regional Science Review, 23*(2), 160–171. https://doi.org/10.1177/016001700761012710
Bruegmann, R. (2005). *Sprawl: A compact history*. University of Chicago Press.
Calthorpe, P. (1993). *The next American metropolis: Ecology, community, and the American dream*. Princeton Architectural Press.
Cantor, M. B., & Rosentraub, M. S. (2012). A ballpark and neighborhood change: Economic integration, a recession, and the altered demography of San Diego's Ballpark District after eight years. *City, Culture and Society, 3*(3), 219–226. https://doi.org/10.1016/j.ccs.2012.05.001
Center for Sport and Urban Policy. (2020). *Publictrack*. www.stadiatrack.org/public
Collins, D., Heere, B., Shapiro, S. L., Ridinger L., & Wear, H. (2016). The displaced fan: The importance of new media and community identification for maintaining team identity with your former hometown team. *European Sport Management Quarterly, 16*(5), 655–674. https://doi.org/10.1080/16184742.2016.1200643
Delia, E. B., & James, J. D. (2018). The meaning of team in team identification. *Sport Management Review, 21*, 416–429. https://doi.org/10.1016/j.smr.2017.09.002
Dixon, D. (2015). Suburban downtowns. In E. Talen (Ed.), *Retrofitting sprawl: Addressing seventy years of failed urban form* (pp. 123–138). University of Georgia Press.
Glaeser, E. L., & Kahn, M. E. (2004). Sprawl and urban growth. In J. V. Henderson & J.-F. Thisse (Eds.), *Handbook of regional and urban economics* (Vol. 4, pp. 2481–2527). Elsevier B.V.
Hart, D., Richardson, C., & Wilkenfeld, B. (2011). Civic identity. In S. J. Schwartz, K. Luyckx, & V. L. Vignoles (Eds.), *Handbook of identity theory and research* (vol. 2, pp. 771–787). Springer.
Hayden, D. (2003). *Building suburbia: Green fields and urban growth, 1820–2000*. Pantheon Books.
Heere, B., & James, J. (2007). Sports teams and their communities: Examining the influence of external group identities on team identity. *Journal of Sport Management, 21*(3), 319–337. https://doi.org/10.1123/jsm.21.3.319
Hyatt, C. G. (2007). Who do I root for now? The impact of franchise relocation on the loyal fans left behind: A case study of Hartford Whalers fans. *Journal of Sport Behavior, 30*(1), 36–56.
Isenberg, D. (2011). *The entrepreneurship ecosystem strategy as a new paradigm for economic policy: Principles for cultivating entrepreneurship*. The Babson Entrepreneurship Ecosystem Project. www.innovationamerica.us/images/stories/2011/The-entrepreneurship-ecosystem-strategy-for-economic-growth-policy-20110620183915.pdf
Jackson, K. T. (1985). *Crabgrass frontier: The suburbanization of the United States*. Oxford University Press.
Kellison, T. (2021). Enduring and emergent public opinion in relation to a suburban stadium district: The case of Truist Park–Battery Atlanta. *Journal of Global Sport Management*. Advance online publication. https://doi.org/10.1080/24704067.2021.1886685
Kellison, T., Kim, Y., & James, J. D. (2020). Secondary outcomes of a legislated stadium subsidy. *Journal of Global Sport Management*. https://doi.org/10.1080/24704067.2019.1604074
Kellison, T., & Mills, B. M. (2020). Voter intentions and political implications of legislated stadium subsidies. *Sport Management Review*. https://doi.org/https://doi.org/10.1016/j.smr.2020.07.003
Kellison, T., Sam, M. P., Hong, S., Swart, K., & Mondello, M. J. (2020). Global perspectives on democracy and public stadium finance. *Journal of Global Sport Management, 5*(4), 321–348. https://doi.org/10.1080/24704067.2018.1531680
Kellison, T. B. (2016). No-vote stadium subsidies and the democratic response. *International Journal of Sport Management, 17*(3), 452–477.
Kellison, T. B., & Mondello, M. J. (2014). Civic paternalism in political policymaking: The justification for no-vote stadium subsidies. *Journal of Sport Management, 28*(2), 162–175. https://doi.org/10.1123/jsm.2012-0210
Kellison, T. B., Newman, J. I., & Bunds, K. S. (2017). Framing democracy: Stadium financing and civic paternalism in Test Market, USA. *Sport in Society, 20*(11), 1548–1564. https://doi.org/10.1080/17430437.2017.1284805
Kerstein, R. (1993). Suburban growth politics in Hillsborough County: Growth management and political regimes. *Social Science Quarterly, 74*(3), 614–630.
Klepal, D., & Schrade, B. (2014, May 28). Cobb approves major stadium agreements: Supporters dominate, criticals shut out at meeting. *Atlanta Journal-Constitution*, A1.

Koschinsky, J., & Talen, E. (2015). From sprawl to walkable: How far is that? In E. Talen (Ed.), *Retrofitting sprawl: Addressing seventy years of failed urban form* (pp. 11–29). University of Georgia Press.

L'Heureux, M.-A. (2015). The creative class, urban boosters, and race: Shaping urban revitalization in Kansas City, Missouri. *Journal of Urban History, 41*(2), 245–260. https://doi.org/10.1177/0096144214563504

Lee, S., Lee, H. J., Seo, W. J., & Green, C. (2012). A new approach to stadium experience: The dynamics of the sensoryscape, social interaction, and sense of home. *Journal of Sport Management, 26*(6), 490–505. https://doi.org/10.1123/jsm.26.6.490

Leslie, K., & Tucker, T. (2013, November 27). Cobb oks Braves move. *Atlanta Journal-Constitution*, A1.

Lewis, M. (2001). Franchise relocation and fan allegiance. *Journal of Sport & Social Issues, 25*(1), 6–19. https://doi.org/10.1177/0193723501251002

Lock, D., Taylor, T., & Darcy, S. (2011). In the absence of achievement: The formation of new team identification. *European Sport Management Quarterly, 11*(2), 171–192. https://doi.org/10.1080/16184742.2011.559135

Lutz, M. (2016, July 31). Some question Boyce's vision for Cobb County: Newly elected chair says he's ready to set the tone of transparency. *Atlanta Journal-Constitution*, B1.

Lutz, M. (2020, November 5). Cobb Republicans lose commission chair amid shift. *Atlanta Journal-Constitution*, B1.

Lutz, M., & Brasch, B. (2017, April 14). SunTrust Park Opening Day: Park pulls Cobb closer to Atlanta: Baseball stadium reflects change in suburb's view of city. *Atlanta Journal-Constitution*, A1.

Mason, D., Sant, S.-L., & Soebbing, B. (2017). The peculiar economics of sports team ownership: Pursuing urban development in North American cities. *Sport, Business and Management: An International Journal, 7*(4), 358–374. https://doi.org/doi:10.1108/SBM-10-2016-0067

Mason, D. S., Washington, M., & Buist, E. A. N. (2015). Signaling status through stadiums: The discourses of comparison within a hierarchy. *Journal of Sport Management, 29*(5), 539–554. https://doi.org/10.1123/jsm.2014-0156

McGehee, G. M., Cianfrone, B. A., & Kellison, T. (2020). Interaction of communication from the sport organization, media, and public perspectives: How does messaging relate and differ? *Journal of Sport Management, 34*(3), 229–239.

Mullin, B. J., Hardy, S., & Sutton, W. (2014). *Sport marketing* (4th ed.). Human Kinetics.

Newman, M. (2006, April 26). The neighborhood that the ballpark built. *New York Times*, 10.

Pancer, S. M. (2015). *The psychology of citizenship and civic engagement*. Oxford University Press.

Phelps, N. A. (2012). The growth machine stops? Urban politics and the making and remaking of an edge city. *Urban Affairs Review, 48*(5), 670–700. https://doi.org/10.1177/1078087412440275

Reifurth, K. R. N., Bernthal, M. J., Ballouli, K., & Collins, D. (2019). Nonlocal fandom: Effects of geographic distance, geographic identity, and local competition on team identification. *Sport Marketing Quarterly, 28*(4), 195–208. http://doi.org/10.32731/SMQ.284.122019.02

Roundy, P. T. (2017). "Small town" entrepreneurial ecosystems: Implications for developed and emerging economies. *Journal of Entrepreneurship in Emerging Economies, 9*(3), 238–262. https://doi.org/10.1108/JEEE-09-2016-0040

Roundy, P. T. (2018). Paying attention to the customer: Consumer forces in small town entrepreneurial ecosystems. *Journal of Research in Marketing and Entrepreneurship, 20*(2), 323–340. https://doi.org/10.1108/JRME-11-2017-0054

Salenger, M. (2015). The personal decisions that govern sprawl. In E. Talen (Ed.), *Retrofitting sprawl: Addressing seventy years of failed urban form* (pp. 81–99). University of Georgia Press.

Seifried, C., & Clopton, A. W. (2013). An alternative view of public subsidy and sport facilities through social anchor theory. *City, Culture and Society, 4*(1), 49–55. https://doi.org/10.1016/j.ccs.2013.01.001

Spigel, B. (2017). The relational organization of entrepreneurial ecosystems. *Entrepreneurship Theory and Practice, 41*(1), 49–72. https://doi.org/10.1111/etap.12167

Sullivan, J. L., & Transue, J. E. (1999). The psychological underpinnings of democracy: A selective review of research on political tolerance, interpersonal trust, and social capital. *Annual Review of Psychology, 50*, 625–650. https://doi.org/10.1146/annurev.psych.50.1.625

Tierney, M. (2014, September 17). To mixed reaction, Braves begin work on stadium outside downtown. *The New York Times*, B14.

Tucker, T. (2018, March 28). Leadoff: Braves say 100 teams have toured The Battery. *Atlanta Journal-Constitution*. www.ajc.com/sports/leadoff-braves-say-100-sports-teams-have-toured-the-battery/mG5WSZakVXeb9qil13W9lL/

Uhlman, B. T., & Trail, G. T. (2012). An analysis of the motivators of Seattle Sounders FC season ticket holders: A case study. *Sport Marketing Quarterly, 21*(4), 243–252. https://fitpublishing.com/content/analysis-motivators-seattle-sounders-fc-season-ticket-holders-case-study-pp-243-252

Wickert, D., & Lutz, M. (2016, July 27). Challenger ousts Cobb chairman: Lee, who lured Braves to county, concedes defeat to retired colonel. *Atlanta Journal-Constitution*, A1.

Williams, M. (2005, October 17). Arena District a blueprint for other cities' development. *Columbus Dispatch.* www.dispatch.com/article/20151017/news/310179728

Xue, H., & Mason, D. S. (2019). Stadium games in entrepreneurial cities in China: A state project. *Journal of Global Sport Management, 4*(2), 185–209. https://doi.org/10.1080/24704067.2018.1531246

Youniss, J., McLellan, J. A., & Yates, M. (1997). What we know about engendering civic identity. *American Behavioral Scientist, 40*(5), 620–631. https://doi.org/10.1177/0002764297040005008

8
Studying Sports Fans Through Ethnographic Methods
Walk a Mile in Their Shoes

Jessica Richards, Keith D. Parry and Daniela Spanjaard

Introduction

Traditionally, sports fans have been studied from a third-person perspective (Smith and Stewart, 2007) with research typically utilising quantitative examinations of fan behaviour to develop a range of defined groups (Campbell, 2017; Madrigal and Chen, 2008; Theodorakis and Wann, 2008; Parry et al., 2014). However, these approaches do not allow for the nuances and interactions of sports fans to be examined in depth and hence perpetuate myths that they are in some way abnormal and/or deviant (Parry, 2012). The authors stress in this chapter the benefits of ethnography and autoethnography as research methods that enable for first-hand observations in the match-day environment, where participants have the opportunity to become co-creators of the phenomenon. This approach responds to Sparkes' (2000) call for emotional and personal approaches to be accepted within academic research on sports fans.

The chapter first defines ethnography and autoethnography by describing some of the key features that constitute the research methods. It then examines the methodological issues associated with their application in the collection and analysis of research on sports fans. Drawing on two case studies, we argue that the value of the ethnographic approach must be more strongly considered when exploring sports fandom as a lived experience. The first case study centres on the match-day interactions of Premier League football team Everton Football Club fans (hereafter Everton FC). Drawing on data collected over a three-year period, the researcher spent over 100 hours in the field and conducted 20 semi-structured interviews. Adopting an ethnographic approach enabled the researcher to gain critical insights by shadowing participants and taking part in their match-day activities. This participation provided an opportunity to observe if what participants recounted in interviews was embellished or understated, minimising distortion, and enhancing the overall research depth and credibility. The second element of the chapter discusses the potential for autoethnography to deepen the understanding of sports fans. Drawing on this method to capture the match-day experience of Everton FC's cross-city rivals Liverpool Football Club (Liverpool FC), the benefits of personal and emotional accounts are detailed. Therefore, this chapter proposes that the use of more emotional and personal qualitative accounts allows readers to develop a greater understanding of, and insight into, sports fans and match-day fan practices.

Ethnographic Methods

Ethnography is a valuable methodological framework because it 'brightly illuminates the relationship between structure, agency and geographical context' (Herbert, 2000: 550). However, defining ethnography is difficult, with Van Maanen (2011) suggesting that this is because of its long evolution, the various techniques employed, and the numerous representational styles involved (that are not always complementary). Despite the multiple definitions that are applied to the term within a variety of research fields, the authors have adopted a definition provided by Ley (1988: 121); ethnography is:

> concerned to make sense of the actions and intentions of people as knowledgeable agents… and attempts to make sense of their making sense of the events and opportunities confronting them in everyday life.

This classification captures the value of the 'everydayness' of football in the lives of the participants who took part in the case studies used throughout this chapter. Blomberg (1995) stresses the significance of ethnography to academic inquiry in its ability to study activities and subjects in their natural setting. Additionally, she notes that it makes valuable contributions and findings because it can be 'difficult for individuals to articulate the tactic knowledge and understandings they have of familiar activities' via interviews (Blomberg, 1995: 177). The core principals of ethnography largely encourage researchers to seek meaning not only in what people say, but also in what they do. Importance is placed not just in how people have seen and understood their environment, but how people do things and behave in those environments (Silverman, 2006).

What particularly separates ethnography from quantitative surveys and structured interviews as a research method is that, typically, ethnographers enter the field more interested in the particular social phenomena being studied with less emphasis on the need to test specific hypotheses (Hammersely and Atkinson, 2007). It also provides a unique avenue to witness life events as they happen, rather than in the artificial settings of other qualitative techniques such as white-room focus groups. The purpose of ethnography is to 'gather whatever data is available to throw light on the issues that are the emerging focus of enquiry' (Hammersely and Atkinson, 2007: 3). This can include using participant and non-participant observation, often in combination with a range of interview techniques (Hammersley, 2018). In addition, sport fandom scholars have also recently adopted digital ethnography, which draws on the practices of traditional ethnography, but applies and modifies these for research studying online sport fan communities (Sturm, 2020; Wegner et al., 2019). As with other qualitative techniques, ethnographers will apply methodological triangulation as one method on its own may not develop adequate robustness to build a meaningful outcome (Flick, 2004). Triangulation also encourages researchers to approach and enter the field with multiple perspectives in mind, which can be placed side by side to better understand the nature of sports fandom (Flick, 2004).

For Van Maanen (2011) it is the conceptual union of fieldwork and culture that represents the answer to how the understanding of others, close or distant, is achieved. In this instance, the ethnographic approach advances its value by providing first a stage to observe and later the principles to write about how sports fans display and perform their fan identity as a lived experience on match-day. Prior ethnographic studies have enabled the complexity of the sports crowd to be illuminated, yielding insider perspectives in an academic field often tainted with controversy (Weed, 2006). As Pearson (2014: iii) notes,

> ethnographic studies on football crowds helps us to overcome the prejudices and misunderstanding that may result from 'outsider' researcher, particularly that carried out by those in authority with vested interest, or by media outlets searching for the sensational.

However, some of the major criticisms of ethnography have been centred on researchers choosing environments that best reflect their aims and purposes, and that these sites serve to reinforce such arguments. For example, Katz (1994: 67) highlights that defining boundaries for a research project can be problematic because:

> when ethnographers discuss 'the field' this is often marked off in space and time, a physical space where the ethnographer is often the one who draws the lines of the field.

We argue that what constitutes the field for ethnographic research remains largely fluid, where researchers studying sports fans are often taken to numerous locations that best epitomise match-day. The tradition of ethnography thus encourages flexible observations at diverse locations, where behavioural variations between the sites, fan groups and the researcher can be better understood. As noted above, the central method of data generation within ethnography has been participant observation, where the researcher becomes the principal research tool (Allen, 2004). Therefore, researchers studying in the tradition of ethnography must also pay attention to issues of their own identity and social status. This involves recognising the significant role they play in the creation of data for research on sports fans; reflexivity is a key element in ethnographic research. In this way, autoethnography extends this reflexive process and offers valuable insights by acknowledging that the individual researcher embodies a number of cultural ideologies and it is these beliefs that serve as a foundation for examining how one interacts with people and places (Anderson, 2006). Through the use of reflexive self-observation this approach presents the researcher as an active and engaged participant in the social world or activity being studied (Anderson and Austin, 2012).

The term autoethnography is a portmanteau of auto- (self), -ethno- (the cultural link), and -graphy (the application of a research process) (Wall, 2006). Autoethnography can take a variety of different forms including 'short stories, poetry, photographic essays, personal essays and fragmented and layer writing' (Ellis, 1999: 673). Anderson (2010) notes that autoethnographies seek to connect what is going on in an individual life to the wider social context. Although its application for research on sports fandom remains in its infancy, researchers using their senses, bodies, movements and feelings to learn about how others experience match-day remains an exciting field of inquiry. Writing about the wider field of fan studies, Evans and Stasi (2014) claim the approach is well suited to scrutinising sports fans because it prioritises the passion of fandom. As such, it also allows researchers to make sense of the tensions and heartaches associated with being a sport fan (Ellis and Bochner, 2006). The authors suggest that researchers employing autoethnography should aim to produce writing that is highly personalised and that tells a story about their own lived experiences of being a sports fan within the broader setting of the crowd. Storytelling is an efficient way to convey information, beliefs and traditions (Suwardy et al., 2013). People tend to remember stories more than facts (Levit, 2009) to such an extent that it provides a lasting method of communication where the blend of verbal and visual educates, informs and entertains. The integration of storytelling with ethnography encourages interaction between the storyteller and the audience, giving opportunity to interpret their own perspectives within the context of their personalised experience.

Knijnik adopted an autoethnographic approach in his research on the Australian association football team the Western Sydney Wanderers (2015). A migrant to Australia himself, his research vividly captured the role football played in his settlement into Australia, whilst acknowledging the challenges faced by many moving to a new country. As supporting a sport team denotes a strong emotional connection between fans (through sharing symbolic and cultural rituals), he argues that personal reflections enable research to be produced that captures the 'hearts and minds' of what it means to be a sport fan (Knijnik, 2015: 36). Sports fans themselves frequently draw on autobiographical stories of players and famous figures from the world of sport, thus revealing the important role that autoethnographic storytelling plays in the lives of fans and society more broadly.

The Value of Using Ethnographic Methods to Understand Sports Fandom

As discussed earlier, there has been a considerable amount of research that has explored sports fandom as an expression of self and social identity. For example, sport marketers have a strong interest in understanding fan psychology and have developed various quantitative models and frameworks to measure sports fan identification (Funk and James 2001; Gwinner and Swanson, 2003; Wann and Branscombe, 1993; Wann, 2006). Wann and Branscombe's (1993) well-cited quantitative model – the Sport Spectator Identification Scale (SSIS) – investigates and measures the extent to which fans feel a psychological connection to a team and view team performance as self-relevant. They specifically focused on the extent to which individuals perceive themselves as fans of the team, are involved with the team, are concerned with the team's performance, and view the team as a representation of themselves (Wann and Branscombe, 1993).

Models of fans also tend to be based on tiered typologies of fandom that rank the nature of the relationship between fans and their involvement with the team (see also Hunt et al., 1999; Mullin et al., 1993; Smith and Stewart, 1999). For example, Mullin et al. (1993) conceptualised fans and their association with the club as being 'highly committed', 'moderately committed' and 'lowly committed'. They consider sport fandom as inherently intangible and subjective in nature, creating various experiences and associated benefits that in turn 'leads to a need to segment sport spectators using specific classifications and frameworks' (Bodet, 2015: 165). Sport marketers have rightfully recognised the heterogeneity of the sports crowd, with the ultimate purpose of their research to attract more fans, funds, and other resources for sports clubs and affiliated organisations.

Quantitative approaches such as these, however, often demand that researchers minimise evidence of their selves and that failing to do so should be regarded as a contaminant in the research process. As such, it has been standard academic practice for the researcher to put 'bias and subjectivity aside in the scientific research process by denying his or her identity' (Wall, 2006: 2). Additionally, quantitative methods are not suited to the study of norms, values, and meanings shared by large aggregates of people (Jonassohn et al., 1981). Sport fandom is not necessarily of the same nature (or influenced by the same causal factors) in which it occurs. Whilst fan cultures of particular sports share common ritual elements, each fan group exhibits distinct forms of prescribed ceremonial behaviour and symbolism (Parry et al., 2014). This distinctiveness is because sports fandom is centred on the emotion and the experience of supporting *your* team. Fans commit time, energy, and in some sense, their self, to the support of their team. The defining feature of a sports fan identity, therefore, is not simply association with a sports team, but rather a distinct identity drawn from membership in a group (Thonhauser, 2015). However, this approach relies on an understanding of fan identity as embedded in both individual and social experiences within the local context of match-day.

A group of scholars based at the Leicester School (notably Eric Dunning, John Williams and Patrick Murphy) significantly shaped how sports fans were theorised and researched. Writing in the early 1980s, they drew from Elias' figurational approach, they understood the roots of football hooliganism and deviant sport fan behaviour as a social problem that evolved from social class tensions (Dunning et al. 1988). However, over time their research methods and the evidence used to support their arguments received widespread critique, with a core wing of this criticism coming from those scholars who favoured ethnographic methods (see Armstrong and Harris, 1991; Giulianotti and Armstrong, 2002; King, 1997; Pearson, 2012). None were more vocal in their criticism than Armstrong and Harris (1991) who described how the Leicester School's use of statistics on employment and criminal convictions as contributing factors in fan violence is problematic.

Quantitative approaches such as these do not allow the lived experiences of sports fans to be examined in depth and hence do nothing to counter the view that these fans are somehow abnormal. For this reason, a substantial number of scholars have turned to ethnographic methods and immersing themselves into the field, where the research is guided by what they observe through 'thick descriptive' analysis (Armstrong, 1998; Giulianotti, 1995; Osborne and Coombs, 2016; Pearson, 2012). Coined by Clifford Geertz, 'thick description' refers to how a researcher's observation of behaviours must be placed in a broader interpretive context, where researchers try and make sense of the native's point of view (Geertz, 1973). As the following case studies illustrate, employing a 'thick-descriptive' ethnographic approach provides clear sense of the match-day routine, which was informed and directed by the very research participants that create and engage with sport fan culture.

Researching in Their Shadow: *Match-day Experiences of Everton FC Fans*

> I guess if I had seen the score a day later that we drew with the Hammers [West Ham United] I would have thought that was a pretty disappointing result. But being there, being at Goodison when Lukaku [Everton striker] equalised in the 90ish minute changed everything. Anyone not at the match would not have felt the atmosphere and excitement… People around me were saying after the match that the result actually felt like a win, which was not what the fans in the pubs afterwards were saying. Feeling the excitement and relief when the flag stayed down and the ball hit the net… I don't think you could have been on the ride if you weren't there… we came back to a pub in Walton buzzing – a buzz that was short lived when we met up with non match-going fans.
>
> *(Fieldwork Note: 6/1/2015 vs. West Ham United)*

Conducting fieldwork and locating the research in environments that best represent the interest of participants remains fundamental to ethnographic research design. In this instance, data for a study on the match-day experiences of Everton FC fans was collected over 22 matches, with 20 semi-structured interviews. Each match generated approximately 4.5 hours of observation (including travel time), totalling approximately 100 hours in the field over three years. The research participants varied considerably in match-day behaviour, in their reasons for following the team, and their reasons for attending live matches. However, a commonality amongst all was the importance each placed on their match-day routines and movements. As such, the locations observed became an important site of analysis and revealed some unexpected insights into the habitual routines of fans.

As part of data capture, the researcher shadowed participants on match-day, usually after they had done an interview. Shadowing in this context meant observations were undertaken in environments guided by the participants, which enabled a stronger understanding of why particular spaces yielded specific significance for some fans. This technique provided comprehensive insights into the variety of practices and meanings fans ascribe to their match-day experience. Additionally, it encouraged them to interact with the researcher through a variety of ways, communicating the rich narratives of their customs and activities. For example, through shadowing, the researcher better understood how certain routes to the stadium yielded historical, social and cultural relevance:

> Was out today with John and Maggie. They walk me down a few laneways that appear to be heading in a different direction and not towards Goodison Park [the Everton FC stadium]. I later find out that they take this route because John would walk this way with his father when he was younger as it involved passing his grandmother's house. He pointed at her house, and although she no longer lived there (she had passed away) this will be the way he gets to the stadium.
>
> *Fieldwork note: 3/9/2013: Everton FC V Newcastle United*

The opportunity to observe if what participants recounted in the interviews was an accurate representation of match-day experiences minimised field distortion and enhanced overall validity. For example, ambiguities to what was discussed in the interviews, at times, varied considerably to match-day behaviour:

> **Jess:** Why wouldn't you go in Lower Gwladys [stand at the stadium]?
> **Tegan:** Because it's where all the young lads go and they're all throwing beer and fighting.
> *Interview*

Like Tegan, many of the fans interviewed expressed that there was something of a 'hooligan wing' at Everton FC, but during three years of observations the researcher never witnessed any behaviour that fitted the traditional descriptions of football hooliganism (i.e. violence between rival football fans or fans and the police). Rather, the only altercation observed was between two Everton FC fans over spilt chips in a takeaway fish and chip shop line prior to a match. Adopting the ethnographic approach therefore allowed for an environment in which non-verbal behaviour could be observed, thus curtailing some of the well-documented 'problems' noted earlier in this chapter by those relying on interviews or surveys as the central method of data collection.

However, the ethnographic approach involves a great deal of reflexivity on behalf of the researcher. For example, building rapport with participants and positioning oneself in a research community can at times be challenging. In practice, access to a research field is not just established at the outset, but is a process of continuing negotiation and explanation (Rowe, 2014). We argue that researchers' accounts and emotions should not be ignored, but become the subject of academic enquiry. As will be shown in the following section, one of the key features of autoethnography is that the researcher's narrative is 'written in' (Chang, 2008) to the research process. Adopting this approach can become a useful pedagogical tool to think about how one's own experiences are linked to wider social and cultural issues associated with being a sport fan.

Situating the Self: *A Football Fan's Autoethnography*

> With the summer here people around me are enjoying the warm weather and looking forward to longer evenings, barbeques, and time spent on the beach. Not me. For me this is a time of pain and suffering. The enforced withdrawal that the end of the football season brings is almost unbearable.
>
> *Reflections, June/July 2009*

Authors who adopt autoethnography use personal reflections, such as the one above, to discuss wider issues in an attempt to 'evoke and provoke emotional responses and identification... in the reader' (Dashper, 2015: 513). Although sports fans experience iconic sporting events together, and perhaps share collective memories of an event, individual fans will also have innately personal experiences and memories. These form the basis of, and the vehicle for, spreading recognisable and 'tellable' stories that often become deeply ingrained in fan culture. One of the benefits of the autoethnographic approach is that it rejects the 'traditional' position of researchers as uninvolved and unobtrusive to their research community (Nash, 2017). It also responds to the call by various scholars for research to move beyond what motivates and satisfies fans, to exploring how people experience sport fandom at an everyday level (Hoeber and Kerwin, 2013).

As with ethnography, it is common for autoethnographers to use *vignettes*, or short stories within research that vividly portray an experience and elicit understanding and emotional identification (Humphreys, 2005). Such an approach has been adopted in some of the admittedly few sports fan autoethnographies to convey the feelings and experiences of the researcher to the audience (see Parry, 2012; Sturm, 2011, 2015). Below is an extract from a diary entry that illustrates the raw emotions, dilemmas and anxieties the author faced when researching the fan experience of Liverpool FC.

> After a hiatus when time has passed all too slowly the much awaited-for start of the season has finally come! I am preparing to put myself through the emotional rollercoaster all over again. I feel my emotions running higher than usual as our first game of the season is being shown live on television, away to Tottenham (a London team) – I hope we beat them, I really cannot stand Tottenham. The sale of midfield maestro Alonso to Spanish giants Real Madrid has left a sense of unease though. We should not be selling our good players; we should have a team filled with the very best players. Rumours abound surrounding the financial plight of my once-great club which also makes me feel unsettled. The arrival of an expensive Italian replacement does not fill the void and, to make matters worse, he is injured and will not feature until October. I have to admit that I am a bit anxious; our squad seems weaker than last season, when we were not good enough; so how can we hope to compete this year? [Written after the match] Sure enough we have lost. I knew it. I said we would. It is going to be another season of disappointment, shattered dreams, and heartache. I know it is. I just know. My pessimism is not shared by fans of all clubs. I have watched interviews with fans from the three clubs newly promoted to the Premier League, who believe that they will easily stay up, confidence in the face of statistics, finances and squad quality. Who are these fans? What do they know?
>
> *Reflections, August 2009*

Diary entries allow the researcher to reflect on their own feelings and experiences at a later point in time and to connect these to wider issues during the write-up of the research.

In autoethnography, they often involve a high degree of reflexivity that situates the researcher methodologically, socially and temporally. The combination of this reflexivity and vivid detail allow the readers to gain an authentic experience of the phenomenon for themselves and to gain insights into fandom that may be ignored in quantitative approaches.

Various scholars in the field of sport have, however, recounted a level of anxiety in using autoethnography (Kerwin and Hoeber, 2015; Kodama et al., 2013). These anxieties are not unfounded, as the approach has been described as a 'self-indulgent practice' (Sparkes, 2002; 211) and 'irreverent, self-absorbed and sentimental' (Ellis and Bochner, 2000: 736). However, we argue that these criticisms overlook its value, particularly its ability to reveal critical insider insights into the culture of sporting organisations. For example, Fleming and Fullagar (2007) drew from the experience of being a player, coach and facility manager of cricket to explore how women constantly have to negotiate gender and power relations. They offer a rich, descriptive and honest account of the personal challenges and dilemmas experienced being involved in a sport historically considered a masculine pursuit and professional domain (Fleming and Fullagar, 2007).

It is this vulnerability and transparency that makes autoethnography not a simple task, but rather a recursive and reflexive process requiring commitment and resolve on behalf of the researcher (Cooper et al., 2017). Validity for autoethnography therefore remains based in its capacity to evoke in readers a feeling or experience that can be described as lifelike, believable and coherent (Ellis et al., 2006). Whilst to date the autoethnographic field within sport remains focused on the past experiences of former elite athletes or those working in management within sport organisations (Drummond, 2010; Sparkes, 2002), we suggest its application for research on sports fandom to be an exciting opportunity to better understand the fan experience.

Conclusion

This chapter has explored the benefits of adopting the methods of ethnography and autoethnography in studies related to sports fandom. Within the context of this chapter, it was the use of 'thick description' by researchers in our two case studies that built depth into their overall research findings, allowing readers to develop a greater understanding of, and insight into, sports fan behaviour. These insights are needed, particularly, to counter accusations that sports fans are in some way deviant and a threat to wider society. The ethnographic approach also provides an opportunity for the voices of fans that have traditionally been excluded and/ or marginalised in the field on sport fandom research (such as women) to be explored. By embracing ethnographic methods, researchers are able to provide a more nuanced description of sports fans that embraces their differences and that does not rely on tiered typologies of fandom alone.

The authors encourage academics studying sports fandom to embrace such methods and to write themselves into their research in order to facilitate understanding of sport fan experiences (Parry, 2012; Richards, 2014). Although there are still relatively few sport fan studies that apply the ethnographic approach, we suggest that both methods provide a high degree of reflexivity that allows the identification of both the beneficial and detrimental effects that come with following a sports fan.

References

Anderson, L. (2006). Analytic autoethnography. *Journal of Contemporary Ethnography*, *35*(4), 373–394.
Anderson, L. Austin, (2012). Auto-ethnography in leisure studies. *Leisure Studies*, *31*(2), 131–146.

Allen, D. (2004). Ethnomethodological insights into insider-outsider relationships in nursing ethnographies of healthcare settings. *Nursing Inquiry*, 11(1), 14–24.

Anderson, L. (2010). Analytic autoethnography. In Atkinson, P. (Ed.) and Delamont, S. (Ed.) (Eds.), *SAGE Qualitative Research Methods* (pp. 374–395). Thousand Oaks, CA: SAGE.

Armstrong, G. (1998). *Football Hooliganism: Knowing the Score*. Oxford, United Kingdom: Berg.

Armstrong, G. and Harris, R. (1991). Football hooligans: theory and evidence. *The Sociological Review*, 39(3), 427–558.

Bloomberg, J. (1995). Ethnography: Aligning field studies of work and design. In A. Monk and N. Gilbert (Eds.), *Perspectives on HCI: Diverse approaches* (175–197). London, United Kingdom: Academic Press.

Bodet, G. (2015). The spectators' perspective. In M. Parent and J. Chappelet (Eds.), *Routledge Handbook of Sports Event Management* (pp. 163–180). Abingdon, United Kingdom: Routledge.

Campbell, E. (2017). 'Apparently Being a Self-Obsessed C**t Is Now Academically Lauded': Experiencing Twitter Trolling of Autoethnographers. *Forum Qualitative Sozialforschung / Forum: Qualitative Social Research*, 18(3). doi:http://dx.doi.org/10.17169/fqs-18.3.2819

Chang, H. (2008). *Autoethnography as Method*: Left Coast Press.

Cooper, J., Grenier, R. and Macaulay, C. (2017). Autoethnography as a critical approach in sport management: Current applications and directions for future research. *Sport Management Review*, 20(1), 43–54.

Dashper, K. (2015). Revise, resubmit and reveal? An autoethnographer's story of facing the challenges of revealing the self through publication. *Current Sociology*, 63(4), 511–527.

Drummond, M. (2010). The natural: an autoethnography of a masculinized body in sport. *Men and Masculinities*, 12(3), 374–389.

Dunning, E., Murphy, P. and Williams, J. (1988). *The roots of football hooliganism: A historical and sociological study*. London, United Kingdom: Routledge.

Ellis, C. (1999). Heartful autoethnography. *Qualitative Health Research*, 9(5), 669–683.

Ellis, C. and Bochner, A. (2000). Autoethnography, personal narrative, reflexivity: researcher as subject in N. K. Denzin and Y. S. Lincoln (Eds.), *Handbook of Qualitative Research* (2nd Ed.). Thousand Oaks, CA: Sage, pp. 733–768.

Ellis, C. S. and Bochner, A. P. (2006). Analyzing analytic autoethnography: An autopsy in *Journal of Contemporary Ethnography*, 35(4), 429–449.

Evans, A. and Stasi, M. (2014) Desperately seeking methods: new directions in fan studies research. *Participations*, 11(2): 4–23.

Fleming, C. and Fullagar, S. (2007). Reflexive methodologies: an autoethnography of the gendered performance of sport/management. *Annals of Leisure Research*, 10(3–4), 238–256.

Flick, U. (2004). Triangulation in qualitative research. In U. Flick, E. Kardorff and I. Steinke (Eds.), *A Companion to Qualitative Research* (178–184). London, United Kingdom: Sage.

Funk, D. and James, J. (2001). The psychological continuum model: A conceptual framework for understanding an individuals' psychological connection to sport. *Sport Management Review*, 4(2), 119–150.

Geertz, C. (1973). *Thick Description: The interpretation of culture*. New York: Basic Books.

Giulianotti, R. (1995). Football and the politics of carnival: An ethnographic study of Scottish fans in Sweden. *International Review for the Sociology of Sport*, 30(2), 191–220.

Giulianotti, R. and Armstrong, G. (2002). Avenues of contestation: Football hooligans running and ruling urban spaces. *Social Anthropology*, 10(2), 211–238.

Gwinner, K. and Swanson, S. (2003). A model of fan identification: Antecedents and sponsorship outcomes. *Journal of Services Marketing*, 17(3), 275–294.

Hammersley, M. (2018). What is ethnography? Can it survive? Should it? *Ethnography and Education*, 13(1), 1–17.

Hammersley, M. and Atkinson, P. (2007). *Ethnography: Principles in practice* (3rd edition). London, United Kingdom: Routledge.

Herbert, S. (2000). For ethnography. *Progress in Human Geography*, 24, 550–568.

Hoeber, L. and Kerwin, S. (2013). Exploring the experiences of female sport fans: A collaborative self-ethnography. *Sport Management Review*, 16(3), 326–336.

Humphreys, M., 2005. Getting personal: Reflexivity and autoethnographic vignettes in *Qualitative Inquiry*, 11(6), 840–860.

Hunt, K., Bristol, T. and Bashaw, R. (1999). A conceptual approach to classifying sport fans. *Journal of Services Marketing*, 13(6), 439–452.

Jonassohn, K., Turowetz, A. and Gruneau, R. (1981). Research methods in the sociology of sport: Strategies and problems. *Qualitative Sociology*, 4(3), 179–197.

Katz, C. (1994). Playing the field: Questions of fieldwork in geography. *Professional Geographers*, 46(1), 67–72.

Kerwin, S. and Hoeber, L. (2015). Collaborative self-ethnography: navigating self-reflexivity in a sport management context, *Journal of Sport Management*, 29(5), 498–509.

King, A. (1997). The lads: Masculinity and the new consumption of football. *Sociology*, 31(2), 329–346.

Knijnik, J. (2015). Feeling at home: an autoethnographic account of an immigrant football fan in Western Sydney. *Leisure Studies*, 34(10), 34–41.

Kodama, E., Doherty, A. and Popovic, M. (2013). Front line insight: an autoethnography of the Vancouver 2010 volunteer experience. *European Sport Management Quarterly*, 13, 76–93.

Levit, N. (2009). Legal storytelling: the theory and the practice-reflective writing across the curriculum. *Journal of Legal Writing Institute*, 15, 259.

Ley, D. (1988). Interpretive social research in the inner city. In J. Eyles (Ed.), *Research in human geography: Introductions and investigations* (pp. 121–138). Oxford, United Kingdom: Blackwell Publishing.

Madrigal, R. and Chen, J. (2008). Moderating and mediating effects of team identification in regard to causal attributions and summary judgments following a game outcome. *Journal of Sport Management*, 22, 717–733.

Mullin, B., Hardy, S. and Sutton, W. (1993). *Sports Marketing*. Champaign, France: IL Human Kinetics.

Nash, M. (2017). Gender on the ropes: An autoethnographic account of boxing in Tasmania, Australia. *International Review for the Sociology of Sport*, 52(6), 734–750.

Osborne, A. and Coombs, D. (2016). *Female Fans of the NFL: Taking Their Place in the Stands*. New York: Routledge.

Parry, K. D. (2012). Game of two passions: A football fan's autoethnography. *Qualitative Research Journal*, 12(2), 238–250.

Parry, K. D., Jones, I. and Wann, D. L. (2014). An examination of sport fandom in the United Kingdom: a comparative analysis of fan behaviours, socialization processes, and team identification. *Journal Of Sport Behavior*, 37(3), 251–267.

Pearson, G. (2012). *An Ethnography of English Football Fans: Cans, cops and carnivals*. Manchester, United Kingdom: Manchester University Press.

Pearson, G. (2014). Playing on a different pitch: ethnographic research on football crowds. In M. Hopkins and J. Treadwell (Eds.), *Football Hooliganism, Fan Behaviour and Crime* (pp. 176–202). London: Palgrave Macmillan.

Richards, J. (2014). 'Which player do you fancy then?' Locating the female ethnographer in the field of the sociology of sport. *Soccer and Society*, 16(2–3), 393–404.

Rowe, A. (2014). Situating the self in prison research: Power, identity, and epistemology. *Qualitative Inquiry*, 20(4), 404–416.

Silverman, D. (2006). *Interpreting Qualitative Data: Methods for analysing talk, text and interaction* (3rd edition). London, United Kingdom: Sage.

Smith, A. and Stewart, B. (2007). The travelling fan: Understanding the mechanisms of sport fan consumption in a sport tourism setting. *Sport & Tourism*, 12(3–4), 155–181.

Smith, A. and Stewart, B. (1999). *Sports Management: A guide to professional practice*. Sydney, Australia: Allen and Urwin.

Sparkes, A. (2000). Autoethnography and narratives of self: Reflections on criteria of action. *Sociology of Sport Journal*, 17, 21–43.

Sparkes, A. C. (2002), *Telling Tales in Sport and Physical Activity: A qualitative journey*, Leeds: Human Kinetics.

Sturm, D. (2011). Masculinities, affect and the (re)place(ment) of stardom in Formula One fan leisure practices, *Annals of Leisure Research*, 14(2–3), 224–241.

Sturm, D. (2015). Playing with the autoethnographical: Performing and re-presenting the fan's voice. *Cultural Studies ↔ Critical Methodologies*, 15(3), 213–223.

Suwardy, T., Pan, G. and Seow, P.-S. (2013). Using digital storytelling to engage student learning. *Accounting Education*, 22(2), 109–112.

Sturm, D. (2020). Fans as e-participants? Utopia/dystopia visions for the future of digital sport fandom. *Convergence: The International Journal of Research into New Media Technologies*. Available online https://doi.org/10.1177/1354856520907096

Theodorakis, N. D. and Wann, D. L. (2008). The relationship between sport team identification and need to belong. *International Journal of Sport Management and Marketing*, 4, 356–374.

Thonhauser, G. (2015 September 24–26). What constitutes being a fan? Towards a social ontology of sports fandom. Paper presented at the Fourth Conference of the European Network on Social Ontology: ENSO IV. University of Palermo, Italy.

Van Maanen, J. (2011). *Tales of the Field: On writing ethnography* (2nd edition). Chicago, United States of America: The University of Chicago Press.

Wall, S., 2006. An autoethnography on learning about ethnography in *International Journal of Qualitative Methods*, 5(2), Article 9.

Wann, D. (2006). Understanding the positive social psychological benefits of sport team identification: The team identification-social psychological health model. *Group Dynamics: Theory, Research, and Practice*, 10(4), 272–296.

Wann, D. and Branscombe, N. (1993). Sports fans: Measuring degree of identification with their team. *International Journal of Sports Psychology*, 24, 1–17.

Weed. (2006). The story of an ethnography: The experience of watching the 2002 World Cup in the pub. *Soccer & Society*, 7(1): 76–95.

Wegner, C., Delia, E. and Baker, B. (2019). Fans as e-participants? Utopia/dystopia visions for the future of digital sport fandom. *Sport Management Review*. Available online https://doi.org/10.1016/j.smr.2019.01.001

9
Media Coverage of Sports Fans
A Framing Analysis

Mark Turner

"Look at it this way."

Here comes the closing salvo of a discussion that likely has seen many twists and turns, digressions and tangents. Perhaps, it's a new angle or maybe a new and clearer example or reference. Either will carry with it the perspective of a person trying to make a point, the point. The aim in that moment is for the listener to see it the way the speaker sees it. Wherever there's communication, be it a discussion over the importance of team success versus personal statistics in picking an MVP or a news report describing a player's post-game conduct or why the team's colors are all wrong, people use references that they hope are the most clear and relevant, so that everyone can share a similar perspective, as different eyes looking through the same lens. This is framing, and it is an inescapable part of life. Look at it this way: Wherever there's communication and someone shares their perspective, there's framing. It seems evident that if something so ubiquitous is happening in society, that the understanding of it becomes important and necessary and the study of it should be occurring widely. Thus, this chapter offers support for why the realm of sports and fandom – as it intersects with news media – should not escape the exacting gaze of framing research. When employed, framing research can help to answer important questions related to how fans process, perceive, and use media content. Areas of framing also may look at the roles those fans play in building frames. Sanderson and Cassilo (2019) explored framing employed by Facebook users in response to the youth football organization Pop Warner eliminating kickoffs in its three youngest age divisions. Using a bottom-up framing approach (Nisbet, 2010), the researchers conducted a thematic data analysis following the announcement. Findings suggested participants framed the policy in one of six ways: "(a) potentially impacting the NFL; (b) overprotecting the players; (c) creating a competitive disadvantage within football; (d) negatively affecting masculinity; (e) providing evidence of America's declining power; and (f) exhibiting legitimate organizational policy" (Sanderson and Cassilo, 2019, p. 8). The study found the public had the ability to introduce alternative frames that could challenge or confirm the frames introduced by media and official sources through the arrival of the internet and social network services.

An analysis of communication research by Bryant and Miron (2004) affirms the growth of framing as one of the most frequently used theories. The concept of framing began its rise to widespread application in the 1970s with Goffman (1974), who asserted that frames were primary means that people used to locate, perceive, and identify events, and to offer meaning, organize experiences, and guide actions. The framing process involves using language to emphasize some issues and not others in an effort to prompt the reader to understand an issue in a specific way. According to Entman (1993), "to frame is to select some aspects of a perceived reality and make them more salient in a communicating text" (pp. 52–53). He added that by doing this, the person communicating promotes a specifically defined problem, causal interpretation, ethical evaluation, or treatment recommendation for the item described. Think of media framing as a window compared to a mirror. Although it is a representation of events and people, it is not a direct representation of the world because some of the context is no longer there. The person who created the window is offering information about the view directly in front of you. It allows for an assessment of the world based on what you see through the window. The media are prolific creators of these windows. For example, media have consistently helped build and shore up the heteronormative window or frame for how sports and athletes are viewed. This frame reflected a systematic intolerance of gays in sport. Researchers found a collective belief that gay men were not playing in the four major U.S. professional team sports (Griffin, 1998; Hekma, 1998). Kian, Anderson, and Shipka (2015) undertook a textual analysis of U.S. media framing of Jason Collins' coming out as the first openly gay active player in the National Basketball Association (NBA). The researchers found that media framed the self-outing as a monumental milestone for U.S. sport. Collins' critics, of whom there were relatively few, were framed as out-of-step with the times. Overall, the study found media used the moment to frame all of sports as becoming more accepting and more inclusive. Noted in the study was journalists' newfound willingness to speak more openly about gays in their content and how this inclusion in the framing of sports culture might have helped to change attitudes among athletes and coaches.

Consider also this area of evolution in sports for further framing research. The NCAA reports that because of the marketing rights, Division I Men's Basketball brings in $867.5 million each year (Van, 2020). The championship tournament, known as "March Madness," is a tournament spanning 21 days. March Madness brings the national spotlight to players and universities. The student athletes' efforts, at least in part, help generate revenue, not to mention attract students to attend the respective schools. The NCAA does not pay student athletes for their names, images, and likenesses and, as the NCAA reports, male basketball players have about a 1 percent chance of making it to the professional leagues. So, with very little promise of future pay, even though their efforts, at least in part, help generate millions of dollars in revenue, millions in other sports tickets and merchandising for the NCAA and their universities. Players, therefore, are campaigning and suing for compensation. Centering these facts, the window an audience looks through in a news report speaks directly to a player's experience. The frame of reference offers information that is touted by sources sympathetic to the plight of student athletes.

Now consider these facts and assertions in a news story: The NCAA (NCAA.org, 2021) awards nearly $3.5 billion in athletic scholarships every year to more than 180,000 student athletes. Many of those scholarships are guaranteed regardless of an athlete's ability to play. The NCAA sponsors a student assistance fund to help Division I athletes with essential needs. Congressional committee members investigating the compensation of student athletes are incredulous about the NCAA's ability to equitably compensate different players who contribute at different levels with different talent and notoriety as well as different sports with varying levels of popularity and revenue. These facts center news coverage of the NCAA pay-for-play debate on elements sympathetic to the NCAA's ongoing practices. The frame of reference is for the organizations' traditions of amateur competition uncomplicated by student income.

Framing and Framing Analysis

The above example speaks directly to the process of framing in news media, a theory at the practical center of journalism practice. While its mechanisms are not expressly stated, framing is employed purposefully with a sense of its impact in mind. Framing is powerful and serves to construct social reality (Reese, 2001; Scheufele, 1999; Tuchman, 1978). In providing a window to the world, framing can inform and influence how the world is understood and navigated. Framing theory suggests that how and what – the frames – media present to the audience influences people's understanding and evaluation of information (Scheufele, 1999).

Scheufele (1999) identifies the study of news framing as encompassing three primary areas: mental framing, group framing, and content framing. Mental frames are the frames individuals have as a result of processing the "content frames" perceived during the consumption of news. Our mental frame acts as a filter on incoming frames to help us organize and form ideas and opinions. To determine the salience of new frames' ability and strength in either altering or reinforcing individual attitudes and beliefs, the complex integration of news frames with individual mental frames must be considered. Group frames are the frames we gather collectively as a culture. They may be expressed as stereotypes, or frames we apply to the information we receive based on how we were raised, where we grew up, and our cultural beliefs. Content frames are the actual language and messages used by media creators, such as presenting a sympathetic view of student athletes seeking compensation or conversely highlighting traditional approaches to amateur athletics.

Gamson and Modigliani (1987) describe a frame as "a central organizing idea or story line that provides meaning to an unfolding strip of events, weaving a connection among them. The frame suggests what the controversy is about, the essence of the issue" (p. 143). In the context of mass media, this circumstance means journalists are providing more than just the facts and an account of events. They are also telling the audience how to understand an event and define an apparent conflict that has made the event valuable in the eyes of those who are creating news reports and selecting events for coverage. The frame or "news value" of controversy or conflict is prevalent in news reports (McGregor, 2002; Bartholomé, Lecheler, & De Vreese, 2018). As noted previously, framing and frames are a ubiquitous element of human communication. The frames that are used by journalists are often already a part of the public discourse (Kinder & Sanders, 1996). This is not to say that media don't have a significant role in the discourse. It is to further affirm that there is a symbiotic interaction of how information is understood and evaluated among media, sources, and audiences. It is to note that journalists are far from lone actors in the framing used in news reports. Kozman (2017) approached the relationship between journalist frames and sources through the coverage of steroid use in professional baseball by traditional and new media. The study focuses on sourcing patterns and found that – counter to research about sourcing in the media – journalists relied heavily on baseball players and less so on officials in forming frames around steroid use. As Schudson (2011) suggests, in order to produce news on a consistent basis, media rely routinely on the same channels of information, at the center of which are the sources who provide reporters with a consistent flow of news and information. The findings suggest that sports, as a subject area on which journalists focus, is different from most other areas. Most studies find government officials as the most authoritative source (Bennett et al., 2006; Hallin, 1986); sports stories put the weight on the players, even in a charged issue such as steroids that saw major societal influences outside the players' circle.

Framing is grounded in media studies surrounding political messages. Research by McCombs and Shaw (1972) and Scheufele and Tewksbury (2007) shows that messages of a political nature communicated through media channels are central to the formation of public opinion. Media may serve as conduits for partisan frames developed by "elite" members of society such as politicians and vocal members of society such as activists who advocate specific issues (Gamson & Modigliani, 1987, 1989). Partisan frames highlight specific information and ideas in order to present specific viewpoints on an issue as being correct and other viewpoints as being wrong. Actors (both individuals and organizations) introduce frames they expect will sway public opinion. The journalist can send these along (frame sending) or intervene (frame setting) with their own or with organizational frames (Bruggemann, 2014). For example, critics of transgender girls and women playing girls or women's sports have justified their opposition by framing the issue as providing an "unfair advantage" for the transgender athletes, whereas supporters have framed the issue as one of inclusiveness (Jones, Arcelus, Bouman, & Haycraft, 2017). Journalists can choose to push either of these frames along in their coverage or highlight other aspects of the controversy including government intervention. Correspondingly, proponents of gay rights have framed these policies as promoting "equal rights," while opponents have framed the policies as promoting "special rights" and undermining "traditional moral values" (Brewer, 2003).

While Bruggemann (2014) touts individual journalists' ability to create or pass along frames, Entman's (2003) Cascading Activation Model (CAM) shows the process by which information is introduced and decisions are made and seeks to explain the overall approach of news media's framing of political events, serving as a macro model for general journalistic processes. Entman suggests framing in the political arena starts at the top level and cascades like a waterfall through multiple levels, including media framing. In using this model of framing to research the use of frames in media coverage surrounding sports, the top-level entity in politics could be substituted for a league commissioner or the owner of a team. Entman (2003) applied his cascading activation model to a study of how the White House framed the events of September 11, 2001, seeking to explore news frames that came directly from the administration. Entman says journalists and individuals are more likely to agree with and pass on the White House's framing of 9/11 if it was congruent with cultural assumptions of the majority of American people. The model shows the circulation of framing up and down the "cascade," which implies that newsroom leaders and staff influence each other's organizational and personal frames. According to Entman, the CAM highlights the interactions of four important variables that influence the activation and spread of the preferred frames: motivations, cultural congruence, power, and strategy. Entman posited that motivations and cultural congruence work internally to "pull" mental associations into individuals' thinking, but that power and strategy operate from the outside to "push" consideration of frames (Entman, 2003).

Entman (2003) asserts that "top editors, correspondents and editorialists" influence the media's audience second only to prominent public officials at the administrative level of his model. News, as well, influences audience ideas and opinions, which in turn influence the way public officials and journalists frame the news. The result is that frames can be challenged (Entman, 2004). "Counterframes" emerge in these instances. They are the frames that are found credible in the public sphere that are against those that originated within the elite level. Entman calls it "framing parity" when a counterframe competes at the same level as a frame that originated at the top of the model and gives the audience an opposing perspective on the story. Social networking sites offer this possibility with fans' voices being heard and amplified to a greater degree. Achieving Entman's idea of parity, however, is uncommon as the frames that are created at the upper tiers of Entman's model flow unchallenged through the model's frames because they tend to align with what the public already deemed true. Framing theory has largely been concerned with the effects of the frames (Scheufele, 1999). This core exploration in framing research is important in understanding the impact media content has on all audiences including sports fans. To be clear, so far, this chapter has referred to framing as a concept and theory. Scholars have also described framing as a paradigm (Entman, 1993; Reese, 2001), a technique (Endres, 2004), a perspective (Kuypers & Cooper, 2005), among other terms. The references all address the power of framing to structure messages and provide meaning for an audience. Most often, the concern centers on the influence framing has on the individual (Druckman, 2001; Goffman, 1974).

Answering Questions about Individual Fans

In his seminal book *Frame Analysis*, Erving Goffman offered context for individual viewpoints using a sports analogy, saying that opposing fans at a football game do not experience the "same" game (Goffman, 1978). Goffman explained that those who rooted for the winning team describe the skilled play of the athletes as the reason for the game's result while those supporting the losing team pick apart the "poor" refereeing in their explanation of the outcome. Entman (1993) has located frames with individuals, news organizations, news sources, news texts, and society, leaving a great deal of space for theorizing about how news framing works and what elements make framing powerful or limited. As such, research into framing effects is built on finding answers to questions such as those suggested by D'Angelo and Kuypers (2010). The authors offer four research areas in the form of questions that can help to guide research into framing effects. The following unpacks these questions.

1. Do news frames shape attitudes of individuals directly by forming opinions or by changing them? This question relates directly to the ongoing examination of just how influential media can be. The question also speaks to the cognitive processes behind how frames work for audience members. Consider a scenario in which fans have read stories framed around the size of contracts for professional athletes during tense trade talks and have begun to think of players as greedy. Within this research context, a researcher might consider if the frames in the stories had swayed fans away from viewing the players as competitive (seeking championship contention or a better team fit) toward viewing players as greedy or if the frames created the first conscious thoughts of a greedy player. The power of media, particularly mass media, has been debated since scholars asserted Hypodermic Needle theory (Laswell, 1927) based on observations of war propaganda and Hollywood films. The theory posited that audiences were powerless against media messages, understanding and acting monolithically after exposure to whatever mass media producers (radio, newspapers) presented. It suggested that media inject content into a passive audience (Laswell, 1927). Though this model has been largely discounted by more recent research showing that mass media's power is only compelling with some people, some of the time using some messages (Katz & Lazarsfeld, 1955; Lazarsfeld, Berelson, & Gaudet, 1944), there is still considerable debate about when and why media are influential. The debate has continued as news media has spread from their traditional platforms to the internet, seen as either adding a layer to the exploration of media strength or demanding a whole new approach to it. Johnson and Romney (2019) studied racial framing – a robust area of media research – on the social network site (SNS) Instagram, a visually based digital platform. The researchers asked whether SNSs reflect racial framing found in sports coverage on traditional platforms. Studies have found that minority athletes are frequently framed along racial stereotypes. Looking at the four major American sports networks – ESPN, FOX Sports, NBC Sports, and CBS Sports – researchers analyzed the posted content of their accounts on Instagram. The study examined nearly 2,000 images and found that significant discrepancies exist between the way black subjects and white subjects were framed. "Black subjects' athletic achievements were overemphasized at the expense of their other virtues and skills" (Johnson and Romney, 2019, p. 12). Black subjects were more likely to be featured in active poses, and are more likely to be featured in strength and team sports. White subjects were less likely than black subjects to be featured as athletes and more likely to be featured in neutral sports, individual sports, and in passive images. The findings correspond to framing studies that show similar patterns that highlight blacks' athletic achievements over non-athletic roles (Hardin, Dodd, et al., 2004).

2. Do frames make certain ideas more salient in the public domain, thus making them more likely to be used by individuals to understand an issue or topic? This question looks at the scope and social impact of frames as they make aspects of specific issues more prominent and important. A researcher might seek to measure the extent that frames centered on protests about sports teams, who have insensitive names and mascots, might be employed by fans to evaluate calls for change. In comparison, the researcher might want to find out whether frames that highlight the diversity of opinions among the group represented by the name or mascot might shape thoughts among fans. These two frames are prominent in media coverage (NAJA, 2003). When critique of these mascots is covered, usually in the form of news coverage of protests, the discussion is often simplistic. Media coverage of news events that surround mascots stereotypically representing indigenous Americans rarely includes either a thoughtful description of the mascots or discussion of the social context that bolsters support for them (NAJA, 2003). The debate over the use of culturally and racially insensitive names and mascots garners a great deal of attention because of the reach of sports and clearly engages social justice movements and political interests. Framing research also investigates the effects of "issue framing" on policy preferences (Chong & Druckman, 2007; Lecheler & deVreese, 2012). Issue framing consists of increasing or decreasing the salience of particular issue aspects in political news (Druckman, 2001; Entman et al., 2009). The idea that subtle differences in the framing of an issue can shape how people evaluate and understand an issue has motivated framing research (Iyengar, 1991; Sniderman and Theriault, 2004; Woods and Arthur, 2017). The effects of issue framing on policy preferences are mostly explored through experiments in which participants are presented with frames that focus on different issue aspects. These studies have demonstrated selecting certain issue aspects in political news can lead individuals to focus on those aspects when forming an attitude about the policy (Kuhne, Weber, & Sommer, 2015).

In a study exploring why some emerging sports communities grow faster than others, Wood (2019) turned to analyzing both the amount of coverage from news media and the issue frames related to normative coverage of mainstream sports. Considering that news media influences the legitimacy and growth of all sports (Aerts and Cormier, 2009; Wonneberger & Jacobs, 2017), Wood sought to answer whether both the size and type of framing of a sport serves as conduits for the sport's legitimacy and growth. Wood used the relatively small sport of disc golf to understand the relationship of legitimacy and growth and the recurrence of certain frames. In keeping with social identity theory (Tajfel and Turner, 1986), people get involved in organized and informal sports communities partly because it benefits their self-concept. Thus, the media's normative framing of a community of fans may influence people's motivation to become members of those communities. Woods identified five types of normative frames – boundary threats, market, social equity, social costs, and social benefits – that may serve as integral to the growth and viability of emerging sports.

3. Do frames activate emotional reactions that mediate cognitive processes through which framing effects occur? This question suggests an examination of both media framings' ability to elicit emotion that further shapes attitudes and beliefs, as well as how framing effects interact with an individual's beliefs and personal characteristics. Kellner (2011) gives the audience a great deal of responsibility for creating its own perceptions. "All texts are subject to multiple readers depending on the perspectives and subject positions of the readers," according to Kellner (2011, p. 13). He points out the areas that influence or contextualize readings including distinct classes, genders, races, nations, regions, sexual preferences, and political ideologies: Media culture provides materials for individuals and communities to create identities and meanings. Controversial and combative issues within the realm of sports carry with them emotionally charged contexts that precede framing usage and may supersede its possible effects. Framing effects are often analyzed through understanding cognitive mechanisms, implying that frames' influences on controversial policy preferences and societal attitudes happen because framing directly impacts how we think about an issue, i.e., the cognitive processes associated with framing (Lecheler & de Vreese, 2012; Price, Tewksbury, & Powers, 1997). Some studies have found the effects of news frames on political ideology could not be solely explained by cognitive processes (Lecheler & de Vreese, 2012) and offered that additional influences of framing effects exist.

One of those possible influences is the cultural relevance of a political issue. To make some issues relevant for people, they have to be properly framed culturally (Gamson and Meyer, 1996; Benford and Snow, 2000). In their 2018 study, Seippel, Dalen, Sandvick, and Solstad sought to discover the relationship between societal factors and the process of sports issues turning into politics. They looked to answer questions such as how cultural factors make a difference in political processes concerning sports, how political opportunity structures contribute to political mobilization of sports issues and which actors are involved when contested sports issues occur? In an experiment, the researchers presented participants with six cases of debated sports issues: gender, sexuality, doping, extreme wages, boxing/violence, and failed talent development. Findings for several of these areas point to a divide between the cultures of Western nations where issues such as gender equality and sexual rights have broad public support and sports organizations implement policies to support them.

> Whereas mobilization around these issues could be relatively straight-forward in some nations, our analyses show, however, that the opportunity structure for these issues is less clear-cut in international elite sports where liberalizing or otherwise critical views face the hurdle of approaching international bodies with vaguely understood political procedures.
> *Seippel and Dalen, 2018, p. 24*

Appraisal theory of emotion (Arnold, 1960) shows that certain frames used by journalists can extract emotional responses, such as anger, fear, or sadness, with these and other emotions elicited through the cognitive assessment prompted by framing (Lazarus, 1991). Like Lazarus in his seminal update of appraisal theory (1991), other researchers suggest appraisal theory of emotion can help interpret how news frames elicit emotions (Gross, 2008; Nabi, 2003). By selecting and emphasizing certain aspects of an issue, news frames suggest certain appraisals or evaluative beliefs that may result in emotional responses (Nabi, 2003). This reasoning indicates that cognitive framing processes can elicit emotional responses: If a news frame produces certain evaluative beliefs about an issue, then emotional responses can result. The evaluations aroused by framing are regarded as assessments or beliefs that reflect the properties of an event, as well as indicate how the event is relevant to the individual (Lazarus, 1991; Smith & Kirby, 2000). Specific emotions result from individual structures of cognitive appraisals. Anger, for example, is elicited when an event is appraised as negative, certain, controllable, and caused by a specific actor (Gross, 2008; Nabi, 2003). Thus, when news framing emphasizes aspects of an issue that are related to emotionally charged cognitive structures and attitudes, this event can cause the automatic and subconscious activation of emotions by the recipient (Leventhal & Scherer, 1987; Smith & Kirby, 2000). Emotion research indicates "it is plausible to assume that framing effects are mediated by cognitive beliefs and emotions and that these processes are influenced by emotion-related moderators" (Kunne, Weber, & Sommer, 2015, p. 262). Sports journalists employ various frames that emphasize specific content in their stories, but knowing the exact amount of influence these frames – particularly in relation to audience beliefs and attitudes – have on fan evaluations of athletes featured within them is not completely clear. Lewis and Weaver (2013) explored some of the factors in the attitude formation process, including features of the media coverage, characteristics of the featured athletes, and characteristics of the processing audience. Those factors specifically were a narrative focus of the stories, religious affiliation of the featured athletes, and dimensions of sports fanship among the processing audience. The researchers found that the character-focused narratives were evaluated more positively than performance-focused narratives. Also, those individuals high in sports fanship evaluated featured athletes more positively when personal attributes were emphasized in a character-focused frame. This finding aligns with sports journalism coverage that now focuses on the cultural aspect of sport. Lewis and Weaver (2013) concluded that sports journalists could increase enjoyment of the content and sway athlete support through framing their narratives for a target audience of fans, emphasizing personal attributes of the athletes.

In the current political environment of awareness and accountability for social injustice, sports fans would have found it difficult to hide from the amount of information and media reports that showed a divided nation in America in terms of race, class, gender, and sexuality among others. Anger and sadness are the emotional fallout of those who have experienced bias and discrimination and those who want to ensure a reckoning comes to address injustices. For others, anger exists in those who see addressing these perceived wrongs as directly challenging a familiar and revered way of life. With these attitudes and emotions swirling around in society, media framing researchers can consider what role, if any, media framing plays in awakening and feeding the anger felt by sports fans who now must contend with socially and politically divisive issues closer to home. An example of an emotionally charged moment of societal discord coming into the realm of sports was when, in 2016, NFL quarterback Colin Kaepernick refused to stand and knelt during the playing of the national anthem before games, sending an intended message about social justice. Coombs, Lambert, Cassilo, and Humphries (2019) found in a framing analysis that media coverage of Kaepernick's kneeling, which intended to highlight social injustice in light of killings by police officers, has been driven more by discussions of his methods of action, kneeling. Framing effects research would seek to further understand whether framing the reports about the manner of protests and less impactfully about the catalyst for the protest influenced how fans thought of Kaepernick's action and message. Another example of an emotional clash of society with sports, which reverberates decades later, is the civil rights turmoil of the 1960s, highlighted by the clenched-fist salutes of Tommie Smith and John Carlos on the victory podium at the 1968 Olympics. The action has been significantly framed as a single, spontaneous act of two isolated athletes, when it was known to be the result of year-long efforts by Smith along with others – including his San Jose State teammate and friend Lee Evans and their sociology instructor Harry Edwards – to organize a Black community boycott of the Games (Cooper, Macaulay, & Rodriguez, 2019).

4. *Are there limits of framing effects; e.g., what levels of partisanship mediate the effects of news frames or must individuals perceive the message or journalist as credible for an effect to occur?* Media effects studies are born out of questions similar to this one. The elements associated with framing, including type of frame, message content, source, and their numerous combinations offer numerous opportunities to discover which relationships are most significant in causing effects. A researcher could consider the political partisanship of an individual fan in weighing the impact of framing effects in a situation that has brought politics to the field of play or politicized the sport in order to understand if strong beliefs might so strongly filter media frames as to deter their effects. Political knowledge moderates the effect of information on opinion formation (Zaller, 1992).

Political messages have a higher probability of providing less knowledgeable individuals with new information than individuals that are already well informed. According to Thorson and Serazio (2018), military support is closely related to fandom. In situations where framing, as has been demonstrated in the Kaepernick media coverage, tends to pit the flag and military service against an athlete, Thorson and Serazio find the military wins the minds of politically partisan Republican fans. Bechtel et al. (2015) asserts citizens may simply hold strong pre-existing beliefs that remain stable even if exposed to personally discordant political messages in the form of different types and combinations of news frames. This idea suggests that the possibility to alter public opinion through framing may be more limited when it comes to controversial policy preferences. Emerging framing analysis seems to lend support to this idea as findings identify the limits to framing effects in competitive information environments (Aaroe, 2012; Jerit and Barabas, 2012).

An Opportunity and a Path

News framing is commonplace throughout the practice of journalism. It is universal behavior that offers vast opportunities to explore long-held questions about the power of media to influence attitudes, beliefs, and behaviors. Framing analysis affords numerous opportunities to understand how instances of news coverage construct meanings. These meanings pervade the descriptions and evaluations of the issues and problems of public life as well as proposed solutions (Entman, 1993).

The opportunities to use framing analysis have grown to include many disciplines and areas of society, since the contexts introduced in Reese's Framing Public Life and certainly since the 1970s landmark studies on framing were published. Consider the large number of general categories of media news stories and related frames. A Pew (2000) study identified 13 prominent frames across news content even as anecdotal and traditional notions suggest the media builds most content around only a couple of storytelling frames, such as conflict and the "horse race." Newspapers front pages showed no dominant frame but offered variety. The frame categories were identified as "straight news account" – no dominant narrative frame other than outlining the expected elements of who, what, when where, why, and how; conflict – a focus on struggle inherent to the situation; consensus – an emphasis on agreement around an issue or event; conjecture – a focus around conjecture or speculation of what is to come; process: an explanation of the process of something or how something works; trend – current craze or what's en vogue; policy explored: a focus on exploring policy and its impact; reaction – response from elite or prominent sources to a newsworthy event; reality check: verifying and legitimizing information; and wrongdoing exposed: uncovering of misdeeds or injustice; personality profile – introducing newsmaker, historical – a comparative focus on how the current news fits into history; horse race – who is winning and who is losing. Using these frames for variables in types and categories in analysis would allow researchers to qualify framing effects in terms of influence in relation to other factors including individual beliefs and characteristics, source credibility, message content and more.

News framing is routine in sports coverage, for instance, conflict between players and owners as policies toward mitigating the health risks inherent in playing professional sports, the trends toward hiring female coaches in traditionally all-male coaching settings such as the NBA and NFL, or of the conjecture presented in the eternal debate about the best player in the game. Framing effects analysis offers a path toward greater understanding of how media coverage – such as those mentioned here and beyond – impacts fandom. In understanding what effects these frames have on fans, not only can scholars comprehend framing effects on attitudes in the sports media but sports journalists can have a better sense of the impact of their content and how it might be made more informative and enjoyable to fans.

References

Aaroe, L. (n.d.). When citizens go against elite directions: Partisan cues and contrast effects on citizens' attitudes. *Party Politics*, 18(2), 215–233. https://doi-org.proxy.library.ohio.edu/10.1177/1354068810380093

Aerts, W., & Cormier, D. (2009). Media legitimacy and corporate environmental communication. *Accounting, Organizations and Society*, 34(1), 1–27. https://doi-org.proxy.library.ohio.edu/10.1016/j.aos.2008.02.005

Arnold, M. B. (1960). *Emotion and personality: Vol. 1. Psychological aspects*. New York: Columbia University Press.

Bartholomé, G., Lecheler, S., & de Vreese, C. (2018). Towards a typology of conflict frames: Substantiveness and interventionism in political conflict news. *Journalism Studies*, 19(12), 1689–1711. https://doi-org.proxy.library.ohio.edu/10.1080/1461670X.2017.1299033

Bechtel, M. M., Hainmueller, J., Hangartner, D., & Helbling, M. (2015). Reality bites: The limits of framing effects for salient and contested policy issues. *Political Science Research and Methods*, 3(3), 683–695.

Brewer, P. R. (2003). Values, political knowledge, and public opinion about gay rights: A framing-based account. *Public Opinion Quarterly*, 67(2), 173–201.

Brüggemann, M. (2014). Between frame setting and frame sending: How journalists contribute to news frames. *Communication Theory*, 24(1), 61–82. https://doi-org.proxy.library.ohio.edu/10.1111/comt.12027

Bryant, J., & Miron, D. (2004). Theory and research in mass communication. *Journal of Communication*, 54(4), 662–704. https://doi-org.proxy.library.ohio.edu/10.1111/j.1460-2466.2004.tb02650.x

Buist, E. A., & Mason, D. S. (2010). Newspaper framing and stadium subsidization. *American Behavioral Scientist*, 53(10), 1492–1510. https://doi-org.proxy.library.ohio.edu/10.1177/0002764210368081

Cacciatore, M. A., Scheufele, D. A., & Iyengar, S. (2016). The end of framing as we know it … and the future of media effects. *Mass Communication & Society*, 19(1), 7–23. https://doi-org.proxy.library.ohio.edu/10.1080/15205436.2015.1068811

Chong, D., & Druckman, J. N. (n.d.). A theory of framing and opinion formation in competitive elite environments. *Journal of Communication*, 57(1), 99–118. https://doi-org.proxy.library.ohio.edu/10.1111/j.1460-2466.2006.00331.x

Coche, R. (2017). How athletes frame themselves on social media: An analysis of Twitter profiles. *Journal of Sports Media*, 12(1), 89–112. https://doi-org.proxy.library.kent.edu/10.1353/jsm.2017.0004

Coombs, D. S., Lambert, C. A., Cassilo, D., & Humphries, Z. (2020). Flag on the Play: Colin Kaepernick and the Protest Paradigm. *Howard Journal of Communications*, 31(4), 317–336. https://doi-org.proxy.library.ohio.edu/10.1080/10646175.2019.1567408

Cooper, J. N., Macaulay, C., & Rodriguez, S. H. (2019). Race and resistance: A typology of African American sport activism. *International Review for the Sociology of Sport*, 54(2), 151–181. https://doi-org.proxy.library.ohio.edu/10.1177/1012690217718170

D'Angelo, P., & Kuypers, J. A. (2010). *Doing news framing analysis: empirical and theoretical perspectives*. Routledge.

Druckman, J. N. (2001). The implications of framing effects for citizen competence. *Political Behavior*, 23(3), 225–256. https://doi-org.proxy.library.ohio.edu/10.1023/A:1015006907312

Druckman, J. N. (2005). The implications of framing effects for citizen competence. *Political Behavior*, 23(3), 225–256. https://doi-org.proxy.library.ohio.edu/10.1023/A:1015006907312

Endres, K. L. (n.d.). "Help-wanted female": Editor & publisher frames a civil rights issue. *Journalism and Mass Communication Quarterly*, 81(1), 7–21. https://doi-org.proxy.library.ohio.edu/10.1177/107769900408100102

Entman, R. M. (2003). Cascading activation: Contesting the White House's frame after 9/11. *Political Communication*, 20(4), 415–432. https://doi-org.proxy.library.ohio.edu/10.1080/10584600390244176

Entman, R. M. (1993). Framing: Toward clarification of a fractured paradigm. *Journal of Communication*, 43(4), 51–58. https://doi-org.proxy.library.ohio.edu/10.1111/j.1460-2466.1993.tb01304.x

Entman, R. M., Matthes, J., & Pellicano, L. (2009). Nature, sources, and effects of news framing, 175–190. In Wahl-Jorgensen, K., & Hanitzsch, T. (Eds.) *The Handbook of Journalism Studies*. Routledge.

Gamson, W. A., & Modigliani, A. (1987). The changing culture of affirmative action. In R. G. Braungart & M. M. Braungart (Eds.), *Research in Political Sociology* (vol. 3, pp. 137–177). Greenwich, CT: JAI Press.

Gamson, W. A., & Modigliani, A. (1989). Media discourse and public opinion on nuclear power: A constructionist approach. *American Journal of Sociology*, 95(1), 1–37. doi: 10.1086/229213

Goffman, E. (1974). *Frame analysis: an essay on the organization of experience.* Harper & Row.
Gross, K. (2008). Framing persuasive appeals: Episodic and thematic framing, emotional response, and policy opinion. *Political Psychology,* 29, 169–192.
Hardin, M., Dodd, J. E., Chance, J., & Walsdorf, K. (2004). Sporting images in black and white: Race in newspaper coverage of the 2000 Olympic Games. *Howard Journal of Communications,* 15(4), 211–227. Iyengar, S. (1991). *Is anyone responsible? How television frames political issues.* Chicago: University of Chicago Press.
Jacobs, S., & Wonneberger, A. (2017). Did we make it to the news? Effects of actual and perceived media coverage on media orientations of communication professionals. *Public Relations Review,* 43(3), 547–559. https://doi-org.proxy.library.ohio.edu/10.1016/j.pubrev.2017.03.010
Jerit, J., & Barabas, J. (2012). Partisan perceptual bias and the information environment. *The Journal of Politics,* 74(3), 672–684. https://doi-org.proxy.library.ohio.edu/10.1017/s0022381612000187
Johnson, R. G., & Romney, M. (2019). Life in black and white: Racial framing by sports networks on Instagram. *Journal of Sports Media,* 13(2), 1–18. https://doi-org.proxy.library.kent.edu/10.1353/jsm.2018.0006
Jones, B. A., Arcelus, J., Bouman, W. P., & Haycraft, E. (2017). Sport and transgender people: A systematic review of the literature relating to sport participation and competitive sport policies. *Sports Medicine,* 47(4), 701. https://doi-org.proxy.library.ohio.edu/10.1007/s40279-016-0621-y
Karimipour, N. (2016). Suicide on the Sidelines: Media Portrayals of NFL Players' Suicides from June 2000 to September 2012. *Journal of Sports Media,* 11(1), 49–80. https://doi-org.proxy.library.kent.edu/10.1353/jsm.2016.0006
Katz, E., & Lazarsfeld, P. (1955) *Personal influence: The part played by people in the flow of mass communications.* The Free Press.
Kellner, D. (2011). Cultural studies, multiculturalism, and media culture. *Gender, race, and class in media: A critical reader,* 3, 7–18.
Kian, E. M., Shipka, D., & Anderson, E. (n.d.). "I am happy to start the conversation": Examining sport media framing of Jason Collins' coming out and playing in the NBA. *Sexualities,* 18(5–6), 618–640. https://doi-org.proxy.library.ohio.edu/10.1177/1363460714550915
Kinder, D. R., & Sanders, L. M. (1990). Mimicking political debate with survey questions: The case of white opinion on affirmative action for blacks. *Social Cognition,* 8, 73–103. https://doi.org/10.1521/soco.1990.8.1.73
Kozman, C. (2017). Who framed the steroid issue in baseball?: A study of the frame-source relationship in traditional and new media. *Journal of Sports Media,* 12(2), 125–156.
Kühne, R., Weber, P., & Sommer, K. (2015). Beyond cognitive framing processes: Anger mediates the effects of responsibility framing on the preference for punitive measures. *Journal of Communication,* 65(2), 259–279. https://doi-org.proxy.library.ohio.edu/10.1111/jcom.12151
Kuypers, J., & Cooper, S. (2005). A comparative framing analysis of embedded and behind-the-lines reporting on the 2003 Iraq War. *Qualitative Research Reports in Communication,* 6(1), 1–10. https://doi-org.proxy.library.ohio.edu/10.1080/17459430500262083
Lasswell, H. (1927). The theory of political propaganda. *The American Political Science Review,* 21(3), 627–631. https://doi-org.proxy.library.ohio.edu/10.2307/1945515
Lazarsfeld, P. Berelson, B., & Gaudet, H. (1944). *The people's choice.* NY. Duell, Sloan, and Pearce.
Lazarus, R. S. (1991). *Emotion and adaptation.* New York: Oxford University Press.
Lecheler, S., & De Vreese, C. H. (n.d.). News framing and public opinion: A mediation analysis of framing effects on political attitudes. *Journalism and Mass Communication Quarterly,* 89(2), 185–204. https://doi-org.proxy.library.ohio.edu/10.1177/1077699011430064
Leventhal, H., & Scherer, K. (1987). The relationship of emotion to cognition: A functional approach to a semantic controversy. *Cognition and Emotion,* 1(1), 3–28. https://doi.org/10.1080/02699938708408361
Lewis, N., & Weaver, A. J. (n.d.). More than a game: Sports media framing effects on attitudes, intentions, and enjoyment. *Communication and Sport,* 3(2), 219–242. https://doi-org.proxy.library.ohio.edu/10.1177/2167479513508273
McGregor, J. (2002, July). Restating news values: Contemporary criteria for selecting the news. In Refereed articles from the Proceedings of the ANZCA 2002 Conference, Coolangatta. Communication: Reconstructed for the 21st Century.
Native American Journalism Association. (NAJA) (2003). *Native American Journalism Association Reading Red Report: A Call for News Media to Recognize Racism in Sports Team Nicknames and Mascots.* Native American Journalism Association. https://najanewsroom.com/wp-content/uploads/2018/11/2003-Reading-Red-Report.pdf

Nabi, R. L. (2003). Exploring the framing effects of emotion: Do discrete emotions differentially influence information accessibility, information seeking, and policy preference? *Communication Research*, 30(2), 224–247. https://doi-org.proxy.library.ohio.edu/10.1177/0093650202250881

Nisbet, M. C. (2010). Knowledge into action: Framing the debates over climate change and poverty. In D'Angelo, P. & Kuypers, J. (Eds). *Doing news framing analysis* (pp. 59–99). Routledge.

Price, V., Tewksbury, D., & Powers, E. (1997). Switching trains of thought: The impact of news frames on readers' cognitive responses. *Communication Research*, 24(5), 481–506. https://doi-org.proxy.library.ohio.edu/10.1177/009365097024005002

Reese, S. D. (2001). Prologue—Framing public life: A bridging model for media research. In S. D. Reese, J. Oscar H. Gandy & A. E. Grant (Eds.), *Framing public life: Perspectives on media and our understanding of the social world* (pp. 7–31). Mahwah, NJ: Lawrence Erlbaum.

Sanderson, J., & Cassilo, D. (2019). "I'm glad I played when the country still had gonads": Pop Warner's kickoff policy change and the framing of health and safety initiatives in football. *Journal of Sports Media*, 14(1), 1–22. https://doi-org.proxy.library.kent.edu/10.1353/jsm.2019.0002

Scheufele, D. A. (1999). Framing as a theory of media effects. *Journal of communication*, 49(1), 103–122. doi:10.1111/j.1460-2466.1999.tb02784.x

Scheufele, D. A., & Tewksbury, D. (2007). Framing, agenda setting, and priming: The evolution of three media effects models. *Journal of Communication*, 57(1), 9–20. https://doi-org.proxy.library.ohio.edu/10.1111/j.0021-9916.2007.00326.x

Seippel, O., Dalen, H. B., Sandvik, M. R., & Solstad, G. M. (2018). From political sports to sports politics: On political mobilization of sports issues. *International Journal of Sport Policy and Politics*, 10(4), 669–686. https://doi.org/10.1080/19406940.2018.1501404

Seltzer, T., & Mitrook, M. (2009). The role of expert opinion in framing media coverage of the Heisman trophy race. *Journal of Sports Media*, 4(2), 1–29. https://doi-org.proxy.library.kent.edu/10.1353/jsm.0.0040

Smith, C. A., & Kirby, L. D. (2000). Consequences require antecedents: Toward a process model of emotion elicitation. In J. P. Forgas (Ed.), *Feeling and thinking: The role of affect in social cognition* (pp. 83–106). Cambridge University Press.

Sniderman, P. M., & Theriault, S. M. (2004). The structure of political argument and the logic of issue framing. In W. E. Saris and P. M. Sniderman (eds), *Studies in public opinion* (pp. 133–165). Princeton, NJ: Princeton University Press.

Tajfel, H., & Turner, J. C. (1986). The social identity theory of intergroup behaviour. In S. Worchel, & W. G. Austin (Eds.), *Psychology of intergroup relations* (pp. 7–24). Chicago: Nelson-Hall.

Thorson, E. A., & Serazio, M. (2018). Sports fandom and political attitudes. *Public Opinion Quarterly*, 82(2), 391–403. https://doi-org.proxy.library.ohio.edu/10.1093/poq/nfy018

Tory Higgins, E., Rholes, W. S., & Jones, C. R. (n.d.). Category accessibility and impression formation. *Journal of Experimental Social Psychology*, 13(2), 141–154. https://doi-org.proxy.library.ohio.edu/10.1016/S0022-1031(77)80007-3

Tuchman, G. (1978). *Making news: A study in the construction of reality*. Free Press.

Van, C. (2020). Pay to play in the NCAA: A data driven playbook on how to compensate athletes. *Sport Journal*, N.PAG. Wood, T. (n.d.). The many voices of business: Framing the Keystone pipeline in US and Canadian news. *Journalism*, 20(2), 292–312. https://doi-org.proxy.library.ohio.edu/10.1177/1464884917717536

Zaller, J. (1992). *The nature and origins of mass opinion*. Cambridge University Press.

10
Rebounding as Praxis
Interrogating Positionality and Proximity in Sporting Fieldwork

Courtney M. Cox

January 2018 | Kazan, Russia

Outside, it is below freezing in Kazan, Russia, but in the gym where Team Kazanochka is finishing up a morning practice, it feels cozy and warm. Under the shoe squeaks and rhythmic bouncing of basketballs, there lies a dull hum of the fluorescent lights that line the ceiling grid. They call this arena the Basket-hall, a clever play on words that tickles me every time I hear it. Cierra, one of the American players, is working one-on-one with the assistant coach, and as others begin heading to the locker room, she calls out to me, "Hey Court! Will you come rebound for me?"

While I don't particularly pride myself on any concrete forms of athleticism, rebounding is easy enough. As she practices shooting the ball in various spots on the court, my job is to grab the ball – whether she makes or misses it – and pass it back to her coach, who resumes the drill. It is a simple act, but one that continues to resonate with me from her initial ask on my first day at practice. Rebounding requires your attention to where the ball is going, and your job, while repetitive, allows the shooter to find a fluidity, a rhythm, based on not chasing down her own ball. My job, seemingly monotonous, is important to the overall point of the exercise. In rebounding for Cierra, I found a parallel to the researcher–participant relationship. I am to be reflexive, responsive, and in the moment, centering her in this action. While I remain on the court and involved, I inevitably change the space I occupy. But it isn't about me. In rebounding for her, I don't try to shoot the ball or dribble a bit to show off my handles.

Acknowledging power in the contextual intersecting relationships between researcher and participants remains a key part of an ethical, accountable praxis. Researchers change space with every interview, focus group or field observation. We enter into the field with various identities, perspectives, and previous experiences that shape how we acquire and analyze data. Rebounding as praxis acknowledges the positionality of the researcher as well as a closeness required to comprehend and contextualize the experiences of those who ground our work. It centers the participant(s) and site of study while remaining attuned to the power dynamics constantly at play both broadly and within the confines of a particular site. It allows for scholarship not limited to the proverbial periphery, but fully engaged on the court, in the stands, or at the bar.

In this chapter, I offer a brief survey of sporting fandom literature, focusing on methodological approaches to the research. I then utilize examples from five years of fieldwork conducted to consider how rebounding might inform sports fandom research, especially those engaging with qualitative methodological approaches. I define rebounding as a research praxis that is at once relational, reflexive, and collaborative.

Approaches to Studying Sport Fandom

Since the initial implementation of the Sport Spectator Identification Scale (Wann and Branscombe, 1993), and later models like the Team Identification Scale (Dimmock & Grove, 2006), scholars continue to find new ways to interrogate how fandom operates within larger social frameworks. While several early studies of sport fans emerged from psychology through surveys with college students, this area of study expanded rapidly over the past three decades, both in methodological approach and area of study. Sport fandom scholarship can now be found in fields as varied as sociology, gender studies, communication, ethnic studies, anthropology, history, kinesiology, and marketing. In order to consider how rebounding as a research praxis might fit into the larger study of sporting fandom, I offer an abbreviated summary of three key themes in sport fandom research, along with the methodological approaches employed by scholars engaged in this work. The majority of recent sporting fandom scholarship falls into one of three categories: identity and sports fandom, fandom as performance, and digital sports fandom.

Identity and Sports Fandom

A significant amount of sport fandom literature published in the last ten years focuses on the relationship between one's fan affiliation and identity, defined broadly. This research focuses on sports fandom as it aligns with political identity (Thorson & Serazio, 2018; Serazio & Thorson, 2020), its relationship to mental health (Wann, Hackathorn, & Sherman, 2017), gendered differences in fandom (Cushen, Rife, & Wann, 2019; James & Ridinger, 2002; Mewett & Toffolotti, 2012; Esmonde, Cooky, & Andrew, 2018), group ideals (Serazio, 2012), and parenthood (Tinson, Sinclair, & Kolyperas, 2017). It is important to note that in each of these areas, the category of fandom is not stable. This can be seen, for example in Sveinson, Hoeber, and Toffoletti's (2019) work on gender and sports fandom, where women who wore pink versions of team merchandise were read as inauthentic fans by others. This policing of fandom shows the range in definitions even within sport fandom groups.

In the same way, an ethnographic examination of a fan ecosystem within a Pittsburgh Steelers bar in Fort Worth, Texas illustrates how the process of becoming an "insider" in the space is predicated upon intimate knowledge of not only the team, but local knowledge of Pittsburgh streets, restaurants, and class dynamics (Kraszewski, 2008). In this way, fandom is not only an identity marker, but constantly performed.

Fandom as Performance

The performance of fandom is both hierarchical and hegemonic, formed by symbolic boundaries and, as Michael Ian Borer writes, continuously reasserted and reinscribed with self-fashioning through merchandise, interaction with other fans, and team/sport knowledge (2009). Abby Waysdorf writes of sporting fandom through Erving Goffman's concept of performance in everyday life (1959), describing her football fandom as "a performance in dressing, acting, and communicating fandom and fan identity. In how I talked about leagues, teams, and players, I performed myself as knowledgeable and authentic, a real fan of the sport" (2015, 2.1) However, she also notes that there is a separation between her online and offline fandom, where she can indulge in "inauthentic" fandom via football fan fiction, where pseudonyms allow for a different kind of fan performance (3.3).

Perhaps one of the most important recent contributions at the intersection of sport fandom and performance is Osborne and Coombs' (2013) fieldwork observing fan behavior at sports bars, tailgates, parties, and games, where they detail nuances of fandom performance not obtainable through survey data. For example, they detail how a woman who regularly attended Steelers watch parties at a local Buffalo Wild Wings was read outside of the fan frame by others due to her attire (being dressed in purple as Pittsburgh took on their division rival Baltimore Ravens). She would appear the next week in a Steelers t-shirt in order to be legible to the group as "one of them," even as she described her own fandom as "personal" and "low key." Here, the authors argue that the binary of public and private fandom does not adequately address the gender dynamics at play within sport fandom. They find that social identity theory, an approach frequently cited in sport fandom literature, cannot capture the full spectrum of fandom. The authors then advocate for the inclusion of identity theory and performative gender theory, two frameworks they conceive together as performative sport fandom. This theory states that individuals become sports fans through performances of fandom that are 1) socially constructed, 2) based on context and audience, and 3) constantly intersecting with other identities such as race, gender, class, or nationality. Their work has impacted other scholars' approach to studying sport fandom performance in football (Humphries & Kucek, 2020), esports (Tang, Kucek, & Toepfer, 2020), family fandom (Grappendorf, Simmons, & Hancock, 2020), and gendered sport consumption (Jakubowska, Antonowicz, & Kossakowsi, 2020), among others. As noted in the Waysdorf example above, the study of fandom extends to online spaces more than ever before.

Digital Sports Fandom

Fandom is experienced in new ways through the digital, whether accessing live games and other content through streaming sites (Rowe, 2014), sports organizations' websites (Meân, 2012), or social media platforms (Toffoletti, Pegoraro, & Comeau, 2019). Digital sports fandom research occupies multiple methodologies – surveys, critical discourse analysis, online ethnography – and often overlaps with previously mentioned themes of identity and performance.

This is of particular importance when considering how online spaces continue to transform fans' relationships to athletes, teams, and leagues. As Sturm (2020) writes, digital approaches to studying fandom often operate within a utopian/dystopian binary. He instead considers how fandom within digital spaces can be described through the fan-as-pseudo-participant (via augmented legacy media practices), fan-as-interactive-participant (generating prosumer content through second-screen engagement), and fan-as-immersed-participant (where digital fandom becomes wholly immersed in the spectacle of mediasport). With the constant influx of new communicative technologies, research in this area must constantly adapt and expand previous research protocols to ensure accurate, ethical work emerges from the data. In studying the sports-media complex through women's basketball over the past five years, I find that the conceptual framework of rebounding serves as a useful methodological praxis, whether engaged in research focused on athletes, spectators, and/or organizations.

Rebounding as Praxis

The fieldwork referenced throughout this chapter is based upon a larger project focused on how Black women and non-binary athletes maneuver through the white heteropatriarchal space of basketball. While my primary participants were athletes, I also spent a considerable amount of time interviewing and observing fans, journalists, team and league employees, and athletes' friends and family members. This project began in California, with a season-long ethnographic study of the Los Angeles Sparks, a Women's National Basketball Association (WNBA) team, and eventually traversed several other sites, including the Russian gym referenced in the opening anecdote, in order to capture the year-round labor of the league's athletes. Early on, I struggled to find a consistent approach to navigating each site or approaching potential participants; my field notes and memos reflected this constant tension. Often, I wrote of how I was unsure when and how often to reveal myself as researcher. I chided myself for engaging too much with "the field," while at other times writing that I did not feel I had conducted "enough" research for a day while observing a practice or game. I constantly carried questions regarding proximity and positionality— in my notes, with fellow researchers, and in my analysis. That day in the gym, engaged on the court in the physical act of rebounding, I found what might be considered a research version of muscle memory that allowed for a relational, reflexive, and collaborative approach to sporting research.

Rebounding as Relational

Early in this project, I realized that fan communities offered rich potential to understand larger questions of identity, representation, and the perceived "value" of women's sports. While working with the Sparks, I assisted the vice president of sales with a new campaign titled #WeAreWomen, an initiative designed to sell out the STAPLES Center, the Sparks home arena for a single game. This season-long initiative required me to engage with fans within the arena during home games and at various outreach events as a Sparks representative. I quickly learned that it would be impossible to understand the "ecosystem" of sporting cultures by limiting my study to athletes and their relation to their team and the league in general. Instead, I would need to approach this research through the various connections, or relations, or each vested group (athlete, team, fan, sponsor, etc.).

In considering how these various groups collide, I employed what Matthew Desmond defines as *relational ethnography*, which moves beyond the study of a group or location, and instead focuses on processes which establish relations between individuals and institutions (2014). Whereas more conventional approaches to ethnography rely upon the static, the permanently situated, Desmond offers the relational in the hopes of broadening and expanding the possibilities of fieldwork. This method requires at least two types of individuals or agencies located in varying positions within a particular social space, bound together through their circumstances (Desmond, 2014, p. 554). It does not focus on comparing these various factions, but rather seeks out the paths and threads which connect them. A relational approach is not invested in the characteristics of organizations or people; it is comprised of the intersections of multiple channels and networks (p. 555).

While working with the Sparks, I often worked the sales table in the atrium of the arena during home games. Here, I constantly interacted with the public, ranging from longtime season-ticket holders (including one woman with a calf-sized tattoo of the team logo) to casual spectators. This post allowed me to both overhear and directly respond to how those attending games identified themselves in relation to the team. Some patrons approached me to complain about concessions or the volume of the arena, while others scavenged for gossip about certain players or offered their own playoff predictions.

Once the doors of the arena opened to the general public, I frequently found myself assisting with large groups with other sales employees. These groups frequently purchased tickets based upon a themed game night and received various pre- and post-game VIP experiences. For example, Native American Heritage Night was scheduled for a game against the Atlanta Dream, a team featuring one of the most visible Indigenous basketball players, Shoni Schimmel. As I brought dozens of Native fans down to the court during shootaround, I observed how fans' relationship to sport and their own cultural identity operated in tandem with the Sparks' sales approach. Several of the fans I spoke to during the Schimmel shootaround had traveled from hundreds of miles away to see her play in person and partake in a themed night that catered to Native culture. This occurred during other games as well, whether the theme was Gospel Night, First Responders Night, or the annual Pride game. The Sparks sales team was less focused on cultivated community around fandom and instead focused on selling large group packages based upon various identity markers. Selling difference became a prominent focus of the sales department that season, a strategy that culminated with the #WeAreWomen game near the end of the season. In utilizing marketplace feminism and neoliberal empowerment logics to sell tickets, consumers "bought in" through the price of admission. However, less than half of the arena was full during a sellout game, revealing the limits of this approach to increasing a fanbase.

After spending a season with the Sparks working in their front office, I shifted the focus of my research to other sites but continued to attend a significant number of their home games for the next few seasons. I frequently encouraged colleagues and friends who had never attended a WNBA game to join me, and recall one particularly poignant moment with a friend, who I'll call Desiree, who saw the invitation (and her subsequent attendance) as a rite of passage as a queer woman. Even before walking into the arena, she read the WNBA as a space of heightened queer visibility, both on and off of the court (and specifically within the fan base), a notion echoing previous literature regarding WNBA games as a space where lesbian and bisexual women find community even as the league itself has struggled to fully embrace its LGBTQ+ athletes and fans (Dolance, 2005; McDonald, 2002; McDonald, 2008; Muller, 2007a; Muller, 2007b). Whether in our seats or walking around the concourse of the arena, she pointed out how different the space felt in comparison to the men's professional sporting events she attended in the past. In many ways, bringing first-time spectators to Sparks games allowed me to "see" the arena with new eyes as well.

My experience with Desiree at her first WNBA game occurred at a moment where the league as a whole began to acknowledge and hesitantly embrace its LGBTQ+ fanbase through leaguewide Pride nights and rainbow-themed merchandise. On one Pride game I attended as a spectator, I waited after the game with a group of friends who were all former classmates of a Sparks player. As she emerged from the locker room, she told us that before we could head to our post-game destination, she needed to "stop by" the Pride afterparty hosted on the roof of STAPLES Center. It was the first event I could think of (in any sport) involving fans and professional athletes mingling together in a social setting following a game. I could sense a bit of anxiety on behalf of the player, a feeling I quickly understood as soon as we walked into the space. As we entered, no barriers existed between fan and athlete, an opportunity many took as an opportunity to approach players, introducing themselves, attempting to engage with their own team and league knowledge, and at times, physical touch. Members of the security team eventually intervened and helped guide the team to a "VIP section," a roped-off area in a corner of the rooftop venue that put the entire roster on full display. After 20 minutes or so of uncomfortable small talk with brave fans who mustered the courage to approach the edge of the VIP area, the majority of the roster swiftly exited the space (including the athlete we accompanied in our group). The obligation of fan/athlete interaction, built into contracts and enforced through themed nights like this one, offered new glimpses into the relational nature of fandom research.

Engaging with multiple groups of participants (often with conflicting interests) requires a certain agility that guides data collection and is attuned to how interview questions might be adjusted (based on the participant's role) or the way field notes are taken (using one's phone may be appropriate in some settings and completely alarming in others). Considering how each group researched might respond is key, just as the researcher's own positionality affects their "court vision."

Rebounding is Reflexive

Regardless of the methodologies we employ, as scholars we must be constantly cognizant of how our own experiences and positionalities affect our work. Given my previous work with the WNBA's Los Angeles Sparks, as well as previous employment with sports media companies, my positionality within this field provides opportunities for access, as well as a range of various biases I must remain aware of during this work.

My own identity as a college-educated Black woman of a certain age studying a league comprised primarily of subjects fitting this exact demographic affected both my approach and access in a dynamic way, which also required my attention. While I may in some ways resemble my participants, I am an outsider in a variety of ways (my position as a researcher and my lack of athletic prowess being two of the most obvious), which will undoubtedly shape this work.

This is perhaps most vivid in my field notes from Russia, where after practice one day I found myself following the players as they trudged towards the locker room, a place dubbed "The Dungeon" (appropriately named for the dark stairs along the route from the gym and an unmistakable dampness in the air). As a researcher attempting to find my place in such an intimate space, I suddenly realize I possess no protocol for how to conduct myself within the locker room. Beyond the typical power dynamics of researcher/participant, I quickly consider how this is now amplified given I am fully dressed as the team undresses, showers, and changes. Once inside, I realize there is a way for me to sit behind a sort of partition comprised of tall lockers which would obscure my view of the team. I would essentially sit next to Alex, the masseuse, as he waits to address any lingering requests post-practice.

I feel this is an appropriate negotiation of involvement without any potential discomfort for anyone involved. I then hear one of Cierra's teammates ask, "Where is your friend? Why isn't she here?" Cierra replies, "She was just going to wait over there with Alex until we're all changed." I hear a murmuring of Russian amongst her teammates and then an indecipherable whisper of English, which leads Cierra beyond the locker wall to me, where she says, "They want you to hang out in here with us." I walk over and several players gesture towards a chair located in the center of the room. As soon I sit, conversation resumes and the locker room emerges as a therapeutic space to decompress after a tough practice or game, make social plans, or complain about coaches. It is a central space of connection for these players; they leave gifts for one another, critique one another's game, and ultimately, bond over basketball. This chair, in many ways, embodies much of my anxiety in conducting this research, navigating how and where my presence changes the environment or imposes upon others unnecessarily. It also represents an opening for considering how to gauge trust and maneuver access and consent, especially amongst research participants whose first language is not my own. I was encouraged by the locker room invitation, an early sign of good standing.

In acknowledging my insider-outsider status and the power I inherently hold as an interviewer, rebounding requires I remain vigilant in my self-reflexivity and in the responsibility I hold as researcher to my participants. I found throughout my time in the field that as a woman studying women and non-binary athletes, I was afforded access because of my gender and/or race. Interviewees offered to let me stay in their apartments overseas to gain further insight, allowed me into the locker room, and shared their struggles to be heard by their male colleagues in ways that highlighted a certain sameness and relatability they felt I would share. I found myself also sharing similar moments of exclusion or reluctant acceptance within either sport or academia, feeling a need to both divulge my own struggles as well as encourage those who shared particularly difficult moments with me where they felt isolated. For this reason, it is also important to acknowledge how research is a collaborative practice, where participants can offer key contributions outside of merely answering questions or completing surveys.

Rebounding is Collaborative

Throughout this research, I employed narrative inquiry as a methodological approach to rebounding, defined by Clandinin and Connelly as "a way of understanding experience. It is a collaboration between researcher and participants, over time, in a place or series of places, and in social interaction with milieus… Simply stated, narrative inquiry is stories lived and told" (2000, p. 20). As a negotiated practice, this approach is rooted in how people live and constitute their experiences. These narratives allow both researcher and participant to make meaning and sense of their existence, drawing upon not only the content of material shared, but the performance of the storytelling itself (Caine, Estefan, & Clandinin, 2013). Data sources for narrative inquiry research include field notes, interviews, autobiographical writing, letter writing, and participant journaling (Savin-Baden & Van Niekerk, 2007, p. 463).

One of the biggest challenges for me (outside of travel logistics) in multi-sited research was identifying potential participants and venues for this work. My field sites were not predetermined; rather, I followed athletes, journalists, and employees who were invested in carving out space for girls and women in the sport wherever they led. My first participant, Cierra, was a rookie for the Sparks in 2015, and later found her way to Kazan, Russia and Las Vegas, Nevada. There were no simple trajectories, no easy flight paths to follow along the way. Instead, I relied upon my participants to not only illustrate their worlds across borders, but to point me in the direction of who I should interview next. In other ethnographic fandom fieldwork, researchers traverse sports bars, private viewings, and team venues as they studied various fan networks.

Elizabeth McIssac Bruce writes that narrative inquiry "offers a potentially liberating approach to research because it acknowledges the importance of grounding education in human subjectivity, emphasizing the importance of claiming one's voice, while also respecting and empowering the human person" (2008, pp. 324–325). Throughout this process, I not only share with my participants my own experiences with basketball and the various leagues around the world I've interacted with but also encourage them to "talk back" to one another, as well as the media coverage surrounding them. Narrative inquiry is particularly useful for several reasons. First, the ease of storytelling for participants, given that we are homo narrans – narrative beings who create our world as a set of stories. Second, the rich data accumulated through this methodology is partially informed by the details provided (or withheld through verbal or non-verbal reactions), allowing for a particular type of truth-telling that does not allow participants to "hide their hand"; the method of telling the story is its own source material (Savin-Baden & Van Niekerk, 2007, p. 467). In using this approach to analyzing interviews, Instagram stories, or autobiographies, the narrative of my work is built in tandem with the self-presentation of the athletes and fans themselves. Other forms of rebounding collaboratively might include member checking, where participants are given copies of their interview transcripts and can clarify, remove, or add as needed. Collaboration can also operate through the presentation or distribution of research findings to participants for feedback before research is made public elsewhere.

Conclusion

In highlighting anecdotes from a broader project located at the intersection of identity, labor, and performance, I offer rebounding as a research praxis that requires constant reflection and adaptation. As I reflect on this process alongside previous sport fandom scholarship, I am reminded of the richness of fan perspectives within the broader sports-media complex. While rebounding is perhaps most useful for scholars conducting qualitative research, I believe it serves as a rich metaphor for a variety of methodological approaches. It reminds us that as we conduct this work, we constantly engage with power dynamics and our own biases every time we take to "the court," whether that is in the presence of fans at a bar, online message boards, or sporting venues. Whether designing, conducting, or analyzing our research, may we find an ethical fluidity, a reflexive rhythm not unlike that day in a chilly, Russian gym.

References

Borer, M. I. (2009). Negotiating the symbols of gendered sports fandom. *Social Psychology Quarterly*, 72(1), 1–4.
Bruce, E. M. (2008). Narrative inquiry: A spiritual and liberating approach to research. *Religious Education*, 103(3), 323–338.
Caine, V., Estefan, A., & Clandinin, D. J. (2013). A return to methodological commitment: Reflections on narrative inquiry. *Scandinavian Journal of Educational Research*, 57(6), 574–586.
Clandinin, J., & Connelly, M. (2000). *Narrative Inquiry: Experience and Story in Qualitative Research*. Jossey Bass Publishers.
Cushen, P. J., Rife, S. C., & Wann, D. L. (2019). The emergence of a new type of sport fan: Comparing the fandom, motivational profiles, and identification of electronic and traditional sport fans. *Journal of Sport Behavior*, 42(2), 127–141.
Desmond, M. (2014). Relational ethnography. *Theory and Society*, 43, 547–579.
Dimmock, J. A., & Grove, R. J. (2006). Identification with sport teams as a function of the search for certainty. *Journal of Sports Sciences*, 24(11), 1203–1211.
Dolance, S. (2005). "A whole stadium full": Lesbian community at women's national basketball association games. *The Journal of Sex Research*, 42(1), 74–83.
Esmonde, K., Cooky, C., & Andrews, D. L. (2018). "That's not the only reason I'm watching the game": Women's (hetero)sexual desire and sports fandom. *Journal of Sport and Social Issues*, 42(6), 498–518.
Goffman, E. (1959). *The Presentation of Self in Everyday Life*. University of Edinburgh Press.
Grappendorf, H., Simmons, J., & Hancock, M. (2020). "I will go to the game, while you stay home with the kids": Gender role expectations and sport fan-family conflict. *Journal of Global Sport Management*, 5(1), 1–18.
Humphries, Z., & Kucek, J. A. (2020). Examining soccer fan performances through performative sport fandom theory: How fans of the Spurs perform their fandom. *Qualitative Research Reports in Communication*, 21(1), 21–28.
Jakubowska, H., Antonowicz, D., & Kossakowski, R. (2020). *Female Fans, Gender Relations, and Football Fandom: Challenging the Brotherhood Culture*. Routledge.
James, J. D., & Ridinger, L. L. (2002). Female and male sports fans: A comparison of sport consumption motives. *Journal of Sport Behavior*, 25(3), 260–278.
Kraszewski, J. (2008). Pittsburgh in Fort Worth: Football bars, sports television, sports fandom, and the management of home. *Journal of Sport & Social Issues*, 32(2), 139–157.
McDonald, M. G. (2002). Queering whiteness: The peculiar case of the Women's National Basketball Association. *Sociological Perspectives*, 45(4), 379–396.

McDonald, M. G. (2008). Rethinking resistance: The queer play of the women's national basketball association, visibility politics and late capitalism. *Leisure Studies*, 27(1), 77–93.

Meân, L. J. (2012). Empowerment through sport? Female fans, women's sport, and the construction of gendered fandom. In K. Toffoletti & P. Mewett (Eds.), *Sport and its Female Fans*. Taylor & Francis Group.

Mewett, P., & Toffoletti, K. (2012). Introduction. In K. Toffoletti & P. Mewett (Eds.), *Sport and its Female Fans*. Taylor & Francis Group.

Muller, T. (2007a). "Lesbian Community" in Women's National Basketball Association (WNBA) Spaces. *Social & Cultural Geography*, 8(1), 9–28.

Muller, T. K. (2007b). Liberty for all? Contested spaces of women's basketball. *Gender, Place & Culture*, 14(2), 197–213.

Osborne, A. C., & Coombs, D. S. (2013). Performative sport fandom: An approach to retheorizing sport fans. *Sport in Society*, 16(5), 672–681.

Rowe, D. (2014). New screen action and its memories: The "live" performance of mediated sport fandom. *Television & New Media*, 15(8), 752–759.

Savin-Baden, M., & Van Niekerk, L. (2007). Narrative inquiry: Theory and practice. *Journal of Geography in Higher Education*, 31(3), 459–472.

Serazio, M. (2012). The elementary forms of sports fandom: A Durkheimian exploration of team myths, kinship, and totemic rituals. *Communication & Sport*, 1(4), 303–325.

Serazio, M., & Thorson, E. (2020). Weaponized patriotism and racial subtext in Kaepernick's aftermath: The anti-politics of American sports fandom. *Television & New Media*, 21(2), 151–168.

Sturm, D. (2020). Fans as e-participants? Utopia/dystopia visions for the future of digital sport fandom. *Convergence: The International Journal of Research into New Media Technologies*, 26(4), 841–856.

Sveinson, K., Hoeber, L., & Toffoletti, K. (2019). "If people are wearing pink stuff they're probably not real fans": Exploring women's perceptions of sport fan clothing. *Sport Management Review*, 22(5), 736–747.

Tang, T., Kucek, J., & Toepfer, S. (2020). Active Within Structures: Predictors of Esports Gameplay and Spectatorship. *Communication & Sport*, 20(10), 1–21.

Thorson, E. A., & Serazio, M. (2018). Sports fandom and political attitudes. *Public Opinion Quarterly*, 82(2), 391–403.

Tinson, J., Sinclair, G., & Kolyperas, D. (2017). Sport fandom and parenthood. *European Sport Management Quarterly*, 17(3), 370–391.

Toffoletti, K., Pegoraro, A., & Comeau, G. S. (2019). Self-representations of women's sport fandom on Instagram at the 2015 FIFA Women's World Cup. Communication & Sport, 20(10), 1–23.

Wann, D. L., & Branscombe, N. R. (1993). Sports fans: Measuring degree of identification with their team. *International Journal of Sport Psychology*, 24(1), 1–17.

Wann, D. L., Hackathorn, J., & Sherman, M. R. (2017). Testing the team identification-social psychological health model: Mediating relationships among team identification, sport fandom, sense of belonging, and meaning in life. *Group Dynamics: Theory, Research, and Practice*, 21(2), 94–107.

Waysdorf, A. (2015). My football fandoms, performance, and place. *Transformative Works and Cultures*, 18.

11
Should We Admire Athletes?

Ben Bradley

Our practices of sports fandom raise some interesting and troubling ethical questions. Here I focus on a question about *admiration*: should we admire athletes? Do they deserve praise and admiration for being good at sports? I will put forward a view about admirability that entails that sporting achievements can be admirable, but also calls into question common practices of admiring star athletes.

Control

To say that someone is admirable is to say they *deserve* admiration, or they are *worthy* of it. There is no question that people do in fact admire athletes; the question is whether that admiration is appropriate. This raises a general question: what can make someone worthy of admiration?

Let's begin with a plausible principle concerning the relevance of *control* to what we deserve. According to this principle, nobody can deserve praise or blame for an outcome if they had no control over it. So, for example, if someone knocks me out and drops my unconscious body onto my neighbor's flowers, my neighbor cannot rightfully blame *me* for the squashed flowers. Although it was my body that squashed them, I had no control over what happened. Perhaps they can blame the person who knocked me out, if that person had control over what they were doing. The same goes for admiration: nobody can deserve admiration for something over which they had no control (Persson, 2005, p. 73).

According to an extreme view, nobody has the slightest bit of control over anything. Everything that happens is determined by previous events, and there is nothing anybody could do to make things go otherwise; we are just like cogs in a great machine. If this is true, then it seems nobody can deserve praise or blame for anything, including athletic achievements. Ultimately, nobody is responsible for their athletic abilities, or any other abilities they have. An individual's abilities are the result of genetics and upbringing, neither of which the individual is responsible for. So you can't be praiseworthy; nor can you be blameworthy. It is luck that you have the genetic makeup and the parents that you have, and you can't be praiseworthy or blameworthy for the circumstances that you lucked into.

In response, you might think: but athletes train hard to become good at their sports! Surely they are responsible for that at least! But why do they train hard? Because their genetics or their upbringing made them the kind of person that will train hard, and they had no control over their genetics or upbringing, so they cannot be responsible for what results from it either, like having a good work ethic.[1]

If this view were true, it wouldn't mean that you can't appreciate or enjoy sporting achievements. You can enjoy them in something like the way you enjoy a sunset, as a beautiful thing that happens sometimes. You just can't rightfully *admire* anyone for such achievements.

Few of us can accept this extreme view. It commits us to thinking that we can't admire a moral saint for her generosity, and that we can't condemn a heinous killer for his brutality. How exactly to account for the possibility of genuine praiseworthiness is difficult, and leads us into questions about freedom of the will. We can't solve such problems here. I am not suggesting that the argument should be dismissed, but for the purposes of this chapter, let's suppose, in accord with common sense, that it is at least possible for us to have some control over some outcomes, so we are sometimes worthy of praise or admiration. (If you disagree with this supposition, then you can consider the rest of the chapter as having a conditional conclusion: if anyone can be admirable, athletes can be.) We can now ask whether sporting ability or achievement is the sort of thing that could make someone praiseworthy or admirable.

According to one more moderate view, we should admire athletes, not for who they are (which is something for which they are not responsible), but rather for what they achieve. We have control over what we do, not what we are. But this view is hard to maintain. There is no sharp line between what we are and what we do. Sometimes, what we achieve just is being a certain way. An athlete may train hard in order to make their body have certain features. Those features are both the thing they achieve and also part of what they are. If we have control over anything, we have control over both what we do and what we are.

Supposing that we do have some control over things, we shouldn't think that control is all or nothing. Control comes in degrees. There are things we have no control over, such as the genetic makeup we were born with. There are things we seem to have a great deal of control over, like whether to throw a fastball or a curveball. Then there are lots of cases that fall somewhere in between; they are a combination of control and luck. If you get no credit for something over which you had no control, then it would make sense to say that you get *more* credit for something the more control you have over it. For example, a good professional baseball player gets a hit not much more than 30 percent of the time. When he does get a hit, it is often in part due to swinging the bat hard in a certain area, which is something he has control over. But it is usually at least in part due to things he has little control over, such as where the ball goes after he hits it. And it is usually due in part to things he has no control at all over: where the fielders are and how they react, mistakes by umpires, interference by fans, gusts of wind, and so on. The amount of praise the hitter deserves seems to vary depending on how much those lucky factors determine the outcome, which would explain why, for example, Derek Jeter gets (or should get) comparatively less praise for his famous fan- and umpire-aided home run in the 1996 playoffs against the Orioles than for some of his other achievements.

This would explain why people are more inclined to praise athletes than winners of games of chance. If I win at roulette, I won't be praised very much, only envied, because I have no control over where the ball lands. I have control over the placing of the bet, but I can do nothing to make it the case that the bet wins. On the other hand, when Roger Federer wins a tennis match, it is the result of years of training and preparation. Federer doesn't have complete control over whether he wins, but he has much more control than the roulette winner. Many cases lie between these. Some sports, like basketball, are simply easier if one is taller. Nobody has control over how tall they are. So while a winning basketball player has control over the bodily movements required to win the game, they don't have control over a factor that plays a large role in determining whether they win. In many sports, excellence is highly dependent on parental resources; the best athletes in sports like tennis or golf often have been trained intensively from an early age, something that is not possible for many people to afford. These factors would all seem to affect the extent to which we should praise someone for their excellence in a sport. To the extent that one's success in sports is the result of things outside one's control, one deserves less praise for one's sporting achievement.

Achievement, Value, and Admirability

A lot of work has been done to understand the nature and value of achievement. In this section I will explain some common and plausible views about achievement. I don't accept these views, but many philosophers do. I'll show that even if we accept these ideas, they do not carry over perfectly to the case of admirability. The best view about the admirability of achievement will be different from the best view about the value of achievement, but will have some features in common.

According to the views of "achievementists," we can broadly divide the components of an achievement into two parts. First there are facts about what the person was doing: how much effort was the person expending? How difficult was it to do what she was doing? How complex was the activity?[2] Second, there are facts about the goal that the person was aiming at: what was achieved? Was it something good or bad? (Hurka, 2006, p. 233)

When a person achieves something, the value of the achievement is determined by these two kinds of facts. The better the goal is, the more valuable the achievement; the more effort it took to achieve the goal, the better the achievement is. If two people expend the same amount of effort into achieving their goals, but one cures a disease while the other counts blades of grass, the disease-curing achievement is better than the grass-counting achievement. Likewise, compare the value of successfully solving a simple math problem when it is done by a grown adult or a three-year-old. On the view we are considering, the child's achievement is more valuable than the adult's.

While achievement is good, failure is bad. If someone expends a lot of effort trying to achieve something, but they fail, this is worse than if they had not expended that effort. This seems to be because they have more invested in the outcome (Portmore, 2007, pp. 6–8). Just consider what a misfortune we think it is when someone fails at their life's work. This is an important feature of the view to which I will return shortly.

As Hurka points out, this view of achievement has important implications for the value of sporting achievement. Sporting excellence often involves performing very difficult actions, and training very hard and very long to do them. This makes sporting achievements or excellences valuable to some degree. But we also value achievements for the value of their goals, and on this measure sporting achievements do not fare as well. An excellent tennis player is very good at hitting a tennis ball with a racket very hard and making it land on certain spots on the ground. There is no inherent value in there being a ball that does this. This is true of every sport. The goal of every sport is something inherently worthless, like getting a ball to go into a hole or through a net. Achieving these sorts of goals has some value, but not as much as achievements with valuable goals, like bettering people's lives, promoting justice or knowledge, or creating or preserving beauty (Hurka, 2006, pp. 233–234).

Now let us return to admirability. A simple way to adapt this view about the value of achievement to the question of admirability would be to say that more valuable achievements are more admirable. This has some initial plausibility. Those who invest a lot of effort into an achievement do seem more admirable than those who don't. And those who direct their efforts at valuable goals do seem more admirable than those who direct their efforts at worthless or evil goals.

Where this simple view goes wrong is in cases of failure. If you think achievements are good, it is nature to think that failures are bad. But failures are not *contemptible* simply for being failures. When someone tries hard to do something good, but they fail, we do not think them worthy of hate or scorn, even if we think it is very bad that they failed. Value and admirability seem to come apart here.

My proposal, then, is that admirability is a function of the effort expended and the value of the goal aimed at, and (unlike value) not at all a function of whether the goal is achieved. This view retains some of the implications of the achievementist view about value. Athletic achievements are admirable due to the amount of effort required to achieve them and the difficulty of achieving them, but due to the triviality of the goals of sports, athletic achievements are generally less admirable, other things equal, than achieving valuable moral, social, or aesthetic goals. We should admire star athletes, but not as much those who achieve more important goals. The reader can decide whether our actual practices of admiration accord with these implications; my own view is that they obviously do not. Now of course, some athletes pursue sporting excellence for the sake of a genuinely worthy goal, such as providing for their family or promoting social justice. Given my proposal, those athletes would deserve more admiration than others. And people do in fact tend to admire athletes for pursuing such goals.

When we combine this view with the considerations about control discussed in the first section "Control", we find other ways in which our practices of admiration are questionable. Suppose that athletes are admirable for the achievements that result from their hard work, but are less admirable for achievements to the extent that those achievements are out of their control. Well, as Torbjörn Tännsjö points out, there are many athletes who work just as hard as, if not harder than, the athletes that have become famous (Tännsjö, 1998, p. 30). Consider how few Paralympic athletes are known to the general public, for example, or consider the relative fame of outstanding female basketball players compared to their male counterparts. And consider Tännsjö's fictional example of the person who enters a world-class racing competition having never trained and somehow wins simply through their "natural" running ability (Tännsjö, 1998, p. 30). Tännsjö suspects, correctly in my view, that such a person would be regarded as a sports hero. This suggests that our admiration practices in fact track high achievements on an objective scale, and have little to do with the extent to which the athlete worked hard for their achievement. If our admiration tracks objective achievement, it will to some extent track genetic traits like height, or otherwise lucky factors such as family wealth, and will to that extent be inappropriate.

Tännsjö's Reversal Test

Tännsjö argues that the admiration of sports heroes is "fascistoid" and, therefore, morally wrong (Tännsjö, 1998). If Tännsjö's argument succeeds, then the view I have put forward here must be wrong, since my view entails that sporting achievement is admirable (even if our actual practices of admiration are often mistaken). So I will use the view I have explained in the second section "Achievement, Value, and Admirability" to explain what I think is wrong with Tännsjö's argument.

Tännsjö's basic thought is that admiring winners involves contempt for losers. But we can understand this thought in different ways, as shown by this passage:

> If we are insincere in our admiration, and we often are, we cannot *help* but feel contempt for the losers. We would be *inconsistent* if we did not feel any kind of contempt for the losers, once we sincerely admire the winner.
>
> Tännsjö, 1998, p. 26

These two sentences express importantly different ideas. The first sentence concerns what people *actually think* about losing competitors. The second concerns what it is *rational* for people to think about them. These two thoughts hang together only to the extent that people are consistent, but we are of course not always consistent. It is possible that we don't actually feel contempt for losers, even though we are somehow committed to such contempt in virtue of having other attitudes. While commentators have focused on the first of these thoughts, and Tännsjö's discussion often focuses on how we in fact feel about athletes, I think the more interesting and plausible argument is based on the second.[3]

As I'll interpret it, Tännsjö's argument goes something like this: admiring athletes involves admiring someone for their strength; admiring someone for their strength rationally requires having contempt for weakness; contempt for weakness is a central characteristic of fascism; we shouldn't be fascists; so we should not admire athletes. Debating the nature of fascism, and what is wrong about fascism, is important, but this is not the best venue for such a debate, as it is likely to shed more heat than light, especially in the current political context. So I would like to consider a version of Tännsjö's argument that does not directly appeal to fascism at all. The argument goes like this: admiring athletes involves admiring people for their strength; admiring strength rationally requires contempt for weakness; contempt for weakness is wrong; therefore it is inappropriate to admire athletes. We could formulate the argument also in terms of achievements rather than traits: winning is not admirable, because to think so would require thinking that losing is contemptible, so we should not admire the winners of sporting events.

To explain Tännsjö's argument, let us start with the first premise: admiring athletes involves admiring strength. Here it is important to understand what Tännsjö means by "strength." He does not here mean simply the ability to lift or move heavy things. Strength, for Tännsjö, might involve other kinds of physical excellence, such as speed, balance, coordination, or flexibility. These are all different kinds of strengths or excellences.

The reason Tännsjö thinks strength is not admirable is that admiring someone for being strong commits us to having contempt for weakness. It is this contempt that Tännsjö thinks is the core of fascism; but again, let us focus on the claim itself rather than the fascism connection. Granting that we should not hate the weak, why should we think that admiring the strong requires us to hate the weak? Why should admiring the winners require us to hate the losers? Here is what Tännsjö says:

> But our value terms are comparative. So if we see a person as especially valuable, because of his excellence, and if the excellence is a manifestation of strength (in a very literal sense), then this must mean that other people, who do not win the fair competition, those who are comparatively weak, are *less* valuable. The most natural feeling associated with this value judgement is—contempt.
>
> Tännsjö, 1998, p. 27

Tännsjö's conclusion here is stronger than he is entitled to. As Persson points out, less excellent does not equal contemptible (Persson, 2005, pp. 71–72). Nothing in the nature of admiration and contempt requires us to have contempt for all but the very best. We could just as easily run the argument in the opposite direction: if we see a person as especially disvaluable because of their weakness, then this must mean that other people, who are comparatively strong, are more valuable; the feeling associated with this value judgment is admiration; thus, we should admire all but the very weakest. This argument has just as much plausibility as Tännsjö's.

Nevertheless, we can construct a plausible argument from Tännsjö's basic materials. Admiration comes in degrees: we admire one person more than another. The same goes for admirability; someone can be more admirable, deserving of higher praise, than another. If strength is grounds for admirability, then someone who is stronger than another is thereby more admirable; or, to put it another way, the person who is weaker is less admirable.

We can also agree with Tännsjö that admirability and contempt lie on the same spectrum. As we admire someone less and less, our feeling turns at some point from admiration to contempt. Since we've established that it is appropriate to admire someone less for being weaker, it is natural to think that someone could be so weak that contempt would be appropriate. Compare how our attitudes operate in the related domain of moral excellence.[4] Moral excellence or virtue is admirable, and the more virtuous you are, the more admirable you are; but if someone is admirable for being excellent on that scale, wouldn't they also be contemptible for rating poorly on that scale? Indeed, that is how we often think of the morally vicious: people deserve contempt for being cowardly, dishonest or cruel.

In this way, we can see how having great admiration for elite athletes – and, of course, less admiration for the less great athletes – might commit us to having contempt for those who are inept at sports (even if it doesn't, as Tännsjö thinks, commit us to having contempt for the second-place finisher). This is a commitment nobody wants to have, whether it is fascistoid or not. But it seems like the commitment follows just from the nature of admiration and contempt. If there is a feature that makes someone admirable, then there is some related feature that makes someone contemptible. This is the core of Tännsjö's objection to admiring sports heroes, and is untouched by extant criticisms of Tännsjö. We might put the main point in the following way. If you think some feature makes someone admirable, then you must ask: would having the opposite trait make someone contemptible? If the answer is no, then you should rethink your position on admirability. Call this "Tännsjö's reversal test."

It is important to reiterate that we do not need to interpret Tännsjö's argument as saying that we in fact do hate those who are bad at sports, though Tännsjö does think we do. Being bad at sports can lead to ridicule or contempt in some settings, as most who endured American physical education classes can attest to. Even making a single mistake can lead to outpourings of hatred, as we see in the case of Bill Buckner, whose error in the 1986 World Series ended up forcing him to move his family thousands of miles from Boston. But most sensible people do not hate anyone for being bad at sports. The interest of Tännsjö's reversal test is that it seems like such hatred would be justified by the same reasons that justify admiring those who are successful at sports. This is the point that commentators on Tännsjö have often overlooked.

To see how easy it is to adopt a view with problematic implications about contempt, recall the simple view of admiration for valuable achievement presented in second section, "Achievement, Value, and Admirability". According to that view, the better an achievement is, the more admirable one is for achieving it. That view seems to have the problematic implication pointed out by Tännsjö. If the value of an achievement determines how admirable it is, and failures have negative value, then, according to Tännsjö's reversal test, sports failures deserve contempt.

Tännsjö's argument is very controversial. It is not quite as extreme as the view that nobody has control over anything, because it is consistent with some people being admirable. But it does seem to very sharply limit the extent of admirability. To respond to this argument, we need a view that entails that it is appropriate to admire sports heroes but not appropriate to hate the inept and the losers.

The view I sketched in the second section "Achievement, Value, and Admirability" is just such a view. We must deny that success is a proper basis for admiration. Failures can be just as admirable as successes. The basis for admiration is exerting oneself towards a worthy goal. So failure is not a reason for contempt. But if we accept Tännsjö's reversal test, there will be some reason for contempt even if my view is true. The reasons for contempt must have to do with either insufficient exertion of effort or having a bad goal.

What would count as an insufficient exertion of effort? This depends in part on the goal. If one's goal is worthless, then exerting no effort to achieve it does not seem like a bad thing. Since sports have worthless goals, not trying to achieve them wouldn't be contemptible. This doesn't mean that when your teammate passes you the basketball you shouldn't try to catch it. Your goal in playing a sport is never merely to achieve the worthless goal of putting the ball in a certain spot. The goal is also to cooperate, have an enjoyable competition, develop skills, and so on. It's hard to enjoy a sport or develop skills if your opponent refuses to try. So refusing to put forth effort when competing in a sport makes one worthy of some measure of ill feeling.[5]

One might also have an unworthy goal in competing in a sport. Some athletes want to win in order to make their opponent feel bad or to get revenge on an enemy. Those are bad goals. Some ill-feeling towards athletes who compete for such reasons is warranted.

So we can accept the general point of Tännsjö's argument, that admiration requires contempt, without being committed to problematic consequences. There are ways of being worthy of ill-feeling in sport, but they have nothing to do with failure; they involve either competing for bad reasons, or failing to compete at all when one ought to be competing.

If we do accept Tännsjö's reversal test, there are implications we need to keep in mind. I have intentionally omitted certain factors from the account of admirability sketched here. Among them are skill and ingenuity. Admiration often tracks features such as these; we admire Federer, for example, because of the great skill he exhibits, even when he loses. But if we accept the reversal test, and we say that skill is admirable, we would have to say that someone who exhibits a complete lack of skill would be contemptible. That is an unacceptable consequence. I would say the same about ingenuity: lack of ingenuity is not contemptible. So if someone wants to say that skillfulness and ingenuity are admirable, they must reject the reversal test. While the view I've presented here doesn't allow me to say that Federer's skill at tennis is admirable, I can say that the effort he put into developing that skill is admirable. Perhaps that is close enough.

Other responses to Tännsjö have been given. Tamburrini argues that elite athletes have traits with important social value, and therefore are admirable, contrary to Tännsjö (Tamburrini, 1998, pp. 44–45). Admiring people for having socially valuable traits does seem appropriate, prima facie. But if we accept the reversal test, we are then committed to saying that having socially disvaluable traits makes one contemptible. Here surely it will depend on the details. Being prone to murder people for no reason is a contemptible trait that is socially disvaluable, but are all socially disvaluable traits contemptible? Furthermore, Tamburrini's claim that "the skills and qualities included in excellence are socially valuable" is clearly an overstatement (1998, p. 44). While it may be true of some of the social skills involved (Tamburrini mentions respect for competitors, for instance), it will not be true of the skills involved in winning a game. There is no social value in hitting a baseball or tennis ball outside of its value in participating in that sport itself. Running fast or lifting heavy things might be slightly more useful, but these days, such abilities have less value than ever. If you want to go fast you are better off driving a car. If you want to lift heavy things there are machines that can do it better than any human. Developing these kinds of abilities might make someone healthier, but that is personal value, not social value. And it is these sport-specific abilities that ground the highest praise from sports fans, not their respect for their competitors.

Conclusion

The view I have defended here is that athletes can be properly admired for their effort and, in some cases, for aiming at a valuable goal. Athletes are generally less admirable, though, than people who devote similar efforts towards more valuable goals. And they are not properly admired for their skills or strengths, or for winning (though they may be admired for the work they put into those things). This view is consistent with the principle that we are not admirable for what is out of our control, and with Tännsjö's reversal test.

Nothing I've said so far entails that people shouldn't *enjoy* sports, either by participating or watching. Enjoyment and admiration are very different. We can enjoy watching someone perform a difficult sporting feat without having any feeling of admiration for that person. (And note, there is no reversal test for enjoyment. If I enjoy something, I don't have to dislike anything else. Enjoying Federer's skill doesn't require me to be annoyed by anyone else's ineptitude.) Taking this kind of enjoyment is one way of being a sports fan. There are many ways to be a fan, and admiring athletes is just one of those.

I close with a puzzle. Does my view entail that putting up unnecessary obstacles, thus requiring more effort, makes one more admirable? If Stephen Curry decides to shoot a free throw with his eyes closed, and he makes the shot, would he really be more admirable than if he had not closed his eyes? There was no reason for him to do that. But it made his achievement much more difficult, so more valuable and more admirable.[6] I think this is an important concern for effort-based views such as the view I've defended, and it might be something that we just have to accept.[7]

Notes

1. For a recent defense of this line of argument in a sporting context, see Persson (2005, pp. 77–80). This line of argument has a long history; for more context and possible responses, see O'Connor and Franklin (2020).
2. These questions are related, but distinct. Different achievementists take different factors to be relevant. For just a few examples, see Keller (2004) for effort; see Hurka (2006) for difficulty and complexity; see Bradford (2015) for difficulty. Portmore (2007) argues that self-sacrifice is what matters, not these other things. In this chapter I am not concerned to make heavy weather over these distinctions.
3. Holowchak, for example, focuses on the first statement when he says "we seldom show contempt for all nonwinners… contempt is too strong a word for the painful disappointment all fans experience when the athletes and teams that they love fail to win it all" (Holowchak, 2005, p. 100). Likewise, Tamburrini focuses on the first sentence when he says: "no matter how contemptuous, the public's attitude towards these athletes does not seem directly related to admiring excellence. Such a complete lack of valuable qualities results on its own in negative reactions" (Tamburrini, 1998, p. 43). Here Tamburrini is clearly talking about how people in fact treat the losers, not how they ought to. And Tamburrini provides no reason to think hatred of the inept would be unjustified.
4. Tännsjö says we should reject the very idea of moral excellence (1998, p. 28), so he would not accept this argument.
5. This ill-feeling need not, contrary to what Tannsjo and Holowchak say, require treating the person as less than a full human being (Tännsjö, 1998, p. 27; Holowchak, 2005, p. 102). More argument would be needed to establish that strong claim. I will just note here that when we have ill-feeling toward the morally vicious, we do not necessarily treat them as less than a person; the same goes for ill-feelings towards exhibitions of poor sportsmanship such as failing to compete.

6 Bradford seems to accept this implication of her view; see Bradford (2015, Ch. 4). Of course, her view is a view about value, not admirability.
7 Thanks to Eric Moore for helpful discussion.

References

Bradford, Gwen. (2015). *Achievement*. Oxford: Oxford University Press.
Holowchak, M. Andrew. (2005). "'Fascistoid' Heroism Revisited: A Deontological Twist to a Recent Debate." *Journal of the Philosophy of Sport* 32(1), 96–104.
Hurka, Thomas. (2006). "Games and the Good." *Proceedings of the Aristotelian Society* 80, 217–235.
Keller, Simon. (2004). "Welfare and the Achievement of Goals." *Philosophical Studies* 121, 27–41.
O'Connor, Timothy and Franklin, Christopher. (2020). "Free Will", *The Stanford Encyclopedia of Philosophy* (Spring 2020 Edition), Edward N. Zalta (ed.), https://plato.stanford.edu/archives/spr2020/entries/freewill/.
Persson, Ingmar. (2005). "What's Wrong with Admiring Athletes and Other People?" In C. Tamburrini and T. Tännsjö (eds.), *Genetic Technology and Sport: Ethical Questions* (pp. 70–81). New York: Routledge.
Portmore, Douglas. (2007). "Welfare, Achievement, and Self-Sacrifice." *Journal of Ethics and Social Philosophy* 2(2), 1–28. Retrieved from https://doi.org/10.26556/jesp.v2i2.22
Tamburrini, Claudio M. (1998). "Sports, Fascism, and the Market." *Journal of the Philosophy of Sport* 25(1), 35–47.
Tännsjö, Torbjörn. (1998). "Is Our Admiration for Sports Heroes Fascistoid?" *Journal of the Philosophy of Sport* 25(1), 23–34.

12
Centering Race in Sport Fan Research
A Call to Action

Anne C. Osborne and Danielle Sarver Coombs

In this book we have tried to highlight the breadth of research on sport fans and fandom, but the reality is that existent research has been dominated by Western scholars and rooted in masculinity and whiteness. In the last several years, numerous researchers, ourselves included, have called out the lack of research on women's fandom, and as a result we have seen considerable advances in the understanding and appreciation of female fans (see e.g. Pfister & Pope, 2018; Toffoletti, 2017; Osborne & Coombs, 2015). Unfortunately, the same cannot be said for research on sport fandom related to BIPOC fans or sport fandom in the global south and Asia. The gap in literature at the intersection of sport, fandom, and race needs to be addressed, particularly as racialized issues continue to feature prominently in sports discourses. In this chapter we outline some of the major areas where race might be centered in future research.

Racist Fans

From the moment sports leagues racially integrated, Black athletes have been subjected to racist abuse. Sometimes these attacks come from other athletes but more often fans are to blame, particularly now that social platforms allow fans to quickly and anonymously fling hatred around.

The 2021 men's European Championship football (soccer) final came down to a penalty shootout. In the end Italy defeated England after three English players, all of whom are Black, missed their shots on goal. Marcus Rashford, Jadon Sancho, and Bukayo Saka were then targeted with racist attacks on social media and a mural of Rushford was defaced with racist graffiti. League officials, the British prime minister, and citizens condemned the attacks, and PM Boris Johnson vowed that those responsible would be banned from future matches (Kirka, 2020).

Unfortunately, instances like this are neither new nor isolated. With only 25 percent of English Premier League players being Black or ethnic minorities while the coaching, ownership, and fanbases remain almost entirely white (Pearn Kandola, 2021), the league has long struggled with a toxic dynamic. At the opening of its 2020 season, the English Premier League sought to directly address racism on and off the pitch. Players' jerseys featured Black Lives Matter arm patches, at times the names on kits were replaced with "Black Lives Matters," and entire teams took a knee at the opening of some matches. The league also launched a system for players and staff to report online abuse. Not all fans supported the leagues efforts. As the *Washington Post* reported:

> Within a week of the mid-June restart, the fuzzy feelings were punctured by a plane, flying over Manchester City's stadium during a match against Burnley, trailing a banner reading "WHITE LIVES MATTER BURNLEY!" The move was quickly decried, but the reminder had been served: Racism has always been—and continues to be—a problem in English football.
>
> *Barshad, 2020*

The market research firm YouGov conducted a survey of 4,500 football fans across nine European countries to assess attitudes and beliefs about racism in football, finding that 90 percent of British fans think racism remains a problem in football and over half (57 percent) think it is a serious issue. Among "ethnically diverse" fans, 79 percent view racism as a serious issue in football. Spain and the Netherlands reported the least concern about racism in football; France reported the greatest level of concern. Fans believe that the leagues and the clubs should do more to combat racism but they also think that fans themselves need to shoulder some of the responsibility. In England, for example, only 20 percent of respondents thought fans were doing enough to end racism; only 10 percent of BIPOC fans agree. More than two-thirds of English fans (68 percent) thought they could do more to stop racism (Sky Sports News, 2021).

Anecdotal evidence also tells us that racist fan behavior takes a very real toll on the players. In recent years, tennis star Naomi Osaka has spoken out about the added pressure and resulting mental health concerns she has faced as a biracial woman competing in front of majority-white fans. She is certainly not alone.

> There is no greater example than Serena Williams, one of the greatest tennis players of all time and also a leading target of racism from the media, fans and social media. In 2001, Serena and her sister Venus Williams were booed and called the N-word during the final of Indian Wells in California. Then in 2015, moments after she won the French Open, hateful comments on Twitter comparing her to a gorilla went viral.... [A former ESPN creative strategist explained], "I think at a certain point, that hate and that anger fuels a player to kind of prove people wrong, but then ultimately it gets to them. We've seen Serena break down on the court, and if you compare her to other white tennis players, they're viewed as passionate and secure about themselves, and that's why they were defending their game. But when it comes to Serena, she's just the angry Black woman."
>
> *Holt, 2021*

Not only does racism affect athletes' mental health, it negatively affects their performance. Researchers in Italy used the fact that fans were barred from attending football matches due to COVID-19 as a natural experiment to examine the relationship between racism and on-the-pitch success. They found, "that players from Africa, who are most heavily targeted by racial harassment during matches, experience a significant improvement in performance when supporters are no longer at the stadium, while the performance of players from other regions does not change" (Caselli & Falco, 2021).

We need more of this kind of research that clearly details the relationship between racism, fandom, and athlete performance. We also need more academic research that investigates how racism targeted toward players affects BIPOC fans. Does animus toward athletes spill over into racial tensions in the stands? To what extent does this racism create barriers to fandom?

Athlete Activists

The previous section explores how white fans treat athletes simply for being Black. What about when those athletes respond to the racism the experience and witness? In 2016, Colin Kaepernick, quarterback for the National Football League's San Francisco 49'ers, took a knee as the national anthem played before a game. Kaepernick was not the first or last athlete to use their platform to address racial oppression, but his actions sparked a heated national conversation about athletes as activists. Kaepernick was protesting longstanding racial injustice in the United States and police brutality targeted toward Black people. Fans were quick to respond with vitriol. Videos showing white fans burning Kaepernick jerseys spread across social media along with posts calling him arrogant, disrespectful of the American military, and unpatriotic. A *Rolling Stone* article explained,

> Kaepernick's protest, just as [Muhammed] Ali's refusal to participate in the Vietnam War, tapped into an entrenched, historical fear of race in this country, that blackness is by default anti-American. This is why when gymnast Gabby Douglas did not place a hand over her heart for the pledge of allegiance during the 2016 Rio Olympics, she was heavily criticized to the point where she released a public apology. Meanwhile, white shot-putters Ryan Crouser and Joe Kovacs kept their hands down at their side and no one questioned them. Whiteness is considered to be intrinsically American; therefore, a white athlete's allegiance to the flag is assumed whereas with black athletes, it is more heavily enforced.
>
> *Jerkins, 2016*

Who does the enforcing? The media play a significant role but largely it's the fans. "When Kaepernick takes a knee during the Star-Spangled Banner, when [Lebron] James wears an 'I Can't Breathe' sweatshirt during warm-ups, when the then-St Louis Rams wide receivers emerge from the stadium tunnel in the 'hands up, don't shoot' pose, they are violating the terms of the white fan's contract" (Freedman, 2016).

It's important to note the power structures at work within most American sports leagues. The US's most popular league, the NFL, has a blindingly white fanbase, 83 percent, while the players are predominantly Black (Jerkins, 2016). Sports such as baseball, hockey, NASCAR, and soccer have similarly white-dominant fans. The National Basketball Association is the only major American sports league that comes close to having a fanbase that resembles the racial make-up of the teams. This may account for the tensions that arise when Black players call out racism. "The white fan begrudgingly tolerates the political engagement of the black athlete. More commonly, though, the white fan treats it as ingratitude, arrogance, defiance, all those variations on the theme of uppity" (Freedman, 2016).

Research bears this out. Content analysis of fan reactions, largely on social media, confirm that fans prefer when players "stick to sports" (see e.g. Chapter 34 in this volume). American sport fans with a strong sense of national identity are more likely to react negatively to player protests (Smith & Tryce, 2019; Smith, 2019). Negative perceptions of player activism is also likely to result in fans purchasing less of that player's merchandise, though team merchandise sales are not affected (Mudrick, Sauder, & Davies, 2019). News media sometimes play a role in fans' perceptions of player activism. News frames (either positive or negative) have little effect on audiences' perceptions of well-known players. However, for unknown athletes, news frames can moderate how fans perceive athlete activism (Park, Park, & Billings, 2020). Fans also respond more positively when white allies support Black player protests (Coombs et al., 2020).

These studies shed light on how fans perceive athletes who engage in social justice causes. They do not, however, tell us much about differences in fans' reactions based on their race, largely because the research has been conducted with predominantly white participants. Research should consider the strong possibility that there are racial and ethnic differences in how fans respond to activism, particularly when it relates to racial justice. It is also worth more deeply exploring the racial attitudes of white fans. As Columbia University journalism professor Samuel Freedman (2016) wrote, "The national conversation about activism by African-American athletes, which itself is part of the larger Black Lives Matter movement, has focused primarily on the participants, on their experiences and motivations. That is only half the discussion that should be taking place. The other part of the sporting equation involves the fan, particularly the white fan."

Motives and Behaviors

Freedman's call for greater consideration of white fandom in relation to activism belies the fact that, generally speaking, we already know a great deal about white fans: their motivations, consumption behaviors, media usage, stadium dining preferences, and sport betting habits. We know far less about the motives and behaviors of BIPOC fans.

In a preliminary study, Wann et al. (1999) compared the motivations of Black and white sport fans on eight factors: eustress (i.e., positive stress), self-esteem, escape, entertainment, economic (i.e., gambling), aesthetics, group affiliation, and family needs. They found that white fans reported significantly higher levels of eustress, self-esteem, escape, and family motivation. Black fans did not score higher than white fans on any of the eight factors, suggesting they are less motivated sport enthusiasts. In subsequent research, Bilyeu and Wann (2002) revised the Sport Fan Motivation Scale to include three additional factors: representation (e.g., people of the same background), similarity (e.g., people they have things in common with), and support/perceived greater equality (e.g., people they want to succeed). They concluded that Black fans indeed have different reasons for their sport fandom than had been identified through research conducted with predominantly white research participants. Other research has found racial differences in sport fan behaviors such as game attendance (Armstrong & Stratta, 2004).

The little bit of research there is that centers race in examining fan motives and behaviors clearly demonstrates the shortcomings of research conducted with only hegemonic white, male participants as well as the problem with measures of fandom that are grounded in the experiences of these same hegemonic sports fans. In order to understand the full diversity of sport fandom the participants in sports fan research need to be diverse.

Global Sport

In addition to research relying heavily on white, male participants, the majority of sport fan research has been conducted by scholars in and from white-dominant countries and has focused on the sports that are most popular there, specifically European and American football. Football/soccer is by far the most popular sport in the world with roughly 4 billion fans so the wealth of research on its fans makes sense. The focus on European football fans does not. According to Nielsen, 80 percent of the United Arab Emirates' population is "interested" or "very interested" in football. Thailand (78 percent), Chile (75 percent), Portugal (75 percent), and Turkey (75 percent) follow in their populations' interest in the beautiful game. The U.K. ranks number 17 with only 51 percent of Brits saying they are interested in football (Nielsen, 2018). The top three countries on Nielsen's list are located in the global south or Asia yet we have very little research on fan cultures from these regions.

There are also sports that enjoy large fanbases in non-Western countries. We should know more about them. Cricket, for example, is the second most popular sport in the world with 2.5 billion fans, largely due to its popularity in India and throughout South Asia. Basketball and table tennis are the most popular sports in China, the world's most populous country. As Western sports such as basketball and American football grow in popularity across the globe it is likely that we will see more research on fans in the global South and East. The concern is that like the early research on female fans and Black fans in predominantly white countries, research is likely to reinforce Western standards and understandings of fandom in non-Western parts of the world.

Conclusion

Whether you like it or not, race permeates all aspects of society and affects the way that people are allowed (or not) to move through the world. Sport is certainly no different. In fact, the influence of race may be even more important given the social nature of sport and sport fandom. It is time for the study of sport fandom to take race seriously, not just as another demographic indicator asked of research participants but as a central construct. This chapter has laid out just a few of the ways that race and sport fandom often intersect or even collide. There are certainly others but we hope with this chapter to provide a jumping off point for more diverse and inclusive research.

References

Armstrong, K. L., & Peretto Stratta, T. M. (2004). Market analyses of race and sport consumption. *Sport Marketing Quarterly*, *13*(1), 7–16.

Barshad, A. (2020, July 31). The English Premier League returned with strong BLM optics. At grass roots, there's skepticism. *Washington Post*. Retrieved from: www.washingtonpost.com/sports/2020/07/30/english-premier-league-racism/.

Bilyeu, J. K., & Wann, D. L. (2002). An investigation of racial differences in sport fan motivation. *International Sports Journal*, *6*(2), 93.

Caselli, M., & Falco, P. (2021). *When the Mob Goes Silent: Uncovering the Effects of Racial Harassment through a Natural Experiment* (No. 2021/01). Department of Economics and Management.

Coombs, D. S., Lambert, C. A., Cassilo, D., & Humphries, Z. (2020). Flag on the play: Colin Kaepernick and the protest paradigm. *Howard Journal of Communications*, *31*(4), 317–336.

Freedman, S. (2016). Needed: The woke white fan. *The Undefeated*. Retrieved from: https://theundefeated.com/features/needed-the-woke-white-fan/.

Holt, B. (2021, July 30). Think winning Olympic gold is tough? Try doing it while coping with racism. *The Guardian*. Retrieved from: www.theguardian.com/sport/2021/jul/30/simone-biles-gymnastics-olympics-tokyo-2020-olympics.

Jerkins, M. (2016). What Colin Kaepernick's National Anthem protest tells us about America. *Rolling Stone*. Retrieved from: www.rollingstone.com/culture/culture-sports/what-colin-kaepernicks-national-anthem-protest-tells-us-about-america-247887/.

Kirka, D. (2021, July 14). UK to ban online racists from games after Euro 2020 uproar. *APnews*. Retrieved from: https://apnews.com/article/euro-2020-sports-government-and-politics-race-and-ethnicity-europe-21265f80b756cb236d020183b5d21fe2.

Mudrick, M., Sauder, M. H., & Davies, M. (2019). When athletes don't "stick to sports": The relationship between athlete political activism and sport consumer behavior. *Journal of Sport Behavior*, *42*(2), 177–199.

Nielsen (2018). Fan favorite: The global popularity of football is rising. Retrieved from: www.nielsen.com/eu/en/insights/article/2018/fan-favorite-the-global-popularity-of-football-is-rising/.

Osborne, A. C., & Coombs, D. S. (2015). *Female Fans of the NFL: Taking their Place in the Stands*. Routledge.

Park, B., Park, S., & Billings, A. C. (2020). Separating perceptions of Kaepernick from perceptions of his protest: An analysis of athlete activism, endorsed brand, and media effects. *Communication & Sport*, *8*(4–5), 629–650.

Pearn Kandola. (2021). Press Release: Lack of diversity found in the leadership of Premier League Football Clubs. Retrieved from: https://pearnkandola.com/press/press-release-lack-of-diversity-found-in-the-leadership-of-premier-league-football-clubs/.

Pfister, G., & Pope, S. (Eds.). (2018). *Female Football Players and Fans: Intruding into a man's world*. Springer.

Sky Sports News. (2021, July 13). Football fans in England and across Europe surveyed on racism in the game. Retrieved from: www.skysports.com/football/news/19692/12354514/football-fans-in-england-and-across-europe-surveyed-on-racism-in-the-game.

Smith, B., & Tryce, S. A. (2019). Understanding emerging adults' national attachments and their reactions to athlete activism. *Journal of Sport and Social Issues, 43*(3), 167–194.

Smith, L. (2019). Stand up, show respect: Athlete activism, nationalistic attitudes, and emotional response. *International Journal of Communication, 13*, 22.

Statista Research Department (n.d.). Share of Sports Fans in 2016, by Country. Retrieved from: www.statista.com/statistics/655880/share-of-sport-fans-by-country/.

Toffoletti, K. (2017). *Women sport fans: Identification, participation, representation*. Routledge.

Wann, D. L., Bilyeu, J. K., Brennan, K., Osborn, H., & Gambouras, A. (1999). An exploratory investigation of the relationship between sport fan motivation and race. *Perceptual and Motor Skills, 88*, 1081–1084.

World Atlas (n.d.). The Most Popular Sports in the World. Retrieved from: www.worldatlas.com/articles/what-are-the-most-popular-sports-in-the-world.html.

Part II
Who Fans Are

13
Sport Fandom
The Complexity of Performative Role Identities

Shannon Kerwin and Larena Hoeber

This identity of the "sports fan" only serves to manipulate. Rather than creating an open and exclusive community, the branded sports fan acts as a gatekeeper, preventing access to the larger group until new members can prove their worth through a properly competitive and exclusionary attitude.

Moore, 2015, p. 1

In sport, the notion of a fan is often associated with positive outcomes of attachment and connection to sport teams, as well as increased sense of community (e.g., Fairley & Tyler, 2012; Heere, 2016; Wann & Pierce, 2003). However, as noted by Moore (2015) sport fandom can be exclusionary, as the very concept of social identification related to fandom highlights the presence of outgroups that are oppressed from and, in some cases, aggressively addressed by the ingroup (Wakefield & Wann, 2006). Heere and James (2007) note that fans of sport teams ultimately see themselves as members of a sport organization and therefore their team identity becomes strong. Heere and James also acknowledge that individuals may hold allegiance to multiple social identities (e.g., based on sport team, sex/gender, ethnicity/race, membership in a local community), and that it is important to recognize how group identity(ies) align with team identity. This multifaceted view requires that we examine sport fan identity from an integrative approach that acknowledges the complexity of constructs interacting across an individual's lifetime to shape their personal, relational, and collective identities (Vignoles, Schwartz, & Luyckx, 2011). Furthermore, the presence of the "dark side" of sport fandom (Wakefield & Wann, 2006, p. 168) emphasizes the importance of recognizing how individuals identify with sport fandom and the impact of that identification on both positive and negative behaviours (e.g., hooliganism, racism, homophobia, abusive parenting).

Relevant to this chapter, Wann and Branscombe (1991) conclude that team identity provides sport fans with a sense of belonging and a connection to larger social structures. However, it is unclear which larger social structure(s) connect with/to team identity (Heere & James, 2007). It is our intent to highlight the relevance of a focused exploration and understanding of larger social structures and culture related to sport fan identity. The goal is to emphasize the multifaceted nature of sport fan identity and the relevance of dissecting behaviours that may result from conflicting and complementing identities.

Multi-Layered Sport Identity

Social identity theory is related to a person's knowledge that they belong to a social group, e.g., the sport team (Hogg & Abrams, 1988). However, this knowledge of social belonging may be informed by, complement, or contrast with other roles or ego identities. Further, as Lock and Heere (2017) suggest, team identity may be closely aligned with (fan) group identity which is more accurately associated with role identity. A recent proposition put forth by Sagas and Wendling (2019) highlights a Multilayer Identity Development System Model (MIDSM) in that team identity connects with multiple identities in a larger social structure, such as work and family life, that ultimately impacts fan behaviour (see Figure 13.1).

Specifically, they indicate the identity construct should be integrated where the focus is on personal, relational, and collective identities, and each focus is related to ego, narrative, role, and social identities (Sagas & Wendling, 2019).

Personal identities are defined by ego and narrative identities that reference an individual's evolving and internalized organization of personal drives, abilities, and beliefs (Marcia, 1980; McAdams & McLean, 2013). For example, an individual's personal identity may be attached to their athletic prowess, how one presents themselves at meetings (e.g., business formal dress), and/or how one behaves at a sporting event (e.g., face painted and jersey worn proud). All of these are constructed by an individual's ego and personal narrative. Inherently in the MIDSM, personal identity is connected to role identity.

Role identities refer to a sense of belonging that is rooted in the positions individuals hold, e.g., board member, father, wife, partner (Caza, Vough, & Puranik, 2018). If we use the example of the individual who paints their face and wears their jersey to a sporting event, that personal identity presentation may be directly linked to one's perceived role identity as a fan. Not every person who identifies as a fan will paint their face. Rather, the individual's personal identity and individual narrative (e.g., where they grew up, who they interact with in sport contexts)

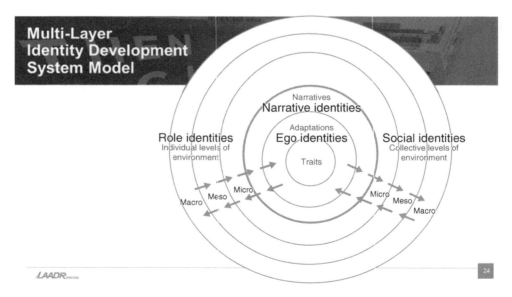

Figure 13.1 Sagas and Wendling (2019) Multi-Layer Identity Development System Model. Permission to reproduce from Michael Sagas.

will inform how they identify and perform the role of fan. The personal meanings that each individual attaches to how the role of fan is performed or lived varies from person to person (Osborne & Coombs, 2013), which adds another layer of complexity and will be explained later in the chapter.

Social identities are an individual's self-concept related to membership in a social group, where membership in the group is linked to value and emotional significance (Tajfel, 1978). Continuing our example, how the sport fan, with the painted face, perceives themselves in relation to the larger social group of sport fans connected to their favourite team defines their emotional tie to being a sport fan of that team. For example, fans of the National Hockey League's Toronto Maple Leafs are a social group that has been historically defined by corporate stoicism while fans of the National Hockey League's Philadelphia Flyers are a social group that has historically been defined by toughness and hegemonically masculine stereotypes. Therefore, individuals who connect with the social group of fans for each team will likely perform their role identity as sport fan in unique ways from one another. This connection to membership in the social group is also based on the role identity attached to personal narratives that each person holds. Therefore, micro, meso, and macro factors within an individual's social world will alter personal identity, which then shape role and social identities (see Figure 13.1).

This comprehensive perspective of identity development is adopted throughout the chapter to highlight the intersection of multiple layers within a system of identity development that influence how and when an individual engages in sport fandom. We begin the chapter with a discussion of the performative nature of sport fan identity and the intersection of identities within the performance of role identities in sport. We then outline the complexity of performative sport fan identity, and conclude by suggesting directions for future research that reflect a multi-layered (e.g., personal, role, social) critical perspective of identity development in relation to performative sport fandom to inform a comprehensive understanding of sport fan behaviour.

Performative Sport Fan Identities

A traditional view of sport fandom suggests there are clear and stable indicators of who is and is not a fan. For example, a real sport fan wears a jersey and attends as many games as possible. This perspective assumes that all "real" fans behave or perform their fandom in the same way. In contrast, Osborne and Coombs (2013) conceptualize sport fandom as performative assuming that all identities are socially constructed, and in turn, individuals determine how they will perform them based on context and audience (Osborne & Coombs, 2013). Their view of sport fandom falls in line with the multi-layered view of identity where the connection between an individual's personal, role, and social identities must be understood when exploring the performance of sport fan identity. Their view recognizes that sport fandom, as an identity, is played out in many different, but individually relevant, ways. For example, Osborne and Coombs (2013) state that knowing how often someone wears or displays a team logo is not as relevant as questioning how and why the act of wearing of a logo fits into the individual's performance as a fan. Within the multi-layered performative fandom lens, if an individual does not attend live sporting events, this does not necessarily mean they are not a fan. The lens challenges researchers to dig deeper to uncover which other identities (as an example) may influence behaviour. In this case, perhaps the individual is a father of a young child and cannot attend live games because of the salience of his fatherhood identity. The multi-layered performative fandom lens allows for the exploration of these nuances.

The questions that may arise out of Osborne and Coombs' work (2013) stem from a recognition of the multiple performative identities that people hold and how they may conflict with other identities thus impacting how fan identity is performed. Therefore, within this chapter we explore the opportunities and barriers that exist when performing sport fandom within the context of multi-layered identity performances (e.g., gender, race, socio-economic status).

The Intersection of Identities in Performative Sport Fandom

Figure 13.1 highlights the link between layers of identity development (Sagas & Wendling, 2019). The work of Osborne and Coombs (2013) provides justification for exploring how different performative identities (personal, role, social) interact to influence how people behave in the sport fandom world. Here we highlight specific connections between identities that have been found in previous research; more specially, an emphasis on social and role identities as these

Table 13.1 Academic Literature Linking Social Identity and Role Identity

Social Identity Target[1]	Role Identity	Select Academic Sources
Identification with a Sport Team	Fan/spectator/consumer/ athlete	Andrijiw & Hyatt, 2009 Delia & James, 2018 Fink, Parker, Brett, & Higgins, 2009 Heere, 2016 Hyatt & Foster, 2015 Inoue, Funk, Wann, Yoshida, & Nakazawa, 2015 Lock & Funk, 2016 Lock, Funk, Doyle, & McDonald, 2014 Lock & Heere, 2017 Lock, Taylor, Funk, & Darcy, 2012 Spaaij & Anderson, 2010 Sveinson & Hoeber, 2016 Wegner, Delia, & Baker, 2020 Wu, Tsai, Hung, 2012
Identification with an Organization	Employee/volunteer/ athlete	Manley, Morgan, & Atkinson, 2016 Ryan, 2018 Swanson & Kent, 2015 Wegner, Jones, & Jordan, 2019
Identification with a Community	Contributing community member	Colombo & Senatore, 2005 Warner, Dixon, & Chalip, 2012
Identification with Family	Mother/father/sister/ brother/grandparent	Hyatt, Kerwin, Hoeber, & Sveinson, 2018 Popovic, 2010 Tinson, Sinclair, & Kolyperas, 2017
Identification with a Religious group	Devote participant in religious actions (e.g., attending religious services)	Mael & Ashforth, 2001
Identification with a Race or Sexual orientation	Activist	Cunningham, Dixon, Singer, Oshiro, Ahn, & Weems, 2019 Mudrick, Sauder, & Davies, 2019

[1] This list is not an exhaustive list, but rather one that focuses on social identity targets that relate to larger social structure(s) that impact sport fans and inherently link to role identities.

identity targets have been most prominent in the development of theory and practice in sport management.

Individuals possess a social identity attached to sport fandom, which is then attached to multiple roles (and role identities) that might align with the sport fan social group (Hyatt, Kerwin, Hoeber, & Sveinson, 2018; Tinson, Sinclair, & Kolyperas, 2017). Inherently, (role) identity theory is intertwined with social identity in that categorization into a social group results in an individual seeing oneself as occupying a role in that social group, where there are meanings, expectations, and performances attached to that role (Stets & Burke, 2000). For example, if an individual identifies with a sport team (social identity) she may see herself as occupying the role of "die hard supporter" or "casual observer." Both role identities function under the sport fan social identity (i.e., team identity), but may have vastly different outcomes for behaviour (i.e., purchase behaviour or game attendance; Stets & Burke, 2000).

Previous research has highlighted situations when one's role identities intersect with and, at times, conflicts with one's social identity as a sport fan. For many adults who are sport fans, their social identity with a sport team exists alongside the role identities of parent and die-hard sport team supporter (Hyatt et al., 2018; Tinson et al., 2017). This intersection leads to a shift in behaviours where an individual will bridge, bond, or balance their competing role identities under the social identity of sport fan (Tinson et al., 2017).

Relevant Identity Targets in Sport

As outlined in the multi-layered conception of identity and the focus on performative identity, the definition of social identity allows for a discussion and summary of multiple social groups that may be relevant in the performance of sport fandom. Specifically, social identity targets could link to the team, organization, community hosting the sport event/program (geography), family, religion, race, ethnicity, gender orientation, and sexual orientation (e.g., Cunningham, Dixon, Singer, Oshiro, Ahn, & Weems, 2019; Hyatt & Foster, 2015; Hyatt et al., 2018; Lock, Taylor, Funk, & Darcy, 2012; Manley, Morgan, & Atkinson, 2016; Warner, Dixon, & Chalip, 2012). Acknowledging social identity targets lends itself to exploring the list of related role and personal identities to each social identity target (see Table 13.1), a phenomenon outlined by Lock and Heere (2017). For example, family identity may be linked to the role identity of mother or sister, and this in turn may influence or interact with an individual's team (social) and fan (role) identity (cf., Tinson et al., 2017). According to Osborne and Coombs (2013), this intersection impacts how an individual will perform their sport fan role. In the example above, a woman may be an L.A. Sparks[1] fan and identify strongly with that role; however, she also identifies as a mother. Given her new-born twin boys go to bed around 7:00 pm (which is game time for the Sparks), she is unable to attend or view the games live. Instead, she watches the game on tape delay. Therefore, she performs her role as a Sparks fan in a unique way to her in-group peers who attended or watched games. Acknowledging the interplay between multiple layers of identity highlights fandom as a dynamic and unstable construct.

Complexity of Performative Sport Fan Identity

Much work has been done on team identity in sport (e.g., Andrijiw & Hyatt, 2009; Lock & Funk, 2016; Lock, Funk, Doyle, & McDonald, 2014; Lock & Heere, 2017; Sveinson & Hoeber, 2016). A growing body of literature has addressed role identity in sport (see Lock & Heere, 2017); however, very few studies have taken a holistic lens to explore multiple layers of identity in relation to performative sport fandom, where the conflict and tension between identities is at the forefront of discussions around sport fan behaviour. Osborne and Coombs (2013) have identified the complexity of sport fandom and the notion that the performance of roles within any identity is impacted by compatible and conflicting alternative identities (i.e., social, role, personal). Further, and perhaps more importantly, we need to recognize that "how individuals manage multiple identities is complicated and varies dramatically, depending on the person and the context" (Mansfield, 2020, p. 10).

In the following section, we draw upon Sagas and Wendling's (2019) framework and Osborne and Coombs' (2013) performative fandom to illustrate how a multi-layered perspective of sport fan identities can challenge our understanding (and inform future research) in this area. Using existing research, we highlight four situations that intersect with team and fan identities: family roles, employee roles, gender identity, and geographic identities.

Performing Fandom with Family Role Identity

The connection between family roles (e.g., parent, grandparent, son, daughter), team identity, and fan identity has typically been thought of in two ways. First, it is assumed that children are socialized into sport fandom by their parents, and that they support the same team as their parents (James, 2001). Porat (2010) alluded to this point when he stated that sport fandom "virtually begins in the cradle and ends in the grave" (p. 282). Second, men, in their roles as fathers, brothers, husbands, and boyfriends, often act as the main socializing agent for others (e.g., mothers, children) into fandom (e.g., Farrell, Fink & Field, 2011; James, 2001). This is because men are assumed to be sport fans, and their duty as men is to educate others about sport. In his study on new parents and sport fandom, Mansfield (2020), recounted that one father "introduced [each of his three children] to fandom practically the day they came home from the hospital" (p. 6).

There is less consensus about how people negotiate their team identity and their family role. Porat (2010) argued that because one's team identity "is a permanent component in the fan's identity profile" (p. 280), there can be tension with their family role. In part, this tension exists because the responsibilities to fandom and families can happen at the same time (e.g., a sport event and a family celebration being scheduled on the same day). People resolve this tension in a variety of ways. Tinson et al. (2017) identified a group of fans, labelled breathers, who used sport as an escape from family. Porat (2010) found that some people prioritized their team identity over family commitments, others were loyal to their family and missed sport events, and some found a compromise, such as attending or watching the game, then showing up late to the family event.

In contrast, some see fan identities and family roles as compatible. Tinson et al. (2017) identified these parents as balancers. Mansfield (2020) found some new parents believed that they can "be a 'good' parent *and* a 'good' fan – and do not view it as a zero-sum proposition" (p. 6; italics in the original). Those individuals saw a unified relationship between family roles and team identity (e.g., "We are a Maple Leafs family") as it contributed to family bonding (Mansfield, 2020; Tinson et al., 2017).

There are also examples of fan and team identities being less stable when people become parents. Hyatt et al. (2018) found some parents who changed their team allegiance to match those of their children. Others adopted secondary teams (i.e., "when my team is not playing, I will cheer for my son or daughter's team"). Some adopted an identity with a new sport (e.g., rock climbing, soccer), as a result of their child's participation in it. Mansfield (2020) and Tinson et al. (2017) also found that some parents spent less time on their sport fandom and more time with their children, particularly when their children were young.

Recent research highlights alternative narratives about the connection between fan identity, team identity, and family roles. Adding to the growing body of literature that recognizes women as sport fans, Hyatt et al. (2018) found a few examples of mothers who were the primary socializing agents for their children into sport fandom. They also found examples of children establishing team identities that were different (sometimes rivals to) to their parents' team identities (Hyatt et al., 2018). This finding suggests that some children have some control over establishing their own team, fan, (and in some cases) sport identities. Further, it may point to changing family norms in certain cultures where children are afforded more independence of choice.

Performing Fandom with Employee Identity

Generally, we would expect little overlap between employee and fan roles because they occur at different times in one's life (employee during work time; fan during leisure). Yet, they can be connected if people bring fandom into work (e.g., watching or betting on sport events while working; Oja, Hazzaa, Wilkerson, & Bass, 2018; Smith & Smith, 2011), or if a sport fan works for a sport organization (Oja et al., 2018; Swanson & Kent, 2015).

There has been limited research on sport fandom in the workplace. Oja et al. (2018) and Smith and Smith (2011) looked at the impact of employees watching and betting on March Madness (a men's college basketball tournament). Oja et al. (2018) observed employees of collegiate athletic departments, while Smith and Smith (2011) surveyed service-industry employees. While the general assumption is that fandom in the workplace is disruptive and lessens employee productivity, as people prioritize fandom over employee roles for a period of time, both studies found that involvement in sport fan activities during work time added to cohesion and did not reduce productivity. However, neither study identified that the individual narratives of the employees will influence if and how their employee and fan identities intersect.

A dominant viewpoint is that people who work for sport teams are also sport fans and/or identify with the team they work for, in part because "sport fandom is a primary motive for pursuing a career in the sport industry" (Swanson & Kent, 2017 p. 461). Swanson and Kent (2015) found that "employees simultaneously and distinctly identify with the overall organization and the affiliated sports team" (p. 472). Interestingly, Oja et al. (2018) noted that not everyone working for the collegiate athletic department watched March Madness games during work or participated in the office pool. This finding emphasizes the need to explore the nuanced intersection between employee identity, fan identity, and individual narratives.

There are some roles in the sport industry that do not endorse employees demonstrating their fandom while working (e.g., reporter, photographer, umpire, game-day staff). For those roles, it is assumed that one performs them in a neutral, objective, and non-biased manner. We can also extend this situation to our careers as sport management researchers. As critical, qualitative researchers we understand that it is difficult to remove or compartmentalize our identities (Kerwin & Hoeber, 2015). When we conducted self-ethnographies on our experiences as women sport fans, we were surprised by how little of our critical and feminist lenses as researchers informed our sport fan practices (Hoeber & Kerwin, 2013). One area that stood out was how our research aimed to be supportive of women in sport, yet our sport fan behaviours and attitudes to some women in attendance were anything but supportive. This juxtaposition emphasized the dynamic interplay (and conflict) between our sport fan identities and critical researcher identities.

Performing Fandom with Gender Identity

Since sport is still strongly associated with masculinity, sport fandom is traditionally connected with men's leisure. The growing body of literature on women's experiences as sport fans challenges this hegemonic masculine view. But it has also highlighted the tensions that many women sport fans experience. As Jones (2008, p. 518) noted, since "fandom is defined in male terms … [how] is it possible to be both a woman and a fan? … [women] must negotiate between their gender and their fan identities." A dominant finding of this body of work is women express their gender identity and sport fandom, and the relationship between them, in a variety of ways (Hoeber & Kerwin, 2013; Jones, 2008; Osborne & Coombs, 2018; Sveinson & Hoeber, 2015, 2016).

Some women downplay femininity, emphasize masculinity, or highlight their sport knowledge in order to blend in and be accepted by men (Jones, 2008; Sveinson & Hoeber, 2016). For them and those around them, the belief is that "femininity and sport fanship are incongruent" (Sveinson & Hoeber, 2016, p. 14). Others refuse to adopt some of the dominant masculine traits of sport fandom, such as booing, excessive drinking, or sexist comments (Jones, 2008; Sveinson & Hoeber, 2015). In contrast, Toffoletti (2017, p. 467) commented on the post-feminist view of "women fans as simultaneously sexy and serious about sport." That is, women who adopt a hegemonic feminine identity (e.g., wearing heels, make-up, close-fitting clothing) and are also highly-identified sport fans.

Sveinson, Hoeber, and Toffoletti's (2019) study of women's perceptions of sport fan clothing demonstrated that they were not a homogenous group. Many professional men's sport teams in North America offer women the option of pink fan clothing. That colour for most women was viewed as incongruent with their sport identities (i.e., pink is not masculine) or team identities (i.e., no team's official colour was pink). Yet, some were willing to wear pink jerseys if it was connected with breast cancer awareness, suggesting that there are other identities (e.g., social causes) that can, at times, be compatible with one's team identity.

Although women's experiences as sport fans is a now a popular research topic, we have not seen much research that explores the dynamic ways men perform their sport fandom. Thus, emphasizing the importance of incorporating individual narratives into the study and understanding of how we perform sport fan identities.

Performing Fandom with Geographic (Community, Nationality) Identity

Narratives that stem from where individuals were raised, currently live, or their nationality are also important identities to consider. The popularity of sports is regionally specific. For example, curling and ice hockey are celebrated in Canada, while Australian Rules Football, rugby, and cricket are cultural icons in Australia. Many sport teams are a manifestation of their geographic community, by adopting colours, logos, and symbols that reflect the history and culture of their community. Further, fans are often "geographically bound" to their teams (Coombs & Osborne, 2018, p. 249). Thus, some people emphasize their nationality and community identities by following certain sports or teams.

The importance of team and sport identity is highlighted with individuals who have moved away from their "homes" (e.g., Kraszewski, 2008; Porat, 2010). Kraszewski's study of Pittsburgh Steelers' fans living in Texas showed that "displaced people … turn to sports fandom to rekindle lost local identities" (p. 155). Media supports the connection to one's original team by showing games on television or streaming. This area of work suggests that team identity is a stable and permanent part of one's life (Kraszewski, 2008; Porat, 2010), regardless of where one lives.

A different perspective exists with non-local or out-of-market fans of sport teams (Andrijiw & Hyatt, 2009; Coombs & Osborne, 2018). In their study of fans of nonlocal National Hockey League teams, Andrijiw and Hyatt (2009) found some individuals favoured the social distinctiveness of following a different team, instead of the sense of community and connectiveness sought by fans of local teams. Thus, their findings highlight unique individual narratives that alter a traditional view of sport fan in some communities (i.e., home to NHL team). As American women researchers following English football, Coombs and Osborne's (2018) narratives also highlighted a negotiation of outsider identity (based on their nationality and gender) and insider status as authentic fans and participant researchers.

Conclusion

The discussion above highlights the need to reflect on and adopt a multi-layered conceptualization of performative sport fan identity in sport management, and the utility of taking a holistic view of recognizing the intersection of narrative/ego identities, role identities, and social identities in our sport management scholarship. For the purpose of this chapter, we focused on several common intersections of identities where individual narratives must be considered. While we highlighted one role or identity (e.g., employee role) that interacted with team and sport identities. In reality, many identities interact together. As a pointed example, Osborne and Coombs' (2018) work illustrates the interaction between nationality, gender, and team identities.

Absent from this summary are several identities that are becoming increasingly important in the sport context, but have received relatively little scholarly attention. For example, are an activist identity and a sport fan identity compatible or in conflict? Or as Agyemang, Singer, and Weems (2020) ask: "Is sport an appropriate forum for activists to engage in political protest?" (p. 1). What happens when athletics do not "stick to sport"? By exploring these questions through a multi-layered lens, we will have a greater understanding of the nature of performative sport identities. To further the example, in North America, sport fans generally are not associated with overt political identities or roles. As noted by Totten (2015, p. 455), "Sport activism represents a radical challenge to the dominant conservative and functionalist social and political values which permeate football [soccer]." One example of compatibility between activism and team identity is fans of FC Sankt Pauli – a football club located in Hamburg, Germany, where the culture of the club is "avowedly libertarian left-wing and profoundly anti-fascist" (ibid., p. 457). People are drawn to this club because the culture is in line with their political ideologies. Their identification with the sport came later. Future research can explore how sport fans manage their political identities (e.g., feminist, liberal, fascist) in relation to their sport and team identities. Interestingly, although sport is typically thought of as apolitical, one could argue that North American sport leagues emphasize conservative values (e.g., military, traditional family units, Christian holidays). Further, some sport leagues, such the National Basketball League's NBA Cares program, are establishing the importance of particular social causes, like environmentalism.

Our main point is that while there are patterns of how identities connect, the dominant conceptualization of sport fandom has not adopted this complex and varied view of sport fan identity. People create their own narratives of how to perform their multiple identities. Therefore, in order to theoretically grasp the complexity of identity within the sport context; the layers of identity must be respected, explored, and understood as unstable and bond by the individual narratives of those who hold them.

Note

1 The Los Angeles Sparks play in the Women's National Basketball Association.

References

Agyemang, K. J. A., Singer, J. N., & Weems, A. J. (2020). "Agitate! Agitate! Agitate!": Sport as a site for political activism and social change. *Organization*, Advance online publication. doi: 10.1177/1350508420928519

Andrijiw, A. M., & Hyatt, C. G. (2009). Using optimal distinctiveness theory to understand identification with a nonlocal professional hockey team. *Journal of Sport Management*, 23, 156–181.

Caza, B. B., Vough, H., & Puranik, H. (2018). Identity work in organizations and occupations: Definitions, theories, and pathways forward. *Journal of Organizational Behaviour*, 39(7), 889–910.

Colombo, M., & Senatore, A. (2005). The discursive construction of community identity. *Journal of Community & Applied Social Psychology*, 15(1), 48–62.

Coombs, D. S., & Osborne, A. (2018). Negotiating insider-outsider status in ethnographic sports research. *Sport in Society*, 21(2), 243–259. https://doi.org/10.1080/17430437.2016.1221938

Cunningham, G. B., Dixon, M. A., Singer, J. N., Oshiro, K. F., Ahn, N. Y., & Weems, A. (2019). A site to resist and persist: Diversity, social justice, and the unique nature of sport. *Journal of Global Sport Management*. Advance online publication. https://doi.org/10.1080/24704067.2019.1578623

Delia, E. B., & James, J. D. (2018). The meaning of team in team identification. *Sport Management Review*, 21(4), 416–429.

Doyle, J. P., Lock, D., Funk, D. C., Filo, K., & McDonald, H. (2017). "I was there from the start": The identity-maintenance strategies used by fans to combat the threat of losing. *Sport Management Review*, 20(2), 184–197. https://doi.org/10.1016/j.smr.2016.04.006

Fairley, S., & Tyler, B. D. (2012). Bringing baseball to the big screen: Building sense of community outside of the ballpark. *Journal of Sport Management*, 26(3), 258–270.

Farrell, A., Fink, J., & Fields, S. (2011). Women's sport spectatorship: An exploration of Men's influence. *Journal of Sport Management*, 25(3), 190–201. https://doi.org/10.1123/jsm.25.3.190

Fink, J. S., Parker, H. M., Brett, M., & Higgins, J. (2009). Off-field behavior of athletes and team identification: Using social identity theory and balance theory to explain fan reactions. *Journal of Sport Management*, 23(2), 142–155. https://doi.org/10.1123/jsm.23.2.142

Heere, B. (2016). Team identity theory. In G. Cunningham, J. Fink, & A. Doherty (Eds.), *Routledge handbook of theory in sport management* (pp. 213–222). New York, NY: Taylor & Francis.

Heere, B., & James, J. D. (2007). Sports teams and their communities: Examining the influence of external group identities on team identity. *Journal of Sport Management*, 21(3), 319–337.

Hoeber, L., & Kerwin, S. (2013). Exploring the experiences of female sport fans: A collaborative self-ethnography. *Sport Management Review*, 16(3), 326–336. http://dx.doi.org/10.1016/j.smr.2012.12.002

Hogg, D., & Abrams, M. A. (1988). Comments on the motivational status of self-esteem in social identity and intergroup discrimination. *European Journal of Sport Psychology*, 18, 317–334.

Hyatt, C., & Foster, W. M. (2015). Using identity work theory to understand the de-escalation of fandom: A study of former fans of National Hockey League teams. *Journal of Sport Management*, 29, 443–460. doi:10.1123/jsm.2013-0327

Hyatt, C., Kerwin, S., Hoeber, L., & Sveinson, K. (2018). The reverse socialization of sport fans: How children impact their parents' sport fandom. *Journal of Sport Management*, 32(6), 542–554.

Inoue, Y., Funk, D. C., Wann, D. L., Yoshida, M., & Nakazawa, M. (2015). Team identification and postdisaster social well-being: The mediating role of social support. *Group Dynamics: Theory, Research, and Practice*, 19(1), 31–44. https://doi.org/10.1037/gdn0000019

James, J. (2001). The role of cognitive development and socialization in the initial development of team loyalty. *Leisure Sciences*, 23, 233–261. doi:10.1080/01490400152809106

Jones, K. (2008). Female fandom: Identity, sexism, and men's professional football in England. *Sociology of Sport Journal*, 25(4), 516–537.

Kerwin, S., & Hoeber, L. (2015). Collaborative self-ethnography: Navigating self-reflexivity in a sport management context. *Journal of Sport Management*, 29(5), 498–509.

Kraszewski, J. (2008). Pittsburgh in Fort Worth: Football bars, sports television, sports fandom, and the management of home. *Journal of Sport and Social Issues*, 32, 139–157. doi: 10.1177/0193723508316377

Lock, D. J., & Funk, D. C. (2016). The multiple in-group identity framework. *Sport Management Review*, *19*(2), 85–96. https://doi.org/10.1016/j.smr.2015.10.001

Lock, D., & Heere, B. (2017). Identity crisis: A theoretical analysis of 'team identification' research. *European Sport Management Quarterly*, *17*(4), 413–435. doi:10.1080/ 16184742.2017.1306872

Lock, D., Funk, D. C., Doyle, J. P., & McDonald, H. (2014). Examining the longitudinal structure, stability, and dimensional interrelationships of team identification. *Journal of Sport Management*, *28*(2), 119–135.

Lock, D., Taylor, T. L., Funk, D., & Darcy, S. A. (2012). Exploring the development of team identification: the contribution of social identity and the psychological continuum model. *Journal of Sport Management*, *26*, 283–294.

Mael, F. A., & Ashforth, B. E. (2001). Identification in work, war, sports, and religion: Contrasting the benefits and risks. *Journal for the Theory of Social Behaviour*, *31*(2), 197–222.

Manley, A., Morgan, H., & Atkinson, J. (2016). "Mzungu!": implications of identity, role formation and programme delivery in the sport for development movement. *International Journal of Sport Policy and Politics*, *8*(3), 383–402.

Mansfield, A. C. (2020). "Count the ways it impacts your life": New parenthood and sport fandom. *Journal of Sport Management*. Advance online publication. https://doi.org/10.1123/jsm.2019-0285

Marcia, J. E. (1980). Identity in adolescence. *Handbook of Adolescent Psychology*, *9*(11), 159–187.

McAdams, D. P., & McLean, K. C. (2013). Narrative identity. *Current Directions in Psychological Science*, *22*(3), 233–238.

Moore, J. (2015, June 19). *We want to believe: The creation of "sports fan" as brand identity*. The Guardian. www.theguardian.com/sport/2015/jun/19/we-want-to-believe-the-creation-of-sports-fan-as-brand-identity

Mudrick, M., Sauder, M. H., & Davies, M. (2019). When athletes don't "stick to sports": The relationship between athlete political activism and sport consumer behaviour. *Journal of Sport Behaviour*, *42*(2), 177–199.

Oja, B. D., Hazzaa, R. N., Wilkerson, Z., & Bass, J. R. (2018). March Madness in the collegiate sport workplace: Cultural implications for sport employees. *Journal of Intercollegiate Sport*, *11*, 82–105. https://doi.org/10.1123/jis.2018-0004

Osborne, A. C., & Coombs, D. S. (2013). Performative sport fandom: An approach to retheorizing sport fans. *Sport in Society: Cultures, Commerce, Media, Politics*, *16*(5), 672–681. http://dx.doi.org/10.1080/17430437.2012.753523

Popovic, M. (2010). A voIce in the rink: Playing with our histories and evoking autoethnography. *Journal of Sport History*, *37*, 235–255.

Porat, A. B. (2010). Football fandom: a bounded identification. *Soccer & Society*, *11*(3), 277–290. http://dx.doi.org/10.1080/14660971003619594

Ryan, C. (2018). Navigating the athlete role: identity construction within New Zealand's elite sport environment. *Qualitative Research in Sport, Exercise and Health*, *10*(3), 306–317.

Sagas, M., & Wendling, E. (2019, May 29 – June 1). *Integrating the identity construct in sport management: The Multilayer Identity Development System (MIDS) Model* [Conference session]. Annual Conference of the North American Society for Sport Management, New Orleans, LA, United States.

Smith, A. A., & Smith, A. D. (2011). March Madness, office gambling, and workplace productivity: An empirical study. *Sport, Business and Management*, *1*(2), 190–206. doi: 10.1108/20426781111146772

Spaaji, R., & Anderson, A. (2010). Psychosocial influences on children's identification with sports teams: A case study of Australian Rules Football supporters. *Journal of Sociology*, *46*, 299–315.

Stets, J. E., & Burke, P. J. (2000). Identity theory and social identity theory. *Social Psychology Quarterly*, 224–237.

Sveinson, K., & Hoeber, L. (2015). Overlooking the obvious: an exploration of what it means to be a sport fan from a female perspective. *Leisure Studies*, *34*(4), 405–419. http://dx.doi.org/10.1080/02614367.2014.923496

Sveinson, K., & Hoeber, L. (2016). Female sport fans' experiences of marginalization and empowerment. *Journal of Sport Management*, *30*, 8–21. http://dx.doi.org/10.1123/jsm2014-0221

Sveinson, K., Hoeber, L., & Toffoletti, K. (2019). "If people are wearing pink stuff they're probably not real fans": Exploring women's perceptions of sport fan clothing. *Sport Management Review*, *22*, 736–747.

Swanson, S., & Kent, A. (2015). Fandom in the workplace: Multi-target identification in professional team sports. *Journal of Sport Management*, *29*, 461–477.

Swanson, S., & Kent, A. (2017). Passion and pride in professional sports: Investigating the role of workplace emotion. *Sport Management Review*, *20*(4), 352–364.

Tajfel, H. (Ed.) (1978). Differentiation between social groups: Studies in the social psychology of intergroup relations. *European Monographs in Social Psychology No. 14*, Academic Press, London.

Tinson, J., Sinclair, G., & Kolyperas, D. (2017). Sport fandom and parenthood. *European Sport Management Quarterly, 17*(3), 370–391.

Toffoletti, K. (2017). Sexy women sports fans: Femininity, sexuality, and the global sport spectacle. *Feminist Media Studies, 17*(3), 457–472. https://doi.org/10.1080/14680777.2016.1234499

Totten, M. (2015). Sport activism and political praxis within the FC Sankt Pauli fan subculture. *Soccer & Society, 16*(4), 453–468. https://doi.org/10.1080/14660970.2014.882828

Vignoles, V. L., Schwartz, S. J., & Luyckx, K. (2011). Introduction: Toward an integrative view of identity. In S. J. Schwartz, K. Luyckx, & V. L. Vignoles (Eds.) *Handbook of identity theory and research* (pp. 1–27). New York, NY: Springer.

Wakefield, K. L., & Wann, D. L. (2006). An examination of dysfunctional sport fans: Method of classification and relationships with problem behaviours. *Journal of Leisure Research, 38*(2), 168–186.

Wann, D. L., & Branscombe, N. R. (1991). The positive social and self-concept consequences of sports team identification. *Journal of Sport and Social Issues, 15*(2), 115–127.

Wann, D. L., Haynes, G., McLean, B., & Pullen, P. (2003). Sport team identification and willingness to consider anonymous acts of hostile aggression. *Aggressive Behaviour: Official Journal of the International Society for Research on Aggression, 29*(5), 406–413.

Wann, D. L., & Pierce, S. (2003). Measuring sport team identification and commitment: An empirical comparison of the Sport Spectator Identification Scale and the Psychological Commitment to Team Scale. *North American Journal of Psychology, 5*(3), 365–372.

Warner, S., Dixon, M. A., & Chalip, L. (2012). The impact of formal versus informal sport: Mapping the differences in sense of community. *Journal of Community Psychology, 40*(8), 983–1003.

Wegner, C., Delia, E. B., & Baker, B. J. (2020). Fan response to the identity threat of potential team relocation. *Sport Management Review, 23*(2), 215–228. https://doi.org/10.1016/j.smr.2019.01.001

Wegner, C. E., Jones, G. J., & Jordan, J. S. (2019). Voluntary sensemaking: The identity formation process of volunteers in sport organizations. *European Sport Management Quarterly, 19*, 625–644.

Wu, S. H., Tsai, C. Y. D., & Hung, C. C. (2012). Toward team or player? How trust, vicarious achievement motive, and identification affect fan loyalty. *Journal of Sport Management, 26*(2), 177–191.

14
Women Sports Fans

Katharine Jones, Stacey Pope and Kim Toffoletti

Introduction

Sports fandom research has typically focused upon the importance of sport for men and constructing men's hegemonic identities. However, there is a growing body of research which seeks to redress this imbalance by centralising the experiences of women as sports fans. This chapter provides an overview of current debates and emergent issues in sport fan research about women. It draws on existing literature in the field, along with findings from a selection of research projects that the authors have conducted in the UK and Australia to map key developments in theorising women's sport fan practices and experiences.

The chapter is divided into three sections. The first section establishes the ways in which women's sport fandom has been characterised relative to men's fandom as 'inferior' and how women have been constructed as 'inauthentic' sports fans. Drawing on a preliminary model of female fandom which examines two broadly drawn female fan types ('hot' and 'cool'), findings are used to challenge perceptions of women as inferior sports fans. The second section explores gender performativity and women's fandom, looking at women's experiences in sport stadiums to understand the ways in which they negotiate gender identities and sport fan identities. We note that the experiences of women fans differ based on their race, sexuality and class positions, but that the ideal-typical woman fan has usually been conceptualised as white, middle class and heterosexual. In the final section, we look at representations of women sport fans in the media, including social media. An analysis of mediated representations of women supporters offers an avenue to consider how discourses of female empowerment and capacity are shaping perceptions of women as followers of sport.

Issues of (In)Authenticity for Women Sports Fans

In January 2020, the management body the Chartered Management Institute made headlines in the UK when it claimed that talking about sport in the workplace served to exclude women. According to company head, Ann Francke, 'A lot of women, in particular, feel left out. They don't follow those sports and they don't like either being forced to talk about them or not being included in the conversation' (Petter, 2020). This account demonstrates the gendered assumptions that typically surround men and women when it comes to their involvement in sport; whereas men are 'naturally' assumed to be fans of sport, women are not. Such stereotypes are also found in media representations of men and women in sport where women are portrayed in highly sexualized roles or assumed to have no knowledge of sport (see final section). These kinds of damaging assumptions that are rooted in allegedly 'natural' differences between the sexes also serve to reinforce perceptions of women as 'inauthentic' sports fans (Pope, 2017a).

The notion that women are inauthentic sports fans is a theme that also runs across the literature on sports fandom. For example, Hoeber and Kerwin (2013) suggest that there is a commonly held belief that women lack knowledge of sport and follow sports for inappropriate reasons, such as to socialise with friends. For Esmonde et al. (2015, p. 35), whereas men are awarded 'legitimate status' based on their gender alone, women are deemed to be 'illegitimate' and are assumed to follow sport for inauthentic reasons, including (hetero)sexual desire or because of a male partners' interest. Thus, there is a gendered hierarchy in sports fandom whereby men are seen as 'authentic' or 'real' fans and women as 'inauthentic' or 'inferior' in their support. This can be largely attributed to how sport has been constructed as a profoundly 'male preserve' (Dunning, 1994; Messner, 2002) and the subsequent links between masculinity and fandom.

Such notions of inauthenticity for women fans of men's sports span across different sports and different continents. For example, 'women [are assumed to attend rugby union] matches because of their interest in men' (Collins, 2009, p. 93) and in UK ice hockey, the term 'puck bunnies' has been applied to women fans, suggesting that these fans lack dedication and only go to matches to 'lust' after male players (Crawford & Gosling, 2004). In the NFL in the US, Osborne and Coombs (2016) found that men are assumed to be more knowledgeable than women, while Chiweshe (2014, p. 220) showed that women who complain about the highly misogynistic culture of Zimbabwean football stadia have been met with accusations of being 'fake fans' from male supporters. In some cases, women's alleged lack of experience in *playing* the sport can lead to questions around their sporting 'capital'; for example, in Australian rules football, Mewett and Toffoletti (2010) found that women were assumed to lack knowledge as a result of allegedly not playing the sport and Danish women football fans are seen as 'football groupies who do not know the rules, want to "score" the players or are only in the stadium to find a boyfriend' (Pfister et al., 2013, p. 858). Likewise, Pope's (2017b) women respondents, fans of football and rugby union in the UK, gave numerous examples of attempts from men to put them on the spot or make them 'prove' their sporting credentials. Thus, women fans must work significantly harder to earn their position as authentic members of a fan group (Dixon, 2015). As fans of *men's* sports, such women may pose a direct challenge to men who seek to use sports fandom to prove that they are 'real men' (Pfister et al., 2013). Being a fan of women's sports can perhaps offer the potential for more welcoming spaces for *some* women; Allison's (2018) research in the US showed that women's football offered a safe space for young girls and heterosexual married women, although lesbian women and adults without children were excluded. This research illustrates the need to complicate the idea of 'women fans' by incorporating feminist notions of intersectionality, as well as attending to transnationality. Below, we challenge perceptions of women as inauthentic sports fans by examining the important role that sports fandom can play in women's lives and identities.

The Importance of Sport for Women: A Model of Female Fandom

Co-author Pope (2017b) interviewed 85 women fans of rugby union and football in the UK to examine the idea that women are inauthentic or inferior sports fans. She measured respondents' level of fandom using responses to a question on whether being a fan of the club was 'an important part of who you are'. Other indicators included whether they are affected when the club wins/loses; the amount of time dedicated to watching or thinking about sport; and if people who knew them related to them as a fan. Pope (2017b) reformulated Giulianotti's (2002) 'hot' and 'cool' axis to incorporate the experiences of women fans. This framework indicates the different degrees the club is central to a fan's project of self-formation: 'hot' forms of loyalty denote intense forms of identification and 'cool' forms involve lower levels of attachment. Pope's (2017b) findings showed two broadly drawn women fan types: 'hot' committed fans for whom the club formed a central interest and an important component of their identity and 'cool', more casual fans for whom the club was not a central life interest and fandom was viewed as one of many leisure activities. There was a continuum between 'hot' and 'cool' with varying levels of fan attachment. Just like men, women fans are a diverse group, despite the insistence that sport is a male preserve (Dunning, 1994; Messner, 2002).

Additionally, women do not simply become fans due to a male partner's interest or their own (hetero)sexual interest in players (Esmonde et al., 2015; Hoeber & Kerwin, 2013); as Pope's (2017b) findings show, sport is central to the lives and identities of many women. Nearly 85 percent of the football fans she interviewed (43/51) and just under half (16/34) of the rugby fans were 'hot' sports fans. For these women, sport was an important aspect of their identity. 'Hot' fans would typically have rooms, or even a home, decorated in club colours and products. Large amounts of their leisure time would be taken up by watching or thinking about sport and results would typically impact their mood, meaning that relations with close relatives were also affected. As the club was such an important part of their lives, it was difficult to organise other activities like weddings around football fixtures. Scholars in Israel and Australia similarly found that sport is a 'way of life' for women fans (Ben-Porat, 2009, p. 890), creating tensions when fixtures clashed with family functions (Mewett & Toffoletti, 2010).

Further evidence of the importance of sport for women's identities can be seen by how some heterosexual 'hot' women fans in Pope's (2017b) study discussed how they would not enter relationships with men who did not support the same club or would threaten to end relationships if male partners did not accompany them to matches. However, for 'cool' fans, sport did not bleed into other areas of their lives in the same manner. The club was not important enough to impact upon personal relationships and watching sport was regarded more as a hobby rather than a central life interest.

Our aim here is not to valorise one type of fandom over another—or construct 'hot' fans as exhibiting a superior form of fandom over 'cool' fans. Indeed, as co-author Jones (2008, p. 518) has noted, fandom has tended to be defined in 'male terms'. Thus, traditional (typically 'masculine') forms of fandom (attending matches in groups, being loud and aggressive, having high levels of passion and a local attachment to the club) are often deemed as superior to other (coded 'feminine') forms of fandom or 'new fandom' (i.e. fans characterised as having a weaker attachment to the club, attending matches with a family group, or following sport through the allegedly weaker platform of the media rather than through live attendance) (Nash, 2000). Our purpose in this section is rather to show that for some women, sports fandom can be one of the most important, if not *the* most important, part of their lives. As well as seeing yourself as a mother, sister or lover, you see yourself as a fan, part of a community where you assume comradeship with all others who love your team. The team's fortunes become your own; you may begin to define yourself in opposition to those who oppose your team; and part of your happiness relates to the success or failure of your team. Thus, how you define yourself is vitally connected to the activities, personnel, and ethos of the team. This is evidenced by the strong connections many women fans express towards sport, the feelings of pleasure they gain through following sport—despite the inequalities that are typically embedded within women's sports fandom and the perceptions of inauthenticity that surround women supporters.

Performativity and Women's Fandom

Fandom and gender scholarship have used the idea of performativity to theorise the relationship between individual fan practices and wider social structures. Performativity, and particularly gendered performativity, emphasises the dailiness and micro-level work done by social actors to exist in the world, to perform a sense of themselves (Butler, 1990; Connell, 1987; West & Zimmerman, 1987). Sport scholars have offered a theory of 'fan performativity' (Osborne & Coombs, 2016; see also Jones, 2008; Sandvoss & Ball, 2018), who understand it to include the behavioural aspects of being a fan. This, according to Osborne and Coombes, allows an understanding of behaviour as relational, contextually situated and open to negotiation. Performativity theory places a sense of self—one's identity—front and centre, operating before the gaze of others. However, being a fan also involves embracing an aspect of the world so strongly that it starts to become a part of you, even when there are no others present. Sandvoss and Ball (2018, p. 292, citing Stacey, 1994) illustrate how this idea of identity also relates to the projection of affect and 'identificatory fantasies'.

For supposedly 'inauthentic' women fans, the issue of performance is tenuous. Women's gender is already viewed as 'the other' in many facets of everyday life, since their bodies are often coded as out-of-place or the sexualised object of the male gaze in public locations of work and leisure (Acker, 1990). In leisure activities, as long as women are accompanied by children or a male partner, they can be infantilised as 'women and children' or devalued as 'wives or girlfriends'. Their femininity has historically been presumed to be antithetical to the hegemonically masculine rough and tumble world of sport (Connell, 1987; Messner, 2002; Pope, 2017b; Toffoletti, 2017) and indeed, research on women's soccer fandom suggests that women have been largely invisible in the public imaginary, and among sports scholars, until recently (Pope & Williams, 2018).

Their invisibility as fans means that the performance of gendered fandom for women sport fans is often contradictory and full of tension. Whether it be in a bar/pub, at a live game, shouting at your television, or simply telling other people that you follow or support a particular team, sport fandom is a performance. Likewise, gender is 'an incessant and repeated action' (Butler, 1990, p. 143). Indeed, although co-author Jones (2008) has previously argued that, like gender, fandom is something you 'do', rather than something you 'are', it seems to be both what you do and who you are. Focusing on performance reminds us that both gender and fandom are social constructs, liable to contestation and challenge even in moment-to-moment engagements. We can note the similarities between gender performance and fan performance: clothing choices and accoutrements like flags, bags or hats; make-up/face-paint; voice pitch (how loudly to sing a song or the way one chants); vocabulary; and other routine or unnoticed actions like when to stand up or sit down, when to sigh at a player and when to swear, even when watching a game alone in the home, let alone when one attends a live match.

Co-author Jones's (2008) research on fans of men's English football shows the ways that women who may see themselves as feminine in their everyday lives can take on the characteristics of hegemonically masculine fan performance when they enter football stadiums, sometimes looking down on women who fail to perform masculine-coded versions of fan practices, like swearing, using sexist or homophobic language, or even simply standing up (see also Pfister et al., 2013). Other research on women who create women-only spaces at football matches confirms this analysis, in that women may separate themselves from women who act in what they see as feminine ways (for instance, giggling or lusting) (Llopis-Goig & Flores, 2018). Women may even resort to violence to prove that they are masculine and should be seen as 'one of the boys' (Pope, 2017b; Radmann & Hedenborg, 2018).

While Sandvoss and Ball (2018) point out that understanding the intersections of gender and fan identities is vital, analysis of how intersectional identities and structures work in terms of other axes of difference has been lacking for women sports fans. As well as considering the *gendering* of fans, we must consider how fans are raced, sexualised, classed, and are also potentially affected by other aspects of identity and structure like ableism, regionalism, nationalism, ethnic bias, sizeism, etc. (and men of course need to be included in this list, since they are also gendered, raced, etc.) (Back et al., 2001, Jones, 2013; 2017; Toffoletti, 2017). This leads to an understanding of fandom and fan performance that incorporates the feminist notion of intersectionality (Combahee River Collective, 2002/1979; Crenshaw, 1991; Jones, 2017; cf. Esmonde et al., 2015; Scraton et al., 2005).

Inviting an understanding of intersectionality into sports fandom helps to explain the experiences of women fans who may not conform to the representations of female fandom that are shown in the media or valorised by marketing teams (see next section). If they are not white, not overtly heterosexual, or not slim or conventionally attractive, they may be subject to different kinds of judgement or abuse. For instance, lesbians that co-author Jones interviewed would not risk holding hands with their lover at football; one lesbian fan had her rainbow flag stolen by straight fans during an away game—and was subjected to homophobic and sexist abuse on a fan forum after she complained (2013). Jones also interviewed veiled Asian and Black women in the early 2000s who were frightened of going to football matches because they were worried about experiencing Islamophobic and racist abuse (see also Ratna (2014) on the experiences of Asian British women at football matches). Thus, it is imperative to recognize that fan performance may mean different things for women of colour and/or lesbian and/or trans and/or differently abled women; combining intersectional theory with performativity theory may be a way to conceptualise the ways agency is constrained or enabled for these women.

Mediated Fandom

Despite a solid body of empirical research documenting women's presence and practices as sport fans, women supporters and fan communities remain underrepresented and misrepresented across traditional and digital media (Antunovic & Hardin, 2015; Wenner, 2012). The lack of images of women sport fans in the mass media consolidates ideas previously raised in this chapter—that the imagined 'typical' sport supporter is male, white and heterosexual, and that women's ardent devotion to sport is an anomaly. Media representations uphold gender differences and inequalities by constructing a narrow picture of the sport supporter, what they should look like and the qualities they should exhibit, which tend to favour white masculine (i.e. 'hot' or traditional) supporter ideals.

When women fans are portrayed in the media, it is often in gender-stereotypical ways, with a handful of studies exploring representations of women's sport fans across Western media and advertising. Sport advertisers have, generally speaking, moved away from depicting women as disinterested 'sport widows' toward representing women as devoted sport fans in their pursuit of new fan markets. Wenner's (2012) examination of a global (but US-centric) database of sport-themed television commercials reveals that, despite growing recognition of women as followers of sport, they are portrayed primarily as wives, mothers, girlfriends or object of male desire. Ads show women fans in gender-stereotypical roles cleaning, shopping and caring for others, and as vulnerable, weak, emotional and passive. By associating women's fandom with socially valorised expressions of femininity, the message remains that fandom and femininity are incompatible. Wenner observes that women's interest in sport is presented primarily in terms of a desire to please men, rather than portraying women's passion for sport (Wenner, 2012,

p. 206). This research indicates that mainstream media accounts rarely represent sport fandom from the perspective of women themselves, instead consolidating restrictive gender expectations socially assigned to women. It also highlights the lack of media portrayals and critical analysis that addresses intersections of race, ethnicity, sexuality, class, and other axes of difference in representations of women as sport fans.

The sexy sport fan is another gender stereotype found in media representations. Research examining television, online and print news reporting of the FIFA men's World Cup identifies the prevalence of hypersexualised images of women fans, which function to delegitimise women's fan performances and consolidate the notion that sport is a male spectacle (Tanaka, 2004; Pope, 2017b; Toffoletti, 2017). By focusing most attention on images and performances of young and conventionally (hetero)sexually attractive women sport fans, media imagery normalises and supports uneven gender relations of power that sustain the privilege of men's sport. These patterns suggest that increased visibility of women fans in the media does not always lead to a transformation in the values and practices that consolidate men's sport participation as the norm (Toffoletti, 2017). Research on representations of women's sport fandom in traditional media reveal enduring societal perceptions of women sport supporters and the requirements expected of those women in the male-dominated sport media. In granting visibility to women sport fans who most closely conform to male-defined ideals, and characterising women's displays of (hetero)sexiness as personal choice, the sport media does little to challenge hierarchies of gender difference in sport.

In some instances, media representations have incorporated more culturally diverse representations of women sport fans. A notable example is the 2015 Men's Cricket World Cup, held in Australia. Billboard advertising for the tournament rejected tropes of 'heterosexy' femininity in favour of images of passionate women supporters from competing nations such as India, The West Indies, Bangladesh and South Africa. Despite appearing progressive, these images do not threaten men's primacy and colonial power in sport. Rather, these representations reinforce myths of sport as a conduit for global harmony, transmitting the perception that sport is devoid of racism, and that cricket can help overcome ethnic and gender divisions so that women can participate fully and freely as sport supporters. Moreover, selling a message of universal female solidarity negates the differences between women, as transnational and intersectional feminists have shown (Mohanty, 2003; Crenshaw, 1991). Transnational feminist scholarship enabled co-author Toffoletti to illuminate how sport media imagery erases the socio-political conditions and cultural expectations of gender, race, class, sexuality and national identity, which shape women's ongoing experiences of gender inequality in sport (2017).

Social Media and Fan Self-Presentations

As well as investigating representations in conventional media, feminist scholarship has also examined women's digital sport fan communities. Research suggests that interactive networked technologies allow women sport fans to bypass sports media that sideline women's voices and experiences and instead support alternative fan representations and performances (Kunert, 2019; Pegoraro et al., 2018). This research indicates that social media can increase the presence and visibility of women as followers of sport, offering an avenue for women sport fans to rework sexist representations that characterise women's supporting modes as lacking authenticity and credibility.

In a recent study, co-author Toffoletti and her colleagues (2020) examined pictures tagged to a major women's sport event—The 2015 FIFA Women's World Cup—on Instagram. Hashtags are an important feature in social media communication, and women sport fans have used hashtags to draw attention to gender issues, to mark virtual conversations about sportswomen and events, and to connect through documenting and sharing their experiences (Antunovic & Linden, 2015; Toffoletti et al., 2020; Pegoraro et al., 2018). By producing their own user-generated content, women sport fans can craft their own representations and forge their own communities. For some women, these self-created communities are preferable to online message boards or official social media pages of sport clubs and leagues, where sexist attitudes discourage women's participation (Kunert, 2019).

Platform-specific capabilities make possible different performances of sport fandom and fan identities. For instance, Toffoletti, Pegoraro and Comeau's research (2020) suggests that women are consciously selecting Instagram because of its platform affordances. It allows them to present their fandom in the context of their lifestyle and identities; to participate in creative forms of fan engagement; and to represent their fan experience from their point of view and in ways that are meaningful and relevant to them. This includes match-day selfies (individual and collective) that share the joys of fandom with a networked audience, and more intimate photos that capture pre-match rituals in private spaces like bedrooms. In contrast to mainstream sport media representations, sexualised displays of femininity are rarely found in women's sport fans self-portrayals (Toffoletti et al., 2020; Toffoletti, 2017). By combining their fan presentation with established Instagram genres (like fitspo, tourism and selfies), women users expand the possibilities of sport fandom, thereby challenging traditional notions of 'hot' and 'cool' fandom, and performing fandom in ways that are different from male-defined norms.

Women's online self-presentations of their fan experiences can support a wider political feminist sports media agenda to increase the visibility of women's sport. User-generated digital content can enable women fans of diverse race, ethnicity, class, ability and sexuality to make their presence felt online, as a means to legitimate their participation in sport communities, communicate fan commitment and authenticity, and challenge perceptions of women's sport fandom as inauthentic. As can be seen in the digital community of women football fans 'This Fan Girl' (www.thisfangirl.com/), the self-imagery being shared does not attempt to attract men or emulate men's fan practices. As such, women fans' self-representations as empowered and agentic social actors prompts a rethinking of femininity and fandom through alternative theoretical frameworks. Co-author Toffoletti has sought to do this by analysing representations of women sport fans in fashion advertising and at women's sport events relative to contemporary formations of postfeminist femininity (2017). This framework pays critical attention to social conditions whereby sport fandom is made appealing to women, and to the changing expectations for women to demonstrate personal empowerment across localised and global sport contexts (Toffoletti et al., 2018). Such critical feminist approaches can help us make sense of socio-cultural transformations in the sport-gender landscape whereby femininity and fandom are no longer considered incompatible. These approaches also provide a critical framework for interrogating how contemporary articulations of 'empowered' fan femininities as they intersect with vectors of difference such as race, ethnicity, class, ability and sexuality, are invoked and managed in sport contexts.

Conclusion

In surveying key developments in the field of women sport fan studies, this chapter identifies a number of ongoing themes of feminist and sociological concern. These include the workings of gendered, sexualized and racialised power in the production of sport fan identities; affective dimensions—feelings of pleasure and connection—women experience through following sport;

and the political potential of alternative fan performances and identities to challenge dominant white heteronormative and male ideals of fandom.

In conclusion, we point to potential research areas warranting further feminist intervention, including (but not limited to) the need for new theoretical and conceptual frameworks for analysing women's sport fan practices that move beyond comparisons to a masculine 'norm'; greater recognition of the meanings of sport fandom for supporters of women's sport, particularly beyond the global north and using intersectional perspectives; transnational encounters and solidarities between women supporters of globalised sports and sport events; women's experiences as sports fans historically which have been largely neglected due to assumptions that sports stadia were spaces for exclusively men; and the relationship between women's fandom and consumer culture in the context of neoliberalism and discourses of empowerment and choice.

References

Acker, J. (1990). Hierarchies, jobs, bodies: A theory of gendered organizations. *Gender and Society*, 4(2), 139–158. www.jstor.org/stable/189609
Allison, R. (2018) *Kicking Centre*. Rutgers University Press.
Antunovic, D., & Hardin, M. (2015). Women and the blogosphere: Exploring feminist approaches to sport. *International Review for the Sociology of Sport*, 50(6), 661–677.
Antunovic, D., & Linden, A. (2015). Disrupting dominant discourses: #HERESPROOF of interest in women's sports. *Feminist Media Studies*, 15(1), 157–159.
Back, L., Crabbe, T., & Solomos, J. (2001). *The Changing Face of Football: Racism, Identity and Multiculture in the English Game*. Berg.
Ben-Porat, A. (2009). Not just for men: Israeli women who fancy football. *Soccer and Society*, 10(6), 883–896.
Butler, J. (1990). *Gender Trouble: Feminism and the Subversion of Identity*. Routledge.
Chiweshe, M. (2014). One of the boys: female fans' responses to the masculine and phallocentric nature of football stadiums in Zimbabwe. *Critical African Studies*, 6(203), 211–222.
Collins, T. (2009). *A Social History of English Rugby Union*. Routledge.
Combahee River Collective. (2002) [1979]. The Combahee River Collective Statement. In B.J. Balliet & P. McDaniel (Eds). *Women, Culture and Society: A Reader* (pp. 15–22). Kendall/Hunt.
Connell, R.W. (1987). *Gender and Power: Society, the Person and Sexual Politics*. Stanford University Press.
Crawford, G. and Gosling, K. (2004). The myth of the 'puck bunny': Female fans and men's ice hockey. *Sociology*, 38(3), 477–493.
Crenshaw, K. (1991). Mapping the margins: Intersectionality, identity politics, and violence against women of color. *Stanford Law Review*, 43(6), 1241–1299.
Dixon, K. (2015). A woman's place recurring: Structuration, football fandom and sub-cultural subservience. *Sport in Society*, 16(6), 636–651.
Dunning, E. (1994). Sport as a male preserve: Notes on the social sources of masculine identity and its transformations. In Birrell, S. & Cole, C. (Eds), *Women, Sport and Culture*. Human Kinetics, pp. 163–179.
Esmonde, K., Cooky, C., & Andrews, D.L. (2015). It's supposed to be about the love of the game, not love of Aaron Rodgers' eyes: Challenging the exclusions of women's sports fans. *Sociology of Sport Journal*, 32(1), 22–48.
Giulianotti, R. (2002). Supporters, followers, fans, and flaneurs. *Journal of Sport and Social Issues*, 26(1), 25–46.
Hoeber, L. and Kerwin, S. (2013). Exploring the experiences of female sport fans: A collaborative self-ethnography. *Sport Management Review*, 16, 326–336.
Jones, K. (2008). Female fandom: Identity, sexism, and men's professional football in England. *Sociology of Sport Journal*, 25, 516–537.
Jones, K. (2013, November 7). 'Unacceptable' words: Are Attitudes Towards Homophobic and Sexist Abuse in English Football Changing? Presented at North American Society for the Sociology of Sport, Quebec City, Canada.
Jones, K. (2017, May 23). Will the Real Fans Please Stand Up? Negotiating Gendered Authenticity in English Football, Invited Presentation at Deakin University, Melbourne, Australia.
Kunert, J. (2019). The footy girls of Tumblr: How women found their niche in the online football fandom. *Communication & Sport*. Online before print. DOI: 10.1177/2167479519860075

Llopis-Goig, R., & Flores, H. (2018). Challenging or Accommodating the Football System? A Case Study of Female Football Supporter Communities in Spain. In G. Pfister & S. Pope (Eds.), *Female Football Players and Fans: Intruding into a Man's World* (pp. 259–278). Palgrave Macmillan.

Messner, M.A. (2002) *Taking the Field: Women, Men, and Sports*. University of Minnesota Press.

Mewett, P. and Toffoletti, K. (2010). Voices from the margins? Women at the footy. *Intergraph*, 3(1), 1–8.

Mohanty, C.T. (2003). *Feminism Without Borders: Decolonizing Theory, Practicing Solidarity*. Duke University Press.

Nash, R. (2000). Contestation in modern football. *International Review for the Sociology of Sport*, 35(4), 465–486.

Osborne, A., & Coombs, D. (2016). *Female fans of the NFL*. Routledge.

Pegoraro, A., Comeau, G., & Frederick, E. (2018). #SheBelieves: Fans' use of social media to frame the US women's soccer team during #FIFAWWC. *Sport in Society*, 21(7), 1063–1077.

Petter, O. (2020). Talking about sport at work excludes women and leads to laddish behaviour, warns management body. *The Independent*, 27 January 2020. Available at: www.independent.co.uk/life-style/women/sport-work-talking-sexist-ban-men-ann-francke-chartered-management-institute-a9303881.html

Pfister, G., Lenneis, V. & Mintert, S. (2013). Female fans of men's football – a case study in Denmark. *Soccer and Society*, 14(6), 850–871.

Pope, S. (2017a). Female fans of men's football. In Hughson, J., Moore, K., Spaaij, R., & Maguire, J. (Eds) *Routledge Handbook of Football Studies*. Routledge.

Pope, S. (2017b). *The Feminization of Sports Fandom*. Routledge.

Pope, S., & Williams, J. (2018). A socio-historical account of female experiences of football's golden age in England. In G. Pfister & S. Pope (Eds.), *Female Football Players and Fans: Intruding into a Man's World* (pp. 157–184). Palgrave Macmillan.

Radmann, A. & Hedenborg, S. (2018). Women's football supporter culture in Sweden. In G. Pfister & S. Pope (Eds.), *Female Football Players and Fans: Intruding into a Man's World* (pp. 241–258). Palgrave Macmillan.

Ratna, A. (2014). 'Who are ya?' The national identities and belongings of British Asian football fans. *Patterns of Prejudice*, 48(3), 286–308. DOI:10.1080/0031322X.2014.927603

Sandvoss, C., & Ball, E. (2018). Gender, play and identity: A longitudinal study of structure and agency in female football fandom. In G. Pfister & S. Pope (Eds.), *Female Football Players and Fans: Intruding into a Man's World* (pp. 279–307). Palgrave Macmillan.

Scraton, S., Caudwell, J., & Holland, S. (2005). 'Bend it like Patel': Centring 'race', ethnicity and gender in feminist analysis of women's football in England. *International Review for the Sociology of Sport*, 40(1), 71–88. https://doi.org/10.1177/1012690205052169

Stacey, J. (1994). *Stargazing: Hollywood Cinema and Female Spectatorship*. Routledge.

Tanaka, T. (2004). The positioning and practices of the 'feminized fan' in Japanese soccer culture through the experience of the FIFA world Cup Korea/Japan 2002. *Inter-Asia Cultural Studies*, 5(1), 52–62.

Toffoletti, K. (2017). *Women Sport Fans*. Routledge.

Toffoletti, K., Pegoraro, A., & Comeau, G. (2020). Self-representations of women's sport fandom on Instagram at the 2015 FIFA Women's World Cup, *Communication & Sport*. Online before print. DOI: 10.1177%2F2167479519893332

Toffoletti, K., Thorpe, H., & Francombe-Webb, J. (Eds.) (2018). *New Sporting Femininities: Embodied Politics in Postfeminist Times*. Palgrave Macmillan.

Wenner, L. (2012). From Football Widow to Fan: Web Narratives of Women and Sports Spectatorship. In A. C. Earnheardt, P. M. Haridakis, & B. S. Hugenberg, (Eds) *Sports Fans, Identity, and Socialization: Exploring the Fandemonium*. Lexington (pp. 203–220).

West, C., & Zimmerman, D. (1987). Doing gender. *Gender & Society*, 1(2) 125–151.

15
The Sports Fanship Lifecycle

Irene I. van Driel, Walter Gantz and Lawrence A. Wenner

Happiness increases with age. Socioemotional selectivity theory (SST; Carstensen, Isaacowitz, & Charles, 1999) attributes this increase to a gradual shift in focus on activities and experiences that are meaningful and positive. Older adults are more strongly motivated than younger adults to engage in activities and relationships that contribute to happiness and to avoid those that do not. Research on happiness shows that increases in life satisfaction are not linear and tend to peak roughly when people reach their sixties (Charles & Carstensen, 2010). If, with age, people become more mindful about how they want to spend their time, this likely has important implications for how sports fanship is experienced across the lifecycle and thus, for core understandings that both scholars and practitioners have about sports fandom.

Indeed, research on the lifecycle of sports fans is gaining traction in the sports industry and the academic world. Based on Nielsen television viewership data of all major sports, the sports fan seems to be aging (Lombardo & Broughton, 2017). This increase in median age seems to be due largely to a drop in the amount of live sports TV viewership among younger generations. Much evidence suggests that millennials are less invested in watching live sports than older generations (Singer, 2017). At the same time, in 2009 ESPN reported that, at least for men, sports fanship becomes less ardent with age (ESPN, 2009). Zooming in on older sports fans, these results suggest two potentially antithetical patterns of change: Nielsen's TV ratings show an aging audience for televised sports whereas ESPN's results suggest that fanship wanes with age.

While tugging in different directions, both patterns have received support. Researchers have found that fanship – or indicators thereof such as the amount of sports media consumption – decreases with age (Brown, Billings, & Ruihley, 2012; Gantz & Lewis, 2021). Yet, other studies have indicated the opposite (Toder Alon, Icekson, & Shuv-Ami, 2019), or displayed mixed results (van Driel & Gantz, 2019). Explanations for a decline in fanship with age center on the decreasing appeal of the emotional intensity of sports and a gradual shift in focus to activities considered more personally meaningful (van Driel & Gantz, 2019). The potential increase in fanship over time is ascribed to the never-wavering strength of the emotional connection and loyalty fans experience with their favorite teams or athletes (Tapp, 2004; Toder-Alon et al., 2019).

In this chapter we will provide an overview of fanship across the adult lifespan and demonstrate how these paradoxical findings may be reconciled with the help of Carstensen's socioemotional selectivity theory (Carstensen et al., 1999). In short, this chapter aims to examine the relationship between sports fanship and aging. In doing so, we will describe changes in fanship across age groups (and thus across generations) and will also document individual-level fanship patterns (within generations). We will investigate how these trends are likely to be dependent on levels of sports fanship.

Sports Fanship and Age

Shifting Patterns of Viewership

Sports fanship comes in all shapes and forms: Some are avid fans of one specific team or sport, others of their college or city's teams, still others follow a multitude of team and athletes across sports as yet again others are fans of anything that allows them to watch with friends (van Driel, Gantz & Lewis, 2019). Changes in levels in fanship with age can thus also be conveyed and assessed in a variety of ways. Typically, the sports industry looks at TV viewership variables and has documented an increase in the average age of the live TV sports viewer (Lombardo & Broughton, 2017). For example, in 2006 the average NASCAR TV viewer was 49 years old. In 2017, that average age increased to 58. The aging viewer also holds true for other major professional, US-based leagues such as the NHL, NFL, MLB and the NBA. It appears that the aging audience for live TV sports is mostly the result of two factors: The first is a decrease in viewership among younger generations and the second is a change in the way people view live televised sports.

Singer (2017) argues that the decline in viewership should not be attributed to a lack of interest in sports among millennials but instead to changing sports consumption patterns. Nielsen ratings showed an increase in overall NFL viewership in 2016–2017 even though total viewing time declined (Nielsen, 2018). These findings suggest that sports viewers have become less likely to watch entire games and instead prefer to drop in and out, with their attention spans shorter and their interests more truncated than before. In particular, many in the younger generation of fans are prone to watch clips and check news and statistics that have become ubiquitous (Singer, 2017). At the same time, Nielsen ratings seem to demonstrate that this viewership pattern is in fact true for all generations. Singer (2017) states that "sports fans of all ages are clicking away from low-stakes or lopsided games." With a plethora of choices at their fingertips, it may be that viewers have grown impatient or, at a minimum, are more willing to multitask, jumping back and forth as games and matches unfold (Lewis, Gantz & Wenner, 2021).

Overall, it seems that audiences have changed their viewing habits and styles, with younger generations' consumption more substantially spread across multiple screens and sports than older generations. An increase in out-of-home viewership among the younger generations may also contribute to skewed data on aging and TV viewing (Nielsen, 2018). Younger fans may be more likely to watch at bars and restaurants and, as a result, be undercounted by ratings companies such as Nielsen. It is difficult to draw clear conclusions on what these TV viewership ratings say about fanship and aging. For example, when comparing the overall sports media consumption of older (55+) and younger adults (18–27), van Driel and Gantz (2019) found older adults consumed less than younger adults. Yet, both groups were equally likely to be sports fans, with fanship avidity similar across age groups. Media consumption in this case was not based on live TV viewing alone, but included both online and traditional ways of following sports.

As we are more interested in fanship levels over time rather than across viewing modalities, we will not distinguish how consumers watch sports (i.e., TV or online) but instead focus on *all* viewing of *live* televised sports.

Theory-Based Explanation

Sports fanship isn't a static, inelastic trait. Anecdotal evidence abounds about those who became fans as adults as well as about those whose ardor may have diminished in response to the increased responsibilities of adulthood (Singer, 2017; Tapp, 2004). Just as there are a variety of motivations that drive sports fanship, there may be a broad array of factors that influence people turning away from following sports. We pose that age-related changes in fanship may be an important intervening factor that can be displayed in diverse ways.

Socioemotional selectivity theory may provide good explanations as to why sports fanship would decline over time. For much of life, physical health and mental health are strongly connected (Charles & Carstensen, 2010). Yet, during old age, a when a decline in physical strength and mobility is almost inevitable, mental well-being remains stable or even increases for many. Carstensen and colleagues (1999) explain that as people age, they become more selective in the (social) activities they undertake and prefer those that contribute to positive feelings and are seen as meaningful. The motivation to optimize emotional experiences is likely driven by an increasing awareness that the time one has left is both limited and precious. A lifetime of experience comes in handy with advancing years to predict which experiences contribute to happiness and which ones do not. As well, there is evidence that older people become less interested in emotional excitement (Charles & Carstensen, 2010). Experiencing intense emotions may be essential for development and identity exploration at a younger age but it is not as much needed at an older age. Media preferences reflect this: Older adults are less likely than younger adults to select programs that bring about emotionally intense experiences (Bartsch, 2012). This change is also visible in the tendency for older adults to favor heartwarming and contemplative programs (Bartsch, 2012).

These findings translate to changes in sports fanship with age in two ways. First, it may be that older adults are less interested in the eustress associated with sports fanship. While the benefits of participating in the "wins" of sporting victory may bring great joy (e.g., the basking in reflected glory [BIRGing]), consuming sports contests also entail taking the risk of experiencing the inherent unknowns and ambiguous outcomes of contests that can be quite unsettling and dispiriting (van Driel & Gantz, 2019).

With age, fanship may lose absolute and comparative meaning over time when other activities may become more important and the attraction to and enjoyment of intense experiences dwindles. Another explanation used by Gantz and Lewis (2021) for potential decreases in fanship with age is based on social identity theory. At a young age, identification with a social group such as fellow fans is important for identity development. Yet, with age, adults will have had the chance to form and explore multiple social identities, thus diminishing the need for this. Theoretically, there is much reason to expect that, *on average*, avidity of fanship would weaken over time.

Several studies support this prediction (Brown, Billings, & Ruihley, 2012; Gantz & Lewis, 2021). Gantz and Lewis found that the majority of the 2,524 adult respondents they surveyed indicated that their fanship levels had decreased over the years. The reasons that respondents provided aligned with Carstensen's SST such as shifting priorities and diminished passion.

Still, we cannot ignore studies that have found evidence of an increase in fanship with age (Gantz & Lewis, 2021; Tapp, 2004; Toder-Alon et al., 2019). Tapp and colleagues found that loyalty to a US Premier League football club was highest for older people, especially if they had been fans of that team for a long time. Toder-Alon et al. (2019) found an increase in overall sports fandom with age among Israeli basketball fans, as assessed by their average score on the Sports Fandom Questionnaire. It is important to note that both investigations only sampled self-acknowledged fans, those of a football club (Tapp, 2004) and those who cared about basketball (Toder-Alon et al., 2019). This means non-fans and former fans were not included in these studies. Tapp and colleagues did compare season ticketholders with lapsed ticketholders and found the reasons for lapsing to be related to perceived rising complexities of life, such as having younger children and shifting financial priorities. Continued ticketholders were more likely to be older, settled fans.

What can it be, then, that explains why some become more avid fans as they enter and pass through middle age? One conceptually plausible explanation lies in the connection that fans experience with their favorite teams and athletes. For example, in the United Kingdom, loyalty to a sports team was found to be stronger than loyalty to religion: 2 percent changed team affiliation across their lifespan while 5 percent switched religion (Performance Communications & Canvas8, 2016). Additionally, 30 percent of those same respondents indicated that religion defined who they are, while 58 percent said sports defined them. This tracks with evidence by Tapp and colleagues (2004) showing that older fans with a history of fanship to that specific club were its most loyal fans. Fanship to the club had become an integral part of their identities. The results of Gantz and Lewis (2021) further support this perspective. Those who increased their fanship over time mentioned the importance of connection with teams, but also with family and friends. Related, Wann (2006) has demonstrated that sport team identification has a positive influence on the social well-being of a fan. Participation in sports, as well as sports spectating, appear to have a positive relationship with short- and long-term well-being (Kim & James, 2019). Results for the relationship between watching *televised* sports and well-being, however, are mixed.

Divergent findings such as these highlight the importance of considering how fanship is measured (e.g., by exposure patterns, self-stated avidity) as variance in such measures seem to affect the outcomes and relationships that scholars find and report. For example, scholars have looked into the possibility that it is not overall sports viewing, but rather the type of game or match that is watched that might differentiate older and younger adults in their sports consumption. Van Driel and Gantz (2019) hypothesized that older adults may avoid games that were anticipated to be highly exciting and had a lot at stake. Yet, older adults were at least equally eager as younger adults to watch highly exciting sports contests of their favorite teams or athletes. At the same time, older adults seem to be less likely to watch sports with the goal to experience and express intense emotions than younger adults (Toder-Alon et al., 2019; van Driel & Gantz, 2019). In order to account for a variety of fan expressions that may change with age, in addition to examining the comparative frequency of watching live sports across the lifecycle, we investigate other indicators of fanship levels such as investment in watching live sports and self-reported fanship as well as the overall importance of sports in life.

Socioemotional selectivity theory (Carstensen et al., 1999) points to the *plausibility* that the relationship between age and fanship may depend on fanship avidity. If being a fan is central to one's self-identity and adds meaning, positive experiences, connection, and happiness to one's life, then it follows that fans would choose fanship activities over other options (van Driel & Gantz, 2019). *Some* older adults may become greater fans with age because fanship is important, personally meaningful and deeply satisfying. The anxiety associated with unknown outcomes and keen disappointment associated with losses is no match to the resultant meaning, connectedness and pleasure that fanship offers. For *other* older adults, particularly where sports fanship was never a central part of their definition of self or core set of activities, the reverse may hold true. Here, their sports fanship may be likely to diminish and this should be marked by decreases in sports viewing that presumably facilitate opportunities to spend more time on activities that bring joy or are seen as more rewarding and meaningful.

In this study we will describe overall changes of fanship across the lifespan, using different fanship measures. In doing so, we will explore how these changes in sports fanship may be related to fanship intensity and address this central question: Does sports fanship increase over time among those who are strong fans and decrease over time among those who are not strong fans?

Method

Procedure

Potential respondents were recruited by Qualtrics through their online research panels. Two inclusion criteria were set prior to data collection. First, the recruitment process was set up to include an equal number of participants into each of six age groups: (1) 18–29, (2) 30–39, (3) 40–49, (4) 50–59, (5) 60–69, and (6) at least 70. Second, quotas were set in sampling to ensure roughly equal proportions of females and males within each age group.

Panelists received a description of the study prior to providing consent to participate. The description stated that the study would be about sports fanship and stated a preference for respondents who, "at least sometimes," watched sports. On average, it took 20 minutes to complete the survey. Respondents who did not correctly respond to all four attention checks distributed throughout the survey were excluded from the final dataset.

Participants

A total of 627 respondents completed the survey and passed the attention checks. The average age was $M = 49.38$ ($SD = 16.92$). The age range for the oldest group was 70 to 87.

Across age groups, education levels were comparable. In terms of self-identified ethnicity, respondents in the youngest age groups had most diverse backgrounds while the oldest age group was least diverse (see Table 15.1). In this study, the diverse backgrounds of the youngest age group versus older age groups is in line with research that shows that younger generations are far more diverse than older generations (Sports Business Daily, 2020). The older age groups in this study overrepresent white adult sport viewers and fans (Silverman, 2020; Gough, 2020). A recent Statista report shows that the ratio of fans and non-fans is similar for white and Hispanic adults and Black adults are more likely to be sports fans and indicate higher fan avidity levels (Gough, 2021). We assessed, but did not find any differences in the levels of fan avidity across ethnic groups among the youngest group of respondents.

Fanship Measures

Overall Fanship. We assessed overall fanship in two ways. First, we asked: Do you consider yourself a sports fan (yes/no)? Then we asked: To what extent are you a fan? with answer options ranging from 0 (not at all a sports fan) to 10 (very strong sports fan). Both questions asked about the current level of respondents' fanship as well as the level that existed when they were in their

Table 15.1 Demographics Across Age Groups

Age	18–29	30–39	40–49	50–59	60–69	at least 70
N	104	105	105	105	104	104
Female (%)	50	50	50	50	50	50
At least some college (%)	63	71	66	65	67	70
African American (%)	14	16	7	7	14	4
Hispanic (%)	16	3	6	1	6	1
Caucasian (%)	59	71	82	80	76	91
Other (%)	11	10	5	2	3	3

20s and 30s (n.b., alternatively here, respondents belonging to the youngest age group (18–29) were asked to think about when they were "younger"). Just about half (51 percent) of our sample of participants said they currently were fans. Just about as many (49 percent) said they were fans when they were younger. On our second fanship measure, the extent of fanship, the corresponding means were 4.85 (SD = 3.62) and 4.52 (SD = 3.81), respectively.

Frequency of Watching Live TV Sports. Respondents were asked how frequently they watched live TV sports (regular or streaming) and were given the following response options: 1 = never; 2 = less than once a year; 3 = about once a year; 4 = a few times a year; 5 = about once a month; 6 = about once a week; and 7 = more often than once a week). Their mean response to this item was 4.74 (SD = 2.38). More than one in five respondents (22 percent) indicated they never watched sports.

Experience of Watching Live TV Sports. Respondents who indicated they watched live TV sports at least sometimes (that is, those who did not select the answer "never," N = 488) received four follow-up questions about their viewing experience. The first question concerned enjoyment of watching sports. The mean response on our 0 (not at all enjoyable) to 10 (very enjoyable) scale was 6.86 (SD = 2.87). Subsequently, they were asked about how passionate they are about watching sports (0 = not at all passionate; 10 = very much passionate; M = 6.32; SD = 3.00) and how personally meaningful watching sports is to them (0 = not at all meaningful; 10 = very meaningful; M = 6.11; SD = 3.11). Finally, respondents rated the importance of the social component of watching sports on a scale of 0 (the social component is not at all important) to 10 (it is very important). The mean response for that item was M = 5.38 (SD = 3.22).

Respondents were also asked about the meaningfulness of watching live sports compared to when they were younger (options ranged from 1 = much less personally meaningful now to 5 = much more personally meaningful now). The mean response here was 3.12 (SD = 1.07).

Due to a mix-up in the skip logic settings of two questions (regular TV viewing and live sports TV viewing) some respondents did not receive the meaningfulness of sports in life questions. This was not discovered until the survey was completed.

Importance of Sports in Life. On an 8-item scale, respondents indicated the importance of sports in their life (0 = no agreement; 10 = total agreement). Illustrative items are *"Following sports brings me great joy," "In the big picture, sports are pretty unimportant in my life,"* and *"When I'm following live sports, I'm totally wrapped up in it."* Respondents answered this set of questions twice, first how they currently felt about sports in their life (M = 4.05; SD = 2.83), and then when they were younger (M = 4.16; SD = 2.84). Cronbach's α = 0.91 and 0.90 respectively.

Results

We will begin by examining responses to our measures (fanship levels, frequency and experience of watching live sports, and the importance of sports in life) based on respondent age groups. We will then examine responses to those measures based on current and past fanship levels (fans and non-fans; none to minimal fans, moderate fans, and avid fans).

Age and Level of Fanship

There were no age group differences in the proportion of respondents indicating they were sports fans. Among our sample of participants, the distribution of fans and non-fans was close to 50–50 across age groups (Table 15.2).

Table 15.2 Percentage of Fans and Non-Fans Across Age Groups

Sports fan	18–29	30–39	40–49	50–59	60–69	at least 70
Yes (%)	51	52	50	52	51	47
No (%)	49	48	50	48	49	53

Table 15.3 Extent of Fanship Across Age Groups

	18–29	30–39	40–49	50–59	60–69	at least 70
Fanship now M (SD)	4.91 (3.75)	4.69 (3.42)	4.87 (3.64)	5.13 (3.71)	4.99 (3.67)	4.53 (3.58)
Fanship then M (SD)	3.90 (3.78)	4.35 (3.72)	5.22 (3.83)	4.70 (4.00)	4.43 (3.80)	4.52 (3.71)

Table 15.4 Frequency of Watching Live TV Sports

Frequency		18–29	30–39	40–49	50–59	60–69	at least 70
(N = 627)	M	4.63	4.90	4.57	4.84	4.87	4.63
	(SD)	(2.46)	(2.25)	(2.37)	(2.37)	(2.30)	(2.42)

Similarly, there were no significant changes in fanship level based on age group (see Table 15.3) or based on age as a continuous variable (F<1 and Pearson r = −0.001, respectively).

We did detect within individual changes over time in fanship levels ($F(1, 5) = 8.80, p < 0.01$). Here, the level of fanship now ($M = 4.85; SE = 0.15$) was reported as higher than when they were younger ($M = 4.52; SE = 0.15$). An interaction effect between age and time ($F(1, 5) = 2.92, p = 0.13$) showed that this difference was significant only for the youngest age group who reported being more of a fan now than they were when they were younger (Table 15.3).

Age and Watching Live Sports

Age was found to be unrelated to the frequency with which respondents said they watched live TV sports ($r = 0.02, p = 0.68$). As well, our assessment of the frequency of live viewing across age groups did not result in any significant differences ($F < 1$; Table 15.4).

Age and the Live Sports Viewing Experience

Older age groups also did not experience watching live sports any differently than younger age groups in terms of level of enjoyment ($F < 1$), passion ($F(1, 5) = 1.22, p = 0.30$), meaningfulness ($F(1, 5) = 1.45, p = 0.21$) or social importance ($F < 1$) (Table 15.5).

Age and the Importance of Sports in Life

Assessments made about the importance of sports in life also did not correlate with age ($r = −0.001, p = 0.97$). As well, we did not find significant differences across age groups ($F < 1$, Table 15.6).

Table 15.5 Enjoyment, Passion, Meaning, and Social Importance of Viewing Live Sports

		18–29	30–39	40–49	50–59	60–69	at least 70
Enjoyment	M	6.78	6.69	7.05	6.57	7.41	6.67
(N = 477)	(SD)	(2.91)	(2.87)	(2.80)	(2.89)	(2.76)	(2.98)
Passion							
(N = 479)	M	6.10	5.96	6.60	6.25	6.93	6.09
	(SD)	(3.02)	(3.12)	(3.83)	(3.12)	(2.61)	(3.15)
Meaning							
(N = 474)	M	5.60	5.77	6.40	6.20	6.73	5.34
	(SD)	(3.15)	(3.26)	(3.08)	(3.26)	(2.67)	(3.07)
Social							
(N = 474)	M	5.04	5.45	5.59	5.22	5.89	5.07
	(SD)	(3.11)	(3.31)	(3.27)	(2.90)	(3.47)	(3.22)

Table 15.6 Importance of Sports in Life Across Age Groups

	18–29	30–39	40–49	50–59	60–69	at least 70
Importance now						
M	4.09	3.91	4.07	4.16	4.37	3.70
(SD)	(2.99)	(2.85)	(2.88)	(2.70)	(2.81)	(2.73)
Importance then						
M	4.84	4.92	5.49	5.37	5.39	4.92
(SD)	(2.93)	(2.79)	(2.75)	(2.84)	(2.94)	(2.78)

Overall, we found no relationship between age and level of fanship, live TV viewing, the experiences of live viewing or the importance of sports in life. Fanship and age seem unrelated and thus overall, fanship does not appear to decrease with age.

Yet, while a main effect of age was not evident for our fanship indicators, the enjoyment, meaningfulness, passion and importance of social context of live TV sports viewing showed an upward trend up to the age of 70 followed by a slight drop (Figure 15.1). This same trend can be seen in Table 15.6 concerning assessments about the importance of sports in life. These results may be indicative of the idea that fanship does indeed contribute to happiness, and thus, engagement through fanship increases (albeit slightly) with age. Still, consistent with evidence that life satisfaction tends to peak around the age of 60, our finding that fanship engagement decreases (as evidenced in the responses by those 70 and over) is also consistent with that which has been postulated by Carstensen.

Changes in Fanship Across Age: Separating Fans from Non-fans

Thus far, we have reported no clear differences in the levels of fanship or indicators of fanship across age groups. The absence of these expected differences may be related to the main premise of this chapter – that is, that fans and non-fans behave differently over time and decreases in sports fanship most hinge on entrenched levels of fanship intensity.

In order to further investigate this expectation we compared fans with non-fans on the extent of their fanship and the importance of sports in their lives now in comparison to the levels reported to be the case when they were younger. An interaction effect of time by fan/non-fan

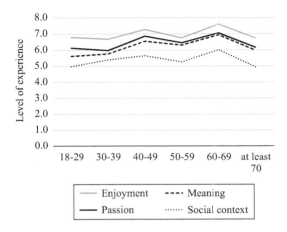

Figure 15.1 Experience of Watching Sports

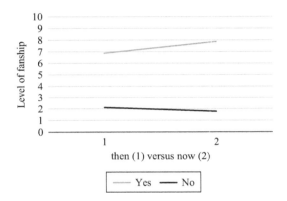

Figure 15.2 Extent of Fanship Then and Now

($F(1, 615) = 36.91, p < 0.001$) revealed that fans reported being more of a fan now ($M = 7.87$; $SE = 0.10$) than when they were younger ($M = 6.88$; $SE = 0.17$) whereas non-fans indicated that they were even less avid in their fanship now ($M = 1.78$; $SE = 0.12$) than they were years ago ($M = 2.11$; $SE = 0.16$) (Figure 15.2). Analyzing fans and non-fans separately, for fans, there was no interaction between age and time. Age groups did not differ on changes in level of fanship over time ($F(5, 311) = 1.81$): for all ages, fanship now was higher than when they were younger. For non-fans, the opposite (also non-significant, $F(5, 304) = 1.58, p = 0.17$) was almost always the case. With the exception of only the youngest age group, the averages indicated that fanship levels were higher when they were younger.

These same trends were found for the importance of sports in life. Fans indicated a significant increase in importance over time (now: $M = 6.27$; $SE = 0.11$; then: $M = 5.84$; $SE = 0.13$), while non-fans indicated a significant decrease over time (now: $M = 1.78$; $SE = 0.09$; then: $M = 2.44$; $SE = 0.12$) (Figure 15.3). Looking at fans only, the interaction effect of time by age was also non-significant ($F < 1$). The direction of the averages showed that all age groups reported to find sports in life more important now compared to when they were younger. For non-fans, again

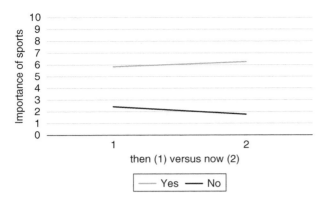

Figure 15.3 Importance of Sports in Life Then and Now

the opposite was true ($F < 1$), with the averages indicating that all age groups reported to find sports more important back in the day compared to now.

One reason for the lack of an interaction effect between age groups and fanship levels may relate to insufficient power in our analyses. For that reason, respondents were split into fans and non-fans again and Pearson correlations were rerun for all fanship variables with age as a continuous variable. The correlations between age and frequency of live TV viewing of fans remained non-significant ($r = 0.05, p = 0.37$), yet the enjoyment ($r = 0.13, p = 0.03$), passion ($r = 0.13, p = 0.03$) and meaning ($r = 0.13, p = 0.02$) of viewing now related positively to age. In line with the previous findings, this same positive relationship was not found for the extent of fanship ($r = 0.02, p = 0.79$) or importance of sports in life ($r = -0.01, p = 0.86$). These results suggest that while fanship levels remain roughly the same, the *experience* of watching live sports changes. For non-fans there was no relationship (also not a negative one) between age and any of these fanship variables.

Subsequently, we investigated whether these relationships may be further dependent on the extent of fanship by comparing non-fans ($N = 129$), minimal fans ($N = 126$), moderate fans ($N = 171$) and avid fans ($N = 201$). A repeated measures mixed ANOVA (time by age group and fanship level) produced an interaction effect for time by fan type on the extent of fanship ($F (3, 603) = 24.43\ p = 0.001$), indicating that non-fans were more of a fan when they were younger compared to now ($M = 0.55; SE = 0.16$ and $M = 0.0; SE = 0.00$, respectively), a tendency evident in minimal fans then when compared to now ($M = 2.80; SE = 0.27, M = 1.88; SE = 0.08$, respectively). On the other hand, evidence shows that moderate fans were less avid in their fanship when they were younger compared to now ($M = 5.07; SE = 0.22, M = 5.80; SE = 0.08$, respectively). The same dynamic was evident even for the most avid fans, who also reported being less of fans then when compared to now ($M = 7.66; SE = 0.21$ and $M = 9.01; SE = 0.06$, respectively, see Figure 15.4 for an overview). No three-way interaction was found for time by age group by fantype ($F < 1$), again likely due to the limited power of the test.

An interaction effect was found for time by fan type on importance of sports in life ($F(3, 603) = 38.37, p < 0.001$), showing that non-fans were more of a fan when they were younger ($M = 1.30; SE = 0.12$) compared to now ($M = 1.03; SE = 0.10$), as were minimal fans then ($M = 2.97; SE = 0.20$) when compared to now ($M = 1.84; SE = 0.12$), while no change was found for moderate fans then ($M = 4.58; SE = 0.18$) compared to now ($M = 4.49; SE = 0.13$). The opposite was true for increasingly avid fans whose fanship became more important now

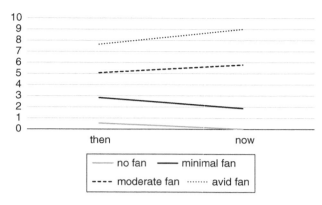

Figure 15.4 Extent of Fanship Then and Now Across Fanship Level

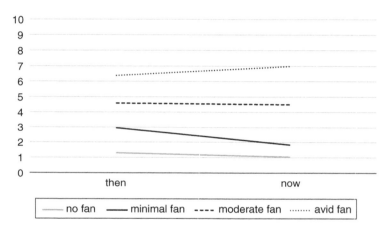

Figure 15.5 Importance of Sports in Life Then and Now Across Fanship Level

than in years past ($M = 6.98$; $SE = 0.12$ and $M = 6.37$; $SE = 0.16$, respectively). Figure 15.5 provides a visual representation of these findings. Again, no three-way interaction was found for time by age group by fan type ($F < 1$).

Discussion

In the past decade, the lifecycle of the sports fan has been a topic of interest for the sports industry as well for scholars. Evidence from previous research has suggested, based on the logic of socio-emotional selectivity theory (Carstensen et al., 1999), that fanship would decrease over time because of shifts in priorities focused on positive experiences later in life (van Driel & Gantz, 2019). Evidence exists for both the fading importance of, as well as a growing love for, sports with age. Our findings could not substantiate the underlying principles associated with SST. No matter how we assessed sports fanship, we were unable to find *uniform* differences solely based on age. Instead, we found that pre-existing fanship levels trumped age as a predictor of current fanship.

Our findings should be interpreted in the context of findings from previous research. Studies that found a *decrease* in fanship over time investigated fans and non-fans across a variety of sports.

Previous research providing evidence for an *increase* in fanship with age only looked at those who identified as fans and thus with firm engagement with sports. Those apparently contradictory findings in fact make sense from Carstensen's perspective. SST holds that older adults prioritize situations and activities that contribute to life satisfaction. Because following sports carries considerable meaning for those with well-developed fanship, following sports likely has become a priority in the same way fine dining is a priority for those who relish good cooking or spending time with grandchildren is important for those who prioritize close, intergenerational family ties. When we compared fans and non-fans and their fanship levels over time, our results supported this interpretation of Carstensen's theory: With age, fanship increased for fans and decreased for those who today identify as non-fans. We observed the same pattern when we divided fanship into four levels. Those who started as non-fans tended to become even more lukewarm with age. Those who were avid fans when they were younger tended to become even more avid as they aged. Similarly, the minimal fan decreased somewhat, and the moderate fan increased somewhat.

Socio-emotional selectivity theory would also predict that for most adults, following sports would become less meaningful with age. People's lives change with different demands and responsibilities that not only take time away from following sports, but also shift priorities in what is experienced as meaningful. The fundamental appeal of following sports – the "who wins" and "who loses" – and the emotional rollercoaster that comes with that might lose meaning and fuel lesser passion as one ages. Although we did not find any significant changes with age across all adults to support that prediction, again when looking at fans only we found a positive relationship between age and the meaningfulness, passion and enjoyment associated with live sports viewing. To our surprise, we did not find this relationship holding for fans with regards to their fanship levels, frequency of viewing or importance of sports in life. It seems that older adults place more emphasis on the meaning, enjoyment and passion of engaging with sports, suggesting that, with age, there is a shift to a less intense, but more meaningful experience of watching live sports. Previous research indeed showed that compared to younger adults, older adults are less likely to watch sports in order to experience and express intense emotions (Toder-Alon et al., 2019; van Driel & Gantz, 2019).

Still, it is not clear why fanship engagement tends to wane when people reach their seventies. Potentially, age-related priorities shift again at this age. Physical health may put more of a burden on their lives, but here we are just speculating. If health issues were at work here, we would expect a less positive outlook – and decreased interest and enjoyment – across all that life offers, and here, interest in sports fanship would seem to be no different than interest in other leisure time activities.

This study shows that findings on the lifecycle of sports fans may depend on the groups being compared. We looked at fans and non-fans as well as their levels of fanship and various indicators thereof. Although others have done so, we did not differentiate on the basis of the sport, team or players fans followed. This may matter, especially across the globe, where passion for one's national football (soccer) team appears to be endemic, where national identities may mesh more clearly with individual identities.

Previous studies also have used a variety of fanship measures. These differences may be of greater consequence than the sport or sports a fan follows. We have demonstrated the importance of going beyond a simple dichotomous choice to ascertain whether one is a fan or not. Both the level and contours of fanship matter. On the other hand, we can rightly be critiqued for the measure we chose to assess exposure to live sports. Our limited and imprecise measure may not have captured differences in the nature and amount of exposure to live mediated sports, as well as the locations and ways in which sports are currently being consumed (e.g., in or out of the home, viewing snippets or entire games and matches, switching across channels and games, watching while using additional screens, multitasking, or socializing). Beyond affecting the overall duration of viewing, these factors may shape the overall investment in, and meaning of, the viewing experience. These shortcomings – along with a sample size that limited the statistical power of our analyses (to test differences amongst groups) – make it challenging for us to say more than our findings still point to the logic and applicability of Carstensen's theory.

Ideally, future research needs to examine the lifecycle of a fan longitudinally to take account of more than mere generational differences. People age differently, and the contexts in which they age (war time, political strife, prolonged recessions and the like) may influence how age intersects with priorities and attitudes. Still, we recognize the longitudinal research often requires more funding than most sports scholars have at their disposal. Perhaps our interests could be incorporated into well-funded, broad-based studies on health and wellness, where thousands are followed for a decade or more of their lives. While we did ask respondents about their fanship levels when they were young to assess changes within respondents, we found similar trends for younger and older adults. Moreover, while our strategy entailed inserting two "then versus now" fanship variables in the study to gain some insight into the changes that come with age, the ability of respondents to make stable assessments of years gone by is not clear.

Further, it seems clear that scholars interested in fandom across the lifecycle need to incorporate more nuanced measures about the nature of the live sports viewing experience.

As SST predicts changes in preferences with age due to the increasing realization that the end of life may be near, it is worth assessing changes in both fanship levels and the nature of live sports viewing experiences across the lifespan based on the extent to which the end is *perceived* to be near. It is often said that age is a state of mind as well as a chronological fact. As the complexities associated with aging are remarkable, perception about where one stands on and negotiates life's timeline may be a much better predictors of the activities adults value and continue to pursue than mere chronological age. These latter considerations suggest that studying sports fandom or other activities and priorities along the lifecycle will require a nuanced approach that draws on broader understandings of both aging and identity. Our study here shows the challenges involved in approaching those understandings.

References

Bartsch, A. (2012). As time goes by: What changes and what remains the same in entertainment experience over the life span? *Journal of Communication, 62,* 588–608. doi:10.1111/ j.1460-2466.2012.01657.x

Brown, N., Billings, A. C., & Ruihley, B. (2012). Exploring the change in motivations for fantasy sport participation during the life cycle of a sports fan. *Communication Research Reports, 29*(4), 333–342. doi:10.1080/08824096.2012.723646

Charles, S. T., & Carstensen, L. L. (2010). Social and emotional aging. *Annual Review of Psychology, 61,* 383–409.

Carstensen, L. L., Isaacowitz, D. M., & Charles, S. T. (1999). Taking time seriously: A theory of socioemotional selectivity. *American Psychologist, 54*(3), 165.

van Driel, I. I., Gantz, W., & Lewis, N. (2019). Unpacking what it means to be—or not be—a fan. *Communication & Sport, 7*(5), 611–629.

van Driel, I. I., & Gantz, W. (2019). The role of emotion regulation and age in experiencing mediated sports. *Communication & Sport,* 2167479519861704.

ESPN. (2009). *The life cycle of the sports fan—2008.* Bristol, CT.

Gantz, W., & Lewis, N. (2021). Sports fanship changes across the lifespan. *Communication & Sport.* doi: 10.1177/ 2167479521991812.

Gough, C. (2020, March 1). *Favorite sport to watch in the U.S. 2020 by ethnicity.* www.statista.com/statistics/ 1108345/favorite-sport-viewers-ethnicity/

Gough, C. (2021, April 6). *Share of sports fans in the United States as of March 2021, by ethnicity.* www.statista.com/statistics/1018817/sports-fans-usa-ethnicity/

Kim, J., & James, J. D. (2019). Sport and happiness: Understanding the relations among sport consumption activities, long-and short-term subjective well-being, and psychological need fulfillment. *Journal of Sport Management*, *33*(2), 119–132.

Lewis, N., Gantz, W., & Wenner, L. A. (2021). What we do when we watch live sports: An Analysis of concurrent viewing behaviors. *International Journal of Sport Communication*, *14*(2). doi: 10.1123/ijsc.2020-0270

Lombardo, J. & Broughton, D. (2017, June 5). *Going gray: Sports TV viewers skew older.* www.sportsbusinessdaily.com/Journal/Issues/2017/06/05/Research-and-Ratings/Viewership-trends.aspx

Nielsen (2018, February 15). *Nielsen's year in Sports Media 2017 Report.* www.nielsen.com/us/en/insights/report/2018/2017-year-in-sports-media/#

Performance Communications & Canvas8 (2016, June 3), What's the future of the sportsfan? www.canvas8.com/blog/2016/06/03/sports-fan.html

Silverman, A. (2020, September 10). *Demographic data shows which major sports fan bases are most likely to support or reject social justice advocacy.* https://morningconsult.com/2020/09/10/sports-fan-base-demographic-data/

Singer, D. (2017, October 2). *We are wrong about millennial sports fans.* www.mckinsey.com/industries/technology-media-and-telecommunications/our-insights/we-are-wrong-about-millennial-sports-fans#

Sports Business Daily (2020, January 13). *Chasing the next generation of fans.* www.sportsbusinessdaily.com/Journal/Issues/2020/01/13/In-Depth/Next-generation.aspx

Tapp, A. (2004). The loyalty of football fans—We'll support you evermore? *Journal of Database Marketing & Customer Strategy Management*, *11*(3), 203–215.

Toder-Alon, A., Icekson, T., & Shuv-Ami, A. (2019). Team identification and sports fandom as predictors of fan aggression: The moderating role of ageing. *Sport Management Review*, *22*(2), 194–208.

Wann, D. L. (2006). Understanding the positive social psychological benefits of sport team identification: The team identification-social psychological health model. *Group Dynamics: Theory, Research, and Practice*, *10*(4), 272–296.

16
The Olympics Sports Fan
A Distinctive Demographic

Andrew C. Billings, Samuel Hakim and Qingru Xu

The Distinctive Demographic: Deciphering the Olympic Sports Fan

The numbers are astounding. Over four billion people watch the Summer Olympics while the Winter Olympics—even with a smaller media footprint—still attracts 1.9 billion viewers every four years ("Global Broadcast and Audience Report," 2018). Many Olympic viewers are sports fans; many sports fans are Olympic viewers—and yet, the people consuming the Olympics represent a demonstrably different demographic from any other sporting event. For instance, women consume roughly one-third of non-Olympic sports media, yet represent the majority of Olympic viewers in many nations (see Elliott, 2008).

This chapter will unfold in three distinct phases: (a) uncovering the differences between Olympic and non-Olympic sports fans, (b) outlining linear (largely television) consumption habits, and (c) advancing knowledge regarding digital/mobile media use in regard to Olympic sports fandom. In doing so, a unique case of overlap will be presented, arguing that while some characteristics of sports fandom match the manner in which people consume the Olympics, other elements are distinctively Olympian, the result of dozens of sports simultaneously being contested in men's and women's disciplines under national flags of interest.

Sports Fans vs. Olympic Fans: Siblings, Not Twins

The difference between a sports fan and an Olympic fan is far from negligible; for instance, there is a reason why ESPN—the self-proclaimed "Worldwide Leader in Sports"—has never launched a successful or even competitive bid for the rights to air the Games. The audiences involved are quite different. Yes, sports fans and Olympic fans overlap, yet three key differences posture the two as related, yet dissimilar in noteworthy manners.

First, there is a wide difference in *familiarity* between the two groups. Sports fans typically know the intricate inner workings of their favorite sport. They know every rule change, strategy, and projected favorite for championships. Sports fans have for decades, constructed and participated in long parasocial relationships with the players involved (Sanderson, 2008); there is very little that a New England Patriots fan could need to know about quarterback Tom Brady, or that an invested soccer/fútbol fan would not know about Cristiano Ronaldo. These teams and players become the fabric of one's continual fandom. An identified fan would buy jerseys or other merchandise to overtly show his/her affiliation (Devlin & Billings, 2018).

Olympic fandom offers a sharp departure from these familiarity traits. An Olympic fan might know relatively little about a sport they are watching beyond basic heuristics for what constitutes excellence. They may know that no splash on a dive, a "stuck" landing in gymnastics, or a puck in a hockey goal is good if your team/athlete is the one who did it. While some athletes such as Michael Phelps or Lindsey Vonn compete in multiple Olympics and facilitate multi-year parasocial relationships, it is just as likely that an athlete a fan had never heard of before the day of competition is nevertheless able to make an Olympic fan swell with emotion. Apparel for Olympic fans often double as patriotism-wear, a sporting surrogate of one's pride in one's own country (Billings, Brown, & Brown, 2013), as Olympic fans will rarely be able to wear such things to an actual Olympic competition. In sum, sports fandom is often about *living* stories (in which one is already familiar) while Olympic fandom is often about *learning* stories (in which one was not familiar until the moment in which they became highly relevant).

Second, the level of *time commitment* to being a fan differs substantially between sport and Olympic fans. If sports fandom were akin to a decades-long committed marriage, Olympic fandom is the two-week love affair happening every other year. The former is more consistent with more breadth; the latter is more immersive with more depth. Consider: an avid football fan may watch their favorite collegiate and professional team play every week. In the regular season, this amounts to 28 total games, or roughly 84 hours of media consumption. Now consider an Olympic fan who watches only the evening primetime telecast of the Games, now 18 days in length. Coverage is often 4.5 hours each evening. This equates to nearly the same number of hours as the football fan, yet it is consumed in two and a half weeks rather than four months. If one includes all other forms of Olympic media coverage, the available amount is staggering. McAdams (2016) reports that NBC offered 6,755 hours of coverage of the 2016 Rio Summer Games, a figure constituting over nine months of 24/7 viewing.

Finally, these two types of fans differ in a level of *urgency* of consumption. Sports fans regularly watch games and contests that could best be classified as mundane or ordinary. A fan of the National Basketball Association, for instance, has 82 regular season games to watch, all while being quite cognizant that most of the games have little effect on their team making the playoffs, as virtually every team with a winning record (and sometimes some with losing records) still advance. Golf fans have four major tournaments dotting a calendar of dozens of other lesser tournaments that nonetheless appeal to a significant segment of their population. In contrast, Olympic fans may have other things to watch between Games (Olympic trials and post-Olympic exhibitions), yet the overwhelming majority of people following the Olympics do so avidly for 18 days and then almost entirely relegate their fandom to nil in the overall priorities of their life over the next two years. Once the Olympic flame is extinguished, fandom generally returns to regularly scheduled sports habituation.

In the end, it is fair to conclude that both sport and Olympic fans share a wealth of other qualities ranging from the types of cognitive, behavioral, and affective motivations offered by Raney (2006). However, it is also proper to conclude that the degree of overlap between Olympic fans and other sports fans is substantially less than the degree of duplicity between baseball and basketball fans or other apt comparisons (see Billings, Angelini, & MacArthur, 2018). The remainder of this chapter will outline the manner in which fans use media almost exclusively to advance and cultivate their Olympic fandom, ranging from the traditional, television-based method to newer mobile and streaming device options that are shifting the Olympic fandom game once again.

Olympic Fan Television Consumption Habits

Within the Olympic Games, there is an unusual television pattern that occurs separately from the "big four" American sport leagues (football, basketball, baseball, hockey): women-led sports are receiving increased media attention. Additionally, in regard to women watching women's sports there tends to be a preference when choosing which sports to consume, however figure skating, tennis, skiing, and gymnastics reign supreme and these sports are usually televised primetime features (Sargent, Zillmann, & Weaver, 1998). The Olympic Games emerged as an anomalous case regarding the media representation of male and female athletes, in which women's sports usually received far more media attention compared to any other non-Olympic periods (Billings, Angelini, & MacArthur, 2018). Although sports media are often accused of providing only a single-digit proportion of the total coverage to women's sports (Billings & Young, 2015), many of these same media entities are frequently applauded for balanced gender representations during the Olympics in which women usually receive media attention commensurate to what men receive (Xu, Billings, Scott, Lewis, & Sharp, 2017). In fact, Arth, Hou, Rush, and Angelini (2018) recently examined NBC's primetime and non-primetime coverage devoted to men and women's sports at the 2018 PyeongChang Winter Olympics, finding that women's sports received 43.2 percent of the total primetime coverage and 37.4 percent of the total non-primetime coverage—more than the men received within primetime (once accounting for paired/mixed-gender events) and far exceeding the media attention that women athletes received in daily practice.

Consumption of Olympic media involves some of the most high-dose viewership anyone could ever find. For instance, in the United States over 150 billion television minutes were consumed during the 18 days of the Rio Summer Olympics, with an additional 4 billion minutes watched via other online and mobile platforms (Billings, Angelini, & MacArthur, 2018). Conversely, television consumption of sports can be something largely driven by perceived cultural norms and gender differences. During the 2018 Super Bowl in the United States, women constituted 49 percent of the 108 million-plus individuals watching the competition (Salkowitz, 2018), although American football is often considered a highly masculine sport (Hardin & Greer, 2009). The Super Bowl is a unique example as it contradicts the "normal" gendered audience while also being culturally one of the most-viewed sporting events in America for a number of reasons beyond the action on the field—i.e., the infamous advertisements and traditionally elaborate half-time performances. The rest of the American sports media diet skews so male that only two sporting events yield a majority female audience: the Kentucky Derby horse race (a single day event each May) and the Olympic telecast (occurring for 18 consecutive nights every two years).

The Olympics are unique compared to the overwhelming majority of sports media products for multiple reasons, including limited viewing opportunities, unusual and/or unfamiliar events (in regard to American audiences), and the increased sense of national identity one may feel via media consumption of the Games. The Olympics offer a range of events such as perceived masculine-natured games like ice hockey to the generally feminine-perceived sport of figure skating (Apostolou, Frantzides, & Pavlidou, 2014). As such, consumption habits may result from culturally based gender stereotypes that are represented by the fan themselves and the sport being consumed and enjoyed.

Sex Differences in Sports Spectatorship

With an increased number of women participating in sports (Women's Sports Foundation, 2020, women currently constitute a significant part of the sports spectator market (Hoeber & Kerwin,

2013). Thus, examining gender differences in sports spectatorship between men and women continues to be a critical area of interest in sports communication (e.g., McDonald, Leckie, Karg, & Zubcevic-Basic, 2018). This area of research is not confined to American borders; a Polish study found that both men and women favored men's sports, but this could have been largely due to the desire to preserve male hegemony under the guise of tradition in this particular sports territory (Jakubowska, 2015). A larger point of discussion can be the impact of cultural norms on consumption patterns. Additionally, there is still the underlying implication for television consumption habits and the media platform. Cooper and Tang (2013) examined sports viewers' multiplatform media use during the 2012 Super Bowl from a lens of gender, revealing that male viewers appreciated athletic competitions more, while female viewers were more likely to enjoy non-athletic elements such as the halftime show. In terms of motivation, scholars found that men's sports consumption was more likely to be driven by entertainment seeking, whereas women's was more apt to be motivated by information seeking and networking with family members (Schallhorn, Knoll, & Schramm, 2017; Whiteside & Hardin, 2011). These findings, overall, pointed out that, although a large number of women consume sports contents, their spectatorship however, may be largely contributed to societal and relationship-based factors such as socializing with friends, family, and partners (Whiteside & Hardin, 2011).

Whiteside and Hardin (2011) examined heterosexual, married women's sports media consumption from a gender roles perspective. Applying focus-group discussions, the authors revealed that women typically assumed more responsibilities on domestic work, leaving limited time for watching sports TV programs or other "free time" activities. Instead of choosing specific sports competitions, their viewing habits were more dictated by their availabilities. As such, their viewing experience was often discontinuous, with a series of interruptions occurring because of other home roles in which they considered themselves to be primary. Moreover, women's viewing preferences were largely influenced and shaped by their husbands because women tended to use sports as a tool for connecting with family members (Whiteside & Hardin, 2011). Examining sports media consumption within the domestic structure, Whiteside and Hardin's (2011) study provided valuable insights into how the traditional gender roles within the dominant social structure influence women's sports spectatorship.

In a similar vein, it is interesting to see how past gendered and cultural norms can guide the viewing consumption of men, but perhaps is even more intriguing for the examination of women. Employing a cross-national comparative approach, Lagaert and Roose (2018) evaluated the relationship between a country's societal gender equality index and its gender gap in sporting events attendance in the European Union, uncovering that although male spectators outnumbered their female counterparts in each country examined, countries with a higher level of gender equality exhibited smaller gender gaps in sporting events attendance. The study indicated that differences in sports spectatorship were significantly influenced by cultural norms and stances on gender equality. Taken collectively with the Whiteside and Hardin (2011) study, the two studies underscore the degree to which sex differences in sports consumption are closely tied with socialization in everyday life.

Of course, there are cases where this is not always accurate, and not all studies that have been conducted have reported salient gender differences in sports spectatorship; instead, some researchers found that, in certain cases, men and women were highly similar regarding sports consumption. For instance, Mehus (2005) examined 399 spectators watching ski jumping and soccer competitions, finding that gender played only a marginal role in affecting sports consumption, particularly when compared to other demographic factors such as age and education. To wit, differences regarding motivation between men and women were minimal among *highly identified* sports fans, echoing Gantz and Wenner's (1991) studies uncovering that, with a similar level of sports interest and fanship, men and women's sports viewing experience could be highly similar.

Preferences in Watching Men and Women's Sports

Among studies exploring sex differences in sports spectatorship, one agenda—men and women's preferences regarding media consumption of sports with male and female athletes—has been in doubt. Assumptions that both men and women viewers prefer to watch men's sports over women's prevail within sports newsrooms, emerging as an important defense for justifying the underrepresentation of women's sports in media (Sherwood, Osborne, Nicholson, & Sherry, 2017). In this sense, the biological sex differences in watching men and women's sports can directly influence sports professionals' decisions on news selections, considering that the majority of sports media institutions are audience-oriented (Billings, 2009).

In prior studies, scholars have reached a wide consensus that male spectators are interested in watching men's competitions in particular sports, except for some highly "feminine" sports that are considered more appealing, including figure skating and gymnastics (Messner, Dunbar, & Hunt, 2000; Sargent, Zillmann, & Weaver, 1998). For instance, Apostolou and his colleagues (2014) recruited participants to explore whether individuals preferred to watch men's sports over women's sports. By surveying participants' willingness to watch 19 sports, researchers asserted that individuals—overall (both men and women)—were more interested in viewing men's competitions.

Regarding biological sex differences in sports spectatorship, researchers also uncovered that men and women tended to hold different preferences toward different *types* of sports. Specifically, Apostolou et al. (2014) explored participants' hypothetical choices in sports consumption, revealing that, among the 19 sports examined, individuals preferred to watch women competing in sports considered to be highly feminine (i.e., gymnastics and aerobics); when it came to the other 17 sports, however, respondents generally held more interest in watching men's sports. Moreover, compared to their female counterparts, men showed more interest in watching perceived masculine sports such as football with less interest in watching any sports seen to be tinged with femininity. The findings indicated that individuals' viewing preferences were highly consistent with traditional gender role beliefs people adopt within daily practice.

However, not all scholars uncovered findings that rigorously concur with the previously conducted research. Angelini (2008) examined interactions between spectators' biological sex and preferences toward different types of sports, revealing that female participants reported higher levels of arousal and positivity when they watched clips featuring female athletes who participated in traditionally masculine sports and clips featuring men who competed in traditionally feminine sports. Through the perspective of social dominance theory, it can be observed that within the membership of the marginalized social group in the sports domain, women tended to favor sports clips that surpassed the traditional, stereotyped gender expectations precisely because the gender transgressions were viewed to be beneficial for women to both legitimate and elevate their status in sport, a domain overwhelmingly typed with masculinity (Angelini, 2008).

Beyond gender differences lie a variety of internally processed (attitude and felt-nationalism) and externally displayed (displayed nationalism and fan identity) fragments that contribute to the contrasts between Olympic and other international sporting events (Billings et al., 2013; Billings & Angelini, 2007). Cultivation theory (Gerbner, Gross, Morgan, & Signorielli, 1986) is an underlying framework for better understanding how television, still to this day the largest mediated device, may transfer to our actual worldly perspectives. There is belief that people retain and internalize information that is seen on television, and with sports being a major component of television, specifically the Olympics, it may come as no surprise that agendas, actions, displays, and performances seen during these events will impact our culture and societal engagements (Billings et al., 2013). Huddy and Khatib (2007) defined three levels of perceived neo-political, internalized political communities: national identity, patriotism, and nationalism (Anderson, 1983). Billings et al. (2013) continued to use the definitions of Huddy and Khatib (2007) and are currently recognized as the following: national identity is seen as common cultural heritage, patriotism as heritage pride, and lastly nationalism as the promotion of one's national identity as superior to other identities, cultures, and countries. While the first two, national identity and patriotism, are seen as more closely tied to that of a typical fan, nationalism may be identified as the negative-bearing performance (and identity) of the three. While nationalism may be seen as negative, it does not seem to handcuff nationalistic displays by sports fans as nationalism was found in some capacity in all countries studied in regard to the Olympics in an early sports communication study (Real, 1989). While other sports may wish to dine at a table that hosts such grand internationally relevant and competitive events, the Olympics tend to display these political communities more clearly. This can be in part due to the extensively long history and tradition the Olympics carry, an open playing field—the opportunity for small countries to take down large countries, Olympian dreams and perks of being an Olympic athlete, and of course the cultivated heroism that is created every two years through the media's meticulously crafted lens (Billings, 2008). In addition, political narratives are created, shared, or in terms of nationally damning events such as war, even halted (Cottrell & Nelson, 2011).

Reeling back to media influence, it is possible to hypothesize how this nationalism is birthed and nurtured. Billings and Eastman (2002) observed that while 51 percent of the athletes mentioned during the 2000 Sydney Olympic coverage were American, the United States only managed to walk away with 11 percent of the total medals awarded. Billings and Eastman (2003) teamed up again to offer additional nationalistic insight by observing that American athletes were distinguished from their international counterparts by being portrayed as courageous and composed, conquering event after event due to their athletic and past Olympic experiences. Interestingly enough, nationalism is not an exclusively American trait. As described by Larson and Rivenburgh (1991) countries airing a national broadcast favored their countrymen and women through clock-time biases and positive athlete depictions. These factors are not exhaustive, however, and it is important to remember that individual, unique factors play a role in television consumption, however those who maintain these political ideologies may be more invested in sports consumption, specifically the Olympics as a breeding ground for potential nationalism, which can then be superseded by arrogance defined as smugness. This internal compete could drive television consumption.

Brand New (Hard to Monetize and Measure) Worlds: Mobile/Streamed Olympic Media Fandom

A plethora of unique and distinctive qualities occur within the billions of Olympic sports fans and consumers ranging from demographic qualities to the modalities of consumption during "the biggest show on television" (Billings, 2008, p. 1). Fans possess layers of motivations ranging from enjoyment and entertainment to passing time and surveillance, each that might take primary or secondary roles depending on tastes and circumstances (Billings, Brown-Devlin, Brown, & Devlin, 2020). Something as simple as an individual's age can influence both *why and how* fans watch sports (Brown, Billings, & Ruihley, 2012). During the 2018 Winter Olympic Games, Deggans (2018) reported the largest variety of mediated sport consumption options to date— including linear television, mobile platforms, on-demand viewing, and over-the-top options along with other forms of legacy media (Bassam, 2018). Due to this increase in consumption via social and mobile media technologies, traditional Olympic viewing has been forever altered in modern mobile device contexts. Second-screen viewing (using a second screen for other gratifications while consuming content on another primary device) and Social TV (using a second screen to interact with content specifically related to what is being rendered on a primary screen) are two relatively new sport media consumption habits (at least when compared to television or print media—see Hutchins, 2019), forming due in part via technological advances and the new opportunities related to social and virtual engagement (Lim, Hwang, Kim, & Biocca, 2015).

A brand-new world—one increasingly difficult to monetize and measure—is crystalizing, revolving around alternative Olympic consumption habits from people around the globe who are unique in both their fanship (defined as "an individual's sense of connection to a sports team"; Reysen & Branscombe, 2010, p. 177) and fandom (defined as "an individual's connection with other fans of a sports team"; Reysen & Branscombe, 2010, p. 177). These Olympic consumers still hold true to three larger elements of sport fan identification: (a) in-group belonging, (b) understanding and cooperating the norms of one's particular in-group, and (c) recognizing the status distinctions between the in-group and other comparable out-groups (Brown, Devlin, & Billings, 2013; Chatman, Bell, & Staw, 1986; Turner, 1985). However, now, instead of traditional television viewing, fans are migrating to social media, streaming websites, mobile device applications, and virtual reality options (IOC, 2018). While the 2018 Winter Olympic Games suffered its lowest NBC *television* ratings to date, this is of diminishing concern in regard to Olympic viewership as consumption is now something increasingly interactive, built on multiple devices and intermittent and diverse media consumption (Otterson, 2018). Moreover, the gender splits between televised and online forms of Olympic media largely mirror each other, as women represent a slight but significant majority across platforms,

An individual's level of enjoyment during consumption of a sporting event is correlated with the entertainment level of the media—the more entertaining the media, the more enjoyment one will feel; thus, understanding the current trend of mobile and streamed Olympic viewership is critical for present and future media insight (Brown, Brown-Devlin, Devlin, & Billings, 2020). For over a decade, social media has contributed to this increased enjoyment, witnessing exponential growth. For example, during the 2018 Olympic Games over 103 million tweets were published, totaling over 33 billion impressions worldwide (Bavishi, 2018). The sheer number of communication messages over a single social media platform has amplified the Olympic conversation to new heights—heights that could not have been achieved previously without mobile internet opportunities.

To provide context to the rate of Olympic-based technological advancement over mobile devices, Onorato (2018) observed a substantial 46 percent increase in mobile device consumption between the 2014 Winter Olympic Games in Sochi and the most recent Winter Games in 2018. Due to this escalating change in consumption habits, NBC can now capture viewer attention (and secure advertising focus) via NBC-affiliated streaming services in addition to the traditional Nielsen television ratings (Brown, Brown-Devlin, Devlin, & Billings, 2020).

Television offers a two-dimensional presentation of sport. Sports megaevents such as the Olympics (see Wenner & Billings, 2017), may be heavily produced by large internationally recognized networks; however, it is difficult to compare passive, yet traditionally entertaining activities (i.e., watching television) to the interactive communities created through social media and the growing development of Social TV (Billings, Brown-Devlin, Brown, & Devlin, 2019).

Entertainment value maintains several characteristics including conflict, suspense, quality of the sporting event, and built drama between opponents (Peterson & Raney, 2008). Through the enactment of these characteristics, the entertainment experience is developed with the desired outcome being overall enjoyment—however, the experience is not solely reliant on the action taking place on the ice, field, or slopes; rather a significant portion of this experience resides in the palm of an individual's hands. For the full entertainment experience to be considered advantageous, outlets such as U.S.-based NBC, must consider avenues that offer "technological and aesthetic appeal to its consumers" in the form of modalities that offer virtual and digital social environments occurring in tandem with the sporting events in competition (Brown, Brown-Devlin, Devlin, & Billings, 2019, p. 105).

Global Involvement

Cultural and nationalistic differences introduce additional layers of difficulty when attempting to assess the Olympic fan's media consumption habits. By breaking down major regions of the globe into representative countries and incorporating new uses and gratifications approaches (West & Turner, 2010), researchers have found recent success in uncovering to determine how people consume the Olympic Games (Billings, Brown-Devlin, Brown, & Devlin, 2019), finding that media consumers make individual decisions that benefit themselves and allow for the highest level of return on their media consumption investment (Brown-Devlin, Devlin, Billings, & Brown, 2018) consistent to understandings of uses and gratifications processes (Ruggerio, 2000; Severin & Tankard, 2000). The modern media consumer has a variety of gratifications to meet including (a) cognitive needs, (b) affective needs, (c) personal integrative needs, (d) social integrative needs, and (e) escapist needs (West & Turner, 2010). Thus, with a menu of sought-after gratifications and comparatively limited *live viewing* opportunities for sporting events (particularly when in television-unfriendly time zones), the Olympic media consumer must utilize a variety of viewing combinations that include TV *combined with* potentially multiple platforms and devices (Billings, Brown-Devlin, Brown, & Devlin, 2019).

In such an environment, fans become their "own media manager" in that individuals are capable of managing multiple platforms and devices depending on consumption goals and needs (Gantz & Lewis, 2014, p. 767). Moreover, recent studies find that fans are likely to assemble the right combination for their needs—such as utilizing a tablet if the fan is attempting to build relationships with family and friends, while also keeping the TV fused upon actual Olympic competition (Billings, Brown-Devlin, Brown, & Devlin, 2019). While major countries such as the United States, China, Canada, and Sweden all participate in technologically layered, multi-screen viewing experiences, some operate at higher levels than others due to the gratifications sought (Brown-Devlin, Devlin, Billings, & Brown, 2018, Billings, Brown-Devlin, Brown, & Devlin, 2019; Brown, Billings, Devlin, & Brown-Devlin, 2020; Wenner & Billings, 2017). What can be established, however, is a significant trend that entertainment has an *inverse* effect on Social TV—an interesting finding, which may indicate that utilizing multiple screens to consume the Olympics is desired, yet not specifically for entertainment-based needs that typically center the sports media experience (Billings, Brown-Devlin, Brown, & Devlin, 2019). Individuals now utilize multiple screens, reducing the level of pure television viewership and simultaneously *bolstering* other interactive and informational desires while *diminishing* entertainment attainment. The opportunity to participate in more textured and rewarding digital-social realms (Biocca, Harms, & Burgoon, 2003) is gradually becoming more appealing for sports fans due to the internet's ability to unite the world through a virtual community (Biocca, Harms, & Gregg, 2001).

Social TV

While increased usage of multiple devices forges new interactive experiences, television still remains at the center of the Olympic media experience—by far the most utilized form of technology for Olympic fans with roughly two-thirds of all Olympic media usage (Brown, Billings, Devlin, & Brown-Devlin, 2020). However, television becomes the basis for more interactive experiences with Olympic media via Social TV—the transformation of passive, entertainment fulfilling television viewing to social fulfillment of engaging relationship and community building through the usage of a second screen (typically a mobile device), while still using television broadcasts as a foundation/consumption screen (Kramer, Winter, Benninghoff, & Gallus, 2015; Cunningham & Eastin, 2017).

Typically, the modality order of Social TV is primarily television and the mobile device is then partnered—however, China has been observed to flip that modality order (Brown-Devlin, Devlin, Billings, & Brown, 2021), with the mobile screen often primary to then pair with other forms of interactive (non-television) content. Incorporated into nearly 33 percent of the Olympic fan's media consumption repertoire (Kramer et al., 2015), Social TV use is rising, especially those who are highly identified with a team, athlete, nation, or sport as those are more likely to engage with sport content through social media, statistical websites, news, and play video games of that sport (Statista, 2019).

The global patterns that can be seen are encouraging and suggest that future consumption through Social TV will increase due—at least in part—to individuals reporting an increase in bridging social capital, enhancing perceived sociability and social presence worldwide, each of which fall into a sought after need of the media consuming individual (Brown-Devlin, Devlin, Billings, & Brown, 2021; Cunningham & Eastin, 2017; Kramer et al., 2015; Sundar & Limperos, 2013).

Conclusion

Frost (2014) opines: "the TV is dead, long live television" (para. 1); the same could be argued for Olympic media as its viewers migrate from legacy media to other content creators (often by the same company) with the net result being the same high engagement found in virtually any form of modern Olympic media offerings. Olympic media fans are increasingly interactive and seeking live/immediate content to bolster their fandom, yet ultimately represent the same laser-focused fans, often watching sports about which they care little until an athlete dons their home nation flag in the process.

Without question, the Olympic fan is demonstrably different than virtually any other fan of mega-sporting events as the fan is more likely to be female, less likely to be a fan of the specific sport being consumed, and more likely to be motivated based on the performances of athletes who, while often unknown, are favorites because of the nation in which they compete with the Games. Technologies increasingly offer the opportunity for global consumption of other forms of sport, which could fuse other nations together. However, realities of time zones and the other requirements of life likely keep the Olympics as a unique form of sports consumption, justifying intense, prolonged media exposure while tabling other life demands because the Games are so big and their frequency so rare.

Billings, Angelini, and MacArthur (2018) contend that the Olympics is "part sporting event, but is also part reality show, part nationalistic emblem, part *Chicken Soup for the Soul*, and part global festival" (p. 1). Indeed, it represents an amalgam of a variety of varied interests arguably unparalleled in modern sports media. Within such a context, it makes sense to conclude that the Olympic fan is just as byzantine an artifact to analyze, drawing non-sports fans to a sporting event for a variety of convoluted (and yet ultimately predictable) premises.

References

Anderson, B. (1983). *Imagined communities*. New York, NY: Verso.
Angelini, J. R. (2008). How did the sport make you feel? Looking at the three dimensions of emotion through a gendered lens. *Sex Roles, 58*(1–2), 127–135.
Apostolou, M., Frantzides, N., & Pavlidou, A. (2014). Men competing, men watching: Exploring watching-pattern contingencies in sports. *International Journal of Sport Communication, 7*(4), 462–476.
Arth, Z. W., Hou, J., Rush, S. W., & Angelini, J. R. (Broad)casting a wider net: Clocking men and women in the primetime and non-primetime coverage of the 2018 Winter Olympics. *Communication & Sport, 1*(1), 1–23. *Advanced online publication*. doi:10.1177/2167479518794505
Bassam, T. (2018). All eyes on PyeongChang: How the Olympic broadcasters are changing the ratings game. *Sports Pro Live*. Retrieved from: www.sportspromedia.com/insight/pyeongchang2018-olympic-broadcast-ratings-total-video.
Bavishi, J. (2018). Recapping the 2018 Winter Olympics on Twitter. *Twitter*. Retrieved from: https://blog.twitter.com/official/en_us/topics/events/2018/Recapping-the-2018-Winter-Olympics-on-Twitter.html.
Billings, A. C., & Eastman, S. T. (2002). Gender, ethnicity, and nationality: Formation of identity in NBC's 2000 Olympic coverage. *International Review for the Sociology of Sport, 37*(3), 349–368.
Billings, A. C., & Eastman, S. T. (2003). Framing identities: Gender, ethnic, and national parity in network announcing of the 2002 Winter Olympics. *Journal of Communication, 53*(4), 369–386.
Billings, A. C. (2008). *Olympic media: Inside the biggest show on television*. London: Routledge.
Billings, A. C. (2009). Conveying the Olympic message: NBC producer and sportscaster interviews regarding the role of identity. *Journal of Sports Media, 4*(1), 1–23.
Billings, A. C., & Angelini, J. R. (2007). Packaging the games for viewer consumption: Gender, ethnicity, and nationality in NBC's coverage of the 2004 Summer Olympics. *Communication Quarterly, 55*(1), 95–111.
Billings, A. C., Angelini, J. R., & MacArthur, P. J. (2018). *Olympic television: Broadcasting the biggest show on Earth*. London: Routledge.
Billings, A. C., Brown, K. A., & Brown, N. A. (2013). 5,535 hours of impact: Effects of Olympic media on nationalism attitudes. *Journal of Broadcasting & Electronic Media, 57*(4), 579–595.
Billings, A. C., Brown-Devlin, N., Brown, K. A., & Devlin, M. B. (2019). When 18 days of coverage is not enough: A six-nation composite of motivations for mobile media use in the 2018 Winter Olympic Games. *Mass Communication & Society, 22*(4), 535–557.
Billings, A., & Young, B. D. (2015). Comparing flagship news programs women's sport coverage in ESPN's *SportsCenter* and FOX Sports 1's *FOX Sports Live*. *Electronic News, 9*(1), 3–16.
Biocca, F., Harms, C., & Burgoon, J. K. (2003). Toward a more robust theory and measure of social presence: Review and suggested criteria. *Presence: Teleoperators and Virtual Environments, 12*(5), 456–480.
Biocca, F., Harms, C., & Gregg, J. (2001). The networked minds measure of social presence: Pilot test of the factor structure and concurrent validity. Paper presented at the Presence Conference, Philadelphia, PA.
Brown, K. A., Billings, A. C., Devlin, M. B., & Brown-Devlin, N. A. (2020, in press). Rings of fandom: Overlapping motivations of sport, Olympic, team, and home nation fans in the 2018 Winter Olympic Games. *Journal of Broadcasting & Electronic Media*.
Brown, K. A., Brown-Devlin, N. A., Devlin, M. B., & Billings, A. C. (2019). The evolution and fragmentation of Olympic media consumption and its impact on the entertainment value of the 2018 Winter Olympics. *Communication Research Reports, 36*(2), 103–113.
Brown, N. A., Billings, A. C., & Ruihley, B. J. (2012). Exploring the change in motivations for fantasy sport participation during the life cycle of a sports fan. *Communication Research Reports, 29*(4), 333–342.
Brown, N. A., Devlin, M. B., & Billings, A. C. (2013). When fan identity levels go extreme: An exploratory study of the highly identified fans of the Ultimate Fighting Championship. *International Journal of Sports Communication, 6*, 19–32.

Brown-Devlin, N., Devlin, M. D., Billings, A. C., & Brown, K. A. (2021). Five rings, five screens?: A global examination of social TV influence on social presence and social identification during the 2018 Winter Olympic Games. *Communication & Sport*, 9(6), 865–887.

Chatman, J. A., Bell, N. E., & Staw, B. M. (1986). The managed thought: The role of self-Justification and impression management in organizational settings. In D. Giola, & H. Sims (Eds.), *The thinking organization* (pp. 191–214). San Francisco, CA: Jossey Bass.

Cooper, R., & Tang, T. (2013). Gender and predictors of multiplatform media uses: A case study of the Super Bowl. *International Journal of Sport Communication*, 6(3), 348–363.

Cottrell, M. P., & Nelson, T. (2011). Not just the Games? Power, protest and politics at the Olympics. *European Journal of International Relations*, 17(4), 729–753.

Cunningham, N. R., & Eastin, M. S. (2017). Second screen and sports: A structural investigation into team identification and efficacy. *Communication & Sport*, 5(3), 288–310.

Deggans, E. (2018, Feb. 21). More ways than ever to watch the Olympics, and fewer are watching in prime time. *The Torch*. Retrieved from: www.npr.org/sections/thetorch/2018/02/21/587205078/more-ways-than-ever-to-watch-the-olympics-and-fewer-are-watching-in-prime-time.

Devlin, M. B., & Billings, A. C. (2018). Examining confirmation biases: Implications regarding sponsorship congruency and fans of the Ultimate Fighting Championship. *International Journal of Sports Marketing and Sponsorship*, 19(1), 58–73.

Elliott, S. (2008, Aug. 18). Olympics draw high percentage of women viewers, and ads intended for them. *New York Times*. Retrieved from: www.nytimes.com/2008/08/19/sports/olympics/19adco.html.

Frost, V. (2014, Dec. 9). The TV is dead, long live television. *The (London) Guardian*. Retrieved from: www.theguardian.com/commentisfree/2014/dec/09/tv-dead-long-live-television-format-consuming.

Gantz, W., & Lewis, N. (2014). Sports on traditional and newer digital media: Is there really a fight for fans? *Television & New Media*, 15(8), 760–768.

Gantz, W., & Wenner, L. A. (1991). Men, women, and sports: Audience experiences and effects. *Journal of Broadcasting & Electronic Media*, 35(2), 233–243.

Gerbner, G., Gross, L., Morgan, M., & Signorielli, N. (1986). *Living with television: The dynamics of the cultivation process*. In J. Bryant & D. Zillmann (Eds.), *Perspectives on media effects* (pp. 17–40). Hillsdale, NJ: Erlbaum.

"Global Broadcast and Audience Report" (2018, June). Olympic Winter Games PyeongChang 2018. *Publicis Media*. Retrieved from: https://stillmed.olympic.org/media/Document%20Library/Olympic Org/Games/Winter-Games/Games-PyeongChang-2018-Winter-Olympic-Games/IOC-Marketing/Olympic-Winter-Games-PyeongChang-2018-Broadcast-Report.pdf.

Hardin, M., & Greer, J. D. (2009). The influence of gender-role socialization, media use and sports participation on perceptions of gender-appropriate sports. *Journal of Sport Behavior*, 32(2), 207–226.

Hoeber, L., & Kerwin, S. (2013). Exploring the experiences of female sport fans: A collaborative self-ethnography. *Sport Management Review*, 16(3), 326–336.

Huddy, L., & Khatib, N. (2007). American patriotism, national identity, and political involvement. *American Journal of Political Science*, 51, 63–77. doi:10.1111=j.1540-5907.2007.00237.x

Hutchins, B. (2019). Mobile media sport: The case for building a mobile media and communications research agenda. *Communication & Sport*, 7(4), 466–487.

IOC (2018). IOC Marketing: Media guide. International Olympic Committee. Retrieved from: https://stillmed.olympic.org/media/Document%20Library/OlympicOrg/Games/Winter-Games/Games-PyeongChang-2018-Winter-Olympic-Games/IOC-Marketing/Media-Guide.pdf#_ga=2.106861511.593821567.1522290134-1545796272.1485819573.

Jakubowska, H. (2015). Are women still the "other sex": Gender and sport in the Polish mass media. *Sport in Society*, 18(2), 168–185.

Kramer, N. C., Winter, S., Benninghoff, B., & Gallus, C. (2015). How "social" is Social TV? The influence of social motives and expected outcomes on the usage of Social TV applications. *Computers in Human Behavior*, 51, 255–262.

Lagaert, S., & Roose, H. (2018). The gender gap in sport event attendance in Europe: The impact of macro-level gender equality. *International Review for the Sociology of Sport*, 53(5), 533–549.

Larson, J. F., & Rivenburgh, N. K. (1991). A comparative analysis of Australian, U.S., and British telecasts of the Seoul Olympic ceremony. *Journal of Broadcasting & Electronic Media*, 35, 75–94.

Lim, J. S., Hwang, Y., Kim, S., & Biocca, F. A. (2015). How social media engagement leads to sports channel loyalty: Mediating roles of social presence and channel commitment. *Computers in Human Behavior*, 46, 158–167.

McAdams, D. D. (2016, Aug. 4). NBC 2016 Rio Olympics by the numbers. *TV Technology*. Retrieved from: www.tvtechnology.com/news/nbc-2016-rio-olympics-coverage-by-the-numbers.

McDonald, H., Leckie, C., Karg, A., & Zubcevic-Basic, N. (2018). Female season ticket holders: How their satisfaction is derived differently from males. *European Sport Management Quarterly, 18*(2), 156–174.

Mehus, I. (2005). Sociability and excitement motives of spectators attending entertainment sport events: Spectators of soccer and ski-jumping. *Journal of Sport Behavior, 28*(4), 333–350.

Messner, M. A., Dunbar, M., & Hunt, D. (2000). The televised sports manhood formula. *Journal Sport and Social Issues, 24*(4), 380–394.

Onorato, A. (2018). Winter Olympics by the numbers: Brands win big on social media. *DMN*. Retrieved from: www.dmnews.com/social-media/olympic-winter games/article/.

Otterson, J. (2018). 2018 Winter Olympics close out as least-watched on record, down 7% from Sochi games. *Variety*. Retrieved from: http://variety.com/2018/tv/news/2018-winter-olympics-ratings-2-1202710137.

Peterson, E., & Raney, A. A. (2008). Exploring the complexity of suspense as a predictor of mediated sports enjoyment. *Journal of Broadcasting & Electronic Media, 52*, 544–562.

Raney, A. A. (2006). Why we watch and enjoy mediated sports. In A. A. Raney and J. Bryant (Eds.). *Handbook of sport and media* (pp. 313–329). Mahwah, NJ: LEA.

Real, M. R. (1989). *Super media: A cultural studies approach*. Newbury Park, CA: Sage.

Reysen, S., & Branscombe, N. R. (2010). Fanship and fandom: Comparisons between sport and non-sport fans. *Journal of Sport Behavior, 33*, 176–193.

Ruggiero, T. E. (2000). Uses and gratifications theory in the 21st Century. *Mass Communication & Society, 3*(1), 3–37.

Salkowitz, R. (2018). Data shows women paid more attention to Super Bowl LII than men. *Forbes*. Retrieved from: www.forbes.com/sites/robsalkowitz/2018/02/05/data-shows-women-paid-more-attention-to-super-bowl-lii-than-men/#4cecaab65c4a (accessed October 3, 2018).

Sanderson, J. (2008). "You are the type of person that children should look up to as a hero": Parasocial interaction on 38.pitches.com. *International Journal of Sport Communication, 1*(3), 337–360.

Sargent, S. L., Zillmann, D., & Weaver III, J. B. (1998). The gender gap in the enjoyment of televised sports. *Journal of Sport and Social Issues, 22*(1), 46–64.

Schallhorn, C., Knoll, J., & Schramm, H. (2017). "Girls just want to have fun?" Sex differences in motives of watching the FIFA World Cup and the UEFA European Championship. *Sport in Society, 20*(9), 1118–1133.

Severin, W. J., & Tankard, J. W. (2000). *Communication theories: Origins, methods and uses in the mass media*. Reading, PA: Addison-Wesley Longman.

Sherwood, M., Osborne, A., Nicholson, M., & Sherry, E. (2017). Newswork, news values, and audience considerations factors that facilitate media coverage of women's sports. *Communication & Sport, 5*(6), 647–668.

Statista (2019, July 23). Number of social network users worldwide, 2010–2021. Retrieved from: www.statista.com/statistics/278414/number-of-worldwide-social-network-users/.

Sundar, S. S., & Limperos, A. M. (2013). Uses and grats 2.0: New gratifications for new media. *Journal of Broadcasting & Electronic Media, 57*(4), 504–525.

Turner, J. C. (1985). Social categorization and the self-concept: A social cognitive theory of group behaviour. In E. J. Lawler (Ed.), *Advances in group processes* (pp. 77–121), Greenwich, CT: JAI Press.

Wenner, L. A., & Billings, A. C. (Eds.) (2017). *Sport, media, and mega-events*. London: Routledge.

West, R. L., & Turner, L. H. (2010). *Introducing communication theory: Analysis and application*. Boston: McGraw-Hill.

Whiteside, E., & Hardin, M. (2011). Women (not) watching women: Leisure time, television, and implications for televised coverage of women's sports. *Communication, Culture & Critique, 4*(2), 122–143.

Women's Sports Foundation (2020). New national report sheds light on girl's sport participation. www.womenssportsfoundation.org/press_release/new-national-report-sheds-light-on-girls-sports-participation/

Xu, Q., Billings, A. C., Scott, O. K. M., Lewis, M., & Sharpe, S. (2017). Gender differences through the lens of Rio: Australian Olympic primetime coverage of the 2016 Rio Summer Olympic Games. *International Review for the Sociology of Sport, 1*(1), 1–19. Advanced online publication. doi:10.1177/1012690217710690.

17
Para Sport Fandom
Fans and Followers of Paralympians

Linda K. Fuller[1]

Introducing Paralympian Fandom

Since first being performed in 1948 by British veterans of World War II, the Paralympic Games were introduced to the world stage in 1960 in Rome,[2] taking place following the regular Olympic Games since 1988 in Seoul. Under the auspices of the International Paralympic Committee (IPC), which was established in 1989 in Dusseldorf, Germany (Fuller, 2016) and initially open only to wheelchair athletes, the Paralympics have expanded to include classifications for those with impaired muscle power or range of movement(s), limb and/or leg length difference(s), short stature, hypertonia, ataxia, vision and/or intellectual impairment. Darcy, Frawley, and Adair (2017: 1) have declared that, "Each successive Paralympic Games has made contribution to this growth: introducing new sports, encouraging more countries to attend, increased scope of broadcasting, record ticket sales, and alternative media channels to promote the event and its athletes." Further, as Mauerberg-deCastro et al. (2016) have noted in their study of the elite disabled athlete paradigm, new performance records are "increasingly and gradually gaining the attention of fans."

The Summer Paralympics include 22 sports and 526 medals, the Winter Paralympics 5 sports and 72 events (Fuller, 2018):

1. Summer: archery, athletics, badminton, boccia canoeing, cycling (track and road), equestrian, football five-a-side, goalball, judo, powerlifting, rowing, shooting, swimming, table tennis, triathlon, volleyball, and wheelchair, fencing, rugby, and tennis.
2. Winter: alpine skiing, para ice hockey, Nordic skiing (biathlon and cross-country skiing), para-snowboarding, and wheelchair curling.

Under the auspices of National Paralympic Committees (NPCs), which are controlled by the IPC, the Paralympics are made up of these associations: African (49), Americas (32), Asian (43), European (48), and Oceania (8). Table 17.1 outlines that history from 1960 to the present:

Importantly, audiences for the Paralympics continue to grow such that 2012 London set a record of drawing a global audience of 3.8 billion and then 2016 Rio attracted a record cumulative audience of more than 4.1 billion people, with another billion engaged via digital media

Table 17.1 Summer and Winter Paralympics

[S=Summer; W=Winter; NPC=National Paralympic Committee]

#	Season	Year	Place	NPCs
1	S	1960	Rome, ITA	17
11	S	1964	Tokyo, JAP	19
111	S	1968	Tel Aviv, ISR	28
1V	S	1972	Heidelberg, GER	41
1	W	1976	Ornskoldsvik, SWE	16
V	S	1976	Toronto, CAN	40
11	W	1980	Geilo, NOR	18
V1	S	1980	Arnheim, NED	42
111	W	1984	Innsbruck, AUT	21
V11	S	1984	Stoke Mandeville, UK and New York, USA	54
1V	W	1988	Innsbruck, AUT	22
V111	S	1988	Seoul, KOR	60
V	W	1992	Tignes-Albertville, FRA	24
1X	S	1992	Barcelona & Madrid, ESP	83
V1	W	1994	Lillehammer, NOR	31
X	S	1996	Atlanta, USA	104
V11	W	1998	Nagano, JAP	31
X1	S	2000	Sydney, AUS	122
V111	W	2002	Salt Lake City, USA	36
X11	S	2004	Athens, GRE	135
1X	W	2006	Torino, ITA	38
X111	S	2008	Beijing, CHI	146
X	W	2010	Vancouver, CAN	44
X1V	S	2012	London, UK	164
X1	W	2014	Sochi, RUS	174
XV	S	2016	Rio de Janeiro, BRA	159
X11	W	2018	PyeongChang, KOR	49

channels. It was covered by more than 154 countries by more than 5,000 hours of broadcasting and more than a billion digital media engagements.

Most recently, Nielsen Sports reported that the 2018 PyeongChang Paralympics broke records for both international broadcast and online viewing for Winter Games outside a host country, selling more than 320,000 tickets and claiming an audience of two million locally and 251.5 million people on the IPC's digital media channels. Some 291.5 million people watched the Opening Ceremony, up 60 million from 2014 Sochi. The USOC reported that the most popular Paralympic social media posts (one million) were for the sled hockey team's three-peat Gold against Canada, while 434 posts dealt with social profiles of medalists Brenna Huckaby (snowboarder, the first Paralympian to appear in *Sports Illustrated*'s swimsuit issue), Oksana Masters (cross-country skier but also a Paralympic rower), and snowboarder Amy Purdy, who collected some 25,000 new followers. Japanese viewers made up 21 percent of the overall audience and, as some 122.8 million Chinese viewers were also tuned in, enthusiasm is even higher for 2022 Beijing. Recognizing that spectators and fans are the lifeblood of both the Olympic and the Paralympic Games, Santiago Manso (2017) emphasizes the role of digital technologies as a means of engaging spectators well before they happen, establishing a "fan engagement methodology" linking technology to both business and the fan experience to enrich "personalized experiences and promote retention and continuous participation."

Still, former President Donald Trump has described the Paralympics as "a little tough to watch too much" (cited in Ioannou, 2018). *The Boston Globe* (Scharfenberg, 2018) bemoans the lack of American audiences' interest, noting how most of its coverage is on secondary stations, with low expectation for ratings:

> There will be no deluge of t-shirt sales. No rash of magazine covers. No major burst of social media activity. Our collective indifference is hard to figure. Americans love spectacle as much as anyone. And the United States has long been a leader on disability rights; indeed, when it comes to legal protections, the country is several steps ahead of many of the nations that have embraced the Paralympics. Yet legal and cultural norms do not move in perfect synch.

Perhaps it is all part of societal approach to difference, not just disability, but this chapter offers an opportunity to dissect the language of fandom and the Paralympics and then outline a number of organizations dedicated to sponsoring and encouraging both athletes and followers. "With a wide variety of sports on their programs, the Olympic and Paralympic Games create possibilities for the realization that we can all be sports fans," Wolfe and Hums (2017) remind us:

> The right combination of hype, energy and visibility opens our eyes to a wide range of sports and activities. We can readily see the potential for a fan-base that wants to engage with women's sports or adaptive sports on a more regular basis.

The Language of "Disability" and the Paralympics

As we continue to learn how far from neutral the language surrounding sport is, that consideration is especially critical relative to Paralympian fandom for the "differently abled," "diffAbled," "people of all abilities," and other euphemisms. For starters, consider the various terms: disabled sports, adaptive sports, and/or para sports, my personal phrase being "grit and glam" (Fuller, 2014). Underpinning this study is the fervent hope that we all use terms describing first the athlete and then his or her category, such as Joe the one-legged gymnast or Jo the vision-impaired Nordic skier. S/he is "a person with paraplegia," not a paraplegic, and the topic is *para sport*.

The term "Paralympics" was thought to be a pun or portmanteau[3] combining "paraplegic" and "Olympic" (Vanlandewijck and Thompson (2011: 8), with the Greek preposition *para* as in "attached to." Jill M. LeClair (2012: 10) cites Article 30 from the 2006 UN Conference on the Rights of Persons with Disabilities: "The historical framing of disability as a social welfare issue, charity-based and medically defined, was replaced by a rights-based approach to support inclusion." Tackling head-on the issue about whether disability is the opposite of ableism, she points out how, historically, "disability has been associated with religious or spiritual punishment and images of evil, so irrational fears led to active policies of discrimination, abuse and even extermination." Activists and athletes alike caution against overusing terms like "amazing" relative to Paralympians' achievements, preferring respectful linguistic terms over labels ranging from "supercrips" (Hardin and Hardin, 2004) and "superhumans" to "exotics." Learning from the LGBT community, Paralympians want to reclaim their true identities.

Stigmas and stereotypes of disabled people nevertheless prevail in mainstream media (Ellis, 2009; Gilbert and Schantz, 2008; Schantz and Gilbert, 2012; Thomas and Smith, 2003), Hodges et al. (2014) summarizing those representations:

- Vulnerable and pitiable: portrayals of disabled people as childlike dependents who need help and charity from others.
- "Supercrip" – inspirational stories of determination and personal courage to overcome "adversity."
- Portrayals of disabled people as less than human, e.g. villains, "freak shows," "exotic."
- Characters primarily defined by their disability rather than other aspects of their identity.
- Disabled people presented as unable to participate fully in everyday life.

But *you* know that they are not "victims," if other-abled, and they adamantly do not want pity or charity, or patronizing language such as being called "inspirational" (Schpigel, 2016).

In something of a double-whammy, female Paralympians typically receive less of the spotlight than their male counterparts (Buysse and Borcherding, 2010; Cheong et al., 2016; Houghton et al., 2017; Thomas and Smith, 2003). Wanting to see how they represent themselves, Kim Toffoletti (2018) generated a list of 67 participants at 2016 Rio from their self-profiles on the Australian Paralympic Committee website, then focused on eight with high public profiles: A paraplegia equestrian, single-legged swimmer, one cyclist with multiple sclerosis and another with vision impairment, a triathlete with right hand limb deficiency, paraplegia athlete, canoeist with Arthrogryposis multiplex congenita, and a table tennis player with Erb's palsy. Her findings:

> Many of these women use social media to offer progressive accounts of women's disability sport, posting images of themselves as autonomous and active sporting subjects who are capable, powerful and successful athletes. These para-sportswomen offer a mixture of active sporting images (riding, running, rolling, paddling, hitting) and more static poses (holding medals or equipment, smiling at cameras, a steeling competitive gaze). They do not shy away from showing their bodies and disabilities.
>
> *p. 263*

Arguing that, "Hyper-visible representations of para-sport could be an important indicator of public representations of, and attitudes towards, people with disabilities," Pullen, et al. (2018) examined how the UK's Paralympic broadcaster, Channel 4, covered the 2016 Rio Paralympics. In a blatant attempt to "hook audiences," albeit claiming they wanted to change public attitudes toward disability, the producers made the commercial decision to emphasize athletes' backstories. Hence, the "super-crip" narrative (re)appeared, repeatedly, simultaneously sensationalizing and personalizing certain stories[4] and re-visiting the notion of able-bodied norms that can cause enormous embarrassment and/or guilt for athletes who feel unable to meet certain expectations.

Cultural considerations also need to be factored in as, while Westerners are encouraged to use "people-first" language relative to disability (e.g., "the woman who is blind" rather than "the blind woman"), while Asians tend to recognize that each individual has a role to play in society and so what might be interpreted as problematic in one culture might be seen as beneficial in another. If we are serious about social justice, we need to add "ableism" to racism, sexism, ageism, and other discriminatory dialect in our speech.

Para Sport Organizations

There are a number of groups dealing with the "disabled"/"variously abled" in sport, all heavily invested in helping their constituents, such as the American Athletic Association for the Deaf, National Foundation of Wheelchair Tennis, National Handicapped Sports, National Wheelchair Athletic Association, Special Olympics International, U.S. Association for Blind Athletes, Wheelchair Sports, USA, etc. Emphasis here, on Paralympic fandom, is concentrated on these para sport organizations: The International Paralympic Committee (IPC), The Agitos Foundation, Paralympic School Days (PSD), and AthletesFirst.

The International Paralympic Committee's Para Sport Fan Zone

> The Para Sport Fan Zone brings together the social media profiles from the whole Paralympic Movement, linking and promoting athletes, National Governing Bodies, National Paralympic Committees and International Federations.
>
> *www.paralympic.org/fan-zone-info*

As delineated above, the Para Sport Fan Zone (www.paralympic.org/fan-zone) is dedicated to the Paralympics and Paralympians, profiling key players and their events. As a platform allowing and encouraging fans to follow and engage with certain favorite athletes, as well as introducing them to many others, it serves as a unique interactive means for interactions with para-athletes via social media. Each day, its "Para sport news" offers information on various athletes and their various sports relative to social media like Facebook postings and Tweets, such as the post that "Jakarta (is) to host Asian Para Games test event: Athletics, badminton, swimming, table tennis and wheelchair basketball to feature at the end of the month." USA, Great Britain, Canada, India, and Australia are the top five countries visiting Paralympic.org.

On any one day, the website offers information on para-athletes and their sports relative to various forms of social media. For 2018 PyeongChang, IPC teamed up with Graybo such that digital media channels reportedly reached some 251 million people, including some 17.4 million video views, Facebook postings (reported by the IPC at 221.5 million) and Tweets (142,096 in 2017). Picture a post that wheelchair rugby between Canada and the United States was taking place, or that Jakarta, Indonesia would soon host an Asian Para Games test event of athletics, badminton, swimming, table tennis, and wheelchair basketball. Instagram also continues to increase its numbers—nearly 20 percent in 2017, when the IPC reported a total of 20.7 million YouTube videos were viewed.

By way of introducing you to some real Paralympians, what follows are brief profiles of the Para Sport Fan Zone's five top "Social leaders"; see Table 17.3, on Fan ranking.

Topping the chart is Italian pro racing driver/para-cyclist **Alex Zanardi**, a CART champion and Formula One racer who, after becoming a double amputee after a serious crash, took up handcycling as his next competition to represent Italy and win Gold at the 2012 London and 2016 Rio Paralympics. Another amputee—dating to when he was five years old, English sprinter **Jonnie Peacock** also earned Gold medals at 2012 London and 2016 Rio and has been

Table 17.2 Overall IPC website visitor numbers 2013–2018

Year	2013	2014	2015	2016	2017	2018
Website visitors	2,061,931	2,807,200	2,784,887	7,728,492	3,151,782	2,149,479

Table 17.3 Rankings by Number of Fans/Followers

Rank	Paralympian	Para-sport	# of fans/followers
1	Alex Zanardi	Handcycling	285,661
2	Jonnie Peacock	Sprint running	102,816
3	Ellie Simmonds	Swimming	87,402
4	Amy Purdy	Para-snowboarding	70,791
5	Hannah Cockroft	Wheelchair racing	51,268

appointed a Member of the British Empire (MBE) for his services to athletics. Born with the genetic disorder achondroplasia that results in dwarfism, British Paralympian swimmer **Ellie Simmonds** began competing at age 13, going on to garner Gold at Beijing 2008, London 2012, and Rio 2016. American actress, author, model, motivational speaker, and clothing designer **Amy Purdy** has been a para-snowboarder since receiving prosthetic legs when she was 19. Co-founder of Adaptive Action Sports, Purdy earned Bronze at 2014 Sochi and again, with Silver, at 2018 PyeongChang; more amazingly, she was a contestant on *Dancing with the Stars*, the television show's first double amputee contestant. "Hurricane" **Hannah Cockroft**, who experienced cardiac arrests and mobility issues soon after birth, is a British wheelchair racer who has won Gold at London 2012 and Rio Paralympic Games 2016 as well as Gold at IPC World Championships at 2011 Christchurch, 2013 Lyon, 2015 Doha, 2017 London, and 2019 Dubai. Her motto: "Those afraid of pain will never know glory."

The real introduction here should/could be to the economics of covering Paralympians in the media, marketplace.org (Wagner, 2018) pointing out how the Games are typically aired at odd times on the major networks, if streamed differently on certain (usually paying) cable channels. Pullen et al. (2018) report how producers of the UK's Channel 4—influenced by notions of sponsorship and broadcast revenues, made their decisions on whom to focus:

> We were following the top trending athletes on social (media) for that period, so we had an automated system that just says, this person was talked about this amount of times, it would just make a leaderboard so we just kind of reference it in both the broadcast and internally for our own use, and sure enough it was doing as we had expected, so Ellie (Symonds), the swimmers go quite early so she was quite up there, she had won the gold medal and going to have a little cry, and also everyone loves a crying athlete … and then I think it was Jonny Peacock next and as expected, these big kind of heroes, being top of the pile and all of a sudden Zinardi went straight to the top, the Italian Formula One racer, and we were sort of like, we knew he was competing but our focus had always been quite partisan, like OK, who from GB has turned up.

As an aside, you may have noted how many of the athletes' names are misspelled in their report, which somehow strikes me as symptomatic of the producers' attitudes toward their subjects.

The Agitos Foundation

A development arm of the IPC established in 2012 and headquartered in Bonn, Germany, The Agitos Foundation (agitosfoundation.org) bills itself as "the leading global organisation developing sport activities for people with disabilities as a tool for changing lives and contributing to an inclusive society for all." Taking its name from the Paralympic symbol of the *Agitos*, a derivation of the Latin verb "to move," the organization works globally to attract philanthropic donations and grants, along with non-financial strategic support to deliver programs and provide grants to the IPC membership with the ultimate goal of enabling people with disabilities to participate in sporting activities. "Convinced that Para athletes make a huge difference to the perceptions of ability and that we can make for an inclusive world through sport," the Agitos Foundation receives support from IPC partners such as Toyota, Panasonic, Allianz, and BP. With a reach to more than 100 countries, it delivers programs such as the NPC Development Programme, I'mPOSSIBLE, Proud Paralympians and Road to the Games along these priority themes:

- **Pathways**: Providing sustainable pathways into grassroots and competitive Para sport.
- **Awareness**: Using the power of sport to help the world to understand disability and embrace inclusion.
- **Representation**: Encouraging worldwide representation and greater diversity within our Movement.
- **Ambassadors**: Empowering athletes to live the Paralympic values in a way that inspires the next generation.

To date, the Agitos Foundation is proud to report that it has distributed grants totaling EUR 3.8 million in 179 projects for 517,500 people through its Grant Support Programme and has recently launched the seventh edition of EUR 650,000 for Para sports projects.

Paralympic School Days (PSD)

An educational program aimed at creating awareness and understanding people with impairments, Paralympic School Day was initiated in 2004 by the IPC (www.paralympic.org/the-ipc/paralympic-school-day) and the European Paralympic Committee (EPC) "to raise schoolchildren's awareness and understanding about people with disabilities around the world." It had the following objectives:

- To increase knowledge and awareness of Paralympic sports.
- To create a better understanding of practical application of inclusion in physical education and activity.
- To inform about the different concepts in disability sports.
- To increase the usage of disability sports for reverse integration.
- To facilitate the change of perception and attitude toward persons with disabilities.
- To promote scholarly research activities and studies about Paralympic education.

Part of the curriculum includes emphasis on respect for sporting achievement, acceptance of individual differences, sport as a human right, and empowerment and social support in sport. Examples might include videos of practicing athletes, stories of inclusion, introductions to adapted equipment, games and quizzes, artistic imaging, coloring sheets, crosswords, learning about Paralympic host cities, wordsmithing, and more. Early on, influenced by the experience of 1996 Atlanta, Wilhite et al. (1997) performed a field study to evaluate PDS in the local schools with 704 students, finding that most respondents were open to participating with one another—if fewer of those with disabilities agreed.

With positive reports from Belgium (van Biesen et al., 2006), Greece (Panagiotou et al., 2008), the Czech Republic (Yang Liu et al., 2010), New York (McKay, 2013, 2015), Brazil

(Borgman and de Almeida, 2015), and Russia (Belousov, 2016), the program demonstrated that attitudes can be changed to be positive toward Paralympians; still, it is obvious that Paralympic Education needs national and international recognition to really make a difference. Recognizing that "Disability awareness programs offer an avenue for raising and changing attitudes toward people with disabilities," McKay et al., 2018) encourage further research in this arena.

AthletesFirst

Established in 2011 from Canada as a blogging site for the disability sport community as www.AthletesFirst.ca, this project was created to allow an online space for discussions by means of what was conceptualized as a participatory action research (PAR) framework (Bundon, 2016). From a beginning with two contributors, it soon expanded to become a six-person blog team that eventually grew to engage a global audience from its first topic of "Language and sport," which established the prefix "para." AthletesFirst visited 9,500+ times by 6,500 readers from 97 countries, their comments filling some 200 printed pages. In addition to creating an important space for conversations among fellow athletes who "spoke the same language" in respectful tones and understood one another's thoughts and feelings, the blog brought together and affirmed solidarity. Here are some examples from posted topics:

1. *Should athletes without disabilities be allowed in parasport?* Responses included comments about how "para sport saved my life (but)… If I had arrived at a program with able bodied people I am not sure I would have felt as able to participate and compete" to rebukes centering on how it could increase numbers and awareness. One thought it a "win-win" while another wondered whether there should be a "disability quota system."

2. *The "supercrip" in advertising*: Recognizing issues such a sponsorships and endorsements and how corporations have predetermined attitudes, discussions dealt with Oscar Pistorius, Nike's use of "wannabe" athletes, false and/or exaggerated representations, and the all-too-often placing of Paralympians on pedestals.

Overall, the real value of the blog was allowing issues such as what determines elite athletes, including more women in the Paralympic movement and, most importantly, just giving voice to this population.

So, Paralympic Fandom

Fortunately, as demonstrated here, there are numerous outlets for the continually growing fan base of the Paralympic Games. We have not even cited the many individual para-athletes who have their own blogs and followers, never mind the 176 National Paralympic Committee (NPC) members[5] and all their numbers. Africa maintains 49 NPCs, The Americas 29, Asia 42, Europe 48, and Oceania 8, but those numbers fluctuate as various constituencies might be suspended or even terminated depending on performances and politics.

Consider: American para sport fans can download the U.S. Paralympics App that offers exclusive, customized news, features, photos, and videos of Team USA's top athletes. Eve Hampton (2016) considers herself their #1 fan, as she herself has had Transverse Myelitis (TM, an inflammation of the spinal cord characterized by neurological dysfunction) since the age of 13; a wheelchair basketball player and mother, she couldn't be happier cheering on the many Paralympians she knows personally. At Rio 2016, the #FillTheSeats crowdfunding campaign organized to send thousands of Brazilian children to the Paralympic Games to fill the stadium left IPC's Craig Spencer with tears streaming down his face, especially when local favorite Daniel Dias won Gold in the 200-metre freestyle swimming meet (Meenaghan, 2016).

The U.S. Olympic & Paralympic Committee maintains a Hall of Fame (Dure, 2019), these Paralympians being the most recent nominees:

- **Cheri Blauwet**, track and field: Seven medals in three Paralympics, several major marathon wins.
- **Candace Cable**, track and field, Nordic skiing, alpine skiing: First American woman to win medals in summer and winter.
- **Muffy Davis**, cycling, alpine skiing: Four medals in skiing before switching to cycling and winning three golds.
- **Bart Dodson**, track and field: Eight gold medals in 1992 alone, 20 medals total over five Paralympics.
- **Greg Mannino**, alpine skiing: Six gold medals and 12 total over five Paralympics.
- **Erin Popovich**, swimming: 14 gold medals and 19 total over three Paralympics.
- **Marla Runyan**, Para track and field, Para-cycling, Olympic track and field: Six Paralympic medals, first legally blind American to compete in Olympics.
- **Chris Waddell**, alpine skiing, track and field: 12 Paralympic medals in skiing, one in track and field.
- **Trischa Zorn**, swimming: 52 medals, including 38 gold, over seven Paralympics.

Para-athletes at the Commonwealth Games and other venues have also been the subjects of disability study (Dickson et al., 2017, McPherson et al., 2016, Misener et al., 2018), but to date none have focused on their fans per se. "Researchers have clearly established the cultural importance of sport fandom in creating unity in communities," Osborne and Coombs (2016: 13) have noted, to which Wolfe and Hums (2017) would add:

> Fan support is important to athletes both with and without a disability. A fan of basketball can be a fan of wheelchair basketball, a volleyball fan can thoroughly enjoy sitting volleyball, and rugby is rugby, whether it's men's, women's or quad rugby, which is often referred to by the intriguing name Murderball. And if you love soccer then you are definitely going to love 5-a-side blind soccer. The most important thing about sports fans is that they stay fans.

Fortunately, we have moved from the medical model of sport and rehabilitation to one that centers on the effects of individual athletic performance for both the para sportsperson and the wider society (Fuller, 2019). We are beginning to do what Purdue and Howe (2012) suggest we do about what they call the Paralympic paradox: "See the sport, not the disability." Or, what *The Guardian* (Editorial, 2016) recommends: "Focus on ability, not disability."

Notes

1. The author would like to acknowledge Nora Varga, Fundraising Assistant of the Agitos Foundation, Craig Spence, Chief Marketing & Communications Officer of the International Paralympic Committee, and Andrea Bundon of the School of Kinesiology, University of British Columbia for their input in this chapter.
2. The first Summer Paralympic Games took place at 1960 Rome, but the first Winter ones began at 1976 Örnsköldsvik, Sweden.
3. The notion of *portmanteau* was recommended to me by Andrea Bundon who, upon reviewing my draft, suggested it as a closer description in combining two terms.
4. See also Bush et al., 2013.

5 Afghanistan, Algeria, Andorra, Angola, Antigua and Barbuda, Argentina, Armenia, Aruba, Australis, Austria, Azerbaijan, Bahrain, Barbados, Belarus, Belgium, Benin, Bermuda, Bhutan, Bosnia and Herzegovina, Botswana, Brazil, Brunei, Bulgaria, Burkina Faso, Burundi, Cambodia, Cameroon, Canada, Cape Verde, Central African Republic, Chile, China, Chinese Taipei, Colombia, Comoros, Congo, Costa Rica, Croatia, Cuba, Cyprus, Czech Republic, Cote d'Ivoire, Denmark, Djibouti, Dominican Republic, DR Congo, Ecuador, Egypt, El Salvador, Estonia, Ethiopia, Faroe Islands, Fiji, Finland, France, Gabon, Gambia, Georgia, Germany, Ghana, Great Britain, Greece, Grenada, Guatemala, Guinea, Guinea-Bissau, Guyana, Haiti, Honduras, Hong Kong, Hungary, Iceland, India, Indonesia, Iran, Iraq, Ireland, Israel, Italy, Jamaica, Japan, Jordan, Kazakhstan, Kenya, Kiribati, Korea, Korea DPR, Kuwait, Kyrgyzstan, Laos, Latvia, Lebanon, Lesotho, Liberia, Libya, Liechtenstein, Lithuania, Luxembourg, Macau, Madagascar, Malawi, Malaysia, Maldives, Mali, Malta, Mauritius, Mexico, Moldova, Mongolia, Montenegro, Morocco, Mozambique, Myanmar, Namibia, Nepal, Netherlands, New Zealand, Nicaragua, Niger, Nigeria, North Macedonia, Norway, Oman, Pakistan, Palestine, Panama, Papua New Guinea, Paraguay, Peru, Philippines, Poland, Portugal, Puerto Rico, Qatar, Refugee Para(lympic) Team, Romania, Russia, Rwanda, Saint Vincent and the Grenadines, Samoa, San Marino, Sao Tome and Principe, Saudi Arabia, Senegal, Serbia, Seychelles, Sierra Leone, Singapore, Slovakia, Slovenia, Salomon Islands, Somalia, South Africa, Spain, Sri Lanka, Sudan, Suriname, Sweden, Switzerland, Syria, Tajikistan, Tanzania, Thailand, Timor-Leste, Togo, Tonga, Trinidad and Tobago, Tunisia, Turkey, Turkmenistan, US Virgin Islands, Uganda, Ukraine, United Arab Emirates, United States of America, Uruguay, Uzbekistan, Vanuatu, Venezuela, Vietnam, Yemen, Zambia, Zimbabwe.

References

Belousov, Lev. Paralympic sport as a vehicle for teaching tolerance to young people. *Procedia—Social and Behavioral Sciences* 233, 2016: 46–52.

Borgmann, Tiago and José Júlio Gavião de Almeida. Paralympic sport at school: A literature review. *Movimento* 21/1, 2015: 49–64.

Bundon, Andrea and L. Hurd Clarke. Unless you go online you are on your own: Blogging as a bridge in para-sport. *Disability & Sport*, 2014: 185–198.

Bundon, Andrea and L. Hurd Clarke. Honey or vinegar? Athletes with disabilities discuss strategies for advocacy within the Paralympic movement. *Journal of Sport and Social Issues* 39/5, 2015: 351–370.

Bundon, Andrea. "Talking my language": The AthletesFirst project and the use of blogging in virtual disability sport communities. In Ellis, Katie and Mike Kent (Eds.) *Disability and social media: Global perspectives*, 241–254. Routledge.

Bush, Anthony, Michael Silk, Jill Porter, and P. David Howe. Disability (sport) and discourse: Stories within the Paralympic legacy. *Reflection Practice* 14/5, 632–647, 2013.

Cashman, Richard and Simon Darcy. *Benchmark games: The Sydney 2000 Paralympic Games*. Walla Walls Press, 2008.

Cheong, Jadeera Phaik Geok, Selina Khoo, and Rizal Razman. Spotlight on athletes with a disability: Malaysian newspaper coverage of the 2012 London Paralympic Games. *Adaptive Physical Activity Quarterly* 33/1, 2016: 15–32.

Brittain, Ian. *The Paralympic Games explained*, 2nd ed. Routledge, 2016.

Buysse, Jo Ann M. and Bria Borcherding. Framing gender and disability: A cross-cultural analysis of photographs from the 2008 Paralympic Games. *International Journal of Sport Communication* 3/3, 2010: 308–321.

Darcy, Simon, Stephen Frawley, and Daryl Adair (Eds.) *Managing the Paralympics*. Palgrave Macmillan, 2017.

deLeseleuc, Eric, Athanasios Pappous, and Anne Marcellini. The media coverage of female athletes with disability: Analysis of the daily press of four European countries during the 2000 Sidney Paralympic Games. *European Journal for Sport and Society* 7/3–4, 2016: 283–296.

Dickson, Tracey J., Laura Misener, and Simon Darcy. Enhancing destination competitiveness through disability sport event legacies: Developing an interdisciplinary typology. *International Journal of Contemporary Hospitality Management* 29/3, 2017: 924–946.

Dure, Beau. Fan voting starts for U.S. Olympic and Paralympic Hall of Fame. nbcsports.com, August 12, 2019. Available: https://olympics.nbcsports.com/2019/08/12/fan-voting-starts-for-u-s-olympic-paralympic-hall-of-fame/

Editorial (2016, September 6). The Guardian view on the Paralympics: Focus on ability, not disability. *The Guardian*.

Ellis, Katie. Beyond the Aww factor: Human interest profiles of Paralympians and the media navigation of physical difference and social stigma. *Asia Pacific Media Educator*, 19, 2009: 23–26.

Fuller, Linda K. "Grit and glam: Female Paralympians' reframing and revisioning of 'disability' in 2012 London." International Association for Media and Communication Research. Hyderabad, India, 2014.

Fuller, Linda K. *Female Olympians: Tracing a mediated socio-cultural/political-economic timeline*. Palgrave Macmillan, 2016.

Fuller, Linda K. *Female Olympian and Paralympian events: Analyses, backgrounds and timelines*. Palgrave Macmillan, 2018.

Fuller, Linda K. Sportswomen in wheelchairs: Doubly discriminated against but duly impressive. In Yuya Kiuchi (Ed.), *Playing on an uneven field: Discrimination and exclusion in sports*, 99–108. McFarland, 2019.

Gilbert, Keith and Otto Schantz. *The Paralympic Games: Empowerment or sideshow?* Maidenhead: Meyer & Meyer Sport, 2008.

Hampton, Eve. How I became U.S. Paralympics number one fan. SRNA. 2016. Available: https://wearesrna.org/how-i-became-u-s-paralympics-number-one-fan/

Hardin, Marie and Brent Hardin. "The "supercrip" in sport media: Wheelchair athletes discuss hegemony's disabled hero." *Sociology of Sport Online* 7/1, 2004.

Hodges, Caroline E., Daniel Jackson, Richard Scullion, Shelley Thompson, and Mike Molesworth. *Tracking changes in everyday experiences of disability and disability sport within the context of the 2012 London Paralympics*. CMC Publishing, 2014.

Houghton, Emily J., Lindsay Pieper, and Maureen Smith. Women in the 2018 Olympic and Paralympic Winter Games: An analysis of participation, leadership, and media coverage. NY: Women's Sports Foundation, 2017.

Ioannou, Filipa (2018, April 27). Trump blasted after calling Paralympics "a little tough to watch." SFGate.com Available: www.sfgate.com/politics/article/Trump-blasted-after-calling-Paralympics-a-little-12870634.php

LeClair, Jill M. (Ed.) *Disability in the global sport arena: A sporting chance*. Routledge, 2012.

Manso, Santiago (2017, December 4). A framework for fan engagement at the Olympic and Paralympic Games. Atos. Available: https://atos.net/en/blog/framework-fan-engagement-olympic-paralympic-games

Mauerberg-deCastro, Eliane, Debra Frances Campbell, and Carolina Paioli Tavares. The global reality of the Paralympic Movement: Challenges and opportunities in disability sports. *Motriz: Revista de Educacao Fisica* 22/3 (July/September), 2016.

McKay, Cathy. Paralympic School Day: A disability awareness and education program. *Palaestra* 27/4, 1–19, 2013.

McKay, Cathy, Martin E. Block, and Jung Yeon Park. The impact of Paralympic School Day on student attitudes toward inclusion in physical education. *Adapted Physical Activity Quarterly* 32/4, 2015: 331–348.

McKay, Cathy, Justin Haegele, and Martin Block. Lessons learned from Paralympic School Day: Reflections from the students. *European Physical Education Review* 25/3, 2018: 745–760.

McPherson, Gayle, Hugh O'Donnell, David McGillivray, and Laura Misener. Elite athletes or superstars? Media representation of para-athletes at the Glasgow 2014 Commonwealth Games, *Disability and Society*, 31/5, 2016: 659–675.

Meenaghan, Gary. #FillTheSeats campaign "a beautiful way to be part of the Paralympic Games." *The National*. September 13, 2016. Available: www.thenational.ae/sport/filltheseats-campaign-a-beautiful-way-to-be-a-part-of-the-paralympic-games-1.229026

Misener, Laura, Gayle McPherson, David McGillivray, and David Legg. *Leveraging disability sports events: Impacts, promises, and possibilities*. Routledge, 2018.

Osborne, A. C., & Coombs, D. S. Female Fans of the NFL: Taking their Place in the Stands. Routledge, 2016.

Panagiotou, Anna K., Christina Evaggelinou, Agapi Doulkeridou, Katerina Mouratidou, and Eirini Koidou, E. Attitudes of 5th and 6th grade Greek students toward the inclusion of children with disabilities in physical education classes after a Paralympic education program. *European Journal of Adapted Physical Activity*, 1/2, 2008: 31–43.

Pullen, Emma, Daniel Jackson, Michael Silk, and Richard Scullion. Giving disability the "Hollywood treatment": Channel 4 and the broadcasting of the Paralympic Games. Paper presented to the International Communication Association, Prague, Czech Republic. 2018.

Purdue, David E.J. and P. David Howe. See the sport, not the disability: Exploring the Paralympic paradox. *Qualitative Research in Sport, Exercise and Health* 4/2, 2012: 189–205.

Schantz, Otto J. and Keith Gilbert (Eds.) *Heroes or zeroes? The media's perceptions of Paralympic sport.* Common Ground, 2012.

Scharfenberg, David (2018, March 1). Why do Americans ignore the Paralympics? *The Boston Globe.* Available: www.bostonglobe.com/ideas/2018/03/01/why-americans-ignore-paralympics/KWWA6u8owaA0V12zDZyDyH/story.html

Schpigel, Ben. "Paralympic athletes' least favorite word: Inspiration." *The New York Times*, 17 September 2016.

Thomas, Nigel B. and Andrew Smith. Preoccupied with able-bodiedness? An analysis of the British media coverage of the 2000 Paralympic Games. *Adapted Physical Activity Quarterly* 20/2, 2003: 166–181.

Toffoletti, Kim. Sport, post feminism and women with disabilities: Female Paralympians on social media. in Toffoletti, Kim, Jessica Francombe-Webb, and Holly Thorpe (Eds.), *New sporting femininities: Embodied politics in postfeminist times*, 253–275. Palgrave Macmillan, 2018.

United States Olympic Committee. Fan engagement through social, digital and broadcast platforms reach new heights during Olympic and Paralympic Winter Games PyeongChang 2018. teamusa.org. Available: www.teamusa.org/News/2018/March/21/Fan-Engagement-Social-Digital-Broadcast-New-Heights-Olympic-Paralympic-Winter-Games-PyeongChang-2018

van Biesen, Debbie, Alycia Busciglio, and Yves Vanlandewijck. Attitudes towards inclusion of children with disabilities: The effect of implementation of A Paralympic School Day on Flemish elementary children. In *European Congress of Adapted Physical Activity* 8, 2006.

Vanlandewijck, Yves and Walter Thompson (Eds.) *The Paralympic athlete.* Wiley-Blackwell. 2011.

Wagner, Tony (2018, March 9). Let's do the numbers on the Paralympic Games. Marketplace.org.

Wilhite, Barbara, Carol Adams Mushett, Lori Goldenberg, and Barbara R. Trader. Promoting inclusive sport and leisure participation: Evaluation of the Paralympic Day in the Schools model. *Adapted Physical Activity Quarterly* 14/2, 1997: 131–146.

Wolfe, Eli and Mary Hums (2017, September 2). We are all sports fans. *The Huffington Post.* Available: www.huffingtonpost.com/eli-wolff/we-are-all-sports-fans_b_11828010.html

Xafopoulos, Georgis, Martin Kudlacek, and Christina Evaggelinou. Effect of the intervention program "Paralympic School Day" on attitudes of children attending international school towards inclusion of students with disabilities. *Acta Universitatis Palackianae Olomucensis. Gymnica*, 39/4, 2009: 63–71.

Yang Liu, Martin Kudláček, and Ondrei Ješina. The influence of Paralympic School Day on children's attitudes towards people with disabilities. *Acta Universitatis Palackianae Olomucensis, Gymnica* 40/2, 2010: 63–69.

18
English Football, Sexuality, and Homophobia
Gay Fans' Perspectives on Governance and Visibility

David Letts and Rory Magrath

Introduction

Men's English football's position as the country's largest spectator sport has frequently led to it being used to highlight a range of political and social issues. Examples of this are witnessed in the sport's efforts to tackle the issues of racism and, more recently, homophobia, both of which have coincided with wider society's increased awareness and resulting attitude changes in these areas (Cashmore & Cleland, 2014). Given the sport's national importance and platform for these wider societal issues, the perspectives of football fans in relation to these issues have received increased academic interest in recent years (Cashmore & Cleland, 2014; Cleland & Cashmore, 2016a, 2016b; Magrath, 2018a).

A significant body of academic research has documented how sexual minority individuals are becoming increasingly accepted in the football industry (e.g., Cashmore & Cleland, 2012; Cleland, 2015; Cleland et al., 2018, 2021; Magrath, 2017a, 2017b, 2018b, 2021; Magrath, Anderson, & Roberts, 2015). While demonstrating improved attitudes amongst the sport's spectatorship is significant, it is important that this attitudinal change is translated into inclusive behavior. Therefore, understanding the lived experience of LGBT+ fans is essential in gauging how the environment – including awareness, attitudes, and action – has altered from their perspective. However, thus far, academic research examining homophobia in the sport has exclusively focused on the attitudes of ostensibly heterosexual male fans, and has, therefore, inadvertently excluded the LGBT+ community's perspective (Cleland & Magrath, 2020).

As such, this chapter aims to address the existing void in academia relating to LGBT+ football fans' perspectives of acceptance and inclusivity towards sexual minorities. In doing so, we present data collected in the first-ever academic research project dedicated to the experiences of LGBT+ sports fans through an examination of the role of governing bodies, professional clubs, and the various interventions in place -- such as the Rainbow Laces movement – designed to make English football a more inclusive space. Focusing on gay male fans, we show that the lack of visibility of governing bodies' work is problematic in that it calls into question their commitment to tackling homophobia. In contrast, however, professional clubs were seen to play a more proactive role in engaging with LGBT+ Fan Groups, thus making these fans welcome in the sport. Finally, while these fans were supportive of the Rainbow Laces movement, they also felt that it lacked a long-term legacy; that it was, at present, too restricted in its overall focus. Accordingly, by focusing on those fans that it affects most – LGBT+ fans – this research is important in that it highlights English football's positive and negative attempts to tackle homophobia.

The Foundations of Football, Masculinity, and Homophobia

While the invention of machinery and transportation necessary for industrialization began in the early 1700s, the antecedents of most of today's sporting culture can be traced to the years of the second Industrial Revolution – the mid-1800s through early-1900s. It was around this time that the organization, regulation, and codification of most dominant sports – including football – occurred (Guttmann, 2000). Around this time, sport – particularly men's competitive team sports – was thought to instill the qualities of discipline and obedience necessary in dangerous occupations (Rigauer, 1981). Factory workers, in particular, were required to sacrifice their time and health for the sake of earning wages at a level required to support their dependent families. Predictably, in service to industrialized interests, participation in sport thus taught boys to reinforce the value of self-sacrifice (Anderson, 2009).

Importantly, the gender segregation conventions of the time enabled sport to play an important role in "masculinizing" – and "remasculinizing" – boys. Given the emergence of an apparent crisis of masculinity – one characterized by a moral panic of the softening of boys' virility (Filene, 1998) – men were forced to demonstrate their heteromasculinity by aligning their "gendered behaviors with an idealized and narrow definition of masculinity" (McCormack & Anderson, 2014). Kimmel (1994) argues that, in this context, idealized attributes included the repression of pain, concealing feminine and/or same-sex desires and behaviors, and simultaneously committing acts of violence against oneself and others. Carter (2006, p. 5), for example, wrote that sport provided a "clear hierarchical structure, autocratic tendencies, traditional notions of masculinity and the need for discipline." This combination of events essentially led to masculinity becoming synonymous with homophobia (Kimmel, 1994).

While sport found cultural value for the first time during this period, this would re-emerge a century later, in the 1980s. At this time, the heightened HIV/AIDS epidemic – which had particular prevalence among gay men – fed the perception that homosexuality was dangerous and illicit (Weeks, 1991). This elevated deleterious cultural attitudes toward homosexuality to an all-time high by the end of the decade. Clements and Field (2014), for example, show that the British Social Attitude Survey reported that 75 percent of the British population believed the same-sex sex was "always wrong" or "mostly wrong" (see also Watt & Elliot, 2019; see Twenge, Sherman, & Wells, 2016, for a discussion of the US context). The existing discriminatory attitudes were also confirmed in law by the Conservative government's introduction of Section 28 in 1988, prohibiting the promotion of homosexuality in British schools (Epstein & Johnson, 1998). Given this hostile environment, it is perhaps unsurprising that LGBT+ individuals either tended to avoid participating in sport or simply hid their sexual identities (Pronger, 1990). Instead, sexual minority participation occurred primarily at amateur levels or in gay-only leagues (Jones & McCarthy, 2010).

Ultimately, the period demonstrated what Anderson (2009) termed *homohysteria*. Here, heterosexual individuals feared being perceived as homosexual and subsequently began to "align their gendered behaviors with idealized and narrow definitions of masculinity" (McCormack & Anderson, 2014, p. 114). As such, during this period, sport provided an important environment for boys and men to prove their masculinity and consequently reduce the likelihood of being perceived as gay (Burstyn, 1999). This resulted in football becoming an increasingly masculinized space, especially for white, working-class males; many of whom were adjusting to increased levels of unemployment and the associated emasculation as a result of no longer being able to provide for their families as they had done previously (Nayak, 2006).

Academic research examining the relationship between sport and homophobia during the 1980s and 1990s highlighted a worrying trend of anti-LGBT+ attitudes in line with broader societal views at the time (e.g., Griffin, 1998; Hekma, 1998; Messner, 1992; Pronger, 1990). Interestingly, although there is no empirical research on English football from around this time, we can draw upon the experiences of Justin Fashanu. Fashanu, who was best known for his playing career at Norwich City and Nottingham Forest, was the world's first openly gay male professional footballer when he publicly came out in 1990 (Cleland, 2015). The result was catastrophic, and Fashanu faced backlash and vilification from fans, fellow players, and even members of his own family. In 1998, having been accused of sexual assault in the US, he took his own life (Gaston, Magrath, & Anderson, 2018).

No active elite (male) player in England has publicly come out since Fashanu, with the negativity surrounding his situation posited as a likely concern for those considering doing so. Indeed, Magrath (2017b. p. 63) has previously described Fashanu as a "trendsetter—symbolic of the fractious relationship between football and homosexuality." This hypothesis also served to be largely accurate throughout the 1990s, as professional footballers remained closeted. Even those who were heterosexual – as evidenced perhaps most notably by former England defender, Graeme Le Saux – were not safe from homophobia. Because of his middle-class background and failure to conform to football's traditional, working-class masculine ideals, Le Saux was routinely abused by teammates, managers, and fans about his supposed homosexuality (Magrath, Cleland, & Anderson, 2020).

The Decline of British Homophobia

Since the turn of the millennium, views regarding homosexuality – and sexual minorities more broadly – improved significantly in the UK and across most of the Western world (Clements & Field, 2014; Watt & Elliot, 2019). This societal advancement has permeated through many facets of modern-day society, perhaps most notably through the introduction of same-sex marriage in a variety of countries across the world.[1] Despite these improved attitudes, however, there are claims that football remains resistant to broader social trends of inclusivity. A 2016 British parliamentary inquiry into homophobia in sport, for example, claimed that, "Despite the significant change in society's attitudes to homosexuality in the last 30 years, there is little reflection of this progress being seen in football" (DCMS, 2017). This narrative has largely been facilitated by a range of non-academic polls and surveys conducted by high-profile organizations. Leading LGBT advocacy British charity, Stonewall, for example, recently claimed that 72 percent of English football fans regularly witness homophobic abuse, and that 20 percent would be "embarrassed" if their favorite player came out.

Critiques of these surveys have highlighted significant methodological weaknesses, a lack of rigor, a lack of restriction on participation measures, and inclusion of "leading" questions (see Magrath, 2020; Magrath & Stott, 2019). Accordingly, surveys of this kind report a "'hearts and minds' study of perceptions and fears, not necessarily reflecting empirical realities" (Anderson, Magrath, & Bullingham, 2016, p. 5). Indeed, when examining scholarly research, the realities are far different.

Evidencing the academic reality, Cashmore and Cleland (2012, pp. 377–378) documented a "new and surprising image" regarding football's growing acceptance of homosexuality.

Specifically, their research showed that 93 percent of 3,500 fans had no objection to an openly gay player being contracted to the team they supported. These fans resented being held accountable for the lack of openly gay players, and almost half believed that clubs, agents, and governing bodies were truly responsible for this trend. Despite these inclusive findings, however, Pearson's (2012) ethnography of "carnival"[2] fans in English football identified use of terms such as "gay" and "queer," and that such language would likely "have made it very uncomfortable for an openly gay fan to join a trip with the carnival fans" (p. 168). Magrath's (2018b) research on "homosexually-themed chanting" further interrogates the complex nature of this language, and that there is no negative intent or effect – something which McCormack (2011) argues is essential when judging this language (see also McCormack, Wignall, & Morris, 2016).

In addition, inclusive attitudes have also been documented on fans forums – which is significant given that this platform allows for anonymity and the potential to voice more honest, yet less widely accepted views. For example, Cleland's (2015) analysis of a fans' forum documented that those who engage with this medium are "displaying more inclusive attitudes towards the presence of gay footballers" (pp. 136–137). And further supporting this, a similar study after Thomas Hitzlsperger's coming out in 2014 demonstrated vastly improved acceptance when compared with Justin Fashanu's coming out some years earlier. The results found that only 2 percent of over 6,000 comments analyzed included pernicious homophobic intent and those holding orthodox views were often confronted by other forum users (Cleland, Magrath, & Kian, 2018).

At least partly responsible for English football's changing culture is the influence of LGBT+ Fan Groups aligned to various professional clubs. These groups have emerged over the past decade to combat English football's traditional hypermasculine environment and to provide greater visibility for sexual minority football fans to network in an environment from which they have traditionally been excluded (Willis, 2015). LGBT+ advocacy groups broadly exist to support sexual and gender minorities in their ongoing pursuit of social and legal equality (Formby, 2017). In football, however, Lawley's (2019) analysis of LGBT+ Fan Groups concludes that they have only limited ability to challenge the overwhelmingly heteronormative culture of English football. This, he argues, is because such groups create "counterspaces which present different norms… [and] they have a limited ability to widen the impact of their change to the mainstream" (p. 9). Accordingly, he calls for the implementation of greater education in order for the central messages of LGBT+ Fan Groups – that of greater overall inclusion and tackling discrimination – to be successfully disseminated.

Finally, English football has also delivered specific initiatives to combat discrimination in this area. The most prominent of these efforts has been through the work of *Kick It Out*, whose remit of tackling racism was broadened around the turn of the millennium to include all forms of discrimination. Since then, initiatives such as The Justin Campaign and Football v. Homophobia have been formed specifically to challenge sexual and gender minority discrimination in football. In addition, the Football Association (FA) – English football's governing body – amended their regulations in 2007 to ensure that they addressed homophobic abuse, placing it on par with FA rules against racist abuse. The FA's most recent policy, *Opening Doors and Joining In*, has been criticized for its lack of clarity and simplistic understandings of discrimination (Magrath & Stott, 2019). Separate analyses also conclude that the FA's discourse on its commitment to LGBT+ inclusion displayed "non-performative institutional speech acts" (Bury, 2015, p. 212). Lastly, Rainbow Laces – a movement introduced by Stonewall in 2013 to raise awareness of LGBT+ inclusion in English football – has been critiqued as tokenistic and ineffective (Bury, 2015).

LGBT+ Fans Project

English professional football has undergone considerable structural and social change over the past three decades (King, 2002). The inception of the English Premier League (EPL) – and its subsequent development into the world's most popular football league (Millward, 2011) – is at least partly responsible for the notable expansion of both domestic and global fan cultures of the English game (Giulianotti, 2002; Pearson, 2012). Interestingly, however, while research has typically focused on English football's "traditional" demographic – heterosexual, white, working-class men (Pfister, Lenneis, & Mintert, 2013) – the diversification of fandom has resulted in a growth of research on under-represented fans' experiences. This includes research on gender (and the apparent "feminization" of fandom) (Pope, 2017; Toffoletti, 2017), ethnicity (Kilvington, 2016), religion (Poulton, 2020; Poulton & Durrell, 2016), and (dis)ability (García, de Wolff, Welford, & Smith, 2016). But despite this diversification of fandom, in addition to the liberalizing of attitudes, LGBT+ fans' voices have been largely overlooked from this body of work.

Against this backdrop, one of us (the second author) embarked on a research project to examine the lived experiences of LGBT+ fans of English professional football clubs. By conducting in-depth, semi-structured interviews with 35 openly gay male fans of various English professional football clubs, it focused on four specific areas: (1) LGBT+ fans' attendance at English professional football matches; (2) General stadium climate for LGBT+ fans; (3) Understanding chanting and language in football; (4) The role of national governing bodies, professional clubs and various interventions in tackling discrimination.

Aside from sexual orientation, participants in this research largely reflected the traditional demographic of English football stadia (Goldblatt, 2014). All were male, all but one was White (the exception was Asian Indian), aged between 19 and 67, and were working-class or lower middle-class (as determined by participants providing their occupation and/or educational status). Additionally, each participant met the project's eligibility criteria, which included: self-identifying as openly gay, lesbian, bisexual and/or transgender; supporting a team who, at the time of data collection, competed in the EPL or English Football League (EFL), and were either season-ticketholders or attended approximately 50 percent of their team's matches, either at "home," "away" or a combination of both. Overall, fans represented 23 separate clubs currently competing in English professional football.

Providing a backdrop to the specifics of governance initiatives discussed later, participants in this research clearly acknowledged that English football had become increasingly acceptant of homosexuality in recent years (Magrath, 2021). Over 74 percent of participants said that they felt "safe" attending matches and that previous feelings of intimidation and anxiety had dissipated in recent years. Furthermore, gay male fans in this research believed that homophobic chanting in stadia had considerably declined in recent years, with all from the youngest two age cohorts (18–24 and 25–35) reporting that they had never witnessed any homophobic chanting. This decline in antisocial behavior supports Cleland and Cashmore's (2016) suggestion that English football – particularly in the EPL – is becoming an increasingly sanitized environment.

The next sections of this chapter outline some of the key findings related to the research project's fourth theme: the role of national governing bodies and professional football clubs in tackling discrimination and promoting inclusion. It is important to note that, for this chapter, we only rely on data focused on the experiences of gay male fans; future publications – including those under review at the time of writing – address the experiences of lesbian, bisexual, and transgender fans, as well as the project's other objectives.

Governance

English football has become an increasingly positive environment for sexual minorities in recent years (Cashmore & Cleland, 2012; Cleland, 2015; Cleland, Magrath, & Kian, 2018; Magrath, 2017a, 2017b, 2018, 2020; Magrath, Anderson, & Roberts, 2015). During the same period, bureaucratic initiatives designed to completely remove homophobia from football have been introduced. High-profile organizations such as *Kick It Out*, *Football v. Homophobia*, and *The Justin Campaign* have been influential in this process; however, the Football Association has been criticized for being too slow to take action (see Caudwell, 2011). The gay male fans in the current research were also critical of the FA for what they saw as a failure to ensure greater levels of LGBT+ inclusion.

Interestingly, countering previous research – which has questioned the FA's commitment to tackling discrimination (Poulton, 2020) – participants in this research acknowledged the organization's work, albeit simultaneously querying its effectiveness. For example, Warren, a life-long West Bromwich Albion fan and season-ticketholder, said that, "I'm pretty sure the FA are doing work on this, but they could definitely be doing more—even if it's just to tell us what they're doing." Similarly, Lionel, a Burnley fan currently attending university, said that, "The FA have done a lot of work recently, but it's still not enough. There are still no openly gay players, so I think there's room for improvement on their part." Wilson, a Reading season-ticketholder, said that, "I think they need to do more, to be honest. They sometimes make good attempts to appear inclusive, but it's just not enough." And Fabio, a Norwich City fan, said that, "They've made steps in the right direction, but I don't think it's been quick enough… More is still needed, particularly as it's the main organization [in English football] we're talking about."

Two-thirds of participants believed that the FA must be more transparent with their efforts to tackle homophobia in English football. David, a Huddersfield Town fan who works in radio, said that, "They can always do more, but it's also about showing more visibility for what they've done already." Similarly, Liam, a Leeds United season-ticketholder, said that, "They should increase their visibility and reach out to the LGBT community a bit better to show that they are making an effort to make the game more inclusive." Nick, a Newcastle United season-ticketholder who also works as a football coach, said that, "It would be good for them [the FA] to show us exactly how committed they are to challenging discrimination." And Jeff, an Arsenal fan, said that, "I'd love to see the FA shouting a bit louder about the stuff that they're doing… I think that's one of the main issues." Moreover, further evidencing the FA's apparent lack of visibility, only one of the 35 gay male fans interviewed for this research were aware of the FA's most recent anti-homophobia policy – *Opening Doors and Joining In* (see also Magrath & Stott, 2019).

To address this lack of visibility, participants in this research made specific recommendations as to how the FA could be more effective. Noel, a West Ham United season-ticketholder, said that, "To deliver the message better, they could use social media a lot more… Post and promote a lot more information about what they're doing." Greater influence on social media was also recommended by Jim, a Sheffield United fan: "Talking more about diversity on social media – especially relating to homophobia – and tagging clubs would be useful." For others, such as Anton, a West Ham United fan, it was the "importance of reaching out to fans and making them aware of their policies… Just saying that they're on the website isn't good enough—they need to be proactive." Finally, Leon, a lifelong Tottenham Hotspur fan, recommended "more of a dialogue between the key groups of people involved… Having a high-profile player from each club would help, too."

According to these fans, then, the FA's attempts to tackle homophobia in football are both weak, and largely invisible, hence the call for greater transparency. Interestingly, however, Bury's

(2015) analysis of FA policy concludes that LGBT+ visibility is important, yet also overlooks institutional power struggles (in an environment apparently dominated by heterosexual white men). But given that the LGBT+ community has made great strides into English football in recent years, we argue that a growth of visibility – particularly from a powerful organization such as the FA – would likely be a positive step for demonstrating their commitment to inclusion.

Clubs

Alongside the FA, professional football clubs have also played a significant role in tackling homophobia (Magrath & Anderson, 2017). LGBT+ fans' presence in English football has been made increasingly visible through the recent emergence of LGBT+ Fan Groups (Lawley, 2019). For example, at the time of writing, almost half (42) of English clubs competing in the EPL or EFL have an officially sanctioned LGBT+ Fan Group. Previous work for this project has acknowledged that these groups are important as they provide visibility, familiarity, and social networking for LGBT+ fans. Here, we outline the gay male fans' assessment of their club's commitment to tackling homophobia in football – showing that there were some mixed perceptions, and that these were dependent on the club in question.

Elliott, a lifelong Leicester City fan who works in recruitment, said that, "The club is doing a good job around LGBT issues. They communicate regularly with the group [Foxes Pride] and listen to our ideas." Similarly, Mason, a Huddersfield Town fan, said that, "They [the club] have been good. They support us regularly in the programme and on social media and are generally pretty visible with everything that's going on." Frazer, a retired Tottenham Hotspur fan, also spoke of his club's engagement with inclusivity on social media: "Spurs have always been great… They've been really supportive and promote the anti-discrimination policies in the programme. They're making steps in the right direction." And Anton, a West Ham United fan, said, "I can't think of anything more the club can do. We've got a lot of recognition and support, and we have good access if there are any issues." These responses typified just over half of the gay male fans interviewed for this research.

In contrast, however, the remainder of participants were less satisfied with their club's efforts at tackling homophobia. Warren, a West Bromwich Albion fan, said that, despite his club's support for Proud Baggies, they could still do more: "We've had a few issues in the past, but the club haven't really done enough to address it. They could definitely do more to approach and tackle homophobic chanting inside the ground." Jason, a Bournemouth season-ticketholder, believed that "accusations of political correctness prevent the club from being more supportive." He also believed that the increase of social media abuse directed toward English clubs (see Kilvington & Price, 2019) was a key reason as to why "they [the club] hardly ever put anything online." And Nathan, a season-ticketholder at Millwall – who, at the time of writing, do not have an LGBT+ Fan Group – criticized the club for "leaving everything like this up to the fans… The club won't set a group up – it's up to us to do anything."

Thus, according to the gay fans in this research, professional clubs – despite having played a key role in the LGBT+ community's growing involvement in football (see Magrath & Anderson, 2017) – are inconsistent in their approach to inclusion. Indeed, while some clubs are actively involved in LGBT+ Fan Groups, others seemingly adopt a more laissez-faire attitude. Coupled with the fact that, despite a rapid recent increase, over half of professional clubs – including some of England's most elite – currently have an LGBT+ Fan Group, this is clearly problematic, and arguably fuels opinions that English football is still failing in its attempts to reach out to minority fans.

Rainbow Laces

Finally, this chapter analyzes gay male fans' perceptions of the Rainbow Laces movement. Introduced by Stonewall in 2013, the Rainbow Laces campaign – a period in the English football season when all professional clubs' players are encouraged to wear rainbow-colored laces – was designed to combat homophobia (and biphobia and transphobia) in sport. While initially restricted to a small number of sports, its take-up has increased each year; indeed, the movement is now regularly embraced by football, rugby union, cricket, darts, cycling, and athletics. It has also grown in visibility, largely thanks to the support of Sky Sports, who have formally backed the initiative since 2016. Despite the movement having previously been critiqued as tokenistic, gay male fans in this research were overwhelmingly positive about the increased prominence of Rainbow Laces.

For example, Adie, a Newcastle United season-ticketholder, said that, "The campaign is a great step in the right direction. I think with Sky's support and it being on TV, people have been made more aware, and that's one of the most important things." Martin, a Crystal Palace fan, said that, "It's such a great idea… It makes people actually discuss homophobia in football, and that's important." And Fabio, a Norwich City fan, answered in a similar vein: "Rainbow Laces has been extremely effective, I think… It's one of the most successful campaigns, because it gets it out in the open." These responses were indicative of all of the fans in this research; indeed, there were no dissenting voices regarding the campaign's presence. That said, however, fans were critical of the long-term legacy of the campaign.

Leicester City fan, Elliott, said that, "The movement is really good… Sadly, every single season it just fizzles out and there's no legacy." Similarly, Grant, a Crawley Town fan, said that, "It's worked in terms of raising visibility, but I'm not sure it's been very effective in the long-run." Wilson, a Reading fan, described the Rainbow Laces movement as having "good intentions" but also "restrictive" due to its relatively short time span. This was raised by almost a third of participants in this research, who felt that the movement was ineffective as a consequence. Other participants – including Leon and Noel – also critiqued the movement for being "too static." Instead, Leon suggested that: "It could be more dynamic – perhaps by doing different things each season. I think people get fed-up with seeing the same thing." And finally, four participants also wanted to see their clubs better engage with the movement as a whole to ensure the overall visibility of Rainbow Laces – and thus ensuring that LGBT+ fans might be more encouraged to attend matches.

Concluding Comments

The findings of this study largely support previous work in this area by demonstrating more inclusive attitudes towards sexual minorities than previously seen in sporting environments (Anderson, Magrath, & Bullingham, 2016) – particularly within British football (Cleland, 2015; Cleland, Magrath, & Kian, 2018). It is evident that the demographic dynamics of football fandom are changing, and previous work has demonstrated that attitudes of heterosexual fans are becoming more inclusive and accepting toward sexual minorities in this environment. Although some research has been critical (e.g., Magrath & Stott, 2019; Poulton, 2020), it is likely that the combination of anti-homophobia initiatives introduced by the sport and social advancements more broadly have aided this development over recent years.

The addition of these findings to the existing armory of academic research provides a new and valuable perspective to understanding the complex relationship between football and societal advancements. It is of critical importance that the findings outlined here illuminate the viewpoint of the minority population themselves, which sets it apart from previous work in this domain. Comprehension of the LGBT+ population's standpoint is essential in understanding how the environment is perceived by those previously marginalized by the sport's heteronormative culture. As explored earlier in this chapter, there have been several developments in tackling LGBT+ abuse and increasing inclusion within English football; the findings here show mixed feelings toward these initiatives.

In summary, the research highlights three broad recommendations for football clubs and governing bodies to address in order to improve upon the foundations currently in place. These include improving awareness of existing policies/initiatives; improving engagement with LGBT+ fan groups; and focusing on improving visibility in this area.

Indeed, supporting previous work, there was a very real lack of awareness regarding the FA's flagship initiative – *Opening Doors and Joining In*. Of the 35 openly gay men included in this research, only one had heard of this campaign; this is an astounding – and, clearly, problematic – statistic, particularly given that the strategy is directly focused on the participant population. If not reaching those who are directly impacted by its intended outcomes, questions arise as to its overall effectiveness. In line with this, the emphasis of responses centered on increased awareness (an area the existing initiative apparently fails on), rather than having policies in place which are not publicized effectively. Accordingly, it is recommended that the FA do more to make these policies visible and ensure that they are active documents rather than tokenistic gestures.

We also evidence mixed perceptions of professional clubs' engagement with LGBT+ inclusion. Central to this process is the increased emergence of LGBT+ Fan Groups – which almost half of the 92 English professional clubs – at the time of writing – had aligned to them. It is evident that the clubs which actively participated and encouraged their associated LGBT+ Fan Group had a significant impact on members' perception of their value – and commitment to the inclusion of LGBT+ fans. Conversely, clubs which failed to engage with these groups (if one existed) left these fans feeling disillusioned and questioning the club's loyalty to them. Therefore, clubs need to make conscious efforts to engage with these groups, and encourage the formation of a group if one does not already exist.

Finally, we acknowledge the role of the Rainbow Laces movement. The gay male fans in this research were critical of the various limitations of this campaign – namely their short-term nature and lack of legacy. They also reported that the publicity of high-profile events is of significant importance to their feeling recognized and accepted within the sport (see also Lawley, 2019). This particular emphasis on the importance of awareness and visibility departs, in some ways, from previous research which has critiqued them as "tokenistic" (Bury, 2015). Clearly, as this research has shown, these visibility initiatives are recognized and appreciated by the LGBT+ community and, as such, should be encouraged throughout the sport. Alongside this, education work for staff and players can add further depth to these actions and embed their value more widely throughout the football industry.

In relation to all of these points, the underpinning premise centers on strengthening the dialogue between both clubs and governing bodies and the sport's LGBT+ population in order to understand the concerns and issues faced first-hand from those experiencing them. English Football has a clear opportunity to utilize the existing LGBT+ community within the sport, which is readily accessible through dedicated fan groups, to build on this research and align further efforts with the sport's LGBT+ fans' perspectives. Policy and action driven from this standpoint will help to ensure the work is appropriate and best addresses the needs of the population in question. This research highlights that the top-down approach seemingly taken up to this point distances initiatives from those they intend to help and risks disillusionment from those within these quarters.

Recognizing LGBT+ fans' perspectives in relation to British football's efforts around sexual minority awareness and inclusion is fundamental to establishing an effective strategy which accounts for the real-life experiences of those within the minority group itself. The initial work here clearly outlines a desire for increased proactive engagement with policies and initiatives, whereby most respondents considered more publicity to be a priority to furthering the effectiveness of work in this area. Additionally, a framework from a central policy could help individual clubs to confidently, and appropriately, engage with LGBT+ supporters' groups; this would help to redress the disparity witnessed across the clubs represented in this study. Future research should aim to explore the experiences of others within the LGBT+ community and broaden the validity of these findings.

Notes

1   More information can be found about the global legality of same-sex marriage here: www.pewresearch.org/fact-tank/2019/10/29/global-snapshot-same-sex-marriage/
2   "Carnival" fans are typically defined as those who take an active role in proceedings at English matches, such as drinking and chanting.

References

Anderson, E. (2009). *Inclusive masculinity: The changing nature of masculinities.* London: Routledge.
Anderson, E., Magrath, R., & Bullingham, R. (2016). *Out in sport: The experiences of openly gay and lesbian athletes in competitive sport.* London: Routledge.
Burstyn, V. (1999). *The rites of men: Manhood, politics and the culture of sport.* Toronto: University of Toronto Press.
Bury, J. (2015). Non-performing inclusion: A critique of the English Football Association's Action Plan on homophobia in football. *International Review for the Sociology of Sport, 50*(2), 211–226.
Carter, N. (2006). *The football manager: A history.* London: Routledge.
Cashmore, E. & Cleland, J. (2012). Fans, homophobia and masculinities in association football: Evidence of a more inclusive environment. *British Journal of Sociology, 63*(2), 370–387.
Cashmore, E. & Cleland, J. (2014). *Football's dark side: Corruption, homophobia, violence and racism in the beautiful game.* Basingstoke: Palgrave.
Caudwell, J. (2011). "Does your boyfriend know you're here?" The spatiality of homophobia in men's football culture in the UK. *Leisure Studies, 30*(2), 123–138.
Cleland, J. (2015). Discussing homosexuality on association football fan message boards: A changing cultural context. *International Review for the Sociology of Sport, 50*(2), 125–140.
Cleland, J. & Cashmore, E. (2016a). Football fans' views of racism in British football. *International Review for the Sociology of Sport, 51*(1), 27–43.
Cleland, J. & Cashmore, E. (2016b). Football fans' views of violence in British football: Evidence of a sanitized and gentrified culture. *Journal of Sport and Social Issues, 40*(2), 124–142.
Cleland, J., Cashmore, E., Dixon, K., & MacDonald, C. (2021). Analyzing the presence of homosexually-themed language among association football fans in the United Kingdom. *Communication & Sport*, doi:10.1177/21674795211005838.
Cleland, J. & Magrath, R. (2020). Association football, masculinity, and sexuality: An evolving relationship. In R. Magrath, J. Cleland & E. Anderson (Eds.). *The Palgrave Handbook of Masculinity and Sport* (pp. 341–357). Basingstoke: Palgrave.
Cleland, J., Magrath, R., and Kian, E. (2018). The internet as a site of decreasing cultural homophobia in association football: An online response by fans to the coming out of Thomas Hitzlsperger. *Men and Masculinities, 21*(1), 91–111.
Clements, B. & Field, C. D. (2014). Public opinion toward homosexuality and gay rights in Great Britain. *Public Opinion Quarterly, 78*(2), 523–547.

Digital, Culture, Media, Culture, and Sport Committee, (2017). Homophobia in sport inquiry—final report. Retrieved November 26, 2020, from UK Parliament website: www.parliament.uk/business/committees/committees-a-z/commons-select/culture-media-and-sport-committee/inquiries/parliament-2015/homophobia-in-sport-15-16/publications/

Epstein, D. & Johnson, R. (1998). *Schooling sexualities.* Buckingham: Open University Press.

Filene, P.G. (1998). *Him/her/self: Gender identities in modern America.* Baltimore, MA: John Hopkins University Press.

Formby, E. (2017). *Exploring LGBT spaces and communities: Contrasting identities, belongings and wellbeing.* United Kingdom: Routledge.

García, B., de Wolff, M., Welford, J., & Smith, B. (2016). Facilitating inclusivity and broadening understandings of access at football clubs. *European Sport Management Quarterly,* 17(2), 226–243.

Gaston, L., Magrath, R., & Anderson, E. (2018). From hegemonic to inclusive masculinities in English professional football: Marking a cultural shift. *Journal of Gender Studies,* 27(3), 301–312.

Giulianotti, R. (2002). Supporters, followers, fans and flaneurs: A taxonomy of spectator identities in football. *Journal of Sport and Social Issues,* 26(1), 25–46.

Goldblatt, D. (2014). *The game of our lives.* London: Penguin.

Griffin, P. (1998). *Strong women, deep closets: Lesbians and homophobia in sport.* Leeds: Human Kinetics.

Guttmann, A. (2000). The development of modern sports. *Handbook of Sports Studies,* pp. 248–259.

Hekma, G. (1998). "As long as they don't make an issue of it..." Gay men and lesbians in organized sports in the Netherlands. *Journal of Homosexuality,* 35(1), 1–23.

Jones, L. and McCarthy, M. (2010). Mapping the landscape of gay men's football. *Leisure Studies,* 29(2), 161–173.

Kilvington, D. (2016). *British Asians, exclusions and the football industry.* London: Routledge.

Kilvington, D. & Price, J. (2019). Tackling social media abuse? Critically assessing English football's response to online racism. *Communication and Sport,* 7(1), 64–79.

Kimmel, M. S. (1994). Masculinity as Homophobia. In: Brod H. and Kaufman M. (eds) *Theorizing Masculinities.* Thousand Oaks, CA: Sage, 119-141.

King, A. (2002). *End of the terraces? The transformation of English football.* London: Bloomsbury.

Lawley, S. (2019). Spaces and laces: insights from LGBT initiatives in sporting institutions. *Journal of Organizational Change Management* (Online First).

Magrath, R. (2017a). The intersection of race, religion and homophobia in British football. *International Review for the Sociology of Sport,* 52(4), 411–429.

Magrath, R. (2017b). *Inclusive masculinities in contemporary football: Men in the beautiful game.* London: Routledge.

Magrath, R. (2018a). Media review: Gareth Thomas: Hate in the Beautiful Game. *International Review for the Sociology of Sport,* 53(2), 250–256.

Magrath, R. (2018b). "To try and gain an advantage for my team": Homophobic and homosexually themed chanting among English football fans. *Sociology,* 52(4), 709–726.

Magrath, R. (2020). Inclusive masculinities of working-class university footballers in the South of England. *Sport in Society* (Online First).

Magrath, R. (2021). Gay Male Football Fans' Experiences: Authenticity, Belonging and Conditional Acceptance. *Sociology* (Online First).

Magrath, R. & Anderson, E. (2017). Football, homosexuality and the English Premier League: A changing cultural relationship. In *The English Premier League: A socio-cultural analysis* (pp. 150–162). London: Routledge.

Magrath, R., Anderson, E., & Roberts, S. (2015). On the door-step of equality: Attitudes toward gay athletes among academy-level footballers. *International Review for the Sociology of Sport,* 50(7), 804–821.

Magrath, R., Cleland, J., & Anderson, E. (2020). Introducing the Palgrave handbook of masculinity and sport. In R. Magrath, J. Cleland, & E. Anderson (Eds.). *The Palgrave Handbook of Masculinity and Sport* (pp. 1–16). Basingstoke: Palgrave.

Magrath, R. & Stott, P. (2019). "Impossible to implement?": The effectiveness of anti-homophobia policy in English professional football. *International Journal of Sport Policy and Politics,* 11(1), 19–38.

McCormack, M. (2011). Mapping the terrain of homosexually-themed language. *Journal of Homosexuality,* 58(5), 664–679.

McCormack, M. & Anderson, E. (2014). The influence of declining homophobia on men's gender in the United States: An argument for the study of homohysteria. *Sex Roles,* 71(3–4), 109–120.

McCormack, M., Wignall, L., & Morris, M. (2016). Gay guys using gay language: Friendship, shared values and the intent-context-effect matrix. *British Journal of Sociology,* 67(4), 747–767.

Messner, M. A. (1992). *Power at play: Sports and the problem of masculinity.* New York: Beacon Press.

Millward, P. (2011). *The global football league: Transnational networks, social movements and sport in the new media age*. Basingstoke: Palgrave.

Nayak, A. (2006). Displaced masculinities: Chavs, youth and class in the post-industrial city. *Sociology, 40*(5), 813–831.

Pearson, G. (2012). *An ethnography of English football fans: Cans, cops and carnivals*. Manchester: Manchester University Press.

Pfister, G., Lenneis, V., & Mintert, S. (2013). Female fans of men's football: A case study in Denmark. *Soccer and Society, 14*(6), 850–871.

Pope, S. (2017). *The feminization of sports fandom: A sociological study*. London: Routledge.

Poulton, E. & Durrell, O. (2016). Uses and meanings of "Yid" in English football fandom: A case study of Tottenham Hotspur. *International Review for the Sociology of Sport, 51*(6), 715–734.

Poulton, E. (2020). Tackling antisemitism within English football: A critical analysis of policies and campaigns using a multiple streams approach. *International Journal of Sport Policy and Politics, 12*(1), 25–47.

Pronger, B. (1990). *The arena of masculinity: Sports, homosexuality, and the meaning of sex*. London: GMP Publishers.

Rigauer, B. (1981). *Sport and work*. New York: Columbia University Press.

Toffoletti, K. (2017). *Women sport fans: Identification, participation, representation*. London: Routledge.

Twenge, J. M., Sherman, R. A., & Wells, B. E. (2016). Changes in American adults' reported same-sex sexual experiences and attitudes, 1973–2014. *Archives of Sexual Behavior, 45*(7), 1713–1730.

Watt, L. & Elliot, M. (2019). Homonegativity in Britain: Changing attitudes towards same-sex relationships. *The Journal of Sex Research, 56*(9), 1101–1114.

Weeks, J. (1991). *Against nature: Essays on history, sexuality and identity*. London: Rivers Oram.

Willis, T. (2015). Kicking down barriers: gay footballers, challenging stereotypes and changing attitudes in amateur league play. *Soccer and Society, 16*(2–3), 377–392.

19
Photography, Autoethnography and Mapping Sporting Transformations
A Discussion of Stuart Roy Clarke's Work on British Football

John Williams

Introduction: Sports Photography and Diego's Little Deception

Photographs in sport can do many things: capture moments of athletic brilliance or physical endurance; evoke memories of sporting affiliation and solidarity – celebrations shared with family and friends in support of a local athlete or club; act as a prism, a rallying point for sporting memories; provide a record of historic socio-cultural events which have a global significance way beyond the sports arena – images of a triumphant Jessie Owens in Berlin, 1936, for example; map significant processes of social change – the emergence of new female sports stars; or chart the transformation, perhaps recorded over time, of a much-loved stadium or venue. They can also be used to symbolise moments of national and international accord or tension, and may help recall emotions of great joy, despair or even redemption. However, analysing and especially *interpreting* photographs in sport has its distinct challenges. In their very construction, of course, photographs have multiple meanings rather than reflect a single beguiling reality – the appearance of history itself. In short, knowing exactly what is going on in a sports photograph – and precisely what it signifies – is, by no quarter, ever an entirely straightforward matter. This is one reason for the limited use of photographs in academic research, linked to the epistemological primacy and historically the supposed greater accuracy given more readily to the written word (Osmond, 2010: 122).

A case in point about the, sometimes troubling, materiality of the photograph in sport is a very famous on-field image of the great Argentinian footballer, Diego Maradona, in action. A world-class player, possibly the best ever, Maradona is captured in all his early pomp on the international stage wearing the traditional pale blue and white striped strip of Argentina. He already seems to be *living* in his number 10 national shirt. The opponents here are Belgium. The match is in the World Cup finals at some point in the 1980s. In this tightly cropped photograph Maradona is pictured centre-stage in a shot taken slightly raised and from behind. There are no other teammates in sight. The Argentinian is hovering on his toes, prancing almost, in those familiar Puma boots of his, caressing the ball on the end of his left foot. Directly in front of him is a tight cluster of *six* red-shirted Belgium defenders in sequence; all eyes are fixed on Maradona. These benighted Europeans look as if they are held in a trance, each preparing for the worst. They appear helpless and fearful in the face of a sporting genius, a man who already has them under his spell.

Years later, Frankie Vercauteren, one of the Belgian players pictured here, challenged the narrative routinely propagated around this photograph. It clearly irked him. The Belgians depicted in this image were actually part of a confident and assured team from the 1982 finals. Vercauteren effectively 'deconstructed' the photograph – it seems obvious on reflection – explaining that an Argentinian free-kick had just been taken and that the Belgian players were so closely packed together simply because they were breaking from their carefully constructed and effective defensive wall. Moreover, far from 'casting his spell' in this game, the inexperienced and young Maradona had played a quiet match and was about to give the ball away in attempting a pass to a team-mate who was just out of shot. Belgium defeated Argentina 1–0 on that day in Barcelona in the 1982 World Cup finals. 'So, for me,' said Vercauteren, in 2017, 'the picture does not show six terrified defenders: it shows our players working perfectly in harmony. It shows how hard we worked that day' (Drury, 2017). Vercauteren's intervention reminds us of the importance of examining the materiality and three-dimensional nature of sports photographs: their forms of publication, consumption and recycling (Barker-Ruchti et al., 2013). Here was a little masterclass, in short, on how a sports photograph, cleverly conceived and re-circulated, can confirm a message already pre-formed in the viewer's mind, no matter the reality. It reminds us that, 'photographs create memories and meanings through the material circumstances in which they are embedded and encountered' (Osmond, 2010: 124).

Which brings me, if a little tangentially, to the work of the independent British football photographer, Stuart Roy Clarke, someone who has been using his camera, professionally and painstakingly, to record and report for more than 30 years on British football, its supporters, and the sport's core places of communion. This, he insists, is a sporting subculture which has been frantically adapting and transforming over the past three decades, but it is also at perpetual risk of collapse. Of course, photographs are never simply taken; they are always *made* by the photographer, both in terms of how and what is shot and what is included and left out. However, Clarke's work offers no obvious Maradona-like memory tricks; he takes single shots, on colour film, nothing cut, staged or filtered. He claims no disguised or hidden meanings. He has, I think, a compelling story to tell about the recent British game and its people.

Hillsborough 1989, and a Chance Meeting

I first met Stuart Clarke – the 'Roy' was actually added much later – in Leicester, in the English east Midlands, very early in the 1990s. Football in England was still emerging from the shadow of the terrible loss of life at the Bradford City stadium fire (56 dead) and the shame of English fan hooliganism which had contributed to the deaths of 39, mainly Italian, fans at the Heysel Stadium in Brussels in that same, grim, month for the English game, May 1985 (Gould & Williams, 2011). This was, without doubt, English football in extremis, a crisis period when politicians and others (including some fans) seemed to question its very existence. Attendances had slumped to a post-war low and were rising again only very slowly. But English football's modest recovery was soon threatened once more, this time by the extraordinary trauma in the spring of 1989 at the Hillsborough stadium in Sheffield, when, on 15 April, 96 Liverpool fans were crushed and suffocated to death, unlawfully killed, as a result of police mismanagement of a penned, standing terrace (Scraton, 2013).

I was sitting that day in the stadium, in the Liverpool seats, looking on aghast as this catastrophe unfolded. I was also working at the time on a fans' research project for a public body called the Football Trust. So, I had the role – not, I can tell you, a very pleasant one – of taking officials around the Hillsborough ground immediately after the stadium was cleared, to try to piece together exactly what had happened. An academic on the front line. There was still grisly debris on the terraces; shoes, scarves and scattered personal objects. The Leppings Lane end perimeter fences, designed to keep fans off the playing field, were now gaping, horribly twisted, where stricken supporters had, only hours before, been dragged out and carried away by fellow fans on emergency stretchers made from advertising hoardings. Senior South Yorkshire police officers were soon showing my 'expert' group the external exit gates – including the infamous Gate C – where 'drunken and ticketless' Liverpool fans had allegedly broken into the stadium and colluded in the killing of their fellow supporters whose corpses, tabloids reported later, they had robbed. None of it was true; in fact, no damage was discernible at all (Williams, 2014). Already, dazed young Liverpool fans, trying to make sense of the enormity of what had happened, were contradicting the 'official' account, telling us that the gates had been opened by the *police* to relieve crowd pressure outside, and that nobody had directed fans into the less crowded parts of the stadium, hence the fatal overcrowding. They showed us their unchecked tickets. The official Taylor (1990) inquiry report into the disaster made clear where the blame lay, but it would take another 23 years for the innocence of fans and the full extent of the police neglect and later press cover-up, to finally be accepted by the British establishment – and by much of the non-footballing public. The definitive findings on this score, produced by a group of experts (including academics) who made up the *Hillsborough Independent Panel*, were finally published only in September 2012. Lives were lost because of neglectful police mistakes. More than 30 years on, however, the Hillsborough families' struggle for 'justice' remained unresolved (Smith, 2019).

Stuart Clarke contacted me soon after Hillsborough and we met in my cramped little university office in Leicester. It was strewn at the time with folders, books and papers. It still is. I had no idea who he was, but Stuart knew I had been doing some research with the Football Trust on fans, and that the Trust was now charged with helping to distribute funds for the national transformation of British football stadia demanded after the 1989 disaster. The English game in the early 1990s was in a state of dynamic flux, with various bodies – the FA, the Football League and the Professional Footballers Association among them – all busily vying for advantage and control of the elite clubs, preparing for a new dawn that would eventually result in the formation of a global cash cow, the English Premier League (Williams, 2006; Elliott, 2017). Clarke showed me evidence of his audacious plan: to capture, in photographs, the story of fans' lives, and some of the distinctive cultural features of British football stadia that may soon be lost. He also wanted to chart the game's as yet uncertain future. It was obvious from the shots he showed me that here was a photographer who had the talent, knowledge and the determination required to do so, but he also clearly needed some help. I was more than happy, in my small way, to oblige.

Neither of us knew back then, of course, quite where the British game was headed; exactly how substantial its social, cultural and material transformation might prove to be. Clarke probably realised that he was recording something important – a valued cultural form in metamorphosis – but he was also clear that he was dealing with something that, for most people, was strangely ephemeral. Naturally, I arranged a meeting for him with representatives from the Football Trust. Who was better placed to photograph for posterity how Britain's historic football venues were now being gutted and 'modernised' to meet the inclusive demands of a new era? Who better to show us how history was being dismantled before our eyes and how all this new investment money from home and abroad was being spent? He got the assignment – I knew he would.

A Fan-Scholar's Life

This may be an apposite moment for me to put my autoethnographic cards squarely on the table, before I return to discuss Stuart Roy Clarke's body of work in a little more detail. His photographs illustrate this chapter throughout, and they chart, both emotionally and analytically, much of my own personal experience as a football supporter, someone who was living through this period of flux and rapid change. I am originally from Bootle, just north of the city of Liverpool. I was a still young academic of 34 in 1989; I am now 67 years old, a rather creaking UK sports sociologist, a fan/scholar, and a long-standing season ticket holder at Liverpool Football Club. This is despite the fact I have lived in Leicester, some 120 miles south-east of Liverpool, for the past 40 years. I have written widely about the club and its fans, both in academic fora and in more popular settings, but always attempting to add some socio-historical insight, whatever the intended audience (Williams et al., 2001; Williams and Hopkins, 2005; Williams, 2010; 2011; 2012). Strangely, this 'double life' has not always made me popular among other academics, those who might prefer the dubious 'objectivity' of the armchair outsider.

Until Covid struck, I sat in the Anfield Kop stand every fortnight, broadly among the same group of people who, like me, have aged but changed in few other ways over the past four decades. Generally, English Premier League crowds are growing older (Premier League, 2015). The locals who occupy the Kop believe that they have a rather 'special' status as peculiarly knowledgeable football fans, a view which goes back at least to the 1930s when a famous Irish Liverpool goalkeeper, Elisha Scott, communed freely with the ranks of supporters crammed behind him on those famous terrace steps (Williams, 2011). I would vouch that there are few places in the world where a football club's history and its connection with place is so revered, or where songs and artefacts in praise of this heritage are created so prodigiously, even in the face of the hyper-commodification and rapid turnover of the current versions of the sport. The American sports sociologist (and Liverpool fan) Grant Farred (2002) has shrewdly claimed that perhaps only three other football clubs in the world – Glasgow Celtic in Scotland, Boca Juniors of Argentina, and FC Barcelona of Spain – rivals Liverpool FC for the depth of its rootedness in local working-class communities and for its local socio-political and ideological importance, beyond mere sport. Reflecting the club's complex (but today largely non-sectarian) Irish heritage, one minute newly written anthems may be pumping out from the Liverpool Kop seats to the rhythms of rousing Irish Republican Catholic choruses, and the next they might come delivered to the strains of deeply Loyalist Protestant hymns. Every sect, every people, has its day.

Football in Liverpool today is a highly mediated, often self-referential text, one which is woven and defined at least as much by the club's supporters as it is by any of its great past players and managers. As the playwright and author, Arthur Hopcraft, famously pointed out more than 40 years ago in his seminal book *The Football Man* (1968), football in Liverpool is not just a sport people take to, like they might do to cricket or to tennis: instead, it incorporates both conflict and beauty and it is inherent in the people. Football is something built into the male British working class urban psyche. In its pomp – astonishingly, the Liverpool Kop alone once accommodated 28,000 people – these great standing terraces in Liverpool and elsewhere acted as giant choral societies, but also as a vast, soft-sided crane, grabbing and lifting its swaying constituents before gently depositing them in another place. In Liverpool, as Hopcraft also puts it, the game and its past really *matters* to the people who live there, as poetry or fine art matters for some people and alcohol does to others.

The standing Kop (if not its humour) had been tamed, its capacity more than halved, long before the Hillsborough disaster occurred (see Figure 19.1). Seats were finally introduced on

John Williams

Figure 19.1 Last Days on the Standing Liverpool Kop, 1992. Photograph used with permission from Stuart Roy Clarke ©stuartroyclarke/homesoffootball

the Kop in 1994 to replace the old standing terraces, as they were at all major British football stadiums around this time, in the name of improved safety following the Taylor inquiry. For a short period, as the conversion was taking place, we Kopites (like other fans) were made to sit out in the rain and snow to watch matches without a covering roof, as Liverpool fans before us would have done in the early 1920s. It felt like the extension of the suffering all 'true' supporters might be expected to endure at British football, a sign of our mulish devotion. Worse, all the nooks and idiosyncratic crannies, the mini-balconies and hidden ledges, that used to feature on many old standing terraces, and which gave the Anfield stadium (and others like it) much of its topophilic attraction, its historic individuality, instantly disappeared as the highly regulated and CCTV-monitored new plastic-seated areas were installed. Younger fans tried valiantly with their customised flags and banners to keep older traditions alive in the new seated areas, but English football grounds became increasingly homogenised and sterile, both in their design and their standardised facilities. These historic local landmarks, which once mapped out generational traditions and synergies with local landscapes, were reconfigured or increasingly erased (Duke, 2002; Bale, 2000).

For a period of at least five years in the early 1990s, the old terraces of major stadia in England were under reconstruction, or simply replaced, as the game played on (See Figure 19.2). Eventually disappearing, too, would be some historic old English stadia, and (from 2007) smoking inside the ground; watching matches through a tobacco fog was commonplace for the first 30-odd years of my own fan career. The relative freedom of the standing terrace at least allowed one

Photography, Autoethnography and Mapping

Figure 19.2 Rebuilding English Football in the Early 1990s: St James Park, Newcastle. Photograph used with permission from Stuart Roy Clarke ©stuartroyclarke/homesoffootball

some sanctuary from particularly acrid chain smokers. As the smoking ban took hold, toilets at British football grounds became the new sanctuary for football's committed puffers, and a profound health hazard for the rest of us.

Also lost in that same year at Liverpool FC – 2007 – was 'Dr Fun', a well-loved local Liverpool character-fan, Lenny Campbell, a man who routinely turned up to the club's home matches wearing a top hat and red tails, carrying a ventriloquist's dummy he had named *Liverpool Charlie*, to entertain fans (see Figure 19.3). No one asked him why, or offered their disrespect. Lenny had watched from the Kop from the age of 13 and he was a children's entertainer in summer holiday camps, where he acquired his nickname and garb, later transferred to the football terraces. Lenny was quite simply part of the cultural fabric of the club and symbolic of its distinctive supporter base. In many ways, in fact, Dr Fun was the very spirit, the resistant soul, of the old standing Kop, and his passing – like that of the unique balconies and walkways of the terrace itself – was deeply felt.

Hillsborough in 1989 constituted a vivid shock, felt especially hard in the city of Liverpool, and some friends and fellow fans stopped attending football as a result. I carried on, partly driven by the requirements of my job, but also because of residual Merseyside family ties. The deep affinity I had with 'home', mediated through football, paradoxically also intensified because of the impact of the disaster. Since the early 1990s, I have spent tens of thousands of pounds, 'lost' thousands of hours, missed important family functions and other events, sitting in endless motorway traffic jams at all hours of the day and night, and I have routinely been engaged in a Darwinian struggle for match tickets; all of this for following my football club at home and abroad. I am far from alone.

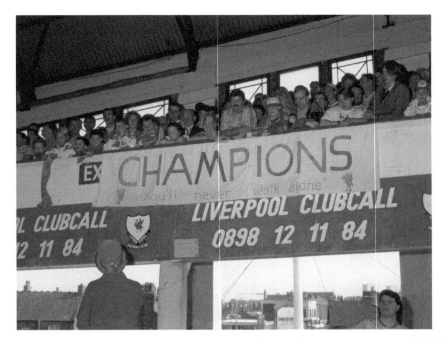

Figure 19.3 Dr. Fun and the Back Balcony on the Standing Kop at Liverpool, 1992. Photograph used with permission from Stuart Roy Clarke ©stuartroyclarke/homesoffootball

However, in the early years of my extended 'career' as an active, if distant, fan, demonstrating my 'long-distance love' as a Liverpool supporter had seemed relatively easy. Liverpool FC routinely won trophies: league championships, FA Cups, League Cups, even European Cups: I was there, tearful, in Rome in 1977, for Liverpool's first ever European Cup win. Indeed, in the 1970s and 1980s it was a crisis season if 'we' won no trophy. But maintaining this connection became more difficult as success dried up. In the same year as Liverpool FC's last Football League title in 1990, the publication of the official Taylor report on events at Hillsborough had surprised the then right-wing Thatcher Tory government by refusing to focus narrowly on the 'facts' of the disaster. Instead, it demonstrated a wider concern with the conflictful and failing governance of the game in England, and in the future of those people who typically watched it, the fans. Me, in fact.

Football culture and the sport's fan base were an incumbrance at best, or a near-complete mystery, to most Conservative politicians at the time. Lord Justice Taylor suggested that English football urgently required improved facilities and better and more coherent leadership. He was right, though dissenting voices remained on both left and right (Brick, 2000). It was rumoured that Taylor's key stadium recommendation – replacing standing terraces with seats – had been pressed on him by Britain's major football bodies, who wanted a completely new direction for a sport long plagued by cultish hyper-masculinity and hooliganism and the associated social exclusion and fan management issues (Robinson, 2010). So now the money had to be found to fund a national stadium modernisation scheme designed to attract new fans, one which was likely to cost more than £500 million in the first year. Crucially, satellite television, itself in financial trouble, was waiting in the arras to invest in top level English football, effectively to save its own skin and English football's future (Williams, 1994). We all know now how that particular marriage of convenience finally worked out.

In fact, around this time and as part of the struggle for the control of the English game, I was invited by Charles Hughes, national football coach and FA guru/theorist, to aid the FA in producing its own new *FA Blueprint for the Future of Football* (1991). Hughes wanted a chapter on fans and the new role I saw for them in the post-Hillsborough era. This 'cloak-and-dagger' FA document was designed, I was assured, to map out a new, improved future for the whole game in England. I saw no other chapters and thought this was some minor, internal report aimed for the FA Council to consider before being shelved. I was reluctant, but the Football Trust thought I should do it. So, I wrote my piece, on supporter engagement and consultation, and moved on. To my surprise, it became a little-discussed section of the published document in 1991 which effectively provided the rationale for the historic breakaway of elite English clubs from the Football League (est. 1888) to form the new Premier League in partnership with satellite TV companies (Millward, 2017; Boyle & Haynes, 2004). I guess you live and learn.

While its rivals from Manchester and London prospered in the new, corporatized Premier League era, Liverpool FC – like the city itself – suffered. My club, once so dominant, fell behind as the game commodified and globalised (Williams et al., 2001). It finally won the Premier League title only in 2020, after a 30-year wait for the top prize, and it had taken just 28 years to conquer the new TV-funded sport-as-soap opera Premier League construction which had been launched back in 1992. In fact, my *wife's* club, unconsidered 5000/1 outsiders, Leicester City, had won the English league title for the first time in *its* history in 2016 (Williams & Peach, 2018). The city I now lived in, and most of my family, was justifiably joyous: frankly, it was hell to experience. But there have also been extraordinary consolations in those lost 30 years for any Liverpool fan. In a remarkable season, in 2001 Liverpool won the FA and League Cups, and in Dortmund claimed the EUFA Cup, by beating Spain's Deportivo Alaves in a coruscating final: I was there, of course, dancing with fellow Reds' fan, Elvis Costello (Williams, 2001). I was also in Istanbul, in 2005, when Liverpool, ridiculously, pulled back three goals to win the Champions League (European Cup) final against the vaunted AC Milan, a victory celebrated by *all* Liverpool supporters in the city and typically captured later by Stuart Clarke (see Figure 19.4). I even co-wrote a book about Istanbul (Williams and Hopkins, 2005). My then partner (now wife) was unusually gleeful on my return in 2005; she insisted that I could now stop attending Liverpool games because: *'You will never see anything quite like that again.'* But I did not listen, and two years later, in chaotic Athens, I watched Liverpool lose in the final, Milan's swift revenge. But my wife was also quite wrong (as I knew she would be): because Liverpool 4, FC Barcelona 0, in the Champions League semi-final, 7 May 2019, was an even more astonishing night than Istanbul.

By now, of course, the finances of the elite English game had irrevocably changed; international owners, preferably billionaires, were routinely required to maintain elite competitiveness, and Premier League clubs had become global investment opportunities (Osborne and Coombes, 2009). In December 2006 Liverpool FC's domestic owners announced that an exclusivity agreement had been struck with Dubai International Capital (DIC), the plaything of Sheikh Mohammed bin Rashid al Maktoum, to buy the club. But the Liverpool board voted for a larger offer from two American speculators, George Gillette and Tom Hicks, who paid £174 million for the club's shares, vowed to pay off £45 million of club debt, and promised £215 million towards the building of a new stadium. In fact, the duo turned out to be squabbling leveraged buyout specialists, venture capitalists who bought businesses on the cheap with borrowed money before selling high for an inflated profit. However, the global financial crisis of 2008 hit the

Figure 19.4 Liverpool, the Day After the Club Won the European Cup in 2005. Photograph used with permission from Stuart Roy Clarke ©stuartroyclarke/homesoffootball

Americans' borrowing commitments hard and, as Liverpool fans protested about their owners' negligence and culpability, by 2010 Liverpool FC was in court and on the brink of administration. The club was rescued only by what seemed, on the face of it, to be (marginally) more stable, new American investors, the Fenway Sports Group (Williams, 2012; Williams & Hopkins, 2011).

Under FSG, the Anfield ground has been modernised and extended, rather than gutted or demolished, and Liverpool FC slowly began to return to its competitive traditions in Europe and at home. Times were good once more. Accordingly, I was in Kiev in 2018, having slept a fitful night outdoors at Warsaw Airport, only to see Liverpool's sophomoric young German goalkeeper, Loris Karius, throw two Real Madrid goals into his own net in a long-awaited Champions League final to ensure supporters, like me, more suffering. No matter. In 2019, under our charismatic coach, the smiling German super-motivator, Jurgen Klopp, Liverpool returned once more to win in the final, in Madrid. It was my *eighth* European Cup/Champions League final following Liverpool – six wins. The league title followed. However, just to prove that ambitious, billionaire super-capitalists can never really be trusted to protect sporting values, in April 2021 FSG turned out to be key figures in a proposed European breakaway league for the super-elite. The project was immediately ditched after universal fan opposition. FSG had its bridges to mend. But at this contentious point, let me rewind a little and get back to photography and Stuart Clarke.

Moving Pictures

In our first meeting, Stuart Clarke had told me that he had been to art college, before getting into photo-journalism for local newspapers in his home town of Watford. But he was now also doing his own thing, taking photographs of Britain's football supporters and stadiums. He was already on what was to become his *Homes of Football* journey charting, through his remarkable images, the extraordinary changes already taking place in the British game and among its people (Clarke, 1999; 2003). Clarke was particularly enthusiastic about the way music and football were synergising in Britain in the 1990s – he regularly took photographs at Glastonbury and other music festivals. I liked him from the start. The football pictures he brought for me to see at that first encounter were like no photographs of the game, its people, and its buildings, that I (or anyone else) had ever seen. They were in colour, large-format, and intimately close to the culture: nothing was staged. They were invariably poignant, often funny, but never intrusive, always respectful of his human subjects. These were mainly of low-level club workers and fans, ordinary men and women making something out of the troubled sport they loved. Or else, Clarke was carefully photographing stadium sheds, walls and stairwells, the buildings and spaces that others could only see as barely functional eyesores, some of them revived as yellow safety staircases on terraces, or blood-red walls; others awaiting likely (and probably deserved) demolition (see Figures 19.5 and 19.6). Clarke's photographs made them look more like listed national monuments. He soon concluded that what was *really* interesting about British football was less the game and more the locations that housed it and the people who watched it from these revered (if often dilapidated) venues.

Clarke, especially, wanted to try to capture the agonies and pleasures of being so deeply involved, the sheer drama acted out on the terraces and the exotic quirkiness of football people. Indeed, it was the creative and respectful *artist's* eye that he brought to a culture and its spaces that had been largely run down, abused and rubbished for many decades, which was so impressive

Figure 19.5 Red Wall, Barnsley FC, 1995. Photograph used with permission from Stuart Roy Clarke ©stuartroyclarke/homesoffootball

John Williams

Figure 19.6 Yellow Brick Road: Bradford City FC, 1992. Photograph used with permission from Stuart Roy Clarke ©stuartroyclarke/homesoffootball

in his work. His photographs, I decided, did much to capture the dignity and wild beauty of a sport and its people on the cusp of its third major transformation, into a new era of elite football's global hyper-commodification (Giulianotti, 2005). The first transformative change in the British game had occurred near the start, as football professionalised in England in the late-1800s, thus finally disentangling itself from its public-school roots, and spreading to working people and the merchant classes in urban areas as the 'football fever' swept north, across the British nation. Patrician industrialists and Muscular Christians funded clubs and hired players, stadiums were rapidly built, and local partisanships were stoked (Korr, 1978). A *national* professional sport was starting to be born. The second great transformation occurred in Britain, surely, in the early 1960s, with the lifting of the maximum wage for players, the emergence of national youth cultures, their influence on player styles and fan practices, and the rise of televised football. All this moulded some elite British footballers, for the first time, into authentic, commercial national celebrities, less contained and constrained by the game alone. A charming, sometimes truculent Irishman, Manchester United's mercurial George Best, was probably the first truly *young* British professional footballer of the new era of youthful consumer culture and increasingly troubled masculinities (Mellor, 2000).

In a way, Stuart Roy Clarke's work in photographs in the early 1990s complemented that of the emerging new football literati in Britain, exemplified by the writer and Arsenal fan Nick Hornby, a man who brought, in the written word, an educated, middle-class sensibility to interrogating the attractions of a post-hooligan English football for 'ordinary' people, particularly young men searching for ways of filling the supermarket masculinity trolley (Hornby, 1992). Like Hornby, the minor public schoolboy Clarke was also a kind of class 'outsider', a flaneur who had the core knowledge, but also the necessary social distance required to unpack and reveal the

Photography, Autoethnography and Mapping

Figure 19.7 The New Huddersfield Town Stadium Grows Wings when Viewed from the Old Leeds Road Ground, 1993. Photograph used with permission from Stuart Roy Clarke ©stuartroyclarke/homesoffootball

deeper meaning and aesthetic appeal of these weekly sporting rituals and the mysteriously idiosyncratic and topophilic places that housed them (Bale, 2000). Clarke inspired others to try to emulate his approach, but I think he remains the standard.

Clarke eventually completed some exceptional work for the Football Trust: elegiac portraits of once loved old terraces being mercilessly crushed by diggers; the steel struts of new stands sprouting up proudly into the sky; entire modern grounds evolving seemingly from nowhere (see Figure 19.7). He also understood implicitly that football fans find real meaning in the detail of their historic grounds and their surrounds: the first sight from a car, coach or train of the floodlight pylon; or the peculiar angle of a grandstand roof; images of bawling programme or fanzine-sellers on the approach to the stadium; a historic PLAYERS AND OFFICIALS ONLY stadium sign; a nailed together ticket-hut, decked out in peeling club colours (see Figure 19.8); the strange beauty of a stadium clock or a Heath Robinson-style half-time scoreboard; the distant view of the corporates in hospitality boxes; and even football graffiti, with its contrary messages of love or abuse. Stadiums that may be eyesores to the faithless are cathedrals to true believers. He discovered that each ground had something distinctive to report and he built up a rich body of photographic art, one that captured the British game at the very moment of its latest transformation. He also managed to portray key aspects of the national condition through the lens of the football watching public.

Clarke almost 'naturally' fused these studies into his wider project of capturing timeless manifestations of British football fandom in its various guises. He included here the working lives of people who were otherwise unnoticed or hidden behind the scenes of the professional game. He understood, intuitively, that photographs can be read to understand nuances

Figure 19.8 Ticket Office, Hull City, 1990. Photograph used with permission from Stuart Roy Clarke ©stuartroyclarke/homesoffootball

of interaction, presentations of self and relations among people to their material environments (Harper, 1988: 61). He spent very little time on what one might describe as the 'glamour' side of the moneyed Premier League; the top players and managers and their lifestyles was of little concern. Instead, he pointed his lens on the tea-ladies and the boot-room volunteers. Occasionally, he turned his attention to the mainly honourable (if often misguided) domestic British football club owners, before the oligarchs, the oil sheikhs, and the international venture capitalists took over. But his focus was mainly on the entrails, the guts, of the sport more than its pampered and powdered surfaces. He enjoyed tracing, before closure, for example, the Accrington brickworks, in Lancashire, which provided the materials to build many northern Victorian football venues at the turn of the nineteenth century.

Because he has worked so exhaustively in football communities across Britain, generating and storing tens of thousands of images, Clarke has arguably been able to observe and record much more than a writer's, or an academic's, account of the reconstruction of British football culture and its spaces could ever reasonably do. His work, in this respect, recalls the words of the great humanitarian photographer David DuChemin that photographing a culture in the here and now often means photographing the intersection of the present with the past. Indeed, rather like a reforming Charles Booth, or the American photo-documentary movement of the 1930s, or else a zealous urban ethnographer of today, Clarke has diligently recorded and reported 'from below' on a culture in flux and under threat: on local sporting communities at risk of falling into disarray. His images of homely merchandise stalls, or of charming, if rickety, structures at football grounds, are matched by his photographs of ordinary working people seeking pleasure, solace and a sense of meaning and belonging through their collective involvement in the game

Figure 19.9 Newcastle United Fans at Ipswich Town, 1990. Photograph used with permission from Stuart Roy Clarke ©stuartroyclarke/homesoffootball

(see Figure 19.9). He is also acutely aware, I think, of the importance of the lives of those working at the margins or behind the scenes in the professional game, usually women. They are included here, too, invariably photographed not with nostalgia but with affection and respect. Local young women serving coffees, pies and emotional labour from a shabby stall or van, can suddenly become vaunted actresses or divas, central characters in an unlikely technicolour drama (see Figure 19.10).

Always with a paternalistic eye for the quirky and absurd, Stuart Roy Clarke has also charted visions of British football's barely hidden, but familiar gentle madness: dogs apparently avidly watching matches; supporters armed in anticipation of glory with party poppers and borrowed toilet rolls; ranks of fans strangely and intensely becalmed, or else in advanced moments of agony or ecstasy; and burly working men in replica-shirted states of drunken joy, or else squeezed into agitated and transgressive forms of fancy dress (see Figures 19.11 and 19.12). Once one sees Clarke's remarkable photographic survey of British football culture at full throttle, the sight of a large, be-whiskered man, dressed as a fairy queen and carrying a sign ostensibly granting his club 'wishes', no longer seems quite so outlandish. Or, indeed, at all out of place. All human life really is here, it is just not obeying the usual rules of social normativity.

A Question of Ethics

In my view, Clarke generally succeeds in capturing, 'naturally occurring or spontaneous behaviour', often a contentious issue in visual social research (Pauwels, 2010: 553). He certainly never stages his settings or edits his results. His recording equipment is always visible to the participants, he photographs in single shots, though his crowd pictures taken in public settings can sometimes

John Williams

Figure 19.10 The Neon Coffee Women: Tranmere Rovers FC, 1992. Photograph used with permission from Stuart Roy Clarke ©stuartroyclarke/homesoffootball

Figure 19.11 Dogged Support: FC United of Manchester Fans at Buxton, 2005. Photograph used with permission from Stuart Roy Clarke ©stuartroyclarke/homesoffootball

Photography, Autoethnography and Mapping

Figure 19.12 Three Wishes: Wolverhampton Wanderers, 2002. Photograph used with permission from Stuart Roy Clarke ©stuartroyclarke/homesoffootball

obscure the sorts of ethical issues routinely faced by academics using visual techniques (Clark et al., 2010). Moreover, the public display, publishing, or wider dissemination of visual data *without* the explicit consent of individuals photographed has been described as ethically questionable for academics (Pink, 2007). Clarke's public exhibitions of his work clearly fall into this equation, though no fan or other subject has ever protested about featuring in Clarke's projects, a sign of his sensibilities. Working with the National Football Museum in Manchester, Clarke has recently organised events to bring together people captured in his images who talk (often movingly) in video installations about the circumstances involved and what the photograph means to them.

'A thing that you see in my pictures,' the lauded rock star photographer Annie Leibovitz once famously said, 'is that I was not afraid to fall in love with these people.' This sort of deep affection, I would argue, is a discernible feature of Clarke's work on football and its fans: everything, and everyone, recorded and exhibited here is deemed to be of value and demands both our attention and respect. In this sense, I would also contend that the necessary ethical reflexivity typically required in research, in terms of awareness and sensitivity and in the degree of honesty and truthfulness involved in dealings with others (Clark et al., 2010: 90), is more than apparent in Clarke's negotiations and interactions with, and representations of, his own football subjects.

Because of all this. I would also claim, I think, that at some deeper emotional level Stuart Clarke understands and identifies with this culture and its socio-spatial significance, especially perhaps in this period of social anxiety about growing feelings of 'placelessness' and ontological insecurity among fans and others (Mainwaring & Clark, 2012). In the late 1980s, many British football grounds may still have seemed Dickensian and run-down, and British (especially English) supporters were not always the best behaved. But in the shadow of wider fragmentations and social dislocations, British football stadiums remain important cultural signifiers, sites soaked in local lore, generational memory and meaningful history. Teams, managers, directors and players may come and go and kits change, but in many cases a club's football ground and its traditions of local support remain a near constant – a recognisable 'home' (Charleston, 2009). This feeling very widely pertained in Britain at least until the early 1990s I would say; that is, until the venues of elite-level football clubs in Britain really *had* to change – and often change radically.

Some Conclusions

Is it happenstance that Stuart Roy Clarke has been around to record what has been a period of rapid change in the British game and, more, that he is a visual transcriber who clearly *cares* about the landscapes and people before his lens? We can say we have an authentic visual memory of British football's recent past – and of the ordinary people who helped make it – in a period when elite, late-modern football can sometimes seem like just another form of managed 'entertainment', played out by impossibly rich, distant and transient global superstars in soulless stadia against the stark background of austerity and an ersatz array of WAGs, influencers and figures drawn from 'celebrity culture' (Webber, 2018; Harris, 2017). More recently, I have worked closely with Clarke on a project to try to describe the early roots of the game – those cranky and violent forms of folk football which are still played by local men on the land and on feast days up and down the British Isles – and the enduring tale of local Sunday morning football, played out on dog-shitted, uncut parks pitches with few decent facilities (Clarke, 2018; 2019). As in some of my own work (Ward & Williams, 2009), Clarke wants to try to insist on making some residual connections, at least in our heads, between the lowest levels of the professional game, parks' play, and the elite few who can now earn millions and have global profiles. It is a tough brief, but he works hard to encapsulate aspects of the local game in all its camaraderie, cultural importance and occasional absurdity, as beer-bellied and aged local men, and determined young women, continue to try to defy space, time and the elements to celebrate sporting sociality and (of course) bring home the points (see Figures 19.13 and 19.14).

Figure 19.13 The Juggler, Regent's Park, 2015. Photograph used with permission from Stuart Roy Clarke ©stuartroyclarke/homesoffootball

Photography, Autoethnography and Mapping

Figure 19.14 The Local Game: The Lake District, 1995. Photograph used with permission from Stuart Roy Clarke ©stuartroyclarke/homesoffootball

More recently, too, although his photographs have never knowingly promoted, in my view, a white hegemonic masculinity, Clarke has been carefully profiling the growing and increasingly diverse role of women in the game in England, unsurprisingly attracted by the thriving local football scene for females and the energy, skill and lack of ego of the top players, even as the elite levels of the women's game have now hurriedly, if belatedly, professionalised in England (Dunn & Welford, 2015). We may yet, as some feminist academics claim, be in a new era for women's involvement in sport in Britain, one which urgently requires its own memories and visual narratives, outwith those tired and irrelevant media comparatives made with men's football (Petty & Pope, 2019). Clarke is already active on this score (see Figures 19.15 and 19.16) and is also encouraging young women photographers to step forward.

Remarkably, in many ways, Stuart Roy Clarke's artist's sensibilities and his knowledge and love for the game and its people at all levels perpetuates, even as he edges into the veteran's career stage. He still travels most weekends all over Britain and to football at all levels, convinced that he has not yet documented it all. He has a restless gaze for continuities but also for something different, for something new to inform football enthusiasts, academics and researchers alike, about how and why we imbibe and play, write and live, key aspects of our lives through the world's most popular team sport. In his most recent work, he and I discuss the game's heritage and condition in a series of conversations, using photographs as our guide (Clarke, 2019). Even today, in his peerless enthusiasm, Clarke still manages to persuade one that he can find *that* image, *that* photograph, or *that* location which can tell the narrative better than any mere scribe can. And generally, I would argue, in the sheer volume, shrewdness, and aesthetic insight and warmth of his imagery, he can make a pretty convincing case.

Figure 19.15 Bradford City Fans in Prayer, 2015. Photograph used with permission from Stuart Roy Clarke ©stuartroyclarke/homesoffootball

Figure 19.16 England's Football Women, 2014. Photograph used with permission from Stuart Roy Clarke ©stuartroyclarke/homesoffootball

Bibliography

Bale, J. (2000) 'The changing face of football: stadium and communities' *Soccer & Society*, 1 (1): 91–101.
Barker-Ruchti, N., Grahn, K. & Annersted, C. (2013) 'Moving towards inclusion: An analysis of photographs from the 1926 Women's Games in Gothenburg' *The International Journal of the History of Sport*, 30 (8): 871–889.
Boyle, R. & Haynes, R. (2004) *Football in the New Media Age*, London: Routledge.
Brick, C. (2000) 'Taking offence: modern moralities and the perception of the football fan' *Soccer& Society*, 1 (1): 158–172.
Charleston, S. (2009) 'The English football ground as a representation of home' *Journal of Environmental Psychology*, 29: 144–150.
Clark, A., Prosser, J. & Wiles, R. (2010) 'Ethical issues in image-based research' *Arts & Health*, 2 (1): 81–89.
Clarke, S. (2019) *The Game Revisited*. Liverpool: Bluecoat Press.
Clarke, S. (2018) *The Game*. Liverpool: Bluecoat Press.
Clarke, S. (2003) *Football in our Time*, Edinburgh and London: Mainstream Publishing.
Clarke, S. (1999) *The Homes of Football: The Passion of a Nation*. London: Little Brown.
Drury, C. (2017) 'Many see the picture as symbolic of Maradona's talent and our terror.' *The Guardian*, 7 July. www.theguardian.com/artanddesign/2017/jul/07/thats-me-in-the-picture-football-belgium-world-cup-1982-maradona
Duke, V. (2002) 'Local tradition versus globalisation: resistance to the McDonaldisation and Disneyisation of professional football in England' *Football Studies*, 5 (1): 5–23.
Dunn, C. & Welford, J. (2015) *Football and the FA Women's Super League*. Basingstoke: Palgrave Macmillan.
Elliott, R. (ed.) (2017) *The English Premier League: A socio-cultural analysis*, London: Routledge.
The FA (1991) *FA Blueprint for the Future of Football*. London: The FA.
Farred, G. (2002) 'Long distance love: Growing up a Liverpool Football Club fan' *Sport and Social Issues* 26 (1): 6–24.
Giulianotti, R. (2005) 'Sport spectators and the social consequences of commodification' *Journal of Sport & Social Issues* 29 (4): 386–410.
Gould, D. & Williams, J. (2011) 'After Heysel: how Italy lost the football "peace"' *Soccer & Society*, 12 (5): 586–601.
Harper, D. (1988) 'Visual Sociology: Expanding sociological vision' *The American Sociologist*, 19 (1): 54–70.
Harris, J. (2017) 'The football star: Celebrity culture and consumption in the English Premier League', in R. Elliott (ed.) *The English Premier League: A socio-cultural analysis*, London: Routledge, pp. 97–111.
Hillsborough Independent Panel (2012) *Hillsborough: the report of the Hillsborough Independent Panel HC 581*. London: The Stationery Office.
Hopcraft, A. (1968) *The Football Man*. London: Collins.
Hornby, N. (1992) *Fever Pitch*. London: Victor Gollancz.
Korr, C. (1978) 'West Ham United football club and the beginnings of professional football in East London 1895–1914' *Journal of Contemporary History*, 13: 211–232.
Mainwaring, E. & Clark, T. (2012) 'We're shit and we know we are: identity, place and ontological security in lower league football in England' *Soccer & Society*, 13 (1) 107–123.
Mellor, G. (2000) 'The genesis of Manchester United as a national and international super club, 1958–68' *Soccer & Society*, 1 (2): 151–166.
Millward, P. (2017) 'A whole new ball game: the English Premier League and television broadcast rights' in R. Elliott (ed.) *The English Premier League: A socio-cultural analysis*, London: Routledge, pp. 33–48.
Osborne, A. & Coombs, D.S (2009) 'Enthusiasts, invaders and custodians: media characterisations of foreign owners in Barclays Premier League' *International Journal of Sports Communications*, 2: 297–318.
Osmond, G. (2010) 'Photographs, materiality and sport history: Peter Norman and the 1968 Mexico City Black Power salute' *Journal of Sport History*, 37 (1): 119–137.
Pauwels, L. (2010) 'Visual sociology reframed: An analytical synthesis and discussion of visual methods in social and cultural research' *Sociological Methods & Research*, 38 (4): 545–581.
Petty, K. & Pope, S. (2019) 'A new age for media coverage of women's sport? An analysis of English media coverage of the 2015 FIFA Women's World Cup' *Sociology*, 53 (3): 486–502.
Pink, S. (2007). *Doing Visual Ethnography* (2nd ed.) London: Sage.
Premier League (2015) 'More of Everyone' http://review.premierleague.com/2014–15/the-fans/full-stadiums.html

Robinson, J. (2010) 'The place of the stadium: English football beyond the fans' *Sport in Society*, 13 (6): 1012–1026.
Scraton, P. (2013) 'The legacy of Hillsborough: Liberating truth, challenging power' *Race and Class*, 55 (1): 1–27.
Smith, R. (2019) 'Families of Hillsborough victims are again left without answers' *New York Times*, 29 November.
Taylor, L. J. (1990) *The Hillsborough Stadium Disaster: 15 April 1989, Final Report*, Cm. 962. London: HMSO.
Ward, A. & Williams J. (2009) *Football Nation*. London: Bloomsbury.
Webber, D. (2018) 'Feasting in a time of famine: The English Premier League, "conspicuous consumption" and the politics of austerity' *Journal of Consumer Culture*. First published online 30 December. DOI: 10.1177/1469540518820948
Williams, J. (2014) 'Justice for the 96? Hillsborough, politics and English football.' In J. Treadwell and M. Hopkins (eds.) *Football Hooliganism, Crime and Crowd Control*. London: Routledge, pp. 273–295.
Williams J. (2012) 'Walking alone together the Liverpool Way: fan culture and "clueless" Yanks' *Soccer & Society*, 13 (3): 426–442.
Williams, J. (2011) 'The Liverpool Way, the matchless Kop and the Anny Road Boys': notes on the contradictions in Liverpool football supporter radicalism.' In J. Belchem & B. Biggs (eds.) *Liverpool: City of Radicals*. Liverpool: Liverpool University Press), pp. 123–139.
Williams, J. (2010) *Red Men: Liverpool Football Club, the Biography*. Edinburgh and London: Mainstream Publishing.
Williams, J. (2006) 'Protect me from what I want: football fandom, celebrity cultures and 'new' football in England' *Soccer & Society*, 7 (1): 96–114.
Williams, J. (2001) *Into the Red*. Edinburgh and London: Mainstream Publishing.
Williams, J. (1994) 'The local and the global in English soccer and the rise of satellite television' *Sociology of Sport Journal*, 11 (4): 376–397.
Williams. J. & Peach, J. (2018): '"We are all Foxes now": Sport, multiculturalism and business in the era of Disneyization' *Sport in Society*, 21 (3): 415–433.
Williams, J. & Hopkins, S. (2011) 'Over here: "Americanisation" and the new politics of football club fandom – the case of Liverpool FC' *Sport and Society*, 14 (2) pp. 160–174.
Williams, J. and Hopkins, S. (2005) *The Miracle of Istanbul*. Edinburgh and London: Mainstream Publishing.
Williams, J. Hopkins, S. and Long, C. (eds.) (2001*) Passing Rhythms: Liverpool FC and the transformation of football*. Oxford and New York: Berg.

20
The Ecosystem of Football Supporter Groups in Brazil
Traditions, Innovation and Hybridity

Ana Carolina Vimieiro

Groups of football fans and fandom practices have been extensively investigated in the literature. From Ian Taylor's classic in the late 1960s, passing by the influential work of the Leicester School in the 1980s, to more contemporary works that analyse, for example, supporters who live in different geographic locations than their clubs (such as Petersen-Wagner, 2017) and digital fan practices (such as Vimieiro, 2017, 2018), we cannot say that the topic has not received the due attention, at least among football researchers. In analysing the contemporary context of football fans in Brazil, however, I came across a difficulty in understanding how diverse, multifaceted and hybrid it is such context. In this chapter, I am calling this environment the *torcidas*[1]' ecosystem.

The approaches that could be called typological, such as that of Giulianotti (2002) and Lever (1983), despite helping to differentiate the characteristics of diverse fans and groups, do not seem to account for the mixtures and the still marked presence of practices and groups that could be seen as quite traditional in contexts that have undergone hypercommodification processes. In some sense, some typologies seem to suggest a certain linearity, in which groups marked by modern characteristics are gradually replaced by fans with postmodern identities.

Studies dedicated to analysing institutionalised groups of fans which often seek to historicise the emergence of certain formations, such as the works of Taylor (1992) and Nash (2000, 2001), also provide important contributions to understand the relationship between fan practices and the cultural and political contexts in which they emerge. However, they also seem to approach such groups from their peculiarities, capturing them in a frozen way, stopped, above all, at the peak of their operation. In addition, how these groups dialogue, conflict and mix with other groups is not exactly explored.

Even in Brazil, where we have a long tradition of studies on football supporters dating back to the 1980s, especially from an anthropological approach, there is a certain difficulty in understanding, for example, how the novelty (the new formations) coexists with continuity. Although we have works that explore different groups throughout history, such as *charangas* (from the 1940s; more about them below), organised fans (from the 1960s), new supporting movements (2000s) and free torcidas (2010s), there are relatively few works that explore the

DOI: 10.4324/9780429342189-22

contemporary scene where groups representing all these types coexist harmoniously, conflict and mix.

This work proposes an analysis of the ecosystem of Brazilian football fan cultures based on the approach of hybrid cultures of the Latin American culturalist Néstor Garcia Canclini to fill some of the mentioned gaps. In my view, Canclini offers an effective contribution to think about the historical developments of fan groups and practices, not as a linear path, but as a path composed of hybridisation cycles in which the new does not replace the archaic, but where traditional and modern mix, giving way to hybrid social practices. As the epigraph of this chapter reveals, in Latin America (and probably also in other regions), traditions have not yet disappeared, and modernity has not completely arrived. Therefore, the development of football fan cultures is no less tortuous than our own history. And it is this non-linear and non-deterministic understanding of history that provides us with the lens for looking at the contemporary context and for understanding the complex football supporting dynamics.

In the following section, I briefly review the literature on football fans developed in the English-speaking world and in Brazil. I end this section, arguing that the hybridisation processes are clearly present in the shaping of Brazilian fan cultures: whether it be in the first fan groups from the early 1940s, which imported and recreated US fan practices to the Brazilian football scene, or in the new supporting movements, which are inspired by South American *barra bravas* at the same time that they combine their practices with those of the traditional organised Brazilian fans, creating new and hybrid practices. The fact that we have fans who are part of different formations at the same time or throughout life strengthens the argument that it is necessary to think about dialogues, mixtures and also what resists to be hybridised. The conflicts between traditional organised fans with feminist collectives and queer groups reveals how antagonistic the values defended by different groups can be, with the traditional, which often is seen as the "authentic", being also very excluding. The last and longest part of the chapter is dedicated to exploring these different formations more closely.

Football Supporter Studies in the Anglo-World and in Brazil

Football supporters have been studied in the anglosphere from a sociological or cultural point of view since late in the 1960s. Especially during the 1970s and 1980s, with the public concern with football hooliganism increasing in the UK, academics found large audiences interested in understanding this type of fan behaviour and sources of research funding, which made this period particularly fertile for this research area (Giulianotti, 1999; Haynes, 1995). For Haynes (1995), football and its culture became objects of serious sociological enquiry with Ian Taylor's work. Adopting a Marxist and "new criminological" perspective, Taylor sought to comprehend the historical changes in the relationship between supporters and the game since the 1960s. For Taylor, rather than gratuitous outbursts, hooliganism was a type of resistance act, resulting from a deep rupture in football dynamics, caused in the first place by complex social and economic changes. These changes had deepened football's commodification, with clubs shifting their "emphasis from satisfying existing 'supporters' to attracting modern 'spectators' or leisure 'customers'" (Giulianotti, 1999, p. 40). For Giulianotti (1999), the major weakness in Taylor's work was its lack of empirical grounding. Taylor has also been criticised for romanticising the conditions of the past (Giulianotti, 2002; Haynes, 1995). On the other hand, both Giulianotti (1999) and Haynes (1995) highlight the importance of Taylor's critical observations regarding the changes in the relationship between supporters and the game.

In the early 1980s, another group of scholars, this time based at the University of Leicester, took the leading position in the debates about football hooliganism. Exponents of the Leicester

School, including Eric Dunning, adopted the figurational approach proposed by the German sociologist Norbert Elias to explain football-related violence. According to Giulianotti (1999), the Leicester School used Elias's conceptual framework to explain football hooliganism in two main aspects: first, they examined how social attitudes towards violence at football matches have changed over time as a result of the civilising process; and second, the researchers attributed fan violence per se to social groups that were not affected by the civilising process. Giulianotti (1999) and Haynes (1995) list a series of critiques that the Leicester School has received over the years. For instance, scholars have pointed out the problematic connections established in the figurationists' work between lower working classes with 'rough' socialisation and hooliganism. Elias's concept of the civilising process has also attracted strong criticism from being a teleological, ethnocentric and inaccurate point of view that misrepresents even the developments of Europe itself (Goudsblom, 1994).

The emergence of what may be called the "fan democracy" line of studies is related somehow to the developments of the football industry in the 1980s and 1990s. Continuing Ian Taylor's concerns about fan dissatisfaction with the modern developments of football, the "fan democracy" agenda has dominated football fandom scholarship since the 1990s, when the intensification of globalisation and commodification processes started a new wave of changes, reinventing at some level the social relations defining the game. Such literature has focused on the emergent social movements and groups with more militant discourses and attitudes that opposed the measures taking place, like the adoption of the all-seater model (Brown, 1998; Haynes, 1995; Nash, 2000, 2001). More recently, a couple of works have analysed the emergence of the so-called movements "Against Modern Football" in diverse countries, such as Italy (Numerato, 2015) and Poland (Gońda, 2013). In these studies, as Crawford (2003) explains, "commercialisation is seen as a perversion of the people's game — leading towards a less dedicated, more fickle supporter base" (p. 221). This resistance approach has one consequence particularly important here, which is the overvaluation of the traditional/authentic fan. This is especially problematic because there are indications that traditions are used by football fans in association with xenophobic, misogynistic and homophobic discourses (Gońda, 2013; Numerato, 2015; Vimieiro et al., 2019a).

More recently, we have seen several studies that, in some way, also problematise such notions of authentic and inauthentic fans based on analyses of online communities and digital fan practices (Wilson, 2007; Ruddock, 2013; Gibbons & Dixon, 2010; Lawrence & Crawford, 2019). We also see, especially from 2010 onwards, a set of studies on women supporters and, among them, many about football. These studies have analysed a variety of phenomena, such as representations of women sport fans on media (Wenner, 2012a, 2012b; Tanaka, 2004); identity formation and forms of sociability between women supporters, especially, through online spaces (Hynes, 2012; Hynes & Cook, 2013; Kunert, 2019); and sports blogs and other media objects produced by women fans (Antunovic & Hardin, 2012, 2013, 2015; Lisec & McDonald, 2012). Some of these studies have also questioned the gender hierarchies supporting the articulation of authentic fandom to working-class masculinity, and inauthenticity to feminised and consumer-related modes of supporting (Toffoletti, 2017).

In Brazil, on the other hand, football has been analysed from sociological and cultural approaches since the 1940s, but it began to consolidate as a field in the 1990s. In the specific case of fans and the relationships they establish with the game, even though Lever (1983) and César (1981) address the issue, it is Toledo (1996) who develops the first work of greater breath and impact when adopting an anthropological approach to examining the sociability patterns of organised fans in São Paulo.

One of the first significant investigations of fans is that of US sociologist Janet Lever, who after working with British sociologist Ian Taylor interviewing fans at the Mexico Cup in 1970, goes to Brazil and interviews more than 200 working-class men in Rio de Janeiro, proposing then a simplified typology of fans. Among his interviewees, 25 per cent fit the weak fan profile, 50 per cent the average fan and 25 per cent the strong fan. From these profiles, Lever (1983) then crosses the data with information about the links of these individuals with family and friends and with the extended community, realising that men who had frequent contacts with friends and neighbours, for example, were five times more likely to be strong fans. The author's conclusion, then, is that football strengthens social ties, especially because rivalries, which could be an obstacle to this, are basically cordial in Brazil.

The work of Lever (1983), although very important, offers us a very general portrait of fans and torcidas, without going into the details of the daily lives of supporters and fan groups. It is the work of Benedito Tadeu César (1981), published a little earlier and also referring to the 1970s context, that will kick-start this line of investigation. César dedicates his master's dissertation to the study of the organised group *Gaviões da Fiel* (of *Corinthians* supporters). He performs an ethnographic work of some length and makes a more sociological analysis, dialoguing particularly with names from the first generation of the Frankfurt School (such as Marcuse and Adorno), Althusser, Gramsci and with currents of anthropology.

Despite the empirical limitations, César's work (1981) maintains a certain validity because of its dialectical reading of football supporter groups. But it is Toledo (1996) who effectively provides a more detailed and systematic account of the multiple practices in which organised fans engage. Toledo's work (1996) is the result of a long three years of ethnography with, initially, eight fan groups from the state of São Paulo which, in a second moment, were narrowed down to two torcidas: *Torcida Tricolor Independente* (*São Paulo* fans) and *Camisa 12* (*Corinthians* fans). Based on discussions of urban anthropology, Toledo (1996) seeks to capture the dynamics of organised fans not only in the stadiums on game days, but also in their headquarters, courts, on their way to the stadium, on trips and caravans and in ordinary activities (more about this below). More recently, we have also seen in Brazil a wave of studies that have analysed gender issues related to ordinary and organised female fans. Topics investigated in this area range from representations of women football fans (Costa, 2007; Bandeira & Seffner, 2018), passing by onsite football fandom practices performed at stadiums by female supporters (Nascimento, 2020; Moraes, 2017), to media objects produced by female fans (Vimieiro et al., 2020), and studies about female sections within the traditional organised football fandom groups and feminist collectives (Vaz, 2014; Pinto, 2017). These studies, which are a minority in fan practices literature, have taken important steps into a closer dialogue with gender studies, seeking to understand, for example, the dominant representations of female supporters present in the media and in social imaginary.

All these perspectives have contributed in some way to the understanding of groups and practices of football fans in the English-speaking world and in Brazil. My difficulty, when looking at the current Brazilian context, is to understand how these different perspectives, practices and groups analysed could converge to enable a comprehension of a multifaceted environment, where groups similar to *Charanga Rubro-Negra*, one of the first known groups in Brazil (more about them below), co-exist with torcidas such as feminist collectives and queer groups, the majority of which are less than five years old. To understand the conflicts, dialogues and this trajectory in which traditional groups are not replaced by new ones (which does not mean that they do not change over time), it was the work of Canclini and his vision of the modernisation process in Latin America that helped me.

Canclini describes the transit of what he calls discrete forms to hybrid forms. For Canclini (1995), hybridisation is a type of sociocultural process in which "discrete structures or practices, previously existing in separate form, are combined to generate new structures, objects and practices" (p. XXV). To characterise the procedural character of these cycles and the usefulness of talking more about hybridisation than about momentary hybridity, Canclini dialogues with Stross's notion of hybridisation cycles, describing, in history, as "we move historically from more heterogeneous forms to other more homogeneous ones, and then to other relatively more heterogeneous forms, without any being 'purely' or simply homogenous" (p. XXV). When modern processes and practices are introduced to football, they do not replace traditional processes and practices. In general, old and new mix and form something hybrid, which, over time, will become more discreet, in the sense of being understood as the "new" traditional. As Canclini says, even though the notion of hybridisation may seem like an excessively kind version of the cultural encounter, it is not: "hybridization is not synonym for fusion without contradiction" (p. XXIV). In this sense, the historical development of fan formations is composed of hybridisation cycles and each of these mixtures often generates conflicts in which the practices gathered may remain incompatible or irreconcilable. In the analysis that follows, I try to highlight the multi and intercultural processes that demarcate the history of football supporting cultures in Brazil. I organised the discussion in a certain typology, dividing it into different groups and supporting practices. However, less than establishing clear distinctions, in each of the sections, I seek to demonstrate precisely the fluidity of this ecosystem.

The Ecosystem of Football Supporter Groups in Brazil

I now proceed to describe in more detail the different groups and practices of football fans still existent in contemporary Brazil, trying to highlight the origins of such groups, points of convergence and divergence and also possible internal transformations (readjustments to different historical moments). This description is made from my fieldwork in some cases (the last two types), together with the work of other Brazilian researchers (especially in the case of the first three).

Uniformed Groups, Charangas and Symbolic Fans

The first known groups of fans in Brazil are dated from the early 1940s. The creation of more or less organised groups of fans coincides with the transformation of football into a mass sport and with the construction of large stadiums in the country that could support the popularity that it had achieved at that time – for example, Pacaembu was inaugurated in São Paulo in 1940 with a capacity for 70,000 people. As Hollanda and Silva (2006) explain, it is at this time that fans began to abandon the elegant dress code of theatre, cinema and opera audiences, with the usual suit and tie, and start to use club shirts, produced in an amateur way, to identify fans of each club. It is not by chance that the first groups are called *torcidas uniformizadas* (uniformed torcidas).

Braga (2010) explains that the early organisation of football fans in Brazil had been copied, to some extent, from the "cinematographic" style of supporting at the US universities. The time was right for this type of cultural exchange. Franklin Roosevelt's Good Neighbour Policy was in effect, and networks of connections were emerging at that time that amplified the similarities between Brazil and the United States. Hollywood cinema, for example, starts to play an important role in spreading the "American way of life" to Brazilians and "among the striking images of [American] life were those that showed university fans" (Braga, 2010, p. 9).

But the Brazilian modernist tradition of incorporating influences, "swallowing" them up and recreating them was present not only in the anthropophagic movement: very soon a Brazilian way of supporting which would reinvent such practices is created in Rio de Janeiro. In 1942, we see the creation of the famous *Charanga Rubro-Negra* (*Flamengo* fans), which was responsible for bringing into the stadium a small musical orchestra with metal, percussion and wind instruments. Hollanda and Silva (2006) state that the innovation was met with resistance, since the presence of musicians inside the stadium seemed a bizarre experience for some: the group's sound quality was doubtful and the out-of-tune noise was used as a strategic resource to support Flamengo as well as to take away the concentration of opponents.

In spite of causing astonishment, the charanga proposed something innovative, "because until that moment music was only part of the celebrations outside the stadium, sometimes in cafes, sometimes on the streets, with car parades imitating the corsairs of carnival" (Hollanda & Silva, 2006, p. 2). It did not take long for typical Brazilian sounds, like sambas and carnival *marchinhas*, to dominate the scene.

The creation of charanga also demonstrates one of the striking characteristics of this initial moment of Brazilian fan cultures: we have the appearance of what some call cheerleaders – even though they are quite dissimilar to US cheerleaders – and other symbolic fans. These figures are commonly known to other fans and important, especially at that moment, in two aspects: coordination of the performances and control of the fans. Hollanda and Silva (2006) explain that symbolic fans like Dulce Rosalina from Vasco, Tarzã from Botafogo and Paulista from Fluminense rehearsed choreographies throughout the week that would be performed in the weekend games. Jaime de Carvalho, creator of Charanga Rubro-Negra, "enlisted children from the neighbourhood of his residence in Niterói to make flags, went to knitting shops in downtown Rio and sought a subsidy from the club's directors to win the fans' tournament" (Hollanda & Silva, 2006, pp. 7 and 8). One of these tournaments was *Duelo das Torcidas* (The Torcidas' Duel), originally launched by the newspaper *Jornal dos Sports* in 1936, which transferred the competitive logic of samba school parades to stadiums. These and other stimuli by the sports press, say Hollanda and Silva (2006), impregnated the games with a carnival atmosphere, with sirens, horns, streamers, confetti, banners and multi-coloured balloons being brought by the crowd to the stadium. It was this spirit that would dominate Brazilian stadiums until the mid-1960s, when we see the emergence of the organised supporters, which will be explored in the next section.

But the charangas and the symbolic fans have not disappeared. In the state of Minas Gerais, the games of Atlético-MG are still animated by *Charanga do Galo*. And there are many symbolic fans in Brazil, such as *Vovó do Galo* (a 100-year-old lady who regularly attends Atlético-MG's matches), *Dona Zuzu* (supporter of América-MG who has been going to the stadium since the 1950s) and *Salomé do Cruzeiro* (who died in 2019, but had been regularly attending Cruzeiro's matches since the 1950s). Nowadays, symbolic fans do not have the function of cheerleaders as in the past, being characters with symbolic rather than coordination functions.

Traditional Organised Groups

In Portuguese, there is a difference between *torcidas uniformizadas* and *torcidas organizadas*. The former means a group of fans that wears a uniform; the latter means an organised group of fans. The term *torcidas organizadas* (TOs from now) is used to characterise associations from the 1960s onwards that are legally formalised as non-profit recreational associations, with complex organisational structures, with actual positions, such as president and director, and a deliberative body. These associations are also registered with the clubs.

All these associations have similar features: they are formed by young fans – in contrast with previous formations, formed mostly by middle-aged adults (uniformed groups and charangas); and also, they are more autonomous and impersonal, with supporters assuming an active position and exerting pressure over club leaders. As Toledo (1996) asserts, these groups were often not welcomed by the clubs, which were used to the passivity of previous groups when these more active organisations emerged.

Such formations arose in the very early days of the military dictatorship government that ruled Brazil from 1964 to 1985. Seen by some as part of the mobilising of opposition forces against the dictatorship system and by others as juvenile gangs whose main form of expression was gratuitous violence (Toledo, 1996), the best way to contextualise the emergence of such groups is perhaps to take into account the broader context. The case of Charanga Rubro-Negra and the formation of *Torcida Jovem do Flamengo*, one of the first TOs in the country, is illuminating. As Hollanda and Silva (2006) explain, this was a time marked by a certain youth unrest and cultural transformation, with student movements such as those of May 1968 in France reverberating around the world, and young members of groups such as charangas starting to claim new forms of participation in the stadiums. There was also a generational conflict, with young people fighting for the right to protest and contest at critical stages of the game (something that uniformed groups and charangas did not do). It is in this context that young people who participated in other groups started to abandon them to create, together with newcomers, the first organised groups, which were constituted from new values, which also expressed this historical moment.

In terms of bureaucratic organisation, participation and visibility in the football scene, such groups consolidated in the 1980s. In the early 1990s, for instance, Gaviões da Fiel's organisational structure included a deliberative body, formed by 40 associates, and three boards of directors: the executive director, the financial director and the Carnival's director (Toledo, 1996). In 1993, Gaviões da Fiel had 23,000 associates; Torcida Tricolor Independente, 15,000; and Palmeiras' *Mancha Verde*, 8,000.

Organised groups have a distinct pattern of sociability and occupy football spaces in a collective way (Toledo, 1996). This distinction is materialised in the routes taken by ordinary fans and organised fans to the stadium on match-days, for instance. The former adopts the home-stadium route, while the latter takes the path from home to the *torcida* headquarters to the stadium. For Toledo (1996), "far from trivial, this difference is evidence of the existence of a fundamental space in the identification and constitution of these supporter groups" (p. 43). The sociability established in the head office, through their parties, celebrations and everyday conviviality, builds ties between individuals from diverse regions in the city, social origins, worldviews and expectations.

In their headquarters, which may differ tremendously depending on the resources and properties owned by each TO, organised supporters generally have remembrance shrines, mostly walls, where fans hang images and photos of memorable matches and victories, conquered titles, beloved players and historic teams. Also, in the headquarters, symbols of the club and of the torcida (all of them have their own logos and emblems) are all over the place, and those supporters who work there, or are passing by, generally wear pieces of clothing and accessories adorned with such signals.

Inside the stadiums, the organised supporter groups are also easily recognised. In Brazil (and in other places as well), they position themselves in the cheapest stands, generally those behind the goals. These groups wear their own customised clothes (not the clubs' branded apparel), they exhibit flags and banners, and they chant anthems, battle cries and songs especially developed by them for their stadium performances. Also, they have a particular physical expressivity that differentiates them from the supporting masses: intense choreographies cadenced by their *bateria* – a kind of simple orchestra of percussion instruments.

These practices discussed above are some of the traditional activities performed by organised supporters. They are still part of their routines and characterise a rather specific type of sociability and aesthetics that constitutes, and is constituted in, such environments. In the current fragmented environment, some organised groups have broken down, with the formation of new organised groups from dissidents of traditional TOs and also with the formation of what has been called new supporting movements. I turn to these now.

New Supporting Movements

Since the early 2000s, Brazilian football culture has witnessed the emergence of new associations of supporters, which some scholars have called *new supporting movements* (Hollanda et al., 2014; Teixeira, 2010, 2013). These new groups are inspired by South American barra bravas, especially the Argentinean ones, and were first formed in Rio Grande do Sul, the southernmost state of Brazil, which borders both Uruguay and Argentina. The first Brazilian barra to get wider visibility was *Geral do Grêmio* (dedicated to *Grêmio*), which was created in 2001 (Rodrigues, 2012). And since then, barras have spread to other places.

These groups often originate from dissidents of TOs, explicitly manifesting a desire to differentiate themselves from the previous organised groups' *ethos* and modes of supporting (Teixeira, 2010). Their absolute devotion to their clubs is expressed through chants – which affirm the club identification over provocation and passion for the torcida itself – and via the support along the whole match (as they say, "always standing and chanting, no matter the scoreboard"). Also, for the new movements, the match is not the time when supporters should protest against players, coaches or club leaders. As a result, protest chants are generally not part of their repertoire. In many of her interviews, Teixeira (2013) identified a type of disenchantment and disappointment experienced by fans that were previously part of organised groups and then became members of new movements. For these dissidents and for the newcomers who reject the traditional organised groups' model, the new movements represent the possibility of collectively living the supporting experience without dangers and risks.

Still, Teixeira (2013) also perceptively indicates that even though such groups self-declare their inspirations in the Argentinean barras, they also make appropriations and new meaning attributions that dislocate such practices from their original contexts. Particularly, supporters interviewed by Teixeira assert that they have removed violence from the repertoire of barra bravas. On the other hand, the new movements also bring inspiration from practices related to organised groups, such as the use of big flags, an element not so much adopted by the South American barras.

For Hollanda and colleagues (2014), the discourses of the new movements converge to what has been advocated by football industry insiders since early in the 2000s in Brazil. Such discourses are related to the growing commodification, the intensification of the repression and surveillance mechanisms inside the sporting arenas, and to the Brazilian winning bid to host the 2014 World Cup (which, especially, pushed the renovation agenda and the mobilisation to end football-related conflicts). In this context, football supporters and insiders have celebrated the return of a festive and familiar environment through the recuperation of chants, uniforms and old-fashioned flags, mimicking supporters from the "symbolic-fan phase". On the other hand, they are criticised for fabricating such "traditions", since they are generally from the middle class, with higher levels of education, representing for some the gentrification of football stadiums and culture in Brazil (Hollanda et al., 2014).

Online Communities and New Supporting Leaders

Football fans in Brazil have been using the internet and digital network systems to talk about sport since the early 1990s (Vimieiro, 2015). In the early 1990s, before the beginning of the commercial operation of the internet, which occurred in 1995, football supporters used Bulletin-board systems (BBBs) to talk to other football enthusiasts in the same geographical area. When the internet arrived in Brazil (i.e. when its use started going beyond universities and research centres) in 1995, these groups migrated to mailing lists. Some of the members of these mailing lists also used to arrange face-to-face meetings to follow games together. That's the case of *lista-atletico*, a mailing list of supporters of *Atlético-MG* that had around 250 members in 1996 and organised its first meeting in April 1997. Soon, some groups formed online became organised groups, such as TIF (*Torcida Internet Flamengo*) and Netg@lo, the "result" of lista-atletico (Vimieiro, 2015).

In previous works, I divided the developments of such communities into three phases (Vimieiro, 2015): 1) the 1990s: restricted use by some fans, young people and students, especially, of BBSs and mailing lists; 2) 2000s: massive and centralised use of Orkut, with club-based communities reaching their peak around 2010/2011, when Orkut started to lose space to other platforms such as Twitter and Facebook; 3) 2010s: from this point onwards, what we have seen is that the fan groups that used to mobilise through a single platform start to disperse, assuming a distributed shape, forming types of multi-sited communities or *networked collectivisms* (Baym, 2010). Today, much of the integration of these diverse spaces is done by key hubs in such groups, who have profiles in many platforms and transfer the information from one to another. The fact that football supporters in Brazil have a relationship with their clubs that is anything but frivolous means that such hubs are generally fans who have been around for a very long time (some since the mailing lists of the 1990s) and who are well known by other fans. I called these hubs new supporting leaders.

In previous works, I demonstrated too how the emergence of such leaders is also linked to the popularisation of decentralised content production tools and to broader changes such as the increasing levels of individualisation and fragmentation typical of post-modernity (Vimieiro, 2018). Such processes resulted in decentralised forms of mobilisation and collective action, where traditional actors such as organised groups have lost organisational centrality and began to share the space with new supporting movements, with new digital leaders and more politicised collectives, which will be explored in the next section.

These digital leaders, in general, (1) dominate much of the conversations about their clubs taking place on platforms such as Facebook, Twitter and YouTube; (2) have been part of such groups and communities for a long time, in addition to often being former members of institutionalised groups of fans like TOs and new supporting movements; (3) they are often producers of popular content about their teams; and (4) are central articulators of the performances and other collective activities that take place "offline", such as campaigns, special actions inside and outside the stadiums, and protests.

In previous research, I interviewed new supporting leaders of Atlético-MG, a top professional Brazilian football club, created in 1908, that has won a variety of regional, national, and international titles. Among my interviewees (11), all but one were regular stadium attendees, including some who did not live in Atlético-MG's hometown, Belo Horizonte (Vimieiro, 2018). They were central nodes (high betweenness centrality) in a network analysis of a large Twitter dataset related to this club (more than 500,000 posts) collected over a three-month period in 2013, which demonstrates how central they were for the Twitter conversations about Atlético-MG during that period (Vimieiro, 2015). They were producers of original media content about their club, maintaining highly popular blogs, YouTube channels, web radios, podcasts among other alternative media projects.

The practices and functions of these new leaders in the context of sport cultures were previously analysed as similar to opinion leaders (Ruddock, 2013). I would say that they play the role of opinion leaders, but they have also assumed the organisational role that the symbolic fans had in the past, when they were cheerleaders. Besides their leadership and organisational functions, these supporters have also engaged in a series of micro-celebrity practices (Marwick, 2010), achieving a type of status within the supporter bases of their clubs. Some have used such status to transfer from alternative media to mainstream media, such as TV channels and the press, or to monetise their media projects, becoming professionals in their own terms. Yet, it is difficult to separate the new supporting leaders from other formations. Some of them were or still are members of TOs and new supporting movements. However, the importance they have as articulators in this ecosystem comes primarily from their digital footprint and not their previous/current involvement with supporter groups.

Feminist Collectives and Queer Groups

The last formation I explore here are the torcidas, collectives, fan movements with a more politicised character that have proliferated in Brazil in the last decade. Since 2013, many groups have formed with an outstanding operation in social networks such as Facebook and calling themselves *torcidas livres* (free torcidas) or *torcidas queer* (queer torcidas). In addition to praising the clubs they support, these groups use such spaces to disseminate content with the purpose of "denaturing misogynistic and homophobic offenses and violence that are constantly reiterated in the football domain and questioning the place of abjection to which women and LGBT people are relegated, deconstructing the idea that football is an exclusive space of cisgender and heterosexual men" (Pinto, 2017, p. 73).

In 2013, fans of Atlético-MG, popularly known as Galo, created *Galo Queer*, the first fan group to present itself as a queer torcida. Created from the discomfort of fans of the club with the homophobic chants sung by its fellow supporters, the group presents itself, according to Pinto (2017), not just as a gay torcida seeking acceptance in a homophobic environment but as an activist group that dialogues with queer activism in general and seeks to refuse violent moral values that institute and enforce the abjection line. The aim is to question this rigid boundary between those who are socially accepted and those who are relegated to humiliation and collective disdain.

After the emergence of Galo Queer, many other groups were created, such as *Palmeiras Livre* and *Bambi Tricolor*. For Pinto (2017), the shaping of such collectives is linked to the political effervescence of 2013 in Brazil and shows the political formation processes of these fans "outside" football. In the speeches of fans involved with these groups, it is clear that many had and have experiences in other political and social movements, especially activism in defence of gender equality and against homophobia, and that these agendas were then brought to sport.

Pinto (2017) sees the roots of these queer collectives in movements of the 1970s, such as the creation of *Coligay*, the first gay group to be present in Brazilian stadiums. Groups with a more feminist agenda were perhaps influenced by the sections or branches within the traditional organised groups dedicated to women. These ramifications, which date from the 1990s, were created in an attempt, by the TOs, to change their images, which were heavily criminalised at the time (Teixeira, 2003). However, in many ways, this incorporation of women was a form of concession, with limits very well imposed by men. There are reports that, for example, women cannot wave flags or play instruments within the organised groups, activities reserved for men (Moraes, 2017). Other reports demonstrate that female fans will often focus their efforts on the social actions of such groups, with a reduced presence in other activities (Nascimento, 2000).

In this sense, collectives started to emerge questioning more directly gender inequalities and violence within the scope of football supporting cultures. One of the first was *Força Feminina Colorada*, a group of women supporters of *Internacional* from Porto Alegre, created in 2009. After them, several other groups emerged, such as *Movimento Coralinas*, of supporters of *Santa Cruz*, *Coletivo INTERfeministas*, also of supporters of Internacional, *Grupa*, from fans of Atlético-MG, and *Movimento Toda Poderosa Corinthiana*, of Corinthians supporters. There are countless reports of conflicts between queer groups and feminist collectives with traditional groups (Pinto, 2017). Queer groups are particularly persecuted by traditional organised groups, strongly marked by hegemonic notions of masculinity, where a large part of sociability revolves around homophobic playfulness.

Conclusion

The tortuous relationships between traditions and modernity in Latin America highlight the difficulty in working with essential notions of fandom practices and groups of fans. As Canclini (1995) states, ordinary citizens and civil society groups may defend traditions as a way of saving them in the face of capitalism impositions – hence the tendency to treat groups formed by supporters of the working classes, as it is the case of TOs, as the "authentic" expression of supporting. However, at other times, the defence of the traditional, in the context of supporting cultures, may imply fascist, sexist and homophobic discourses, as in the conflicts identified between traditional groups and politicised collectives in Brazil, and conservative positions defended, for example, by fans who identify themselves with movements against modern football.

Other authors, such as Eric Hobsbawn and Raymond Williams, already pointed to the constructed character of traditions. The analysis presented above demonstrates how what is seen as "traditional" in Brazilian fan cultures (TOs, for instance) are groups that are formed from dissidents of uniformed groups and charangas, thus constituting hybrid practices, since certain routines were maintained (such as the presence of music, uniforms and adornments), while other elements were renewed (such as the most questioning posture, the most intense body movements in the stands, among others). If we were to work on the basis of essentialisations, the new supporting movements of the 2000s could be seen in some sense as more "authentic" than the TOs, since they have revived various slogans and attitudes of the groups of the 1940s.

Thus, addressing football supporter cultures from hybridisation, which generates both productive dialogues and irreconcilable conflicts, seems quite enriching precisely because it does not approach the historical developments of these cultures in a linear perspective. Not everything that is traditional should be forgotten. Not everything that is modern should be adopted. The traditional can be outrageous and exclusive, and the new, progressive and disruptive (and not passive as the new forms of fandom are sometimes treated in the literature). The current ecosystem of Brazilian fan groups is very fragmented and dispersed, which is viewed with suspicion by some researchers. However, there is something liberating about fragmentation, insofar as dissonant and counter-hegemonic identities (such as those of feminist collectives and queer groups) find fertile space to germinate.

Note

1 A Portuguese expression used with three meanings: the stadium crowd, the whole body of supporters of a club (which includes fans who are not stadium attendees, that is, the supporter base), and a group of organised fans. *Torcida* comes from the verb *torcer*, which originally means "to turn"; however, in the football context, it came to mean "to root for". *Torcer* generated the two Portuguese expressions that designate the crowd, *torcida*, and the supporter itself, *torcedor* or *torcedora*.

References

Antunovic, D., & Hardin, M. (2012). Activism in women's sports blogs: Fandom and feminist potential. *International Journal of Sport Communication*, 5, 305–322.

Antunovic, D., & Hardin, M. (2013). Women bloggers: Identity and the conceptualization of sports. *New Media and Society*, 15(8), 1374–1392.

Antunovic, D., & Hardin, M. (2015). Women and the blogosphere: Exploring feminist approaches to sport. *International Review for the Sociology of Sport*, 50(6), 661–677.

Bandeira, G. A., & Seffner, F. (2018). Representações sobre mulheres nos estádios de futebol. *Mosaico*, 9(14), 285–301.

Baym, N. K. (2010). *Personal connections in the digital age*. Cambridge: Polity.

Braga, J. L. B. (2010). As Torcidas Uniformizadas (Organizadas) de Futebol no Rio de Janeiro nos anos 1940. *Esporte e Sociedade*, 5(14), 1–24.

Brown, A. (1998). United we stand: some problems with fan democracy. In A. Brown (Ed.), *Fanatics! power, identity and fandom in football*. London: Routledge.

Canclini, N. G. (1995). *Hybrid cultures: Strategies for entering and leaving modernity*. Minneapolis: University of Minnesota Press.

César, B. T. (1981). Os Gaviões da Fiel e a Águia do Capitalismo ou o Duelo. (Master's thesis, Unicamp).

Costa, L. M. (2007). O que é uma torcedora? Notas sobre a representação e auto-representação do público feminino de futebol. *Esporte e Sociedade*, 2(4), 1–31.

Crawford, G. (2003). The career of the sport supporter: the case of the Manchester storm. *Sociology*, 37(2), 219–237.

Gońda, M. (2013). Supporters' Movement "Against Modern Football" and Sport Mega Events: European and Polish Contexts. *Przegląd Socjologiczny*, 62, 85–106.

Goudsblom, J. (1994). *The theory of the civilizing process and its discontents*. Paper presented at Zesde Sociaal-Wetenschappelijke Studiedagen, Amsterdam.

Gibbons, T., & Dixon, K. (2010). "Surf's up!": A call to take English soccer fan interactions on the Internet more seriously. *Soccer & Society*, 11(5), 599–613.

Giulianotti, R. (1999). *Football: a sociology of the global game*. Cambridge: Polity Press/Blackwell Publishers Ltd.

Giulianotti, R. (2002). Supporters, followers, fans, and flaneurs: a taxonomy of spectator identities in football. *Journal of Sport & Social Issues*, 26(1), 25–46.

Haynes, R. (1995). *The football imagination: the rise of football fanzine culture*. Aldershot: Arena.

Hollanda, B. B. B., & Silva, M. F. (2006). No tempo da Charanga. *Esporte e Sociedade*, 2(4), 1–8.

Hollanda, B. B. B., Azevedo, A. L., & Queiroz, A. L. (2014). Das torcidas jovens às embaixadas de torcedores: uma análise das novas dinâmicas associativas de torcer no futebol brasileiro. *Recorde: Revista de História do Esporte*, 7(1), 1–37.

Hynes, D. (2012). "Jaysus! Is Janno a bird?" A study of femininity and football fans in online forums. In R. Krovel, & T. Roksvold, *We Love to Hate Each Other: Mediated Football Fan Culture* (pp. 189–205). Goteborg: Nordicom.

Hynes, D., & Cook, A. M. (2013). Online belongings: Female fans experiences in online soccer forums. In B. Hutchins, & D. Rowe, *Digital Media Sport: Technology, Power and Culture in the Network Society* (pp. 97–110). New York: Routledge.

Kunert, J. (2019). The footy girls of Tumblr: How women found their niche in the online football fandom. *Communication & Sport*.

Lawrence, S., & Crawford, G. (Eds.). (2019). *Digital Football Cultures: Fandom, Identities and Resistance*. Abington: Routledge.

Lever, J. (1983). *A loucura do futebol*. Rio de Janeiro: Record.

Lisec, J., & McDonald, M. G. (2012). Gender inequality in the new millennium: An analysis of WNBA representations in sport blogs. *Journal of Sports Media*, 7(2), 153–178.

Marwick, A. E. (2010). *Status update: Celebrity, publicity and self-branding in Web 2.0* (Doctoral dissertation, New York University).

Moraes, C. F. (2017). As torcedoras querem torcer: tensões e negociações da presença das mulheres nas arquibancadas de futebol. Paper presented at the Seminário Internacional Fazendo Gênero 11 & 13th Women's Worlds Congress, Florianópolis.

Nascimento, M. L. (2020). *Torcida, substantivo feminino: interações e relações de gênero nas torcidas do clássico Remo x Paysandu*. (Master's thesis, Universidade Federal do Pará).

Nash, R. (2000). Contestation in modern English professional football: the Independent Supporters Association Movement. *International Review for the Sociology of Sport*, 35(4), 465–486.

Nash, R. (2001). English football fan groups in the 1990s: class, representation and fan power. *Soccer & Society*, 2(1), 39–58.

Numerato, D. (2015). Who says "no to modern football?" Italian supporters, reflexivity, and neo-liberalism. *Journal of Sport and Social Issues*, 39(2), 120–138.

Petersen-Wagner, R. (2017). The football supporter in a cosmopolitan Epoch. *Journal of Sport and Social Issues*, 41(2), 133–150.

Pinto, M. R. (2017). *Pelo direito de torcer: das torcidas gays aos movimentos de torcedores contrários ao machismo e à homofobia no futebol.* (Master's thesis, Universidade de São Paulo.)

Rodrigues, F. C. S. (2012). *Amizade, trago e alento. A Torcida Geral do Grêmio (2001-2011) da rebeldia à institucionalização: mudanças na relação entre torcedores e clubes no campo esportivo brasileiro.* (Master's thesis, Universidade Federal Fluminense.)

Ruddock, A. (2013). "Born on Swan Street, Next to the Yarra": Online Opinion Leaders and Inventing Commitment. In B. Hutchins & D. Rowe (Eds.), *Digital Media Sport: Technology and Power in the Network Society* (pp. 153–165). New York: Routledge.

Tanaka, T. (2004). The positioning and practices of the "feminized fan" in Japanese soccer culture through the experience of the FIFA World Cup Korea/Japan 2002. *Inter-Asia Cultural Studies*, 5(1), 52–62.

Taylor, R. (1992). *Football and its fans.* London: Leicester UP.

Teixeira, R. d. C. (2003). *Os perigos da paixão: visitando jovens torcidas cariocas.* São Paulo: Annablume.

Teixeira, R. d. C. (2010). *Torcidas jovens e novos movimentos de torcedores no Rio de Janeiro: sentidos atribuídos à paixão futebolística e às manifestações torcedoras.* Paper presented at the I Simpósio de Estudos sobre Futebol, São Paulo.

Teixeira, R. d. C. (2013). Futebol, emoção e sociabilidade: narrativas de fundadores e lideranças dos movimentos populares de torcedores no Rio de Janeiro. *Esporte e Sociedade*, 8(21), 1–16.

Toffoletti, K. (2017). *Women sport fans: Identification, participation, representation.* New York, NY; London, England: Routledge.

Toledo, L. H. d. (1996). *Torcidas organizadas de futebol.* Campinas: Autores Associados/Anpocs.

Vaz, L. A. C. (2014). Em nome da garra, do amor e da paixão: uma análise das marcas coletivas de grupos femininos nas torcidas organizadas do clube de regatas do Flamengo. *Esporte e Sociedade*, 23, 1–16.

Vimieiro, A. C. (2015). *Football supporter cultures in modern-day Brazil: Hypercommodification, networked collectivisms and digital productivity* (Doctoral dissertation, Queensland University of Technology.)

Vimieiro, A. C. (2017). Sports journalism, supporters and new technologies: Challenging the usual complicity between media and football institutions. *Digital Journalism*, 5(5), 567–586.

Vimieiro, A. C. (2018). The digital productivity of football supporters: Formats, motivations and styles. *Convergence*, 24(4), 374–390.

Vimieiro, A. C, Petersen-Wagner, R., D'Andrea, C. F. B., Queiróz, A., Maldini, G., & Martins, M. C. (2019a). Despolitização e re-politização do futebol: em análise, a defesa das "tradições" pelos movimentos contra o futebol moderno no Brasil. Paper presented at the 42° Congresso Brasileiro de Ciências da Comunicação, Belém.

Vimieiro, A. C., Queiróz, A., Maldini, G., & Martins, M. C. (2019b). A economia cultural do futebol brasileiro no século XXI: comodificação, hibridez e contradições. *Recorde: Revista de História do Esporte*, 12(1), p. 1–34.

Vimieiro, A. C., Clementino, A. V. Q., Silva, A. Q., Carmo, G. M. S., Quintela, G. P., Alves, L. E. C., & Andrade, M. C. G. M. (2020). É mais que preconceito! Dimensões da opressão de gênero no esporte a partir da análise do Podcast das Marias. Paper presented at the 43° Congresso Brasileiro de Ciências da Comunicação, online.

Wenner, L. (2012a). Reading the commodified female sports fan: Interrogating strategic dirt and characterization in commercial narratives. In K. Toffoletti, & P. Mewett, *Sport and Its Female Fans* (pp. 135–151). New York and London: Routledge.

Wenner, L. (2012b). From football widow to fan: Web narratives of women and sports spectatorship. In A. C. Earnheardt, P. M. Haridakis, & B. S. Hugenberg, *Sports Fans, Identity, and Socialization: Exploring the Fandemonium* (pp. 203–220). Lanham, MD: Lexington.

Wilson, W. (2007). All together now, click: MLS soccer fans in cyberspace. *Soccer & Society*, 8(2–3), 381–398.

21
Disabled Athletes' Use of Social Media to Cultivate Fandom

Joshua R. Pate and Robin Hardin

Athletes use social media platforms to provide unprecedented access to fans by offering up-close and personal views of their experiences. Conversely, social media allows access to information and perspectives that traditional media outlets are unable to provide (Sanderson, 2011). Traditional media have served as a filter for communication and exposure between athletes and fans, leaving athlete voices to only be heard through press conferences or arranged media gatherings. The establishment and growth of social media, particularly in sport, has eradicated those filters and gatekeepers, offering more exposure to fans than ever before. This open gateway has since allowed athletes to use social media to communicate with followers about life outside of their sport (Hambrick et al., 2010), which ultimately gives them control of building their own voices and audiences through their personal brand (Pegoraro, 2010).

In Goffman's (1959) *The Presentation of Self in Everyday Life*, he presented the concept that individuals perform frontstage and backstage. Frontstage refers to calculated performances that are prepared for the general public—a created image—whereas backstage refers to performances or conversations that would typically occur behind the curtain and present a more realistic and complete image. Social media, in the words of Goffman (1959), provides backstage access to the lives of the athletes in addition to the frontstage portrayals that come through traditional media outlets. Athletes can select which part of their identity to portray to the public and whether or not to reveal their backstage presentation, which is often a more private and personal presentation (Papacharissi, 2002).

Social media gives athletes the ability to control their own message, personas, and ultimately market value (Brazeal, 2008; Hull & Lewis, 2014). Social media can be used to better engage sport fans, in part, due to athlete self-presentation, or how the athlete is crafting the message to followers (Hull & Lewis, 2014). Taking control of their own messages, then, provides athletes with a choice on how they want to craft and deliver their messages for fans. The athlete decides on the presentation they deliver to their followers, rather than a media relations gatekeeper. The athlete may even interact with fans and followers. Therefore, fans have greater access to the real, unfiltered lives of their favorite athletes and even sport executives rather than a filtered version.

The power to choose what message is sent and how it is crafted is vital to creating and building the voice of the athlete, and this is supremely important for those athletes from underrepresented or traditionally oppressed minority groups. Harnessing such power is critical for the disability community and athletes with disabilities partly due to how that demographic has been portrayed through traditional media coverage over the years.

The purpose of this chapter is to demonstrate how athletes with disabilities can grow their fan base as well as enhance emotional attachment with existing fans by using self-presentation through social media. Elite athletes with disabilities can use self-presentation to bypass the lack of traditional media coverage and serve as their own marketing arm to enhance fandom through frontstage and backstage presentations. Traditional media coverage of disability sport is severely lacking and has been sparce for years (Pate & Mirabito, 2014). Social media, however, provides athletes with disabilities the opportunity to stay in the public eye, interact with fans, promote their sport, and increase fandom due to self-presentation despite a lack of traditional media coverage. It is first important to examine media's evolving role in establishing sport within our culture, building fandom, and allowing athletes to take control of their own messaging.

Backstage Access through Presentation of Self

Goffman (1959) proposed the concept that individuals are always performing for others in his book *The Presentation of Self in Everyday Life*. He suggested that frontstage performances occur when we present as an actor in a play, producing calculated performances that are filtered and reveal edited versions of our true selves to the general public. These portrayals are manufactured images that provide a produced message to an intended audience. Conversely, our backstage performances imitate those images and conversations that would take place behind the curtain. These performances, Goffman argued, reveal a more realistic image of ourselves because they are often unfiltered without concern or thought for who receives the message.

Social media has developed as an avenue for individuals to present frontstage to followers and fans (Bullingham & Vasconcelos, 2013). Anecdotally, we see social media feeds flooded with posed photos of smiles, staged scenarios of friends and families, and carefully edited posts that share information and opinion of current events. The individual, then, becomes their own gatekeeper by choosing their performance and how it will be conducted in order to build an image or avoid an image (Miller, 1995; Papacharissi, 2002).

Much of the prior research on self-presentation and social media has focused on narcissism and self-esteem (Mehdizadeh, 2010; Ong et al., 2011), personality traits (Michikyan et al., 2014; Rosenberg & Egbert, 2011), and the social benefits (Kim & Lee, 2011). That body of work primarily focused on how individuals use social media to perform, realizing that most participants were private individuals. Social media allows athletes to choose which identity they want to portray, either the carefully crafted frontstage performance or the more personal, private, and realistic backstage performance. The frontstage performance is one where an athlete can use social media for actions such as sponsorship mentions or when speaking about or on behalf of their team/teammates. The backstage performance, however, is one where an athlete can reveal their true identity by disclosing imagery or communicating with fans.

Athletes are considered to be public figures, so these frontstage images, appearances, statements, and soundbites are often edited or supervised to protect an image created by the athlete. It is a modern version of the traditional gatekeeper approach, only the athlete serves as his or her own gatekeeper. We argue, however, that social media provides athletes the opportunity to display backstage performances, by Goffman's (1959) definition, to then build stronger personal brands and therefore stronger fandom among followers. When athletes choose to display backstage performances, it allows the fan and follower to step behind the curtain and be part of a public figure's world that is typically guarded and locked. Social media, then, provides backstage access to a new world in sport that had previously been inaccessible to most fans: The personal lives of the athletes.

Our argument is supported by Lebel and Danylchuk's 2012 study that found 77 percent of athlete tweets were backstage performances, which helped solidify the athletes' personal brands due to direct communication with fans and followers. Findings from Pate et al. (2014) slightly differed, showing that Paralympic athletes used a mix of frontstage and backstage performances via Twitter. In their findings, frontstage performances helped educate followers on Paralympic events by explaining different sports, showing videos from competition, and reporting on results. The backstage performances helped dispel stereotypes about disability by revealing that the athletes lived out normal elements of life with their disability, such as socializing and communicating with family back home.

Researchers have explored self-presentation through the social media platforms of Facebook and Twitter in a variety of contexts (Clavio & Kian, 2010; Hambrick et al., 2010; Kassing & Sanderson, 2010; Kim & Lee, 2011; Lebel & Danylchuk, 2012; Mehdizadeh, 2010, Michikyan et al., 2014; Rosenberg & Egbert, 2011; Van Der Heide et al., 2012). Hull and Lewis (2014) argued that Twitter was an ideal platform for athletes' self-presentation because they gain control of their own messages and can shape their market values. This, they suggested, allows athletes to use Twitter in a way that supplants more traditional media formats such as television and radio.

Researchers, however, have scarcely explored how self-presentation can be used to specifically benefit minority athletes due to a lack of traditional media coverage. Thus, athletes with disabilities are prime candidates for using self-presentation through social media outlets for multiple reasons, such as brand building, education, activism, and building fandom. Athletes with disabilities can use social media to create a "transparent curtain that separates frontstage and backstage" performances (Pate et al., 2014, p. 145).

Twitter—and other social media platforms that have challenged or surpassed it in popularity and use—allows the user to present both frontstage and backstage, all at the discretion of the user. Such an option is not new for social media users. What is relatively new and important to identify is that minority athletes such as athletes with disabilities can use this power of choice to craft their own unfiltered messages and imagery rather than have society dictate it through stereotyping and labelling, which has often been the case through traditional media coverage.

Communication through Traditional Media

The beginning of sport being included as part of the media landscape began in the mid-1800s as magazines provided the first sport coverage (Sloan, 2002). This initial coverage by magazines led newspapers to begin to include sport in their regular coverage of the events of the day, which eventually led to the creation of the first newspaper sports department by Joseph Pultizer at the *New York World* in the 1880s (Mott, 1962). Sports departments eventually spread through the newspaper industry and were generally accepted as part of a newspapers news-gathering operations by the 1920s (McChesney, 1986; McGregor, 1989).

Other events in the 1920s also led to an increase in sports coverage as well as an increase in sports interest in general. Technological advances in communications (i.e., telephone, telegraph, typewriter, printing press) allowed sports journalists to create content more efficiently. Other changes were occurring in American society as well that led to an increase in newspaper popularity. The move from a rural to urban society, a switch from agrarian professions to industrial professions, transportation improvements, shorter working hours, and increased literacy rates all led to higher consumption of newspapers, which of course contained sports news. This increase in sports coverage, in turn, created more interest in sport, and soon sport became part of the social fabric of the United States (Coakley, 2017).

The technological advances in regards to communications continued to develop during the 1920s, and soon the radio was a common item in the American household as the number of radio stations and number of homes with a radio increased dramatically in the early 1920s. This influx of stations and a growing audience gave sports another way to reach the public. The World Series was first on the airwaves in 1921 as Grantland Rice provided the play-by-play commentary, and by the end of the 1920s, radio networks had organized sports divisions. Radio firmly entrenched itself as a sport communication medium with the broadcasting of the 1936 Olympic Games from Berlin (Sloan, 2002).

Next up on the technological front was the advent of television. Television was widely introduced after World War II as it slowly began to develop programming and audiences throughout the 1950s and 1960s. It became a staple of the communications industry by the early 1970s. There were only three commercial networks during this time, but sport was very much a part of the content of the networks. Baseball, football, basketball, boxing, and other sporting events made their way into American households across the country (Sloan, 2002).

The issue at hand through all of these communication media was that consumers had little choice in what information they were able to read, hear, or watch. Media acted as gatekeepers by choosing what was available to sports fans. The notion of media as gatekeepers was first introduced by Lewin (1947), who stated information had to flow through "gates" and at each gate decisions were made as to what information was to be included or excluded in the news coverage of the event, issue, or person. Reporters, editors, producers, photographers, and other news professionals were making decisions as to what information passed through the "gate" and was available to the public. These people informed the public on what was important in society and what was not important (Shifflett & Revelle, 1994), taking control of all messages.

Agenda Setting and Framing

Traditional media (magazines, newspapers, radio, and television) were the main conduits by which consumers received information about leagues, teams, and athletes (Shultz & Arke, 2016). Media were powerful forces in American society with the ability to influence public opinion as well as the perception of athletes. McCombs and Shaw (1972) conceptualized this phenomenon with the development of agenda setting theory. This theory posits that journalists, reporters, and producers "play an important part in shaping ... reality. (Consumers) learn not only about a given issue but how much importance to attach to that issue" from the amount and prominence of the coverage of the issue (p. 176). Agenda setting was later refined with the emergence of framing theory. This was developed by Entman (1993), who said frames "call attention to some aspects of reality while obscuring other elements" (p. 55).

Goffman (1959) maintained that people classify, organize, and interpret life experience to make sense of them. The interpretations are labeled as frames, and allow people to perceive, identify, and label events and information. Gitlin (1980) defined framing as the persistent selection, emphasis, or exclusion of information. Framing is conceptualized differently among scholars but it is generally accepted that framing is the perspective a person applies to define or make sense of an event, issue, or person. Entman (1993) contended framing involves the selection and highlighting of some information and the exclusion of other information.

How media frame an issue can influence how the public perceives it (Hardin & Zuegner, 2003). The angle or slant that is presented by media to the news can influence how the public thinks about that issue (Ghanem, 1997). Thus, media coverage of an issue or lack of coverage can influence how the public perceives the issue or person. Now, media are not a "magic bullet" that automatically creates a person's perception of an event, issue, or person. Dependency theory postulates that media do have an influence but the perception is also dependent on a person's own relationships, experiences, demographics, and interpretation of the news (Severin & Tankard, 1992).

Individual experiences with media have evolved as media has grown. The shift from traditional sport media coverage began in the 1980s with the development of cable television and pay-per-view sporting events (Shultz & Arke, 2016). Consumers had many options in which to view sports and did not have to entirely rely on the national networks of ABC, CBS, and NBC for their sports coverage. Cable television continued to grow as more and more viewing options became available for consumers. But the advent and widespread accessibility of the internet completely altered how people consume sport media and seek out information about sport. It also has impacted the role media had in the framing of sports news and athletes, therefore reshaping the means by which fandom is developed.

Sports fans no longer passively consume information from media as they now can control what information they receive, when they receive it, and can also directly communicate with organizations, teams, and athletes. Organizations, teams, and athletes also directly communicate with fans. Media no longer play a gatekeeping role in regards to what information is available to fans and how that information is being presented to fans.

Communication and the Social Media Revolution

The widespread availability of the internet allowed organizations, teams, and athletes to directly communicate with fans. Media no longer played a gatekeeping role, and the availability of information was somewhat overwhelming. A fan had the ability to obtain information about their favorite team or athlete directly from the source. Technology continued to develop and soon social media platforms began to develop, leading to the introduction of current platform leaders Facebook, Twitter, and Instagram. Other social media platforms have been introduced and faded away but those three have become the mainstays in the social media revolution.

Social media is instant communication that may be used as one-way communication for fans or two-way communication between fans and athletes or teams without any sort of filter in place. Social media allows an ongoing and sometimes live conversation between fans and athletes. Fans who had been shut out the sport communication process are now an integral part of the process.

The other aspect of social media that has impacted fandom is that athletes can now directly share their thoughts with fans without having to rely on traditional media channels to deliver that message. This once again has changed the dynamic in fandom as athletes have direct access to their fans, and fans have direct access to athletes. The availability of access is astounding as 70 percent of the adult population in the United States uses Facebook, 37 percent are Instagram users, and 22 percent are Twitter users (Pew Research Center, 2019).

Addressing Gaps in Disability Sport Media Coverage

It is important for athletes with disabilities to be able to craft their own messages and imagery because that has historically been nonexistent or distorted through traditional sport media coverage. Tynedal and Wolbring (2013) examined Paralympic coverage appearing in the *New York Times* between 1955 and 2012 and found that coverage of the summer Games increased over time but that the overall amount of coverage was minimal. They found that just 246 articles were printed during the 62-year data collection period. Such a lack of coverage on disability sport or even the elite level of Paralympic sport may leave the general public unaware that it even exists.

Comparisons between Paralympic and Olympic sport coverage has been extensively examined within the literature, showing that the Olympic sport coverage was much greater than Paralympic sport coverage despite the events occurring in the same years and within the same host cities (Bruce, 2014; Chung & Ahn, 2011; Pappous, Marcellini, & de Leseleuc, 2011). Golden (2003) explored the difference in coverage of the two mega-events and suggested the discrepancy was primarily due to a lower number of journalists covering the Paralympic Games. Surveying the journalists, Golden found they were not covering the Paralympic Games for three reasons: (1) lack of audience interest and appeal, (2) logistical challenges of covering both Olympics and Paralympics, and (3) the Paralympics were not perceived as real competition, or not the highest level of competition in comparison to the Olympics.

Even when disability sport is covered within traditional media, it appears as a human interest story rather than a sports story. Portrayal of Paralympic athletes has most prominently been viewed through a medical model lens. The medical model is a lens through which disability is viewed as an individual's problem that can be corrected or rehabilitated. Shakespeare (2017) argues that medical model thinking focuses solely on impairment and reduces "complex problems of disabled people to issues of medical prevention, cure, or rehabilitation" (p. 197). In this context, Thomas and Smith (2003) found that journalists used medicalized descriptions of disability and compared them to athletes without disabilities. Their findings also revealed that photos within the coverage often hid any physical impairments of the athletes.

Medical model coverage of Paralympic sport situates it in dePauw's (1997) category of Visibility of Disability, where disability sport is inferior to other categories of sport. The medical emphasis categorizes disability sport as a story of rehabilitation, inspiration, or overemphasizing successes (Cottingham & Pate, 2012; Hardin & Hardin, 2004). Through the rehabilitation lens, athletes and their stories are framed as overcoming their disability and still finding success in sport.

As an example, in the 2012 Paralympic Games, U.S. swimmer Brad Snyder won the gold medal in the 400-meter freestyle exactly one year after losing his sight in combat as a U.S. Navy SEAL in Afghanistan. Journalists are taught to cover "the story," and the story was the one-year anniversary behind such a rebound. However, Snyder's athletic story was minimalized. Snyder won four gold medals in the 2012 Warrior Games a month before the Paralympics. Prior to his 400-meter victory, Snyder had already won gold in the 100-meter freestyle and bronze in the 50-meter freestyle. Following his well-documented rehabilitation that came full-circle, Snyder won three gold medals at the 2015 International Paralympic Committee (IPC) World Championships in Glasgow (50-meter freestyle, 100-meter freestyle, and 400-meter freestyle). He later won gold in all three of his events at the 2016 Rio Paralympic Games. Traditional media coverage of Snyder's athletic successes has been limited.

Through the inspirational or overemphasizing successes lens, athletes and their stories are framed toward a supercrip label. The supercrip label is applied to people with disabilities whose actions become heroic by performing feats others may consider impossible for those individuals (Berger, 2008; Hardin & Hardin, 2004). Those feats are sometimes regular and daily activities but the general public may be unaware that people with disabilities can and do accomplish those actions. The supercrip lens frames unlikely successes as surprising, major accomplishments (Clogston, 1991).

The supercrip portrayal has been commonplace among Paralympic Games media coverage, reinforcing the medicalized stereotype and tragedy of disability (Brittain, 2010). For example, athletes with disabilities winning medals in competition or even the mere act of competing on an international stage surpasses any expectation society may have had for that individual due primarily to their disability. Howe's (2008) research examined how journalists covered the Paralympic Games, which revealed a focus on overcoming hardships related to their disability while displaying courage in the name of competition. This type of media coverage of Paralympic sport and disability overall is problematic, according to Tynedal and Wolbring (2013). They suggest the supercrip portrayal stymies the disability movement because it does nothing to further discussion of inclusion and the future of disability sport; it merely positions disability as a feel-good story.

Athletes with disabilities have been clear that the supercrip lens may engage audiences, but the courtesy coverage is not preferred by the athletes (Hardin & Hardin, 2004). Instead, they desire their elite athletic accomplishments to be the focus of media attention. Going back to the Snyder example, the preference would be covering his athletic achievements rather than the heartwarming story of "overcoming" blindness.

One could argue that skewed portrayal of disability through traditional media has limited the growth of fandom within disability sport—at least beyond the population of people who are directly connected with the disability community. One bright spot is that viewership and attention toward disability sport and the Paralympic Games have significantly increased recently.

The 2012 Paralympic Games became known as a monumental moment for the disability movement because of the extensive media coverage both in the United Kingdom as well as internationally (Carew, Noor, & Burns, 2018). The IPC reported that 3.4 billion people worldwide watched the 2012 Paralympic Games, which was a 37 percent increase from the 2008 Games (Sky News, 2012). Much of that increase may be attributed to the Paralympics being held in London, close to the original site of the Stoke Mandeville Hospital, where Ludwig Guttmann organized 16 athletes using wheelchairs for an archery competition on the same day as the Opening Ceremony of the 1948 Olympic Games. This tiny competition is recognized as the start of the Paralympic movement. More than 60 years later, Channel 4's unprecedented Paralympic coverage leading up to and during the 2012 London Games was a monumental turning point for fans following elite sport for people with disabilities. Sport feature shows and live competition in primetime television slots took the Paralympics into homes at a rate similar to Olympic coverage while a blanket advertising campaign called "We're the Superhumans" took disability sport before mainstream consumer pockets.

Increased coverage paralleled a shift in the way athletes with disabilities were portrayed through media as well, at least during the 2012 Paralympics. Media coverage sometimes used a supercrip lens, but primarily focused on successes and abilities of the athletes (Beacom et al., 2016). However, even in large markets of successful Paralympic teams, traditional media coverage has lagged. In the United States, as an example, media coverage has grown from near non-existence to at least an educational moment for American viewers and readers.

Media coverage of the 2012 Paralympics in the United States was limited to 5.5 hours of delayed television coverage (Dumlao, 2012) and criticized by supporters of the Paralympic movement (Associated Press, 2012). In a country that finished sixth in medal count and tallied 31 gold medals at the 2012 Games, spectators had to stumble upon television footage while the competition actually took place. NBC and its affiliate stations increased Paralympic coverage to more than 70 hours for the 2016 Games, but that also included online streaming. The 2016 Paralympic Games overall broke television audience records with more than 4.1 billion viewers across 154 countries (International Paralympic Committee, 2017). The viewership represents a 127 percent increase since the 2004 Paralympics in Athens.

While coverage has steadily increased, it pales in comparison to media coverage of other global major sporting events, including the Olympic Games. Paralympic coverage embodies the role of gatekeeper traditional media can play in crafting and sending messages to fans. A limited or skewed message may shape fandom, or stymie it. The lack of traditional media exposure to

Paralympic sport and disability in general has left athletes and sport teams using social media to fill that gap. Social media allows athletes with disabilities to promote their sport accomplishments and be seen as human, neither of which have historically been accurate in traditional media coverage.

Using Self-Presentation to Educate and Enhance Fandom

Self-presentation gives individuals the choice of whether to filter the way they present themselves to the public or to allow a more transparent portrayal of their image. Particularly using social media, under-represented populations such as athletes with disabilities can use frontstage performances to fully inform followers about their elite-level athletic performances. Pate et al. (2014) examined Paralympic tweets during the 2012 London Games and found frontstage performances typically highlighting their own or even other Paralympic events. Athlete Roy Perkins, for example, tweeted "Knocked 1.03 seconds off my 50 fly American record in prelims with 34.53. Just .2 from world record. Final: 11:21 PST paralympic.org." The tweet served as a performance that informed fans of the athlete's swimming performance and when and where they could watch the final. It took the place of traditional journalism by merely informing followers with the possibility of developing fandom. Similarly to their findings, rugby athlete Seth McBride used frontstage performance to build fandom for his sport and the events by tweeting, "Rugby starts tomorrow, first game: 2 pm London time vs. GB, watch us at http://paralympics.org #london2012 #usawcrugby." These frontstage performances served as a baseline foundation that can build fandom.

Backstage performances give athletes with disabilities the power to lift the curtain on their day-to-day lives, which in turn works to break down long-established stigma. Findings from Pate et al. (2014), for example, showed cyclist Megan Fisher tweeted: "Headed over to the Pringle for @London2012 #velodrome women's C4 500m Time Trial. Go Team USA!!!!" The backstage performance simply allowed fans to know Fisher's actions within the Olympic and Paralympic Village, documenting daily actions. Other athletes revealed backstage performances through interactions with peers and fans. Lex Gillette retweeted a congratulatory post from someone else expressing pride in his performance and the Paralympians. Paralympic swimmer Colleen Young expressed backstage performance through a conversation on Twitter with Olympic swimmer Natalie Coughlin. Coughlin tweeted congratulations to Young, and Young responded in her tweet, "@NatalieCoughlin THANK YOU! I'm a young Paralympic swimmer! Huge fan! Your support is awesome!" The conversation allowed fans to see and experience a conversation that otherwise would have been hidden. It further strengthens opportunity for fandom by exposing Coughlin's fans to Young.

Combined, using self-presentation through social media educates followers to grow a fanbase. Poor traditional media coverage is beyond the control of the athletes, so frontstage performances become the social media SportsCenter that is told first-person with facts and statistics, equipping the athletes themselves to promote their sport, disability sport overall, and disability as a movement. Even in a period where traditional media coverage of disability sport has increased slightly, the stories are either heightened periodically through annual or semi-annual events or skewed toward an inspirational tone fit more for a lifestyle feature than a sports story.

If traditional media introduces the athlete with a disability to the public, then self-presentation through social media gives the athlete a choice to remain in the public's eye and craft their story in their own words. We argue that a combination of both frontstage and backstage performances strengthen that control for the athlete.

Frontstage performances through social media channels align more closely with the traditional media coverage of athletes with disabilities, although it removes the gatekeepers and allows the athletes themselves to tell their own stories. It allows the athletes to inform their followers about the nuances, rules, expectations, outcomes, successes, and failures within their sport that traditional media has not done.

Backstage performances through social media channels can serve to break down strong and sometimes inaccurate stereotypes of under-represented populations such as athletes with disabilities. The backstage performance removes the veil for the athlete, allowing for and promoting interaction between athlete and fan. It reveals a human side of disability that is either hidden in traditional media or hyper-glamourized in traditional media as a story of overcoming adversity. The real story may simply be about an athlete who trained hard and won a medal. Yet, a backstage performance of an athlete tweeting her conversation with a relative in their home country or an athlete posting an Instagram photo from the belly of the stadium before the Opening Ceremony begins brings life to the person in control of the account.

Such a grassroots effort to establish and enhance fandom among athletes with disabilities both advances the disability movement and tears down public stigma that people with disabilities are unapproachable, abnormal, or different. Frontstage and backstage performances through social media shifts the locus of control away from traditional media gatekeepers and into the hands of the athlete with a disability, which are increment steps toward transitioning the way disability is portrayed through a sport setting.

References

Associated Press. (2012). Full TV coverage for Paralympics, just not in US. *ESPN*. Retrieved from http://sports.espn.go.com/espn/wire?id=8295913

Beacom, A., French, L., & Kendall, S. (2016). Reframing impairment? Continuity and change in media representations of disability through the Paralympic Games. *International Journal of Sport Communication, 9*(1), 42–62.

Berger, R. J. (2008). Disability and the dedicated wheelchair athlete: Beyond the 'supercrip' critique. *Journal of Contemporary Ethnography, 37*, 647–678.

Brazeal, L. M. (2008). The image repair strategies of Terrell Owens. *Public Relations Review, 34*(2), 145–150.

Brittain, I. (2010). *The Paralympic Games explained*. London: Routledge.

Bruce, T. (2014). Us and them: The influence of discourses of nationalism on media coverage of the Paralympics. *Disability & Society, 29*, 1443–1459.

Bullingham, L., & Vasconcelos, A. C. (2013). The presentation of self in the online world: Goffman and the study of online identities. *Journal of Information Science, 39*(1), 101–112.

Carew, M. T., Noor, M., & Burns, J. (2018). The impact of exposure to media coverage of the 2012 Paralympic Games on mixed physical ability interactions. *Journal of Community & Applied Social Psychology, 29*(2), 104–120.

Chung, Y. L., & Ahn, C. W. (2011). How much is too much? Newspaper coverage of the 2008 Beijing Paralympic and Olympic Games. *International Journal of Human Movement Science, 5*, 161–182.

Clavio, G., & Kian, T. (2010). Uses and gratifications of a retired female athlete's Twitter followers. *International Journal of Sport Communication, 3*(4), 485–500.

Clogston, J. S. (1991). Disability coverage in American newspapers. In J. A. Nelson (ed.), *The disabled, the media, and the information age* (pp. 45–58). Westport, CT: Greenwood Press.

Coakley, J. (2017). *Sports in society: Issues and controversies* (12th ed.). New York: McGraw-Hill Education.

Cottingham, M., & Pate, J. R. (2012, November). A lasting impression: Examining "inspiration" as it is used in disability sport. Paper presented at the *North American Society for the Sociology of Sport 33rd Annual Conference*, New Orleans, LA.

dePauw, K. (1997). The (in)visibility of disability: Cultural contexts and "sporting bodies." *Quest, 49*, 416–430.

Dumlao, R. (2012, August 14). U.S. Paralympics finally get TV coverage on American soil. *Denver Post*. Retrieved from http://blogs.denverpost.com/sports/2012/08/14/paralympics-finally-coverage-american-soil/23193/

Entman, R. (1993). Framing: Toward clarification of a fractured paradigm. *Journal of Communication*, *43*(4), 51–58.
Ghanem, S. (1997). Filling in the tapestry: The second level of agenda setting. In M. McCombs, D. L. Shaw, and D. Weaver (Eds.), *Communication and democracy: Exploring the intellectual frontiers in agenda-setting theory* (pp. 3–14). Mahwah, NJ: Lawrence Erlbaum Associates.
Gitlin, T. (1980). *The whole world is watching: Mass media in the making and unmaking of the new life*. Los Angeles: University of California Press.
Goffman, E. (1959). *The presentation of self in everyday life*. New York: Anchor Books.
Golden, A. V. (2003). An analysis of the dissimilar coverage of the 2002 Olympics and Paralympics: Frenzied pack journalism versus the empty press room. *Disability Studies Quarterly*, *23*(3/4). Retrieved from www.dsq-sds.org/article/view/437/614
Hambrick, M. E., Simmons, J. M., Greenhalgh, G. P., & Greenwell, T. C. (2010). Understanding professional athletes' use of Twitter: A content analysis of athlete tweets. *International Journal of Sports Communication*, *3*(4), 454–471.
Hardin, M., & Hardin, B. (2004). The "supercrip" in sport media: Wheelchair athletes discuss hegemony's disabled hero. *Sociology of Sport Online*, *7*(1). Retrieved from http://physed.otago.ac.nz/sosol/v7i1/v7i1_1.html
Hardin, R., & Zuegner, C. (2003). Life, liberty and the pursuit of golf balls: Magazine promotion of golf in the 1920s. *Journalism History*, *29*(2), 82–90.
Howe, P. D. (2008). From inside the newsroom: Paralympic media and the "production" of elite disability. *International Review for the Sociology of Sport*, *43*, 135–150.
Hull, K., & Lewis, N. P. (2014). Why Twitter displaces broadcast sports media: A model. *International Journal of Sport Communication*, *7*(1), 16–33.
International Paralympic Committee. (2017). Rio 2016 Paralympics smash all TV viewing records. *Paralympic.org*. Retrieved from www.paralympic.org/news/rio-2016-paralympics-smash-all-tv-viewing-records
Kassing, J. W., & Sanderson, J. (2010). Fan-athlete interaction and Twitter tweeting through the giro: A case study. *International Journal of Sport Communication*, *3*(1), 113–128.
Kim, J., & Lee, J. R. (2011). The Facebook paths to happiness: Effects of the number of Facebook friends and self-presentation on subjective well-being. *Cyberpsychology, Behavior, and Social Networking*, *15*(6), 359–364.
Lebel, K., & Danylchuk, K. (2012). How tweet it is: A gendered analysis of professional tennis players' self-presentation on Twitter. *International Journal of Sport Communication*, *5*(4), 461–480.
Lewin, K. (1947). Channels of group life. *Human Relations*, *1*, 143–153.
McChesney, R. (1986). *Sport, Mass Media and Monopoly Capital: Toward a Reinterpretation of the 1920s and Beyond*. Unpublished Master Thesis, University of Washington.
McCombs, M. E., & Shaw, D. L. (1972). The agenda-setting function of the mass media. *Public Opinion Quarterly*, *36*(2), 176–187.
McGregor, E. (1989). Mass Media and Sport: Influences on the Public. *The Physical Educator*, 46 (1), 52–55.
Mehdizadeh, S. (2010). Self-presentation 2.0: Narcissism and self-esteem on Facebook. *Cyberpsychology, Behavior, and Social Networking*, *13*(4), 357–364.
Michikyan, M., Subrahmanyam, K., & Dennis, J. (2014). Can you tell who I am? Neuroticism, extraversion, and online self-presentation among young adults. *Computers in Human Behavior*, *33*, p. 179–183.
Miller, H. (1995). The presentation of self in electronic life: Goffman on the internet. Paper presented at *Embodied Knowledge and Virtual Space Conference* in London, UK.
Mott, F. (1962). *American journalism, a history 1690-1960* (3rd ed.). New York: The MacMillan Company.
Ong, E., Ang, R., Ho., J., Lim, J., Goh, D., Lee, C., & Chua, A. (2011). Narcissism, extraversion and adolescents' self-presentation on Facebook. *Personality and Individual Differences*, *50*(2), 180–185.
Papacharissi, Z. (2002). The presentation of self in virtual life: Characteristics of personal home pages. *Journalism & Mass Communication Quarterly*, *79*(3), 643–660.
Pappous, A., Marcellini, A., & de Leseleuc, E. (2011). From Sydney to Beijing: The evolution of the photographic coverage of Paralympic Games in five European countries. *Sport in Society*, *14*, 345–354.
Pate, J. R., Hardin, R., & Ruihley, B. J. (2014). Speak for yourself: Analysing how US athletes used self-presentation on Twitter during the 2012 London Paralympic Games. *International Journal of Sport Management and Marketing*, *15*(3/4), 141–162.
Pate, J. R., & Mirabito, T. (2014). Spirit in motion: An exploration of NBC's broadcast coverage of the 2012 Paralympic Games. Paper presented at the *2014 North American Society for Sport Management Conference* in Pittsburgh, PA.

Pegoraro, A. (2010). Look who's talking—athletes on Twitter: A case study. *International Journal of Sport Communication, 3*(4), 501–514.
Pew Research Center (2019). Share of U.S. adults using social, including Facebook, is mostly unchanged since 2018. Retrieved from www.pewresearch.org/fact-tank/2019/04/10/share-of-u-s-adults-using-social-media-including-facebook-is-mostly-unchanged-since-2018/
Rosenberg, J., & Egbert, N. (2011). Online impression management: Personality traits and concerns for secondary goals as predictors of self-presentation tactics on Facebook. *Journal of Computer-Mediated Communication, 17*(1), 1–18.
Sanderson, J. (2011). *It's a whole new ballgame: How social media is changing sports.* New York: Hampton Press.
Severin, W., & J. Tankard (1992). *Communication theories: Origins, methods, and uses in the mass media* (3rd ed.). New York: Longman.
Shultz. D., & E. Arke (2016). *Sports media.* New York: Focal Press.
Shakespeare, T. (2017). The social model of disability. In L. J. Davis (ed.), *The disability studies reader 5th Ed.* (pp. 195–203). New York: Routledge.
Shifflett, B., & Revelle, R. (1994). Gender equity in sports media coverage: A review of the NCAA news. *Journal of Sport and Social Issues, 18*(2), 144–150.
Sky News. (2012, November 28). London 2012 Paralympics a TV ratings winner. *Sky News.* Retrieved from http://news.sky.com/story/1017490/london-2012-paralympics-a-tv-ratings-winner
Sloan., W. D., (2002). *The media in America: A history* (5th ed.). Los Angeles: Vision Press.
Thomas, N., & Smith, A. (2003). Preoccupied with able-bodiedness? An analysis of the British media coverage of the 2000 Paralympic Games. *Adapted Physical Activity Quarterly, 20*(2), 166–181.
Tynedal, J., & Wolbring, G. (2013). Paralympics and its athletes through the lens of the New York Times. *Sports, 1,* 13–36.
Van Der Heide, B., D'Angelo, J. D., & Schumaker, E. M. (2012). The effects of verbal versus photographic self-presentation on impression formation in Facebook. *Journal of Communication, 62*(1), 98–116.

22
Engaging the Non-Local Sport Fan

Dorothy Collins

The modern sport industry is undeniably one of the most global industries in existence, driven by sport fans in every corner of the world. Across the globe, there is perhaps no other industry that is so pervasive; almost everyone has, at some point in their life, engaged with the sport industry—as a player, a spectator, a fan, or a parent. As such, sport has come to define both individuals and communities. This influence is so strong that sport is increasingly being used by individuals as a way to create a sense of community with other individuals. This sense of community has been found to be critical for individuals to become highly identified fans of a sport team (Heere & James, 2007), and is tied to high levels of consumptive behavior (Shapiro, Ridinger & Trail, 2013).

Traditionally these fan communities have been stoked through live attendance at sporting events; making tickets sales, and the fans that buy those tickets the trunk of the sport revenue tree. Their strong feelings of identification with sport organizations has led to the development of a robust business enterprise, that, as of 2019 generated more than 73 billion dollars, in the North American market alone. Globally, the sport industry is valued at nearly $500 billion dollars, with approximately half that being generated by the spectator sport sector of the industry.

Traditionally, the sizeable share of the sport industry that can be attributed to the spectator sport sector has centered around fans that live with relative geographic proximity to their favorite teams, and therefore are able to attend sporting events with some sort of regularity. Unsurprisingly, research has demonstrated that individuals will often attach, early in life, to the team that is most geographically relevant, thereby explaining the popularity of professional sport in the Northeast where these teams proliferate, as opposed to athletics in the Midwest and South, where due to lesser population density there are not as many professional sport organizations.

The Rise of the Non-Local Fan

While the trunk of this revenue tree remains ticket sales and live event attendance, the way that people consume sport has changed over the past 25 years. As a result, there is an increasing opportunity for a team's fan base to include a significant number of fans that are not located within the geographic proximity of the team. There are three factors that have led to the rise of the highly identified, highly engaged, non-local sport fan. First, the population has become increasingly mobile, with large numbers of people relocating from the hometown in which they were raised. Second, the decline in traditional social supports such as civic organizations and religious groups has led to individuals looking for new ways to connect with others. Finally, the rise of technology has allowed fans that reside out of the team's primary geographic market to more effectively consume the sport product and associate with other fans.

While there was a time that very few people moved from their hometowns, today people settle far from home. Team identification, however, is a very durable power. It is well understood that team identification is passed from generation to generation and is not easily changed, simply because someone moves from the area where their favorite team plays (James, 2001). Furthermore, it is well understood that team identification for many people is so strong that it contributes to their sense of identity, and their fandom helps define who they are as individuals (Branscombe & Wann, 1991). In addition, the search for ways to connect with other fans of the same team is universal, even when fans live far from their favorite team and when it is difficult to find such connections (Andrijiw & Hyatt, 2009). This combination of a sense of team identification that is both durable and central to an individual's identity, as well as an increasingly large group of people who do not live where they are originally from, has resulted in a substantial number of people following teams that have no relevance to their current geographical location.

There has also been a societal shift away from traditional social constructs like churches and civic organizations that people have used to create a sense of community for themselves (Putnam, 2000). Because many people are living far afield of their families and childhood social connections, they are forced to seek out new ways of connecting with others. In many cases, instead of joining more traditional social civic organizations—long the caretakers of community building—they choose to join smaller, more narrowly focused special interest groups. This has been the driving factor in the development of sport fan groups, centered on an interest in a specific sport, team, or player. Until recently, these groups tended to have a mostly local flair; however, the fact that many people no longer live where they are originally from, and the fact that there is more knowledge of sport outside one's physical location has led to a rise in groups that represent teams and sports that are not in geographic proximity to where the teams they support exist. The rise of these groups has encouraged the non-local fan to be not only highly identified, but also highly engaged, a key prerequisite for high levels of consumptive behavior (Collins & Heere, 2018; Shapiro, Ridinger & Trail, 2013).

While the increasingly mobile population and the decline of traditional social supports set the stage for the rise of the non-local fan, it can be surmised that ultimately, it was the rise in technology that has been the final piece of the puzzle, necessary to bring these fans together and make them a force which cannot be ignored, from both a social and a fiscal standpoint. The rapid growth of technology in the last two decades has allowed sport fans to consume sport in a more robust manner, making in-person game attendance decidedly less important. Prior to the rise of internet streaming, while it was possible to still feel a sense of connection to a sport organization, it was very difficult to successfully consume the sport itself. Over time, therefore, it became difficult for individuals to remain engaged with their favorite non-local sports teams. The rise of technology, however, that could bring games and team experiences to fans wherever they may be, it became increasingly easy for non-local individuals to not only claim to be identified with their favorite team, but to increasingly remain engaged with these teams. As such, over time, these non-local fans began to create communities for themselves that are not based on the geography associated with their favorite team, but on a combination of identification with the team itself, and their current geography. The creation of communities—often referred to as brand communities—centered on these sports organizations has therefore led to a rise in the number of non-local sports fans that are able to remain highly identified with their favorite team. As such, these non-local fans have gained an increasing amount of power, with regard to their willingness to invest money in experiences related to their favorite sport organization.

The advent of a myriad of entertainment technologies means that today's sports fan consumes sport via a variety of remote platforms. These platforms include both cable and satellite television options, as well as a host of internet-based platforms, including livestreaming, social media, and a host of team and sport-specific content, created by everyone from analysts to teams to fans. The rise of these new methods of consuming sport has led to an experience that is both enjoyable and affordable, and therefore has opened new doors for fans that do not live within geographic proximity to maintain stronger ties to those teams. It is well understood that in order for a fan to remain highly identified with a team, it is important for that fan to also remain engaged with that team. While certainly there have always been non-local fans, prior to the rapid rise of technology that has taken place in the last 25 years, it was difficult for these fans to remain engaged with their favorite non-local teams.

Today, however, not only have subscription services like NFL Sunday Ticket made it easy for non-local fans to watch their favorite teams, there are also a wide array of live streaming and pay-per-view options that allow non-local fans to watch sport programming from all corners of the globe, for both the world's most popular sports, as well as for a host of niche and special interest sports, leagues and teams. Today, fans are able to easily and regularly view sport competitions from around the world, often without ever having visited the regions from which the broadcasts emanate.

In addition to the ability to watch sport competitions, the proliferation of user-generated media has made it easier for these fans to remain engaged with other fans of the team or sport. For example, today's fan can engage with other fans via message boards and blogs, and with players and the organization itself, via social media platforms like Twitter and Instagram. In addition to engagement with the team that is fostered watching the team play, the internet has allowed this non-local fan to remain highly engaged with the team or sport by having easy and meaningful interactions with other fans of the team. Today, there is an increasing number of opportunities for fans to participate in fan groups. Some of these groups are completely virtual, with online message boards and real-time chats that allow fans to interact with other fans that they are unlikely to meet in person. It has, however, been found that these online fan groups are often significant enough in the lives of these individuals to generate the type of socialization and social capital that helps fans remain not only engaged, but highly identified (Palmer & Thompson, 2007).

In addition to these solely online fan groups, there are other fan groups that employ an online presence as a way to advertise their group and its meetings, but that are primarily focused on in person, face-to-face interaction between fans of the same organization. For teams with national or international following, these groups have sprung up in virtually every city and town across the country, meeting at local sports bars to watch games together. Proximity to the team does not appear to have any influence on the strength of these groups, or the identification of the fans that belong to them (Collins et al., 2016). These groups allow the non-local fans to not only engage with their team through viewing the game, but also to engage with the fans in an environment that is, in fact, very similar to the way in which live-game attendance allows a fan in geographic proximity to the team to engage with other fans. Some of these groups go so far as to encourage non-local fans to travel together to see their favorite team play live.

Now that it is possible to engage these fans through both technology and in person interaction with other fans, these non-local individuals are more likely to remain highly identified than they would have a generation ago. As such, because they are both engaged and highly identified, these individuals are more likely to spend money for products and services connected to their favorite team than they would otherwise be. As a result, in addition to the costs surrounding viewing of games, these non-local fans contribute revenue to the industry through merchandise sales (most frequently independent of event attendance). There is no shortage of sport-related merchandise, with North American sport industry merchandise accounting for nearly $15 billion dollars of revenue. It is a well-understood fact that fans that are proud of their team's performance are more likely to wear merchandise that shows their affiliation with the team (Cialdini, Borden, Thorne, Walker, Freeman, & Sloan, 1976). Because fans are engaged with other fans and in some cases the team itself through social media, there are ample opportunities for these non-local fans to "show off" their team identification by wearing team-branded merchandise and placing other types of team-branded merchandise in their homes, workplaces, and vehicles as a way to signal their fan affiliation to other individuals. Regardless of where these fans live with relation to their favorite sport organizations, because they have been able to remain highly identified fans, they certainly play a part in the explosion of the sport industry as a global business enterprise.

Types of Non-Local Fans

The ability of the non-local fan to remain increasingly engaged with their favorite sport teams has led to both the increased visibility and importance of these fans. The umbrella term "non-local fans" is a generic term that encompasses individuals that support sport that do not align with their current geographic locations (Reifurth, Bernthal, Ballouli, & Collins, 2019). While we have discussed why non-local fans have become increasingly important to the sport industry, it is also important to acknowledge that there are several different types of non-local sport fans. For example, there is the displaced fan, defined as a fan that once lived in the geographic area represented by their favorite team. These individuals have often moved from their hometown in pursuit of career or personal opportunities, but continue to retain a strong sense of identification with their "hometown" team (Collins et al., 2016). This segment of fans continues to grow, as society becomes increasingly mobile. In fact, more than 10 percent of the United States population moves to a new state each year, which means that this is a sizeable group of people. For many of these individuals, there is still a strong sense of connection to the town or geographic area in which they were raised, or lived as a young person. In some cases, they identify more strongly with this location than with the location in which they currently reside.

Displaced fans use identification with their hometown team as a way to maintain ties to their hometown. This has been found to occur even when individuals have been gone from their hometowns for decades, or live very far away from the hometown. In fact, research has shown that neither time removed from the hometown nor distance from the hometown has a significant impact on a displaced fan's level of team identification (Collins et al., 2016). What has been found, however, is that in order for these individuals to maintain a strong sense of identification with their favorite team, they must also maintain a strong sense of identification with their hometown itself (Collins et al., 2016). In addition, it has been found that these individuals use their identification with the hometown team to ensure commonalities with the social supports, such as family and friends remain, despite the individual no longer living in the same geographic region.

Research has also demonstrated that while the displaced fan may use high levels of identification with the hometown team to support their identification with the hometown itself, as well as a way to bolster connections to individuals still in that hometown, it has also been found that these individuals may use their fandom with the hometown team as a way to integrate themselves and make connections within their new community. In fact, Collins and Heere (2018) found that some individuals joined fan groups in their new cities and develop such strong bonds with the individuals in those groups that, over time, social capital develops and the displaced fans gain valuable social and practical benefits within the new community. For example, there is a group of New York Jets fans that have been watching football together in bars in Columbia, SC for more than 20 years. This group is made up of various types of non-local fans, with those individuals new to South Carolina drawing on the experience of those who have been part of the community for longer.

These displaced fans often demonstrate very high levels of identification (Collins et al., 2016), which appears to be highly durable, as it is often found to be passed down from one generation to the next, much as traditional fans of local teams do (James, 2001). In fact, it has been found that a displaced fans passes his or her sense of team identification with the hometown team down to children and grandchildren as fans of teams that are geographically connected to their place of residence do. As such, a subset of the displaced non-local fan has been created. That group is characterized by non-local fans who have no personal connection to the geographic location represented by the team with which they are identified, but have developed that connection through a family member.

These second-generation displaced fans demonstrate how durable team identification is. In fact, it has been demonstrated that there is economic potential for a wide array of sport organizations, particularly outside the major league sport teams. In fact, a qualitative data analysis of attendees at Minor League Baseball games conducted during the summer of 2019 found that there are many individuals who use the minor league affiliates of their favorite, far away major league teams. This then becomes a way to develop and maintain a strong level of team identification in their children, with a team that the children neither grew up in geographic proximity to, nor currently live near (Collins & Reifurth, 2020). For many of these individuals, attendance at their favorite major league park is often impractical due to distance and financial concerns. As such, these fans represent a particular opportunity for smaller sport organizations to draw larger numbers of fans, first by marketing to people who hail from the same geographic location that their parent organization represents, and second by paying special attention to the affiliations of visiting teams, particularly when those teams represent large market teams (Collins & Reifurth, 2020).

Displaced fans and their descendants are, however, not the only the only non-local fans that have the potential to bring revenue to sport organizations. In addition to the displaced fan, there are non-local fans who develop team identification with a non-local team for various other reasons. These are individuals that have no connection to the geographic location represented by their favorite team, but have found some other point of connection with a team that does not share geographic relevance with the individual. Other individuals have chosen to support a non-local team as a result of a desire to be different from their peers (Andrijiw & Hyatt, 2009). Some people are fans of sports that they play, that do not have a high level of popularity in the spectator sector where they are located. Finally, there are some people who have attached to a non-local team for what appear to be superfluous reasons, for example the team's aesthetic or image. Finally, everyone loves a winner, and there is always a sub-section of non-local fans that attach to a team, often early in their lives, due to competitive success. While some of these fans are considered "bandwagon" fans, in some cases the identification forms strongly enough to withstand periods of less competitive success.

Research has demonstrated that there are not, in terms of identification, vast differences between these types of fans. For example, distance from the favorite team had no impact on level of team identification for any type of non-local fan (Reifurth, et al., 2019). Additionally, team identification was found to be strong enough that the presence of local teams in the same or different sports did not diminish the team identification amongst any of the non-local fans, suggesting that non-local fans are a valuable population segment within any market (Reifurth et al., 2019). Furthermore, both Collins, et al. (2016) and Reifurth, et al. (2019) support the notion that geographic identity and team identification, are connected, and therefore it is in a team's best interest to encourage this type of identification amongst non-local fans.

Non-local Fans: Sense of Community and Social Capital

While at one time the word community had a strongly geographic connotation, in recent years this has changed. Today, while community sometimes still has a geographic component, more often communities are defined by the existence of some point of connection between members of a group. Often, these connections are not based on surface commonalities like geography, but on shared interests or beliefs. The same forces that have led to the rise of the non-local sport fan, have led to a shift in the definition and makeup for modern communities. Identification with a sport organization that represents that geographic location is one way in which some individuals have helped to continue to maintain a connection to their geographic roots. This has led to the opportunity for non-local fans to create and join communities that focus on their favorite sport team, as a way to both remain highly engaged and enmesh themselves in a new community. While this action may help them become part of the larger community in which they now reside, in some cases the fan group itself becomes a community.

While there is no doubt that there is a proliferation of non-local sport fans and groups that have sprung up to support them, there has been some question about whether or not sport fandom is a strong enough force to create sustainable communities that provide tangible and intangible benefits to their members. Because it has been found that being a part of a community of like-minded fans is critical to the ability to remain highly identified fans, it is critical that this question be considered. There is considerable debate about the extent to which some groups are actually communities, groups based on shared interest in a sport organization is undeniably strong enough to create long-lasting bonds that become a central part of people's social identity (Heere et al., 2011). Shared social identity, defined as one's sense of self, as defined by the groups of which an individual is a member (Tajfel, 1978), is a powerful and durable link between individuals. If affiliation with a sport team is strong enough to create part of an individual's social identity, then it is a strong enough bond for a group based on this social identity to consider that they might constitute a community. While there has been considerable question about the ability of sport to create positive social capital, there is an emerging body of research that suggests that fans of sport organizations may be particularly well suited to become brand communities (Underwood, Bond, & Baer, 2001; Grant, Heere, & Dickson, 2011)—that is, communities based on interest or use of a specific product (Muniz & O'Guinn, 2001). It is also well understood that brand communities provide opportunities for consumption and thus the generation of revenue for an organization (Muniz & O'Guinn, 2001).

While the literature is fairly consistent in the idea that non-local fans have strong levels of social identity (Collins et al., 2016; Reifurth et al., 2019), taking this a step further to argue that these fan groups are significant enough in the lives of individuals to generate social capital has been more widely debated. Social capital can be defined as benefits—either tangible or intangible—that one derives specifically from membership in that group (Coleman, 1988). The generation of this type of social capital has long been considered the domain of traditional civic organizations such as churches and community based social-civic organizations. While it is known that not all organizations are equally capable of generating social capital, there is increasing evidence that non-traditional groups do, at least in some circumstances, have the potential to create social capital and thus can be considered communities (Collins & Heere, 2018; Palmer & Thompson, 2007).

While sport fan groups have become very widespread, sport organizations have not paid a great deal of attention to such groups. If, however, one considers these groups to be communities that are capable of generating social capital and keeping fans not just identified with teams, but also engaged with those teams, it becomes clear why this is not a sound business practice. In order to maximize the potential for revenue, however, it may be necessary to create experiences and marketing materials that are targeted specifically at these fans (Collins et al., 2016). For example, research suggests that since a displaced fan's team identification is strongly tied to his sense of city or state identification, it may be important to remind these fans not only that do they love the team, but they love the city or state represented by the team. Furthermore, any opportunities the team can offer to make the experience of group membership extend beyond game day is particularly critical to building not just identification, but taking it one step further to create social capital for these individuals. For example, because these fans have to travel to attend local games, it may be beneficial to offer them bundled packages that include both travel and ticket options.

While there are not a large number of examples of sport organizations working with fan groups, there are a few. One example of such a partnership is the NY Mets and the 7 Line Army. The 7 Line Army is a group of NY Mets fans that include both local NYers and Mets fans from across the country. The group offers opportunities for group members to cheer at local games at CitiField, as well as several trips around the country to cheer for the Mets at other ballparks. The impact of this for non-local fans is two-fold. First off, this encourages non-local fans who may be visiting NY (or may visit specifically for a game) to attend games by giving them a guaranteed group to be part of while at that game, even if they do not have local individuals to attend the game with. On the flip side, when the group travels, it allows fans in, or closer to, the cities in which they visit to attend games to cheer for the Mets in an environment in which they are surrounded by like-minded fans, and therefore gain the socialization benefits that is a primary benefit of sport event attendance for fans. In addition to offering the opportunity for socialization for non-local fans of all types, the group includes exclusive merchandise for those individuals purchasing tickets through the group that increases a sense of belonging with the group. Finally, the group offers supplementary ticketing options, such as relevant tours or happy hour experiences. While the Mets do not sponsor or directly fund the group, they do work with the group to allow individuals to purchase tickets in the 7 Line Army section at CitiField for the games they attend as a group, directly through the team's ticket office. While some people might question the benefit of supporting a group like this, it is clear that the benefits outweigh any costs. It is a guaranteed sale of tickets for the team, and, beyond that, it helps keep non-local fans engaged. There is also a benefit for the away games' venue, as the group buys often upwards of 1000 tickets to a game, which it then redistributes to its members.

While the focus of groups like the 7 Line Army is in fact in-person game attendance, there are other types of non-local fan groups that focus less on game attendance and more on keeping fans engaged through a robust social experience while viewing games at a third-place location via satellite or cable television. For example, there is a loosely organized group of NY Jets fans (currently known as the Gotham City Jets Group) that has been watching NY Jets Football together in Columbia, SC for more than two decades. The group's members are very diverse, and comprise a variety of types of non-local fans from displaced NYers, to native South Carolinians that have been Jets fans since childhood. Group members rarely, if ever, attend games in person; however, they are all long-term, highly engaged Jets fans. They are a tight-knit group, often gathering for events outside football games. In fact, in recent years a member left his truck to the group's president upon his passing (Collins & Heere, 2018); suggesting that groups such as this are well able to build social capital for members. Most groups like this have no official (or unofficial) tie with the teams they support; however, research that demonstrates that these fan groups are stable enough to keep non-local fans engaged suggests that sport organizations might benefit from providing some sort of support to these groups. It is well established that engagement is necessary to promote high levels of identification with a team, and that highly identified fans are more likely to spend money. As such, any group that helps individuals stay highly engaged with their favorite team is beneficial to the sport organization.

In addition, these fan groups that have large numbers of non-local provide the potential for revenue generation by a variety of businesses beyond the sport organization itself. For example, groups of non-local sport fans that meet at third-place locations provide opportunity for consistent and loyal business for the third-place locations at which they meet. In some cases, these locations have jumped on the bandwagon by offering these groups special discounts on food during games or the opportunity to reserve prime space in the dining room for the game. Beyond this, support of these groups may encourage group members to visit the locations for dining outside of game times, as there is a positive association created by the location's support of the fan group (Collins & Heere, 2018).

While live sport attendance is certainly still important, the way individuals consume sport has begun to evolve (Fairley & Tyler, 2012; O'Shea & Alonso, 2011), and it is important that sport organizations acknowledge the challenges created by this fact. With the rise of technology, many individuals today place less importance on live game attendance than other forms of consumption. This trend is particularly strong with the non-local fan, particularly as the expense of attending sporting events has continued to grow. This has led to many individuals who actually prefer to watch sporting events at these third-place locations, including everything from movie theatres showing sporting events to more traditional places like sports bars, making geographic proximity to the stadium less relevant.

In addition, modern sport fans seek an active sport consumption experience using technology like on-demand streaming, social media interaction, virtual reality, and fantasy sport. These methods of consumption allow fans to remain highly identified without necessarily requiring geographic proximity. No discussion of non-local fans would be complete without a discussion of the role in fantasy sport, and the growing preference of individuals to be able to engage with their fantasy teams, while watching sport. Individuals can play fantasy sport regardless of actual geography, and remains another way of keeping non-local fans highly engaged at both the sport and the team level. This type of active consumption is critical to creating highly identified fans. It is also important to note that fantasy sport itself may help create non-local fans, as individuals may begin to identify not just with teams, but with individual players, based on the performance of those individuals on the fantasy team.

As a result of these factors, today's sport landscape includes a critical mass of non-local fans that display high levels of team identification, despite the lack of geographic proximity to their favorite teams (Collins et al., 2016). These fans often use modern technology to allow a more robust sport consumption experience, and therefore are able to maintain high levels of team identification, even without the experience of live sport attendance. While technology allows the non-local fan to remain highly identified with teams outside his geographic area, the non-local fan's desire to remain highly identified is often rooted in an attachment to the city the team represents (Collins et al., 2016; Collins & Heere, 2018).

Previous research has shown that there is a positive correlation between identification and consumptive behavior among sport fans (Fink, Trail, & Anderson, 2002). In fact, it has even been suggested that these non-local fans create social capital based on their team identification, suggesting the importance of the relationships between fans of the same non-local team (Collins & Heere, 2018). Consumption of sport by non-local fans therefore provides an opportunity for sport organizations, third-place locations, and other providers of sport experiences to reap financial gains.

Furthermore, as technology continues to advance the way individuals consume sport, it is likely that the experience of the non-local fan will also evolve. An understanding of how to use the latest technology to tap into the sociological factors and motivations that keep non-local fans both engaged and identified with their favorite teams will likely lead to an experience that is both personal and immersive for the non-local fan. Augmented reality, for example, is a highly interactive three-dimensional viewing experience that combines the superimposing of computer-generated elements on top of real-world situations. In the last few years, this technology has moved into the sport industry. This moves the already popular VR experience beyond a self-contained computer experience, into a decidedly more realistic experience in which geographic location is nearly irrelevant. While some initial studies on the use of AR in the stadium suggest mixed results for fan engagement and satisfaction (Rogers, Strudler, Decker, & Grazulis, 2019), this is only an emerging area of research as it applies to sport. The AR technology sector is rapidly growing, and as this technology becomes more accessible, it seems likely that it will have vast out-of-stadium reach, a trend pushed by the COVID-19 pandemic and the need to keep all fans engaged without in-person attendance (Goebert, 2020). This has allowed for better understanding of how to effectively use AR to enhance the fan experience. Early research suggests that effective AR implementation must be visually appealing, provide an immersive experience for the fan, and must serve as a complement to the sport product itself (Goebert, 2020). It is the ability of AR to provide an immersive experience that suggests it may become another strategy for teams and sport marketers to use to keep the non-local fan not only identified, but highly engaged with their favorite teams, even without geographic proximity. This is yet another way in which the continued exploration of the unique characteristics of non-local fans and their fandom demonstrates that they are a largely untapped market for the creation of new revenue streams.

References

Andrijiw, A. M., & Hyatt, C. G. (2009). Using optimal distinctiveness theory to understand identification with a nonlocal professional hockey team. *Journal of Sport Management, 23*(2), 156–181.

Branscombe, N. R., & Wann, D. L. (1991). The positive social and self concept consequences of sports team identification. *Journal of Sport and Social Issues, 15*(2), 115–127.

Cialdini, R. B., Borden, R. J., Thorne, A., Walker, M. R., Freeman, S., & Sloan, L. R. (1976). Basking in reflected glory: Three (football) field studies. *Journal of personality and social psychology, 34*(3), 366.

Coleman, J. S. (1988). Social capital in the creation of human capital. *American Journal of Sociology, 94*, S95–S120.

Collins, D. R., Heere, B., Shapiro, S., Ridinger, L., & Wear, H. (2016). The displaced fan: The importance of new media and community identification for maintaining team identity with your hometown team. *European Sport Management Quarterly, 16*(5), 655–674.

Collins, D. R., & Heere, B. (2018). Sunday afternoon social capital: An ethnographic study of the Southern City Jets Club. *European Sport Management Quarterly, 18*(4), 439–458.

Collins, D. R., & Reifurth, K. N. (2020) Where in the World are the Minor League Fans? Effects of Proximity and Competition on Minor League Baseball Attendance. *Conference Presentation, NASSM 2020 Virtual Conference.*

Fairley, S., & Tyler, B. D. (2012). Bringing baseball to the big screen: Building sense of community outside of the ballpark. *Journal of Sport Management, 26*(2), 258–261.

Fink, J. S., Trail, G. T., & Anderson, D. F. (2002). An examination of team identification: Which motives are most salient to its existence? *International Sports Journal, 18*, 39–50.

Goebert, C. (2020). Augmented reality in sport marketing: Uses and directions. *Sports Innovation Journal, 1*, 134–151.

Grant, N., Heere, B., & Dickson, G. (2011). New sport teams and the development of brand community. *European Sport Management Quarterly*, *11*(1), 35–54.

Heere, B., & James, J. D. (2007). Sports teams and their communities: Examining the influence of external group identities on team identity. *Journal of Sport Management*, *21*(3), 319–337.

Heere, B., Walker, M., Yoshida, M., Ko, Y. J., Jordan, J. S., & James, J. D. (2011). Brand community development through associated communities: Grounding community measurement within social identity theory. *Journal of Marketing Theory and Practice*, *19*(4), 407–422.

James, J. D. (2001). The role of cognitive development and socialization on the initial development of team loyalty. *Leisure Sciences*, *23*, 233–261.

Muniz, A. M., & O'guinn, T. C. (2001). Brand community. *Journal of Consumer Research*, *27*(4), 412–432.

O'Shea, M., & Alonso, A. D. (2011). Opportunity or obstacle? A preliminary study of professional sport organisations in the age of social media. *International Journal of Sport Management and Marketing*, *10*(3/4), 196–212.

Palmer, C., & Thompson, K. (2007). The paradoxes of football spectatorship: On-field and online expressions of social capital among the "Grog Squad". *Sociology of Sport Journal*, *24*(2), 187–205.

Putman, R. (2000). *Bowling Alone: The collapse and revival of American community*, New York: Simon and Schuster.

Reifurth, K., Bernthal, M. J., Ballouli, K., & Collins, D. (2019). Nonlocal fandom: Effects of geographic distance, geographic identity, and local competition on team identification. *Sport Marketing Quarterly*, *28*(4).

Rogers, R., Strudler, K., Decker, A., & Grazulis, A. (2019). Does augmented reality augment the experience? A qualitative analysis of enjoyment for sports spectators. *Media Watch*, *10*, 664–674.

Shapiro, S. L., Ridinger, L. L., & Trail, G. T. (2013). An analysis of multiple spectator consumption behaviors, identification, and future behavioral intentions within the context of a new college football program. *Journal of Sport Management*, *27*(2), 130–145.

Tajfel, H. E. (1978). *Differentiation between social groups: Studies in the social psychology of intergroup relations*. Academic Press.

Underwood, R., Bond, E., & Baer, R. (2001). Building service brands via social identity: Lessons from the sports marketplace. *Journal of Marketing Theory and Practice*, *9*(1), 1–13.

Part III
What Fans Do

23
Digital Sport Fandom

Heather Kennedy, Josh Gonzales and Ann Pegoraro

The Rise of Digital Sport Fandom

The advent and growth of the internet exponentially increased the number of opportunities for sport fans to interact with other fans, teams, and athletes. Early avenues of interaction, which included message boards and social network sites (e.g., Facebook), allowed fans to engage in fandom-related activities online. The 2012 London Olympics was generally considered a major turning point for digital platforms in sport and is dubbed the "first social media Olympics" (Pegoraro & Lebel, 2021). The global scale of the London Olympics showcased both the power and scope of emergent technologies with athletes and fans from around the world gathering to engage via social media platforms (Humphreys, 2012). Six years later, the 2018 World Cup generated 115 billion impressions (i.e., views on Twitter) during the tournament (Bavishi & Filadelfo, 2018). Today, coaches, athletes, fans, sport organizations, and journalists alike all maintain accounts on various digital platforms and interact with one another (Browning & Sanderson, 2012; Sanderson & Kassing, 2011).

As each new sporting event unfolds, digital platforms consistently generate new record-breaking traffic, fueled by the persistent growth of the user base. While the total number of all social media users in 2010 was just under one billion, that number grew to over 3.6 billion by 2020 (Tankovska, 2021). The sport industry reflects this general mass popularity of digital platforms; over 60 percent of sport fans follow sport accounts on social media (Ivana, 2020). Thus, this chapter explores the relationship between digital fandom and the sport industry. It begins with an examination into why sport fans embrace digital media, with an emphasis on social media due to its near ubiquitous state in both society and the sport industry. Next, this chapter discusses digital engagement, highlighting its role and use in the fan experience. The chapter then acknowledges that digital fandom is not always positive by discussing the dark side of sport fandom. Finally, this chapter concludes with an overview of the future of digital fandom, including new technologies and what that means for sport practitioners and scholars alike.

Theorizing Digital Sport Fandom

Originally, digital platforms were envisioned to operate as virtual communities that allowed users to participate in designing, publishing, editing, and sharing in a dynamic environment (van Dijck and Poell, 2013). These digital platforms were embraced by fans as channels to display their fandom (Pegoraro et al., 2018). The motives of gathering information and technical knowledge, together with receiving entertainment and diversion, were found when examining digital media use from a sport perspective (Hur, Ko, & Valacich, 2007; Seo & Green, 2008). The capacity of digital platforms to foster self-expressions among users provided instantaneous connectivity and helped to break down geographic and communicative boundaries for sport fans allowing them to interact with their favorite athletes and teams with relative ease (Pegoraro, 2013). The potential of digital media was further realized with the advent and adoption of social media platforms. These new opportunities for engagement by fans and sport consumers have garnered significant attention from sport researchers. A frequent focus of sport researchers looking to understand digital fandom has been investigating why fans use digital media, or their motivations.

Why Fans Use Digital Media

For sport fans, following digital media of sport figures, organizations, and media has become a popular past-time. Consequently, there has been a significant shift in the sports communication paradigm (Hambrick et al., 2010), with social media being a dominant medium embraced by sport fans and organizations alike. Sport organizations have embraced digital media including social media to provide fans with information updates, online marketplaces to purchase sport-related products and services, and interaction opportunities such as message boards and blogs (Hardin et al., 2012). Meanwhile, sport fans use social media for interactivity, information gathering, entertainment, fandom, and camaraderie (Filo et al., 2015). More broadly, social media has been found to complement or enhance the sport consumption experience (Kassing & Sanderson, 2010), such as sport fans using a second screen (e.g., using a smartphone or computer while watching a sport game on TV) for their excitement, need to obtain information, and its convenience (Hwang & Lim, 2015).

Existing sport management scholarship has identified motives driving social media use. For example, Clavio and Kian (2010) found that an important motivating factor for following an athlete's Twitter was the perception of the athlete as an expert, with followers' motives captured under three categories: organic fandom, functional fandom, and interaction. Other research has considered social media more broadly, finding 12 motives associated with usage among sport fans: arousal, passing time, camaraderie, entertainment, self-expression, habitual use, escape, information surveillance, building a virtual community, companionship, coolness, and maintaining relationships (e.g., Billings et al., 2019; Lewis et al., 2017). Overall, these motives have been summarized as interactivity, information gathering, entertainment, fandom, and camaraderie (Filo et al., 2015). Evidently, by this summary of drivers of social media usage, fandom is an important component.

Digital media, and social media more specifically, play an important role in digital fandom as it facilitates the opportunities for sport fans to (i) express their fandom and (ii) strengthen their fandom. First, digital media allows fans an additional way to express their fandom, with fandom often being a driving factor of social media usage (e.g., Mumcu & Lough, 2017; Witkemper et al., 2012). Prior to digital media, the ability for fans to effortlessly express their fandom was limited; for instance, they could wear a team's jersey following a win or call up a friend to discuss the win, but it was difficult to broadcast their fandom. Now, with digital media, it is possible for a fan to continuously post throughout a game, essentially having a megaphone to broadcast their fandom digitally. Consequently, existing research indicates that fans use social media to balance and express various sport identities (Larkin & Fink, 2016) and express their passion and identification (Wakefield, 2016). This chapter will further discuss how digital media facilitates fandom expression in the next section on digital engagement when it looks at how digital media, particularly social media, is used to reinforce and perpetuate offline fandom behaviors.

Second, digital media helps to strengthen fandom. As we know from existing literature, there are various antecedents of fandom including: the need to belong, the need for distinctiveness, socialization into fandom, presence of rivals, proximity to a team/stadium, perceived similarity with the team, player attributes, and the team's history (Koch & Wann, 2016). Social media helps to facilitate opportunities for these antecedents, which in turn can strengthen fandom. For example, digital media can help to overcome geographic differences, artificially increasing the proximity to a team or stadium and increasing fandom (Collins et al., 2016). Social media can enhance the similarity to and sense of connection with sport teams and athletes since it can provide fans with additional information on and access to their favorite sport entities. For instance, when Clavio and Kian (2010) explored motives for following a retired LPGA player, there was a motive of affinity towards the athlete, such as interest in the athlete and affinity for the athlete's writing. Similarly, for athletes who feature two-way, social communication with fans on their accounts, fans were motivated to follow them for consumption, admiration, promotion, and community (Frederick et al., 2012). Social media is designed to connect fans, allowing them to feel a sense of belonging and connection to other fans and sport entities they might not have access to otherwise. Consequently, interaction is often a motive of social media usage (e.g., Gibbs et al., 2014) and fans often use social media to build a virtual community (e.g., Billings et al., 2019; Lewis et al., 2017). Therefore, by examining why sport fans use social media, we can understand its role in facilitating expression and strengthening of digital fandom.

Digital Engagement

Scholars have investigated how different types of content prompt consumers to engage or interact, moving them from passive to active consumers on digital platforms. Thompson et al. (2014) found consumers most often interacted with content that poses questions and provides behind-the-scenes content opportunities. Boehmer and Tandoc (2015) found retweets of sport news by students were impacted by perceptions of credibility and likability of the source. Respondents were influenced by a tweet's originality, informativeness, and style when deciding what types of content to retweet. Characteristics of the users, including their interest in the tweet's topic, the relevancy of the tweet's topic to the user, similarity in opinion, and impact on the user's followers, all impacted users' decisions on whether they would retweet a post. Engaging with content was also found to be influenced by students' perceptions of their own Twitter followers' interests (Boehmer & Tandoc, 2015).

As digital platforms and their user bases have matured, scholars have re-focused their attention to issues beyond why people follow and what prompts engagement, to studies that investigate the different types of outcomes that digital interaction can provide to sport consumers. At the same time, there has been a rise in social television (TV), or second screen experiences. Each live sporting event draws significant attention on digital platforms – the 2018 Super Bowl, for example, generated 4.8 billion tweets around the event (Cohen, 2018). Cunningham and Eastin (2017) found that 79 percent of participants used second screens for social media interaction while watching sports (e.g., posting and commenting on Facebook or Twitter) and 65 percent looked online for information related to the game or sport while it was being played.

Recognizing that sports fans are increasingly turning to Twitter to experience events and receive commentary, Smith et al. (2019) surveyed fans to measure how Twitter might influence their enjoyment of viewing live and mediated sporting events. Respondents in this study were found to focus on American football and they primarily reported using Twitter to augment their consumption of sports. When asked about how Twitter use impacted their enjoyment level while consuming live and broadcast sports, heavy Twitter users reported higher enjoyment levels when using the platform to watch sports (Smith et al., 2019). Practically speaking, this research shows that engagement with content and posting of one's own content on Twitter can be important drivers of consumer enjoyment of digital sport viewing.

Research has also considered traditional sport consumer behavior, such as BIRGing (Basking in Reflective Glory) and CORFing (Cutting off Reflective Failure), online. In analyzing nearly 100,000 tweets posted during two of England's 2018 World Cup games, it was evident that English fans tended to BIRG when England was leading or victorious and tended to CORF when England was trailing or defeated (Fan et al., 2020). Sport fans' online engagement increased with the excitement level of the game, such as sharing and exchanging opinions and information more during more exciting game moments (Lee et al., 2014). Overall, this illustrates how fans use digital platforms to extend traditional fan behaviors during live sport events.

Similarly, researchers have investigated rivalry on digital platforms as rivalries have long been a part of sport consumer behavior. The convenience to engage in expressions of rivalry – to commiserate, celebrate, as well as antagonize by interacting with teams and fans – has reached an unprecedented degree of flexibility and freedom on digital platforms. Watanabe et al. (2019) measured the number of Twitter posts by individuals about US college football teams to model how often fans create content during game days. After controlling for a number of factors, including the type of rivalry game, results indicated that fans post more during traditional rivalries. Furthermore, newer rivalry games had less impact on the amount of content posted about a team. Previous research on the effect of conference realignment on attendance (Szymanski & Winfree, 2018), revealed the loss of rivalries were estimated to only have a negligible impact on attendance at games, sometimes accounting for only half a percent change in attendance demand. Therefore, the study demonstrated that rivalries may play a more substantial role in driving consumer interest for college football teams in the digital realm, compared to actual physical attendance (Watanabe et al., 2019). Thus, not only does digital fandom represent a replication of offline fandom behaviors, but there is also an additional importance of digital fandom.

Role of Digital Fans

The engagement of fans online has allowed them to experience a shift in their role – no longer just fans, rather they are increasingly involved in the design and production of the sport experience. For example, sport attendees can form online fan communities and leverage these fan communities to demand change from sport organizations or content providers, like when the United Kingdom's Parliament agreed to discuss the possibility of letting fans return to watching live matches in stadiums following the Covid-19 global pandemic after an online petition amassed over 190,000 signatures. Digital media provide sport fans the tools to call for change. It connects fans to other like-minded fans, lets them congregate, discuss and demand change, and facilitates the collection of opinions/signatures/signs of support to amplify fans voices, often at no financial expense. This allows fans to be, or at least feel, increasingly involved in the fan experience.

Digital media has also given rise to the notion of value co-creation. Using social media can increase the flow of information and comments of stakeholders, particularly those coming from fans (Zagnoli & Radicchi, 2010). The use of social media by sport fans can raise awareness of sport events or unique experiences, in turn having fans act as a marketer for that sport event. When David Ayres, a 42-year-old Zamboni driver and operations manager in Toronto, was called into the Carolina Hurricanes' net as the emergency goalie against the Toronto Maple Leafs in a regular season game, he became an internet sensation due to social media attention from various stakeholders. The Hurricanes then capitalized on his internet popularity, designing t-shirts in his honour. Overall, this example demonstrates the value the online community was able to create around the unique event. Effectively, digital fandom not only facilitates additional, online opportunities for fans to express and experience their fandom (such as tweeting their BIRGing and CORFing), but also increases their role in the sport experience, letting them take on a more active role and call for change in the industry.

Dark Side of Digital Fandom

Thus far, this chapter has painted digital fandom in a positive light. For example, we have examined the opportunities that digital media allows for fans, such as highlighting how social media can be used to complement and enhance the fan viewing experience (Kassing & Sanderson, 2010) or demand and facilitate social change. However, it is important to acknowledge the dark side of digital fandom to paint a balanced picture of the reality of sport fandom in a digital age. Therefore, this chapter will briefly overview three negative aspects to digital fandom: (i) how digital media can reinforce offline inequities, (ii) negativity on digital media, and (iii) privacy concerns related to data collection and usage.

Digital Media as an Equalizer

The advancement of digital media was thought to be a disrupting force that could help balance and equalize the sport industry as well as society more broadly. For example, due to its ability to lower the threshold for civic engagement and increase the awareness of and opportunities for social justice, the internet and social media have been dubbed great equalizers (Xenos et al., 2014). Conventionally, offline civic behavior has been reserved for men (Putnam, 2000), with women being less politically interested and informed (Verba et al., 1997). Though some researchers are optimistic with respect to social media's ability to stem or reverse patterns of civic inequality (e.g., Xenos et al., 2014), other researchers find evidence that gender inequities are perpetuated and reinforced on social media (e.g., Brandtzaeg, 2017).

Traditionally, women's sports have struggled to receive media coverage compared to men's sports (Cooky et al., 2015) and the coverage that is received is often gendered, portraying women athletes as women who play sports as opposed to simply athletes (Meân & Kassing, 2008), and often overly sexualizing women or branding them as mothers (Cooky et al., 2015). Digital media has the potential to disrupt this narrative and provide sport fans with a more equitable quantity and quality of sport coverage. Digital media also has the potential to provide sport teams and athletes with more of a voice and control of their own narrative; just as it has with sport fans. However, emerging scholarship on digital media's ability to challenge offline inequalities is mixed. Some research suggests that the inequalities are still perpetuated; for example, digital coverage of the 2008 Olympics was 1.6 times more likely to feature men than women (Jones, 2013) and self-presentation of athletes on social media (e.g., Twitter) indicates a persistence of hegemonic values (Lebel & Danylchuk, 2014). Conversely, other scholarship finds that social media has the potential to be leveraged to promote women athletes positively; for example, Pegoraro et al.'s (2018) study following the #SheBelieves for the US Women's Soccer team during the 2015 World Cup found a positive framing of women as athletes. Effectively, the evidence of digital media challenging and disrupting offline inequalities versus perpetuating and reinforcing them is mixed. Thus, a potential dark side of digital media is that, without purposeful efforts to change narratives surrounding inequities, digital media might continue to exasperate them.

Online Negativity

Another dark side of digital fandom is related to the negativity that can be experienced by users. Since all social media users have the ability to comment and react to posts, social media can become toxic and negative for some users. For example, the racist and discriminatory online comments directed towards Ethan Bear, an NHL player from the Ochapoace Nation in Saskatchewan and the first player to have his name printed on his jersey in Cree syllabics, became so bad that the Confederacy of Treaty Six First Nations Chiefs and the Federation of Sovereign Indigenous Nations released statements calling for the NHL to address racism and hate towards First Nation people in the league. While digital media can provide a voice for individuals and organizations to support individuals such as Ethan Bear in this example, it also provides the same voice to individuals seeking to spread hate and negativity. This can negatively impact social media users who are on the receiving end of bigotry or observing it.

Negativity or the fear of receiving a negative backlash can stifle the voices of users; for example, women athletes report receiving unwanted direct messages and rude public messages on their social media which has a silencing effect as they expressed concern about post reception, resulting in them rethinking and shying away from certain post content (Geurin, 2017). This can make it difficult for athletes to be authentic and fully leverage their online brand. As athletes speak out, such as NBA athletes who have leveraged their social media accounts to express social justice causes like Dwayne Wade and LeBron James posting pictures of themselves and their team respectively wearing the apparel a victim wore when he was shot by the police (Demby, 2012), there is a responding conversation by stakeholders, with some critics going so far as to say that athletes should "stay in their lanes". Digital media, and particularly social media, makes it increasingly easy for angry or upset fans to vocalize or express their negative emotions, with less sense of consequence as people can experience anonymity online. Overall, negativity on digital media can hurt those receiving it and those reading it.

Privacy

The final dark side of digital sport fandom discussed in this chapter is related to privacy, with a particular emphasis on the amount of data fans are knowingly or unknowingly giving away in the name of fandom. The rise of digital fandom parallels other advancements in technology including big data and machine learning; namely, tools and techniques sport organizations can use to collect and analyze fans' data. For example, a sport team and their newly upgraded digital stadium might use an online ticket process and an app in their stadium to improve fan experiences such as providing mobile ticketing, real-time information about parking or traffic, coupon and discounts for in stadium purchases, etc. However, for fans to embrace these improved, digital fan experiences, it is often at the expense of providing data such as their demographics, purchase history, in-stadium behavior, and/or credit card information. Moreover, in the wake of Covid-19, fans may be required to provide sensitive health information to enter a venue. Failing to properly secure data can lead to data breaches and security concerns for consumers, particularly for health data that sport organizations are not used to handling.

Fitness apps, such as Strava, are another area of potential privacy issues as they track, store, and often make available collected data. Fitness apps represent a great tool in digital fandom, a way for athletes to track and share their workouts and even connect with other users. Moreover, the competition element, such as apps allowing users to set up challenges with and against other users, can help to drive and increase fandom. However, providing all this information can have unintended consequences. For individual runners or cyclists, the Strava Flyby feature showed who they've passed on a run or bike ride, intended to help connect athletes and build a community. However, the unintended consequence of this data collection was the ability to document the routines of a user, including where they lived, worked, and exercised.

In response to fans moving their consumption online, sport management scholars have also moved to online research techniques, such as digital media content analysis. When fans converse in a digital world, such as posting online in groups or on social media, they are likely doing so without realizing their posts may be collected and analyzed without their knowledge. This raises many discussion points when academic researchers leverage publicly available social media data: "Did the participants know they were going to be a part of a research study? Would the comments be different if people knew their responses were going to be used in an academic setting? How can permission be obtained to use the posts or comments on the website?" (Ruihley & Hardin, 2014, p. 4). Effectively, as fans increasingly move to digital spaces, they are consciously or unconsciously providing more data and information about themselves to the general public which may be collected, stored, analyzed, or applied in a way that they might not be comfortable with. Moreover, major data breaches, such as an attack on a sport organization to obtain fan information such as credit card numbers, have the potential to significantly and negatively impact all sport stakeholders involved. Thus, privacy, or more accurately the lack thereof, is a dark side of digital fandom that needs to receive significant attention.

The Future of Digital Sport Fandom

So, what is next in the digital world of sports fandom? There is no doubt that new digital trends will continue to permeate and disrupt the sports industry, providing many future avenues for research. We conclude this chapter by broadly reviewing a few potential areas we believe offer promising opportunities: (i) new social media platforms, (ii) new technologies, and (iii) women's sports.

New Platforms

Currently, platforms such as Facebook, YouTube, WhatsApp, and Instagram maintain dominance (Tankovska, 2021). However, new platforms are constantly introduced to vie for digital market share. Two new platforms that are growing in popularity and have the potential to become common place in digital sport consumption are TikTok and Clubhouse.

TikTok is a social media platform that allows users to upload videos that can be anywhere from 15–60 seconds long and share them to a feed that is aggregated and displayed based on user preferences. TikTok recently sprung up in popularity, boasting 689 million users as of January 2021 (Tankovska, 2021). If teams or athletes want to engage with fans in a short-form video format, TikTok provides a good avenue to do so. Due to its relative novelty compared to more established platforms, few studies have yet to analyze TikTok's impacts on fan engagement (although see Su et al., 2020). While TikTok does nothing inherently new, it is yet another social media platform fans can use to express or strength their digital fandom.

Clubhouse is another platform that has recently gained momentum. Unlike other digital platforms that primarily make use of video and text, Clubhouse relies solely on audio. Creators on the platform carry out convention-style panels, allowing designated speakers to engage in conversation with other prominent figures. The platform also allows users to digitally "raise their hand," and – if chosen by moderators – they are offered the chance to ask questions. The NFL partnered with Clubhouse to have live conversations about their most recent player draft

(Bloom, 2021). This format allows fans the opportunity to interact with multiple athletes and prominent figures directly and would give unique opportunities for digital fandom.

While TikTok and Clubhouse exemplify new platforms that have gained traction and have the potential to facilitate digital fandom, there is no guarantee that they will continue to grow into sustainable channels nor be adopted by sport industry stakeholders. Consequently, it is important for academics and practitioners alike to continually monitor different platforms to understand their evolving role in digital fandom. Additionally, social media companies are continually restricting the data available from their platforms. Therefore, even though there may be more platforms for fans to use in their digital fandom, there may be barriers to researching their usage within the sport consumption experience.

New Technologies

Social media platforms are well-established within the digital ecosystems and there exists many use cases for sports researchers with those tools. However, digital innovation is not limited to social media – other technologies provide different avenues for researchers to explore digital sport fandom. We outline two potential opportunities: (i) AR/VR and (ii) NFTs.

AR and VR. Augmented reality (AR) is a technology that provides a composite view of the world by super-imposing computer-generated images over a consumer's real-world view. While AR has long since been embraced by the sport industry to improve consumers' viewing experiences (e.g., the first down line superimposed in TV broadcasts of American football), it has the potential to continue to advance and be embraced in various aspects of the sport industry. Virtual reality (VR) is the natural evolution of AR as it goes a step further and completely replaces a consumer's visual field with a digital experience through electronics. Both technologies offer exciting opportunities for the sport industry, potentially providing fans with more digital or virtual fandom opportunities. For example, in 2017 FC Bayern Munich used their own team app to create an interface where fans could virtually insert themselves into selfies with the team's star players (Srivastav, 2017). This immersive experience is reported to have increased the club's revenue, while providing an additional way for fans to express their fandom. The MLB has also added AR to its At Bat app with the aim of enhancing the game that fans are watching on the field (Newman, 2017).

Overall, we have learned that digital or virtual environments provide fans with additional opportunities to express their fandom; for example, after your team wins a game, not only can you wear their jersey to show your support, but you can now post pictures and videos with it online to broadcast your support to a wider audience and share in the moment with others online. AR and VR are the natural extensions of the ability to experience and express fandom. Since AR can enhance a traditional experience, such as providing real-time player statistics by holding an app up to a game, it has the possibility to strengthen fandom. VR has the potential to provide fans with immersive experiences they would not otherwise have, like sitting courtside at a game, again facilitating fandom opportunities. As these technologies are adopted by the sport industry, it will provide academics with interesting research opportunities including: whether fans truly enjoy these augmented experiences; how AR/VR experiences impact digital fandom; are fans more likely to engage with teams that use AR/VR; and do these digital immersive experiences lead to increased attendance or purchases.

NFTs. Another new technology that facilitates unique ways for fans to interact with their favorite teams and players are non-fungible tokens (NFTs). Most sports fans are familiar with the concept of trading cards and other collectibles. NFTs essentially act as digital extensions of this collectible market. What makes them special is that they use blockchain technology to create immutable digital receipts of object authenticity. Additionally, a royalty payment can be attached to any future sale of the NFT, meaning a creator can make income on the work in perpetuity.

Athletes have already begun to sell NFTs independently of the sports they participate in, as evidenced by releases by athletes such as Megan Rapinoe and Sue Bird (Caron, 2021). This means athletes can offer a very singular experience directly to their fans. Moreover, the NBA uses this technology to sell "moments", which are NFTs of specific in-game instance of an NBA season sold on a platform called Top Shot. This means fans get the chance at digital ownership of the league and its players. One moment of LeBron James has sold for $208,000; this is evidence that NFTs can provide a completely new income streams for athletes and sports leagues. NFTs represent an opportunity to continue to migrate fandom to a digital space; for instance, why own a physical poster or a trading card when you can have an NFT? Since NFTs are still in their infancy, it is unclear the degree to which they will be adopted by the sport industry or the role they will play for fans. Will fans migrate to a digital fandom completely, with NFTs serving the role of collectibles, or will NFTs only resonate with the most extreme fans who would have always invested in expensive paraphernalia? These represent important areas of inquiry for academics and practitioners alike as NFTs gain traction in the industry.

Women's Sports

Neilson (2018) surveyed 1,000 individuals in eight of the most commercially active sports markets: United States, United Kingdom, France, Germany, Italy, Spain, Australia, and New Zealand. The report found that 84 percent of all general sport fans showed interest in women's sport and 66 percent reported watching at least one women's sport. It also found that 63 percent of respondents felt brands should invest in women's sport, 75 percent could recall at least one brand that is involved in women's sport, and 20 percent said they were more influenced by brands associated with women's sport than ones associated with men's sport. These figures reveal not only the public's interest and appetite for women's sport, but also the opportunity for digital fandom.

Women's sports represent a unique opportunity for digital fandom due to their historical underrepresentation in sport media. For example, unlike the NBA that has long-standing contracts with broadcasters, the WNBA leverages numerous broadcast medium including traditional broadcast avenues like ESPN and non-traditional like Twitter and mobile apps. Without the baggage of traditional structures, women's sports have an opportunity to be an industry leader with respect to digital fandom. Namely, women's sports can disrupt the industry and leverage new technologies to reach their existing fans and cultivate new fans. As women's sports challenge existing status quos, there are exciting research opportunities to explore the impact on digital fandom. For instance, Pegoraro et al. (2021) examined the role of broadcast medium on game day social media engagements, finding that Twitter broadcasts were associated with lower engagement levels than other broadcast avenues. Overall, women's sports are keenly positioned to leverage opportunities for digital fandom.

It is also important going forward to ensure that digital fandom is a safe and accepting place for women and women's sports. When discussing the dark sides of fandom, the points of digital media as an equalizer and online negativity were raised; specifically, discussing how digital media can perpetuate and reinforce offline inequalities or be unsafe and negative for users. Just Not Sports released a YouTube video that featured men reading mean tweets about women sport reporters directly to these reporters, illustrating the unsafe online feedback women can receive. In this video, the men were visibly uncomfortable by the comments that had been directed towards the women reporters. While digital media can serve as an equalizer, giving women ample opportunities to engage with sports media, it can also be a megaphone for negativity. Furthermore, this chapter briefly highlighted how the negative backlash women receive online can be stifling for them, resulting in them rethinking and shying away from certain post content (Geurin, 2017). Going forward, it is important that digital fandom, particularly around women's sports, is developed in such a way to encourage positivity and inclusion, rather than reinforce inequities and negativity.

Conclusion

In conclusion, this chapter provided an overview of digital fandom. First, it discussed how, although sport fans use digital media for a variety of reasons, it serves an important role in fandom expression and strengthening. The chapter then discussed digital engagement, explaining how fans exhibit offline behaviors online, such as BIRGing and CORFing or engaging in rivalries. This research can inform sport marketers who might take note of the fact that fans who use digital platforms to follow sport more frequently exhibit high levels of enjoyment when watching both televised and live sport. Next, this chapter overviewed the shifting role of sport consumers with respect to their digital fandom, highlighting how sport fans have become increasingly involved in value co-creation. This chapter concluded by acknowledging potential dark sides of digital fandom and discussing the future of digital fandom. Collectively, this chapter overviewed more than a decade of digital sport consumer behavior research to provide many salient contributions to inform both academic literature and industry practitioners.

References

Bavishi, J., & Filadelfo, E. (2018, July 17). Insights into the 2018 #WorldCup conversation on Twitter. *Twitter*. https://blog.twitter.com/en_us/topics/events/2018/2018-World-Cup-Insights.html

Billings, A. C., Broussard, R. M., Xu, Q., & Xu, M. (2019). Untangling international sport social media use: Contrasting US and Chinese uses and gratifications across four platforms. *Communication & Sport*, 7(5), 630–652.

Bloom, D. (2021, April 25). NFL partners with social audio app Clubhouse ahead of draft. *Forbes*. www.forbes.com/sites/dbloom/2021/04/25/nfl-partners-with-social-audio-app-clubhouse-ahead-of-draft/

Boehmer, J., & Tandoc, E. C. (2015). Why we retweet: Factors influencing intentions to share sport news on Twitter. *International Journal of Sport Communication*, 8(2), 212–232.

Brandtzaeg, P. B. (2017). Facebook is no "Great equalizer": A big data approach to gender differences in civic engagement across countries. *Social Science Computer Review*, 35(1), 103–125.

Browning, B., & Sanderson, J. (2012). The positives and negatives of Twitter: Exploring how student-athletes use Twitter and respond to critical tweets. *International Journal of Sport Communication*, 5(4), 503–521.

Caron, E. (2021, April 27). Rapinoe, Bird and female stars come together in limited NFT collection. *Sportico*. www.sportico.com/business/commerce/2021/uswnt-wnba-olympic-athletes-nft-collection-1234627493/

Clavio, G., & Kian, T. M. (2010). Uses and gratifications of a retired female athlete's Twitter followers. *International Journal of Sport Communication*, 3(4), 485–500.

Cohen, D. (2018, February 5). What drove discussion during Super Bowl LII on Twitter, Facebook, YouTube? *AdWeek*. www.adweek.com/performance-marketing/super-bowl-lii-wrap-twitter-facebook-youtube/

Collins, D.R., Heere, B., Shapiro, S., Ridinger, L., & Wear, H. (2016). The displaced fan: The importance of new media and community identification for maintaining team identity with your hometown team. *European Sport Management Quarterly*, 16(5), 655–674.

Cooky, C., Messner, M. A., & Musto, M. (2015). "It's dude time!": A quarter century of excluding women's sports in televised news and highlight shows. *Communication & Sport*, 3(3), 261–287.

Cunningham, N.R., & Eastin, M.S. (2017). Second screen and sports: A structural investigation into team identification and efficacy. *Communication & Sport*, 5(3), 288–310.

Demby, G. (2012, March 23). LeBron and the Miami Heat: We Are Trayvon Martin. *HuffPost*. www.huffpost.com/entry/lebron-heat-trayvon-tweet_n_1375831

Fan, M., Billings, A., Zhu, X., & Yu, P. (2020). Twitter-based BIRGing: Big data analysis of English national team fans during the 2018 FIFA World cup. *Communication & Sport*, 8(3), 317–345.

Filo, K., Lock, D., & Karg, A. (2015). Sport and social media research: A review. *Sport Management Review*, 18(2), 166–181.

Frederick, E. L., Lim, C. H., Clavio, G., & Walsh, P. (2012). Why we follow: An examination of parasocial interaction and fan motivations for following athlete archetypes on Twitter. *International Journal of Sport Communication*, 5(4), 481–502.

Geurin, A. N. (2017). Elite female athletes' perceptions of new media use relating to their careers: A qualitative analysis. *Journal of Sport Management*, 31(4), 345–359.

Gibbs, C., O'Reilly, N., & Brunette, M. (2014). Professional team sport and Twitter: Gratifications sought and obtained by followers. *International Journal of Sport Communication*, 7(2), 188–213.

Hambrick, M. E., Simmons, J. M., Greenhalgh, G. P., & Greenwell, T. C. (2010). Understanding professional athletes' use of Twitter: A content analysis of athlete tweets. *International Journal of Sport Communication*, 3(4), 454–471.

Hardin, R., Koo, G.-Y., Ruihley, B., Dittmore, S.W., & McGreevey, M. (2012). Motivation for consumption of collegiate athletics subscription web sites. *International Journal of Sport Communication*, 5(3), 368–383.

Humphreys, L. (2012, August 22). Social media & the Olympics. *Culture Digitally*. https://culturedigitally.org/2012/08/social-media-the-olympics/

Hur, Y., Ko, Y. J., & Valacich, J. (2007). Motivation and concerns for online sport consumption. *Journal of Sport Management*, 21(4), 521–539.

Hwang, Y., and Lim, J. S. (2015). The impact of engagement motives for social TV on social presence and sports channel commitment. *Telemat. Informat.* 32, 755–765.

Ivana. (2020, May 26). The growing impact of social media on sports. *Bettingmate.uk*. https://bettingmate.uk/sports-on-social-media/

Jones, D. (2013). Online coverage of the 2008 Olympic Games on the ABC, BBC, CBC and TVNZ. *Pacific Journalism Review*, 19(1), 244–263.

Kassing, J.W., & Sanderson, J. (2010). Fan–athlete interaction and Twitter tweeting through the giro: A case study. *International Journal of Sport Communication*, 3(1), 113–128.

Koch, K., & Wann, D. L. (2016). Team identification and sport fandom: Gender differences in relationship-based and recognition-based perceived antecedents. *Journal of Sport Behavior*, 39(3), 278–300.

Larkin, B. A., & Fink, J. S. (2016). Fantasy sport, FoMo, and traditional fandom: How second-screen use of social media allows fans to accommodate multiple identities. *Journal of Sport Management*, 30(6), 643–655.

Lebel, K., & Danylchuk, K. (2014). An Audience Interpretation of Professional Athlete Self-Presentation on Twitter. *Journal of Applied Sport Management*, 6(2), 16–36.

Lee, H., Han, Y., Kim, K. K., and Kim, Y. (2014). "Sports and social media: Twitter usage patterns during the 2013 super bowl broadcast," in *Proceedings from International Conference on Communication, Media, Technology and Design*. Presented at the Istanbul, Turkey (Istanbul).

Lewis, M., Brown, K. A., & Billings, A. C. (2017). Social media becomes traditional: Sport media consumption and the blending of modern information pathways. *Journal of Global Sport Management*, 2(2), 111–127.

Meân, L. J., & Kassing, J.W. (2008). "I would just like to be known as an athlete": Managing hegemony, femininity, and heterosexuality in female sport. *Western Journal of Communication*, 72(2), 126–144.

Mumcu, C., & Lough, N. (2017). Are fans proud of the WNBA's pride campaign? *Sport Marketing Quarterly*, 26(1), 42–54.

Neilson. (2018, March 10). The rise of women's sports: Identifying and maximizing the opportunity. www.nielsen.com/eu/en/insights/report/2018/the-rise-of-womens-sports/#

Newman, M. (2017, October 10). MLB takes AR to next level for fans at ballpark. *MLB.Com*. www.mlb.com/news/mlb-to-use-augmented-reality-to-enhance-data-c258179374

Pegoraro, A. (2013). *Sport fandom in the digital world* (P.M. Pedersen, Ed.). Routledge.

Pegoraro, A., Comeau, G.S., & Frederick, E.L. (2018). #SheBelieves: The use of Instagram to frame the US Women's Soccer Team during #FIFAWWC. *Sport in Society*, 21(7), 1063–1077.

Pegoraro, A., Kennedy, H., Agha, N., Brown, N., & Berri, D. (2021). An analysis of broadcasting media using social media engagement in the WNBA. *Frontiers in Sports and Active Living*.

Pegoraro, A. and Lebel, K. (2021) Social Media and Sport Marketing in Butterworth, M. L. (Ed) *Handbook of Communication and Sport*, Mouton de Gruyter.

Putnam, R. D. (2000). *Bowling alone: The collapse and revival of American community*. Simon & Schuster.

Ruihley, B. J., & Hardin, R. (2014). Sport fans and online data collection. *Journal of Applied Sport Management*, *6*(3), 1–15.

Sanderson, J., & Kassing, J. (2011). Tweets and blogs: Transformative, adversarial and integrative developments in sports media. In A. C. Billings (Ed.), *Sports media: Transformation, integration, consumption* (pp. 114–127). Routledge.

Seo, W. J., & Green, B. C. (2008). Development of the motivation scale for sport online consumption. *Journal of Sport Management*, *22*(1), 82–109.

Smith, L. R., Pegoraro, A., & Cruikshank, S. A. (2019). Tweet, retweet, favorite: The impact of Twitter use on enjoyment and sports viewing. *Journal of Broadcasting & Electronic Media*, *63*(1), 94–110.

Srivastav, T. (2017, October 18). FC Bayern Munich rolls out augmented reality feature to offer fans personalised selfies with players. *The Drum*. www.thedrum.com/news/2017/10/18/fc-bayern-munich-rolls-out-augmented-reality-feature-offer-fans-personalised-selfies

Su, Y., Baker, B. J., Doyle, J. P., & Yan, M. (2020). Fan engagement in 15 seconds: Athletes' relationship marketing during a pandemic via TikTok. *International Journal of Sport Communication*, *13*(3), 436–446.

Szymanski, S., & Winfree, J. (2018). On the optimal realignment of a contest: The case of college football. *Economic Inquiry*, *56*(1), 483–496.

Tankovska, H. (2021). *Most used social media 2021*. Statista. www.statista.com/statistics/272014/global-social-networks-ranked-by-number-of-users/

Thompson, A.-J., Martin, A., Gee, S., & Eagleman, A. (2014). Examining the development of a social media strategy for a national sport organisation: A case study of tennis New Zealand. *Journal of Applied Sport Management*, *6*(2), 42–63.

van Dijck, J., & Poell, T. (2013). Understanding social media logic. *Media and Communication*, *1*(1), 2–14.

Verba, S., Burns, N., & Schlozman, K. L. (1997). Knowing and caring about politics: Gender and political engagement. *The Journal of Politics*, *59*(4), 1051–1072.

Wakefield, K. (2016). Using fan passion to predict attendance, media consumption, and social media behaviors. *Journal of Sport Management*, *30*(3), 229–247.

Watanabe, N. M., Pegoraro, A., Yan, G., & Shapiro, S. L. (2019). Does rivalry matter? An analysis of sport consumer interest on social media. *International Journal of Sports Marketing and Sponsorship*, *20*(4), 646–665.

Witkemper, C., Lim, C. H., & Waldburger, A. (2012). Social media and sports marketing: Examining the motivations and constraints of Twitter users. *Sport Marketing Quarterly*, *21*(3), 170–183.

Xenos, M., Vromen, A., & Loader, B. D. (2014). The great equalizer? Patterns of social media use and youth political engagement in three advanced democracies. *Information, Communication & Society*, *17*(2), 151–167.

Zagnoli, P., & Radicchi, E. (2010). The football-fan community as a determinant stakeholder in value co-creation. *Sport in Society*, *13*(10), 1532–1551.

24
Online Performances of Fandom
Selective Self-Presentation, Perceived Affordances, and Parasocial Interactions on Social Media

Kathryn Coduto

The Los Angeles Lakers' official Twitter account has approximately 9.3 million followers. Their star player, LeBron James, has 48.2 million followers on his personal account. The NBA's Twitter account boasts 31.6 million followers, and the NBA on ESPN Twitter account has 6.7 million followers. If you are a Lakers fan, you may follow all of these accounts, you may follow some of these accounts. As a fan, you can reach the team, your favorite player, or the media covering your team with a few clicks and a 280-character message.

Social media continue to increase access to figures previously deemed unreachable. We often characterize these figures as celebrities. Not long ago, a reply from LeBron James would have been unthinkable. Now, a dedicated fan might send a tweet to LeBron and get a "like" or even a reply on it. A Lakers fan might tweet directly to the @lakers account, and the team may respond. In fact, publications ranging from *Complex* to *Forbes* have ranked the best Twitter accounts of professional sports teams. These rankings are based on original content, replies, and the use of memes and GIFs—signaling a team's ability to stay-up-to-date and personable.

Athletes, their teams, and organizations are not limited to Twitter, either—this is just one example of the many platforms available for these kinds of interactions. The NBA has a presence on Facebook, Instagram, YouTube, even Reddit and Snapchat. LeBron James goes live on Instagram and shares updates on Facebook in addition to his lively Twitter account.

Fans of teams and athletes also have these options available to them. Fans can use social media to perform their fandom. This might be by posting regularly about their favorite teams and players; using the team's logo or imagery as part of their profiles (such as a Facebook or Twitter banner); even including the name of the team in their handle (such as @cavskaty on Twitter or Instagram). Fans can weave in and out of players' lives by posting to them directly. All of this is enabled by taking advantage of the affordances of the platforms available.

This chapter explores the performance of fandom and the engagement that stems from such performative behaviors. First, the ability to selectively self-present online is explained as a mechanism for this performance. Then, affordances of platforms are explored to further develop the idea of both fandom performed and fandom engaged. This then extends to an exploration of parasocial interactions and relationships enabled by social media platforms, both with players individually and teams broadly.

Selective Self-Presentation of Fandom

The performance of fandom online is a form of strategic self-presentation. The internet enables selective self-presentation; individuals can highlight whatever characteristics of themselves they want, while hiding others (Walther, 1996). Online daters, for example, can carefully select certain photos of themselves for dating profiles to highlight their most desirable aspects and to downplay those that might be seen as less than desirable (Heino et al., 2010). Not only can online daters choose photos, but they can write short bios, set their location, and alter their age—all of which can showcase the "best" version of themselves, if not the true version (Ellison et al., 2006). These showcasing abilities are not limited to online dating. Sports fans can use these same strategies to demonstrate the depth and seriousness of their fandom, both to other serious fans and to more casual observers. Through this process, they can make a sports team a significant part of their identity.

Think about being a fan of a team: Maybe you are a diehard Ohio State Buckeyes football fan. If you want to show off your Ohio State dedication as part of your identity, you could showcase numerous aspects of this on your social media channels. You might make the block "O" your profile picture on Twitter; your profile picture on Facebook could be you with the script Ohio, wearing Ohio State gear. Your bio might include information about why you love Ohio State so much (you could be a student, your parents might be alumni, etc.). Your posts on social media might reflect your current feelings about the team, the team's prospects for a coming season, regret over a (rare) loss, and so on. Each piece of this online identity is building up you as an Ohio State fan. You can choose what parts of that are highlighted or hidden. If Ohio State has a particularly bad season, you could remove the profile photos or edit your bio. You have the power to selectively self-present your Ohio State fandom.

Typically, when we think about selectively self-presenting, we think about the use of photos and the use of text-based posts. These two elements together can help a dedicated sports fan build their fandom into their online identities.

The Use of Photos in Online Self-Presentation of Fandom

Consider first how fans may select photos for their online profiles, like you did as an Ohio State fan. In the case of Twitter, fans are limited to only one profile photo, and no one can access previous profile photos (unlike Facebook, for example). In this instance, a fan can choose either to

1. Post a picture of themselves in the team's gear or at the team's home field or even with a player or coach.
2. Use the team's logo as their own profile photo.
3. Use a photo of a team player(s) as their profile photo.

Each profile photo choice broadcasts the individual's dedication to the given team and communicates something about that person. Particularly because profile photos are limited (you can only have one at a time), the single photo picked will be seen on one's profile, attached to one's tweets, including their tweet replies, and in their direct messages, and thus will be seen the most. This holds true across platforms: Instagram, Facebook, and so on limit how many profile photos are visible at one time. Though you might be able to scroll back through someone's previous profile photos on Facebook, only one photo is seen with regular commenting and engagement. Choosing one's profile photo can thus announce one's fandom and is a critical step in the development of that performed fandom. Other profile aspects can be included, but the photo is often the first cue about someone in these online spaces.

Photos can also be shared to individuals' social media platforms, beyond as a profile photo (Kofoed & Larsen, 2016). The profile photo is the first cue but is not the last chance for photographic fandom. Individuals who attend team games or other events (such as a championship parade) can snap photos and share those to their social media platforms. Thus, not just attending the event, but the sharing of that event allows for an individual to further adopt a team into their personal identity and sense of self.

Not only does photo-sharing about sports teams and their events allow for fans to identify with those teams, but it also facilitates connections and communication with other like-minded fans. A recent study investigated how fandom was expressed during the 2015 FIFA Women's World Cup (Toffoletti et al., 2019). Fans posting about the cup on Instagram used specific hashtags to drive conversation and create communities where they could not only share opinions about the sport, but also help to legitimate a women's sport. Thus, not only are individuals creating a sense of self through photo sharing in sports fandom, but they are also supporting the sports of interest. Building a community through shared photos helps individuals to not only engage with a sport, but to further see themselves as fans of the sport, the team(s), and the player(s).

Text-Based Expressions of Self-Presented Sports Fandom

Of course, photos are not the only vehicle for self-expression related to one's sports fandom. Across social platforms, individuals also have the ability to express their fandom through text-based posts and comments. This could include a caption on an Instagram post or stand-alone Facebook and Twitter posts. The words individuals choose to express their fandom are often just as revealing as the photos they choose to share (Walther, 2007). Word choice and word ordering may both offer insight into how an individual feels about a team, a player, or a league.

Posting about a team may take different forms. Consider the earlier example: A Lakers fan may be able to post about the team on their Facebook or Twitter. That same fan could reply to the Lakers' accounts more directly, including through tagging them or through a retweet of one of the Lakers' tweets. A fan might express excitement at a new season; concern about a player; disdain for a team's recent performance. In posting on one's own channels in particular, a fan can show their investment in a given team, all while contributing to their sense of self. Photos provide powerful self-presentation cues, but text-based posts can reveal even more information, especially about one's feelings.

Text-based information can also take the form of comments on other fans' posts. Research on fandom within popular music has explored how communities are able to form through commenting on a celebrity's posts (Bennett, 2014). Similar to how photo-based posts drew attention to the FIFA WWC, text-based posts can draw attention to celebrities, the issues they care about, and inspire community formation. Similar activities can occur via text-based posting in sports fandom.

Finding individuals with similar interests and investments in a team can further support one's fandom and how one presents online. An individual who posts in support of a team and then gets comments demonstrating more support should make that individual feel even stronger about the team (Walther et al., 2011). This is known as a *feedback loop* that supports *identity-shift*. In this, the selective self-presentation that has been enacted online is supported by further engagement from one's community and thus the self-identity created is shifted and/or cemented in place. If the same fan were to post about a team and receive *negative* feedback on the post, this may change the fan's strategy to posting as well as their relationship to the team.

Think about how a Cleveland Browns football fan might feel following the 2017–2018 season compared to the 2020–2021 season, and how these feelings would translate to posts and possible feedback loops. Prior to the 2020–2021 season, the Browns were mostly known as a losing team (Labbe, 2020), including a season that saw them lose all 16 possible games they played (the 2017–2018 season, McManamon, 2017). Individuals with their identity tied to being a Browns fan might have (rightly) had a difficult time expressing that fandom when there was not even one win to speak of. In continuing to lose, the Browns didn't offer fans much to express joy about, and thus what fans might have chosen to self-present in referral to their fandom would be difficult at best. The event they may have captured photos of and shared would have been the first ever 0–16 parade (Breech, 2018). Considering the feedback loop, too, Browns fans who posted about the team during the 2017–2018 season might have had negative aspects of the team and their support of the team reinforced. If you're a Browns fan when the team loses all 16 games, what does that say about you?

Fast-forward, now, to the 2020–2021 season. In the 2020–2021 season, the Browns played in their first AFC Divisional Round matchup since *1994* (Gribble, 2021). The divisional playoff followed a 12-win season, clearly an improvement over the 0 wins from just a few seasons before. Fans who strongly identified with the Browns may have had a vastly different posting experience: The Browns gave their fans a lot to talk about and a lot of potential photo opportunities that were not of a losing parade. What Browns fans were able to share in the 2020–2021 season likely led to more positive feelings about the team—again, the feedback loop here would solidify the positivity of the season as a whole. A Browns fan expressing their fandom on Facebook, for example, likely got a lot of positive support from other fans as well as outsiders who like an underdog story. This would reinforce the fan's feelings about both the team and themselves as a fan of that team.

Thus, in expressing fandom, individuals can have their fandom further supported – their identity can be shifted and solidified through what they post, including both text-based posts and photos that are shared. Together, cues from photos and text-based posts can inform us as to how dedicated an individual is, how deep their fandom goes. Yet, these posts alone are not the only cues we may have about one's fandom. Further cues may be inferred from the channels individuals choose to use and the perceived affordances of those channels.

Affordances for Selective Self-Presentation and Engagement

Social platforms have affordances that influence how users engage with each channel. An affordance of a technology is what it offers to the user; the term was originally coined to explain the complementary relationship between an object and an actor interacting with the object (Gibson, 1979). Different people may interact with different objects in different ways. While you may use a mug as a container for a hot drink, another person may use a mug as a paperweight. You experience the affordances of warmth and containment; another person takes advantage of the affordance of weight. Both uses are valid; they are also not mutually exclusive. It is simply up to you as an actor to interact with the object (mug) in whatever way seems most correct for you.

This translates to social media platforms and the uses they offer to their online users. When thinking about social media platforms, we can consider both *technological* affordances and *social* affordances (Wellman et al., 2003). A technological affordance is related to the technology specifically; what does the technology itself enable? Here, though, we will focus on social affordances: How different channels allow us to interact and connect with others in different ways (Wellman et al., 2003).

Fox and McEwan (2017) conceptualize social affordances of communication technology as *perceived* social affordances. This makes it clear that the affordance itself is up to the user of the technology; again, what is relevant and useful to you may not be as relevant to someone else. Therefore, as we consider the affordances that may help an individual build their selective self-presentation online, we are talking about perceived social affordances of a technology.

Affordances can be used both in the creation of one's online self as well as in how individuals engage with individual players and sports teams. We will thus break this section into affordances for selective self-presentation and affordances for fan engagement.

Affordances for Selective Self-Presentation

Editability. Social channels vary in the affordance of editability: How much one feels they can edit (or not) their social profiles (Fox & McEwan, 2017). Most social channels include a profile component. To be able to perform an authentic fandom for a team, you need to be able to edit your profile to reflect that fandom. Facebook is a highly editable platform: You can change your profile photo as well as your cover photo; you can update information related to your location, job, education, birthday, and contact information; you can post and edit posts after they have been published. Twitter affords editability differently; you can change your profile photo and cover photo, much like Facebook, and you can also edit your general information. But once a tweet is posted, you cannot edit the tweet. The only option is to delete the tweet and rewrite it. This also means you can't update a tweet that you posted when you were angry (like when a team was losing) after you get over it (the team comes back). Editability is critical for a fan to be able to express their fandom; without the opportunity to edit one's profile and content, the selective self-presentation cannot happen. Editability assumes the individual is an active part of the creation of their online identity.

Persistence. Social channels may or may not keep information available for long periods of time; the affordance of persistence is how long information stays on a website or social channel (Treem & Leonardi, 2013). Snapchat has less persistence than Facebook, for example. When you send a Snapchat to a friend, the photo disappears after they have opened it. If you send a text message within Snapchat, though, that may have greater persistence: You or your friend could choose to save the text chat for later. Once the text chat is saved, it lasts until one of you decides you do not need or want it anymore.

Facebook, on the other hand, automatically saves all of your posts and photos for as long as you leave them there. You can scroll back for years on Facebook, if you so choose (and maybe you have!). Facebook and Instagram can also remind you of their persistence with tools like "On This Day," where posts from years past on the same day are brought back up.

Persistence, then, can also help to solidify one's fandom. If you went to a baseball game for your favorite team four years ago, Instagram might remind you of that on the exact anniversary. You could then re-share that post, demonstrating the longevity of your fandom. If you are no longer a fan of that team, you may want to go back and delete the post, so no one else can see your previous support of that team. Persistence can be a hard affordance to manage in this way; sometimes, you want information to remain visible. But often, as we age and mature, our interests change and update. Thus, as a sports fan, you might need to revisit old posts and sometimes delete those posts, for the sake of consistency with the selective self you have chosen to craft and present.

Visibility. Similar to persistence is visibility. Social channels can make information visible or not; visibility refers to how much information about an individual is *readily* visible on the platform. You might think of visibility by answering this question: How easy is it to find information about someone? When information is hard to find, or when we perceive it is hard to find, we are less motivated to attempt to seek it out (Treem & Leonardi, 2013). What information is visible on social media? Social media helps us to make our preferences and behaviors visible. Information that we originally, in face-to-face settings, would have had to work hard to uncover and understand is now often readily posted on social channels. Thus, this is why visibility matters to presenting as a sports fan.

Say you are really active on a Miami Heat basketball fan page on Facebook. You post a lot of your own thoughts as well as commenting on others' posts. Visibility would first be you expressing your thoughts and feelings; those are readily available to others in the group. But others in the group might want to see more about you or understand why you care so much. They could click on your profile link and see more information about you that is readily visible. They could then see that you have lived in Miami your whole life, and thus further understand your investment in the team. These individuals don't have to work hard to find that information; instead, the profile and the channel hosting the profile make that information easily available for others to consume.

Anonymity. As you likely know, individuals do not have to be themselves online. Individuals can choose how anonymous they wish to be or not when they are online; someone could choose to be a blank slate or fully themselves (Fox & McEwan, 2017). Certain channels afford greater anonymity than others. On Twitter, you can be an egg profile photo, with a name that has no part of your real name. Your display name does not have to be your real name, and you do not need to include any highly personal information. Reddit is similar; you can customize your Reddit avatar, but it does not have to look like or reflect you at all. In this way, you could be anonymous on Twitter or Reddit if you so desired.

Facebook does not afford anonymity the way Reddit or Twitter do. You cannot have a fake name on Facebook; the platform continues to increase verification of who people are. You can limit information about yourself or choose photos that aren't of you, but key aspects of yourself have to be verified for you to be a Facebook user. It is much harder to pretend to be someone else or to be a blank slate on Facebook.

Thus, on Twitter, you can *only* be a fan of a team or player if that is what you wish to express. You do not have to use your real name ever; your Twitter handle might be "@ohiostatefan1991," and your display name could just read "Go Bucks." As discussed before, you could use a block O as your profile photo; you don't need a photo of yourself. Your location could be "The Shoe," the stadium where Ohio State plays. None of these pieces reveal information about you except your dedication to this team. You can be anonymous, or at least not your true self, and still be active on the site.

Personalization. Critical for selective self-presentation is the ability to personalize the channel, particularly one's profile on the channel. Combined with the visibility of information and the persistence of information, these pieces can work together to fully show a developed fandom identity. An editable channel needs to be editable in a way that you can make it your own. If you can't personalize, you cannot express your fandom. If you can only edit your name, age, and location, this does not necessarily give you a level of personalization that leads to fandom expressed. You need to be able to make the channel your own, whether through posts, photos, links, or however you want to express the fandom you are experiencing.

Affordances for Engagement with Others

Editability. Editability is critical not just for profile creation, but also for managing messages and comments on others' posts. Being able to edit means being able to take the time to consider what to say. Think of it like this: You can edit your photos and your posts so that they perfectly reflect who you are as a sports fan. When you comment on others' posts, then, you also need to be able to edit and to think about what you might say.

Perhaps you are a fan of a high-school baseball team. The team is close to you, the games are easy to go to, and so you find it easy to get invested. You might know a player or even be related to one. When the team is victorious, they post about it on Facebook. You can comment on their Facebook post to congratulate them or talk about their big win. Editability is the affordance at play here: You are able to think about how you might congratulate them and even type out different versions before posting. Do you go with a simple "Congratulations!" Maybe you want to call out a specific player who did well—you would erase the "Congratulations!" and edit that into a more personal comment. The channel allows you to edit before posting. On the flip of this, Facebook also allows you to edit after you have already posted. So, if you comment and spell something wrong, for instance, you can go back and fix your spelling mistake.

Some channels offer more editability in this way than others do. Once you reply to someone on Twitter, you cannot edit the message. If you make a typo when replying to the Lakers' Twitter, the typo is there forever, unless you delete the tweet and try again. Snapchat messages are not editable; once you have sent the message, it is out there. Editability is important for being able to send messages and write comments to others, but you have to consider *how much* editability is truly afforded by the channel when you engage in these kinds of posting behaviors.

Asynchrony. Asynchrony and editability go hand in hand. Asynchrony is how much time-shifting is possible within a channel (Giesbers, Rienties, Tempelaar, & Gijselaears, 2014). If you receive a message, is a response required immediately and in real time, or can you take time to respond? Face-to-face communication is typically synchronous: We expect that, when we talk in-person with someone else, we will respond to each other immediately. You can probably think of conversations where an extended pause was awkward or uncomfortable: That's because face-to-face contact affords us real-time responses and thus, we expect those responses. Social media channels, on the other hand, usually afford us *asynchrony*: We don't expect instant responses in most of those online channels.

You can see how editability and asynchrony go together: The more time you have to respond, the more you can edit. If you watch old highlight reels of your favorite sports team on YouTube and see someone comment something negative, you might get into a comment fight with them. The asynchronous nature of these fights means you can take time to write your comments and develop your argument. However, if you perceive that the person you are arguing with is waiting for you to respond or is typing faster than you, this may change your perception of asynchrony. You might start typing faster and editing less to get the next comment or word in—you might sacrifice your spelling or overall accuracy to be quicker.

Channels like Facebook, Twitter, and Instagram are generally asynchronous. You upload a post and wait for comments and likes to come in. You respond to them when you can, and no one has an expectation that you are immediately available to respond. Instant messenger is different: It's instant, and so we feel like responses should be quicker in this context. Chatting with a group of fans of your team in an online forum is more likely to be asynchronous than chatting with one of those fans in a direct message. Asynchrony is time-shifting; the immediateness of your response is dependent, in part, on whether the channel affords you this shifting.

Network association. Network association is how much you are able to access or otherwise find new network members through the social channel (Fox & McEwan, 2017). Are new people available to you? Network association often means seeing friends of friends through the given social channel. When you are on Facebook, you are recommended potential friends that you have not connected with. More often than not, these people are recommended because you already have a friend (or more!) in common. Twitter and Instagram both use similar principles: If you have a lot of followers in common with someone else, Twitter will probably recommend that you follow that person, and Instagram will recommend the same.

Network association can help you to find fans of your same team and sport, especially if you have overlaps in other areas of your life (such as work, school, or family members). Consider how network association might work if you move to a new city, for instance. Perhaps you moved for a job, and so your coworkers have added you on Facebook. You might try to find another fan of the Pittsburgh Steelers, so you have someone else to watch football games with. You can see if, in your new recommended friends, anyone has those obvious symbols of fandom we talked about earlier, such as a profile picture. You could then ask the mutual friend about that person and subsequently be connected with them. The association within your current network allows you to expand your network to include another fan, someone you can then express your fandom with.

Searchability. When connecting with other fans, the affordance of *searchability* is also important (Eismann, 2021). While network association might readily show you fans "near" your own network, not every person you might want to connect with is readily available in or near your network (you might not have shared friends, for example). Sometimes, you might want to search for someone to chat with about sports specifically; even more likely, you might search for your specific team or player. Social media that lets you search for other people and conversation topics is searchable (Zappavinga, 2015).

Facebook is searchable in that it allows you to search for potential friends as well as groups to join. A search for "Chicago Cubs" might not just present you with the team page, but also with groups you could join to talk about the team (like a "Cubs Fans Only" group). On the other hand, you might have a new coworker who is a Cubs fan, but no one else is friends with them on Facebook yet. You could search their name on Facebook, find them, and add them to start (or continue) your conversation about the Cubs.

Searchability on Twitter, though, is a little different. You could search for people or teams, but Twitter also utilizes hashtags (Zappavinga, 2015). As we mentioned earlier, hashtags were important for community formation and discussion around the FIFA WWC. Hashtags start with the # symbol before a word or phrase, like #gocubs. When you are on Twitter, every tweet that includes #gocubs will be grouped together. In this way, you can join a conversation about the Cubs without just having the ability to search for them, their players, or other fans. Twitter makes these conversations more visible to you and easier to join through this grouping.

Social presence. Social presence refers to whether or not you perceive other users as actually being present with you (Weidlich & Bastiaens, 2019). Does the channel allow you to feel like others are interacting with you? FaceTime might have more social presence than a tweet, for example. When you FaceTime with a friend, you can see their facial responses in addition to hearing what they are saying. You can see where they are, and you get real-time responses—so social presence is often perceived alongside synchrony. A tweet may feel more limited when it comes to social presence; unless you see the tweet posted in real time, you probably don't feel like the person is close to you or even currently online.

Social presence may encourage you to use certain channels more if you perceive that people are *with* you or approximating real-world contact. If you are watching a football game and commenting online, you are probably getting more enjoyment out of commenting if others are commenting back as the game goes. An especially exciting game is probably one you'd rather talk about more instantaneously with people you perceive as active on the channel—talking about a fumble hours after it happened is different than expressing and sharing feelings in the moment. You can probably think of times where this has happened; experiencing it in-game is very different from later on, when you know the outcome of the game.

Accessibility. The *accessibility* of a channel is essentially how easy it is to use that channel (Fox & McEwan, 2017). If you do not know how to use the channel or otherwise experience difficulty in finding it, none of the previous affordances matter much! To be able to build your selective self-presentation or to connect with other fans, you need to be able to access the channel.

Access can come in the form of where the channel is available: Do you access Facebook via your mobile phone or via a computer? If you don't have a desktop computer, Facebook remains accessible via the app option on your phone. If you don't have a phone, on the other hand, you could still access Facebook, Twitter, and Instagram through desktop versions. But without a phone, Snapchat becomes a lot harder to use. Accessibility is key for you to be able to pick and choose the channels where you post and connect with others. Imagine the online expression of your fandom if social media channels weren't available for you—you probably wouldn't express much online!

From this overview, you can hopefully see how social affordances of different channels can support the expression and development of fandom online. This is not an exhaustive list; other affordances exist, and you may have already thought of other ways that you use social media to build your online fan persona. Now that you have a general understanding of affordances, though, we can talk about not just the expression of fandom, but the development of relationships with players and teams virtually.

Parasocial Relationships with Players and Teams

Do you have a certain player that you follow on social media, regardless of what team they are on? Maybe you are a Cleveland Cavaliers fan who still follows LeBron James, despite his moves away from the team. Or maybe you can't get enough of Olympic gymnast Simone Biles and you're curious what her day-to-day is like. If you have a specific sports figure that you follow, you might have a *parasocial relationship* with that person (Dibble, Hartmann, & Rosaen, 2016). A parasocial relationship can occur when you develop an imaginary relationship with someone, typically a celebrity or other mediated persona, and then work to maintain that relationship—like continuing to follow them on social channels (Brown, 2015).

Horton and Wohl (1956) first proposed the idea of parasocial interactions and relationships, arguing that people felt like they got to know TV news broadcasters in the 1950s. This is because the same broadcasters were on at the same time every night, and there wasn't much media choice available at the time (no Twitter to check for news in the 1950s!). So, people who watched the evening news regularly could expect the same person to be talking to them, and it felt like a friend. Thinking about a sports figure that you follow now, maybe you feel similarly: You might open Instagram and expect a post from Tom Brady or an update from Tony Hawk. You have been given insight into their lives via social media, and you could come to expect more updates from them as a result.

Social media has furthered what could be considered a parasocial relationship. When Horton and Wohl (1956) were doing their research, it was hard to imagine a time when news broadcasters or any other celebrity figures could respond to their viewers and fans. Now, of course, we know that exactly that can happen. If you post an especially interesting tweet, there's a chance that

LeBron James could like it, retweet it, or even respond to it—you could have one of the biggest basketball stars respond directly to you! But this also begs a question: Because LeBron responded to you, does that mean that you two now have a relationship? Is there a connection between you and LeBron, maybe a friendship?

Unfortunately, that seems unlikely. Parasocial relationships were proposed as one-way relationships, with viewers having to do all of the relationship maintenance (Horton & Wohl, 1956; Horton & Strauss, 1957). And, just because you can get a response today, your relationship with any celebrity is probably still one-sided (Hartmann, 2008). That response to your tweet does not open an ongoing communication channel between you and LeBron (though you may wish it did!).

Thus, a parasocial relationship with a sports figure is still a one-way relationship, but it may be accentuated by the social media channels that you follow them on. You aren't limited to seeing Simone Biles on your TV or Francisco Lindor in a magazine spread. You may follow a sports figure who posts at a certain time every day or who goes live on Instagram with glimpses into their life or who posts insightful Twitter threads. Even though you don't know them, you might feel like you have a better understanding of their lives. You might really understand what it's like to be Tony Hawk—think of all the memes about his mistaken identity!

Your parasocial relationship may not be limited to a specific athlete, either. Many major league sports teams have social media channels that they post on. As different teams cultivate their voices and post, you might feel like you have a direct relationship with the team, too! In spring 2021, for instance, the Arizona Diamondbacks baseball team Twitter helped someone find his roommate during the game—and it turned out the roommate was on a first date (Marcus, 2021). The Diamondbacks Twitter helped keep the conversation going, even getting other Arizona teams to help with future dates. Using this opportunity, the Diamondbacks were able to hone their voice and likely start new relationships with a number of people. Even if you were a fan of a team across the country, you might have wondered what the Diamondbacks would do and say next!

Social media, through different affordances, allow fans the opportunity to develop relationships with players and teams beyond what many people would have ever thought possible. These relationships are one-sided, but they still exist. We should also ask: Just because a relationship is one-sided, does that mean it's bad? When thinking about parasocial relationships, the answer is: Not necessarily! Parasocial relationships can be good for those who engage in them (Hartmann, 2016). Creating bonds with teams and players could make for better experiences at games or in interactions with other fans. In research I have done, I have found that people with parasocial relationships feel less social anxiety as a result of having someone online to have a relationship with (Coduto, 2019). If you're thinking about your own parasocial relationships at this point, you should be thinking about the positives of them! Perhaps the next time you see your favorite team tweet, you'll engage with it, and then have a great experience at the next game you attend, too.

Parasocial Relationships, Affordances, and Online Fandom

Putting everything together, having a parasocial relationship with a certain athlete or team may further your own sense of fandom. Taking advantage of the affordances we talked about, you might connect with other fans as well as the players and teams themselves. A player liking your tweet may strengthen your performance of your fandom. A team sharing your photo on Facebook may strengthen your performance of fandom. The more you have your selective self-presentation confirmed by others, the more likely you are to continue to engage in those behaviors (Walther, 1996). If you have modeled yourself online as an Ohio State fan, every like related to that will tell you to continue performing that type of fandom. As you develop a parasocial relationship with Ohio State's online channels, you may feel even more solidified in the performance of that fandom.

As we said, this can have positive effects for you. It might help you have better real-life experiences with teams; it might also help you to find community online. The next time you go to edit your profile, take a minute to think about your fandom and how you are reflecting it. What affordances are you using? What are you saying about yourself with your profile? You might be surprised who you connect with next.

References

Bennett, L. (2014). Tracing textual poachers: Reflections on the development of fan studies and digital fandom. *The Journal of Fandom Studies*, 2(1), 5–20.

Breech, J. (2018, January 6). Look: The Browns 0-16 parade gets just as crazy as you thought it would. *CBS Sports*. Retrieved from www.cbssports.com/nfl/news/look-the-browns-0-16-parade-gets-just-as-crazy-as-you-thought-it-would/

Brown, W. J. (2015). Examining four processes of audience involvement with media personae: Transportation, parasocial interaction, identification, and worship. *Communication Theory*, 25, 259–283. https://doi.org/10.1111/comt.12053

Coduto, K. D. (2019, May 24–28). *Parasocial relationships with celebrities predict preference for online social interaction for socially anxious individuals* [Paper presentation]. International Communication Association 69th Annual Meeting, Washington, D.C., United States.

Dibble, J. L., Hartmann, T., & Rosaen, S. F. (2016). Parasocial interaction and parasocial relationship: Conceptual clarification and a critical assessment of measures. *Human Communication Research*, 42, 21–44. doi:10.1111/hcre.12063.

Eismann, K. (2021). Diffusion and persistence of false rumors in social media networks: Implications of searchability on rumor self-correction on Twitter. *Journal of Business Economics*. https://doi.org/10.1007/s11573-020-01022-9

Ellison, N. B., Heino, R. D., & Gibbs, J. L. (2006). Managing impressions online: Self-presentation processes in the online dating environment. *Journal of Computer-Mediated Communication*, 11, 415–441. https://doi.org/10.1111/j.1083-6101.2006.00020.x

Fox, J., & McEwan, B. (2017). Distinguishing technologies for social interaction: The perceived social affordances of communication channels scale. *Communication Monographs*, 84(3), 298–318. https://doi.org/10.1080/03637751.2017.1332418

Gibson, J. J. (1979). *The ecological approach to visual perception*. Boston, MA: Houghton Mifflin Harcourt.

Giesbers, B., Rienties, B., Tempelaar, D., & Gijselaers, W. (2014). A dynamic analysis of the interplay between asynchronous and synchronous communication in online learning: The impact of motivation. *Journal of Computer Assisted Learning*, 30(1), 30–50. https://doi.org/10.1111/jcal.12020

Gribble, A. (2021, January 17). Browns' comeback comes up short, memorable 2020 season comes to an end in Kansas City. *Cleveland Browns*. Retrieved from www.clevelandbrowns.com/news/browns-comeback-comes-up-short-memorable-2020-season-comes-to-an-end-in-kansas-c

Hartmann, T. (2008). Parasocial interactions and paracommunication with new media characters. In E. A. Konijn, S. Utz, M. Tanis, & S. Barnes (Eds.), *Mediated interpersonal communication* (pp. 177–199). Lawrence Erlbaum Associates.

Hartmann, T. (2016). Parasocial interaction, parasocial relationships, and well-being. In L. Reinecke & M. B. Oliver (Eds.), *The Routledge handbook of media use and well-being: International perspectives on theory and research on positive media effects* (pp. 131–144). Routledge/Taylor & Francis Group.

Horton, D., & Wohl, R. R. (1956). Mass communication and para-social interaction: Observations on intimacy at a distance. *Psychiatry: Interpersonal and Biological Processes*, 19, 215–229. doi:10.1080/00332747.1956.11023049

Horton, D., & Strauss, A. (1957). Interaction in audience participation shows. *The American Journal of Sociology*, 62(6), 579–587.

Heino, R. D., Ellison, N. B., & Gibbs, J. L. (2010). Relationshopping: Investigating the market metaphor in online dating. *Journal of Social and Personal Relationships*, 27(4), 427–447. https://doi.org/10.1177/0265407510361614

Kofoed, J., & Larsen, M. C. (2016). A snap of intimacy: Photo-sharing practices among young people on social media. *First Monday, 21*(11). https://doi.org/10.5210/fm.v21i11.6905

Labbe, D. (2020, January 2). Cleveland Browns 2019 season review: The defining moments, highlights and lowlights from all 16 games. *Cleveland.com*. Retrieved from www.cleveland.com/browns/2020/01/cleveland-browns-2019-season-review-the- defining-moments-highlights-and-lowlights-from-all-16-games.html

Marcus, R. (2021, May 6). YouTuber tracks friend's date at Arizona Diamondbacks game and captivates Twitter. *ESPN*. Retrieved from www.espn.com/mlb/story/_/id/31374830/youtuber-tracks-friend-date-arizona- diamondbacks-game-captivates-twitter

McManamon, P. (2017, December 31). Cleveland Browns make losing an art in forgettable 0-16 season. *ESPN*. Retrieved from www.espn.com/nfl/story/_/id/21926596/cleveland- browns-complete-0-16-season-forgettable-losers

Toffoletti, K., Pegoraro, A., & Comeau, G. S. (2019). Self-representations of women's sport fandom on Instagram at the 2015 FIFA Women's World Cup. *Communication & Sport,* OnlineFirst. https://doi.org/10.1177/2167479519893332

Treem, J. W., & Leonardi, P. M. (2013). Social media use in organizations: Exploring the affordances of visibility, editability, persistence, and association. *Annals of the International Communication Association, 36*(1), 143–189. https://doi.org/10.1080/23808985.2013.11679130

Walther, J. B. (1996). Computer-mediated communication: Impersonal, interpersonal, and hyperpersonal interaction. *Communication Research, 23*(3), 3–43. https://doi.org/10.1177/009365096023001001

Walther, J. B. (2007). Selective self-presentation in computer-mediated communication: Hyperpersonal dimensions of technology, language, and cognition. *Computers in Human Behavior, 23*(5), 2538–2557. https://doi.org/10.1016/j.chb.2006.05.002

Walther, J. B., Liang, Y. J., DeAndrea, D. C., Tong, S. T., Carr, C. T., Spottswood, E. L., & Amichai-Hamburger, Y. (2011). The effect of feedback on identity shift in computer- mediated communication. *Media Psychology, 14*(1), 1–26. https://doi.org/10.0180/15213269.2010.547832

Weidlich, J., & Bastiaens, T. J. (2019). Designing sociable online learning environments and enhancing social presence: An affordance enrichment approach. *Computers & Education, 142*. https://doi.org/10.1016/j.compedu.2019.103622

Wellman, B., Quan-Haase, A., Boase, J., Chen, W., Hampton, K., Diaz, I., & Miyata, K. (2003). The social affordances of the Internet for networked individualism. *Journal of Computer- Mediated Communication, 8*(3). https://doi.org/10.1111/j.1083-6101.2003.tb00216.x

Zappavigna, M. (2015). Searchable talk: The linguistic functions of hashtags. *Social Semiotics, 25*(3), 274–291. https://doi.org/10.1080/10350330.2014.996948

25
The Construction of Sports Fandom by Sports Betting Companies

Jason Kido Lopez

Sports fandom might seem to be obviously aligned with practices of sports betting, as in the case of a fan of the Los Angeles Dodgers placing a bet on them to win the championship. Yet there are also ways that the activities and interests of sports betting might contradict our assumptions about sports fandom, such as when sports bettors eschew fannish loyalty in order to root for their bets. This chapter explores the complex relationship between sports fandom and sports betting by investigating the corporations and digital platforms that facilitate gaming experiences for fans. Though the game of sports betting has certain general structures and common rules across its variations, it is important to think about the particularities of the contexts in which the games are played. In this way, betting on sports is just like any other engagement with sports in that it happens in a particular legal, economic, technical, and social context. To understand how people choose to express themselves, it is crucial to understand the possibilities that are allowed, encouraged, and foreclosed upon by those surrounding structures. In particular, this chapter analyzes how the game of sports betting is instantiated on the DraftKings and FanDuel websites. While there are many other opportunities to bet on sports (e.g., physical locations and other internet-based options) these two websites are popular and highly marketed avenues for American sports fans and bettors.

This research asks what specific fannish and gaming experiences are afforded and foreclosed upon by the game of sports betting offered by DraftKings and FanDuel. This chapter carries out a discursive interface analysis (Stanfill, 2015) of these two websites guided by Halverson and Halverson's (2008) notion of *competitive fandom*. Halverson and Halverson explore how this concept reveals a wide variety of fan and gaming engagements for fantasy sports, and this chapter will apply this framework to sports betting on DraftKings and FanDuel. While there are meaningful potential overlaps between sports fandom and sports betting, the websites of DraftKings and FanDuel also promote a kind of sports fan gaming experience that de-emphasizes fannish values such as community connection and team loyalty in favor of prioritizing the neoliberal values of capitalization and financial gain.

Conceptualizing Sports Betting

Sports betting cannot be understood in isolation from other games played around sports. In particular, sports betting, season-long fantasy sports, and daily fantasy sports have rich conceptual, historical, and industrial connections. At their most abstract, fantasy sports and sports betting both offer opportunities for fans and other interested parties to do more than watch sporting events; they organize play around them. As such, they can be conceived of as *second-order games* that are built upon a first-order sporting event or set of events. So, while it is conceptually possible to have the first-order sport without any second-order gaming, second-order games are logically dependent on first-order sporting events. Without them, there would be no second-order sports betting or fantasy play. It is not unhelpful to think about second-order games as gamifying sports. While there are many disagreements about the exact definition of what it means to *gamify* something or its usefulness as a concept (Bogost, 2014), and one could question whether it fully describes the relationship between the two orders of games, these second-order games do indeed make a game out of watching the first-order sport.

While sports betting usually focuses on the overall outcomes of the first-order event (like the final score) and fantasy tends to center around the performances of individual athletes (like which player scores), both games are built upon making predictions and then seeing whether those predictions are accurate. In this way, second-order games play with the epistemic uncertainty of the first-order sport. Though one could use methods of prediction that are random, like choosing based on a coin flip or jersey colors, it is possible for players to use information to overcome epistemic uncertainty to some degree. For this reason, these are information games (Scott, 1968), in which research and analysis constitute play. Second-order games are blends of *alea* (games of chance) and *agon* (games of skill). The former comes from the fact that players have no control over the events that play out in the first-order sport, and the latter from the research used to predict those events despite the lack of control.

While both games are second-order, predictive information games, their legal histories are very different despite being bound together. Second-order gaming on first-order sports is as old as first-order sports themselves; in any first-order competition it is pretty simple for two people to disagree about its results and place a wager. However, some began to worry as individuals and organizations began to profit from accepting bets from a betting public (the former sometimes called *bookmakers* or *bookies*, and the latter *sportsbooks*). Due to the perceptions that those with financial interests fixed games, and that betting brought an unruly and undesirable crowd to sporting events, sports betting was rendered illegal in most states. Sports leagues and media companies also distanced themselves from the game for similar reasons, and didn't acknowledge the largely illegal and yet vibrant betting communities organized around the sporting events they covered.

In this vacuum of legalized second-order gaming, sports fans organized a different game in the late twentieth century known as fantasy sports. Defined as "an interactive team management activity based on statistics accrued by athletes of real-life professional sports organizations and/or college athletics" (Ruihley & Hardin, 2011, p. 233), fantasy sports were largely a niche game reserved for superfans. Participating in early fantasy leagues involved doing research without fantasy-specific resources, and running a league demanded pouring over box scores to calculate fantasy results by pen and paper. As a consequence, it was extremely time consuming to play. However, the development of Web 2.0 allowed sports media companies to offer a more accessible fantasy product to sports fans. This was a profitable decision, as it was discovered that fantasy play increased interest and engagement with sports (Karg & McDonald, 2011; Randle & Nyland, 2008).

Gaming online caught the interest of lawmakers, however, as the same technology that afforded easy online fantasy play also enabled online poker games and betting with offshore sportsbooks. While the 1992 Professional and Amateur Sports Protection Act prohibited states from legalizing sports betting, it was the 2006 Unlawful Internet Gambling Enforcement Act that banned online sports betting and poker in states in which the games were illegal. Yet it also explicitly stated that wagering on fantasy was exempt from this prohibition. If the purpose of the legislation was to protect people from the supposed ills of betting, fantasy represented a lesser threat than sports betting or poker. These games, due to their accessibility and speed, allowed the possibility for players to lose money consistently and quickly. Fantasy was a slower, season-long competition in which the opportunities to play were usually restricted by how many other willing players could be found in one's social circle.

Yet a loophole in this legislation was quickly identified; if playing fantasy sports for money was permitted, the only thing stopping a company from significantly profiting off that play is how often people can play and place bets. On this principle, daily fantasy sports (DFS) were born. Startups including DraftKings and FanDuel offered a fantasy betting game that lasted anywhere from a week to an afternoon. With classic sports betting being largely illegal, DFS became a craze that was visible in a flurry of marketing for DraftKings and FanDuel. In response, some states moved quickly to pass their own legislation prohibiting DFS. This led the companies to surveil their players to make sure they are playing in states that permit DFS play (Lopez, 2018).

In 2018, the federal government overthrew the Professional and Amateur Sports Protection Act, thereby allowing any state to decide for itself whether to legalize sports betting. States with heavy casino presences, like New Jersey, already had structures in place to get sports betting up and running. However, not all states had these facilities. With considerable economic and technological resources at their disposal, DraftKings and FanDuel were quick to enter the betting market. As of 2021, both companies run branded physical sportsbooks and offer online versions of their games through websites and mobile applications in states that have legalized sports betting. Just as with their DFS products years earlier, these two companies popularize their games through partnerships with sports media companies and sports leagues. Due partially to the effort of companies like this, sports betting is coming out of the shadows and becoming more and more popular (Purdum, 2020; Silverman, 2019).

Competitive Fandom and DFS

Although sports betting predates fantasy sports, there has been considerably more academic research on fantasy sports due to the fantasy boom of the 2000s. A useful framework that emerged from the research on fantasy sports is Halverson and Halverson's (2008) conception of *competitive fandom*, as it can be used to analyze the way that sports fans engage with DraftKings' and FanDuel's websites. Competitive fandom involves two modes of engagement: as a fan and as a gamer. Relying on the work on fandom by media and cultural studies scholars, Halverson and Halverson (2008) note the dual planes of activities of *fans*: the consumptive and the productive (p. 292). The consumptive realm involves regular engagement with the fan object, and the subsequent obtaining of knowledge about that object. The familiarity with the first plane allows fans to participate in the second: to produce media and engage with fan cultures. Examples of this plane are making mashup media and fanfiction (Halverson & Halverson, 2008, p. 293). Both planes are found in fantasy: fans gain knowledge through media consumption and then use that knowledge to construct a fantasy team. Competitive fandom is more than just fan expression, though; it is fan expression through *gaming*. Because they are games, fantasy sports consist of artificial rules that lead to quantifiable outcomes (Halverson & Halverson, 2008, p. 294). In the context of competitive fandom, these structures are used to determine who knows more about the fan object. For many fantasy sports, this involves an element of role-play in which fan knowledge is expressed by pretending to be a team franchise owner, general manager, or head coach. By drafting a hypothetical team, players partake in the *fantasy* of fantasy sports.

It is crucial to acknowledge that not every fantasy player is interested in competitive fandom. While some players might be fans of the first-order sport and interested in proving their skills through gamified role-play, not all engage in the same way. For this reason, Halverson and Halverson (2008) provide a framework that organizes reasons for player engagement. While it is probably most accurate to think of this framework as a scale, we can roughly organize fantasy players into four categories that relate to the two conditions of competitive fandom:

1. High fandom/high gaming: This is the realm of competitive fandom. Any gamer who falls in this category is a fan of the sport and interested in proving it through the role-playing game of fantasy.
2. High fandom/low gaming: A fantasy player in this category plays fantasy, but does so without much interest in the second-order game. These players prefer to keep their fandom of the first-order sport at the forefront, and don't engage with game as much as those in either of the high gaming groups.
3. Low fandom/high gaming: These are people who like gaming, and happen to find an opportunity in fantasy sports. These players are not attached to sports in a fannish way, and yet still compete in the second-order game.
4. Low fandom/low gaming: These would be people who aren't interested in either aspect of the game and yet play it anyway. Halverson and Halverson's (2008) study didn't interview any subjects who put themselves in this category. The reason is fairly obvious; if you don't care much about sports and gaming, fantasy sports' demand that players regularly engage with the game over an entire sports leagues' season would be formidable. However, the possibility remains that people who aren't fans and aren't drawn to gaming might still play fantasy for other reasons.

Competitive fandom, therefore, does more than explicate a particular way of engaging with the game of fantasy sports, it reveals a wider framework of motivation for fantasy play. While Halverson and Halverson (2008) use interviews to substantiate their claims, it is important to note that their way of conceiving of how fans and non-fans engage with the game of fantasy is born out of connecting theories about fandom and gaming to the particular rules and structures of the game of fantasy sports. That is, the game of season-long fantasy sports affords a particular set of fan and gaming experiences. We can use these structures to study other games like DFS and sports betting.

DFS represents a conceptual middle-ground between season-long fantasy and sports betting. While both DFS and season-long fantasy involve roster building (and therefore some degree of fantasy role-play), DFS shares certain qualities with sports betting as well. First, even though DraftKings and FanDuel allow its users to make and invite friends, the majority of games are played against strangers (sometimes numbering in the thousands). So, while those in the two high gaming categories might still be interested in challenging others through DFS, it is usually expressed differently than in season-long. The number of competitors lessens the possibility for community building; a DFS players will know few, if any, of those they play against. For this reason, DFS players' decisions are made in a vacuum, independent of engagement with other players. So, despite (usually) playing massively multiplayer games, DFS players choose their own team and then see how their choices compare to unknown others who made their decisions in an identical vacuum. This differs greatly from the friendships and community often found around season-long fantasy (Serazio, 2008).

DFS's focus on money also helps us better understand sports betting. While it is possible to play DFS without risking money, the vast majority of games involve financial risk. In examining the web interface of DraftKings and FanDuel DFS, we see that a principle way of organizing the games is through money (Lopez, 2018, p. 304). One can sort and search based on how much money players can win and, more importantly, how much it costs to play. The latter is crucial, of course, as some players cannot or will not pay the entry fee for particular contests (sometimes thousands of dollars). The design of these virtual platforms emphasizes the role of financial risk that marks engagements with DFS. That isn't to say that season-long fantasy players don't risk money, or that it isn't gambling; they do and it is (Bernhard & Eade, 2005). DFS, however, foregrounds financial capital.

This focus on money opens up a possible engagement that season-long fantasy sports cannot support: professionalization. Professionals might be fans of the sports they play and therefore engage in competitive fandom. However, with the potential ability to accrue regular financial profits from play, those in the high gaming categories can be drawn to it. During the DFS boom, think pieces about professional DFS players were common (e.g., Bales, 2013; Lewak, 2014). Discourse from this kind of journalism painted a picture of data-driven, Excel sheet wielding, number-crunching mathematicians. While personal fandoms might be mentioned, it was clear that the competition and the desire to profit from it drove these players. This is an expression of low fandom/high gaming more novel to DFS. While season-long players might be driven to win money and use data in that pursuit, the fact that DFS affords people an opportunity to make a living can completely remove DFS play from the realm of playful expression of fan knowledge. The competitive gaming becomes work in these cases.

Sports Betting, Fandom, and Competition

We are now in a position to see how applying Halverson and Halverson's (2008) fan/gaming framework to an interface analysis (Stanfill, 2015) of the DraftKings and FanDuel websites reveals specific forms of engagement. In particular, we will view the websites' "interfaces as both reflecting social logics and non-deterministically reinforcing them" (Stanfill, 2015, p. 1060). While fans and gamers can play through the websites in a multitude of ways, there is "unequal power between industry and site visitors" (Stanfill, 2015, p. 1062), and that power differential shapes norms and expectations of the game. The interface analysis below will attend to how the websites shape the fan/gaming framework from Halverson and Halverson (2008), and explore the wider ideologies novel to this particular second-order game.

To start, the game of sports betting is usually composed of discrete decisions the player can make. These are normally based around the results of a particular first-order competitive event. While the terms can change greatly depending on the first-order sporting event, the most common bets offered usually revolve around choosing which competitor will win or how many total points will be scored by both competitors combined. The bettor chooses from a menu of bets laid out by the gaming companies. This means that the game consists of two main decisions: which bets to select and how much money to wager. Money, therefore, is not an incidental add-on to the game (as it is with season-long fantasy sports) and is not simply foregrounded on the website (as it is with DFS). Money is an essential component to the game; without money there is no sports betting. While the companies determine maximum and minimum bet amounts, and while the bettors must limit their wagers to the pre-established menu, we will see that the games allow for a great diversity of play.

The front pages of DraftKings and FanDuel lead straight to the game. DraftKings put opportunities to bet on games currently happening as their frontpage content, and FanDuel highlighted games popular with American sports fans (e.g., college football on a Saturday). While these bets were based on a fairly limited number of first-order sporting events, the front material also displayed a very diverse selection of other first-order competitions. Both websites provide a hyperlinked list of sports in a sidebar on the left side of the page. Some are popular with American fans (like basketball, football, and mixed martial arts), but others are less so (like Australian-rules football, cricket, cycling, and darts). By selecting one of these sports, the user gets taken to a page that offers a list of different leagues running that first-order game. For example, selecting "soccer" on a weekend filled with soccer games leads users to a page in which it is possible to choose between different countries and leagues; FanDuel, for instance, had 22 countries and a few leagues and cups listed (like the Champions League and Copa America). Clicking on the countries reveals the leagues running within it (e.g., both sites had four leagues and cups listed for British soccer). Popular American sports leagues, like the National Football League, NCAA football and basketball, Major League Baseball, and the National Basketball Association, got their own links. Both of the sites are almost exclusively text and hyperlinks, offering lists of possible bets and links between bet menus.

Another major component of DraftKings and FanDuel's online sports betting product is their promotions. Like the specific bets offered, the details of the promotions change depending on the first-order sport they are based around. However, despite this, some general observations can be made. First, the promotions are ways to highlight certain kinds of bets. The first way this is done is through advertising the bets. These are basically intra-site banner ads that, when selected, lead to a special page that lists these bets. Second, these bets almost always change the terms of the bet to the bettor's favor. They commonly offer "insurance" on particular bets (in which, if the bet is lost, the bettor's money is partially or fully returned) or boosts to the amount of money the bettor could win.

The competition of the game appears to be between the bettor and the gaming companies; the possible bets are set by the companies, and the bettors wager their money against the companies'. This differs greatly from the DFS products offered by DraftKings and FanDuel, in which players compete directly against each other and their wagered money is distributed to the winners (with a service fee taken out by the companies). For sports betting, no other bettors are represented; there is only the individual bettor and that bettor's bets. While this has important consequences for bettors, the impression that the game is a one-player game or a two-party game (the players vs. the sportsbook) is misleading. Instead, sports betting must be recognized as a massively multi-player game. The terms of the bets are, at the end of the day, selected by the gaming companies, but sportsbooks use information generated by their other players and available from other books to set their bets. There is an entire betting market because skilled bettors will shop between sportsbooks for the best betting terms. Sportsbooks, therefore, have to shift with the way the markets move in order to avoid being taken advantage of by savvy bettors. This means the play on DraftKings and FanDuel for each individual bettor has been determined by a host of other entities: other bettors on their websites, other bettors on other websites, and other sports betting companies. While it might appear to bettors they are making their bets in a vacuum, they are actually partaking in an entire ecosystem which shapes the very nature of the game.

When viewed from Halverson and Halverson's (2008) fan/gaming framework, these details from the interface analysis of DraftKings and FanDuel allow for comparative examination of fantasy sports and sports betting. To start, while fan expression and competition usually happens around communities of people who know each other in season-long fantasy, and while DFS allows for friending and competing against other players, the game of sports betting as offered on DraftKings and FanDuel doesn't allow for direct, interpersonal competition. Despite the fact that players are involved in a vast, multi-player game/economy, their play through the websites is completely solitary. Of course, one could play with others by having a joint account or pooling money, but the design of the sites themselves forecloses upon interpersonal interaction through the game. This means that the communities established around fandom and gaming are disallowed in sports betting.

The game's structures also have profound implications for those interested in competitive fandom. On this front, we see opportunities very similar to DFS and season-long fantasy. Like both of these games, the information-based competition rewards fans' knowledge of their object of fandom. Good bettors use information gleaned from their fandom to predict the results of first-order sporting events. Yet there is one major difference between this expression of fandom and fantasy's: it doesn't operate through role-playing. As we saw above, fantasy allows sports fans to pretend to be in certain sports roles: managers, coaches, and so on. These games allow fans to explore, at least in their minds, whether they have the knowledge actually to participate in their object of fandom. This is different from sports betting, as there is no role in sports or the sporting industry akin to the sports bettor. While similar analytic predictions might be used by sports teams and sports bettors, there is no role to play for the sports bettor.

If fans are not demonstrating their knowledge through building fake rosters and teams, the novelty of sports fan expression comes mainly in the kind of predictions used to play the game and how the game is represented. Again, while noting that there is an incredible diversity of bets, on the whole they are really simple decisions: will team X or Y win, or will more or less than Z points be scored? Bettors who make these choices can use all sorts of information and analytics to win their games. Like both varieties of fantasy, sports betting allows sports fans the opportunity to use their engagement with and knowledge of their fan object to demonstrate their knowledge through competition. As noted above, within the game itself there are no other players represented, so this demonstration can't be for the other players also playing on DraftKings and FanDuel. Despite lacking this in-game communal experience, knowledge is rewarded through competition in sports betting.

This aspect of the game has similar effects on the high fandom/low gaming and low fandom/high gaming groups. Because those in the low fandom/high gaming category aren't as interested in demonstrating their fan knowledge, the distance from the other players in sports betting is irrelevant or even desirable. Sports betting allows for those interested in information games and/or winning money to play in a vacuum, and put fandom aside. On the other hand, it also allows those in high fandom/low gaming category to use the game to support and identify with their team further. As sports fandom is a matter of constructing personal identity by connecting oneself with one's fan object (Sandvoss, 2003), putting money on one's team gives a further reason to attach oneself to the outcome of a first-order sporting event. This can happen through fantasy sports as well (players can try to draft players from their favorite team, for instance), but betting on one's favorite competitor *directly* aligns one's rooting interests with one's gaming/financial interests.

Finally, the betting products offered by DraftKings and FanDuel also offer novel possibilities in the low fandom/low gaming category. The time commitment of season-long fantasy might make those in this category less likely to play. Furthermore, that both season-long and daily fantasy revolve around knowing a host of individual players might make the barriers to entry too rigorous for more casual fans. However, the simplicity of the game of sports betting results in a much less intimidating game. Even though the game is incredibly difficult, the websites represent it as simply as possible. It is easy to locate a first-order sport (or have one suggested), choose one of the possible bets, and decide how much money to wager. While there are certainly aspects of the game that will not be apparent to the novice bettor/fan (e.g., why one might have to wager $110 to win $100), the discrete, menu-like construction of the game makes for simple play.

If these potential bettors are neither fans nor gamers, the incentives must be clearly communicated by the companies seeking to draw in participants. For sports betting, the apparently simple 50/50 odds of winning most bets could seem like an easy way towards financial gain. Despite the fact that the companies profit from making the odds steeper than 50 percent, the game is often presented as a coin flip: either Competitor A wins or loses. Furthermore, recall the roles of promotions in these websites. These are designed to increase traffic and engagement with the game. For those in the low fandom/low gaming category (and for the high fandom/low gaming group as well), these promos are meant to make the game seem even less intimidating by reducing risk or increasing the benefits of winning.

In all, the sports betting game as offered by DraftKings and FanDuel allows for the kinds of fandom and gaming expressions as outlined by the fan/gaming framework, but with their own particularities due to the construction of the game.

1. High fandom/high gaming: Competitive fandom is allowed, but without the role-playing and community of season-long fantasy.
2. High fandom/low gaming: Fans less interested in the gaming component can easily match up their fannish rooting interests with their financial interests by betting on their favorite team. The wide selection of possible events to bet on gives many opportunities for these kinds of bets.
3. Low fandom/high gaming: Gamers who are uninterested in fandom, but who are out to compete or make money, could treat the game as an information-crunching pastime or job. Rather than competing against other individuals, the game is represented as being between the player and the game companies.
4. Low fandom/low gaming: Those uninterested in competition or fandom might still try to make money through the apparent simplicity and approachability of the game. It is easy to find the sites, deposit money, and play. The promotional bets add to the approachability.

Second-order gaming, in general, affords fans and non-fans the opportunity to play with their connection to sports, and the sports betting game offered by DraftKings and FanDuel affords its own possible engagements due to the particularities of the game. The focus on money, the invisibility of other players, and the relative ease of entry into the game all construct a set of novel possibilities for fans and gamers.

These unique components of the game support ideologies particular to sports betting. The idea that it is possible for individuals, all on their own, to find financial success supports the neoliberal good of "liberating individual entrepreneurial freedoms and skills within an institutional framework" (Harvey, 2007, p. 2). In this case, fandom and even play can get reduced to a set of potentially profitable financial decisions made by an atomic individual. The games, therefore, are an instantiation of a general tenant of neoliberalism to "bring all human action into the domain of the market" (Harvey, 2007, p. 3). In this case fan knowledge, production, and gaming are subsumed under the wider neoliberal ideologies.

Second-order connection to sports is reoriented away from community-based role-playing fandom and towards an individualistic money-making venture. While it again is important to recognize that not every sports bettor plays in this way, it should also be understood this novel engagement encouraged by DraftKings' and FanDuel's betting games. In this way, this chapter adds to work analyzing the ideological possibilities of first-order sport and second-order games, and the spectrum of ways that neoliberalism can be expressed through and around sports (Andrews, 2012).

Conclusion: Competitive Fandom in the Sports Media Complex

This analysis of the websites of DraftKings and FanDuel doesn't tell us about the individual motivations for any particular fan or gamer to play these games. However, fandom and gaming always occur in a particular context and, in the contemporary sports and sports media world, this context is often partially determined by media and gaming companies that have the resources to build opportunities for fan expression and/or play. This calls for a sensitivity to the institutional and mediated structures built around fandom and gaming cultures. In this case, this involves an examination of the construction of the game of sports betting and a comparative analysis to other forms of second-order gaming around sports.

Season-long fantasy, DFS, and sports betting all encourage engagement with sports in a similar way; they allow fans to demonstrate their fan knowledge through competition and allow gamers to play a second-order, information-based prediction game. All three games afford a diverse array of possible gaming and fannish engagements with first-order sports, and the game of sports betting on DraftKings and FanDuel afford novel expressions of those engagements. The framework above helps us understand how and why sports betting, more so than DFS and season-long fantasy, simultaneously affords high-level, professional play and more mundane interactions with the game as a player and/or fan. It also, and again unlike both fantasy games, forecloses upon community building through the game itself. These novelties situate fandom and gaming within neoliberal ideologies: the game becomes a market in which an atomic individual can find financial success through skill and hard work.

These insights generated from the application of Halverson and Halverson's (2008) framework to the DraftKings and FanDuel websites hopefully lay the ground for future research on the intersection of fandom and gaming broadly, but also on the particularities of second-order games. This chapter demonstrates that the framework's dual planes of activity give structure to an analysis of how sites like DraftKings and FanDuel shape fandom, play, and their interplay. In a similar vein, it would be worthwhile to consider how the particular context of play on other platforms (e.g., mobile applications), other websites (e.g., offshore sportsbooks), other modalities (e.g., physical sportsbooks), and other second-order games (e.g., March Madness brackets) all shift the interplay of fandom and gaming in novel ways.

References

Andrews, D. (2012). *Sports and Neoliberalism: Politics, Consumption, and Culture*. Philadelphia: Temple University Press.
Bales, J. (2013). Here's What it Takes to Make a Living Playing Fantasy Sports. BusinessInsider.com. www.businessinsider.com/how-pros-play-fantasy-sports-2013-11
Bernhard, B. & Eade, V. (2005). Gambling in a Fantasy World: An Exploratory Study of Rotisserie Baseball Games. *UNLV Gaming Research & Review Journal*, 9(1), 29–42.
Bogost, I. (2014). Why Gamification is Bullshit. In S. Walz & S. Deterding (Eds.), *The Gameful World: Approaches, Issues, Applications* (pp. 65–80). Cambridge: MIT Press.
Halverson, E. & Halverson, R. (2008). Fantasy Baseball: The Case for Competitive Fandom. *Games and Culture*, 3(3–4), 286–308.
Harvey, D. (2007). *A Brief History of Neoliberalism*. Oxford: Oxford University Press.
Karg, A. & McDonald, H. (2011). Fantasy Sport Participation as a Compliment to Traditional Sport Consumption. *Sport Management Review*, 14, 327–346.

Lewak, D. (2014). The Men Who Make 6 Figures Off Fantasy Football. *Nypost.com*. https://nypost.com/2014/11/20/meet-the-men-who-make-a-luxe-living-off-fantasy-football/

Lopez, J. (2018). DraftKings: Daily Fantasy Sports Leagues, Legality, and Shifting Mobile Spaces. In J. Morris and S. Murray (Eds.), *Appified: Culture in the Age of Apps* (pp. 299–207). Ann Arbor: University of Michigan Press.

Purdum, D. (2020). Sports Betting's Growth in U.S. 'Extraordinary'. *ESPN.com*. www.espn.com/chalk/story/_/id/29174799/sports-betting-growth-us-extraordinary

Randle, Q. & Nyland, R. (2008). Participation in Internet Fantasy Sports Leagues and Mass Media Use. *Journal of Website Promotion*, 3(3/4), 143–152.

Ruihley, B., & Hardin, R. (2011). Message Boards and the Fantasy Sports Experience. *International Journal of Sport Communication*, 4, 233–252.

Sandvoss, C. (2003). *A Game of Two Halves: Football Fandom, Television and Globalization*. New York: Routledge.

Scott, M. (1968). *The Racing Game*. Chicago: The Aldine Publishing Company.

Serazio, M. (2008). Virtual Sports Consumption, Authentic Brotherhood: The Reality of Fantasy Football. In L. Hugenberg, P. Haridakis, & A. Earneardt (Eds.), *Sports Mania: Essays on Fandom and the Media in the 21st Century* (pp. 229–242). Jefferson, North Carolina: McFarland & Company, Inc., Publishers.

Silverman, S. (2019). Legalized Sports Gambling Passes $10 Billion, Likely Just Tip of the Iceberg. *Forbes.com*. www.forbes.com/sites/stevesilverman/2019/08/29/legalized-sports-gambling-passes-10-billion-likely-just-tip-of-the-iceberg/?sh=62774c31c223

Stanfill, Mel. (2015). The Interface as Discourse: The Production of Norms through Web Design. *New Media and Society*, 17(7), 1059–1074.

26
Fandom in the Realm of Fantasy Sport

Brody J. Ruihley and Robin Hardin

Introduction

Fantasy sport is an interactive team or athlete management activity utilizing player statistics from actual competitions as individuals compete against one another (Ruihley & Hardin, 2011). This once niche activity has now carved out a significant place with sport fans and has firmly entrenched itself into the fabric of sport in the United States. Participation in fantasy sport in the United States and Canada has seen annual increases during the past two decades, as the number of participants has grown from less than one million in the mid-1990s to 59.3 million by 2019 (Fantasy Sports & Gaming Association, 2020). Many developments led to this dramatic increase in fantasy sport participation including, but not limited to (a) technological advancements, (b) inclusion and acceptance of fantasy sport information in mainstream sport media, and (c) the explosion of daily fantasy sport competition (Billings & Ruihley, 2014; Billings, Ruihley, & Yang, 2017; Weiner & Dwyer, 2017).

As a major development worldwide, technology advancements have influenced sport media consumption in a variety of facets and the continued growth in fantasy sport participation is just one of the impacts of this. Thanks to the fertile environment of the World Wide Web, many of the top sporting news organizations (i.e., ESPN, CBS Sports, CNNSI), as well as professional sport organizations such as the National Football League (NFL), Major League Baseball (MLB), Professional Golfers' Association Tour (PGA), offer opportunities to participate in fantasy sport leagues and competitions. The influx of available statistics and analytics, which is at the core of fantasy sport participation, has aided tremendously in the growth of fantasy sport participation. The ease at which fantasy sport can be consumed and used via smartphone and tablets has drastically raised convenience. In fact, when asked by Ruihley and Billings (2019), ESPN's Kevin Ota confirmed a report about fantasy sport use on mobile devices. Previous estimates showed an 80/20 mobile-to-desktop percentage split, Ota claimed the figured to be closer to a percentage of 88/12.

A second major development revolves entirely around information acceptance and accessibility. Providing the means to participate is one important aspect, but also delivering *the information necessary* for success is a perfect combination for many of the media outlets. As outlined further in this chapter, it is quite common to have a host like ESPN or Yahoo! provide the platform for the game, offer fantasy sport updates on fantasy-specific and non-fantasy-based shows, and have expert opinion and advice readily available in regard to the potential top fantasy sports performers in a specific competition. The type of information needed for fantasy sport users is deep and wide – meaning that the analysis is statistically detailed, containing many data points, and cutting across a variety of sports with many athletes.

Daily fantasy sport (DFS) is a third major development shaping the fantasy sport experience. DFS is an accelerated version of traditional fantasy sports held over short time periods such as a single-day competition rather than during the course of the entire season. DFS is typically structured in the form of paid competitions, thus providing a unique way to gamble on live-sporting contests. In 2015, DFS companies, FanDuel and DraftKings, lit the sports world on fire with a barrage of advertisements highlighting daily fantasy contests. With the promotion of competition and the chance at large monetary prizes, the attention on the activity quickly turned to legality. During the course of the next three years, the (then named) Fantasy Sports Trade Association fought state by state seeking allowance of the activity. Their efforts are ongoing, but have been successful, as favorable state legislation is forming in many regions. Even with the recent development and legalization of state-specific sports betting and continued legal push for DFS play, the popularity of DFS continues to climb and bolster an already booming fantasy sport industry.

Technology advancements, acceptance and consumption of fantasy sport information, and the increased attention to the activity have all aided in the growth of the fantasy sport phenomenon and led to the creation of a different type of sports fan. This fan may be concerned with what team wins a sporting contest, but they are equally as interested in which player rushes for 100 yards, scores a touchdown, hits five three-pointers, grabs 12 rebounds, strikes out 10 batters, or scores a hockey goal. They are concerned with statistics, analytics, and individual performance. They are playing games within the game (Billings & Ruihley, 2014). This has led to the development of an amplified fan known as a fantasy sport user. Joining aspects of competition, sport knowledge, and socialization into one activity, fantasy sport activities have created sport fans that are informed, attentive, dedicated, social, and competitive. Fantasy sport users control their own rosters and simply participating does not require much effort or knowledge. But to be competitive, having knowledge of the sport, the athletes involved, matchups, and trends is crucial. Part of this knowledge concerns player or team statistics because knowing the finer points of player and team performance is vital when analyzing roster adjustments or player selection strategies. Fantasy sport users are actively seeking information, spending more than 20 hours per week devoted to sports consumption (Billings & Ruihley, 2020), and gathering information from a variety of channels including social media, website/app usage, television, and podcasts (Bell & Ruihley, 2019). This is a unique and coveted type of fan. With that, this chapter examines fantasy sport user fandom addressing motivations of the fantasy sport participant, media consumption, fantasy-sport-based media offerings, and the fantasy sport industry. Examining the fantasy sport user, as a segment of the sport consumer population, is valuable and imperative to sport-media and sport-information-based organizations.

Motivation for Play

Examining motivation for fandom, sport viewing, and sport participation has led to many findings that have contributed greatly in understanding more about sport-specific fandom and consumption. Wann, Grieve, Zapalac, and Pease (2008) stated that learning more about spectator and fan motivation can be viewed as a "psychographic segmentation method that can result in more effective marketing campaigns" (p. 7). This can then lead to effectively reaching constituents and creating specific campaigns that could ultimately drive attendance and consumption (p. 17). Understanding sport fan motivation has been an important foundation for many subsequent research findings expanding to traditional and new forms of communication technology. Heavily cited, Wann's (1995) sport fan motivation scale outlined many areas of sport fandom. Outlined in his work were motivational areas of eustress, self-esteem benefits, escape, entertainment, economic, aesthetic, group affiliation, and family needs. These findings help explain many of the motives that fantasy sport users tend to possess.

While difficult to imagine in today's sport media climate, Gantz (1981) examined motivation and behavior associated with televised sport as a response to sports programming expanding to "prime time as well as afternoons, weekdays as well as weekends, all year round" (p. 263). There is even mention of a new network, ESPN, offering "hours of sports daily" (p. 263). In this work, underlying motivations were labeled as four dimensions: (1) to thrill in victory, (2) to let loose, (3) to learn, and (4) to pass time. Gantz continues, and in an odd appropriateness to the fantasy sport context, states that among the motives, "there should be the anticipation of the intrinsic, transitory experiences associated with exposure and fantasy participation in the game or activity broadcast" (p. 264). Gantz and Wenner's (1995) further exploration of fanship and television viewing led to their emphasizing the "fan" in the word fanatic. Their "findings... speak to the term fan as a derivative of fanatic. Compared to... nonfans, fans were clearly more intense and enthusiastic, certainly not 'couch potatoes' who passively watch one game after another" (Gantz & Wenner, 1995, p. 70). They go on to say that fans were clearly more invested, involved, responsive, emotional, prepared, and expressive than the non-fan counterparts." Watching televised sports for nonfans "appears to be an activity engaged in without much passion or zeal, an activity that, when over, is easily discarded for the next activity on the agenda" (Gantz & Wenner, 1995, p. 70). Expanding on this idea of preparing for and exiting a sport event, Gantz et al. (2006) state that "sports fans are strikingly different from all other types of fans in their pre-viewing and post-viewing behaviors [as they] stretch out rituals associated with viewing sports as long as possible" (p. 114). Additional discovery and discussion align well with the forthcoming motives for fantasy play, with this statement on sport fans:

> They begin early, thinking about an upcoming game, searching for information about it on the Web and in print, talking about it with their friends, and planning their schedules so as not to miss any of the action. Even after the game ends, the game continues to play an important role in the sports fan's media diet. Sports fans watch news and recap programs and read about the outcome on the Web and in print. Unlike any other type of fan, sports fans relive the game again and again.
>
> *Gantz, et al., 2006, p. 114*

Research on sport participation and commitment to sport have important connections to fantasy sport play. Examining sport enjoyment, Scanlan et al. (1993a) identified several factors including perceived ability, sport enjoyment, positive team interactions and support, positive parental involvement, effort and mastery, and positive coach support and satisfaction. The Sport Commitment Model (Scanlan et al., 1993b) was created to help determine athletes' continued participation in sport. Initially the model included factors such as sport enjoyment, involvement alternatives, personal investments, social constraints, and involvement opportunities. Other factors, like social support and desire to excel, have since bolstered the model (Scanlan et al., 2016). Milne, Sutton, and McDonald (1996) cited personal improvement, sport appreciation, and social facilitation as reasons why people participate in sport. In later work, McDonald, Milne, and Hong (2002) expanded the previously mentioned areas to include participation factors of physical fitness, risk taking, stress reduction, aggression, affiliation, social facilitation, self-esteem, competition, achievement, skill mastery, aesthetics, value development, and self-actualization.

Fantasy sport entered the scene as a quasi-combination of many of the aforementioned elements. Gantz's (1981) motivations of letting loose, learning, experiencing the thrill of victory, and passing time are all applicable to fantasy sport consumption. Fantasy sport users mirror and amplify Gantz and Wenner's (1995) discussion on sport fans being actively engaged and being emotional, responsive, prepared, and expressive. Additionally, how and why people participate and stay in the activity are reflected in the participation factors set forth by McDonald, Milne, and Hong (2002). Not only are fantasy sport users participating in a competition, they are also consuming much of the same sport media offerings of traditional sport fans. Based on the aforementioned research, as well as other findings, it is important to understand *fantasy-sport-specific* motivation and consumption. Research has uncovered many of the following areas as motives for participation.

- *Control* and *ownership* are major parts of fantasy sport participation because of the freedom participants have to create, shape, and build their own team. Billings and Ruihley (2014) state it best: "For those wishing to test their roster management and ownership skills in the areas of drafting, trading, adding, or dropping players, and controlling a myriad of other player-personnel decisions, fantasy sport is a perfect conduit to fulfill these desires" (p. 22). This motivational area differs from sport fandom for the obvious reason: sport fans don't control their team's transactions, rosters, or lineup decisions. Fantasy play is built upon this one factor.
- *Camaraderie* is one part of the socialization aspects of fantasy sport. This motive only focuses on the relationship-side of socialization. Similar to sport fandom providing commonality amongst people, fantasy sport provides a space for common interests, competition, and discussion to take place (Billings & Ruihley, 2014; Ruihley & Hardin, 2011). The second part of the socialization aspect of fantasy sport is called *social sport*. The key aspect of this motive states that fantasy sport provides a conversational starting point. The act of discussing league results, the draft, strategy, general sport results, fantasy team or player performance, or any other fantasy-relevant topic is what makes this motive part of the social aspects of play. (Ruihley & Hardin, 2011)
- *Competition* in fantasy sport is the desire for your team performance and roster strategy to win over other competitors. While competition is undoubtedly a part of sport fandom, fantasy sport competition adds an additional element… choice. Fantasy sport users are in charge of their own team, their own roster formation, and compete as manager or owner, and not only as a fan. Naturally, this leads to a top motive in fantasy sport play.
- *Self-esteem* in fantasy sport comes into the picture when the participant feels "better or worse about oneself as it relates to a fantasy sport outcome" (Ruihley, Billings, & Rae, 2017). Sports fandom has a lot of emotion and pride. Whether it be one's city, college, or lifelong team, fans carry wins and losses with them. Fantasy play has the same effect with the addition of the aforementioned control one has over the roster, making the wins and losses even more personal.
- *Surveillance* in the fantasy sport context is the gathering of information to assist with fantasy sport decisions. This primarily includes information about one's roster or draft strategy and is sought out through expert opinions, pre-season draft guides, and player performance breakdowns to gathering information on matchups, weather, statistical projections, and much more (Billings & Ruihley, 2014; Hur, Ko, & Valacich, 2007; Seo & Green 2008). While sport fandom allows people to learn (Gantz, 1981), the information gathered does not necessarily lead to action, unless one is gambling on sport, then the information is quite useful.

- *Arousal* is defined as the positive stress and is part of the emotional nature of being a sport fan (Billings & Ruihley, 2014; Wann, 1995). Related to fantasy sport, arousal is the stimulation generated from the competition, player performance, or exciting outcome associated with participation. In the same way sport fandom includes highs and lows of consumption, fantasy sport provides pleasure and pain while following the performances of real athletes impacting a fantasy sport competition (Ruihley & Grappendorf, 2019).
- *Escape* is a term describing how participants disengage from a daily reality, routine, or worry by participating in fantasy sport (Billings & Ruihley, 2014; Hur, Ko, & Valacich, 2007; Seo & Green, 2008). This is similar to sport fandom in that consuming, talking, or identifying sport can provide people with a needed mental break from other parts of life.
- *Passing time* in sport fandom, as well as fantasy sport play, simply means to participate in an activity or consume sport in a way that allows the time to move without much effort. This is an action that has the "goal for nothing major to occur, seemingly to [relax or have a] mind-clearing effect" (Billings & Ruihley, 2014, p. 23).

Participant Consumption

Fantasy sport is a unique product in that it is consumed, as well as an activity that requires participation. Participation in fantasy sport is comes in many different shapes and sizes and can be completely lax or intensive as the participant desires. Fantasy sport play is offered in season-long, weekly, or daily varieties. Even when a sport season has concluded, fantasy sport keeps the attention of participants thinking about off-season roster moves or next season draft preparation. In several examinations of the motives driving this activity, several have risen to the top, including self-esteem, competition, social interaction, arousal, entertainment, and surveillance (Billings & Ruihley, 2014; Dwyer & Kim, 2011; Ruihley, 2018). These top motives help explain fantasy sport users as a type of elevated sports fan. Drafting and preparing a lineup takes time, energy, and research (surveillance). This is all in preparation to compete with others in a league on a daily, weekly, or seasonal basis (competition and arousal), showing off one's roster management skills and where the results of competition are taken personally (self-esteem and arousal), and as a result of fantasy play, participants know more about the sport, consume a wide-range of players and results beyond their local team, and are able to discuss sport more (surveillance and social sport).

Consumption takes place in a myriad of ways including preparation for a fantasy draft, deciding on lineup decisions, adding or trading players, consuming team performance, and evaluating team performance. Related to the motive of surveillance, fantasy sport participation requires an elevated level of attention to sports news, expert advice, matchup analysis, statistical breakdowns, player information, injury reports, and even the weather. In addition, fantasy sport users are consuming more live sports to follow the action of their fantasy sport roster. For example, someone in the Atlanta Falcons fan base and broadcast market will still tune into the Seattle Seahawks and San Francisco 49ers game because they have the quarterback for the Seahawks and kicker for the 49ers employed on their fantasy roster (and this is just two of their players). This increased consumption has grabbed the attention of major media outlets and researchers alike. An early example of this comes from a 2010 report where ESPN's Department of Integrated Media Research indicated that a non-fantasy sport viewer consumes, on average, more than seven hours of ESPN media each week. The fantasy sport user consumed over *three times* that amount, averaging 22 hours and 40 minutes per week (Billings & Ruihley, 2013; ESPN's Department of Integrated Media Research, 2010). A second example comes from an examination of similarities and differences between sport fans and fantasy sport users. Billings and Ruihley (2013; 2014) found fantasy sport users consume twice as much sport programming per week than traditional sport fans (9.6 hours compared to 18.0 hours) and have a 60 percent increase in sport consumption when examining gender-specific findings related to non-fantasy sport to fantasy sport users. In recent findings, fantasy sport-specific consumption is holding steady throughout the years between 7.5–9.2 hours per week (Billings & Ruihley, 2014, 2020; Ruihley, 2018).

A final example of media companies taking note of fantasy sport consumption is highlighted in Ruihley and Billings' (2019) exploration of fantasy sport as it relates to ESPN. While many interesting findings came out of this research, a few statistics emphasize the importance of fantasy sport participation and consumption. First, on NFL Sundays, 50 percent of all minutes across ESPN digital platforms are fantasy sport related. Second, ESPN reported 20 million unique fantasy sport users with a staggering 88 percent of traffic coming from mobile devices. Finally, ESPN created new content for television/app/web consumption with their fantasy football marathons lasting 28 consecutive hours. This programming was designed to inform, persuade, and generate interest in the fantasy sport product. The efforts paid off with 1.75 million teams drafted in 2016, 2 million teams in 2017, and 1.9 million teams in 2018 (Ota, 2018; Ruihley & Billings, 2019).

Fantasy Sport Media Offerings

As a result of the enhanced consumption, fantasy sport fandom has created pressure and opportunity for many sport media outlets to meet the informational needs of sport fans by considering the amount and types of information presented. This includes the presentation of box scores, bottom line scrolls, altered programming or even new programming. In one example of the fantasy sport fan altering the way things are presented, Fox Sports' Jim Bernard spoke to Billings and Ruihley (2014) and described a time when he told the graphics department that fantasy sport users want more than just the scores, they need information that is relevant to the fantasy sport experience. This includes providing information regarding the statistical leaders in rushing yards, passing yards in relation to football or leaders in scoring or rebounds in regard to basketball. Another example is the decision ESPN made when they decided to counter-program their Sunday staple, *NFL Countdown*, with a fantasy-specific show called *Fantasy Football Now*. In this bold move, ESPN recognized that the fantasy sport consumer needed more than just a breakdown of the day's games. They need start/sit advice, weather reports, injury statuses, matchup analysis, and elevated statistics. This move was made again when consumers drove ESPN to create another fantasy-sport-based show with *The Fantasy Show with Matthew Berry*. Again, this show was counterprogramed against ESPN's key shows of *Around the Horn* and *Pardon the Interruption*. These two examples are only a sampling of how fantasy sport users are driving coverage, demanding more content, and are important enough to matter. Whether it is a column in *USA Today*, front-page coverage on Yahoo!'s website, web shows, podcasts, or 30 seconds on ESPN's SportsCenter, all are trying to provide information and content to draw the attention of this type of sport fan.

Fantasy sport activities have even spawned the creation of two new, fantasy sport-specific media outlets. First SiriusXM created a station devoted exclusively to fantasy sport discussion and shows. About the creation of this station, Scott Greenstein, Sirius XM's President and Chief Content Officer, stated:

> We've created a unique destination for fantasy sports fans. Our listeners get live play-by-play from the NFL, MLB, NASCAR, NHL, NBA, PGA, soccer and more that allows them to follow all their fantasy players or teams in real time. Now they have a dedicated fantasy

sports channel that they can tune into 24 hours a day that will give them the stats, injury news and expert advice they'll need to dominate their fantasy sports leagues.

Sirius XM, 2010, para. 5

This station rose quickly to popularity and in an interview with Billings and Ruihley (2014), Sirius XM's Steve Cohen states, "[Almost instantly,] we got more listeners calling our talk shows on our fantasy sports channel than we did on any other Sirius XM produced sports channel. [By December 2011] we had an average of over 28,000 calls a day" (p. 67).

The second media outlet created for fantasy sport play was the appropriately named FNTSY Sports Network. In 2014, this network was created to provide content and information to fantasy sport users via television, video and audio streaming, and radio. This network is widely available providing traditional and contemporary access via 35 North American cable providers, streaming services like Apple TV, Roku, Amazon Fire TV, Pluto TV, Fubo TV, and Twitch (FNTSY, 2019). Audio streams are available in outlets consisting of iHeartRadio, TuneIn, and the FNTSY Sports Radio Network App.

In addition to SiriusXM and FNTSY Sports Network, there have been other television changes, potentially catering to the fantasy-sport-minded consumer, providing more games and contests. Specifically, stations and offerings like DirecTV Sunday Ticket and My Players feature, the NFL RedZone, NBA TV, and MLB.TV all are providing greater access to their sport, their games, and individual player performance (Ruihley, In Press). With these advancements, fantasy participants are no longer tied to the local team or the selection of the broadcast network. As mentioned, part of the appeal of the fantasy sport experience is following a constructed team's performance. Appropriate for the fantasy sport user, the NFL RedZone (N.D.) touts that fans will see "every touchdown from every game Sunday afternoon" (N.D., para. 2). The marketing of this channel self-describes as the "perfect fantasy companion" (N.D., para. 2). Additionally, DirecTV also provides the NFL Sunday ticket and a feature directed towards the fantasy sport user or sports better. Their My Players feature instructs consumers to "add your favorite players within the NFL Sunday Ticket app. Once added, you'll have easy access to their stats and highlights and receive alerts when one of your favorites makes a big play" (DirecTV, N.D., para. 1). These features and channels are examples of media outlets providing content to make the fantasy sport experience more enjoyable as fantasy owners can have easy access to the live action and results of their managerial decisions.

Fantasy Sport Industry

The fantasy sport industry is made up of many different organizations and businesses created to serve, provide content, operate games, and provide information for the fantasy sport user. The field is made up of writers, designers, statisticians, computer engineers, information providers, individual entrepreneurs, and large media conglomerates. Major hosts of fantasy play (i.e. providing the online space for play) include media outlets like ESPN, Yahoo!, CBS Sports, and Fox Sports. Also offering play are individual professional leagues and associations like the NFL, National Basketball Association, PGA, National Hockey League, MLB, NASCAR, and Indy Car. In the past decade, two other organizations, not associated with mainstream broadcasting companies, joined the mix and have taken the fantasy sport world by storm. The aforementioned FanDuel and DraftKings were created initially to offer DFS contests. Along with their success and the political haze concerning gaming and gambling, these companies continue to grow their consumer base, continue to push the line on fantasy sport and gambling legislation, and continue to expand their offerings to the fantasy sport user.

Answering the call to provide pertinent information to fantasy sport enthusiasts, companies like NBC Sports/Rotoworld and Rotowire are dedicated outlets providing fantasy sport information and up-to-the-minute player updates. Comprised of fantasy sport writers and analysts, these organizations provide supplementary player information, player profiles, matchup predictions, and expert advice for their own subscribers and also as an outsourced partner with many of the aforementioned fantasy sport providers. Going even further into the intel provided to fantasy sport users, companies like FantasyPros, numberFire, and Fantasy Labs examine information about the fantasy sport experience even further. FantasyPros describes their operation as providing "fantasy advice from around the web to make it easy for you to make the best decisions. We promote the best experts based on one simple question, '*How good is your advice?*'" (FantasyPros, 2020, para. 1). numberFire uses advanced analytics to provide more information to their clients stating, "We take the unstructured and misleading data that exists all around sports and mine it for unprecedented insight that allows us to predict player and team performance better than any competitor" (numberFire, 2020, para. 1). Created specifically for daily contexts, FantasyLabs "provides daily fantasy sports players with proprietary data and tools to test theories, quickly create and backtest models, and ultimately construct profitable DFS lineups" (FantasyLabs, 2020, para. 1).

The industry is overseen by a formidable trade association. As a way to band together, create legitimacy, and protect the legal rights of the activity, the Fantasy Sports Trade Association was created in 1998. During the past two decades, this organization has provided industry conventions, political and legal support for legislative battles, and a place for professionals in the field to come together as one organization. In 2019, the Fantasy Sports Trade Association changed its name to the Fantasy Sports & Gaming Association. The move came "in response to a mandate from its membership to expand the association's focus to include sports gaming as well as embrace the rapid legal and technological changes facing the broader sports industry" (Fantasy Sports & Gaming Association, 2019a, para. 1). Protecting the organizations involved and ensuring a lasting product for the fantasy sport user, the values of this organization revolve around being pro-business, embracing innovation, seeing the long-term picture, supporting lawful participation in sports gaming, and providing protection to consumers (Fantasy Sports & Gaming Association, 2020).

Conclusion

Sport fans typologies have been developed in attempts to classify fans and levels of fandom for many years (Hunt, Bristol, & Bashaw, 1999; Stewart, Smith, & Nicholson, 2003; Samra & Wos, 2014). With fandom in sport varying in consumption, priority, motivation, team loyalty, and desire to consume, there is no worry about the sport fan competing in and consuming fantasy sport. From their motives, sport consumption, need for information, and sheer size, fantasy sport users are literally changing the way fans view, consume, and experience sport. Written in 1981, long before the rise of fantasy sport popularity, Gantz offered this description of fandom and after reading his description it is difficult to imagine he was not writing this about the contemporary fantasy sport user:

> *Being a fan serves fantasy and escape functions and can be a pleasurable experience, particularly when one's player or team performs well. Fans can vicariously experience the struggles and successes of the athletes. Being a fan fulfills needs of sharing, feeling, and belonging. It provides an acceptable outlet for exhibiting emotions and feelings. Moreover, being a fan can be a relatively low risk proposition. When*

a player or team does well, the fan shares the success and may feel him/herself to be a contributing agent. Associated with success are feelings of satisfaction and self-worth. In lean times, the fan can reduce feelings of association or come up with scapegoat reasons lifting the onus of defeat from him/herself. Failure may be turned into success if actual game strategies employed were not consistent with those thought of by the fan while being an "armchair" quarterback or manager. The fan may have the best of both worlds.

Gantz, 1981, p. 264

The fantasy sport user is a fan that *has* the best of both worlds. Consuming a sport, regardless of *real* team wins and losses, while actively participating and competing based on individual player outcomes. This new type of fan has certainly emerged in the sport marketplace and is one that cannot be overlooked. Their level of fandom is elevated, and they have interest in not only how teams and athletes are performing in general but in the minute details in which they have a fantasy sport interest.

References

Bell, T., & Ruihley, B.J. (2019). Media dependency and the fantasy sport draft. *International Association for Communication and Sport*. Boise, ID.

Billings, A. C., & Ruihley, B.J. (2013). Why we watch, why we play: The relationship between fantasy sport and fanship motivations. *Mass Communication & Society, 16*(1), 5–25.

Billings, A. C., & Ruihley, B. J. (2014). *The fantasy sport industry: Games within games*. London: Routledge.

Billings, A.C., & Ruihley, B.J. (2020). Why some fantasy players don't gamble on sports…and how to get them to try it. *Fantasy Sports & Gaming Association Winter Conference*. Las Vegas, N.V.

Billings, A.C., Ruihley, B.J., & Yang, Y. (2017). Fantasy gaming on steroids?: Contrasting perceptions of traditional and daily fantasy sport participants. *Communication & Sport, 5*(6), 732–750.

DirecTV. (N.D.). Features: What is the my players feature? Retrieved from https://nflsthelp.directv.com/hc/en-us/articles/204503649-What-is-the-My-Players-feature-.

Dwyer, B., & Kim, Y. (2011). For love or money: Developing and validating a motivational scale for fantasy sport participation. *Journal of Sport Management, 25*(1), 70–85.

ESPN Department of Integrated Media Research. (2010). ESPN top ten list for sport research. Paper presented at the Broadcast Education Association Research Symposium, Las Vegas, NV.

FantasyLabs. (2020). Est. 2015. Retrieved from www.fantasylabs.com/about/.

FantasyPros. (2020). About. Retrieved from www.fantasypros.com/about/.

Fantasy Sports & Gaming Association. (2019a). Fantasy Sports & Gaming Association officially launches. Retrieved from https://thefsga.org/fantasy-sports-gaming-association-officially-launches/.

Fantasy Sports & Gaming Association. (2020). Industry demographics: Actionable insights & insightful data. Retrieved from https://thefsga.org/industry-demographics/.

Fantasy Sports & Gaming Association. (2020). Who we are. Retrieved from https://thefsga.org/about-the-fsga.

FNTSY Sports Network. 2019. Fantasy Sports Network (FNTSY). Retrieved from https://fantasysportsnetwork.com/about_us/.

Gantz, W. (1981). An exploration of viewing motives and behaviors associated with television sports. *Journal of Broadcasting & Electronic Media, 25*(3), 263–275.

Gantz, W., Want, Z., Paul, B., & Potter, R. F. (2006). Sports versus all comers: Comparing tv sports fans with fans of other programming genres. *Journal of Broadcasting Electronic Media, 50*(1), 95–118.

Gantz, W., & Wenner, L. A. (1995). Fanship and the television sports viewing experience. *Sociology of Sport Journal, 12*(1), 56–74.

Hunt, K. A., Bristol, T., & Bashaw, R. E. (1999). A conceptual approach to classifying sports fans. *Journal of Services Marketing, 13*(6), 439–452.

Hur, Y., Ko, Y. J., & Valacich, J. (2007). Motivation and concerns for online sport consumption. *Journal of Sport Management, 21*(4), 521.

McDonald, M. A., Milne, G. R., & Hong, J. (2002). Motivational factors for evaluating sport spectator and participant markets. *Sport Marketing Quarterly, 11*(2), 100–113.

Milne, G, Sutton, W., & McDonald, M. (1996). Niche analysis: A strategic measurement tool for managers. *Sport Marketing Quarterly, 5*(3), 17–21.

NFL Redzone. (N.D.) About RedZone. Retrieved from www.nfl.com/qs/redzone/about-redzone.jsp.

NumberFire. (2020). About us. Retrieved from www.numberfire.com/info/about-us.

Ota, K. (2018). Fans draft nearly 2 million teams during ESPN's fantasy football marathon. Retrieved from https://espnpressroom.com/us/press-releases/2018/08/fans-draft-nearly-2-million-teams-during-espns-fantasy-football-marathon/.

Ruihley, B.J. (In Press). Communicating fantasy sport. In M. Butterworth (Ed.) *Handbook of communication and sport*. Berlin: De Gruyter Mouton.

Ruihley, B.J. (2018). Fantasy sport participants: Profile update 2017. *Fantasy Sports Trade Association Winter Conference*. Los Angeles, C.A.

Ruihley, B.J., & Billings, A.C. (2019). Ascending as the fantasy giant: ESPN fantasy, mainstreaming fantasy gaming, and the role of Goliath. In G. Armfield, J. McGuire, & A. Earnheardt (Eds.) *The ESPN after effect and the changing sports media marketplace*. Peter Lang.

Ruihley, B. J., Billings, A. C., & Rae, C. (2017). Not sport, yet defining sport: The mainstreaming of fantasy sport participation. In Klein, S., (Ed.) *Defining Sport*. London: Lexington Books.

Ruihley, B. J., & Grappendorf, H. (2019). Women sports fans' opinion of fantasy sport activity. *Journal of Contemporary Athletics, 13*(4).

Ruihley, B. J., & Hardin, R. L. (2011). Beyond touchdowns, homeruns, and 3-pointers: An examination of fantasy sport participation motivation. *International Journal of Sport Management and Marketing, 10*(3/4), 232–256.

Samra, B., & Wos, A. (2014). Consumer in sports: Fan typology analysis. *Journal of Intercultural Management, 6*(4), 263–288.

Scanlan, T. K., Carpenter, P. J., Lobel, M., & Simons, J. P. (1993a). Sources of enjoyment for youth sport athletes. *Pediatric Exercise Science, 5*(3), 275–285.

Scanlan, T. K., Carpenter, P. J., Simons, J. P., Schmidt, G. W., & Keeler, B. (1993b). An introduction to the sport commitment model. *Journal of Sport and Exercise Psychology, 15*(1), 1–15.

Scanlan, T. K., Chow, G. M., Sousa, C., Scanlan, L. A., & Knifsend, C. A. (2016). The development of the sport commitment questionnaire-2 (English version). *Psychology of Sport and Exercise, 22*, 233–246.

Seo, W. J. & Green. B. C. (2008). Development of the motivation scale for sport online consumption. *Journal of Sport Management, 22*, 82–109.

Sirius XM. (2010). SIRIUS XM to launch "SIRIUS XM Fantasy Sports Radio," 24/7 fantasy sports channel available nationwide. http://investor.SiriusXM.com/investor-overview/press-releases/press-release-details/2010/SIRIUS-XM-to-Launch-SIRIUS-XM-Fantasy-Sports-Radio-24-7-Fantasy-Sports-Channel-Available-Nationwide/default.aspx.

Stewart, B., Smith, A., & Nicholson, M. (2003). Sport consumer typologies: A critical review. *Sport Marketing Quarterly, 12*(4), 206–216.

Wann, D. L. (1995). Preliminary validation of the sport fan motivation scale. *Journal of Sport and Social issues, 19*(4), 377–396.

Wann, D. L., Grieve, F. G., Zapalac, R. K., & Pease, D. G. (2008). Motivational profiles of sport fans of different sports. *Sport Marketing Quarterly, 17*(1), 6–19.

Weiner, J., & Dwyer, B. (2017). A new player in the game: Examining differences in motives and consumption between traditional, hybrid, and daily fantasy sport users. *Sport Marketing Quarterly, 26*(3), 140–152.

27
Understanding Sport Videogames
The Extensions of Fan

Steven Conway

Introduction

Number is the ruler of forms and ideas, and the cause of gods and daemons.
                    quote attributed to Pythagoras (C.570–495 BCE)

Arriving home from the office, I commit a sin common to information workers within a post-industrial economy: I open up my laptop and refresh my email. This habit is a consequence of the tight coupling between a person and their various technologies; as Marshall McLuhan ruminated (1964), perhaps a better term than coupling is "extension". As Marie-Luise Angerer outlines, the "algorithms of affective computing have long begun to intervene to link up man and machine in affective and thus psycho-cybernetic ways" (2018, p. 241). Refreshing email, checking various social media for updates and responses, an affective economy reigns: a tight loop of anticipation, excitement and abatement long established in regular users' neural pathways (Peper & Harvey, 2018). I move through my task list, feeling a rush of accomplishment each time I tick off a chore. Seven emails still require an immediate response.

At the top of my inbox, an unnerving, forthright admonishment from my bosses. They are unhappy with my recent performance, deploying the tyrannical fidelity of numbers to prove their case: here was my goal, here is my failure. They warn, in the most formal, oblique manner, that if I do not change things soon, I will be looking for another job. Anxiety-ridden now, I scan next week's schedule. It's going to be a hard slog. I scan across reports on the employees I directly manage, sighing. My organisation has invested enormous amounts of labour, and no doubt finances, creating an exhaustive portfolio on each aspect of my staff's performance and potential. Composure, Leadership, Teamwork, Concentration, Vision, Aggression, Anticipation, and many more parameters. All available for perusal, attached to a definitive numerical score per worker.

This is a clear example of the "quantified self", a contemporary cultural paradigm entangled with various technologies of surveillance concordant with the neoliberal demand for self-dependency, regulation and responsibility: the "self" is an investment to be continuously monitored, quantified and optimised against standards set by external agencies (e.g. a "health" standard immanent within a daily calorie goal tracker). In consumer-oriented products we see this in devices such as the "Fitbit", or task management software such as *EpicWin*. As Whitson explains, "The digitization of data gathering permits new kinds of accumulation and scorekeeping, detailing and chronicling… New technologies enable us to measure, chart, and quantify what was previously unquantifiable… We… track and measure, display and share all of this heretofore unknown data" (Whitson, 2013, p. 168).

This trend also has a distinctive, futural accent. Media theorist Richard Grusin terms this "premediation" (2010), as Blackman explains, "[this term] refers to strategies that anticipate what might happen in the future, as well as exploring how the past and therefore possible futures are always in the present" (2018, p. 228). The ideological purity of the number, the sheer discursive power of mathematics in contemporary society, delineates and delimits the future. Anything outside of its predictions is discarded as an anomaly, an error, absurd in its most literal sense (i.e. deaf to comprehension, see Conway (2016)).

As I gaze over the various statistics and projections available regarding my staff, one particular employee stands out whom, through his own competence, has saved my position more than a few times. Yet one alarming number glowers above all else: *A match sharpness of 35 per cent*. I bury my head in my hands; I may well be looking for another position come Sunday morning.

The World of Form(ulae)s

This panoptical nightmare is of course not a description of the author's University workplace, but his other, more challenging one, existing within *Football Manager 2019* (Sports Interactive, 2018). The terror of the system is, curiously, an outcome of its subscription to the Platonic ideal (inherited, it is often commented, from Pythagoras (Riedweg, 2005)): in this digital world, the transcendent certainty of numbers rules, permeates, indeed, *is* everything. The algorithm is the philosopher-king of this realm, and it rules the Ship of State with absolute authority.

Of interest for this chapter are the consequences engagement with such games have upon subject formation, i.e., the shaping of one's sense of self. In this regard we are conducting a post-phenomenological investigation, as Rosenberger and Verbeek outline, such approaches perceive technology "in terms of the *relations between human beings and technological artifacts*, focusing on the various ways in which technologies help to shape relations between human beings and the world. They do not approach technologies as merely functional and instrumental objects, but as mediators of human experiences and practices" (2015, p. 9, italics in original). Further, through this approach post-phenomenology "does away with the idea that there is a pre-given subject in a pre-given world of objects, with a mediating entity between them. Rather, the mediation is the *source* of the specific shape the human subjectivity… can take in this specific situation" (2015, p. 12, italics in original).

This sense of self firstly emerges in affect; as an embodied, felt significance. Simply, playing these games encourages certain moods, feelings, emotions, translating into specific motoric and cognitive dispositions and habits. To be clear, this is not an Internalist position, i.e., that affect is generated purely by an internal subject, but instead posits affect as a relational process. This view is summarised by Röttger-Rössler & Slaby:

> We understand affect not as processes "within" a person, but as social-relational dynamics unfolding in situated practices and social interaction. Affect is formative of human subjects as it binds them into shared environmental (e.g., social, material and technological) constellations, which in turn shape modalities of agency, habit and self-understanding.
>
> *Röttger-Rössler & Slaby, 2018, p. 2*

This chapter interrogates how, then, the sports digital game *as* digital game shapes subjectivity, and therefore affords certain performances of sports fandom, a signifier undergoing transformation in contemporary times. This emphasis on medium affordances is key since, whilst sometimes overlooked in sports studies literature, the distinct attributes of the digital medium shape the ontological and epistemological limits of sports fandom; from fans' understanding of the sport, to the rituals they regularly engage with, to their very identity *as* fan.

The Float(ing) Fan

In *A Game of Two Halves: Football, Television and Globalization* (2003), Cornel Sandvoss articulates an insightful, emphatic, and largely damning indictment of the future of sports fandom. Placing the blame firmly within the machinations of a global economy and its attendant features of mass consumerism and rationalization, Sandvoss conceptualises the contemporary fan as a "DIY" fan, i.e., a fan-consumer undertaking a cyborgian incorporation of a football club, establishing a chimeric identity:

> While fans interact and choose between various discourses of the public sphere through their fandom, and thereby articulate and form identity and DIY citizenship, the ground upon which their fandom is constructed is firmly positioned within the ideological apparatus of mass consumerism, rationalization and industrial capitalism. Football, then, remains an interface between the macro transformations of an increasingly global economic, social and cultural system and individuals and their ability to position themselves in today's world through acts of consumption, negotiation and indigenization.
>
> *Sandvoss, 2003, p. 176*

In Sandvoss's view, this self-image, built of floating signifiers, hyperreal and placeless, allows a soccer club's semantic content to become uniquely accessible to the fan-consumer's desires: the fan picks and chooses as if at a buffet, exchanging and deciding between clubs and features as suits. This segues entirely with the computation of sport, as numbers are, by their nature, floating signifiers, the "placeless" sign par excellence. As Lev Manovich (2002) has discussed, due to its numerical basis, and therefore eminent configurability, automation, and variability, digital media engenders the move from mass standardisation to mass customisation; the dominant cultural paradigm has shifted from narrative to database. Rather than engaging with content as a linear sequence of beginning, middle, end, one jumps in and out at various points within a rhizomatic structure (e.g. creating playlists on iTunes; engaging with the Marvel "universe" across film, television, comics and digital games).

The sport fan might, similarly, follow *this team* in *this league* or just *this player*; they might engage only through television, or websites, or solely know teams through their digital game emulation. Indeed, all of the digital games discussed herein allow the creation of one's own custom club, selecting everything from team name, to colours and player constitution. Sandvoss ruminates:

> The less clubs have a meaning of their own, the better they function as spaces of self-projection to a large number of fans. This self-reflection forms the modus operandi of football fandom. To return to the Narcissus myth, it is on plain water that Narcissus sees his reflection. Precisely such even, semantically empty surfaces are fostered by the application of formal rationality and its postmodern consequences in the realm of football.
>
> *Sandvoss, 2003, p. 174*

Invoking the myth of Narcissus, the "Ur-Myth of Media" (Jenkins, 2016), is appropriate, as Jenkins ruminates, the allegory is:

> [C]oncerned primarily with the relationship between self and perception through the mediation of water and offering lessons about the dangers and desires of images powerful enough to spawn "deceit," "delusion," and even death. Thus, the myth introduces fundamental issues related to media, especially the ambiguous and potentially problematic reality status of mediated representations.
>
> *Jenkins, 2016, p. 648*

The sheer liquidity of digital media, its unmatched capacity to remediate (Bolter & Grusin, 1999) any existing medium, to transduce binary code into representational format, has a totalising effect upon one's subjectification within that experience. As touched upon in the opening, it delimits, contours, and, as we now turn to, produces one's interactions as fan.

The Media Makes The Fan

The relationship between the Narcissus myth and the media is perhaps most famously pondered by Marshall McLuhan (1964). McLuhan describes the impact of media upon the human sensorium as engendering a "narcosis", a numbing effect whereby Narcissus (i.e. anyone using media) "became the servomechanism of his own extended or repeated image" (1964, p. 51). This has immediate psycho-physiological consequences for the person, similar to Don Ihde's "magnification/reduction" structure (Ihde, 1990). For example, looking at a mobile phone diminishes one's larger awareness of the immediate environment, or (to paraphrase Ihde's famous example), looking at the moon through a telescope renders the planetary satellite into an isolated object of scientific scrutiny, and thus removes its larger context within the firmament as religious or poetic phenomenon.

Such engagement also has larger socio-cultural ramifications of course. Jenkins is once more helpful here, applying McLuhan's insight to television:

> Narcosis spells a bleak outcome, perhaps resulting in something similar to the psychosis known as parasocial relationships, in which the viewer falsely believes they have a personal relationship with a screen celebrity. Narcissus experiences a parasocial relationship with the image reflected in the water, mistaking the intimacy and involvement of the (televisual) image for reality and thereby becoming paralyzed.
>
> *Jenkins, 2016, p. 653*

One of the key affordances of the sport digital game is interaction with, indeed *control* over well-known athletes, from simulations of Cristiano Ronaldo to even retired players such as Diego Maradona. As I have articulated previously, the "existence of these rare celebrity avatars creates for the player a form of metagame following the aesthetics of collectible card games, whereby they attempt to collect as many uniquely gifted star players as possible" (Conway, 2018, p. 145). Preceding, perhaps "premediating" (Grusin, 2010) the "Big Data" trend in sport (Hutchins, 2015), these games become cycles of collecting and improving athletes-as-quantifiable-commodities; their existence reduced, flattened to a set of statistics. Compressed into numbers, these athletes become eminently fungible; transferable, replaceable across settings. Thus it is entirely unsurprising the athlete-as-commodity emerges as the dominant paradigm for many interactions, from video games to Fantasy Sport (e.g. Fantasy Football leagues) to expert analysis and commentary to the professional athlete's very contract with a club. This is made most explicit in Fantasy Sport leagues and digital games' multiplayer modes where players compete to bid, purchase and trade players based solely on the statistics they proffer, and thus "value" they embody.

Such understanding ties in with Sandvoss's pessimism regarding fandom:

> As vision acts as the fundamental dimension of perception in contemporary football, other dimensions of experience have been impoverished. In light of the increasingly standardized and pasteurized semiotic structure of contemporary football, DIY citizenship is progressively transformed into "IKEA citizenship" in which fans merely choose between interchangeable, ever similar, stereotypical messages and discourses, rooted in a pseudo-creative and pseudo-participatory environment.
>
> *Sandvoss, 2003, p174*

Thus we find ourselves back at the original vision, Plato's purest idea (from the Greek *idein*, "to see"): the number. As we will discuss, users of contemporary sports digital games, regardless of the individual sport, are largely tasked with managing, configuring, and swapping numbers. It is apt here to remember McLuhan's later, playful reworking of his early dictum, "the medium is the message" (1964), into "the medium is the massage" (1967). Simply, as the medium extends us, it *works upon us*, shaping our affective, cognitive and motoric sensitivities, capacities, and habits. McLuhan's understanding of affect is here very much in line with contemporary phenomenology, as mentioned earlier (Röttger-Rössler & Slaby, 2018). How then, does the sports digital game work upon us?

Hook and Pull

Before we delve into how people engage with these games and their effects, we should briefly outline how habitual play is encouraged and formed within many mainstream digital games' eco-systems. Nir Eyal's work on habit formation, summarised in his book *Hooked: How to Build Habit-Forming Products* (Eyal & Hoover, 2014) outlines four phases involved in the sedimentation of product use into habit. His work abounds with examples from digital media, especially social media and digital games, since this is where he finds the model applied most effectively. The four phases, in sequence, are Trigger, Action, Reward, and Investment. This model is cyclical, thus the last stage is designed to instantiate new Triggers for the next round of user engagement, as frequent use is essential to solidifying habit (Eyal & Hoover, 2014).

Triggers are either internal or external. For example, an internal trigger is feeling hungry, whilst an external trigger is an advertisement for McDonalds. The goal for any company is for external triggers to be enmeshed with internal triggers, e.g., the internal trigger of hunger becomes automatically associated with McDonalds; the trigger of boredom translates into playing *FIFA* (EA Sports, 2020). Triggers exist across three broad categories: biological (e.g. hunger), psychological (e.g. anxiety), and social (e.g. status). These often overlap, as for example using a social media app one might access to reduce a sense of loneliness, simultaneously felt as anxiety, concurrently experienced as a coiled tightness in the stomach. For digital games, internal triggers might exist as the removal of boredom, or a desire for accomplishment or status (such as in multiplayer rankings). External triggers can range from the narrative of a game (a character asking "Help!") to the game's marketing campaign ("will you be the hero?").

Action designates the process a person undertakes to satiate the Trigger, achieving a Reward. Generally the less effort required (the removal of "friction" in user-centred design terminology), the better for habit formation. Rewards are defined in an Epicurean manner: satiation is the reduction of some kind of pain. Eating is the reduction of hunger, playing a digital game is the reduction of boredom, logging on to Facebook is the reduction of loneliness (whether, and how these succeed, is another question).

This raises an interesting issue for game design, since all games are premised upon the introduction of absurd constraints, as Suits coyly summarises, "aside from bureaucratic practice, in anything but a game the gratuitous introduction of unnecessary obstacles to the achievement of an end is regarded as a decidedly irrational thing to do, whereas in games it appears to be an absolutely essential thing to do" (Suits, 2005, p. 39). For example, in golf the goal of placing a ball in a hole is complicated immeasurably by the restriction of using only a club to do so.

Yet this conundrum is solved if one takes the position that the motivation of many players is the pursuit of a sense of autonomy, competence, and relatedness (Conway & Elphinstone, 2019). The immediate feedback loop and clarity inherent to the ontology of games, whether in the mechanics (such as striking a ball) or representational corollaries (such as a score board), provides a sense of progression and independence rare in other activities. Thus obstacles are a necessary and expected pre-condition for any heightened sense of competence.

Taking their cue from the behaviourist school of psychology, Eyal and Hoover postulate that variability is the key to a reward becoming habit-forming. This is often referred to as the "Skinner box" model, after B.F. Skinner's famous lab experiments with rats in a maze. This format has been adopted widely within the game industry, as variable ratio (based on amount of user actions) or variable interval (based on amount of time the user has engaged) rewards. For example, a variable ratio reward might exist as "every x amount of monsters killed reward the user with y weapon", where both x and y are randomised. A variable interval is similar, but simply interchanges actions with time: "every x amount of time reward the user with y weapon". As we will discuss, soccer digital games have adapted these variable rewards in many ways.

Finally, the investment stage reifies memory within the product. This can be as simple as having one's efforts visible in the artefact's end-state; once more we can refer to IKEA vis-à-vis the well-known "IKEA effect", where consumers value the furniture they've put together over pre-built items (Norton et al., 2011). Or we can cite loyalty cards, air miles, and in digital games, customisable avatars, experience points, attributes, decision trees, "loot" and so on. The key is that the product must remember the consumer and acknowledge this memory in some conspicuous, perceptible manner.

A Game of Two Systems

Data Management

The labelling of a videogame as "sports" is, as with any genre classification, slippery and rhizomatic. Whilst there are many, widely varying interpretations of sports within the history of digital games, contemporary versions often share the motif of two interlinked, but separate, layers of user interaction. Whether identified as part of the "manager" sub-genre, such as the *Football Manager* series (Sports Interactive, 2004–present), the "televisual" sub-genre (Conway, 2010), such as EA Sports' *FIFA* series (1993–present) or Konami's *Pro Evolution Soccer*[1] (Konami, 1995–present), or the "Arcade" interpretation seen in the sporadic *FIFA Street* series ((EA Vancouver, 2005–2012) revitalised as the *Volta Football* mode in *FIFA 20* (EA Sports, 2019), or the critically acclaimed mobile game *New Star Soccer* (2012–present)). Regardless of genre, most contemporary iterations confront the player with a distinct binary ouroboros: data management and data processing, each feeding into the other.

Data management tasks the user with manipulating and configuring their team, squad, or player-avatar towards a speculative optimal. External triggers (Eyal, 2014) abound here, directing the user's attention through various conventional design techniques: notifications and color-coding of important data for the user's attention; particle effects drawing the eye towards key issues; and temporal "parenting" within the interface (the user is asked to make a selection in one window before the next window, or game sequence is "born"). The user schedules training sessions, tactics and team talks in *Football Manager 2019* (Sports Interactive, 2018); configures formation, defensive attitude and passing tendencies in the *FIFA* series (EA Sports, 1993–present); or spends "Style Points" to increase the statistics of their "Virtual Pro" within *FIFA Street 4* (EA Vancouver, 2012).

All focus upon cognitive tasks familiar to any white collar information worker such as organisation of information, abstract assessment, and detailed scheduling (Paas and Van Merriënboer, 1994). The variability of the Reward here so keenly stressed by Eyal and Hoover (2014) is built into the very game dynamic. The sheer complexity of handling hundreds of different statistics, across various domains, all intersecting in the black box of the game algorithm, percolate, generating a sense of excitement and expectation. The user does not yet *know*, but they *hope* they have managed the various data points correctly, a tingling sense of expectation familiar to any fan.

Data Processing

Once the data management is completed to the user's satisfaction, the next phase, data processing, is enacted. Though the official moniker for this phase varies product to product, the colloquial term from football fandom would simply be "match day". This is where the user's careful data management is processed in real-time via a digital representation of the sport-in-play. In the *Football Manager* series (Sports Interactive, 2004–present), as the name implies, the game's design leans heavily towards the data management phase. Thus the data processing on "match day" is limited to managerial duties such as changing tactics, making substitutions, or performing "shouts" at the players (such as "Show Some Passion" or "Focus").

Whilst, as the name indicates, data management is prominent within the manager sub-genre, within the televisual and arcade sub-genres, data processing is the primary phase. This aspect takes the form of a spectacular remediation of the sport's televisual representation (Conway & Finn, 2013): multiple camera angles, action commentary, replays, highlights, photo lens effects and so on. This remediation is allied to a conspicuous, verisimilitudinous implementation of physics, so that the soccer ball bounces, slides, and swerves in a convincing manner under various conditions such as rain, snow, high wind and so on.

The user must control avatars in real time to process the data (i.e., the numerous statistics embodied in the virtual athlete), to win the match. The challenge is not only to navigate the avatars-as-numbers, but also the various calculations introduced by the ground, weather and ball-as-numbers. The vertiginous excitement afforded by pressing the "shoot" button whilst in control of an avatar with 99 "shot power" is wrapped up in the promise of witnessing a technological marvel, in watching the physics engine pushed to an extreme, in spectating the spectacle of the algorithm. Thus, as we will discuss further below, the data processing phase is both action and reward (Eyal & Hoover, 2014).

Arithmomania

The ways in which the player's data management decisions interact with the algorithms of the game system (i.e. encoded ruleset) are, fundamentally, about surveillance. Better yet, to tie in with Sandvoss's view on fandom (2003), the "quantified self" trend, and the above-mentioned IKEA effect, we can refer to this as *Ikeaveillance*, as Mantello explains, "an Orwellian co-opting of Mann's (2002) *sousveillance* (human-focused, bottom up, individualistic approaches to the monitoring of authority). *Ikeaveillance* encourages citizens to… participate in the do-it-yourself, reward-centered, pro-active, networked and… gamified versions of automated governance" (2016, p. 2, italics in original). As the user inspects the system, makes decisions, they are not only aware the system surveils them, governs them; they actively participate in it.

Whilst the system veils the rules and dynamics under which it operates, it conversely maintains complete, transparent access to all the user's decisions. Indeed this is the *sine qua non* of the computing medium: all output first requires input. Thus not only are users aware of the system's intrusive quantification of their actions, they yearn for judgment. Angerer captures this sentiment well discussing the relation between a person and an operating system in the Spike Jonze film *Her*. The digital system:

> [I]s more than himself. Here we can also refer to… Lacan's… definition of desire as something that addresses itself not to the other or others, but to the great Other, to the authority that always sees more and knows more than oneself, that always sees through one, without one ever being able to attain this state, this position of knowledge.
>
> *Angerer, 2018, p. 245*

This style of governance, as in the most efficient systems, chooses discipline over punishment (Foucault, 1995). As we discuss in the next section, the user never encounters the whiplash of a "game over" screen in sports digital games, but is better disciplined, coerced, reformed through play. The very obfuscation of the system's workings is central to its pleasure: the crushing shock of a match loss, the *fiero* sensation (Lazzaro, 2004) of overcoming a more prestigious opponent, are ultimately only achievable as components of the game's affective structure through a designed opacity.

In a scopophilic culture, it is vision(-as-surveillance) that dominates mainstream game design; a logic of voyeurism inculcating exhibitionism. The system within sports digital games offers many forms of voyeuristic gaze. Indeed it could be argued that dominant practices within digital game design premediated (Grusin, 2010) the logic of the "quantified self" trend by many years. There are numerous examples from the history of the digital game medium, from high score boards to more contemporary "achievements" (drawing upon the history of sport, also known as trophies or badges), content "unlocks", and the well-known design trope of "levelling up", i.e. as mentioned earlier, "earning" some form of currency through game activities, used to increase the attributes of a player-avatar. This is emphasised through certain features within the televisual genre such as the "Career" mode, allowing the user to create a custom avatar they then take sole control over, from unsigned youth player to (after many, many in-game seasons), World Cup star.

Whilst the quantification of progress is essential to the ontology of any game (as opposed to play), a hyperactive, granular quantification of progress is essential to the Reward (Eyal, 2014) of the core game loop in sports digital games. The user (embodied in their avatar/s) is rated in a neurotic manner: from physical attributes such as stamina and speed, to mental attributes such as composure and awareness, to learned skills such as defending or finishing. After managing this data, the user enacts the data processing as outlined earlier. Depending upon their performance, they are then rewarded with new data to manage: an increase in the avatar's physical attributes, a newly-learned skill, a wage demand, and so on. This tight coupling of anticipation-excitement is analogous to the phases of data management-data processing, generating a subjectivity wholly desirous for more numbers, bigger numbers, pursuing the "digital sublime" of "Big Data" so prevalent in contemporary sports (Hutchins, 2015), seeking the perfect equation.

The Capricious Machine

As mentioned, due to imperfect information, i.e., the designed obfuscation of rules and processes, there is always a degree of capriciousness for the user experience (of course, from the system's perspective, this is wholly deterministic). As Whitson reminds:

> [W]e cannot open up the black box of the software that hides the rules from us. We cannot see why and how and when some of our actions are deemed successful and rewarded versus others that are not. We want to assume that these value judgements are achieved in a fair and impartial manner, but this is not always the case. There is no space in these systems for the mutual negotiation and agreement upon the rules.
>
> *Whitson, 2013, p. 175*

Following the Hook model (Eyal & Hoover, 2014) outlined in the section "Hook and Pull", this aleatory experience is embedded in a few key design features. Depending upon the sub-genre, there are various facets that build in a degree of randomness. The televisual genre offers a player "form" variable, such as the "condition" arrow in the *Pro Evolution Soccer* series, indicating either a boost or penalty to avatar performance (the degree is unspecified by the game interface). More recent features such as "Player Emotion" add to this, transforming an avatar's performative capacity based upon match-day events such as scoring a goal or making a disastrous tackle.

Within the Manager sub-genre, a stochastic veneer permeates the entire data processing phase. The user interacts and makes decisions such as performing "team shouts" and giving half-time "team talks" without any feedback from the system on the impact of such actions: choosing to berate a player-avatar, make a substitution, or yell at the team to "Focus" are left unmoored to any clear feedback loop within the user interface. Instead the player simply watches the match itself progress and is left alone to interpret the success or failure of their interventions.

Random reward mechanisms (RRMs) dominate the televisual genre, seen for example in the *FIFA* series' "card packs". These are in-app purchases (IAPs) users can enact to collect player-avatars for a team they can use online against other players. Again, there is a longer history here traceable to Japanese "gacha toys", baseball cards, and nineteenth century collectible picture cards packaged with cigarettes (Nielsen & Grabarczyk, 2019). Much like their predecessors, the *FIFA* card packs come in an assortment of rarity types and sizes, e.g. a "prime" pack affords a greater possibility to "unwrap" a star player than a "normal", a "jumbo" allows users to buy more players at once than a "small" permits, and so on. The unpacking ritual itself is fully articulate within the series; tactile sounds, elaborate animations and spectacular particle effects bombard the user's audio-visual system as each card is pulled from the pack and salivated over.

Aligned with the audio-visual spectacle, the rhythm of anticipation, excitement and abatement is similar here to gambling and games of chance in a casino; it is of course no coincidence that the variable reward design of *FIFA*'s card packs mirrors that used in slot machines and has recently come under scrutiny as such. PEGI (Pan European Game Information, responsible for the age rating system applied to digital games within Europe) has required an "In-Game Purchases" label to be applied to games with such features since 2018. Meanwhile the *FIFA* series is currently the focus of a court case in France, where the lawyers directly offered the analogy, "[T]he developers of this game mode have created an illusionary and particularly addictive system… We believe that a gambling game has been integrated into this video game because buying packs is nothing more than a bet. It is the logic of a casino that has entered their homes" (Usher, 2020, online). This last line is, perhaps, rather naïve: the affective loop of the digital game has for many years rested upon the variability embedded in the casino. It is simply that the casino's crude implementation has undergone a sophisticated transformation within the digital game.

Conclusion: Numerology

The sports digital game, much like its analogues, has no conclusion. The user is encouraged to play endlessly, each season's end signalling the start of a new transfer window, building towards the next season, fresh opportunities to satiate their arithmomania; the now compulsive need for more numbers, bigger numbers, to infinity. There emerges in this affective loop a numerological compulsion, a worship of and desire for the perfect number, the absolute solution to satisfy the fickle algorithm of the *deus ex machina*.

Both core loops of data management and data processing within any current sport digital game take the computational nature of the medium and perform a substantial transfiguration: the binary ones and zeroes of the computer processing unit (CPU) become decimals, core attributes of an athlete-avatar, characteristics of a formation and playing style, or the physics engine's calculation of collisions. These undergo yet another transformation in the user experience: these attributes become a sense of hard-earned physical prowess, an appreciation of mental acuity, a desire for rare skills. Then a final act of transubstantiation, as the representational veneer of web design, or office software, or televisual convention is varyingly incorporated, and the user answers emails from the board; organises a training session to improve endurance and defensive coordination; or fights against the wind and rain on a miserable winter's day match in northeast England.

The user's sense of fandom is constrained, confined, and yet in the first instance, enabled by these stages of mediation. The emphasis on quantification, the ability to capture in numerical high fidelity every aspect of sport, of performance, of mental competence, of rituals such as team talks, press conferences, and player routine, leads the user to gorge on a sense of efficiency; a flattening of participation, achievement and identity to the white collar work of database configuration and maintenance. Fandom, in a very literal sense, becomes a numbers game.

Note

1 Recently retitled *eFootball Pro Evolution Soccer* to align with Konami's goal of making the series a staple of the eSports industry.

References

Angerer, L. (2018). Intensive bondage. In B. Röttger-Rössler & J. Slaby (Eds.), *Affect in Relation*. London: Routledge.
Blackman, L. (2018). Affect and mediation. In B. Röttger-Rössler & J. Slaby (Eds.), *Affect in Relation*. London: Routledge.
Bolter, J. D., & Grusin, R. (1999). *Remediation: Understanding New Media*. Cambridge: MIT Press.
Conway, S. (2010). "It's in the Game" and Above the Game: An Analysis of the Users of Sports Videogames. *Convergence: The International Journal of Research into New Media Technologies, 16*(3), 334–354.
Conway, S. (2016). An earthless world: the contemporary Enframing of sport in digital games. *Sport, Ethics and Philosophy, 10*(1), 83–96.
Conway, S. (2018). Avastars: The Encoding of Fame within Sport Digital Games. In R. A. Brookey & T. P. Oates (Eds.), *Playing to Win: Sports, Video Games, and the Culture of Play* (pp. 133–151). Indianapolis: Indiana University Press.
Conway, S., & Elphinstone, B. (2019). Towards gameworld studies. *Journal of Gaming & Virtual Worlds, 11*(3), 289–307.

Conway, S., & Finn, M. (2013). Carnival Mirrors: Sport and Digital Games. In B. Hutchins & D. Rowe (Eds.), *Digital Media Sport: Technology, Power and Culture in the Network Society*. London: Routledge.
EA Sports (1993–present). *FIFA* series [numerous]. Redwood City, CA: EA Sports.
EA Vancouver (2012). *FIFA Street 4* [PlayStation 3]. Redwood City, CA: EA Sports.
Eyal, N., & Hoover, R. (2014). *Hooked: How to Build Habit-Forming Products*. Nir Eyal.
Foucault, M. (1995). *Discipline & Punish: The Birth of the Prison*. New York: Vintage Books.
Grusin, R. (2010). *Premediation: Affect and Mediality after 9/11*. Basingstoke and New York: Palgrave.
Hutchins, B. (2015). Tales of the Digital Sublime: Tracing the Relationship Between Big Data and Professional Sport. *Convergence: The International Journal of Research into New Media Technologies*, 22(5), 494–509.
Ihde, D. (1990). *Technology and the Lifeworld: From Garden to Earth*. Indianapolis: Indiana University Press.
Jenkins, E. S. (2016). Updating Narcissus, the Ur-myth of Media, for Digital Gaming. *Games and Culture*, 11(7–8), 647–666.
Konami (1995-present). *eFootball Pro Evolution Soccer* [numerous]. Tokyo, Japan: Konami.
Lazzaro, N. (2004). Why We Play Games: Four Keys to More Emotion Without Story. *Player Experience Research and Design for Mass Market Interactive Entertainment*. Retrieved from www.xeodesign.com/xeodesign_whyweplaygames.pdf
Manovich, L. (2002). *The Language of New Media*. Cambridge, MA: MIT Press.
Mantello, P. (2016). The machine that ate bad people: The ontopolitics of the precrime assemblage. *Big Data & Society*, 3(2), 1–11.
McLuhan, M. (1964). *Understanding Media: The Extensions of Man*. New York: Mentor.
McLuhan, M. (1967). *The Medium is the Massage*. (Q. Fiore, Ed.). London: Penguin Books Ltd.
Nielsen, R. K. L., & Grabarczyk, P. (2019). Are loot boxes gambling? *Transactions of the Digital Games Research Association*, 4(3), 171–207. Retrieved from www.eurogamer.net/articles/2017-10-11-are-loot-boxes-gambling
Norton, M. I., Mochon, D., & Ariely, D. (2011). *The "IKEA effect": When Labor Leads to Love* (No. 11–091). Boston, MA. Retrieved from www.hbs.edu/faculty/Publication Files/11-091.pdf
Paas, F. G. W. C., & Van Merriënboer, J. J. G. (1994). Instructional control of cognitive load in the training of complex cognitive tasks. *Educational Psychology Review*, 6(4), 351–371.
Peper, E., & Harvey, R. (2018). Digital addiction: Increased loneliness, anxiety, and depression. *NeuroRegulation*, 5(1), 3–8.
Rosenberger, R., & Verbeek, P.-P. (2015). A Field Guide to Postphenomenology. In R. Rosenberger & P.-P. Verbeek (Eds.), *Postphenomenological Investigations: Essays on Human-Technology Relations* (pp. 9–41). New York, NY: Lexington Books.
Riedweg, C. (2005). *Pythagoras His Life, Teaching, and Influence*. Ithaca: Cornell University Press.
Röttger-Rössler, B., & Slaby, J. (2018). Introduction. In B. Röttger-Rössler & J. Slaby (Eds.), *Affect in Relation*. London: Routledge.
Sandvoss, C. (2003). *A Game of Two Halves: Football, Television and Globalization*. London: Routledge.
Sports Interactive (2004–present). *Football Manager* series [Mac]. Tokyo, Japan: Sega Games Co.
Suits, B. (2005). *The Grasshopper: Games, Life and Utopia*. Ontario: Broadview Press.
Usher, T. (2020). *Does Fifa Ultimate Team risk turning players into gambling addicts?* Retrieved from www.theguardian.com/commentisfree/2020/feb/04/fifa-ultimate-team-gambling-french-lawsuit-ea-video-game-card-packs
Whitson, J. R. (2013). Gaming the Quantified Self. *Surveillance & Society*, 11(1/2), 163–176.

28
Sports Fans Hunt for Women's Games
Beyond News Media Coverage

Anji L. Phillips and Dunja Antunovic

In the United States, women's sports have seen tremendous growth over the last half-century. Title IX of the Educational Amendments passed by Congress in 1972 paved the way for an increase in opportunities for women and girls to play interscholastic and intercollegiate sports by prohibiting "discrimination on the basis of sex in any federally funded education program or activity" ("Overview of Title IX," 2015, para. 1). Since the 1970s, new leagues, sponsorships, and pay have expanded women's opportunities in professional sport with inconsistent success (Antunovic, 2016). The late 2010s have seen substantial marketing investment and visibility of women's sport despite women's professional leagues struggling to make a profit (Lough & Geurin, 2019).

Sport media outlets, however, persistently underrepresent women's sport. ESPN, a commercial sports channel launched in the fall of 1979, provided unprecedented access to coverage of men's sports (Vogan, 2015), but dedicates comparatively little attention to women's sport (Cooky et al., 2015). Online-only platforms created new opportunities for fans to connect over women's sport—both to consume and produce content (Lough & Geurin, 2019). Although increasingly available, broadcasts of women's sport remain constrained to limited choices of channels that offer sporadic women's sport content. Additionally, women's sport is not offered in a consistent basis in various online platforms. For example, a women's professional hockey game could be "broadcast" on YouTube in one week, and Twitter the next week, which makes the hunt by fans for women's games difficult at best (Phillips & Antunovic, 2019).

This chapter examines the challenges and opportunities that fans of women's sport encounter to access games and engage in mediated fandom. Sport media scholars have dedicated much attention to the study of sports fans, including women who are sports fans (e.g., Esmonde et al., 2015; Osborne & Coombs, 2015; Pope, 2013; Toffoletti, 2017), but substantially less research has been done on fandom and media consumption of women's sport (Mumcu et al., 2016; Whiteside & Hardin, 2011). Therefore, there is relatively little empirical knowledge on the technological, socio-cultural, and economic conditions that structure fandom of women's sport.

In order to examine the process through which fans "hunt" for women's sport, we begin by identifying the ways in which media and technology have fostered and eroded fandom of women's sport. Researchers have extensively documented the scarcity of news coverage of women's sport (Billings & Young, 2015; Cooky et al., 2015; Kian et al., 2008; Roessner & Whiteside, 2016; Tuggle, 1997; Wolter, 2015), and the low production quality of women's sports broadcasts (Billings et al., 2002; Greer et al., 2009). We extend this literature to account for the availability of women's sports competition broadcasts—or lack thereof—in the development of fandom. Next, we identify dominant narratives about fans of women's sport and illustrate how sociological research challenges these narratives and brings light to gendered social structures. In the last section, we point to recent data and to the shifts in the business of women's sport to suggest potential avenues for change (Lough & Geurin, 2019). In the conclusion, we suggest three future areas of research, including the need to center women's sport in sport fandom research, challenge masculinist conceptualizations of fandom and fanship, and build bridges across disciplinary boundaries.

The Media's Role in Fostering and Eroding Fandom of Women's Sport

The media's role in sports has changed for fans of both men's and women's sports over time. Early on men's sports and their fans benefited from broadcasts of competition and coverage during the Golden Age of radio and television. The primary role of media for fans between the 1920s and 1950s in the United States, aside from coverage of competition by reporting scores to fans who could not attend, was to broadcast competitions first over terrestrial radio, and later on broadcast television.

Men's collegiate sport broadcasts became ubiquitous over the last few decades. Broadcast rights for NCAA member schools were restricted between the 1950s and the 1980s to limit the quantity of games broadcast nationally, which did limit fan access. Additional restrictions by the NCAA between 1982 and 1985 were "intended to reduce the adverse effect of live television upon football game attendance" (*NCAA v. Board of Regents of the Univ. of Okla.*, 1984, p. 85). The Supreme Court ruled the NCAA's restrictions on member schools negotiating broadcast rights for national games violated the Sherman Act, and constituted "price fixing" (*NCAA v. Board of Regents of the Univ. of Okla.*, 1984, p. 86). The decision by the Supreme Court in 1984 against the NCAA controlling broadcast rights led to the first exclusive national television broadcast contract between Notre Dame and NBC in 1990 (Gullifor, 2001). Notre Dame was able to extend their fan base due to the availability of their televised games on a national level with competition more easily accessible by fans.

Alternately, a lack of women's sport competitions whether collegiate, semi-professional, professional, or otherwise being programmed by traditional terrestrial network television was limited when ABC, NBC, and CBS were still the household mainstays of television prior to the increase in cable and later satellite subscriptions, and were reflective of those individuals programming the networks. According to Real (2005), "In the first decade of major television sports in the 1950s, the producers and executives in charge of sports television decision making were white males" (p. 346). The thought process by television programmers during this time was that "Sunday afternoon programming was unimportant," and sports like men's golf that did not bring in large ratings, were preferred by programmers, because the executives liked golf, and potential television viewers were out watching "polo matches" (Real, 2005, p. 346).

Fans of women's sport, however, have not been able to rely on the terrestrial networks or even cable and satellite media to program women's sport competitions for fans to watch. Fans still have to hunt for women's sport competitions outside of network, cable, and satellite television, but more choices are being found both domestically and globally with an increased use of websites, apps, and social media platforms to stream women's sport competition content (Phillips & Antunovic, 2019). The LPGA, for example, "secured the long-term extension of the

LPGA/GOLF Channel partnership (2022–2030)… [and] maintains control of all of its media rights outside the United States and receives expanded digital content rights," with additional competitions to air on both legacy NBC and CBS networks (LPGA, 2020). This means the LPGA still has avenues to be able to offer fans outside the United States access to view competition, and still provides LPGA's use of various social media platforms to highlight women's competition to their fans. The LPGA contract, however, shows how the media can both foster fandom of women's sport by providing access to competition, but also fails fans by not providing equal access to women's competition. In contrast, the PGA maintains agreements with both NBC and CBS, while also expanding access with Disney and ESPN+ (LPGA, 2020). The representation of women's competition is still not on parity with men's competition, which hinders access for fans.

Traditional or legacy media (radio, broadcast television, cable, and satellite) then play a dual role in both fostering and eroding fandom of women's sport. Traditional or terrestrial (e.g., over-the-air radio and broadcast television) media, and cable television have the power to broadcast women's sport competitions. It is evident that broadcasts of women's sport have been/are relegated to secondary or tertiary outlets for traditional broadcast organizations such as ESPN where one would expect to find men's sport competition, as an example (Wolter, 2015). More concerning, however, is the absolute lack of televised broadcast outlets for women's sport competition at all. To be clear, women's sport is oftentimes not just relegated to a broadcast with fewer viewers or poor watch times compared to traditional men's teams. An entire season of women's competitions (outside of the Women's National Basketball Association (WNBA)), for example, are not broadcast at all, or only on streaming platforms. Availability of a full season of games is not consistent across women's sport. The WNBA still offers a streaming package to view games from the entire season on their website to make sure their fans have access except for local and national blackouts (WNBA, n.d.). The National Basketball Association (NBA) also offers fans options to view games both online and on demand (NBA, n.d.). The main difference between the two leagues is the price and availability for fans. A WNBA league pass is less than $5, and the NBA league pass has a base price of almost $30, with add-ons for all teams commercial free reaching nearly $125. The $5 league pass is great for fans of women's basketball, but less profit reinforces the stereotype that women's games are not as profitable or as valuable as men's games. Hegemony has its privileges.

Alternately, women's hockey is a sport with no support on broadcast television. Women's first hockey game is documented as taking place in 1891 near the same time as documentation of men's first hockey game (McFarlane, 1994). The modern Olympic games began just five years later in 1896. The International Ice Hockey Federation (IIHF) did not sanction the first official World Championship, however, until 1990 (Etue & Williams, 1996), and it wasn't until 1998 that women's hockey was considered an official sport in the Olympics (Theberge, 2002). Men, however, have been able to compete on the international stage in hockey since 1920. Therefore, women were not offered the legitimacy of the Olympic national stage in ice hockey until almost 80 years after their male counterparts despite their humble beginnings at nearly the same time. The length of time to establish and maintain professional opportunities for women in hockey has stalled with the Canadian Women's Hockey League (CWHL) folding in 2019, along with the ability of women's hockey to gain a footing in traditional radio and television broadcasting compared to their male counterparts (CWHL, 2019). Again, there is no media institutional structure for broadcasts of women's games.

Women's hockey fans have previously had to access games with low production quality via YouTube and Twitter (Phillips & Antunovic, 2019). The 2019–2020 season is the first time the National Women's Hockey League (NWHL) broadcast games on Twitch (NWHL, n.d.). The use of the streaming platform is the first time the league had a single cohesive place for fans of women's hockey to watch without scouring multiple online platforms to find a game. Twitch users can also "co-stream" by directing the NWHL stream to their own account where they can supply their own commentary, and play-by-play. Twitch fosters the fandom of women's sport by providing live access to games, which can then be "rebroadcast" on YouTube for additional consumption and commentary. These opportunities provide potential additional revenue streams through fan donations, and advertising revenue, which strengthens the finances of the organization.

Ultimately, examples of women's basketball and hockey show how traditional media have the ability to both foster and erode fandom of women's sport by broadcasting some, but not other women's sport competitions. The drought of women's competition beginning in early radio and television, and even the addition of satellite radio has created a disconnect in parity between men's and women's sport organizations, and thus, eroded the ability of fans to access competition. Newer niche platforms have the ability to level the playing field previous exclusion by broadcasters created. The evolution of new media platforms, however, often begins with access to men's sport first. For example, on SiriusXM satellite radio you can find play-by-play and sports talk for Major League Baseball (MLB), NBA, National Football League (NFL), and National Hockey League (NHL), but not for professional women's teams in 2020 (SiriusXM, n.d.).

Niche theory, adapted from ecology, and long applied in media, "concern… how populations compete and coexist on limited resources in an ecological community" (Dimmick & Rothenbuhler, 1984, p. 105). There is a finite audience for media consumption in general (Guo, 2019), and sports media in particular. Fans of women's sport niche content is further splintered by the consistent introduction of new niche online media platforms (e.g., YouTube, Twitter, Twitch, etc.). These same platforms have provided much needed access to fans of women's sport, but traditional media outlets of men's sport are also utilizing these same platforms to increase their television and radio share among platforms that stream content over the internet.

Media ecology theory is the foundation for trying to understand "what roles media force us to play, how media structure what we are seeing or thinking, and why media make us feel and act as we do" (Scolari, 2012, p. 205). The disparity felt by women's sport fans is also present for women's sport fans in the gaming community. For example, "When NBA 2K20 was released in 2019, it was the first time the annual game – that premiered in 1999 – featured WNBA players" (Salvado, J., 2020, para. 4). The 2020 release features "The W" mode, which "allows players to create their own WNBA player for the first time" (Salvado, J., 2020, para. 7). Alternately, the NWHL continued to use Twitch as the only platform for "broadcasting" their actual games for 2020–2021 season, while the NHL uses the Twitch platform to livestream the fan-playable NHL game made for the PlayStation and Xbox by EA Sports (NWHL, n.d.; NHL, n.d.).

Thus, fandom of women's sport can be enhanced by traditional media through the normalization of women's sport through consistent and regular broadcasts of competition, and the introduction of women's sport into popular culture through gaming. The current trend of "ghosting" or excluding women's sport competition from traditional over-the-air, cable and satellite broadcasts may give the appearance of eroding or nonexistent fans of women's sport; however, technology in the form of emerging online streaming platforms, and the popularity of eSports has created access for some fans, by providing alternative media outlets for the "broadcast" of women's sport competition.

Dominant Narratives about Fans of Women's Sport

In the context of portrayals of sports fans, both dominant cultural narratives and academic scholarship have rendered fans of women's sport to a marginalized position. As evident from this chapter, traditional broadcast and legacy media have historically eroded opportunities for fans to engage with women's sport content. Following market logic, the industry has put the blame on fans, rather than on structural issues and systemic lack of investment (Lough & Geurin, 2019). Sport industry leaders have constructed at least three cultural narratives surrounding mediated fandom of women's sport: 1) no one is interested in women's sport, 2) women who played sports should/will be watching women's sport, and 3) sex sells women's sport ("Media Coverage," n. d.). Deducting from this narrative, fans of women's sport have been portrayed as nonexistent, or—if they are out there at all—as former female athletes or misogynist men who don't care about women's sport. Feminist sport scholars have responded to these cultural narratives with audience research that disrupts gendered assumptions about women's sport coverage and challenges perceptions about fans of women's sport. Yet, as we argue, sport scholars ought to also consider the ways in which normative conceptualizations of fandom obscure the complex media consumption practices in relation to women's sport.

For decades, sport industry professionals claimed that "no one is interested in women's sport" to justify the lack of media coverage, sponsorship, and financial support. To counter the narrative, researchers have published empirical evidence that indicates an increase in attendance, viewership, and revenue (Lough & Geurin, 2019; "Media Coverage," n.d.). Cultural narratives and representations have primarily focused on fans of men's sport—including female fans—but scarcely on fans of women's sport. Indeed, Wenner (2015) observed a persistent gap by stating that "fanship norms, for female and male fans, disproportionally follow and celebrate male sporting performance," which has rendered fanship of women's sport "exceptional and elusive" (p. 631). However, as we discuss in the final section, interest in women's sport is very much there and fans of women's sport need more consistent empirical attention.

Early scholarship on audiences of women's sport responded to the pattern that, despite the increase in girls' and women's participation in sport, media continued to marginalize and trivialize women's sport. Studies that rely on content or textual analysis on stereotypes in media coverage operated under the assumption that audiences will internalize stereotypes in media coverage without actually conducting studies on audiences. In response, Bruce (1998) took a cultural studies approach to illustrate how contextual factors shaped women's interpretation of televised women's basketball and found that viewers engaged in a complex process of negotiating dominant narratives that devalue women's sport. Contextual factors included previous athletic experience and the structure of the domestic sphere.

By the early 2000s, the continued increase of girls' and women's participation in sport expanded a cultural narrative around audiences of women's sport. Namely, women's sports advocates lamented the lack of support for newly emerged women's professional leagues and argued that women who played sports will and should watch women's sports on television. This argument is based on the women-supporting-women idea. In response to this assumption, Whiteside and Hardin (2011) examined women's motivation to watch sports within the context of leisure in the home. The study based on interviews with married heterosexual women found that watching sports on television for these women was a form of "emotion labor," structured and constrained by the everyday of domestic life (Whiteside & Hardin, 2011, p. 138). Other studies with women who watched sport found that women were expected to adhere to the leisure demands of the men in their lives (e.g., fathers, husbands, sons), who tended to invest time and resources into watching men's sports, but not women's sports (Farrell et al., 2011). The domestic space was a structural factor, for women who had power to control television choices and, thus, watched women's sport (Bruce, 1998). The findings of these studies based on a small sample of interviews cannot be overgeneralized, but the conceptual frameworks reveal structural barriers to women watching women and complicate the dominant cultural narratives surrounding televised consumption of women's sport.

The third cultural assumption in relation to mediated fandom of women's sport is that sex sells. Even an advocacy-oriented documentary by ESPN on the promotion of women's sport concluded that audiences tune in to watch athletes who meet dominant cultural standards of beauty and femininity (Ewing & Grady, 2013). In response, Kane and Maxwell (2011) turned to audience research to examine how audiences interpreted the types of images media most often use to depict women's sport. The findings of the study explicitly disrupted the cultural narrative that sex sells women's sport by providing evidence that audiences (both men and women) expressed the highest level of interest in attending women's sporting events after viewing images associated with athletic competency, rather than sexual objectification (Kane & Maxwell, 2011).

As evident from the research above, audiences of women's sport engage in a complex negotiation of gender, which structures their availabilities and approach to fandom. These negotiations are also evident from research on collectives in the blogosphere, where women carve out space to talk about sport participation, advocate for women's sport, and engage in fandom (Antunovic & Hardin, 2012; Antunovic & Hardin, 2015; Hardin, 2011). Thus, we reiterate recommendations from previous studies that advocate for the critical reflection and disruption of masculinist notions of fandom and that of sport, which have historically excluded both women's sport and fans of women's sport.

Business Imperatives and their Effect on Mediated Fandom

In a 2018 report, Nielsen observed that "Sports must work harder than ever to obtain, retain and grow their fan bases and revenue streams" (Lovett, 2018, para. 5). The main concern among businesses that negotiate media rights, sponsor teams, spend advertising dollars, and even those who own media rights to teams, "is whether media rights revenues will hold up as the traditional TV business is disrupted" (Lovett, 2018, para. 9). The increase in the number of fans cutting the cable cord, and abandoning satellite in exchange for a small return to free over-the-air (OTA) terrestrial broadcasts is on the rise. Overall less expensive over-the-top (OTT) streaming services such as Amazon Prime, Netflix, and Hulu have changed the financial trajectory of all parties who benefit from broadcasting men's and women's sport (Prince & Greenstein, 2017; Sussman, 2017).

Multichannel video program distributors (MVPDs) such as cable, and direct broadcast satellite (DBS) providers are losing subscribers, which reduces the amount of money channels like ESPN receive from MVPDs in return to then both secure media rights and distribute games through subsequent carriage on an MVPD or DBS. ESPN, however, is "well positioned as any cable network to withstand the possibility of further viewer erosion" (Sussman, 2017, p. 461). The loss of subscribers, however, means less money by networks who have typically broadcast sports competition available to secure media rights, which translates to less money paid to teams who are selling these rights by legacy sports channels. Additionally, fewer subscribers also mean less money paid by advertisers to traditional broadcasters, because fewer viewers are watching those same broadcasts and commercials on MVPDs, DBS, or even OTA network television. The rise of multiple online platforms for distribution of sport competition is changing where these finite advertising dollars are being spent, and where fans are accessing games.

Mega events are one place where legacy OTAs, MVPDs, and DBS broadcasts show women's games, and fans turn out to watch. Fox Sports held media rights for the 2015 FIFA Women's World Cup, and U.S. Soccer provided a list of where fans could watch games on various platforms

(Haldane, 2015). The United States Women's National Team (USWNT) Women's World Cup final win over Japan in 2015 "was seen by 25.4 million viewers on FOX—a record for any soccer game, men's or women's, shown on English-language television" in the United States (Sandomir, 2015, para. 1). Another $1.3 million Spanish viewers watched the women's final on Telemundo, in addition to the primary broadcast on FOX (Sandomir, 2015). The 2019 USWNT still drew more legacy television viewers during the day than the 2018 United States Men's National Team (USMNT), in addition to, increasing "the average minute audience of 289,000 viewers… [which is up] 402% from the 2015 Women's World Cup—making it the most-streamed women's final in history" (Hess, 2019, para. 7). Overall, the USWNT garnered 22 percent more viewers than the 2018 USMNT in their respective world cup finals (Hess, 2019),

Yet, the political economy of women's sport remains different from men's (Zill, 2015). The argument often presented to justify the systemic marginalization of women's sport is that fans of women's sport do not buy tickets, or buy merchandise to support their teams. This cyclical nature of treating women's sport as an afterthought erodes financial opportunities businesses may gain from broadcasting women's sport and connections from fans that support women's sport. In fact, "Nike didn't start making and selling USWNT jerseys for men until" the spring of 2015 (Zill, 2015, para. 12). In direct contrast, "according to Nike, the 2019 women's stadium home jersey is the top-selling soccer jersey, men's or women's, ever sold on Nike.com in one season" (Hess, 2019, para. 9). Gear for women's sport is generally difficult to find even after national championship titles (Gibbs, 2019). As marketing research suggests, fans of women's sport care about excitement and product price, which means that "sport marketers should stimulate fans' emotions and build emotional connections between fans women's sports and female athletes" (Mumcu, Lough, & Barnes, 2016, p. 14). Building emotional connections is certainly hard to do when merchandise availability is an issue.

Women's sport is not new to the idea of adapting to the "shut out" or exclusion from the traditional media marketplace on radio or television. Women's sport had/has to continuously seek out new ways to provide fans access to games (Phillips & Antunovic, 2019). Rights holders, brands, and legacy/new media are trying to figure out ways to increase revenue with these new business models, and simply provide fans access to their games. Men's sports are adapting to the changing marketplace of multiplatform access to games the same as women; men are just paid more in these new spaces with increasingly more access (NBA, n.d.; WNBA, n.d.).

Companies such as YouTube launched YouTubeTV to act as a direct competitor to existing MVPDs and DBS platforms (Levenson & Cohen, 2020; YouTubeTV, n.d.). These new streaming spaces do not provide more access to women's games, because the existing programming will carry over from each channel. The channels that were previously limited to outlets and contracts on MVPDs and DBS are providing access to their existing content on a different platform. The price of almost $50 per month is less expensive than many cable and satellite packages, but users will still have to factor in the cost of access to the internet (Levenson & Cohen, 2020). Women's sport will continue to carve out a space for themselves in the growing streaming marketplace. The greater access to men's sport on these platforms has the potential to exclude women's sport in the few places women's sport found a home for games.

Industry data and scholarly work increasingly points to the viability of women's sport and the presence of fans of women's sport (see Lough & Guerin, 2019). In a 2018 sport research report, Nielsen proclaimed that "global interest in women's sport is on the rise," supported by empirical evidence that "84% of sports fans are interested in women's sports" (Nielsen, 2018, para. 1–2). Based on data collected in the U.S., U.K., France, Italy, Germany, Spain, Australia and New Zealand, the report found that 49 percent of the fans interested in women's sport are female and 51 percent are male. Nielsen (2018) positioned women's sport as "untapped potential and new commercial opportunities for rights holders, brands and media" (para. 1). According to the Global Managing Director of Nielsen Sports, Glenn Lovett (2018), diversity issues are on the rise, and so are "new women's sports formats" (para. 2). This tone is notably different from the broader cultural narratives that have dominated conversations about women's sport surrounding the economic downturn in securing and selling media rights. The broadcast and streaming success of women's sport supports the claim that women's sport has untapped potential with regard to fans tuning in to watch women play (Hess, 2019).

The fractured marketplace of multiplatform sports broadcasting will continue to splinter audiences. The question becomes how fast can "broadcasters" on all platforms both produce and procure content using these new mediums to keep up with the changing media landscape in the digital location of their fan base. This new multiplatform media landscape allows fans more power and control over the date, time, and location of their game-watching experience regardless of gender if women are not shut out.

Conclusion: Challenges and Opportunities for Researchers

In an article for the *Huffington Post*, freelance journalist and co-host of the feminist sports podcast *Burn It All Down*, Jessica Luther (2018) wrote:

> It is not fair that to be a fan of women's sports, you have to do this work. We need much more sustained coverage for women's sports, and sports media needs to do better. For that moment, though, this is what we have. So, do what you can today. Don't miss out.
>
> *para. 18*

While this quote addresses fans of women's sport, the lack of sustained coverage raises challenges for researchers of women's sport as well.

To account for changes in the distribution and consumption of women's sport, we offer several potential areas of research. First, simply put, sports media scholars need to pay more attention to fans of women's sport. Since the 1970s, hundreds—if not thousands—of studies have examined the media coverage of sportswomen in a variety of contexts (Bruce, 2016). While numerous studies on sports fandom take gender as an independent variable (Gantz & Wenner, 1995) and/or focus on women who are fans of men's sport (e.g., Osborne & Coombs, 2015; Toffoletti, 2017), fewer place women's sport at the analytical center (Mumcu et al., 2016). Thus, despite the overview we provide in this chapter, scholars have much more to learn about fans of women's sport.

One question the sport media scholars could ask is: How do fans of women's sport access content? What does the process entail? This area presents a methodological challenge because of the relative instability of contracts and the multiplatform nature of women's sports competition broadcasts and fans' sport consumption habits. Technological changes have created new spaces for women's sports, which has significantly shaped availabilities and challenged constructions of fandom. While "new media" continue to center men's sport, women's sport organizations and fans of women's sport have carved out spaces to stream events and provide commentary. Not all of these fractured spaces are communal, but the evolution of niche platforms like Twitch and subsequent distribution on YouTube open up additional revenue streams, and additional places for fans of women's sport to congregate online. As such, consumption of women's sport requires awareness of changes and multiplatform engagement. Various theoretical approaches could be utilized to examine this process, including channel repertoire and uses and gratifications (Sundar & Limperos, 2013; Taneja et al., 2012). The inequity regarding availability of women's sport requires that fans subscribe to multiple platforms. As such, studies ought to take into account financial strains on accessing women's sport content, and in particular how socio-economic status shapes fandom of women's sport. Entertainment price is a key factor in women's fans consumption intentions (Mumcu, Lough, & Barnes, 2016). As such, the affordability of women's sports content should be examined both from a sport marketing perspective and a political economy approach regarding the ownership structures.

Second, sports media scholars need to nuance the measurements of "fanship" and challenge the "generic," yet deeply gendered, constructions of fandom. We, likewise, ought to be careful not to assume that those who *consume* mediated women's sports are *fans* of women's sports. Rather, scholars could build upon the work of van Driel et al. (2019), who argue that "fanship is a multidimensional concept" (p. 626), and use multiple measures to gain conceptual clarity on the dynamics of fans and non-fans. Subsequently, a closer look at the relationship between attitudes towards women's sport, consumption intentions, and intention to seek mediated content is warranted (Mumcu & Marley, 2017).

Further, critical approaches are necessary to examine how, if at all, fandom of women's sport disrupts the male-centered and masculinist associations of sport. Ethnographic work, in particular, would provide depth and complexity to understand how fans negotiate socio-cultural norms and gender ideologies (Esmonde et al., 2015). While this chapter focused only on the U.S. context, future studies could focus on other geopolitical contexts with a particular attention on the media philosophies/landscapes, socio-cultural and political role of sport, national identity, and gender norms that shape mediated fandom.

Finally, in our observation of reviewing this literature, the disciplinary boundaries and citation practices remain surprisingly rigid considering that—regardless of the epistemological and ontological approach—scholarship on fandom of women's sport appears to align on at least one axiological dimension: To change the landscape for women's sport for the better. Subsequently, it would make sense to intentionally build bridges across multiple disciplines and continue the utilization of a variety of theoretical and methodological approaches in this area of study. An interdisciplinary approach that draws on feminist theory, sport sociology, social psychology, sport management and media effects would substantially further theorizing fandom in the context of women's sport. To use Luther's (2018) words, "Do what you can today. Don't miss out."

References

Antunovic, D. (2016). "You had to cover Nadia Comaneci": "Points of change" in coverage of women's sport. *The International Journal of the History of Sport, 33*(13), 1551–1573. https://doi.org/10.1080/09523367.2016.1254623

Antunovic, D., & Hardin, M. (2012). Activism in women's sports blogs: Fandom and feminist potential. *International Journal of Sport Communication, 5*(3), 305–322. https://doi.org/10.1123/ijsc.5.3.305

Antunovic, D., & Hardin, M. (2015). Women and the blogosphere: Exploring feminist approaches to sport. *International Review for the Sociology of Sport, 50*(6), 661–677. https://doi.org/10.1177/1012690213493106

Billings, A. C., Halone, K. K., & Denham, B. E. (2002). "Man, that was a pretty shot": An analysis of gendered broadcast commentary surrounding the 2000 men's and women's NCAA Final Four basketball championships. *Mass Communication & Society, 5*(3), 295–315. https://doi.org/10.1207/S15327825MCS0503_4

Billings, A. C., & Young, B. D. (2015). Comparing flagship news programs: Women's sport coverage in ESPN's SportsCenter and FOX Sports 1's FOX Sports Live. *Electronic News, 9*(1), 3–16. https://doi.org/10.1177/1931243115572824

Ewing, H., & Grady, R. (Directors). (2013, August 27). Branded. (Season 1, Episode 9) [TV series episode]. In J. Dahl, R. Roberts, J. Rosenthal, C. Schell, & B. Simmons (Executive Producers), *Nine for IX*. ESPN Films.

Bruce, T. (1998). Audience frustration and pleasure: Women viewers confront televised women's basketball. *Journal of Sport & Social Issues, 22*(4), 373–397. https://doi.org/10.1177/019372398022004004

Bruce, T. (2016). New rules for new times: Sportswomen and media representation in the third wave. *Sex Roles, 74*, 361–376. https://doi.org/10.1007/s11199-015-0497-6

Cooky, C., Messner, M. A., & Musto, M. (2015). "It's dude time!": A quarter century of excluding women's sports in televised news and highlight shows. *Communication & Sport, 3*(3), 261–287. https://doi.org/10.1177/2167479515588761

CWHL. (2019). *Canadian women's hockey league*. www.thecwhl.com/

Dimmick, J., & Rothenbuhler, E. (1984). The theory of the niche: Quantifying competition among media industries. *Journal of Communication, 34*(1), 103–119. https://doi.org/10.1111/j.1460-2466.1984.tb02988.x

Esmonde, K., Cooky, C., & Andrews, D. L. (2015). "It's supposed to be about the love of the game, not the love of Aaron Rogers' eyes": Challenging the exclusions of women's sports fans. *Sociology of Sport Journal, 32*(1), 22–48. https://doi.org/10.1123/ssj.2014-0072

Etue, E., & Williams, M. (1996). *On the edge: Women making hockey history*. Second Story Press. https://secondstorypress.ca/adult/on-the-edge

Farrell, A., Fink, J. S., & Fields, S. (2011). Women's sport spectatorship: An exploration of men's influence. *Journal of Sport Management, 25*(3), 190–201. https://doi.org/10.1123/jsm.25.3.190

Gantz, W., & Wenner, L. A. (1995). Fanship and the television sports viewing experience. *Sociology of Sport Journal, 12*(1), 56–74. https://doi.org/10.1123/ssj.12.1.56

Guo, M. (2019). Social television viewing with second screen platforms: Antecedents and consequences. *Media and Communication, 7*(1), 139–152. https://doi.org/10.17645/mac.v7i1.1745

Gibbs, L. (2019, November 4). Missing in DC: Washington Mystics WNBA championship gear. *Power Plays*. www.powerplays.news/p/missing-in-dc-washington-mystics

Greer, J. D., Hardin, M., & Homan, C. (2009). "Naturally" less exciting? Visual production of men's and women's track and field coverage during the 2004 Olympics. *Journal of Broadcasting & Electronic Media, 53*(2), 173–189. https://doi.org/10.1080/08838150902907595

Gullifor, P. (2001). *The fighting Irish on the air: The history of Notre Dame football broadcasting*. TaylorTrade Publishing. https://rowman.com/ISBN/9781888698398/The-Fighting-Irish-on-the-Air-The-History-of-Notre-Dame-Football-Broadcasting

Haldane, L. (2015, July 5). Women's world cup: How to watch and follow the 2015 tournament. *U.S. Soccer*. www.mlssoccer.com/post/2015/07/05/womens-world-cup-how-watch-and-follow-2015-tournament

Hardin, M. (2011). The power of a fragmented collective: Radical pluralist feminism and technologies of the self in the sports blogosphere. In A. C. Billings (Ed.), *Sports media: Transformation, integration, consumption* (pp. 40–60). Routledge. www.routledge.com/Sports-Media-Transformation-Integration-Consumption-1st-Edition/Billings/p/book/9780415703321

Hess, A. (2019, July 10). US viewership of the 2019 Women's World Cup final was 22% higher than the 2018 men's final. *CNBC*. www.cnbc.com/2019/07/10/us-viewership-of-the-womens-world-cup-final-was-higher-than-the-mens.html

Kane, M. J., & Maxwell, H. D. (2011). Expanding the boundaries of sport media research: Using critical theory to explore consumer responses to representations of women's sports. *Journal of Sport Management, 25*(3), 202–216. https://doi.org/10.1123/jsm.25.3.202

Kian, E. M., Vincent, J., & Mondello, M. (2008). Masculine hegemonic hoops: An analysis of media coverage of March madness. *Sociology of Sport Journal, 25*(2), 223–242. https://doi.org/10.1123/ssj.25.2.223

Levenson, J., & Cohen, S. (2020, February 28). What is YouTube TV? Here's everything you need to know. *Digital Trends*. www.digitaltrends.com/home-theater/what-is-youtube-tv/

Lough, N., & Geurin, A. N. (2019). Introduction. In N. Lough, & A. N. Geurin (Eds.), *Routledge handbook of the business of women's sport* (pp. 1–5). Routledge. www.routledge.com/Routledge-Handbook-of-the-Business-of-Womens-Sport-1st-Edition/Lough-Geurin/p/book/9781138571617

Lovett, G. (2018). Top 5 global sports industry trends. *Nielsen Sports*. https://nielsensports.com/reports/commercial-trends-sports-2018/

Luther, J. (2018). Everyone loses when women's sports are ignored. *Huffington Post*. www.huffpost.com/entry/opinion-luther-watch-women-sports_n_5af9dee9e4b044dfffb4ea9d

LPGA Communications. (2020, March 9). The LPGA tour and PGA tour announce new media rights portfolio. *LPGA*. www.lpga.com/news/2020-new-television-contract-for-lpga-and-pga-tour

McFarlane, B. (1994). *Proud past, bright future: One hundred years of Canadian women's hockey*. Stoddart Publishing.

Media Coverage + Female Athletes. (n.d.). *The Tucker Center for Research on Girls and Women in Sport, University of Minnesota*. www.cehd.umn.edu/tuckercenter/projects/heresproof.html

Mumcu, C., Lough, N., & Barnes, J. C. (2016). Examination of women's sports fans' attitudes and consumption intentions. *Journal of Applied Sport Management, 8*(4), 25–47. https://doi.org/10.18666/JASM-2016-V8-I4-7221

Mumcu, C., & Marley, S. (2017). Development of the Attitude towards Women's Sport Scale (ATWS). *International Journal of Sport Management, 18*(2), 183–209. www.americanpresspublishers.com/IJSMContents2017.html

NBA. (n.d.). *NBA league pass*. www.nba.com/watch/pricing

NCAA v. Board of Regents of the Univ. of Okla., 468 U.S. 85 (1984). www.loc.gov/item/usrep468085/

NHL. (n.d.). Official channel of the NHL. *Twitch*. www.twitch.tv/nhl

Nielsen. (2018, October 3). Global interest in women's sports is on the rise. *Nielsen*. www.nielsen.com/us/en/insights/article/2018/global-interest-in-womens-sports-is-on-the-rise/

NWHL. (n.d.). Official channel of the NWHL. *Twitch*. www.twitch.tv/nwhl

Osborne, A. C. & Coombs, D. S. (2015). *Female fans of the NFL: Taking their place in the stands*. Routledge. www.routledge.com/Female-Fans-of-the-NFL-Taking-Their-Place-in-the-Stands/Osborne-Coombs/p/book/9781138067875

Overview of Title IX of the Education Amendments of 1972, 20 U.S.C. A§ 1681 ET. SEQ. (n.d.). *The United States Department of Justice*. www.justice.gov/crt/overview-title-ix-education-amendments-1972-20-usc-1681-et-seq

Phillips, A. L., & Antunovic, D. (2019). "Seeking a storybook ending": Examining the future distribution of women's sporting events. In G. G. Armfield, J. McGuire, & A. Earnheardt (Eds.), *ESPN and the changing sports media marketplace*., Vol. 2. Communication, Sport, and Society, pp. 269–287. Lang Publishing, Inc. https://doi.org/10.3726/b15990

Pope, S. (2013). "The Love of my Life:" The Meaning and importance of sport for female fans. *Journal of Sport and Social Issues, 37*(2), 176–195. https://doi.org/10.1177/0193723512455919

Prince, J., & Greenstein, S. (2017). Measuring consumer preferences for video content provision via cord-cutting behavior. *Journal of Economics & Management Strategy, 26*(2), 293–317. https://doi.org/10.1111/jems.12181

Real, M. (2005). Television and sports. In J. Wasko (Ed.), *A companion to television* (1st ed., pp. 337–360). Blackwell Publishing Ltd.

Roessner, A., & Whiteside, E. (2016). Unmasking Title IX on its 40th birthday: The operation of women's voices, women's spaces, and sporting mythnarratives in the commemorative coverage of Title IX. *Journalism, 17*(5), 583–599. https://doi.org/10.1177/1464884915572868

Salvador, J. (2020, November 25). WNBA players: New NBA 2K21 features for women's game "just surreal". *USA Today*. https://doi.org/10.17645/mac.v7i1.1745

Sandomir, R. (2015, July 6). Women's World Cup Final was most-watched soccer game in United States history. *New York Times*. www.nytimes.com/2015/07/07/sports/soccer/womens-world-cup-final-was-most-watched-soccer-game-in-united-states-history.html

Scolari, C. (2012). Media ecology: Exploring the metaphor to expand the theory. *Communication Theory, 22*(2), 204–225. https://doi.org/10.1111/j.1468-2885.2012.01404.x

SiriusXM. (n.d.). *SiriusXM sports*. www.siriusxm.com/sports?intcmp=RC_NA_www:sports_ViewallSportsChannels#channelgroup-1550769689918

Sundar, S. S., & Limperos, A. M. (2013). Uses and grats 2.0: New gratifications for new media. *Journal of Broadcasting & Electronic Media, 57*(4), 504–525. https://doi.org/10.1080/08838151.2013.845827

Sussman, D. W. (2017). Are our pastimes past their time? How will the media industry disruption and changes to the legal environment affect the sports industry? *Syracuse Law Review, 67*, 449–514. https://heinonline.org/HOL/LandingPage?handle=hein.journals/syrlr67&div=20&id=&page=

Taneja H., Webster J. G., Malthouse E. C., & Ksiazek, T. B. (2012) Media consumption across platforms: Identifying user-defined repertoires. *New Media & Society, 14*(6), 951–968. https://doi.org/10.1177/1461444811436146

Theberge, N. (2002). Challenging the gendered space of sport: Women's ice hockey and the struggle for legitimacy. In S. Scraton, & A. Flintoff (Eds.), *Gender and sport: A reader* (pp. 292–302). Psychology Press.

Toffoletti, K. (2017). *Women sport fans: Identification, participation, representation*. Routledge. www.routledge.com/Women-Sport-Fans-Identification-Participation-Representation-1st-Edition/Toffoletti/p/book/9781138189270

Tuggle, C. A. (1997). Differences in television sports reporting of men's and women's athletics: ESPN SportsCenter and CNN Sports Tonight. *Journal of Broadcasting & Electronic Media, 41*(1), 14–24. https://doi.org/10.1080/08838159709364387

van Driel, I. I., Gantz, W., & Lewis, N. (2019). Unpacking what it means to be—or not be—a fan. *Communication & Sport, 7*(5), 611–629. https://doi.org/10.1177/2167479518800659

Vogan, T. (2015). *ESPN: The making of a sports media empire.* Urbana, IL: University of Illinois Press. www.press.uillinois.edu/books/catalog/65gtw7be9780252039768.html

Wenner, L. A. (2015). Communication and sport, where art thou? Epistemological reflections on the moment and field(s) of play. *Communication & Sport, 3*(3), 247–260. https://doi.org/10.1177/2167479515584781

Whiteside, E., & Hardin, M. (2011). Women (not) watching women: Leisure, time, television, and implications for televised coverage of women's sports. *Communication, Culture & Critique, 4*(1): 122–143. https://doi.org/10.1111/j.1753-9137.2011.01098.x

WNBA. (n.d.). *League pass.* https://leaguepass.wnba.com/packages

Wolter, S. (2015). A critical discourse analysis of espnW: Divergent dialogues and postfeminist conceptions of female fans and female athletes. *International Journal of Sport Communication, 8*(3), 345–370. https://doi.org/10.1123/IJSC.2015-0040

YouTubeTV. (n.d.). Watch live TV from 70+ channels. *YouTube.* https://tv.youtube.com/welcome/

Zill, Z. (2015, July 16). Soccer's sexist political economy. *Jacobin.* www.jacobinmag.com/2015/07/womens-world-cup-fifa-hope-solo-wages/

29
Twitter Discourse in the Southeaster Conference
The Nick Saban Effect

Vincent L. Benigni and Lance V. Porter

After seeing its football program register just three winning seasons in the previous seven, the University of Alabama lured Nick Saban away from the NFL's Miami Dolphins in 2007. University administrators hailed Saban as the catalyst to help Alabama become a national university (Brady, Berkowitz & Schnaars, 2017).

Saint Nick has delivered the goods, bringing six national championships to Tuscaloosa while winning an astounding 88 percent of his games. He is credited for transforming the academic and physical infrastructure of the university, while fomenting a cultural revolution within both city and state. Saban's $9 million annual salary (excluding lucrative incentive bonuses) is considered a bargain given that applications, student grade-point averages and entrance exam scores have skyrocketed since his arrival. He recently signed a contract extension that runs until 2028.

Saban personifies the modern CEO (Brady et al., 2017), and brings significant return on investment (Hurt, 2017). In doing so, he generates a "staggering number of (media) headlines with his thoughts on the state and future of the game... as the greatest coach of all time" (Braziller & Kussoy, 2019, para. 5). His unprecedented success has also spawned a cottage industry of fan and media engagement, particularly on Twitter. Here we take a close look at a decade's worth of those tweets through the lens of cultural studies and field theory to understand Saban's effect on the commodification of sport.

SEC Football Fandom – Media, Money and Mobilization

To examine commodification in college football, it is instructive to first examine where the money is: television. For the 2019 season, the *SEC on CBS* – the prime scheduling television block for college football on Saturday fall afternoons – averaged a 4.32 rating (up 24 percent from 2018) and 7.10 million viewers, ranking as the network's most-watched college football package since 1990 (Paulsen, 2019). The conference has produced 11 of the last 15 college football national champions. Such prestige begets profound pressure, particularly on the SEC's head coaches, the best compensated in the country at an average of $5 million annually.

The SEC's "dump truck" (Towers, 2017, para. 17) of $45 million in revenues doled out per school in 2019 is largely funded through big media. ESPN, which paid $2.2 billion to launch the SEC Network in 2013, is expected to outbid CBS in 2023 for exclusive rights to Saturday afternoon football games (15 to 17 games annually) at an estimated annual price of $330 million, dwarfing the current $55 million per annum in the 15-year CBS contract (Ourand, 2019). ESPN's current contract for the remaining games was extended through 2034. The new revenues should move annual payouts (per SEC university) to $63 million, surpassing the Big Ten's per-school disbursement of $52 million (Cobb, 2020). Furthermore, ESPN's plethora of digital platforms allow for more targeted smartphone content in a hyper-commodified sports landscape (Hutchins, 2019).

Football commodification began to gather steam in 1990 (Walsh & Giulianotti, 2001), and similarly, SEC coffers have ballooned in that timeframe. Conference commissioner Roy Kramer green-lighted the inaugural SEC title game in Birmingham in 1992, and since moving to Atlanta two years later, the annual event has brought more than $1 billion in economic impact to Georgia (Burns, 2015). Current SEC commissioner Greg Sankey and ESPN president Jimmy Pitaro join Nick Saban as the sport's three biggest influencers (Braziller & Kussoy, 2019).

While traditional media pulls purse strings in SEC football circles, emergent fans seek more interactive outlets than TV and talk radio. They have been mobilized to digital and social platforms to gain influence (Benigni, Porter & Wood, 2013; Porter, Wood & Benigni, 2011). Social identification is gleaned from both obsessive and harmonious fan passion, dictating social media behavior related to the team (Wakefield, 2016). College football yields the most social media fervor (Syme & Dosh, 2015), forges more tribalism than other consumer audiences (Steinbach, 2009), and elicits an array of constructive and destructive emotions (Porter et al., 2011). Social media engagement in sport efficiently advances customer–organization interactions (Abeza, O'Reilly, Seguin & Nzindukiyimana, 2015) through a branded, "backstage sensation" which drives revenues (Hipke & Hachtmann, 2014, p. 517).

Newer fans prefer a more virtual relationship because of more competition for their time and money (Moor, 2007). Despite some critique of Twitter as a site of sports research that reflects overall public opinion (Wenner, 2014a), Twitter is the dominant social media platform in sport (Browning & Sanderson, 2012). Deprez, Mechant and Hoebeke (2013) note that the blurring between professional and personal communication allows Twitter to serve as a platform for dialogue, and to build a newsmaker brand (for both fan and pundit). Wenner (2014b) has postulated that as today's social media has transitioned into the mainstream, it has merely served to prop up legacy media and the traditional institutions of sport instead of supplanting them.

Through opinion-centric platforms such as social media and podcasting, college football print journalists leverage institutional theory and news ecology to fortify work routines and instrumental behaviors. In particular, the second-screen focus and appeal of Twitter provides an entertaining social gathering space; this brand alternative is critical given that writers are now judged on number of followers and retweets, instead of having the last word (Roberts & Emmons, 2016). Previous researchers have theorized that story ideas in sport emanated from followers, the new gatekeepers (Sheffer & Schultz, 2010), resulting in a flattened media hierarchy and more connectedness between fan and sport entity (Gibbs & Haynes, 2013). This development provides a more even playing field for smaller market teams (such as SEC cities) with resource constraints in line with economic demand theory (Watanabe, Yan & Soebbing, 2015).

Twitter's second-screen sporting utility (Hull & Lewis, 2014) allows for filtered fan opinion along with critical, objective analysis that can sustain print journalism in the social media age (Price, Farrington & Hall, 2013). Consumers still value the truthfulness of mainstream over social (Stoldt, Noble, Ross, Richardson & Bonsall, 2013), and sports reporters now integrate significant daily value to the Twittersphere (Burns, 2015).

Clavio, Burch and Frederick's (2012) study of Big Ten football teams cited systems theory to analyze traditional media-operated Twitter "hubs." Many interactive tweets from fans are directed toward traditional media, whose accounts tend to interact greatly with each other, while non-traditional accounts (blogs, message boards, etc.) appear to possess users focused on mutual interactivity.

Thus, the intersection of traditional and emerging media in college football supports Jhally's (1984) sports/media complex with regard to capitalism – a Marxist-informed analysis of generational sporting love highlighted by spectacle and accumulation. This notion infers a culture of promotion that Carson and Rinehart (2010) see as a toxic potion… a commodity fundamentally changing the role of athletics on campus. Wenner (1998) coined the term "mediasport" to describe how sports and mass communication have been combined to exploit the lucrative multimedia markets that sports offer. Certainly, the SEC has delivered on that promise.

Bourdieu offers an instructive lens through which to view mediasport and how social and mobile media may be accelerating the commodification of sport. His theories of capital, habitus and field have further informed the study of power relations in digital media (Ignatow & Robinson, 2017; Daniels, Gregory & Cottom, 2016; Lupton, 2014; Marres, 2017; Orton-Johnson & Prior, 2013) as well as the field of sport (see, for example, Duncan, 2016; 2018; English, 2016). According to Bourdieu (1990; 1993; 1994), different social groups struggle to compete within various fields such as education, the arts, law, politics and the economy to earn social, cultural, symbolic and economic capital. Capital represents any form of power that enables citizens to participate in a field of society to gain further power, thereby improving their positions within a field. Bourdieu examines this power by asking who consumes culture and to what effect (Sardar & Van Loon, 2010).

Such capital comes in many forms. According to Duncan (2016), social capital represents resources such as relationships and networks of influence or support. Similarly, cultural capital represents non-financial social assets that promote social mobility and the ability to read cultural codes such as education, knowledge and skills. In contrast, symbolic capital represents resources such as prestige, honor or recognition. Perhaps most importantly to this study, economic capital represents one's command over financial resources. Bourdieu believed that economic capital tended to dominate the other fields. As citizens compete with one another to gain economic capital, all fields begin to resemble the economic field and consequently, one another. While Bourdieu places sports in the arts and entertainment field, he (1993), along with Duncan (2016; 2018) and Wenner (1998), found that economic and media factors have begun to dominate the play aspects of the field of sport. In fact, Duncan (2018) described sport as having moved inside the media field, which is already inside the economic field,

> The role and influence of the media field, already influenced by the economic field, has also merged with the sport field, utilizing play as a product to market and sell to a mass consumer audience to generate profit.
>
> *p. 21*

To understand a field requires examining the ideology of that field. Habitus represents the historical system of responses and dispositions or "feel for the game" that individuals develop in the field in which they are competing (Bourdieu, 1990, p. 52). In other words, habitus represents ideology, or how citizens within a field see themselves and each other. Digital media researchers have developed methods of defining and measuring habitus through sentiment analysis along with likes and favorites (Ignatow & Robinson, 2017). Here we will use an algorithm that categorizes tweets to understand the patterns and responses over the course of 10 years. In addition, we will use likes and favorites as a proxy for understanding users' values and ideology around Nick Saban.

Brothers in Arms

Because college players are not paid, commodification often plays out in the form of an arms race for facilities and resources designed to attract both player and fan. Ten of the top 25 football facilities reside in SEC institutions (Crawford, 2020), and from 1999 to 2012, all 14 SEC schools underwent significant facilities upgrades (Farner, 2016). Player amenities include nutrition centers, ventilated lockers, customized player pods, hydrotherapy pools, TV screens above every sink/mirror, and video game arcades. And at South Carolina, alum Darius Rucker funded a sound recording studio (Crawford, 2020).

The southern football arms race stems from a wartime resource mentality (Moran, 2019; Dyer, 2019) and an instant-veneration culture (Steinbach, 2011) where stagnation can mean disaster (Pope, 2019). While the Big Ten is the only comparable conference regarding football payouts to its schools (Berkowitz, 2019), Texas A&M (8th) and Vanderbilt (24th) are the only SEC schools among the nation's Top 30 endowments, while the Big Ten has five (Barham, 2019). SEC schools do benefit from their bucolic locations and limited entertainment options (Santesteban & Leffler, 2017).

Leveraging its fandom and football prowess, the University of Alabama established The Crimson Standard, a 10-year plan to enhance the student-athlete experience, recruiting efforts and game-day experience (McNair, 2019) for fans. The $600-million project, launched in 2018, includes new club and box seats at Bryant-Denny Stadium, and a sports science center (Martin, 2020). And of course, crimson strobe lights for pre-game introductions (Crawford, 2020).

The SEC Coaching Carousel: Nick Saban as Coach Whisperer

This arms race also contributes to a pressurized coaching environment. There have been 36 head coaching changes in the SEC during Saban's tenure, including five coaches who won national championships while at SEC schools. Athletic directors and university presidents are pressed to fire coaches based on fan/donor pressures, exacerbated through the hyper-charged nature of social and digital media platforms. Contract buyouts of SEC head coaching contracts routinely cost more than $10 million to member schools, with most occurring in state-funded institutions. The rationale to recalibrate is understandable… a school cannot afford to retain a bad coach (Cox, 2017).

Coaching hires spawn renewed optimism, even though only five of the conference's 14 member schools have won SEC titles in the last 21 years. Conference decision makers covet talent from the Saban coaching tree, a dizzying development that some consider his greatest achievement (Pinak, 2019). In recent years, seven Saban protégés have been hired as head coaches in the SEC. In 2017, Texas A&M lured former Saban/LSU assistant Jimbo Fisher from Florida State with a record $75 million contract. Two years prior, Alabama defensive coordinator Kirby Smart was tabbed at Georgia. Even the Tide's celebrated strength coach, Scott Cochran, was poached by Smart in 2020 to become UGA's special-teams coordinator (Talty, 2020).

Saban's dynasty begs imitation, a bandwagon (Kwon, Trail & Lee, 2008) blueprint reshaping an entire sport, in hopes of replicating the inimitable (Scarborough, 2018). Saban's disruptive style is being embraced and imitated (O'Keefe, 2018), and coaching turnover is linked to his domination (McFadden, 2017). The league's bandwagon outlier is Auburn, whose coach (Gus

Malzahn) has no Saban ties, and enough wins (a record-tying three over Saban) to satiate the individualistic, dissonant and rebellious nature (Campbell, Aiken & Kent, 2004) of a bitter in-state rival.

The Sisyphean quest to stem the Tide has yielded some bizarre consequences. After firing former Saban assistant Derek Dooley in 2017, Tennessee announced it would hire respected coaching veteran Greg Schiano. However, his hiring was derailed by an orchestrated social media smear campaign led by influential sports media provocateur (and Tennessee native) Clay Travis. Notable football pundits characterized the chaotic chorus – which included high-profile politicians on Twitter – as "delusional… a social media mob" (Staples, 2017, paras. 7, 8), "weaponized… unprecedented (in) speed and tenor" (Auerbach, 2020, para. 31), "internet vigilantes… bullying… rubes" (Forde, 2017, para. 4), and "the craziest day in the history of the coaching carousel… nuclear" (Schlabach, 2017; paras. 5, 7). The Volunteers would (of course) eventually hire Jeremy Pruitt, Saban's defensive coordinator, who lasted just three years in Knoxville before being fired in 2020.

Whether it's seen as a mob mentality or a copycat culture, SEC fans, coaches and media continue to stalk Nick Saban, the existential epicenter of college football for a generation. Channels for this aggression are evolving, with social media platforms (especially Twitter) emerging as a more accessible and mobilizing alternative in an increasingly disintermediated landscape. Given that Twitter is the main stage for this discussion, and that Saban is the dominant figure in the most successful conference, we will examine how the discussion of Saban on Twitter furthers the commodification of college football. Therefore, we propose the following research questions:

> RQ1: What is the habitus regarding Saban around the sports, media and economic fields?
> RQ2: Who are the influencers gaining social capital through this conversation?

Methods

Data

Social media allows researchers to view fields, habitus and capital in the data that users leave behind. Digital researchers have used methods such as word clouds, mind maps and path diagrams to observe and define fields (Ignatow & Robinson, 2017; Viégas & Wattenberg, 2008; Wheeldon & Åhlberg, 2012). We used Crimson Hexagon (CH), a social media analytics tool that offers access to the Twitter firehose (Hitlin, 2013; Hopkins & King, 2010) to gather tweets from January 1, 2010 until June 9, 2020, mentioning the word "Saban" and at least one of approximately 80 other football-related terms such as "coach," "Alabama," or "SEC." Academic researchers have used CH in the past to examine issues in social media such as frames and messaging (McGregor, Lawrence & Cordona, 2016; McGregor, 2014; Williams & Gonlin, 2017). After examining preliminary results, we excluded any terms that were unrelated to Nick Saban. This search yielded 6,291,871 tweets for analysis.

Algorithm Training

We used the CH Brightview machine learning feature to train an opinion monitor to code tweets related to sports, media and economic fields from this data. Examining a random sample of tweets in this monitor, we hand coded exemplar tweets belonging to several recurring categories related to these fields, allowing the CH algorithm to learn to categorize relevant data.

The algorithm requires a minimum of 20–45 tweets unambiguously representing each category to code properly. We trained 154 tweets for the following categories: *coaching tree, hiring/firing, arms race, media impact*, or *off topic*. The *coaching tree* category involved tweets that mentioned Saban along with any other coach who was part of his staff as compiled in articles in the popular press about the Saban coaching tree (Cannon, Berkowitz & Sergent, 2018; Pinak, 2019) or the words "coaching tree." *Hiring/firing* involved tweets that mentioned the words "hired" or "fired" along with Saban and another coach's name. *Arms race* involved the mentioning of the words "facilities," "budgets," "recruiting" or the words "arms race." *Media impact* involved tweets mentioning words such as "media," "press," and "journalist." *Off topic* included other topics not related to commodification such as in-game coaching analysis. After we completed training, the algorithm classified the full corpus of tweets based on the training data.

Social Capital Analysis

We randomly selected and exported 10,000 tweets for further analysis, using the Twitter Capture and Analysis Tool (TCAT) to fetch additional data from those tweets not provided by CH. The TCAT data allowed us to isolate and export @mentions for further network analysis to observe and measure social capital by seeing who was driving these conversations. In addition, we were able to see how often each tweet was favorited and retweeted so that we could see the implications of these tweets.

We used Gephi, a social network analysis tool, to visualize social networks tweeting about Saban by @mention of the top 500 users in this group. Gephi allowed us to use algorithms to further classify these users into specific communities who were @mentioning each other (Blondel, Guillaume, Lambiotte & Lefebvre, 2008). In addition, we used Gephi to calculate eigenvector centrality, which measures influence, taking into account both the number of times each user is @mentioned and also the influence of who they are @mentioned by. Users who are @mentioned more by users who also are highly mentioned, have higher eigenvector scores (Hansen, Schneiderman, Smith & Himelboim, 2019). In other words, eigenvector centrality measures not only how many you know, but who you know. We coded all influencers with eigenvector scores into the type of user (institutional, fan, media, etc.) by researching their individual Twitter accounts.

RQ1: What is the habitus regarding Saban around the sports, media and economic fields?

The habitus of Twitter conversation around Saban was dominated (61 percent) by economic concerns, mostly mentions of his coaching tree, followed by discussions of media impact, the arms race, and hiring and firing (see Figure 29.1).

The tweets cycled in predictable patterns each year, culminating in spikes (see Figure 29.2) around each year's national championship game and the weeks following the end of the season.

As coaches were hired and fired, discussions on Twitter centered mostly around media posts regarding the economic implications of programs hiring head coaches from the Saban coaching tree. Figure 29.3 provides a word cloud that illustrates the most common words in the coaching tree category. The most prominent names in the word cloud represent NCAA personnel, coaches from the Saban tree, and athletic directors in the SEC and competing conferences.

Off-topic tweets tended to reference pre-game, second screening and post-game analysis, recruiting prospects, and fans reacting emotionally to the outcome of individual games and seasons. Figure 29.4 shows the top 10 retweets over the past decade. These tweets are often

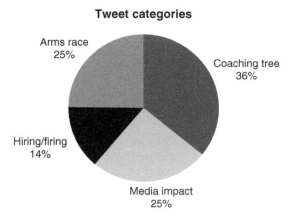

Figure 29.1 Commodification Tweet Categories
*Note: excludes 39% of tweets Off Topic

humorous (including several from a noted Nick Saban impressionist), and posted during times of peak fan interest (such as recruiting season) as referenced in Figure 29.2.

To further analyze the habitus of these tweets, we conducted one-way analyses of variance with a Tukey post hoc test to compare the number of times tweets were favorited and retweeted in each category. Tweets that were off topic were favorited significantly more (M = 18.79) than tweets about the arms race (M = 3.28), hiring/firing (M = 2.46), or media impact (M = 4.39, F (5, 10233) = 3.91, p=.002). Favorited tweets about the coaching tree category (M = 7.98) were not significantly different from other categories. Differences among these categories' retweets were not significant.

RQ2: Who are the influencers gaining social capital through this conversation?

Out of the top 100 users with eigenvector centrality scores, media accounts were most influential among users tweeting about Saban. Of the top 100 most influential users, media comprised 64 of these accounts, with 28 fan accounts, six institutional accounts, one athlete and one coach making up the balance. Media users were split among 20 broadcast, 31 online media accounts and 11 print media accounts. In terms of national versus regional, national media led the list with 37 users, compared to 27 regional media users. Figure 29.5 illustrates the most significant national pundits (e.g., former Alabama quarterback and current SEC analyst Greg McElroy and CBS Sports national writer Barrett Sallee), and regional media influencers (e.g., longtime Alabama newspaper beat writer Cecil Hurt, along with @TideSports). Colors represent communities who @mention each other, with lines showing connection. The circumference of the nodes represents eigenvector centrality or influence. The smaller, illegible nodes on the right of the illustration are mostly fans with little influence.

Discussion

In the Saban Twittersphere, economic and media fields dominate the sport field in terms of influence and social capital because that's what influential media members are interested in

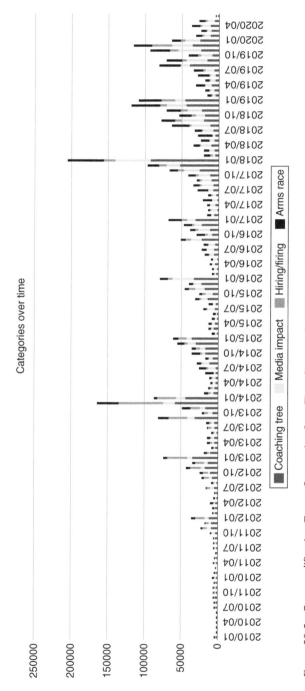

Figure 29.2 Commodification Tweet Categories Over Time (January 1, 2010–June 9, 2020)
*Note: excludes 39% of tweets Off Topic

Figure 29.3 Word Cloud: Coaching Tree Category

discussing with each other. Wenner's conception of mediasport certainly holds true here. Over the past decade, as social media has become more mainstream and Twitter the dominant forum, traditional institutions of sport are the main players here. Despite print media giving way to online forms, we still see print and broadcast journalists holding positions of gatekeeping and social power here within these networks alongside their online counterparts. Our work rejects previous notions of flattened hierarchies and more connectedness between fans and their chosen institution. We find no evidence that fans have gained extensive social power in these networks.

Even so, because 39 percent of the conversation is about subjects other than commodification, and that fans are more interested in favoriting non-commodification topics, Bourdieu's notion of the play field still occupies an important part of the Twitter discourse. Gameday and second-screening conversations are favorited more than commodification topics, confirming that fans see utility in sharing their opinions with each other and with the media (Clavio et al., 2012). The network visualization (Figure 29.5) clearly shows less influential fans clustering around Alabama football, conversing with each other more about play/game results, while media influencers talk mainly to each other about commodification topics.

Retweet	Occurrences	Original Author
Nick Saban out here recruiting his ass off 😂😂😂😂😂 https://t.co/aevlvnni94 (1/28/19)	21000	Aj_Marshall17 (AJ Marshall)
Nick Saban pulling in the driveway as we speak https://t.co/Ppmsuhwppy (3/22/19)	20000	ChickenColeman (Depressed Cowboys Fan)
Nick Saban recommends I play 59 minutes and 59 seconds instead. (1/1/13)	11000	NatePlay60 (Play 60 Kid)
Nick Saban after opening Christmas gifts https://t.co/gnqHPDlowH (12/25/19)	11000	JoeyMulinaro (Joey)
Nick Saban and the Tide after getting the final spot in the playoff... https://t.co/A4XPUONdGN (1/3/17)	9800	BleacherReport (Bleacher Report)
Coach O calls Nick Saban before the #CFBPlayoff https://t.co/0BknVQc6ow (12/27/19)	8800	JoeyMulinaro (Joey)
Mrs. Saban prepping thanksgiving "Honey, what side should we bring?" Nick Saban: https://t.co/GL9vs1jNO6 (11/27/19)	8000	JoeyMulinaro (Joey)
Nick Saban doesn't mess around 😂😂 https://t.co/SjGNKJPdPA (11/13/19)	5700	ILiveForFball (I Live For Football)
The debate is over. Nick Saban is the greatest coach in college football history. (1/9/18)	5500	finebaum (Paul Finebaum)
Nick Saban got emotional when asked about Jalen Hurts' comeback https://t.co/3N2Xrtr00b (1/2/18)	5300	BleacherReport (Bleacher Report)

Figure 29.4 Top 10 Saban Retweets from January 1, 2010–June 9, 2020

However, the coaching tree category offers an exception to this finding. Of the four commodification topics, the coaching tree is most closely related to Saban and his coaching abilities, and is therefore more attributable to play-oriented discussions. Perhaps fans agree with the regional and national media that hiring one of Saban's protégés is the key to winning, because both entities strongly believe that Saban's influence is the primary catalyst for the program's dominance. This exception may portend why commodification is now inextricably part of sport. The economic field dominates a "win at all costs" sport field.

Conclusion

Prominent southern college football media personality Paul Finebaum noted that Saban's value to Alabama, even during the COVID-19 pandemic, is $100 million per year (Bratton, 2020). But at 70, can Saban hold off legacy threats such as Clemson head coach Dabo Swinney, who has twice defeated the Crimson Tide in recent national-title games? Will Saban continue to dictate a competitive landscape that now includes player compensation rights and cultural upheaval?

Our work is not without limitations. We examined a fraction of the discussions around Nick Saban over the past 10 years. Twitter may be the dominant forum for sports discussion, but most

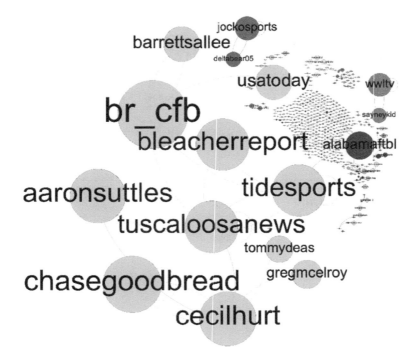

Figure 29.5 Network Visualization of Influence by Eigenvector Centrality

Americans (including Saban) do not use the platform. In addition, to identify and categorize users, we relied solely on information from Twitter bios. With the prominent media dominating this conversation usually having verified Twitter accounts, this method was appropriate here. However, to get a true gauge of fan opinion and sentiment, more work is required to better identify and classify these users, such as surveys and interviews. Future research could combine social media data from other platforms and sports communities with surveys to provide a richer picture of the commodification of sport.

References

Abeza, G., O'Reilly, N., Seguin, B. & Nzindukiyimana, O. (2015). Social media scholarship in sport management research: a critical review. *Journal of Sport Management*, 29, 601–618.
Auerbach, N. (2020, Feb. 20). The reintroduction of head coach Greg Schiano. The Athletic. https://theathletic.com/1621672/2020/02/20/greg-schiano-rutgers-head-coach-career/
Barham, J.A. (2019, Sept. 13). The 100 richest universities: their generosity and commitment to research. The Best Schools. https://thebestschools.org/features/richest-universities-endowments-generosity-research/
Benigni, V.L., Porter, L.V. & Wood, C. (2013). The new game day: fan engagement and the marriage of mediated and mobile. In Billings, A.C. and Hardin, M. (Eds.) *Routledge Handbook of Sport and New Media* (pp. 225–236). New York: Routledge.
Berkowitz, S. (2019, May 15). Big Ten Conference had nearly $759 million in revenue in fiscal 2018, new records show. *USA Today*. www.usatoday.com/story/sports/2019/05/15/big-ten-revenue-hit-nearly-759-million-fiscal-2018/3686089002/
Blondel, V., Guillaume, J., Lambiotte, R. & Lefebvre, E. (2008). Fast unfolding of communities in large networks. *Journal of Statistical Mechanics: Theory and Experiment* 2008 (10), P1000.
Bourdieu, P. (1990). *The Logic of Practice*. Cambridge: Polity Press.

Bourdieu, P. (1993). How can one be a sportsman? In Bourdieu, P. *Sociology in Question*. London: Sage, 117–131.

Bourdieu, P. (1994). Raisons pratiques. Sur la théorie de l'action. Paris: SEUIL.

Brady, E., Berkowitz, S. & Schnaars, C. (2017, Oct. 25). Is Nick Saban underpaid at more than $11 million this season? *USA Today*. www.usatoday.com/story/sports/ncaaf/sec/2017/10/25/nick-saban-underpaid-more-than-11-million-season/794275001/

Bratton, M.W. (2020, July 21). Paul Finebaum doesn't believe Nick Saban needs to take a pay cut at Alabama, says Tide coach is worth $100 million a year. *Saturday Down South*. www.saturdaydownsouth.com/alabama-football/paul-finebaum-nick-saban-100-million-value-crimson-tide-pay-cut/

Braziller, Z. & Kussoy, H. (2019, Aug. 27). The 20 most powerful people in college football. *The New York Post*. https://nypost.com/2019/08/27/the-20-most-powerful-people-in-college-football/

Browning, B. & Sanderson, J. (2012). The positives and negatives of Twitter: exploring how student-athletes use Twitter and respond to critical tweets. *International Journal of Sport Communication*, 5, 503–521.

Burns, M.J. (2015, Dec. 4). How much is the SEC championship worth to the city of Atlanta? *Forbes*. www.forbes.com/sites/markjburns/2015/12/04/how-much-is-the-sec-championship-worth-to-the-city-of-atlanta/#50baeaa254be

Campbell, Jr., R.M., Aiken, D. & Kent, A. (2004). Beyond BIRGing and CORFing: continuing the exploration of fan behavior. *Sport Marketing Quarterly*, 13, 151–157.

Cannon, J., Berkowitz, S. & Sergent, J. (2018, Oct. 3). Nick Saban's coaching tree grows in size, title and compensation. *USA Today*. www.usatoday.com/story/sports/2018/10/03/nick-saban-coaching-tree/1434787002/

Carson, L.C. & Rinehart, M.A. (2010). The big business of college game day. *Texas Review of Entertainment & Sports Law*. 12(1), 1–12.

Clavio, G., Burch, L.M. & Frederick, E.L. (2012). Networked fandom: applying systems theory to sport Twitter analysis. *International Journal of Sport Communication*, 5, 522–538.

Cobb, J.C. (2020, Jan. 30). Is college football selling out its future? Zocalo Public Square. www.zocalopublicsquare.org/2020/01/30/is-college-football-selling-out-its-future/ideas/essay/

Cox, J. (2017). The SEC arms race: With $40 million pouring in to each program, no buyout is too big. *Saturday Down South*. www.saturdaydownsouth.com/sec-football/big-money-means-no-buyout-too-big-to-pay/

Crawford, B. (2020, Jan. 31) – Updated: college football's 25 best facilities in 2020. *24/7 Sports*. https://247sports.com/LongFormArticle/college-football-recruiting-2020-facilities-Alabama-Clemson-Ohio-State-LSU-Texas-Georgia-Florida-142838731/

Daniels, J., Gregory, K. & Cottom, T.M. (2016). *Digital sociology in everyday life*. Bristol, UK: Policy Press.

Deprez, A., Mechant, P. & Hoebeke, T. (2013). Social media and Flemish sports reporters: a multimethod analysis of Twitter use as journalistic tool. *International Journal of Sport Communication*, 6, 107–119.

Duncan, S. (2016). Interpreting Huizinga through Bourdieu: a new lens for understanding the commodification of the play element in society and its effects on genuine community. *Cosmos & History*, 12(1), 37–66.

Duncan, S.K. (2018). The Business of Sport, Sledging and the Corruption of Play – an Interpretation through a Huizingian-Bourdieu Lens. *Physical Culture & Sport. Studies & Research*, 80(1), 15–26.

Dyer, K. (2019, Sept. 9). College football arms race: Georgia football announces new $80 million building. *Fox Business*. www.foxbusiness.com/features/university-of-georgia-football-new-facilities

English, P. (2016). Mapping the sports journalism field: Bourdieu and broadsheet newsrooms. *Journalism*, 17(8), 1001–1017.

Farner, K. (2016). Best facilities in college football. *Saturday Down South*. www.saturdaydownsouth.com/sec-football/best-facilities-college-football/

Forde, P. (2017, Nov. 26). Coaching carousel winners and losers (yes, Tennessee is definitely a loser). *Yahoo! Sports*. https://sports.yahoo.com/coaching-carousel-winners-losers-yes-tennessee-definitely-loser-022637752.html

Gibbs, C. & Haynes, R. (2013). A phenomenological investigation into how Twitter has changed the nature of sport media relations. *International Journal of Sport Communication*, 6, 394–408.

Hansen, D.L., Schneiderman, B., Smith, M.A. & Himelboim, I. (2019). *Analyzing social media networks with NodeXL: insights from a connected world*, Second Edition. Amsterdam: M. Kaufmann.

Hipke, M. & Hachtmann, F. (2014). Game changer: a case study of social media strategy in Big Ten athletic departments. *International Journal of Sport Communication*, 7, 516–532.

Hitlin, P. (2013, Nov. 4). How Crimson Hexagon works. Pew Research Center. www.journalism.org/2013/11/04/methodology-crimson-hexagon/

Hopkins, D. & King, G. (2010). A method of automated nonparametric content analysis for social science. *American Journal of Political Science*, 54(1), 229–247.
Hull, K. & Lewis, N.P. (2014). Why Twitter displaces broadcast sports media: a model. *International Journal of Sport Communication*, 7, 16–33.
Hurt, C. (2017, May 2). Is Nick Saban worth new contract extension? Tidesports.com. www.tidesports.com/cecil-hurt-nick-saban-worth-new-contract-extension/
Hutchins, B. (2019). Mobile media sport: the case for building a mobile media and communications research agenda. *Communication & Sport*, 2019, 7(4), 466–487.
Ignatow, G. & Robinson, L. (2017). Pierre Bourdieu: theorizing the digital. *Information, Communication & Society*, 20(7), 950–966, https://doi:10.1080/1369118X.2017.1301519
Jhally, S. (1984). The spectacle of accumulation: material and cultural factors in the evolution of the sports/media complex. *Insurgent Sociologist*, 12(3), 41–57.
Kwon, H.H., Trail, G.T. & Lee, D. (2008). The effects of vicarious achievement and team identification on BIRGing and CORFing. *Sport Marketing Quarterly*, 17, 209–217.
Lupton, D. (2014). *Digital sociology*. Oxon, UK: Routledge.
Marres, N. (2017). *Digital sociology: The reinvention of social research*. Cambridge, UK: Wiley.
Martin, T. (2020, Jan. 9). The Crimson Standard initiative reaches over halfway point of $600 million fundraising goal. SI.com (Bama Central). www.si.com/college/alabama/bamacentral/alabama-crimson-standard-greg-bryne-reaches-over-halfway-point#:~:text=University%20of%20Alabama%20 athletic%20director,the%20%24600%20million%20fundraising%20goal.
McGregor, S.C. (2014). The press and public on Twitter: shared space, disparate discussion. Paper presented at the Association for Education in Journalism and Mass Communication, Montreal, Quebec.
McGregor, S., Lawrence, R. & Cardona, A. (2016). Personalization, gender, and social media: gubernatorial candidates' social media strategies. *Information, Communication & Society*, DOI: 10.1080/1369118X.2016.1167228
McFadden, W. (2017). How many SEC coaches have been fired since Nick Saban arrived at Alabama? *Saturday Down South*. www.saturdaydownsouth.com/sec-football/how-many-sec-football-fired-since-nick-saban-arrived-alabama/
McNair, K. (2019, June 5). No end in sight in athletics facilities arms race. *CBSSports.com*. www.cbssports.com/college-football/news/no-end-in-sight-in-athletics-facilities-arms-race/
Moor, L. (2007). Sport and commodification: a reflection on key concepts. *Journal of Sport & Social Issues*, 31(2), 128–142.
Moran, J. (2019, Apr. 23). "You win wars with resources" – New LSU AD Scott Woodward understands the war for SEC superiority is an arms race. *Tiger Rag*. www.tigerrag.com/you-win-wars-with-resources-new-lsu-ad-scott-woodward-understands-the-war-for-sec-superiority-is-an-arms-race/
O'Keefe, B. (2018, April 23). How Nick Saban keeps Alabama football rolling. *Fortune*. https://fortune.com/2018/04/23/nick-saban-coach-university-of-alabama-football/
Orton-Johnson, K. & Prior, N. (2013). *Digital sociology: Critical perspectives*. Hampshire, UK: Palgrave Macmillan.
Ourand, J. (2019, Dec. 20). SEC football leaving CBS after 2023, likely for ESPN/ABC. *Street & Smith's SBJ Newsletters*. www.sportsbusinessdaily.com/SB-Blogs/Breaking-News/2019/12/SEC.aspx
Paulsen (2019). Rout sinks SEC title game, but ratings still big: caps most-watched college football season on CBS since 1990. *Sports Media Watch*. www.sportsmediawatch.com/2019/12/sec-championship-ratings-lsu-georgia-cbs/
Pew Research Center (2014). Social networking fact sheet. www.pewinternet.org/fact-sheets/social-networking-fact-sheet/
Pinak, P. (2019, Dec. 26). Nick Saban's coaching tree may be his greatest achievement. *Fanbuzz*. https://fanbuzz.com/college-football/sec/alabama/nick-saban-coaching-tree/
Pope, K. (2019, March 22). The SEC Effect – South End Zone Project exemplifies SEC's unrelenting arms race. Missourian. www.columbiamissourian.com/sports/mizzou_sports/south-end-zone-project-exemplifies-secs-unrelenting-arms-race/article_196c565e-4b4e-11e9-9866-ff6ca0db6f2f.html
Porter, L.V., Wood, C. & Benigni, V.L. (2011). From analysis to aggression: the nature of fan emotion, cognition and behavior in internet sports communities. In Billings, A.C. (Ed.), *Sports media: Transformation, integration, consumption* (pp. 128–145). New York: Routledge.
Price, J., Farrington, N. & Hall, L. (2013). Changing the game? The impact of Twitter on relationships between football clubs, supporters and the sports media. *Soccer & Society*, 14(4), 446–461.

Roberts, C. & Emmons, B. (2016). Twitter in the press box: how a new technology affects game-day routines of print-focused sports journalists. *International Journal of Sport Communication*, 9, 97–115.

Santesteban, C.J. & Leffler, K.B. (2017). Assessing the efficiency justifications for the NCAA player compensation restrictions. *The Antitrust Bulletin*, 62(1), 91–111.

Sardar, Z. & Van Loon, B. (2010). *Cultural Studies, A Graphic Guide*. London: Icon.

Scarborough, A. (2018, Aug. 5). The Saban effect: how one coach's unrelenting process has sculpted college football. *ESPN.com*. www.espn.com/college-sports/story/_/id/24258666/how-alabama-coach-nick-saban-unrelenting-process-sculpted-college-football

Schlabach, M. (2017, Nov. 27). Why the craziest coaching carousel day ever is just the beginning. *ESPN.com*. www.espn.com/college-football/story/_/id/21582719/tennessee-volunteers-coaching-search-takes-bizarre-turn-backs-away-greg-schiano

Sheffer, M.L. & Schultz, B. (2010). Paradigm shift or passing fad? Twitter and sports journalism. *International Journal of Sport Communication*, 2010, 3, 472–484.

Staples, A. (2017, Nov. 27). The lessons and warnings of Tennessee's Greg Schiano saga. *SI.com*. www.si.com/college/2017/11/28/greg-schiano-tennessee-coach-protest-penn-state

Steinbach, P. (2009, October). Twitter rivals: Social media is revolutionizing how sports are consumed, as well as how schools, conferences and fans interact. *Athletic Business*, 60–63. www.athleticbusiness.com/Web-Social/social-media-revolutionizing-how-sports-are-consumed.html

Steinbach, P. (2011, April). SEC experiencing statuary arms race. *Athletic Business*. www.athleticbusiness.com/sec-experiencing-statuary-arms-race.html

Stoldt, G.C., Noble, J., Ross, M., Richardson, T. & Bonsall, J. (2013, March). Advantages and disadvantages of social media use: perceptions of college athletics communicators. *CoSIDA E-Digest*, 62–67.

Syme, C. & Dosh, K. (2015, January). CoSIDA social media survey results & analysis: Part I. *CoSIDA E-Digest*, 31–32.

Talty, J. (2020, March 3); Scott Cochran takes pay cut to head to Georgia. *AL.com*. www.al.com/alabamafootball/2020/03/scott-cochran-takes-pay-cut-to-head-to-georgia.html

Towers, C. (2017). UGA needs to wage war in SEC's 'facilities arms race'. *DawgNation (AJC.com)*. www.dawgnation.com/football/opinion/georgia-football-kirby-smart-facilities-lag-against-sec

Viégas, F. & Wattenberg, M. (2008). TIMELINES: Tag clouds and the case for vernacular visualization. *Interactions*, 15(4), 49–52.

Wakefield, K. (2016). Using fan passion to predict attendance, media consumption, and social media behaviors. *Journal of Sport Management*, 30, 229–247.

Walsh, A.J. & Giulianotti, R. (2001). This sporting mammon: a normative critique of the commodification of sport. *Journal of the Philosophy of Sport*, 2001, XXVIII, 53–77.

Watanabe, N., Yan, G. & Soebbing, B.P. (2015). Major League Baseball and Twitter usage: the economics of social media use. *Journal of Sport Management*, 29, 619–632.

Wenner, L.A. (Ed.) (1998). *Mediasport*. London: Routledge.

Wenner, L.A. (2014a). Much ado (or not) about Twitter? Assessing an emergent communication and sport research agenda. *Communication & Sport*, 2(2), 103–106. https://doi.org/10.1177/2167479514527426

Wenner, L.A. (2014b). On the limits of the new and the lasting power of the mediasport interpellation. *Television & New Media*, 15(8), 732–740.

Wheeldon, J. & Åhlberg, M. (2012). *Visualizing social science research: Maps, methods, & meaning*. Los Angeles, CA: Sage.

Williams, A. & Gonlin, V. (2017). I got all my sisters with me (on Black Twitter): second screening of How to Get Away with Murder as a discourse on Black Womanhood. *Information, Communication & Society*, 20(7), 984–1004.

30
Football Fan Reactions to Video Assistant Referee
No More Hand of God

Yuya Kiuchi

Introduction

Football fans of all ages continue to talk about the "hand of god" by Maradona during the 1986 World Cup match between Argentina and England. Or they may discuss more recent cases: France's Thierry Henry deliberately handling the ball and the play immediately leading to a goal on a 2010 World Cup qualifying match against Ireland. Or some English fans may still hold the sour memory from the World Cup in South Africa, during which Frank Lampard's goal against Germany was disallowed even though the ball had clearly crossed the goal line. In all of these cases, the referee crew on the respective match was unable to make the correct decision for various reasons. Fans and pundits claimed that technology, including video replay technology, would have helped the referees make the right decision.

In other instances, technology could have proven that a referee made a correct decision despite what fans might have thought. An American referee, Esse Baharmast, correctly made a penalty kick call on the 1998 World Cup game between Brazil and Norway. Because of the goal scored from this penalty kick by Norway, Morocco, which was in the same group with the two teams at the game, was eliminated from the tournament. Baharmast remembers, "On the field of play there was no problem and at the end of the match there was no problem with the teams. It wasn't until the journalists and reporters got into it and it became a conspiracy against African nations and things of that nature." After the game, Baharmast suffered "abuse from various publications and news outlets denouncing him as a racist, incompetent and a player in a scandal and conspiracy against Morocco." It was only a day and a half later that a Swedish television station published a picture and a video that supported Baharmast's call (U.S. Soccer, 2019). Video replay technology would have confirmed the accuracy of Baharmast's call immediately, saving him what he calls "36 hours of agony," which "[he] wouldn't wish it on [his] worst enemy" (U.S. Soccer, 2019).

Both FIFA (Fédération Internationale de Football Association), the governing body of football, and IFAB (International Football Association Board), the body in charge of the Laws of the Game, as well as their affiliates have closely examined different ways to improve football officiating. Several academic projects, with or without collaboration with these organizations, have also examined what factors affected officiating quality. A series of studies in recent years examined how the quality of a referee's decisions might be affected by the referee's physical strain (Samuel et al., 2019), distance and angle from the play (Hossner, 2018), and the referee's height (McCarrick et al., 2020). In the age of replays, Spitz et al., (2017) examined how viewing a replay at a slower speed could affect the perception of a foul compared to viewing it at natural speed.

As technology developed and studies on the impact of technology were conducted, it was just a matter of time for football to adopt the use of video technology to assist referees. The FIFA World Cup events in 2010 in South Africa and in 2014 in Brazil both saw significant television technology development. After the World Cup in 2006 where high-definition broadcasting was first introduced, the 2010 event witnessed the use of high-definition broadcasting coupled with internet streaming and 3D broadcasting. Four years later, the ultra-high-definition broadcasting arrived (Gounden, 2010; Bojanova, 2014). With better quality images and more cameras surrounding the field, the environment for the technology, known as Video Assistant Referee (VAR), was set. However, its implementation was by no means trifling for the sport. It turned out to be one of the most dramatic and controversial changes to football in its recent history. Although the video replay had long existed with numerous other popular sports including tennis, American football, baseball, judo, and rugby just to name a few, and several technologies had been used to assist football referees to improve the accuracy of their calls (e.g. the Goal Line Technology), various stakeholders from team owners and coaches to referees and players have expressed varying opinions about the VAR.

Reviewing how fans have reacted to decisions involving the VAR enables a glance at the relationship between fans and football's technology. Examining fan tweets on several controversial incidents on major football matches reveals fans' psychological conflicts. On one level, they have an idea what football is supposed to be like. Football traditionalists and purists are vocal. After all, the sport had resisted video replays so long, even when blatant errors had been made by officials. When a goal is canceled for an attacker being offside by a centimeter or two, it compromises the human nature of football, these traditionalists argue. On another level, many fans are primarily fans of a particular team. Impartial views on the decisions made by a referee or a VAR are difficult to reach when one is overwhelmed with frustration or joy because of officials' decisions.

Refereeing 2.0

By the beginning of the 2010s, football was under severe pressure to update itself. While the sport is proud of its history, roots, and simplicity, as the most popular sport in the world, football's traditionalist attitude was under scrutiny. It was particularly the case because of technological developments. On many professional and international matches, over a dozen cameras would surround the field of play and capture the game. This allowed fans to see a football star's play not only from multiple angles but also with zoomed-in slow-motion without compromising the resolution of the image. While these technological advancements made the game even more exciting, they also put referees on the field at a serious disadvantage. They had only one opportunity to make a correct call when their view of a play could be blocked by another player or an incident might simply be too close to tell with human eyes.

For a long time, many professional football leagues did not allow a replay video clip to be shown on the jumbotron in the stadium after a questionable call. When fans watching a game at home or at a pub saw replays and noticed the referee's error, that was one thing. But when tens of thousands of fans in the stadium did the same, it was another. Referees were not allowed to change their decision based on what was shown on the jumbotron. When a technical operator at Saitama Stadium 2002 accidentally replayed a goal on the stadium's jumbotron on May 11, 2013, it was clear that the goal should not have counted because of the goal scorer having been in an offside position. Defending team players pointed at the jumbotron to urge the referee to watch the replay while he could do nothing other than manage the players and resume the game with a kickoff, i.e. allowing the goal to stand. Today, even if the stadium jumbotron remained blank and silent, the advancement in communication technology enabled fans in the stadium to see a replay on their smartphones. The referees were truly left alone without an opportunity to review their calls.

In order to utilize the available technology, assist referees with technology, and improve football, the Royal Netherlands Football Association (KNVB) launched Refereeing 2.0, or a project to "reinvent refereeing" (Medeiros, 2018). Lukas Brud, the secretary of the IFAB expressed the pressure football was under by stating, "With all the 4G and Wi-Fi in stadia today, the referee is the only person who can't see exactly what is happening and he's actually the only one who should" (Medeiros, 2018). KNVB tested the use of the VAR during its 2012–2013 season on its Eredivisie—the topflight league in the country—games. Based on its experimental results, in 2014, KNVB encouraged the IFAB, the body that was responsible for establishing and amending the Laws of the Game, to officially consider introducing the VAR to the sport.

After the departure of Sepp Blatter who was a vocal advocate against the use of VAR from his FIFA president role, the debate to introduce the VAR gained momentum under the new president, Gianni Infantino. Its experimental use was approved in many competitions across the world. About five years after the KNVB's original testing, the VAR's associate protocols and mechanisms had developed sufficiently to the point that it could be used in the largest football event in the world, the FIFA World Cup, in 2018.

VAR Today

Since the VAR was formally introduced in the Laws of the Game in 2018, IFAB has been clear that the VAR should only be used in specific circumstances. IFAB (2019) states that the VAR "may assist the referee only in the event of a 'clear and obvious error' or 'serious missed incident' in relation to goal / no goal, penalty / no penalty, direct red card … [and] mistaken identity" (p. 139). It is also important to note that referees are not allowed to ask the VAR what to call. The referee must make a decision first before the VAR is able to assist the referee. In all other instances, a referee is not allowed to solicit input from the VAR. IFAB (2019) writes, "the referee must always make a decision, i.e. the referee is not permitted to give 'no decision' and then use the VAR to make a decision" (p. 139). It is also important to note that the VAR is only expected to be involved for a "clear and obvious error" or "serious missed incident" (IFAB, 2019, p. 139).

Once a game starts, the VAR automatically checks all reviewable incidents, i.e. situations that fall under one of the four categories listed above. This is why players and bench personnel are not allowed to, but also do not need to, request a review. All reviewable plays such as a possible red card offense, a possible goal, a possible penalty kick, and others are checked by the VAR regardless. When the VAR supports the decision of the referee, the game simply continues. It is only the referee crew that hears, "Check complete," from the VAR on their earpiece, indicating that the decision on the field stands. If the VAR needs extra time to ensure the accuracy of the original call, he or she may tell the referee not to restart a game. Once the decision is confirmed, the VAR tells the referee, "Check complete," to have the match restarted.

When a referee's decision cannot be validated, one of the two scenarios happen. When there is a factual error, the VAR simply tells the referee what had happened so that the proper action can be taken. Examples include a missed goal or an offside situation. In these instances, the referee has no reason to watch the replay to make a correct decision. However, when a possible error is not factual, the VAR recommends the referee to undertake an on-field review (OFR). Whether or not a foul was serious enough to deserve a red card or whether or not a foul that would result in a penalty kick should be called fall under this category of reviews and are different from the aforementioned goal or offside situations in nature.

IFAB's approach to the VAR is summarized concisely as "maximum benefit with minimum interference" (FIFA, 2018). This approach appears to be successful. During the Annual General Meeting in March 2018, IFAB distributed study findings about the VAR experiment since March 2016. During the two-year experiment, 972 competitive matches used the VAR. On average, a game had 5 instances which the VAR checked, with each instance taking 20 seconds at median. Referees' decisions within the reviewable category of situations had 93 percent accuracy without the VAR. With the VAR, accuracy went up to 98.8 percent. The VAR resulted in on average 55 seconds of time lost per match (IFAB, 2018).

Fan Reactions

By the time the VAR was formally launched and utilized for the first time at the FIFA World Cup in 2018, the VAR experiment had undergone over two years of preparation and over 1,000 games in which the system was adopted. As noted above, the accuracy of game-changing decisions, which was already high, now is near 100 percent. The VAR, at least according to the data, appeared to be making the game fairer and more accurate. Fan reactions, however, have been mixed.

Fact-based VAR Involvement

On the one hand, some of the calls that the VAR is involved in, such as a possible violent conduct, a possible penalty kick, and the like, require the referee on the field to review the replay to make the final decision. Ultimately, it is the referee on the field who determines the call. Although referees go through much training to normalize their officiating standard including the assessment about the severity of an offense, it still leaves room for subjective interpretation of the situation. A dozen or so referees who work on the top-flight domestic professional league do not always agree with each other when they are shown a gray-zone offence.

On the other hand, if the question is whether or not a player was in an offside position or whether or not a foul happened inside or outside the penalty area, the referee on the field has no reason to watch a review. The VAR is able to simply check the replay to determine the correct decision. In theory, these decisions are black and white. There is no room for argument or controversy.

Judging whether or not a player is in an offside position is simple. The Laws of the Game published by IFAB (2019) states, "A player is in an offside position if any part of the head, body or feet is in the opponents' half (excluding the halfway line) and any parts of the head body or feet is nearer to the opponents' goal line than both the ball and the second-last opponent" (99). In addition, arms and hands of any player are not taken into consideration in determining an offside position. This means, if a part of an attacking player's body is ahead of the second-to-last defending team player's body, even by a millimeter, the attacker is considered to be in an offside position.

An offside decision in itself is not within the purview of the VAR, according to IFAB. However, because many offside decisions are connected to a goal decision, the VAR ends up being involved in numerous offside cases. After a goal is scored, there may be up to a minute of hesitant celebration by the attacking team while the VAR is checking for a possible offside. Joyous fans may be told by the VAR that the goal would not stand. It is in these instances when even a black-and-white decision may become controversial, at least in the mind of fans.

When a player is offside by a meter or more and when players are moving slowly, making an accurate offside decision is relatively easy. However, at the professional and international levels and above, attackers and defenders are often moving in opposing directions. The second to last defender is not always the same player. The flash-lag effect also interferes with the perception of an assistant referee, making an onside player appear offside (Helsen et al., 2006). Even though professional league assistant referees undergo intensive training, it is next to impossible to know if someone's head was ahead of another player's heel by a few centimeters, let alone closer distance.

Technology helps referees make accurate close offside decisions beyond the ability of human eyes. For example, Hawk-Eye's virtual offside line technology can draw virtual lines parallel to the goal line across the pitch on a TV monitor. The lines can be moved so that a line is located with the second-last defending team player. When an attacker is offside or onside by several centimeters or more, this gridline technology is often sufficient to make a correct decision.

When an offside situation is closer, the 3-D line technology is employed. Zooming into the attacking player in question and the second-to-last defender and determining which part of each player's body was the closest to the goal line, a computer draws a virtual line that is vertical from the body part to the pitch. These two vertical lines—one for the attacker and one for the defender—are only one pixel wide. A line parallel to the goal line is drawn for each vertical line. If the attacker's line is behind or completely overlaps the defender's line, the player is deemed onside. If the attacker's line is close to the goal line than the defender's line, the player is offside. This means that a player may be deemed offside by a pixel on the VAR's computer screen.

One of the offside-related VAR involvements at the 2018 FIFA World Cup, the first World Cup where the VAR was used, took place on the seventh day of the tournament. At the 64th minute of the match, Iran's possible equalizer to make the game 1–1 against Spain was called offside. FOX Soccer (2018) tweeted, "Iran thought they had equalized but VAR ruled it was offside!" A tweet by Kirsten Schlewitz (2018) was more concerning, "VAR better watch his back." In response to the canceled goal, Minoo Taheri tweeted, "It was unfair judgement from the referre [sic] and VAR part! It was an absolut [sic] score on Iran's behalf! Was the decision based on politics?" Another fan (Rosenblatt, 2018) rhetorically asked, "Has anyone considered the possibility that VAR might not be great?" The video replay shows that a clear offside offense had been made by an Iranian attacker before the goal. But some fans continued to believe that the Iranian goal was mistakenly taken away, possibly for political reasons.

In reality, despite what some fans tweeted, the offside decision was originally made by an assistant referee. The VAR simply confirmed the accuracy of the call. Some fans (Castro, 2019; Harris, 2018; Mizen, 2018) who correctly acknowledged that not allowing the goal was the correct decision nonetheless wrongfully argued that the VAR had made a right call. James Tyler (2018), Senior Editor of ESPNFC, also wrote, "a VARy, VARy big decision there." However, the VAR had no impact on the referee's call to begin with. It simply confirmed that the assistant referee had made the right call.

Even a more controversial offside decision was made a year after, during the FIFA Women's World Cup. At the 68th minute of a semi-final match, England's Ellen White seemingly have scored an equalizer against the U.S., only to have it overturned by the VAR. In this instance, unlike the aforementioned Iranian case, the referee crew originally awarded a goal. It was after the review by the VAR that the goal was canceled. The game ended 2–1 for the United States, which moved on to the final and eventually won the tournament. According to the replay, White was offside by a very small margin. Even though the call was correct, controversy was inevitable, especially with a match between two high-profile teams.

Many fans, probably supporting England, reacted to the canceled goal disapprovingly. The replay showed that White was offside albeit marginally. Viewing how close the offside call was, Blakey (2019) reflected the sentiment of many that the goal should have counted because White was barely offside. He wrote, "#VAR getting beyond ridiculous now, you can't be overruling goals because a players toe is half a centimetre offside." Smith ITFC (2019) also tweeted, "I think VAR is good as it gets rid of really bad decisions changing the outcome of matches. However, it should be for changing CLEAR AND OBVIOUS errors and not marginal ones. Being offside by an inch … shouldn't be changed for the sake of it." When it comes to offside, however, "there [is] no such a thing as almost offside," as FIFA's Referee's Committee Chair, Peirluigi Collina stated (Hays & Hamilton, 2019). There is one correct answer and the other answer is clearly and obviously incorrect.

Some fans remained unconvinced that White was actually offside. The Cold End (2019) tweeted, "The #VAR debate goes on. I don't think Ellen White was offside last night—look at her foot!" Similarly, Efhymiou (2019) commented, "That was not offside … shame … Ellen White did score … stop helping US … #VAR is a big mistake because it is not used properly … SHAME." Hough (2019) hinted that the referees were biased and intentionally made a wrong call against England, by tweeting, "Lots of people who never watch soccer but following #USAvENG on Twitter are wondering 'Who does #VAR play for?'"

Aside from those who discredited what the replay showed and continued to claim that White was not offside, frustrated fans generally argued that White was offside by a margin too small for human eyes to detect. For these fans, accuracy interfered with their enjoyment of the game. Lionheart Sport (2019) shared its sorrow by noting, "Right decision but it's so marginal, it's kinda hard to take seeing goals taken away like that." Fisher (2019) echoed by tweeting, "Her foot was offside? Ridiculous. Margin is too fine. #VAR is killing the game." King's (2019) tweet summarizes these fans' emotions well, "#VAR is ruining football!" Even Ellen White herself admits that she still cringes at the memory of the incident. She commented, "I do sit at home at night and say, 'ahhh, I just can't stand VAR'" (Edwards, 2020).

These controversies about tight offside calls have not been limited to the World Cup tournaments. For example, the English Premier League has had numerous instances in which the VAR's input resulted in the referee invalidating a goal. During the 2019–2020 season, as of early February, 25 goals have been ruled out by the VAR (Lipton, 2020). One such situation involved Liverpool's Roberto Firmino whose armpit, after a video review, was deemed offside, on the match against Aston Villa on November 2, 2019. Or on December 28, 2019, another "armpit offside" happened to Crystal Palace against Southampton. After a few more goals were canceled after VAR reviews on the same day, Chris Sutton (2019) concisely but poignantly tweeted, "VAR worst day ever…."

In response to these "armpit" offside decisions, the Premier League teams have asked Mike Riley, the head of the PGMOL (Professional Game Match Officials Limited), to replace the one-pixel wide offside line to a thicker line that is equivalent of 10 centimeters on a football pitch. This will allow an attacker who is marginally offside by almost up to 10 centimeters to be considered level with the second-last defender, i.e. onside. Lipton (2020) reports that Riley admitted that the 10-centimeter line would have allowed 9 out of 25 aforementioned disallowed goals to stand. The change has not been made because the vertical line specification is not determined by a league. But both the frustration among players and coaches, as well as the implication of such a change on the number of goals, are evident.

VAR with Penalty Area Incidents

Penalty area incidents have major repercussions for the outcome of a match. A foul by a defender results in a penalty kick, which about three-quarters of the time results in a goal (Staley, 2018). A foul by an attacker prior to a goal results in the goal being canceled. These foul-related decisions are different from judging if an attacker was in an offside position. They are less black and white. Because a match has only one final decision maker, i.e. the referee, the referee must watch a replay to either confirm or overrule their own original decision. The VAR only recommends a review for a possible clear and obvious error. For example, what appeared to be a reckless push by an attacker in a penalty area might have looked as such because of an embellishment by the defender. The penalty kick decision may have to be canceled. Or what appeared to be an innocuous contact between two players might have been initiated by a defender's tripping offence which was only caught by a camera behind a goal. Regardless of the nature of the incident, because such a decision leaves more grey area, fans have more opportunities to disagree with the referee's final decision.

During the semi-final match between England and the U.S. in which Ellen White's equalizer was canceled, the VAR was also involved in a penalty kick decision. With about 10 minutes left in the match, American defender Becky Sauerbrunn and White collided in the American penalty area. Even though a penalty kick was not originally awarded by the referee, after checking the pitch-side monitor for a replay following the recommendation by the VAR, the referee awarded a penalty kick. Not all fans were in favor of this decision. Yip82 (2019) tweeted, "If a touch in the box merits a penalty, then expect a shed load of penalties to be awarded in the #PremierLeague next season!" Similarly, Oliver (2019) wrote, "Shocking penalty it wasn't a penalty anyway. #VAR strikes again. All wrong." Smith ITFC (2019) who did not agree with the cancelation of White's earlier goal also characterized the decision as "dodgy."

IFAB (2019) is clear that the referee should spend as much time as needed to watch the replay in order to ensure that the final decision is correct. It states, "There is no time limit for the review process as accuracy is more important than speed" (p. 140). However, some fans criticized the fact that the referee, Edina Alves Batista of Brazil, had spent over two minutes reviewing the replay. Siegel (2019) tweeted, "If it takes you over 20 replays to decide if it's a penalty, it's not a clear and obvious error…" Another referee, Katalin Kulcsar was also subject of criticism when she spent over four minutes to confirm a penalty kick decision between the U.S. and Spain. Collina has defended the referees by stating, "It's matter of time versus accuracy….You cannot be accurate and be fast. This does not mean we are happy to be slow. We are trying to do things very quickly, but sometimes you need to check more things" (Baxter, 2019).

Another high-profile involvement of the VAR on a penalty area incident took place during the Women's World Cup Final between the Netherlands and the U.S. At the 58th minute, after a collision between Dutch defender, Stefanie van der Gragt, and American attacker, Alex Morgan, Stéphanie Frappart, the referee, did not immediately call a PK. Rather, she signaled for a corner kick. Before the kick was taken, however, the referee was recommended to review the replay and the corner kick decision was reversed. Unsurprisingly, American media generally supported this decision. Writing for CBS Sports, Roger Gonzales (2019) called the foul "clear."

Not all fans agreed with the penalty decision, though. Marco H. (2019) compared Morgan with Neymar, a Brazilian player known for exaggerating the severity of fouls, and wrote, "Alex Morgan is another Neymar." Gundlach (2019) echoed by tweeting, "Terrible call. She was playing the ball and missed. Not a dangerous play. Terrible to have this decide World Cup." Boehm (2019) wrote, "for VAR to give a pk in a World Cup final for that is bullshit." These examples show that when a black-and-white decision like offside can be controversial, less black-and-white foul decisions are very much likely to be highly controversial.

Not Knowing the Laws while Supporting Your Team

One may not like or agree with the Laws of the Game, but the VAR's decisions are, in general, very accurate. Of course, accuracy simply means that a decision aligns with the Laws, and does not mean it is a popular one among fans, players, and coaches. A universally popular call, after all, is impossible to achieve when two teams do not share the same interest while playing against each other. Nonetheless, at the conclusion of the group stage of the FIFA World Cup in 2018, referees' decisions on game critical situations had 95 percent accuracy for a total of 335 incidents where the VAR checked the referee's call. Once the VAR was engaged, the accuracy went up to 99.3 percent (Associated Press, 2018; Chacksfield, 2018).

Fans' negative reactions to the VAR, despite the statistical evidence that the accuracy of referee decisions is near 100 percent—which to begin was very high at 95 percent—partly come from their lack of knowledge about the Laws of the Game. An example of such knowledge gap may explain the discussion about another goal by Ellen White that was canceled during the Bronze Medal match between England and Sweden. At the 33rd minute of the match, White seemingly scored a goal. However, when she chested the ball down to her foot, the ball slid against her arm. According to the 2019/2020 version of the Laws of the Game, any contact between the attacker's arm and the ball—no matter how accidental or minor—is a foul if it leads to a goal or creates a goal scoring opportunity. No other points of consideration matter to call a handling offence by an attacker who scored a goal or who created a goal scoring opportunity after a contact between their arm or hand and the ball. For this reason, White's goal was rightfully canceled. Sweden went on to win the match to earn the bronze medal. White's handling left no room for a debate. The contact between her arm and the ball was clear on the replay. Understandably, the football community had not always been supportive of this law change because even a very minor and accidental contact could cancel a goal. But the law was properly applied. This was another black-and-white decision for the referee, without any room for a discussion.

Not understanding the instructions given to assistant referees for a close offside decision also leads to fan frustrations. On a match to which the VAR is appointed, assistant referees are instructed not to raise their flag for a close offside case until the possession of the ball changes or the ball goes out of play. This ensures that an attack is not stopped for an erroneous offside decision when the attacker was actually onside. If a goal is scored, the assistant referee raises their flag to indicate offside and the VAR confirms the decision, as was the case on the aforementioned Iranian game. If a goal is not scored, the assistant referee raises their flag, and the referee stops play to restart with an indirect freekick. This procedure creates seeming goals when the assistant referee was only allowing the play to continue just in case he or she was wrong. This new protocol allows more goals to be scored only to be canceled later.

Fans are not always familiar with these law changes and procedural instructions. Tweets during the Women's World Cup revealed that a lack of knowledge or misunderstandings about the laws often resulted in criticism about the VAR. This explains why fans reacted positively when Christina Unkel, a FIFA Referee at the time, served as a rule analyst for FOX Sports during the Women's FIFA World cup. As a current FIFA referee, she provided insights to how calls were made and explained the reasons behind referees' decisions. Ward (2019) expressed her appreciation to her by tweeting, "kudos to @ChristinaUnkel for the follow up explanation!" Similarly, Matt (2019) wrote, "Christina Unkel gives way clearer and more descriptive explanations than [another rules analyst]. Can we please use her for both men and women @

FOXSoccer??" Listening to Unkel's explanation, fans at least realize that the referee had made a correct decision, even if they may not like it.

Conclusion: The VAR is for Accuracy not for Satisfied Fans

During a football match, the ultimate goal for referees is to apply the Laws of the Game accurately. Fairness, according to IFAB (2019), is "a crucial foundation of the beauty of the 'beautiful game'" (p. 11). For players, it is to win. It is the same for the manager, coaches, and other bench personnel. For many fans, it is to see their favorite team win or their favorite player perform well. Goals are the culmination of football excitement. Although all parties are present to enjoy this beautiful game, in reality, each party has its own vested interests.

Fans feel that only the skills and performance by the players on the field—the protagonists of a football match—should determine the outcome of the game without the interference of anything else. It may be more so when it is a high-stake match such as the World Cup final. case (2019) tweeted, "Nobody wanted to see a pk given from var in a World Cup final." Similarly, Hoogenraad (2019) was frustrated, commenting, "A World Cup Final should never be decided by a PK given for incidental contact thru VAR." Boehm (2019) wrote, "I get it. Studs are high but for VAR to give a pk in a World Cup final for that is bullshit." These fans suggest that the VAR is tarnishing the beauty of football. Although the VAR or referee's lack of involvement after an offence also means that their absence impacted the outcome the match, officials' active involvement catches fans' attention more. Barry (2019) summarized well when he wrote, "VAR is ruining soccer. Can't have any genuine moments anymore."

From time to time, the VAR decisions negatively impact a fan's favorite team. Other times, the VAR decisions benefit them. The lack of impartiality among fans also explains how they react. In 2010, at the FIFA World Cup in South Africa, England's Frank Lampard's shot famously hit the goalpost, bounced downwards, hit the ground behind the goal line (i.e. goal), and came back on to the field of play. Although the ball had clearly crossed the goal line, the assistant referee was caught off guard by the speed of the shot and was unable to determine if the ball had fully crossed the line (FP Sports, 2018). England went on to lose the match against Germany 1–4. Understandably, English fans asked for technology to be used to prevent such a clear and obvious error.

Nine years later, it was almost ironic that England had two goals canceled because of technology. Cunnigham (2019) not only pointed out these incidents as ironic but also discussed the psychology of many fans. He wrote, "Remember when Lampard was disallowed a goal against Germany and all of England wanted video assistance but now it is used against them they want rid of it?" The Down Podcast (2019) also tweeted, "they wanted var@so bad after lampards disallowed goal against Germany. Careful what you wish for." Ponndonkey (2019), an English Twitter user, was critical of the VAR and its offside decision during the Women's World Cup semifinal between England and the U.S. However, less than 10 minutes after her tweet criticizing the VAR, England received a PK against the U.S. thanks to the replay. She tweeted, "Ignore my last tweet. I love #VAR." During men's World Cup, Kanpp (2018) also echoed and wrote, "I hate VAR when it works against the result I want I don't care that it was the right call." When the PK decision was made on the Women's World Cup final, Dupree (2019) tweeted, "some of ya'll are so blind because its your Nation playing. stop watching trough [sic] your Fan glasses."

The VAR technology has clearly impacted football (Carlos et al., 2019). It has also changed how fans experience matches. While technology has helped make the accuracy of critical calls by referees near perfect, it has not created more satisfied fans. Baker (2018) tweeted, "Seriously VAR. Its a fuzzy, fussy, muddled, complicated, bloated, hopeless fudge of a con foisted onto the game.

It does not make things better or clearer or decisive. Fuck off Var and all your supporters." This sentiment is likely to remain, as football embodies balancing of traditionalism and modern technology, as well as visceral emotions of joy and sorrow that can never be enhanced or appeased by technology.

References

Associated Press. (2019, June 29). *VAR decisions at World Cp 99.3 percent accurate*. ESPN. www.espn.com/soccer/fifa-world-cup/story/3550678/var-decisions-at-world-cup-993-percent-accurate-fifa

Baker, D. [@prodnose]. (2018, June 25). *Seriously VAR. Its a fuzzy, fussy, muddled, complicated, bloated, hopeless fudge of a con foisted onto the game. It does not make things better or clearer or decisive. Fuck off Var and all your supporters*. [Tweet]. Twitter. https://twitter.com/prodnose/status/1011336840417300480

Barry, D. [@DaveBarry_]. (2019, July 6). *VAR is ruining soccer. Can't have any genuine moments anymore*. [Tweet]. Twitter. https://twitter.com/DaveBarry_/status/1147538201243992065

Baxter, K. (2019, June 27). Soccer World Cup notes: Reviews are mixed for new video assistant referee plan. *Los Angeles Times*.

Blakey, D. [@DomBlakey]. (2019, July 2). *#VAR getting beyond ridiculous now, you can't be overruling goals because a players toe is half a centimetre offside #USAvENG*. [Tweet]. Twitter. https://twitter.com/DomBlakey/status/1146154468683259908

Boehm, J [@Justin_Boehm]. (2019, July 7). *I get it. Studs are high but for VAR to give a pk in a World Cup final for that is bullshit. Morgan was not going to doing anything with that ball when she received it. Needs to be taken into consideration*. [Tweet] Twitter. https://twitter.com/Justin_Boehm/status/1147905665169575936

Bojanova, I. (2010). IT enhances football at World Cup 2014. *IT Professional*, 16(4), 12–17.

Carlos, L-P., Ezequiel, R., & Anton, K. (2019). How does video assistant referee (VAR) modify the game in elite soccer? *International Journal of Performance Analysis in Sport*, 19(4), 646–653. https://doi.org/10.1080/24748668.2019.1646521

case [@case_cap]. (2019, July 15). *Nobody wanted to see a pk given from var in a World Cup final*. [Tweet]. Twitter. https://twitter.com/case_cap/status/1018520494084063232

Castro, G. [@germanecastro]. (2018, June 20). *But… it was correct*. [Tweet]. Twitter. https://twitter.com/germanecastro/status/1009518183911510017

Chacksfield, M. (2018, June 30). *What is VAR?: The controversial star of World Cup 2018 decoded*. TechRader. www.techradar.com/news/what-is-var-the-controversial-star-of-world-cup-2018-decoded

Cold End, The [@thecoldend]. (2019, July 3). *The #VAR debate goes on. I don't think Ellen White was offside last night - look at her foot! And I don't think the penalty decision was a penalty*. [Tweet]. Twitter. https://twitter.com/thecoldend/status/1146308592271859712

Cunningham, A [@a-m-cunningham]. (2019, July 2). *Remember when Lampard was disallowed a goal against Germany and all of England wanted video assistance but now it is used against them they want rid of it? #Var #USAvENG*. [Tweet]. Twitter. https://twitter.com/a_m_cunningham/status/1146173477197680640

Downturn Podcast, The [@DownturnThe]. (2019, July 6). *Coulda woulda shoulda they wanted var@so bad after lampards disallowed goal against Germany. Careful what you wish for*. [Tweet]. Twitter. https://twitter.com/DownturnThe/status/1147532773126803458

Dupree, R [@Simmi0312]. (2019, July 2). *some of ya'll are so blind because its your Nation playing. stop watching trough your Fan glasses … both are running, she was in the shooting motion, and the US Player was crossing her way… she did touch her, while shooting … without that, she has an empty goal-> clear PK*. [Tweet]. Twitter. https://twitter.com/Simmi0312/status/1146156986138005506

Edwards, L. (2020, March 3). Ellen White: "I Just Can't Stand VAR…. It Reminds Me of England's World Cup Defeat to USA." *The Telegraph*. www.telegraph.co.uk/football/2020/03/03/ellen-white-really-cant-stand-var-reminds-world-cup-defeat-usa/

Efthymiou, N [@NEKTINA]. (2019, July 2). *That was not offside… shame… Ellen White did score… stop helping US… #VAR is a big mistake because it is not being used properly… SHAME #USAvENG #FWWC2019*. [Tweet]. Twitter. https://twitter.com/NEKTINA/status/1146153251680768000

FP Sports. (2018, June 11). FIFA World Cup moments: When Frank Lampard's disallowed Goal against Germany provided impetus for goalline technology." *FP Sports*. www.firstpost.com/sports/fifa-world-cup-moments-when-frank-lampards-disallowed-goal-against-germany-provided-impetus-for-goalline-technology-4504535.html

FIFA. (2018, April 24). *Inside look into the VAR review process*. FIFA. www.fifa.com/news/inside-look-into-the-var-review-process

Fisher, A [@AlanFisher]. (2019, July 2). *Her foot was offside? Ridiculous. Margin is too fine. #VAR is killing the game #USAvENG*. [Tweet]. Twitter. https://twitter.com/AlanFisher/status/1146153926061961218

FOX Soccer [FOXSoccer]. (2018, June 20). *Iran thought they had equalized but VAR ruled it was offside!* [Tweet]. Twitter. https://twitter.com/FOXSoccer/status/1009517428475191296

Gonzales, R. (2019, July 7). *Women's World Cup final: USWNT's Megan Rapinoe opens the scoring, makes history with penalty kick goal*. CBS Sports. www.cbssports.com/soccer/world-cup/news/womens-world-cup-final-uswnts-megan-rapinoe-opens-the-scoring-makes-history-with-penalty-kick-goal/

Gouden, F. (2010, May 22). It's going to be the best Cup broadcast ever, FIFA promised: There will be 24-hour coverage and all 64 matches will be in high-definition TV. *The Saturday Star*.

Gundlach, H. [@Hank4438]. (2019, July 7). *Terrible call. She was playing the ball and missed. Not a dangerous play. Terrible to have this decide World Cup*. [Tweet]. Twitter. https://twitter.com/Hank4438/status/1147920457439617026

Harris, N [@NathanIHarris]. (2018, June 20). *It worked there*. [Tweet]. Twitter. https://twitter.com/NathanIHarris/status/1009518076943978496

Hays, G., & Hamilton, T. (2019, July 2). *Press, Morgan score to lead USWNT past England and into Women's World Cup final*. ESPN. www.espn.com/soccer/fifa-womens-world-cup/story/3890943/pressmorgan-score-to-lead-uswnt-past-england-and-into-womens-world-cup-final

Helsen, W., Gills, B., & Weston, M. (2006). Errors in judging "offside" in association football: Test of the optical error versus the perceptual flash-lag hypothesis. *Journal of Sports Science*, *24*(5), 521–528. https://doi.org/10.1080/02640410500298065

Hoogenraad, L. D. [@danluvzmelissa]. (2009, July 7). *A World Cup Final should never be decided by a PK given for incidental contact thru VAR. #worldcupfinal*. [Tweet]. Twitter. https://twitter.com/danluvzmelissa/status/1147904088987713536

Hossner, E-J., Schnyder, U., Schmid, J., & Kredel, R. (2018). The role of viewing distance and viewing angle on referees' decision-making performance during the FIFA World Cup 2014. *Journal of Sports Sciences*, *37*(13), 1481–1489. https://doi.org/10.1080/02640414.2019.1570898

Hough, J [@leftcoastbabe]. (2019, July 2). *Lots of people who never watch soccer but following #USAvENG on Twitter are wondering "Who does #VAR play for?*. [Tweet]. Twitter. https://twitter.com/leftcoastbabe/status/1146157510312652801

International Football Association Board. (2018). *Media package: Information on video assistant referee (VAR) and experiment results*. IFAB.

International Football Association Board. (2019). *Laws of the game 2019/20*. IFAB.

King, S. (2019, July 2). *VAR is ruining football! #VAR #USAvENG*. [Tweet] Twitter. https://twitter.com/stephenking82/status/1146156626019323905

Knapp, K. [@TheKaylaKnapp]. (2018, June 20). *I hate VAR when it works against the result I want I don't care that it was the right call #WorldCup*. [Tweet]. Twitter. https://twitter.com/TheKaylaKnapp/status/1009517230629900288

Lipton, M. (2020, February 7). We can thicks video woe: Premier League to make VAR lines thicker to help stop controversial offside decisions after outrage this season. *The Sun*. www.thesun.co.uk/sport/football/10916949/var-premier-league-thicker-lines/

Lionheart Sport [@LHSport_21_]. (2019, July 2). *Right decision but it's so marginal, it's kinda hard to take seeing goals taken away like that #VAR #WomensWorldCup #USAvENG*. [Tweet]. Twitter

McCarrick, D., Brewer, G., Lyons, M., Pollet, T.V., & Neave, N. (2020). Referee height influences decision making in British football leagues. *BMC Psychology*, *8*(4). https://doi.org/10.1186/s40359-020-0370-4

Marco H. [@_mrcoh312]. (2019, July 7). *Alex Morgan is another Neymar*. [Tweet]. Twitter. https://twitter.com/_mrcoh312/status/1147905610429553360

Matt [@BartsNewGlasses]. (2019, July 6). *Christina Unkel gives way clearer and more descriptive explanations than Dr. Joe. Can we please use her for both men and women @FOXSoccer??* [Tweet]. Twitter. https://twitter.com/BartsNewGlasses/status/1147532227468808193

Medeiros, J. (2018, June 23). *The inside story of how FIFA's controversial VIA system was born*. Wired. www.wired.co.uk/article/var-football-world-cup

Mizen, K [@KyleMizen]. (2018, June 20). *it worked properly?* [Tweet]. Twitter. https://twitter.com/KyleMizen/status/1009517750564409351

Oliver, S. [@Loftboy63]. (2019, July 2). *Didn't watch the #USAvENG game but just saw the penalty. Shocking penalty it wasn't a penalty anyway. #VAR strikes again. All wrong*. [Tweet]. Twitter. https://twitter.com/Loftboy63/status/1146177869661593600

Ponddonkey [@ponddonkey]. (2019, July 2). *Ignore my last tweet. I love #VAR #Lionesses #USAvENG #WomensWorldCup2019 #WomensWorldCup #roarforthelionesses*. [Tweet]. Twitter. https://twitter.com/ponddonkey/status/1146156217498251269

Premier League (2020, February 18). *How offsides are determined by VAR*. Premier League. www.premierleague.com/news/1488423

Rosenblatt, R [@RyanTosenblatt]. (2018, June 20). *Has anyone considered the possibility that VAR might not be great?* [Tweet]. Twitter. https://twitter.com/RyanRosenblatt/status/1009517636017782784

Samuel, R. D., Galily, Y., Guy, O., Sharoni, E., & Tenenbaum, G. (2019). A decision-making simulator for soccer referees. *International Journal of Sports Science & Coaching, 14*(4), 480–489. https://doi.org/10.1177/1747954119885896

Schlewitz, K [@kdschlewitz]. (2018, June 20). *VAR better watch his back*. [Tweet]. Twitter. https://twitter.com/kdschlewitz/status/1009517244332822529

Siegel, S [@sarah_seagull15]. *If it takes you over 20 replays to decide if it's a penalty, it's not a clear and obvious error... #USAvENG #var*. [Tweet]. Twitter. https://twitter.com/sarah_seagull15/status/1146156690557034512

Smith ITFC, N [@nici_smith49]. (2019, July 2). *I think VAR is good as it gets rid of really bad decisions changing the outcome of matches. However, it should be for changing CLEAR AND OBVIOUS errors and not marginal ones. Being offside by an inch and a dodgy pen shouldn't be changed for the sake of it. #var #USAvENG*. [Tweet]. Twitter. https://twitter.com/nick_smith49/status/1146158359781003265

Spitz, J., Put, K., Wagemans, J., Williams, A. M., & Werner, F. H. (2017). Does slow motion impact on the perception of foul play in football? *European Journal of Sport Science, 17*(6), 748–756. https://doi.org/10.1080/17461391.2017.1304580

Staley, O. (2018, July 3). *The problem with penalty kicks in soccer*. Quartz. https://qz.com/1319419/world-cup-2018-the-problem-with-penalty-kicks/

Sutton, C. [@chris_sutton73]. (2019, December 28). *VAR worst day ever....* [Tweet]. Twitter. https://twitter.com/chris_sutton73/status/1211011749228556289

Taheri, M. [@minoo2009]. (2018, June 20). *It was unfair judgement from the referre and VAR part! It was an absolut score on Iran's behalf! Was the decision based on politics?* [Tweet]. Twitter. https://twitter.com/minoo2009/status/1009615704398721026

Tyler, J. [@JamesTylerESPN]. (2018, June 20). *a VARy, VARy big decision there*. [Tweet]. Twitter. https://twitter.com/JamesTylerESPN/status/1009517021661450241

U.S. Soccer. (2019, December 12). *Esse Baharmast's big call: ESPN reviews Esse Baharmast's big call during the 1998 FIFA World Cup*. U.S. Soccer. www.ussoccer.com/stories/2019/12/esse-baharmasts-big-call

Ward, J. [JameyWard17]. (2019, July 6). *Once again they get it right kudos to @ChristinaUnkel for the follow up explanation!* [Tweet]. Twitter. https://twitter.com/JameyWard17/status/1147531660176572416

Yip82 [@yipmann82]. (2019, July 2). *If a touch in the box merits a penalty, then expect a shed load of penalties to be awarded in the #PremierLeague next season! #USAvENG*. [Tweet]. Twitter. https://twitter.com/yipmann82/status/1146161668180893696

31
Reconfiguring Transnational Fan Experience Through Digital Media
European Football in China

Yuan Gong

Introduction

Since the opening-up of its entertainment and sport market in the 1980s, China has seen the growth of a considerable fan base for European professional male football. Consisting largely of young middle class in urban China, European football fans have been forming both online and offline communities to collectively watch and discuss football competitions of their favorite European clubs usually from the so-called "big five" leagues. Central to this phenomenon is those fans' active use of digital media in the organization of various activities that showcase their identity and productivity. Their reliance on Weibo, WeChat and other local online platforms in the engagement with European football reflects the ubiquitous presence of digital technology in the contemporary landscape of global sports fandom.

In a broader sense, the Chinese fandom of European football embodies the vibrant experience of transnational football consumption that has been increasingly digitally reconfigured in late modern capitalism where sports fan identity is less determined by social class and locality (Giulianotti, 2002; King, 2003). Comprised of media representations and consumer goods (Crawford, 2004), twenty-first-century sports have appropriated the emerging technologies to create new spaces where cross-cultural fans can interpret sporting texts, connect to each other and perform diverse identities. Digital media have contributed significantly to the formation of transnational sports fandom by offering easier access to overseas sports representations and commodities as well as binding dispersed, disembodied supporters virtually together.

In this chapter, I draw from my exploration of the European football fans in China to offer an overview of how sports fandoms are reconfigured by digital technology in the global and transnational contexts. Building upon the poststructuralist approach to understanding sports consumption as part of everyday life, the chapter first reviews the key literature in transnational and digital sport fan cultures. I then examine the use of digital media by the Chinese fans of European football based on the ethnographic evidence about their core practices – game viewing, community building and online discussions. My analysis shows that this transnational football fandom is negotiated between the globalized sporting text from the West and the local technological arrangements driven by China's transitions to authoritarian digital capitalism.

Sports Fandom, Football Consumption and Everyday Life

In response to the theoretical shift in both audience research and sports sociology, recent scholarship in sports fandoms has transcended the "incorporation/resistance" paradigm (Abercrombie & Longhurst, 1998) that understands media reception in relation to structure and agency and sees fandom as either a response to or an outcome out of social reproduction. Moving towards a poststructuralist approach to cultural consumption, a growing body of sports fan research echoes the interests of the "third-wave" fan studies in the saturation of fans' readings, tastes and practices in "the overarching social, cultural, and economic transformations of our time, including the dialectic between the global and the local" (Gray, Harrington, & Sandvoss, 2007, p. 8). This paradigm has illuminated fruitful accounts of sports fandom scrutinizing the fabrics of fans' lifeworlds and its relations to late modernity and global capitalism. In *Consuming Sport: Fans, sport and culture*, Crawford (2004) questions the dualities between real/resistant fans and inauthentic/passive consumers and urges for a relocation of sports fandom within the wider context of consumer culture. For him, late modern sports form principal cultural commodities upon which fans become performers of their identities. Accordingly, resistance to the established economic structures of professional sports occurs in more isolated and short-lived manners, usually based on improving specific consumer interests rather than radically undermining power relations. As part of this broader trend, football fan cultures across the globe and Europe in particular have seen the thriving of fleeting, performative "communities" motivated by the sense of temporality and consumerist desire for belonging (Crabble, 2008), as well as self-reflexive fan-consumers who can choose identity "from a range of opportunities in mediasphere and communication through acts of football consumption" (Dixon, 2013). In his account of football fandom as an important aspect of the everyday life in the historical context of industrial modernization, mediatization, and globalization, Sandvoss (2003) notably argues that football fan practices are integral to these individuals' self-reflexive project in which they appropriate the increasingly "contentless" mediated texts of football clubs to reflect on their own social identities and conditions.

Transnational Football Fans

This paradigm shift has raised the attention to the significant role of digital technology in sports fan formations in an increasingly globalized and mediatized world. On the one hand, the poststructuralist conceptualization of sports spectatorship beyond locality and proximity has triggered interests in dispersed, disembodied fans who follow football teams cross-culturally. Resonating the efforts of global fan studies to reconcile the political economic analysis of global media production and the reception analysis of local audience (Harrington & Bielby, 2007), the scholarship in transnational football fandom has revolved around the debate over whether the growing global popularity of European football is consequential to cultural imperialism or heterogenization.

Scholars approaching this phenomenon from the premise of cultural imperialism emphasize leading European football clubs' endless expansion to overseas markets through integral presence in the "banal cosmopolitanization of football" (Giulianotti & Robertson, 2007). In their eyes, transnational sports consumption is far less a simple constitution of mutual cultural exchanges than an imbalanced process led by neocolonial Western domination that eventually benefits the commercial interests of elite European teams. Across the spectrum lies the perspective of cultural heterogenization, which celebrates the localized agency of overseas supporters who follow European football in distinct ways from the proximate and embodied fans. This view suggests that football consumption has provided global fans with distinctive cultural resources for reflecting upon identities, enacting creative practices, and constructing a meaningful social life in local settings (Manzenreiter, 2004; Toffoletti, 2017). A notable concept to resolve these opposing views is "glocalization" (Giulianotti & Robertson, 2009), which sees sports as global processes mutually constitutive of and deeply recontextualized in the local cultures. For example, the English Premier League (EPL) has been seen as "a nationally based competition that has transmuted into a hybrid of local and global reflecting the dynamics of power in the global media sports complex" (Rowe, 2011, p. 90). Transnational football consumption is thus a crucial site where homogenization and heterogenization coexist and interact.

This debate is especially evident in the studies of the burgeoning fanbase of EPL in Asia. From the cultural imperialist perspective, Rowe and Gilmour (2010) refer to EPL as an example of Western media sport that has dominated in Asia and experienced little significant and intraregional exchange. They point out that Western sports interests are complicit with the transnational media corporations to privilege European- or American-based sports leagues and marginalize the spectatorship of the local Asian sports. On the contrary, as evidence of cultural heterogenization, Satoshi (2004) has found that East Asian fans follow star players more closely than EPL teams, thus reflecting a different supporting style from their European counterparts. Similarly, Millward (2011) reveals that Malaysian fans of Manchester United critically interpret the meanings of club's "red devil" badge on the basis of their local religious beliefs. Foregrounding the framework of glocalization, my own analysis of Chinese Arsenal fans' online discourses (Gong, 2016) demonstrates a mid-way, redefining these fans' discursive constructions of fluid masculine identities as a negotiation between the globalized EPL culture and the local meanings about Chinese masculinities.

Digital Sport Fan Practices

On the other hand, the poststructuralist approach has redirected the academic focus onto the centrality of new media in forming sports fandom as an everyday process. As it has become one of the main forces shaping our life experiences, digital technology has generated tremendous transformative impact on fan practices. As Tussey (2013) argues, digital media, by allowing fans to tailor sports consumption to their daily work and life, have remolded the forms and space of sports fandom through the creation of a link between multitasking spectatorship and modern connected labor in the global network economy. Shedding light on the longstanding utopian/dystopian trope of new technology, the existing literature has explored digital football fan practices threefold.

The first line of research looks at the digital impact on football fans' mediated game viewing. As broadcasting channels, live streaming sites are widely considered as an improved replacement for traditional telecast, providing audiences alternative accesses to live football games (Kirton & David, 2013). As second screens, social media supplement and reshape the televised football spectatorship into a participatory experience. Not only do social networking sites become extensions of sport television and catalysts for increased viewer attention (Hutchins & Rowe, 2012) but they also enable football fans to lessen their dependency on a single screen (Kroon, 2017; Rowe & Baker, 2012) and play a more active role as reflexive spectators (Gong, 2020).

Second, football supporters' digital practices have been examined in relation to the formation of fan communities. Divergent findings show the various ways in which football fans have formed cyber communities characterized "by fluidity, occasional gatherings and dispersal" (Crabble, 2008). Virtual fan communities are regarded to be liberating and empowering in their democratic potentials for not only mobilizing resistance to the status quos in football (Millward,

2013; Levental, Galily, Yarchi, & Tamir, 2016), but also facilitating fans' decision-making about club operation (Hutchins, Rowe, & Ruddock, 2009; Ruddock, Hutchings, & Rowe, 2010). Meanwhile, other scholars point out the commercial nature of online football communities, stressing that fans' dependence on technology in football viewing and discussion has become part of the branding project of football clubs and the mediated sports economy (Checchinato, Disegna, & Gazzola, 2015; Popp & Woratschek, 2016).

Finally, recent inquiries have enriched a critical consideration as to whether digital media have the deliberative and participatory capacities for football fans to construct productivity and subjectivity through discursive and creative practices. The optimistic view represented by Ruddock (2013) contends that online discussions are part of the materiality of football fandom, "allowing the democratized 'fabrication' of a tradition to be an authentic and rationalized means of finding pleasure and community in a heavily commodified world" (p. 164). Nevertheless, other digital media critics present a dystopian scene through the findings about the persistence of unequal power relations in digital football spaces. They urge for a critical reflection on the limitations in active participation and social inclusion in digital football fandom. For instance, Hynes and Cook (2013) have addressed the prevalence of heteronormative notions of masculinity in online football forums, which force female football fans to regulate the expression of their gender identity to fit into this male-dominated culture.

The literature in transnational football consumption and digital sport practices has raised important questions regarding how they are intersected. What is the role of digital technology in shaping and maintaining transnational sports consumption? How has digitization penetrated and transformed the viewing, communicative, and deliberative experience of cross-cultural sports fan subjects and in turn distinguished them from the conventional, localized, and embodied followers? How have the different affordances of digital technology contributed to this transformative process? Chinese fans' digitized engagement with European football provides a unique, non-Eurocentric perspective for exploring these questions.

Chinese Fans' Digitized Consumption of European football

Before I delve into European football fans' lively experiences, it is necessary to first contextualize them in China's rapid technological development and social transformation. Under the Xi Administration, the Chinese state economy is enforcing an upgrade from labor-concentrated manufacturing to information-based services in an attempt to expand domestic market and achieve sustainable development. Consequently, digital platforms developed by domestic conglomerates of information and communication technology, such as Sina Weibo and WeChat, are prospering and penetrating the fabrics of everyday life in China. Apart from its social and communicative functions, these sites serve commercial and entrepreneurial motives and substantially perpetuate the neoliberal structure and ideology. Despite its endorsement of digital technology for its role in capitalism and mass surveillance, the Chinese authority is alert to those platforms' potentials for political deliberations and civil engagement, thus making a remarkable effort to monitor and censor online interactions (Huang and Sun, 2014; Wang, 2016). Such ambiguous attitude mirrors China's transition to what I call "authoritarian digital capitalism" in which the state relies on digital technology to maintain and negotiate between economic neoliberalism and political totalitarianism. It is within this wider context that Chinese fans' consumption of European football has closely intertwined with their everyday communication through local digital media.

In the following section, I use my ethnography in the Chinese fandom of European football to provide an account of how digital technology, with a variety of affordances, has reconfigured transnational sports consumption. My in-depth interviewing and participant observations with both individual and organized fans in Shanghai have revealed Chinese fans' appropriation of a variety of local online platforms including Weibo, WeChat, QQ and public sports forums to organize fan activities. Their everyday consumption of European football revolves around three core practices facilitated by digital technologies: mediated game viewing, fan community building, and online discussions, through which their identities and relationships have been reformulated across virtual and real-life spaces.

Televised Spectatorship and Social Media

While most Chinese fans regard viewing European football competitions on television as the primary practice of supporting their favorite clubs, digital media use plays a crucial part in transforming the nature of such televised spectatorship. During game viewing, those fans are able to recontextualize the globally standardized telecast of European football in the local sociocultural settings by conducting information search and thoughts sharing on social media including Sina Weibo and WeChat. Used as a second screen supplement to the primary screen, these mobile networking apps work to make up for the limitations of television and enhance fans' viewing experience. My participants often switch to the second screen when a live match is stuck with some "boring periods" when key scenes are left out of the screen due to the limited scope of the televised representation of football. Social media use is also considered as an effective way to evade tedious TV commercials during half-time breaks. Therefore, fans' versatile engagement with Weibo and WeChat based on their distinct affordances represents their activeness to rework and improve their televised spectatorship.

Weibo is a microblogging website that can be accessed through mobile applications. It allows users to follow other users; create and repost texts, images, music, and videos; add hashtags; mention or talk to other users using "@UserName" formatting; and verify the accounts if run by celebrities or organizations. The Weibo content regarding European football is mainly created and disseminated by 1) the official accounts created by the leagues, clubs, and footballers with the purpose of promoting themselves to the Chinese market; and 2) the accounts of fan organizations and key opinion leaders (hereafter KOL) among individual fans. Through the posting of live updates, statistics, analysis, jokes, and backstage stories during live games, both types of accounts produce multi-perspective content that supplements the limited angles and storage of television representation. As a result, Weibo becomes a reliable source for Chinese fans to catch up on what they have missed from the television screen or to access those parts of the field not covered by the broadcasting cameras. It is creatively treated as an extension of television that offers fans additional textual and audio/visual resources enriching their understanding of the game. Furthermore, individual fans tend to share and communicate the game updates from those official or KOL accounts by Weibo's affordances of "reposting" and "hashtag". By reposting the updates of the same game under a communal hashtag, these fans, even with limited direct conversations, pass through their team's highs and lows during the game together and sequentially achieve a unique mode of "imagined collectiveness". In this sense, the use of Weibo in televised football viewing might facilitate a stronger sense of community among fans of the same club.

On the other hand, the cross-platform instant messaging app WeChat mainly attracts European football viewers with the function "Moments", which allow texts, images, and videos about the live matches to be shared as updates in their private social circles. Despite its instant messaging function, WeChat primarily offers football supporters this asynchronized space to discuss their viewing experience with other fans they know in person. In Moments, they cheer for the goals, champion the victory, mourn for the loss, as well as express emotions to other dramatic incidents on the field. As Moments allows a form of asymmetrical communication that can be freely initiated, joined, and left at any time during a game, WeChat successfully affords European football fans' needs for contingent, discontinued, fragmented interactions and emotional expression to accommodate the ups and downs of their televised spectatorship. Fans can thus reinscribe the collective celebration of feelings and sympathy embedded in the organic, in-situ football spectatorship which has been disrupted by the individualized and rationalized viewing style enforced by television. It is worth noting that Chinese supporters tend to use WeChat to discuss live football games with family members, friends, colleagues, or at least acquaintances in real life. Compared to the imagined collectivity of unknown fans on Weibo, the viewing community enabled by WeChat sees fans socialize and connect in more private and intimate manners.

More importantly, Chinese fans' active appropriation of Weibo and WeChat occurs alongside both individual viewing of European football in private settings and collective televised spectatorship at public events. Digital second-screening generates a new form of mediated football spectatorship that breaks the boundaries between the individualistic and the collective, the rational and the emotional, and the public and the private. For dispersed fans who watch European football at home, switching between television and social media screens enables them to virtually view the games together, as well as to integrate the collectivist, emotional, and active traditions of in-situ spectatorship to the individualized, rationalized, and passive nature of televised football. Social media use is also a norm at the organized game viewing gatherings where the collective televised football spectatorship is constantly destabilized by fans' engagement with information search on Weibo or thoughts sharing via WeChat. The limited interactions among physically proximate fans at the viewing events *reflects* the prevalence of "absent presence" at social occasions caused by the obsessions with mobile communication. In this sense, the impact of social media on Chinese fans' televised spectatorship of European football is complicated, if not contradictory, thanks to their engagement with the social media.

Fan Community Building Through Digital Platforms

Chinese fans of European football have also appropriated digital technology to establish and maintain local communities that connect both online and offline spaces. As an important sector of this cross-cultural fandom, supporter organizations for European clubs have thrived in large cities such as Shanghai, Guangzhou and Chengdu. My fieldwork in Shanghai uncovers two prominent examples of this kind – *Barcelona Fan Association* (*BFA*) and *Reds in Shanghai* (*RIS*), an association for Manchester United fans. Aiming at hosting in-person gatherings for game viewing, fan interactions, and football competitions, these fan associations provide abundant opportunities for individual fans to connect with each other and conduct collective practices. Yet these face-to-face activities are only possible because of the organizers' active digital networking and publicity. Indeed, the local supporter organizations are built principally via different forms of social media including QQ, Weibo, and WeChat that help connect and mobilize dispersed fans into a union. To a large extent, the founding and expansion of these associations in Chinese urban spaces reflect the frequent interweaving of European football fans' virtual and real-life communications, networks, and practices.

Interestingly, my observations of *BFA* and *RIS* have chronicled the synchronization of the development of these organizations with the evolution of various Chinese social media. In particular, QQ, Weibo, and WeChat have all contributed to the current structures and routines of the communities revolving around those two fan associations. Both *BFA* and *RIS* started from QQ chat groups a decade ago when this desktop-based program was the most popular instant messaging tool in urban China, and then expanded their networks on the mobile apps of Weibo and WeChat. The rudimentary format of the fan organizations was a closed QQ chat group composed of a small number of fans who followed the same European team and often had certain real-life connections (e.g. university peers, colleagues). Entry mainly through personal references, such chat group created a clearly bounded community that later extended virtual interactions to face-to-face meetings. The growth of openly accessed Weibo since 2010 has allowed the organizations to transcend the boundary of the initial QQ groups and make themselves formally known to a wider audience. Both *BFA* and *RIS* use Weibo to announce, publicize, and record the fan gatherings and other team-related events they host. In spite of its embedded interactivity, Weibo is strategically revised by fan organizations as a one-to-many channel to circulate event information among potential participants. With more than 200,000 followers, the Weibo accounts enable the fan associations to mediate an extended "imagined" fan community across greater geographical locations. In more recent years, WeChat gradually becomes the predominant social platform for the local football fan associations to redefine and rebound their communities. My investigation reveals three WeChat functions that *BFA* and *RIS* often appropriate to connect with their members – private contact between the organizers and fans, group discussions coordinated by the organizers, and official public accounts with regular feeds of event information, club news, and match analysis. With these communicative tools of varying degrees of reach and openness, WeChat enables the local fan organizations of European football to rebuild communities that are smaller than the Weibo audience but much larger than the original QQ chat groups. It especially revives the exclusivity and sense of community of the original QQ groups that have been lessened by Weibo. Yet compared to the real-life social and spacial proximities implanted in the QQ groups, the WeChat-based community incorporates a broader range of fans whose common interests in the European team are prioritized to their real social identities.

Given the respective role of QQ, Weibo, and WeChat in the emergence, expansion, and rebounding of the local fan organizations, the communities they build have witnessed various changes in their boundaries and become increasingly hybrid in nature. Such fluid structure allows members of the fan communities to play with their identities across virtual interactions and real-life gatherings. Indeed, most supporters maintain a consistent virtual identity through a pseudonym in all the online and offline contexts provided by the fan associations. For some fans, such identity enables them to highlight their collective interests in European football and separate their fan enjoyment from real life often fraught with restrictions and struggles. For others, using pseudonym in offline gatherings creates appropriate distance between themselves and peer fans, which protects their privacy in these embodied situations where their gender, age, and class are easily disclosed.

The presence of such hybridized fan identity in the organized activities subsequently leads to contingent and unstable relationships between members of the same fan association. In other words, regardless of the in-person collectivity they sometimes facilitate, the digitized fan communities are convenient and flux by nature. The predominance of social media in the coordination of these fan communities has created reluctance among the members to develop closer private relationships with their peers. In spite of their frequent online interactions with other members of the fan organizations, most of my participants lack trust in this digitally saturated community as a reliable source for constructing more solid, real-life friendship. They tend to agree that the hybrid, virtual identity and the contingent interpersonal connections sustained by social media imply uncertainties about other fans' worldviews, social positions, and material conditions which they consider as more important factors for forming real life solidarity than the common interests in European football.

Online Deliberations

In addition to game viewing and community building, digital technology has offered a vital site for Chinese fans to produce and circulate texts and discourses regarding European football. While social media such as Weibo and WeChat prevail in many other aspects of this fandom, online fan discussions continue to aggregate on Chinese public forums which afford the participants to deliberate on social and political issues beyond European football in a "virtual sphere" (Papacharissi, 2002). A representative of such sports forums is *Hupu*, a comprehensive bulletin board system that comprises a section for the discussions around European football leagues. While each of the "Big Five" leagues has its own discussion board, the most visited board in the section is one called *Football Topics* (足球话题区), where European football fans come together for general communication regardless of club preferences. The *Football Topics* board welcomes all sorts of talks about leagues, clubs, and players, which range from match analysis, club reformations and transfers, to out-of-field gossip. My everyday reading of these discussion posts during the fieldwork has revealed European football fans' heated debates over race and sexuality, two remarkable social issues that have been largely overlooked in the mainstream media and public discourses in China.

Chinese football fans' collective deliberations around race on *Hupu* are twofold. The first category critically reacts to the notorious incidents of racism that occur in European football competitions. Chinese fans' conversations have drawn specific attention to the on-the-field racism towards Asians which has not obtained sufficient European media coverage. Notably, fans' deliberations initiated from the racial problems in European football often extend to the critique of racism in the local society. The second type of posts dealing with race include those championing the significant contributions that players of color have made to elite European football leagues. These discussions allow Chinese fans to reflect on the ways in which the global racial hierarchy is simultaneously perpetuated and challenged by the trans-continental migration of footballers of color as well as their rise to stardom in European leagues.

In the meantime, the debates over sexuality regularly emerge from fans' considerations of both football leagues and individual players. News coverage of the campaigns in support of LGBT groups in European football culture is frequently shared on the forum, which inspires *Hupu* users to deliberate on the biological and sociocultural roots of desires and to defend the legitimacy of diverse sexual identities. Another thread of interactions endorses equal rights for LGBT by imaginatively associating footballers with non-normative sexualities. These discussions present two polarized views about the queered imagination of European football: one sees it as discriminative due to its irrelevance to football skills whereas the other regards it as emancipatory because its accentuation of alternative sexualities already resists heteronormativity. These conflicting yet insightful views produce further deliberations on how promoting equal rights and contesting heteronormativity can be accomplished in everyday football talks.

Chinese fans' critical reflections through the online discussions about European football are culturally and politically progressive in the local context because of their explicit critique of racism and homophobia. The mainstream political and entertainment discourse in China has not only kept both race and sexuality as marginalized topics but shows how racial and sexual minorities are stigmatized, mocked, and sometimes uncannily commercialized. Rational, serious deliberations on race and sexuality are barely visible in many other online platforms. Yet the *Football Topics* section on *Hupu* permits a wide range of imaginations about European football, a sporting text with rich cultural and symbolic resources for reckoning on these issues. It thus becomes one of the rare discursive sites in China where race and sexuality are explicitly considered, where racism and homophobia in both football and the wider society are spotlighted and criticized, and where the profound origins and consequences for these discriminative processes are debated. In fact, Chinese fans' awareness of and consensus on the advocacy for equal rights across different races and sexualities drawn from European football discussions have questioned the dominant state rhetoric which is designed to mute and suppress critical conscience on those issues.

Furthermore, the technological affordances of the *Hupu* discussion boards have facilitated a virtual sphere where European football fans can advance their cultural and political deliberations. From the Habermasian perspective (1989) of the public sphere, *Hupu* provides some key conditions for an ideal speech situation comprised of equal participation, public interests, rational thinking, and discursive democracy. First, the *Football Topics* board is inclusive of topics encompassing different European leagues, clubs, and players; it therefore supports fans' equal participation by breaking the boundaries between club-based communities. Such openness and inclusiveness allow the discussion board to attract fans with varying tastes, experience, and thoughts to collectively form communicative actions. Second, thanks to *Hupu*'s unlimited storage and presentation of content, Chinese fans' eloquent and serious deliberations on social issues on *Hupu* surpass the public imagination of football supporters' mania and demonstrate rational communicative processes that foreground the presentation of evidence and theory in addressing topics relevant to public interests. Third, the *Football Topics* section makes relatively democratic exchanges of discourses possible because the implicitness of European football's socio-political implications compared to other foreign cultural texts has made this sporting text a somewhat tolerated subject whose online discussions can obtain more autonomy from state censorship. However, this virtual sphere does not guarantee the continuity of fan deliberations until consensus or mutual understanding is reached. Neither can the collective speech actions encouraged by online football talks develop into more substantial engagement with local activism for race and sexuality. In this sense, the deliberative democracy embodied by *Hupu* users has limited impact on the advancement of political transformations in China.

Conclusions

Chinese European football fans' digital practices entail the significant roles that local digital platforms have played in shaping transnational sports consumption and fandom in reforming China. The use of digital technology in mediated football spectatorship, fan community building and online football discussions allows my participants to achieve a unique form of collectivity that transcends the real and virtual spaces. However, as an epitome of the contradictory nature of transnational digital sports consumption, this fan collective carries such individualistic characters as fluid identity, flexible relationships, and convenient participation. These characters are prone to dissolve football fans' solidarity and sense of community, thus preventing them from taking more substantial collective actions with potentials for formal political movements in real life. Facilitated by local social networking sites and public forums, this individualized virtual collectivity among European football fans is compatible with the state's authoritarian capitalist strategy that shapes Chinese digital technology as an entrepreneurial and consumerist vehicle containing limited possibilities for ideological contestations and civic engagement.

Through these individualized collective formations, Chinese fans' transnational consumption of European football are digitally reconfigured in both online and offline spaces. It is yet important to note that this process is not solely driven by the affordances of the local digital sites but also intertwined with fans' engagement with the globalized text of European football as well as their situation in the socio-economic context of reforming China. This case reflects the broader trend of sports consumption in China where digital media have served as key sites for cross-cultural fans to perform productivity, collectivity, and subjectivity. In spite of its lack of direct and explicit political appeals, the collective activeness of European football fans constructed through digital practices still conveys a progressive message about the potentials of transnational sports fandom in response to China's increasing integration of digital technology into authoritarian neoliberal capitalism.

References

Abercrombie, N., & Longhurst, B. (1998). *Audiences*. Cambridge: Polity.
Checchinato, F., Disegna, M., & Gazzola, P. (2015). Content and feedback analysis of YouTube videos: Football clubs and fans as brand communities. *Journal of Creative Communications*, 10(1), 71–88. 10.1177/0973258615569954
Crabble, T. (2008). Postmodern community and future directions – Fishing for community: England fans at the 2006 FIFA World Cup. *Soccer & Society*, 9(3), 428–438. doi: 10.1080/14660970800200905
Crawford, G. (2004). *Consuming sport: Fans, sport and culture*. London: Routledge.
Dixon, K. (2013). *Consuming football in late modern life*. Burlington, VT: Ashgate Publishing.
Giulianotti, R. (2002). Supporters, followers, fans, and flaneurs: A taxonomy of spectator identities in football. *Journal of Sport & Social Issues*, 26(1), 25–46.
Giulianotti, R., & Robertson, R. (2007). Recovering the social: Globalization, football and transnationalism. *Global Networks*, 7(2), 144–186. doi: 10.1111/j.1471-0374.2007.00163.x
Giulianotti, R., & Robertson, R. (2009). *Globalization and football*. London: Sage.
Gong, Y. (2016). Online discourse of masculinities in transnational football fandom: Chinese Arsenal fans' talk around "gaofushuai" and "diaosi". *Discourse & Society*, 27(1) 20–37. doi: 10.1177/0957926515605964
Gong, Y. (2020). Virtual collectivity through second screen: Chinese fans' WeChat use in televised spectatorship of European football. *Television & New Media*, 21(8) 807–824. doi: 10.1177/1527476419857199
Gray, J., Sandvoss, C., & Harrington, L. (2007). Introduction. In J. Gray, C. Sandvoss, & L. Harrington (eds.) *Fandom: Identities and communities in a mediated world* (pp. 1–16). New York: NYU Press.
Harbermas, J. (1989). *The structural transformation of the public sphere: An inquiry into a category of bourgeois society*. Trans. by T. Burger and F. Lawrence. Cambridge: MIT Press.
Harrington, C. L., & Bielby, D. B. (2007). Global fandom/global fan studies. In J. Gray, C. Sandvoss, & L. Harrington (eds.) *Fandom: Identities and communities in a mediated world* (pp. 179–197). New York: NYU Press.
Huang, R., and Sun, X. (2014). Weibo network, information diffusion and implications for collective action in China. *Information, Communication & Society*, 17(1), 86–104. doi: 10.1080/1369118X.2013.853817
Hynes, D. & Cook, A. (2013). Online belongings: Female fan experiences in online soccer forums. In B. Hutchins & D. Rowe (eds.) *Digital media sport* (pp. 97–110). New York: Routledge.
Hutchins, B., & Rowe, D. (2012). *Sport beyond television: The internet, digital media and the rise of networked media sport*. New York: Routledge.
Hutchins, B., Rowe, D., & Ruddock, A. (2009). "It's fantasy football made real": Networked media sport, the Internet, and the hybrid reality of MyFootballClub. *Sociology of Sport Journal*, 26 (1), 89–106. doi: 10.1123/ssj.26.1.89
King, A., (2003). *The European ritual: Football in the new Europe*. Aldershot: Ashgate.
Kirton, A. & David, M. (2013). The challenge of unauthorized online streaming to the English Premier League and television broadcasters. In B. Hutchins & D. Rowe (eds.), *Digital media sport* (pp. 81–94). New York: Routledge.
Kroon, Å. (2017). More than a hashtag: Producers' and users' co-creation of a loving "we" in a second Screen TV sports production. *Television and New Media*, 18(7), 670–88. doi: 10.1177/1527476417699708
Levental, O., Galily, Y., Yarchi, M., & Tamir, I. (2016). Imagined communities, the online sphere, and sport: The Internet and Hapoel Tel Aviv Football Club fans as a case study. *Communication and the Public*, 1(3), 323–338. doi: 10.1177/2057047316668364
Manzenreiter, W. (2004). Japanese football and world sports: Raising the global game in a local setting. *Japan Forum*, 16(2), 289–313. doi: 10.1080/0955580042000222664
Millward, P. (2011). *The global football league: Transnational networks, social movements and sport in the new media age*. Hampshire, UK: Palgrave Macmillan.

Millward, P. (2013). Fan movements in the network society: Project, resistance and legitimizing identities among Manchester United supporters. In B. Hutchins & D. Rowe (eds.), *Digital media sport* (pp. 139–152). New York: Routledge.

Papacharissi, Z. (2002). The virtual sphere: The internet as a public sphere. *New Media & Society*, 4(*1*), 9–27. https://doi.org/10.1177/14614440222226244

Popp, B., & Woratschek, H. (2016). Introducing branded communities in sport for building strong brand relations in social media. *Sport Management Review*, 19(*2*), 183–197. doi:10.1016/j.smr.2015.06.001

Rowe, D. (2011). *Global media sport: Flows, forms and futures*. London: Bloomsbury Publishing.

Rowe, D., & Baker, S. A. (2012). Truly a fan experience? The cultural politics of the live site. In R. Krøvel & T. Roksvold (eds.) *We love to hate each other: Mediated football fan culture* (pp. 301–317). Göteborg: Nordicom.

Rowe, D., & Gilmour, C. (2010). Sport, media, and consumption in Asia: A merchandised milieu. *American Behavioral Scientist*, 53(*10*), 1530–1548. doi: 10.1177/0002764210368083

Ruddock, A. (2013). "Born on Swan Street, next to the Yarra": Online opinion leaders and inventing commitment. In B. Hutchins & D. Rowe (eds.), *Digital media sport* (pp. 153–165). New York: Routledge.

Ruddock, A., Hutchins, B., & Rowe, D. (2010). Contradictions in media sport culture: The reinscription of football supporter traditions through online media. *European Journal of Cultural Studies*, 13 (*3*), 323–339. doi: 10.1177/1367549410363200

Sandvoss, C. (2003). *A game of two halves: Football, television and globalization*. London: Routledge.

Satoshi, S. (2004). Football, nationalism and celebrity culture: Reflections on the impact of different discourses on Japanese identity since the 2002 World Cup. In W. Manzenreiter & J. Horne (eds.) *Football goes East: Business, culture, and the people's game in China, Japan and South Korea* (pp. 180–194). Abingdon: Routledge.

Toffoletti, Kim (2017). Sexy women sports fans: Femininity, sexuality, and the global sport spectacle. *Feminist Media Studies*, 17(*3*): 457–472. doi: 10.1080/14680777.2016.1234499

Tussey, E. (2013). Desktop day games: Workspace media, multitasking and the digital baseball fan. In B. Hutchins & D. Rowe (eds.), *Digital media sport* (pp. 37–51). New York: Routledge.

Wang, X. (2016). *Social media in industrial China*. London: UCL Press.

32

The Commodification and Mediatization of Fandom

Creating Executive Fandom

Brett Hutchins, David Rowe and Andy Ruddock

Introduction: Alienation from the 'Sportsbiz'

The sports fan, while having much in common with other types of fan (Gray, Sandvoss & Harrington, 2007), differs from them in key respects. All fans are expected to be 'fanatical' – that is, passionate about some aspect of a cultural form: a text, a practice, a practitioner and so on. But few bear the wide-ranging responsibilities of the dedicated sports fan who, especially when living in the same city and community as the sporting club they support, is given many duties. They are expected routinely to pay to enter the 'home ground' and travel to distant sporting contests throughout the season; they are pressured to purchase and wear a particular style of sport-related clothing, and acquire other branded merchandise displaying the symbols of allegiance to the team and its history; and learn a specific mode of behaviour, including moving, chanting and (sometimes) singing. In the process, they are compelled to submit to the televisual gaze as a pivotal aspect of the mediated sport spectacle that is expensively bought and sold, sometimes on a global scale (Wenner & Billings, 2017). Fan loyalty is frequently 'rewarded' by being placed under close surveillance and control by the authorities in and around stadia. All this activity, expense and unpaid labour is dedicated to a cultural form and set of social and media practices built around an 'illusion' that it somehow '*matters* who wins the game' (Serazio, 2019: 31, emphasis in original). The result is that access to the intermittent social and affective pleasures of sports fandom is predicated on voluntarily entering into a contract that, in law, would likely be considered 'unconscionable, harsh or oppressive' – an arrangement that is unfair, unequal and exploitative.

Not all sports fans accept these arrangements. Indeed, many have sought to create social meaning for themselves and others by representing themselves as the 'true custodians' of sport, despite the significant levels of control exercised by so-called 'sportswashing' repressive states and commercial corporations, speculative investors, franchising strategists, celebrity owners, sponsors and media companies (Ronay, 2019). The assertion of rights by sports fans in the face of their alienation from the 'sportsbiz' (Rowe, 1995: 104) can be regarded as an attempt to enhance cultural citizenship at a time when the idea of the informed, active citizen is subordinated to that of the targeted, reactive consumer (Miller, 2007). The concept of citizenship involves both rights and responsibilities (Wenner, Bellamy & Walker, 2014), and citizen-fans have declared the importance of actively contributing to the operation, conduct and governance of sport, rather than accepting or rejecting what is offered to them as interested 'outsiders' (Millward, 2011). This declaration has led to a proliferation of sports fan federations, trusts and groups that have intervened in sport by running media campaigns and communicating their interests to journalists and publics. Heavily publicised fan interventions include those targeted at saving their sport club from financial collapse and/or protesting to stop the relocation of their team to other areas and cities. Historically, various ownership, control and governance precedents exist that enable fans, as members with a financial stake in sporting organisations, to have an impact on the clubs and teams that they support in the fullest sense. The corporatisation of sport, though, has often rendered even this fan involvement impotent, reducing it to a phatic process of periodic consultation, market surveys and online supporter polls.

Executive Fandom Explained

A notable problem for fans who wish to have a greater impact on the running of sport and sports clubs is that they are relatively isolated from each other. Unlike the owners and those professionals with formal roles within sporting organisations, most fans see each other only intermittently, if at all, and communicate mainly through the meetings of voluntary associations, and via social media, websites, email listservs and online bulletin boards. In the twenty-first century, however, the flourishing of digital and mobile media has enabled sport fans to engage in more regular and efficient methods of assembly. Placing these communicative tools in the hands of fans has fostered what Rowe (2011: 77) terms *executive fandom*. This form of fandom is a product of the interactive affordances of digital and mobile media, and makes large-scale synchronous and asynchronous communication between large numbers of geographically dispersed fans possible (Hutchins & Rowe, 2012). This concept captures a longstanding aspiration of many dedicated fans to participate actively in the running of teams and sports – to make their voices heard and to see their wishes acted upon. It is an ambition grounded in a seductive 'fantasy construct' (Hermes, 2005: 37): 'real' fans coming together and mobilising *through media* to take back control and ownership of sport from 'out of touch' business executives and the 'corrupting' forces of corporate capital (which, ironically, intervened in sport because of growth in media technologies, audiences and markets) (Ruddock, Hutchins & Rowe, 2010: 325). This construct imagines an ideal of media-based participatory democracy that, in practice, delivers the unruly, cacophonous and contingent features of the demotic (Keane, 2010; Turner, 2010). There is rarely any agreed upon systematic agenda or workable plan of action developed among groups of fans online – only a consistently expressed *desire* to exercise greater control of, and ownership over, their team or sport. As this chapter outlines, the aspiration of fan control relies on a community- and participation-based model of digital media and communication that, at best, is realised infrequently and, at worst, is illusory. Furthermore, the executives, administrators and professionals who own and run media sport show no sign of handing significant decision-making control to fans, except under highly circumscribed conditions designed to deliver marketing opportunities, valuable consumer data and/or growth in revenue (although exceptional cases such as MyFootballClub [2019] do exist – see below). Executive fandom, therefore, describes how the promise of fan empowerment in media sport is structurally organised to deliver instead technological novelty, publicity and data harvesting through digital and mobile media.

The authors have published previously on the audacious-but-failed experiment of MyFootballClub in the United Kingdom (Hutchins & Rowe, 2012; Hutchins, Rowe &

Ruddock, 2009; Rowe, 2011; Rowe, Ruddock & Hutchins, 2010; Ruddock et al., 2010), a venture that began in 2007 as the 'world's first and only web-community owned football club' under the motto 'Own the club, pick the team'. In turning fans living anywhere in the world into owner/members for a modest annual fee (£35/$US46), the club pooled its funds to choose and purchase a controlling stake in a small English association football (referred to as soccer in this chapter) club, Ebbsfleet United. Like a 'real-life' version of the soccer management simulation video game, *Championship Manager* (Crawford, 2006), member-fans could then vote via a web poll on matters including contracts with sponsors; the price of entry, merchandise, food and drink; player uniform colour and design; and incoming and outgoing player transfers. The most striking decision-making area of all – the composition of the team and its tactics – was, though, never carried beyond non-binding advice to the team's coach. MyFootballClub, riven with disagreement among its member-fans, lost most of its once substantial membership (at its peak over 30,000 worldwide, but falling to below 1,000), sold out of Ebbsfleet United, and moved to a mere sponsorship role at another small club, Slough Town. Nonetheless, along with several other instances in world sport – especially soccer (García & Zheng, 2017) – it provides a useful pointer to executive fandom in action. Fans act on the promises and possibilities of digital media to contest the dependency and passivity of commercially prescribed fan roles.

A sense of technological novelty pervades the evidence presented in this chapter. However, the social and cultural significance of executive fandom also needs to be recognised. Two factors stand out in this regard. First, the advent and growth of executive fandom speaks to how media sport directs the politics of leisure via its audiences. Media attain political significance by offering audiences easy access to social pleasure. Fan culture may initially have represented a popular, 'imaginary' solution to the inequities of mass culture, but it is arguably now a model for monetising pleasure and attention by transforming this 'resistance' into commodified labour (Fiske, 1987; Soha & McDowell, 2016; Terranova, 2000). Resistance refers to interpretative processes through which audiences use corporate mass media content to critique the 'raced', classed and gendered exclusions of capitalist societies. MyFootballClub, for example, significantly resisted soccer's transformation into a global media phenomenon, dominated by a select few brands; Barcelona, Real Madrid, Manchester City and the like. Ironically, such resistance only drew fans further into media dependency. This transformation is increasingly achieved through targeted and mass advertising, data collection, crowd-sourced media content and the building of subscription- and 'freemium'-based online communities at scale. Executive fandom represents, perpetuates and intensifies this trend. Second, changing modes of fandom highlight the expansion of mediatisation processes in sport and in the wider social world. In reflecting on these trends, we argue that executive fandom is indicative of deep-seated changes in media practice and the ways in which sociality is enacted and understood in mediatised societies.

This chapter examines the changing modes of fan interaction and activity in media sport facilitated by digital, mobile media, gaming and video streaming technologies, and the communities of dynamic scale and geography organised in and through the networks made possible by them. Building on previous research analysing the rise of executive fandom in the context of English soccer and supported by a new case study of American football, we show that fans and supporters are engaging in an increasingly sophisticated and routinised range of mediatised interactions with teams, leagues, competitions and events. Mostly evident in the Global North, these initiatives represent the ongoing mutual constitution of media, gaming and sport, and are underpinned by 'everyware media' (Miller, 2014: 107; Taylor, 2018) – that is, computing and screen-based devices (smartphones, tablets, laptops and desktop computers, handheld and console gaming technologies, wearable media devices, video displays and touch screen monitors) and wireless and telecommunications networks and broadband technologies (varying forms of cellular mobile, Wi-Fi networks, distributed antenna systems, cabled and mobile internet, near-field communication, local area networks and sensor-based technologies). These interactions are also the product of media sport industry strategies that capitalise on the interests, activities and emotions of fans by accumulating attention, data, commercial revenue, advertising and publicity. As such, these diffuse socio-technical processes materialise an historical trend in which commercial media constitute publics and define the terms of social interaction.

Cultural Participation: Directing the Politics of Leisure via Crowds and Audiences

Attention now turns to soccer in order to examine how cultural participation, fan practices, public spaces and digital media intersect. Soccer fandom, in particular, underwrites the discursive repertoire of executive fandom, adapting and reinventing cultural storylines rooted in the traditions of locally embodied folk cultures, particularly in the United Kingdom and Europe. The notion that there is an essential form of authentic fandom rooted in physical presence remains the underlying myth of fan interaction (Brown, Crabbe and Mellor, 2008). Intriguingly, current practices 'keep the faith' by reversing the myth's polarity. In traditional and 'newer' territories and markets such as the United States and Australia, this sport shows how digital media practices are used to create fan identities and communities that then manifest as publics in stadia (Lunt & Livingstone, 2013; Ruddock, 2013). Apparent throughout are the ways in which fans seek to influence the politics and appearance of sport via their collective presence and voice.

Soccer fandom produces visible political effects when the broader politics of leisure stimulate the energy of the crowd. The ability of fans to gather in large numbers in a stadium and adjacent public space is still championed as the essence of their power (Guschwan, 2016a). The pleasures of contemporary *media* sports fandom originate in the disruptive potential of cultural or institutional practices that become the focus of communication and enable people to experience and deploy culture's *congregational* power (Thompson, 1963). The physical location of people who consciously adopt and perform particular identities in specific places also means that politics can never be eradicated from stadia (Guschwan, 2016b).

Physical co-presence in the stadium remains important to fans and those institutions that seek to organise them, and the power of the crowd has fuelled explicitly political fan actions in recent years. For example, in 2013 rival fans from Turkish sides Beşiktaş, Fenerbahçe and Galatasaray marched together through the streets of Istanbul to protest against a government crackdown on environmental protestors (Erhart, 2014). Scandinavian women's supporter groups have made themselves visible at games as a distinct cohort, with their presence seen as vital to rewriting soccer's gender narrative and 'staging femininity in a man's world' (Mintert & Pfister, 2014: 1640). The willingness of Ghanaian fans to travel to, and be seen at, World Cup tournaments has also been hailed as significant to national development (Alber & Ungruhe, 2016). There is also a clear relationship between 'being seen' and live television sport. Television allows millions of viewers to feel the pleasures of community at a distance, and adds to one of broadcast media's signature appeals: the thrill of 'being there' as history happens (Bourdon, 2000; Dayan & Katz, 1992; Guschwan, 2016c). The appeal of live television is tied to the power of the crowd given that stadium crowds enhance soccer as a media spectacle (Abercrombie & Longhurst, 1998). The crucial importance of the physical crowd was dramatically emphasised when, in 2020, the Covid-19 pandemic forced major sport events to be played in empty stadia. The resultant television sport spectacle was so degraded there was a resort to the use of cardboard cut-out fans, crowd noise sampled from earlier contests, and screen projections of spectators on Zoom and other services previously used only for video conferencing (Al Jazeera, 2020). Many fans recognise their commercial power as people who are important to be seen and, therefore, demand that their role as actors – not just as spectators – in soccer cultures be taken with corresponding seriousness. Implicit in the bargain struck between fans, teams and the media industries is an acknowledgement that soccer should be about more than the international brands and content that appeal to global markets (Gerke, 2018).

Soccer's capacity to spark debates about racism, sexism and homophobia has turned online fora and social media into places where fans 'do' politics by posting, liking and commenting (cf. Poulton & Durell, 2016). On occasion, these media practices produce identifiable change by serving as a barometer of fan and/or consumer satisfaction. For example, in 2005 English club Birmingham City moved to sign England international Lee Bowyer from Newcastle United. Bowyer was a player with a history of disciplinary problems, and the trade was abandoned in the face of a hostile online fan petition. This was a relatively early sign of soccer's new mediatised reality – online fora and networks offer an opportunity for fans to have their voices heard by those running the game (Ruddock, 2005). These voices can be hard to ignore when those speaking attend games, chant in the stands, purchase season tickets and buy cable and satellite television subscriptions.

Executive fandom is the final destination in a narrative where digital media practices have exposed the simplifications at play in notions of passive audiences and armchair fans (Gibbons & Nuttall, 2016). The process of mediatisation retains the idea that these practices 'bend' cultural expression toward commercial interests. Yet, as Bolin (2012) argues, digital culture has a two-speed economy where resistance and incorporation coexist comfortably because they work off and through each other. Importantly, the diffusion of digital and mobile technologies has rendered media use a requirement of committed fandom. Online communities are vital to keeping the game alive in nations where soccer is a relatively new phenomenon, as it cannot justify its appeal or even existence through recourse to local traditions. In the United States, professional soccer matters to many as a code despite a 'fragmented culture' compared to more established sports like American football, baseball and basketball (Wilson, 2007: 381). Given the challenges of distance and comparatively low live game attendances in some locations, the active online presence of American Major League Soccer (MLS) fans has been crucial to the game's survival and growth (Wilson, 2007).

A symptom of a mediatised society is that people sometimes congregate as media users before they become publics (Lunt & Livingstone, 2013). A fledgling Australian A-League team, Melbourne Heart (now Melbourne City and owned by the Abu Dhabi United Group for Development and Investment-controlled City Football Group), offers an instructive example here, particularly as soccer competes with larger and more popular football codes in Australasia (Australian rules football, rugby league and rugby union). Heart fans engaged in online storytelling practices to energise feelings of commitment before the new club kicked a ball in 2010 (Ruddock, 2013). The prospect of live games as spectacles relied upon the development of an active supporter group, Yarraside. The group invested considerable energy in narrating its identity online in the weeks and months before Heart took to the field. These stories drew heavily on widely accessible global soccer hooligan histories available through film, television and bestselling biographies (Poulton, 2006; Redhead, 2004). Such stories offered a rationale for fans to enter the stadium, a recipe for how to behave once they were there, and a logic with which to form relationships with other fans and with the club itself. Yarraside is a vivid example of how conventional fan practices – embodied, present and hostile toward the commercial taming of soccer – are entwined with media pleasures, commercial practices and marketisation (Ruddock, 2013). Now well established and playing in its eleventh season, the club is subject to familiar complaints made by soccer fans in online fora: a lack of on-field success, poor team selections and signings, inept coaching and club management ignoring the wishes of fans.

The next section presents evidence of how executive fandom is manifest in the digital and mobile media sport industries. It demonstrates that the historical emphasis discussed above – on crowd congregation, public space and the wider politics of leisure and history – is conspicuously lacking. While leveraging the ideal of fan empowerment, the mediatised modes of engagement on offer remain strictly within the confines of branded media experiences, are parasitical on video game cultures, and emphasise the affordances of technical connectivity over social connection or political expression.

Interactivity is not Control

The urge of fans to influence control over competitions has deep historical roots. As Richard Gruneau (2017: 40) identifies, the ancient Roman gladiatorial arena (from approximately 105 BCE to 404 CE) was a site where a 'potentially lethal' form of spectatorship held sway. The crowd's judgement played a decisive role in whether a defeated gladiator lived or died based on an assumed level of bravery shown during a fight. The uncertainty of a fight's final outcome dramatised and magnified the power of 'the public' in Roman society, albeit mediated through a high-ranking public official in a physical setting where the power of the state ultimately held sway (2017: 40). Efforts by fans to shape the features and course of physical contests continue over 1,500 years later, but the centrality of citizenship and publics to these efforts has long since given way to the dramatisation of media sport consumption in the pursuit of data and profit.

The following case study of the Fan Controlled Football League (FCFL) exemplifies two interrelated dynamics of executive fandom: heavily-hyped experiments in fan-controlled sporting competition and the structuring of 'sport *as* media' – that is, the ways in which digital and mobile technologies are materially and experientially constitutive of many contemporary media sport practices and events (Hutchins & Rowe, 2012; Hutchins et al., 2009). The FCFL was selected from a range of available cases, including the aforementioned MyFootballClub; Formula-E motor racing (a fan-voted Power Boost for drivers and the live Ghost Racing mobile game); National Association for Stock Car Auto Racing (NASCAR) motor-racing and experiments with gamification, augmented reality and the scouting of new driver talent; rugby fans in Christchurch, New Zealand, voting to continue with their team's name, the Canterbury Crusaders, following a mass shooting in a city mosque; multiple examples of fans helping to determine team line-ups in various sports (e.g., All Star games in Major League Baseball [MLB], Major League Soccer [MLS], the National Basketball Association [NBA] and the National Football League [NFL]); various fan-voted player-of-the-match initiatives; and fans deciding the uniforms and colours worn by teams (e.g., the Australian cricket team's one-day international uniform). These examples sit alongside a growing number of social media influencer- and platform-led sporting activities that respond to subscriber, viewer and algorithmically determined preferences (e.g., Spencer Owen and Hashtag United FC, and widely covered boxing matches between KSI and Logan Paul) (Hutchinson, 2020).[1]

The Fan Controlled Football League

Fan engagement and interaction are primary objectives of professional sporting teams and leagues worldwide. The popularity and accessibility of mobile media, social media services, apps, video platforms and websites have helped to transform these objectives into *deeply mediatised* practices and processes (Couldry & Hepp, 2017; Frandsen, 2020). As a result, the social dimensions of fan engagement and interaction are increasingly sublimated into data-driven systems, algorithmic logics, computational and telecommunications infrastructures, targeted advertising and commercial transactions (Andrejevic, 2020; Couldry & Mejias, 2019). The apotheosis of this pattern in media sport (at the time of writing) is the Las Vegas-based FCFL.

The FCFL has successfully mobilised the discursive promise of executive fandom. Despite not having staged a game, the FCFL has achieved widespread news media coverage (including by *CBS Sports*, the *Wall Street Journal* and the *Washington Post*), significant corporate investment (the Amazon-owned Twitch and IMG) and high-profile celebrity involvement (including Mike Tyson, Richard Sherman, Bob Menery and Greg Miller). In a striking parallel with the early days of MyFootballClub, the FCFL promotes a live video game-like experience:

> A new pro football league where the fans call the shots. The Fan Controlled Football League (FCFL) is exactly what it sounds like, a real world sports league where the Fans are in charge. It's like Madden in real life. All FCFL games will be live-streamed on Twitch, the world's leading social video service and community for gamers and eSports, available on mobile, desktop, and tablet. The FCFL has also teamed up with IMG Original Content who will be supporting the league with their unparalleled expertise in sports and entertainment.
>
> *FANchise LLC, 2019*

The antecedent of this four-team league was the Utah-based Salt Lake Screaming Eagles, which competed in the 2017 Indoor Football League (IFL) and attracted national media attention (Balk, 2017; Flynn, 2016; Moxley, 2017; Stevenson, 2017).

Controlled by the operators of the FCFL, Project Fanchise, the Screaming Eagles won five matches, lost 11 and finished fourth in their five-team conference. The presentation and organisation of the team resembled a mix of the Madden NFL video game and fantasy sports (Oates, 2014). The team's players were sourced from social media and by amateur fan scouts, and the squad line-up was decided through a combination of fan and coach selections. Fans chose the team's name and uniform, resulting in a garish red, white and blue design. The distinctive feature of the Screaming Eagles' in-game tactical decisions was that fans, in real time during games, decided the plays run by the team via a selected menu of options and a popular vote. Votes were made through a mobile app for Android or Apple iOS that resembled the Madden NFL interface in its presentation. Off the field and online, fans celebrated plays when they were successful, argued when they failed and complained about poor player execution, such as 'I don't remember "drop the ball in the end zone" as a play option in the app' (cited in Stevenson, 2017). The coach complained about fans calling too many passing plays when running may have been a more effective tactical option (Balk, 2017). The ever-present threat of mobile disconnection and technological failure was realised when the stadium Wi-Fi network crashed during a game, meaning neither fans nor coaching staff could use the app for a short period (Moxley, 2017). But, the 'first fan-run football team' was successful in other ways (Flynn, 2016). Crowds for games sometimes doubled the League average and the mobile app was reportedly popular in all 50 US states, as well as being downloaded in countries such as Mexico, Germany and Australia (Moxley, 2017). The Screaming Eagles were, in effect, 'a proof of concept' that made both the FCFL and its high-profile streaming rights deal with Twitch possible:

> Project Fanchise isn't exactly about sports – it's a business, and one perfectly suited to our atomized, everybody-has-a-voice, Silicon Valley-spawned era. More than 200,000 people streamed the team's first game, making it one of the most-watched in IFL history.
>
> *Moxley, 2017*

Following this success, the team left the IFL at the end of the 2017 season and its owners announced the launch of a new Interactive Football League, later renamed the FCFL.

The most significant feature of the FCFL is arguably its rights deal with the video game streaming platform Twitch, which Amazon purchased for US$970 million in 2014 (Amazon's market capitalisation presently sits at over US$850 billion). This platform already streams live NFL games (Thursday Night Football), the NBA's G-League, and the National Women's Hockey League (NWHL), as well as myriad e-sports competitions and channels devoted to sport video games such as Madden NFL and NBA2K (Hutchins, Li & Rowe, 2019). In conjunction with these competitions and games, the FCFL signifies the rise of 'networked broadcasting' (Taylor, 2018: 10). According to Taylor, this concept denotes the interweaving of streaming platforms, video game cultures, sports products and media entertainment, with this process both reflecting and contributing to a wider set of transformations across the global media industries. In the context of live sport, this interweaving is triggering a proliferation of interactive possibilities and media experiences for fans that further constitutes sport *as* media:

> Via an interactive video overlay on Twitch or in the FCFL app, fans will call all the plays in real time for the 8 teams in the new league. The outcome of each fan vote will be relayed to the quarterback and executed on the field. In addition to play calling, the FCFL is putting fans in the General Manager role for the first time in sports, allowing them to determine each team's name, logo, coach, and the players that make the roster via a fan-run draft. It's a video game brought to life, and it's what every football fan has been waiting for … The Twitch platform enables the FCFL to deliver a cutting edge fan experience with interactive overlays enabling fans to deep dive into player analytics and call plays live for their team. Fan Captains will co-stream their team games to provide their insight on what play calls and roster moves they want their team's fans to make in real time.
>
> *FANchise LLC, 2019*

Caution is recommended when considering the promotional hype here, especially as at time of writing (November 2020) no FCFL game has kicked off (the six-week game schedule being scheduled to commence in February 2021). Much like MyFootballClub before it and the phenomenon of executive fandom more generally, the FCFC is built on the *promise* of fan control. Cascading interactive options generated via streaming video, digital interfaces and mobile apps do not, however, constitute control of sport. Rather, the FCFL seeks to entertain and engage fans by manufacturing video game-like decision-tree structures in football – that is, a set of mobile media-dependent options and fast-moving popular votes. These options may initially deliver novel experiences, but the strictures and patterns of platform capitalism mean that they will quickly become routinised, habituated and copied when (or if) their viability is demonstrated (Fordyce, 2019; Mosco, 2017; Srnicek, 2017). Actual control over the conditions and terms of fan engagement – technical features and menus, competition rules and design, tactical options, team ownership, intellectual property and branding, player recruitment and labour, user data and privacy, revenue and technology – is the preserve of Project Fanchise and its investors, FCFL corporate partners, and Amazon as the holder of media and data rights. The achievement of the FCFL so far has been to formulate and market a participation-based media sport business model that animates the discursive promise of fan empowerment. Its ultimate success relies on the continued use of novel technologies and entertaining experiences to divert attention from the fact that the main game being played is the appropriation of fan labour, commodification of fan attention, and datafication of fan interactions.

Conclusion: Executive Fandom Reconsidered

Despite our analytical scepticism, this chapter has not sought to represent executive fandom as some form of mediated false consciousness, whereby fans are duped into feeling a sense of power over their inherited or acquired 'deep fan' attachment (Real, 1996). It is certainly the case that fan power is exaggerated and even in some respects illusory, especially when tied to the development, promotion and sale of new digital technologies and services. But, as noted above, it can also be efficacious in selected instances, although usually over conspicuous issues involving public protests and boycotts rather than continuing, systematic organisational governance. This situation is hardly surprising given that executive fans are overwhelmingly volunteers and 'amateurs', not remunerated career specialists. In any case, treating cultural practices involving judgements and commitments of taste (Bennett et al., 2020) as exemplars of pure reason is its own illusion. Being a fan in sport or in any other cultural domain is to embrace to a substantial degree the non-rational, without which fandom itself would not exist. However, executive fandom in sport inevitably constitutes an unequal contest between the massive economic and technological forces arrayed against those who, quite legitimately, aspire to assert greater collective control over their objects of fan desire.

We have examined here the ways in which this aspiration, whether romantic or instrumental, is routinely thwarted. We have shown how the very mediatised technological affordances that invite a sense of unprecedented fan agency operate in ways that enmesh aspiring executive fans in a network of commercial, informational and mediated relations from which they cannot escape. This is not an argument against resisting fan manipulation and exploitation, but a recognition of what such resistance is up against. In their discussion of transmedia engagement focused mainly on fiction fandom, Jenkins et al. (2013: 150–1) refer to *obsession_inc's* (2009) distinction between 'affirmational fandom' and 'transformational fandom'. If translated to sport, this distinction could be described as the difference between traditional, passive forms of fandom and modern, active executive fandom. These authors are at pains not to treat it in hierarchical terms, but it is apparent that those who practise executive fandom do tend to see it as such – or they would probably not intervene in sport processes in the first place. We, by contrast, have argued that to seek to transform sport via information and media-enhanced collective fan action is, by turns, to challenge and affirm its current structure of power. Those who seek to assert fan power in sport should be acutely aware that, in the very act of doing so, they are producing the data that may be appropriated for very different, less liberating purposes.

Acknowledgements

Evidence presented in this chapter was collected as part an Australian Research Council Future Fellowship awarded to Brett Hutchins, 'The Mobile Media Moment: Investigating the Pivotal Role of Sport in Mobile Media Content, Markets and Technologies' (FT130100506).

Note

1 These examples and the selected case study are drawn from a searchable trade press database produced from stories published by major sport business and technology media outlets in the United States, United Kingdom, Europe and Australia. Maintained weekly since 2 January 2014, it is organised by theme, key words, sport, nation/region and key quotations, and contains 3,531 items at the time of writing (17 November 2020). Trade press and related industry sources represent 'a crucial resource' for researchers investigating the strategies, discourses and narratives that shape new technologies and markets (Wilken, 2014: 1089).

References

Abercrombie, N. & Longhurst, B. J. (1998). *Audiences: A sociological theory of performance and imagination*. London: Sage.

Al Jazeera (2020). 'Sports TV: Faking spectators & spectacles'. 26 September, www.youtube.com/watch?v=0AlD63s26sQ&feature=youtu.be&t=827. Accessed 25 November 2020.

Alber, E. & Ungruhe, C. (2016). Fans and states at work: A Ghanaian fan trip to the FIFA World Cup 2010 in South Africa. *Soccer & Society*, 17(1): 18–39.

Andrejevic, M. (2020). *Automated media*. New York: Routledge.

Balk, T. (2017). Tasked with play-calling, Salt Lake Screaming Eagles fans can't resist the pass. *Sports Illustrated*, 2 May, www.si.com/ifl/2017/05/02/salt-lake-screaming-eagles-play-calling-pass-verlon-reed. Accessed 19 November 2019.

Bennett, T., Carter, D., Gayo, M., Kelly, M. & Noble, G. (eds) (2020, in press). *Fields, capitals, habitus: Australian culture, inequalities and social divisions*. London and New York: Routledge.

Bolin, G.R. (2012). The labour of media use. *Information, Communication & Society*, 15(6): 796–814.

Bourdon, J. (2000). Live television is still alive: On television as an unfulfilled promise. *Media, Culture & Society*, 22(5): 531–56.

Brown, A., Crabbe, T. & Mellor, G. (2008). Introduction: Football and Community – Practical and Theoretical Considerations. *Soccer and Society*, 9(3): 303–12.

Couldry, N. & Hepp, A. (2017). *The mediated construction of reality*. Cambridge: Polity Press.

Couldry, N. & Mejias, U.A. (2019). *The costs of connection: How data is colonizing human life and appropriating it for capitalism*. Stanford, CA: Stanford University Press.

Crawford, G. (2006). The cult of Champ Man: The culture and pleasures of Championship Manager/football manager games. *Information, Communication & Society*, 9(4): 496–514.

Dayan, D. & Katz, E. (1992). *Media events: The live broadcasting of history*. Cambridge, MA: Harvard University Press.

Erhart, I. (2014). United in protest: From 'living and dying with our colours' to 'let all the colours of the world unite'. *International Journal of the History of Sport*, 31(14): 1724–38.

FANchise LLC (2019). About us. *FCFL*, www.fcfl.io/about-us. Accessed 15 November 2019.

Fiske, J. (1987). *Television culture*. London: Routledge.

Flynn, E. (2016). How the first fan-run football team was born. *Sports Illustrated*, 6 June, www.si.com/ifl/2016/06/07/project-fanchise-indoor-football-league-fans. Accessed 19 November 2019.

Fordyce, R. (2019). 'Bandersnatch': That game we all played. *Overland*, 5 February, https://overland.org.au/2019/02/bandersnatch-that-game-we-all-played/comment-page-1. Accessed 19 November 2019.

Frandsen, K. (2020). *Sport and mediatization*. Abingdon, UK: Routledge.

García, B. & Zheng, J. (eds) (2017). *Football and supporter activism in Europe: Whose game is it?* Basingstoke: Palgrave Macmillan.

Gerke, M. (2018). 'Supporters, not consumers': Grassroots supporters' culture and sports entertainment in the US. *Sport in Society*, 21(6): 932–45.

Gibbons, T. & Nuttall, D. (2016). 'True fan = watch match'? In search of the 'authentic' soccer fan. *Soccer & Society*, 17(4), 527–39.

Gray, J., Sandvoss, C. & Harrington, C.L. (eds) (2007). *Fandom: Identities and communities in a mediated world*. New York: New York University Press.

Gruneau, R. (2017). *Sport and modernity*. Cambridge: Polity Press.

Guschwan, M. (2016a). Fandom face to face. *Soccer & Society*, 17(3): 274–89.

Guschwan, M. (2016b). Performance in the stands. *Soccer & Society*, 17(3): 290–316.

Guschwan, M. (2016c). Broadcast media: Live and in-person. *Soccer & Society*, 17(3): 332–50.

Hermes, J. (2005). *Re-reading popular culture: Rethinking gender, television, and popular media audiences*. Oxford: Wiley-Blackwell

Hutchins, B., Li, N. & Rowe, D. (2019). Over-the-top sport: Live streaming services, changing coverage rights markets, and the growth of media sport portals. *Media, Culture & Society*, 41(7): 975–94.

Hutchins, B., & Rowe, D. (2012) *Sport beyond television: The internet, digital media and the rise of networked media sport*. Abingdon: Routledge.

Hutchins, B., Rowe, D. & Ruddock, A. (2009). 'It's fantasy football made real': Networked media sport, the internet and the hybrid reality of MyFootballClub. *Sociology of Sport Journal*, 26(1): 89–106.

Hutchinson, J. (2020). Digital first personality: Automation and influence within evolving media ecologies. *Convergence*, 26(5–6): 1284–1300.

Jenkins, H., Ford, S. & Green, J. (2013). *Spreadable media: Creating value and meaning in a networked culture*. New York, NY: New York University Press.

Keane, J. (2010). *The life and death of democracy*. Sydney: Pocket Books.

Lunt, P. & Livingstone, S. (2013). Media studies' fascination with the concept of the public sphere: Critical reflections and emerging debates. *Media, Culture & Society*, 35(1): 87–96.

Miller, J. (2014). Intensifying mediatization: Everyware media. In A. Hepp & F. Krotz (eds), *Mediatized worlds: Culture and society in a media age*. Basingstoke: Palgrave Macmillan, 107–22.

Miller T. (2007). *Cultural citizenship: Cosmopolitanism, consumerism, and television in a neoliberal age*. Philadelphia, PA: Temple University Press.

Millward, P. (2011). *The global football league: Transnational networks, social movements and sport in the age of new media*. Basingstoke: Palgrave Macmillan.

Mintert, S. & Pfister, G. (2014). The female Vikings, a women's fan group in Denmark: Formation and development in the context of football and fan histories. *International Journal of the History of Sport*, 31(13): 1639–55.

Mosco, V. (2017). *Becoming digital: Towards a post-internet society*. Bingley: Emerald.

Moxley, M. (2017). The great fan-run football experiment. *GQ*, 26 October, www.gq.com/story/fan-run-football-experiment. Accessed 19 November 2019.

MyFootballClub (2019). Teams, www.pitchero.com/clubs/myfootballclub/teams/150211. Accessed 23 February 2019.

Oates, T.P. (2014). New media and the repackaging of NFL fandom. In T.P. Oates & Z. Furness (eds), *The NFL: Critical and cultural perspectives*. Philadelphia, PA: Temple University Press, 80–100.

obsession_inc (2009). Affirmational fandom vs. transformational fandom. Blog, 1 June, https://obsession-inc.dreamwidth.org/82589.html. Accessed 9 December 2019.

Poulton, E. (2006). 'Lights, camera, aggro!' Readings of 'celluloid hooliganism'. *Sport in Society*, 9(3): 403–26.

Poulton, E. & Durell, O. (2016). Uses and meanings of 'yid' in English football fandom: A case study of Tottenham Hotspur Football Club. *International Review for the Sociology of Sport*, 51(6): 715–34.

Real, M. (1996). *Exploring media culture: A guide*. Thousand Oaks, CA: Sage.

Redhead, S. (2004). Hit and tell: A review essay on the Soccer Hooligan Memoir. *Soccer & Society*, 5(3): 392–403.

Ronay, B. (2019). Sportswashing and the tangled web of Europe's biggest clubs. *The Guardian*, 15 February, www.theguardian.com/football/2019/feb/15/sportswashing-europes-biggest-clubs-champions-league-owners-sponsors-uefa. Accessed 9 December 2019.

Rowe, D. (1995). *Popular cultures: Rock music, sport and the politics of pleasure*. London: Sage.

Rowe, D. (2011). *Global media sport: Flows, forms and futures*. London: Bloomsbury Academic.

Rowe, D., Ruddock, A. & Hutchins, B. (2010). Cultures of complaint: Online fan message boards and networked digital media sport communities. *Convergence*, 16(3): 298–315.

Ruddock, A. (2005). Let's kick racism out of football – and the lefties too! Responses to Lee Bowyer on a West Ham web site. *Journal of Sport and Social Issues*, 29(4): 369–85.

Ruddock, A. (2013). 'Born on Swan Street, next to the Yarra': Social media and inventing commitment. In B. Hutchins & D. Rowe (eds), *Digital media sport: Technology and power in the network society*. New York: Routledge, 153–65.

Ruddock, A., Hutchins, B. & Rowe, D. (2010). Contradictions in media sport culture: 'MyFootballClub' and the reinscription of football supporter traditions through online media. *European Journal of Cultural Studies*, 13(3): 323–39.

Serazio, M. (2019). *The power of sports: Media and spectacle in American culture*. New York: New York University Press.

Soha, M.S. & McDowell, Z.J. (2016). Monetizing a meme: YouTube, content ID, and the Harlem Shake. *Social Media + Society*, 2(1): 1–12.

Srnicek, N. (2017). *Platform capitalism*. Cambridge: Polity Press.

Stevenson, S. (2017). That was my play! *Slate*, 17 February, https://slate.com/culture/2017/02/the-salt-lake-screaming-eagles-a-football-team-controlled-by-fans-with-smartphones.html. Accessed 19 November 2019.

Taylor, T.L. (2018). *Watch me play: Twitch and the rise of game live streaming*. Princeton, NJ: Princeton University Press.

Terranova, T. (2000). Free labor: Producing culture for the digital economy. *Social Text*, 18(2): 33–58.

Thompson, E.P. (1963). *The making of the English working class*. New York: Pantheon Books.

Turner, G. (2010). *Ordinary people and the media*. Thousand Oaks, CA: Sage.
Wenner L.A., Bellamy, R.V. & Walker, J.R. (2014). Selling out: The gaming of the living room seat for the US sports fan. In J. Scherer & D. Rowe (eds), *Sport, public broadcasting, and cultural citizenship: Signal lost?* London: Routledge, 74–95.
Wenner, L.A. & Billings, A. C. (eds) (2017). *Sport, media and mega-events*. London: Routledge.
Wilken, R. (2014). Places nearby: Facebook as a location-based social media platform. *New Media & Society*, *16*(7): 1087–1103.
Wilson, W. (2007). All together now, click: MLS soccer fans in cyberspace. *Soccer & Society*, *8*(2/3): 381–98.

33
Football Fans and Food
Feeding the Desire

Keith D. Parry and Jessica Richards

Introduction

Restrictions on fans attending games in person during Covid-19-enforced lockdowns around the world have not only stretched the finances of leagues and clubs but have also highlighted the significance of matchday attendance, for both clubs and fans. Yet even before this hiatus, with the amount of sport that is available on television and via the internet increasing, some sports teams and codes were struggling to encourage an increasingly sedentary population to attend live events (Parry et al., 2018). Mediated consumption of sport has become the most common method for fans to engage with professional sport. It is now more usual for fans from regions such as Europe, North America, and Australia to watch sport via some form of media rather than to attend a venue in person (Parry, Jones, & Wann, 2014). The emergence of new "players" in the media sport market, such as Amazon Prime Video, have rewritten the schedules of many sports leagues, moving games to satisfy television audiences – to the frustration of many fans – but to the joy of those who are happy to spend hours on end watching numerous matches. Covid-19 lockdowns further impacted match schedules and allowed leagues and broadcasters to fill even more hours with live broadcasts.

The reasons for falling attendances are varied, but the rising cost of attending cannot be ignored. There are concerns that the high prices (when tickets, food, and transport are considered) at some stadia may be pricing "the common person", particularly those with families, out of attending sports matches (Sutton, 2017). Indeed, the BBC Price of Football survey reveals the high prices that are now charged by many football clubs in England and Europe, identifying how much tickets, food, and drinks cost at each club. The cost for a family of four to attend an English Premier League football match is likely to be at least £150 (U.S. $200/€175) when transport and food are taken into consideration.

Moreover, it has been argued that mediated consumption is unhealthy for consumers as it encourages sedentary behaviour. Guidelines on sedentary behaviour and physical activity have been established in many countries, aiming to minimise time spent sitting generally and the time that populations spend in front of screens (Parry et al., 2019). As such, the greater availability and enhanced quality of mediated sport may have a detrimental impact on health by encouraging prolonged bouts of sedentary behaviour while watching sport. Therefore, a greater understanding of the relationship between fans and food and drink is becoming increasingly important.

It has been shown that the price of food and drink is not the only culinary frustration for many fans (Parry, Hall, & Baxter, 2017). Closed concession stalls, long queues, poor service, and a lack of food options are issues that impact on the fan experience and that may deter revisitation intentions. The tendency for venues to outsource their catering also puts them in a difficult position. Sports teams who relinquish control over their offerings can make every effort to provide a high-quality matchday experience, but even when the team wins fan satisfaction can be marred by poor service quality and low-quality, high-priced offerings. Although it has been noted that food and alcohol are the primary purchases that sports fans make when they attend sports matches (Jones, 2002), this element of sport consumption has, until recently, been largely overlooked in academic research into the actual offerings in stadia (Carter et al., 2012).

Amid questions on the suitability of stadia for place-based health interventions (Parry et al., 2019) we refocus attention on the food and drink consumption behaviours of fans. We present findings from a series of ethnographic studies into fandom in both Australia and the United Kingdom, along with insights from our earlier work in this area to examine the role of food and drink within the sports fan experience. In doing so, we provide valuable insight for both practitioners and academics and may provide solutions for those wishing to encourage fans to return to stadia.

Fan Experience and Journey – Eating on the Way and Drinking in Pubs

The sports stadium is often conceived as "the place in which sport is produced, consumed and delivered to sport fans" (Westerbeek & Shilbury, 1999: 2). As a result, research on sports fans generally begins and ends in an analysis from inside of the stadium, making little or no mention of the surrounds or processions fans pass to reach their home sports stadium. When such is considered, it usually sits docile in the background of work focused on the "football hooligan" fan identity, or as a backdrop to deviant fan behaviour (Richards & Parry, 2019). Yet, as with the fan experience more generally, matchday food and beverage consumption often also begins outside of the stadium.

Stadia have, historically, been built within densely populated, lower-socioeconomic areas of towns and cities and so the routes that fans take to these venues often have a plethora of takeaway shops, grocers and, perhaps most importantly for fans, public houses (pubs) along the way. The ongoing popularity of these venues emphasises the importance placed on eating and drinking but may also be indicative of frustrations with the existing offerings at venues. Increasingly, clubs and venues are recognising how important food and beverages are to fans on a matchday and have looked for ways to encourage fans to eat and drink more in the venue or the immediate vicinity by setting up fan zones. These have been defined as "bounded spaces external to the stadium that are set aside for family-friendly fan engagement activities" (Richards & Parry, 2019: 4) and it is common to see food trucks or barbeques as part of the engagement activities. These sites add to the atmosphere and environment around the stadium with the smell of fast food and sound of sizzling of burgers tied to what Gaffney and Bale describe vividly as "sensing the stadium" (2004). By this they are referring to the smells that fans experience en route to and inside a stadium, which, they argue, evoke responses that familiarises them with sport (Gaffney & Bale, 2004). Smells, just like familiar landmarks, anchor fans spatially on match-day by triggering in the minds of fans a return to the stadium. This in turn evokes feelings of routine, comfort, and familiarity. While eating at home symbolises intimacy and family, eating out prior to a football match symbolises festivity, excitement, and builds atmosphere for the upcoming fixture (Richards, 2015). The following fieldwork note, which was part of a study into the matchday experience at Everton Football Club, emphasises the role that the senses play in the food and beverage experience:

> As I walked down Goodison Road today [towards the club's stadium], I passed flags on my right of the timeline of the club's history. I could smell and hear the burgers and onions sizzling away.
>
> *Fieldwork Notes: 15/9/2012 vs. Southampton*

Our research has found that passing or meeting at take-away shops or pubs, which are often endowed with personal memories, anchors fans on their matchday journey. These spaces are locations for social interaction and are often where the match-day atmosphere begins developing. We argue that the spaces inhabited prior to the match remain spatially configured to encourage the consumption of certain types of food and drink that are tied to interactions and engagements between fans. Therefore, eating and drinking on matchdays becomes a key element in creating a strong bond between fans and the locations that they occupy by connecting them not only to each other, but also to the overall local community (such as shop owners).

Our observations have also shown that pre-match stops at pubs are as important, if not more so, than the match itself for many fans and particularly males (Richards & Parry, 2019). The relationship between association football (although it is equally applicable to many other sports), alcohol and male bonding has been described as "the holy trinity" (Weed, 2007), emphasising how important alcohol is in the fan experience. While pubs have been spaces for male bonding on match days (Brown, 2010; Wenner & Jackson, 2009), they are also becoming spaces for families and female fans, albeit within a gendered and spatial hierarchy (Richards & Parry, 2019).

The Inextricable Link with Beer

As noted at the start of this chapter and above, beer remains a key purchase for many fans attending sports matches. The (excessive) drinking of alcohol gives rise to a variety of fan behaviours, including the creation of "beer snakes" at cricket matches, which are created by stacking a large number of empty plastic beer cups to form a long "snake". Although this activity is frowned upon and regulated by security staffs and stewards, fans still attempt to build these creations with the building of snakes taking place in secret, hidden from the eyes of the stewards and police, and then the separate sections of the creation are brought together. Once the snake is revealed to spectators there is often a rain of plastic cups (mostly empty) being thrown towards the snake's creators to help it grow with the accompanying song "feed the snake and it will grow", which is set to the tune of the traditional hymn *Bread of Heaven* adding to this element of the spectacle.

In some countries, drinking beer while attending games is the de facto norm and a symbolic representation of masculinity. Alcohol-fuelled fights, tales of drunken exploits, and spectator boasts over the number of beers that they will be able to drink are commonplace during sports matches (Parry, 2014). Wedgwood (1997: 26) highlights that cricket crowds in Australia in the late 1990s celebrated and exhibited hegemonic masculine displays through behaviours that included drinking excessively, noting that at cricket matches at this time, "the more beer/alcohol one drinks publicly, the more masculine one is considered". This attitude that the consumption of beer by fans is linked to masculinity is not confined to Australia or to cricket. Observations at association football matches in England reveal a similar pattern, as highlighted by the following fieldwork note from a match between Everton and Aston Villa:

> I overheard a male fan decline a beer, with his friend calling him "soft" and "weak" and suggesting that he was "unworthy" of being an Everton fan.

Yet in Australia, players have also elevated drinking large volumes of beer into a national "sport". Until recently, Australian cricketers vied with one another to set an unofficial "world record" for the number of cans of beer consumed on the flight from Sydney to London with cult figure David Boon overtaking Rodney Marsh and setting a record of 52 cans (McKay, Emmison, & Mikosza, 2009. With players setting such examples it is unsurprising that fans also associate watching sport with drinking and the price of beer at venues is often a primary concern for fans and the media alike, so much so that increases in the price of beer can make headline news (Parry & Hughes, 2016).

As a further example of the hegemonic masculinity associated with fandom, a number of Australian sports have recently clamped down on the unsavoury presence of so-called "beer wenches". As reported in a variety of media outlets, an advert posted on the listing site Gumtree sought young women who were "easy on the eye" to attend a cricket match with a group of male fans, dressed in a "serving wench" outfit in order to queue up for beer and then serve them during the day. The post, which promised to pay AU$20 per hour and the price of admission, drew outrage and was criticised for being "sexist and demeaning". This practice has been reported at other events previously but in recent years it has been banned by venues who cite an inability to monitor the drunkenness of the fans as the primary reason for outlawing the practice. In this instance, the venue in question stated that "there are rules on the responsible consumption of alcohol that are very clear to everyone throughout the venue and on our website" (*Queensland Times*, 2015).

Given the perceived desire to consume alcohol to excess at sporting matches, the drinks served in general bar areas at stadia (in Australia in particular) are often low-strength or non-alcoholic, and limits are imposed on the number of alcoholic drinks that can be bought at a time – typically four. However, many North American venues go further and allow no more than two alcoholic drinks per single sale, with Soldier Field in Chicago only selling one beer per purchase in their seating areas during NFL games (Lenk et al., 2010). Due to alcohol-related issues, the Sydney Cricket Ground introduced a "low alcohol beer policy for public concourse areas at international cricket fixtures", and dedicated non-alcohol seating areas in 1998 (Sydney Cricket & Sports Ground Trust, 2017). In the United Kingdom, football fans have been banned from drinking alcohol in the stands during matches, a result of earlier spectator violence. Images of drunken (male) fans fighting and causing disruptions at major sporting events also help to cement the association between fans and alcohol into the psyche of the wider population. These restrictions serve to propagate views that fans are in some way deviant, needing to be controlled (Richards & Parry, 2019). Nevertheless, the link between sport and alcohol is hard to shake.

Even in countries that have more conservative views on the consumption of alcohol, the role that beer plays in the fan experience is recognised. Qatar, a Muslim state and host of the 2022 FIFA World Cup has strict laws on the consumption of alcohol. It is normally only available at licensed hotel restaurants and bars while expatriates living in Qatar are only able to buy alcohol via a permit system. According to the US Department of State (2018), penalties for alcohol-related offences "are severe, including immediate arrest, heavy fines, imprisonment, and/or deportation". In 2019 Qatar introduced a so-called "sin tax" as part of a series of measures to target "health-damaging" goods (Osborne, 2019). The move involved a 100 per cent tax on alcohol, which effectively doubled the already steep price of beer. These measures added to the worries of sports fans and administrators, even those who seem more willing to overlook more significant human rights violations. FIFA has long attempted to allay the fears of fans that the choice of Qatar as host nation would result in a different, more restricted experience, but in 2016 it was reported that the public consumption of beer, including in public squares and in stadia, would be banned during the tournament (Payne, 2016). However, in another example of the power-wielding of FIFA (and other sports bodies), a nation state has adapted its laws to satisfy the demands of fans (or the commercial imperatives of the sport). At the recently completed 2019 FIFA Club World Cup in Qatar, which was viewed as somewhat of a test event ahead of the World Cup, a fan zone was set up at Doha Golf Club so that fans would be able to enjoy a traditional match day fan experience with fewer of the typical Qatari restrictions on alcohol. As part of this change, beer was subsidised and cost "only" $7 instead of the $10 that is typically seen in Doha (Robinson, 2019). This move is likely to be replicated at other locations during the World Cup and, in addition, hotel happy hours are to be extended and alcohol will be available in more locations or the World Cup itself. The chief executive officer of the 2022 World Cup, Nasser al-Khater is quoted in the *Guardian* (Ingle, 2019) as saying:

> Alcohol is not part of our culture. However, hospitality is. Alcohol is not as readily available here as in other parts of the world but for the World Cup we want to ensure it is accessible for fans who want to have a drink, so we are trying to find designated locations for fans to have alcohol, other than traditional places such as hotels and so forth… We recognise there is an issue with the price and it is something we are looking into. We are looking at finding ways to reduce the price of alcohol.

Again, the "important" relationship between sport fandom and alcohol is recognised and ordinary rules are deemed to no longer apply. As we note, for many fans drinking alcohol has been the most important aspect of attending sports matches, again making it difficult to change behaviours and encourage healthier and more inclusive practices.

In Stadia Food Options

Given their enclosed nature and with increasingly strict security measures to control who may enter, stadia are effectively physically sealed off from the outside world, much like airports, providing the kind of commercial domain that allows food and beverages to be controlled by a monopoly or oligopoly of caterers. A small number of suppliers pay a premium to provide a limited offering to the fans at a high mark-up. The economic reality of such a system has, until recently, encouraged catering companies to offer food that is quick to prepare/cook and that has a low initial cost (typically due to its lower quality). As has been noted previously, recently enhanced security checks when entering sports venues not only ensure the safety of attendees but also stop attendees from entering with "those [food and drink items] that may 'injure' the profit margins of the suppliers of hospitality" (Parry et al., 2017: 220). "Trapped" inside these spaces, fans have little option but to pay the price. As far back as the mid-1990s, stadium food prices were identified as an area of dissatisfaction for many sports fans (Wakefield & Sloan, 1995), and a number of more recent studies suggest that many sport attendees are still not satisfied with stadium food and beverages (Ireland & Watkins, 2010; Martin & O'Neill, 2010; Parry, Hall, & Baxter, 2017; Sukalakamala, Sukalakamala, & Young, 2013).

Based on the supposedly healthy nature of sport, it may be expected that sports stadia could/should act as sites for health promotion. However, one of the juxtapositions of modern professional sport is that the majority of people (including those who can afford to attend live matches) spend a large amount of time sat watching a small minority exert themselves for their viewing benefit. Moreover, the tendency for sports venues, clubs and leagues to "partner" with fast food, soft drink and alcohol companies means that spectators and viewers are bombarded with messages for unhealthy food and drink choices (not to mention unhealthy lifestyle choices such as gambling and previously smoking). Any health promotion messages can, therefore, be lost amidst the background noise of these sponsors. Spectators are left perplexed at the lack of promotion for healthier foods (Ireland, Chambers, & Bunn, 2019) and there is growing concern at the connection of such products with sport (Piggin, Tlili, & Louzada, 2017).

More so, technological developments and the increased proliferation of internet-enabled mobile devices have resulted in enhancements such as the San Francisco 49ers' stadium app that shows the length of queues for beverages, reducing the time that fans need to wait. In addition, there is also a greater availability of in-seat delivery, whereby food is pre-ordered and then delivered straight to the fan in their seat. App-based companies such as *Seat Serve* now allow fans to order food from the concession stands closest to their seats and receive it during the match. Another "enhancement" to the fan experience is the introduction of all-you-can-eat food promotions, which in the United States may only add an extra U.S.$15–20 onto the price of a ticket (Parry et al., 2019). Such a promotion clearly encourages fans to over-indulge and this practice can also be seen at corporate levels where hospitality packages often include unlimited food and drink.

The services listed above may provide a greater degree of ease and convenience for those attending games, but they also raise questions concerning the ethical practices of sports clubs and stadia and the extent to which they have a responsibility to promote healthy behaviours. Both of the all-you-can-eat options above are contrary to best practice in nutrition with regards to eating smaller portions more often. Browsing the selection of food available through the apps noted above reveals that what is on offer typically conforms to traditional views of stadium food; pies, chips, burgers, chocolate, and alcohol are commonly found. While it is not easy to find a clear definition of healthy foods, it is typically those that are low in fat, sugars and cholesterol that are considered healthy. Stadia sell vast quantities of foods but these are generally high in fats, sugars and cholesterol In addition, in-seat delivery reduces the physical activity levels of match going fans, increasing sedentary behaviour. Fans are therefore "encouraged" to embrace unhealthy practices when attending sports matches. As noted earlier, fans of all ages are widely exposed to advertising of unhealthy food and drinks with children able to recall these unhealthy sponsors (Ireland, Chambers, & Bunn, 2019). Significantly, it has been found that exposing younger fans to unhealthy food and drink environments can influence behaviour patterns in later life, shaping their food choices (Koenigstorfer, 2018) so the proliferation of unhealthy choices should be of concern.

It should, therefore, not be surprising that the food available through in-seat delivery apps is unhealthy as it has been shown that stadia generally provide very few healthy options for fans (Parry, Hall, & Baxter, 2017) and those that are available are often over-priced. Although a growing number of fans do want healthier options at sports matches (Parry, Hall, & Baxter, 2017), it is often difficult for them to find any at a reasonable price. Healthy options have previously included frozen yogurt, teriyaki bowls and fresh fruit (Roan, 1997). Newer venues now offer healthier food options including pizzas made on whole-wheat pitas, wraps, grilled sandwiches, and low-fat organic parfaits (Fabricant, 2005). A greater variety of food and beverages are also appearing on the menu of many stadia and, as noted previously (Parry, Hall, & Baxter, 2017), the New York Yankees serves Latin food (while retaining the "compulsory" hot dogs, popcorn, and Cracker Jack) while Miami's Sun Life Stadium have handmade turkey empanadas, baked potatoes, and a "Pizza Dog" – a foot-long hotdog baked in pizza dough on their multicultural menu. In Australia, redevelopments at a number of their iconic venues have included better quality food options, which spectators appear to have embraced. It is now common to find à la carte restaurants specialising in local seasonal food and local beverages, and the 2012–2014 Sydney Cricket Ground Northern Stand redevelopment included a "food court" style food area and a microbrewery bar. This food court offers higher quality and healthier food options with a number of higher end brands. The newly constructed Western Sydney Stadium also has gourmet options including a Korean fried chicken burger on a charcoal bun. It also offers healthier choices such as poke bowls, salads, and wraps with both gluten free and vegetarian options. In England, eighteen of the twenty Premier League clubs had invested in plant-based or low-carbon foods and most clubs were reducing or removing single use plastic from their food and drink offerings. For example, Liverpool Football Club have removed plastic straws and single-use plastic food packaging, replacing the latter with compostable palm leaf and maize trays (Sport Positive, 2019). In a survey of these clubs, food options include; three-bean Mexican wrap, Sticky Korean glazed vegetable, Veggie Chilli Cheese Fries at Arsenal; beetroot burgers, hot jackfruit sandwiches, Tofu Katsu curries, and beer battered tofu at Tottenham Hotspur and vegan hot dogs and burgers with non-gluten bread offered at Southampton (Sport Positive, 2019).

It is common to find either organic gardens or farms, which grow food both to use in the venues' catering outlets and often make donations to the local community in North American stadia. For instance, Fenway Park (home of the Boston Red Sox baseball team) has a 5,000-square-foot rooftop farm and San Jose Earthquakes' Avaya Stadium has an "edible garden" which includes fruit trees (Johnston, 2015). At the time of writing in 2020, some Australian venues were also planning to adopt this initiative (Rolfe & Frost, 2019). North America also has a long tradition for tailgating, where fans set up portable grills or barbeques in stadium car parks and cook their own food as an alternative to eating within the stadia. This practice has grown from its historic association with College football in south-eastern states of North America (Keaton, Watanabe, & Gearhart, 2015). Food and socialising are important elements of this practice and a varied menu is likely to be found that may include ribs, steaks, and seafood (Russell, 2011). However, a variety of historical and societal factors may mean that healthy eating initiatives may not be accepted by fans.

Fan Food Preferences

Stadia have historically been built in the less affluent areas of cities and towns. In these regions, particularly where there are food-insecure populations (Puppephatt et al., 2020) even when individuals value eating healthily they are often not able to afford healthier options as they cost significantly more than less healthy choices (Ashton et al., 2016). The higher cost, in addition to factors such as the greater accessibility of fast-food shops and viewing healthy eating as not masculine mean that those living in these areas may have little option but to opt for fast food and lower-priced, unhealthier options (Ashton et al., 2016; Puddephatt et al., 2020). Potentially due to a combination of these factors, the higher-quality, healthier options that we highlight above are often only available in sections of stadia that are reserved for members or corporate attendees. In this way, societal inequalities are reinforced and stereotypes are perpetuated. Moreover, consuming fast food has symbolic meanings attached to it as well, where meanings tied to particular types of food are reflective of and attached to match-day experiences and traditions. Blumer (1969) notes that the nature of an object (such as food) consists of the meanings that are created by the person and also how the group the individual is interacting with at the time defines it. Sports fans often see stadium food as a guilty pleasure to indulge in during their time in the stress-free stadium environment. Attending sports matches is often seen as a "release" for fans from their everyday life, resulting in them engaging in indulgent behaviour that can include excessive alcohol consumption and unhealthy fast food – termed the "football fan diet" by Ireland and Watkins (2010) in their study into association football fans. As part of our research on Everton Football Club, Stacey stated that she only let her child Callum and his cousin consume fast food on match-day. She considered the practice of consuming fast food at a sporting fixture a treat, and subsequently tied to the experience of match-day:

> Well, my Callum is allowed to eat that type of, like deep-fried, type, food like, only on match-day. Only before the match, with his cousin, like a treat. Usually he doesn't eat it… well I don't know, I don't let him eat it other times.
>
> *Interview: Stacey, 30–40*

Fans are resistant to changes in their matchday routines and habits, which can hinder attempts to introduce less traditional or healthier options. For example, corporate fans were famously described by former Manchester United football player Roy Keane as individuals who watch the game while eating a prawn sandwich (Davis, 2015). Because of this comment, corporate fans and/or those who do not consume the "traditional football fan diet" have been dubbed the "prawn sandwich brigade" by the wider football community. It is not surprising then that clubs/venues that break from the norm and attempt to innovate with their food and beverage offerings can often come in for criticism. Parry et al. (2019) detail the example of Forest Green Rovers Football Club who became the first vegetarian, and then, in 2015, the first vegan football club in the world as part of a wider push to promote healthier and sustainable living. While their meat-free policy was initially introduced for the players, it was subsequently applied to the whole stadium. The response from fans and the media was largely negative in the first instance and drew on stereotypical views on vegetarian and vegan food. The vegan diet of the players was blamed for poor performances and it was common to find reports of resistance from players initially. While "home" supporters have now embraced the menu, opposition fans are more likely to complain when they visit Forest Green's New Lawn stadium. Parry et al. (2019: 193) examined fan reviews of the matchday experience on the *Football Ground Guide* and *TripAdvisor* websites and note numerous comments on the club's food. They conclude that, for opposition fans, "the fan experience is adversely affected by perceptions of the poor-quality". However, food can play a major role in uniting sporting communities through change. For example, we observed how Everton Football Club celebrated the (recently appointed at the time) manager Roberto Martinez through a Spanish cultural food day in the "fan zone" precinct at their home stadium prior to a match (see below for more on fan zones). Spanish cuisine was on offer to local fans as a way of building a connection between them and the international manager at a time when some fans were uncertain about his appointment.

Moving Forward

Despite our above note of caution on stadium-based health promotion, there is some evidence that stadia and clubs are truly embracing healthier food options. There is also an expanding network of academics and practitioners that are working to improve the quality and healthiness of stadia food (and all aspects of stadia). In Europe, the Health Stadia Network has developed a series of guidance documents and toolkits to facilitate the development of stadia as health-promoting environments, which may also include healthy eating policies. Their guidance has focused on achieving tobacco-free stadia, promoting active travel, and a benchmarking tool for healthy matchday catering, which is supported by the British Heart Foundation. This tool includes a "Healthy Match Mark" award for compliant venues and focuses on the sale of healthier food options; food preparation and healthier cooking techniques; the control of portion size and condiments; the supply of healthier beverages; pricing; and the promotion of healthier options. As such, Healthy Stadia, are defined as:

> those which promote the health of visitors, fans, players, employees and the surrounding community… places where people can go to have a positive healthy experience playing or watching sport.
>
> *Philpott & Seymour, 2011: 69*

In addition, we, along with our earlier co-authors (see Parry, Hall, & Baxter (2017) and Parry et al. (2018)) have added a number of recommendations in this area including offering healthier drinks, offering healthier food options such as sushi rolls, providing nutritional information (particularly nutrient values) for stadium food at the point of sale, and more widespread use of designated driver programmes. However, for these changes to be accepted, a cultural shift in the attitudes of and towards sports fans is needed. Rather than major sporting events (and whole countries) accommodating sports fans it may be time for fans to alter their behaviours. With the advent of new norms, driven by changing demographics of sports fans, it is possible to marginalise traditional practices and create alternative, inclusive environments.

As we have detailed, food and drink are a significant factor in the fan experience and may be able to increase repatriation intentions by creating emotive responses and comforting memories. At a time when clubs are desperate for fans to return to stadia, the significance of this factor should not be overlooked. With the cost of attending sport rising, the quality of the in-stadium experience needs to be enhanced to appeal to a greater range of fan demographics. Therefore, the cultural shift in fan attitudes that we identify above will need to be matched by similar challenges to issues such as the economically driven practices of stadium catering, the restriction of higher-quality, healthier options to member and corporate sections, and the tendency for clubs and venues to partner themselves with sponsors associated with unhealthy lifestyle choices. Clubs and stadia cannot continue with established practices that reinforce social inequalities and impact both the pocket and the health of fans.

References

Ashton, L. M., Hutchesson, M. J., Rollo, M. E., Morgan, P. J., & Collins, C. E. (2016). Motivators and barriers to engaging in healthy eating and physical activity: A cross-sectional survey in young adult men. *American Journal of Men's Health*, 11(2), 330–343. doi:10.1177/1557988316680936

BBC. (2017, 15 November). Price of Football: Full results 2017. Retrieved from www.bbc.co.uk/sport/football/41482931

Blumer, H. (1969). *Symbolic Interactionism: Perspective and Method*. Berkeley: University of California Press.

Brown, A. (2010). Come home: The stadium, locality and community at FC United of Manchester. In: S. Frank and S. Steets (eds) *Stadium Worlds: Football, Space and the Built Environment*. London: Routledge, pp. 163–179.

Carter, M-A., Edwards, R., Signal, L., & Hoek, J. (2012). Availability and marketing of food and beverages to children through sports settings: a systematic review. *Public Health Nutr.*, 15(8), 1373–1379. doi:10.1017/S136898001100320X

Davis, L. (2015). Football fandom and authenticity: a critical discussion of historical and contemporary perspectives. *Soccer & Society*, 16(2–3), 422–436. doi:10.1080/14660970.2014.961381

Fabricant, F. (2005, 27 April). Healthier Food Lineup at New Stadium. Retrieved from www.nytimes.com/2005/04/27/style/dining/food-stuff-healthier-food-lineupat-new-stadium.html

Gaffney, C., & Bale, J. (2004). Sensing the stadium. In P. Vertinsky and J. Bale (eds). *Sites of Sport: Space, Place, Experience*. London: Routledge, pp. 25–38.

Ingle, S. (2019, 26 September). Alcohol set to be subsidised and more available at 2022 World Cup in Qatar. Retrieved from www.theguardian.com/football/2019/sep/26/alcohol-2022-football-world-cup-qatar

Ireland, R., & Watkins, F. (2010). Football fans and food: A case study of a football club in the English Premier League. *Public Health Nutrition*, 13(05), 682–687. doi:doi:10.1017/S1368980009991765

Ireland, R., Chambers, S., & Bunn, C. (2019). Exploring the relationship between Big Food corporations and professional sports clubs: A scoping review. *Public Health Nutrition*, 22(10), 1888–1897.

Johnston, M. W. (2015). Sports Teams Build Food Recovery Awareness. *BioCycle*, 56(5), 34. Retrieved from www.biocycle.net/2015/06/18/sports-teams-build-food-recovery-awareness/

Jones, C. (2002). The Stadium and Economic Development: Cardiff and the Millennium Stadium, *European Planning Studies*, 10(7), pp. 819–829.

Keaton, S. A., Watanabe, N. M., & Gearhart, C. C. (2015). A comparison of college football and NASCAR consumer profiles: Identity formation and spectatorship motivation. *Sport Marketing Quarterly*, 24(1), 43–55.

Koenigstorfer, J. (2018). Childhood experiences and sporting event visitors' preference for unhealthy versus healthy foods: Priming the route to obesity? *Nutrients*, 10(11).

Lenk, K. M., Toomey, T. L., Erickson, D. J., Kilian, G. R., Nelson, T. F., & Fabian, L. E. A. (2010). Alcohol Control Policies and Practices at Professional Sports Stadiums. *Public Health Reports* (1974–), 125(5), 665–673. doi:10.2307/41434823

Martin, D. S., & O'Neill, M. (2010). Scale development and testing: A new measure of cognitive satisfaction in sports tourism. *Event Management*, 14(1), 1–15.

McKay, J., Emmison M., & Mikosza J. (2009). "Lads, Larrikins and Mates: Hegemonic Masculinities in Australian Beer Advertisements", in L. Wenner and S. Jackson (eds) *Sport, Beer, & Gender: Promotional Culture and Contemporary Social Life*, Peter Lang, New York, pp. 163–179.

Osborne, S. (2019, 1 January). Qatar raises cost of 24-pack of beer to £82 three years ahead of World Cup. Retrieved from www.independent.co.uk/news/world/middle-east/qatar-alcohol-price-increase-tax-double-100-per-cent-world-cup-2022-a8706846.html

Parry, K. D. (2014, 26 December). Boxing Day Test: sunny spectacle on a stadium-sized stage. Retrieved from https://theconversation.com/boxing-day-test-sunny-spectacle-on-a-stadium-sized-stage-34300

Parry, K. D., Jones, I., & Wann, D. L. (2014). An examination of sport fandom in the United Kingdom: A comparative analysis of fan behaviors, socialization processes, and team identification. *Journal of Sport Behavior*, 37(3), 251–267.

Parry, K. D., & Hughes, B. (2016). *The price is not right: how much is too much for a beer at sporting events?* Retrieved from https://theconversation.com/the-price-is-not-right-how-much-is-too-much-for-a-beer-at-sporting-events-69708

Parry, K. D., Hall, T., & Baxter, A. (2017). Who ate all the pies? The importance of food in the Australian sporting experience. *Sport in Society*, 20(2), 202–218. doi:10.1080/17430437.2016.1173916

Parry, K. D., Rowe, D., George, E. S., & Hall, T. J. (2018). Healthy sport consumption: Moving away from pies and beer. In D. Parnell & P. Krustrup (Eds.), *Sport and Health: Exploring the Current State of Play* (pp. 219–237). London: Routledge.

Parry, K. D., George, E. S., Richards, J., & Stevens, A. (2019). Watching Football as Medicine: promoting health at the football stadium. In P. Krustrup & D. Parnell (Eds.), *Football as Medicine: Prescribing Football for Global Health Promotion*. London: Routledge.

Payne, M. (2016, 9 November). Alcohol banned from stadiums, streets at 2022 World Cup in Qatar. Retrieved from www.washingtonpost.com/news/early-lead/wp/2016/11/09/alcohol-banned-from-stadiums-streets-at-2022-world-cup-in-qatar/

Philpott, M. & Russel Seymour, R. (2011). The European healthy stadia network: Sports stadia, public health and sustainability. In J. Savery & K. Gilbert (Eds), *Sustainability and Sport*. Champaign, IL: Common Ground.

Piggin, J., Tlili, H., & Louzada, B. H. (2017). How does health policy affect practice at a sport mega event? A study of policy, food and drink at Euro 2016. *International Journal of Sport Policy and Politics*, 9(4), 739–751.

Puddephatt, J.-A., Keenan, G. S., Fielden, A., Reaves, D. L., Halford, J. C. G., & Hardman, C. A. (2020). "Eating to survive": A qualitative analysis of factors influencing food choice and eating behaviour in a food-insecure population. *Appetite*, 147, 104547. doi:https://doi.org/10.1016/j.appet.2019.104547

Queensland Times. (2015, 25 November). "Wanted: Beer wenches" – Cricket fans' bad taste Gumtree ad. Retrieved from www.qt.com.au/news/wanted-beer-wenches-cricket-fans-bad-taste-gumtree/2852295/

Richards, J. (2015). Which player do you fancy then?: locating the female ethnographer in the field of the sociology of sport. *Soccer and Society*, 16(2–3), 393–404.

Richards, J., & Parry, K. D. (2019). Beers and blurred boundaries: The spatial and gendered organisation of pre-match venues for English football fans. *International Review for the Sociology of Sport*. doi:10.1177/1012690219835487

Roan, S. (1997, 11 June). Buy Me Some Peanuts and Yogurt? Food: Survey Finds Healthy Choices Have Become Available at All Major League Stadiums. *Los Angeles Times*.

Robinson, J. (2019, 18 December). Qatar's World Cup Dress Rehearsal. Retrieved from www.wsj.com/articles/qatars-world-cup-dress-rehearsal-11576676594

Rolfe, P., & Frost, A. (2019, 26 October). MCG and Melbourne Park bosses consider rooftop stadium gardens inspired by Boston Red Sox Fenway Park scheme. Retrieved from www.heraldsun.com.au/news/victoria/future-melbourne/mcg-and-melbourne-park-bosses-consider-rooftop-stadium-gardens-inspired-by-boston-red-sox-fenway-park-scheme/news-story/5591d7692dd9c5dacdb70239367d2351

Russell, N. E. (2011, 21 September). Forget Stadium Food – Just Eat up at the Tailgate. Retrieved from www.dailycomet.com/article/20110921/WIRE/110929934

Sport Positive. (2019). EPL Sustainability Table. Retrieved from www.sportpositivesummit.com/epl-sustainability-table/

Sukalakamala, P., Sukalakamala, S., & Young, P. (2013). An Exploratory Study of the Concession Preferences of Generation Y Consumers. *Journal of Foodservice Business Research*, 16(4), 378–390. doi:10.1080/15378020.2013.824278

Sutton, M. (2017, 22 February). *Adelaide Oval's 'ridiculous' food prices and ticket costs making it 'untenable' for families: punters*. Retrieved from www.abc.net.au/news/2017-02-22/prices-at-adelaide-oval-becoming-untenable-for-families/8289382

Sydney Cricket & Sports Ground Trust. (2017). Alcohol Policy. Retrieved from www.sydneycricketground.com.au/news/2014-ashes-media-kit/faq-crowdpolicies/alcohol-policy/

US Department of State. (2018, 26 December). Qatar International Travel Information. Retrieved from https://travel.state.gov/content/travel/en/international-travel/International-Travel-Country-Information-Pages/Qatar.html

Wakefield, K. L., & Sloan, H. J. (1995). The Effects of Team Loyalty and Selected Stadium Factors on Spectator Attendance. *Journal of Sport Management*, 9(2), 153–172.

Wedgwood, N. (1997). "Spewin', mate!" A day at the cricket [Observations of the crowd at a cricket match between Australia and Pakistan.]. *Social Alternatives*, 16(3), 26–30.

Weed, M. (2007). The pub as a virtual football fandom venue: An alternative to "being there"? *Soccer & Society*, 8(2–3), 399–414.

Westerbeek, H. M., & Shilbury, D. (1999). Increasing the Focus on "Place" in the Marketing Mix for Facility Dependent Sport Services. *Sport Management Review*, 2(1), 1–23.

Wenner, L. A., & Jackson, S. J. (2009). *Sport, beer, and gender: promotional culture and contemporary social life*. New York: Peter Lang.

34
Fan Reactions to Athlete Activism
"Stick to Sports"

Stephen Warren

In the summer of 2016, NFL quarterback Colin Kaepernick, then of the San Francisco 49ers, bent to one knee during the United States national anthem prior to a preseason game. He later said he did so to protest a recent string of incidents involving black men being killed by police officers (Schmidt et al., 2019). The near-immediate response among many was that of nationalism: he was being anti-American and disrespectful to the United States and the U.S. Army. Though the first, he was not the only athlete to kneel during the anthem, as several other football players began to join him around the league. Outside of the sport, U.S. Women's National Team soccer player Megan Rapinoe began kneeling during the national anthem in September of that year as a gesture towards Kaepernick and to bring to light her own concerns of oppression of marginalized groups (Schmidt et al., 2019).

One year earlier, on November 8, 2015, after several racialized incidents involving the school, University of Missouri football players (supported by the rest of the team and coaching staff) stated they would boycott their games until the university president, Tim Wolfe, stepped down. He did so the next day. Obviously, there were a lot of opinions shared on both sides about this event. But, one of the most common sentiments in comments posted to the official University of Missouri Athletic Department Facebook page was the idea that advocacy and sports did not mix. In other words, the players should "stick to sports" (Frederick et al., 2017, p. 27).

In the chapter that follows, how and why sports fans respond to activism and political statements the ways they do will be examined. Additionally, this perceived separation of sports and politics will be explicated to show that it has never truly existed. In fact, there is quite a longstanding relationship. However, there does appear to be a current increase in the salience of this relationship, largely due to the role of social media within sports media, which will be discussed. Then, the chapter will explore exactly how and why sports fans react so strongly, often negatively, to these often-laudable political statements to attempt to explain those reactions.

The Rise of Sports and/in Politics: Don't Call It a Comeback

"Stick to sports." This phrase is often the response heard whenever a professional athlete – particularly in the United States – makes any type of political statement. This call for keeping politics off the field asks the professional athletes to not complicate the games that billions of sports fans seek out for entertainment on a daily basis. In a time when seemingly every aspect of people's daily lives has turned political in some way, many want to be able to spend a lazy Sunday watching NFL games and eating Buffalo wings.

Yet, even when athletes have not been outwardly making political statements, sports have never really been *apolitical*. Politics can be defined in myriad ways. In fact, some of the more explicit ways in which sports have invoked politics are more accepted. From betting to broadcast rights, governments often develop public policy with regard to sports. Indeed, the sheer economic impact of sports around the world makes it privy to public policy issues, with team owners trying to garner interest to publicly fund new stadiums in part using residents' taxes (Gift & Miner, 2017). More implicitly, even the Olympics have built-in ideological messages, with sports drumming up strong nationalism as spectators watch athletes from their home countries compete against athletes from other countries (Gift & Miner, 2017). Likewise, besides simply consisting of a group of players/coaches/fans/etc., local sports teams "might also symbolize or represent other communities (e.g., geographic, vocational, ethnic, etc.)" (Heere & James, 2007, p. 324). Take the New Orleans Saints of the NFL. In 2009 – only a few years after Hurricane Katrina devastated New Orleans – the Saints had their most successful season ever. And, this success was seen by many in the city as a symbol that the city would recover after the disaster (Burns, 2014).

As for individual athletes, they are often expected to use their fame and resources to start charitable foundations, something that many team executives are in favor of for financial purposes (Babiak et al., 2012), regardless of their expertise or knowledge about those causes (Gift & Miner, 2017). Few would argue that these athletes' charity and activism are not political in some way. Similarly, seemingly bipartisan (from an American political frame) issues like bringing attention to men struggling with eating disorders (Mitchell et al., 2018) or NBA players dealing with depression and anxiety (Parrott et al., 2019) can be thought of as political in the sense of advocating for awareness and the de-stigmatization of these important health issues. Both of those types of concerns usually have sympathetic reactions from all ideological perspectives.

In fact, politics and sports have quite the symbiotic relationship, with the two topics having been discussed together since the ancient Greeks and Romans, and through the Middle Ages and Renaissance (Gift & Miner, 2017). Alternatively, the notion of sports being "separate and distinct from political turmoil" (Whannel, 1992, p. 181) dates back to the British Empire. Often, this relationship is more implicit or outside of the actual sporting events themselves. One could even argue that women's sports, in and of itself, is political. In twentieth-century America, the most frequent of these issues were regarding Black/White relations, starting with athletes like Olympian Jesse Owens and black athletes breaking the color barrier, to players speaking out about issues at stake in the Civil Rights era (Edwards, 2016) and hall-of-fame athletes including Jim Brown and Bill Russell voicing support for Mohammed Ali's protests, marking what some call a "pivotal moment in athlete activism" (Vasilogambros, 2016, p. 1). For on-the-field protests, the iconic example is when Tommie Smith and John Carlos raised their fists on the podium during the national anthem in the 1968 Olympics to protest racism and segregation in American sports and society more generally (Rorke & Copeland, 2018). Moreover, other athletes have made similar statements, like tennis player Arthur Ashe refusing to play a match in South Africa during Apartheid unless the crowd was allowed to be racially mixed (Perry, 2019).

Even simply the popularity of sports, and the public broadcasting that sports garners, can be enough to spark political statements or activism. For example, Korean protestors used the 1988 Seoul Olympics as a stage to demonstrate without the worry of being punished, simply because of the attention and exposure towards the country during that time (Gift & Miner, 2017).

In sum, sports have been politically involved for a long time. But despite this history, there does seem to be an increase in just how political sports have become. Incidents like Barack Obama commenting on NBA players wearing "I can't breathe" shirts during pre-game warmups (in reference to the death of Eric Garner by New York City police) (Galily, 2019), as well as Fidel Castro's death inciting commentary about his influence on Major League Baseball (Gift & Miner, 2017), are now daily news stories. Most recently, the NBA painted "Black Lives Matter" on their courts for the remainder of the 2020 season in the Disney quarantine campus in response to the protests and anger in the wake of several incidents including the video depicting the death of George Floyd – a Black man – who died from a white police officer putting his knee on Floyd's neck for over eight minutes (Andrews, 2020).

Some opine that part of the reason for the rising levels of racial issues in sports leagues is that the main issue for many athletes – inequality – also takes shape in their sport. For example, in the National Football League, 70 percent of players in 2018 were Black, yet only 22 percent of head coaches were (not to mention zero Black owners) (Stratmoen et al., 2019). Others suggest that in the 1980s and 1990s, there were fewer social ills for players to concern themselves with than the decades prior (or since), and athletes hesitated to speak out due to the perceived threat of financial fallout from their potentially controversial statements. The epitome of this is Michael Jordan's, most likely apocryphal, anecdotal quote in response to why he chose not to endorse a black candidate in the racialized 1990 North Carolina senate race: "Republicans wear sneakers, too" (Coombs & Cassilo, 2017). Now, even Jordan did not remain silent during the 2020 protests in the wake of the death of George Floyd: "I stand with those who are calling out the ingrained racism and violence toward people of color in our country. We have had enough" (Jordan, 2020).

However, another potential reason for this increase in salience of politics is the proliferation of social media in the past ten years and the widespread influence it has had on sports.

How Social/New Media has Amplified the Sports/Politics Complex

From the turn of the twentieth century, media technologies have been influential and crucial in the publicizing and consumption of sports. The telegraph allowed newspapers to be more timely in their reporting of sporting event results. Likewise, fans could see sport clips on newsreels in movie houses in the 1920s, increasing the prominence of athletes (Bryant & Holt, 2006). And obviously, live broadcasts on radio and television have allowed sports to become the popular mainstay that they are today. More recently, the rise of social media has amplified the relationship between sports, sports fans, and politics in three distinct ways: (1) greater social awareness through social media use/exposure; (2) increased fan/producer/athlete interaction and perceptions of closeness; and (3) sports media's increasing use of and competition with social media platforms. Combined, these developments have spurred the recent influx of athletes expressing political opinions and fans responding to them.

Greater Social Awareness through Social Media Use/Exposure

Traditionally, mass media tends to reinforce existing structures, since much of their content is controlled by large, economically driven companies (Galily, 2019). This is not in and of itself bad. The point is that companies are looking to profit, and the most efficient way is typically to rely on proven strategies. Social media, however, does not inherently build up existing power dynamics. The difference is that audiences or users are often the content creators, and "the connectivity offered by social media platforms also enables people to find community around issues of interest" (Sanderson et al., 2016, p. 305). For fans, there is a narrowing in the "time-space barrier between spectators and sports" (Bowman & Cranmer, 2014, p. 213), allowing social media to become the perfect place for all those involved in the SocialMediaSport complex – fans, athletes, organizations, sports journalists, etc. – to interact with one another about anything they desire. This also means that there has been a "disintermediation" of the barriers for publication, with reporters now routinely tweeting out play-by-play of sporting events they cover in real time.

Prior to social media, fans had to wait for the TV cameras or sports reporters to bring awareness to any athlete wishing to speak out or make a political statement. Today, athletes can reach millions at any time through social media. So, when polarizing events occur, athletes will not shy away from expressing their feelings. For example, when George Zimmerman was found not guilty of attempted second-degree murder of Trayvon Martin, a Black seventeen-year-old, athletes' posts ranged from critiques of the American justice system and social institutions to expressions of shock and offers of support for the family of the victim (Schmittel & Sanderson, 2015). And, these responses to events or statements of support have reached beyond simply social media. National Basketball Association (NBA) player Lebron James' tweet in which he called President Trump a "bum" in response to Trump's false claim that he uninvited the Golden State Warriors team from visiting the White House garnered major non-sports news coverage, leading to a Fox News host responded directly with "shut up and dribble" (Galily, 2019).

LeBron James is a quintessential example of how social media can expose fans to issues and topics that they may not have been aware of in previous generations. He has been able to utilize Twitter as a platform for raising issues about institutionalized racial injustice, something an average basketball fan might not be privy to (Galily, 2019). He so regularly speaks out that it has gotten to a point where he is almost expected to weigh in on issues concerning racial injustice (Coombs & Cassilo, 2017). Compare this to a similarly outspoken NBA player from the 1990s, Craig Hodges. In 1992, he expressed disappointment in the Bush administration's lack of focus on racial issues and criticized Michael Jordan for not using his platform to bring more awareness to social causes. Following his comments, no team offered him a contract, and he eventually sued the NBA for "blackballing" him, the same case that Colin Kaepernick had against the Nation Football League. Hodges lost his case, whereas Kaepernick settled. One noticeable difference in these situations: social media access. And a lot more people know the name Kaepernick now than Hodges (Galily, 2019).

Even the qualms about echo chambers online – with people selectively choosing content and interacting with people primarily with whom they already agree (Colleoni et al., 2014) – can be placated by athletes' use of social media. Sports fans are especially susceptible to sports media content (Meân, 2014). With traditional or legacy media, "these discussions are programmed, are often one-directional, and rarely incorporate audience feedback" (Sanderson et al., 2016, p. 316) Thus, their influence on sports fans tends to reinforce existing beliefs. "Through channels such as Facebook and Twitter, however, the intersection of group cultural values is ongoing, and participation is not limited to media producers" (Sanderson et al., 2016, p. 316). As such, fans are exposed to athletes who may provide them with ideas and perspectives different from their own, potentially becoming more informed in the process. Seventy-five percent of respondents from thirty-three different countries agreed that "sports bring different groups and races… closer together" (Seippel, 2018, p. 334). So, athletes have the potential to be a vehicle that allows fans to bridge the political gap and help break down echo chambers (Galily, 2019). And, this notion is especially important considering the newfound closeness that fans now perceive towards athletes.

Increased Fan/Producer/Athlete Interaction and Perceptions of Closeness

Another reason for the recent uptick in athletes expressing political views is the perceived closeness with each other that digital media provides. Though "Fan-Based Internet Sports Communities (FBISCs)" – spaces like blogs, forums or Reddit (Benigni et al., 2014) – have allowed significant interaction between fans and facilitated the blurring of the boundaries between fan and content creator for years, newer media platforms offer an environment where sports fans can express and talk about their support for teams and players more often and with more people than has ever been possible with traditional media (Gantz & Lewis, 2014). Not to mention, participation in online discussions about sport (or really, anything) is not limited by time or space – these discussions can be asynchronous (Sanderson, 2010). Social media allows people to talk about their opinions, thoughts and team fandom to a wide group of people using several platforms (Filo et al., 2015). And, it is this "ability of new media to help acquire and distill information coupled with its facility to draw people closer together across time and distance [that] makes it a powerful medium for enabling [fan-athlete interactions]" (Sanderson & Kassing, 2014, p. 249).

For athletes, the shift in dynamic between themselves and others has greatly increased the potential for interaction. Athletes can now talk to reporters, fans, or their teams directly, including in confrontational ways (Benigni et al., 2014; Novick & Steen, 2014). Even a decade ago, athletes understood the interpersonal aspects of Twitter. A 2010 content analysis of U.S. professional athletes' tweets found that over one third of the tweets – the largest category – were posted with the purpose of engagement with fans and other athletes (Hambrick et al., 2010). Now, fans can learn interesting and unique things about any of their favorite players: "typically, only the highest profile and most popular athletes participate in extensive interviews in which they can reveal in-depth information about their personal lives. Twitter makes the process more democratic" (Hambrick et al., 2010, p. 464). Indeed, there are countless moments of athletes responding to and arguing with fans through social media, going back as early as 2009, with Shaquille O'Neil conducting scavenger hunts for his followers to find him at the mall (O'Neal, 2009).

There is some criticism that these interactions online are still very distant and detached: "no one actually meets; no one actually makes contact" (Novick & Steen, 2014, p. 125). Supporting this idea, findings from a cross-sectional survey suggested social networking sites were more useful for college football fans in developing *weak* ties to a large array of people to share ideas (bridging social capital), than they were for nurturing and deepening relationships (bonding) (Phua, 2012). Thus, it is likely more appropriate to discuss these online interactions in mediated – not interpersonal – terms.

However, as these newer technologies allow for fans and athletes to foster deeper "relationships," there is potential for athletes and sports leagues to persuade fans into taking action in support of athletes (Sanderson & Kassing, 2014). After all, social media combines "the collective perspectives of athletes, fans and organizations into sports media content" (Benigni et al., 2014, p. 233). Traditional sports media outlets have also turned to social media to harness some of this power for their own success, despite that power sometimes being a direct challenger to legacy media.

Sports Media's Increasing Use of and Competition with Social Media Platforms

For many fans, actually spectating a game is simply the beginning of how they consume sports. Information seeking and discussion are things sports fans yearn for: "they want to understand, prognosticate, and pontificate. They want to express glee, indignation, and sadness. For all of this, they turn to newer media" (Gantz & Lewis, 2014, p. 24).

Often, newer media technologies force more established technologies to alter their utility. For example, when radio first became a success for sporting events, newspaper editors and writers were forced to focus on the aspects of sports coverage that broadcasts were not well equipped for: analysis and depicting the personalities of athletes (Bryant & Holt, 2006). And while social media has not necessarily deterred spectators from traditional media – the Super Bowl continues to break television ratings records, for example (Boehmer, 2016) – social media has influenced what aspects of sports are talked about. In addition, those actively using Twitter have been found to use other media significantly more, including television, suggesting a complementary role to the more consumption practices (Boehmer, 2016). In other words, there is a greater presence of sports content online that fans interact with, but "this tends to be *in addition to* traditional media consumption rather than *instead of* it" (Billings & Hardin, 2014, p. 1). In fact, use of online media has been found to be the most impactful media type on the strength of association between college team fan identification and collective self-esteem (Phua, 2010). So, online media has become essential for sports coverage.

When this new relationship between traditional and social media teams up with the notions that social media can increase awareness of societal issues, and help fans and athletes develop closer relationships than previously, it looks like a perfect incubator for politically active athletes. An example of how influential social media can be is the case of the University of Missouri athlete protest. Within a day of players from the football team declaring that they would not play until the University President resigned, major media outlets like CNN and ESPN reported on the story. As a result of that increased exposure, more people became aware of the protest, and the University President resigned within two days. Researchers used geographic mapping and cluster analysis to determine exactly how impactful Twitter was for the football players at the school when they coordinated their strike. They found that the people's concerns spread considerably more after the players went on strike (Yan et al., 2017). Any sort of opinion expressed by athletes, especially online, has the potential to result in hundreds of thousands, if not millions, of people engaging with the opinion, at which point mainstream media can feel the need to pick up the story. Prior to social media, the mainstream media would have had to first decide whether they wanted to even cover that type of story. Now, players themselves can influence the gatekeeping process.

In sum, social media has facilitated increases in social awareness and fan/athlete interaction, as well as helped foster new and continued interest in sports in concert with traditional sports media. With the increase in social awareness and outspoken athletes, the argument that politics should not be mixed with sports may not be about the mixing per se, but rather about the specific political statements themselves. Some argue that not allowing players to speak out is a form of politics, and others go so far as to say that cheering for one team over another, singing of the national anthem, or the playing of *God Bless America* at baseball games following the 9/11 terrorist attacks show that free speech is, in fact, encouraged at sporting events (Perry, 2019). The question that remains is why are these acts deemed acceptable – even encouraged – while other political statements are derided?

Sports Fan Reactions to Politics/Activism

In attempting to answer how and why sports fans respond to political statements made by athletes, the "how" is examined categorically more often in the existing research. As will be seen below, this is most likely due to the descriptive nature of looking at how people respond. For example, analyzing comments via social media is much easier to do than analyzing the motivation – the "why" – behind such comments. Instead, the value in the "how" is seeing the trends in responses to political statements over time, as well as what types of statements motivate responses. To fully understand what the reactions are from sports fans regarding athlete activism and political expression, it is helpful to look at the extant research on the subject.

How Sports Fans Respond to Politics/Activism

Often, research regarding responses from fans focuses specifically on responses via social media. One common technique is to look at comments on news stories or team homepages on Facebook. For example, Frederick and colleagues (2017) looked at the reaction to the protest by the University of Missouri football players by analyzing the comments on news links posted on the official Missouri Athletic Department Facebook page to see how the activism was framed and how the comments challenged or reinforced the "dominant ideology around racism in sport" (Frederick et al., 2017, p. 18). In the 473 comments, they found themes that included trivializing racism; encouraging advocacy; and criticism of the relationship between advocacy and sports (i.e. the "stick to sports" objection) (Frederick et al., 2017). Similarly, comments on the Facebook pages of Colin Kaepernick and Megan Rapinoe (two athletes who have knelt in protest during the national anthem) involved discussions of race, American values, and whether or not athletes should engage in politics (Schmidt et al., 2019). An examination of the responses to St. Louis Rams' players protesting the Ferguson shooting revealed that racial commentary was only the *third* most frequent topic discussed on the "Boycott the St. Louis Rams" Facebook page, behind people renouncing their fandom and those suggesting players should be punished (Sanderson et al., 2016). People on Facebook even respond to non-protest statements, like when several NBA players spoke at the ESPY's in 2016 on the topic of police brutality and racial divides. Again, the plurality of comments discussed race (Frederick et al., 2018).

Others have examined comments posted under news articles on sports and non-sports media sites. After the St. Louis Rams' protest, the comments on various news articles about the protesting actually revealed a mostly even split of positive and negative reactions from commenters. The 1,200 comments ranged from support for the athletes and continued activism, to seeking punishment for the players and directly ignoring evidence in the matter (Gill Jr., 2016). Another study found that, in response to articles about former NBA player Charles Barkley criticizing Auburn University for hiring a White coach that many deemed inferior to a Black candidate, many of the 9,000 commenters minimized the role of racism in modern society and accused Black people of using racism as an excuse. At the same time, others acknowledged that the lack of diversity in college football coaching was problematic, exhibiting the possibility of non-mainstream concepts being promoted in the digital media space (Sanderson, 2010).

Something that many of these studies reveal is that these discussions are often categorized or framed into two competing perspectives. For example, some argued that Kaepernick was protesting American values by kneeling, whereas others thought he was doing his civic duty to bring to light the injustice he was seeing in the country. Similarly, Megan Rapinoe's Facebook comments revealed dividedness among discussions of representing America, American freedom, and whether or not athletes should engage in politics (Schmidt et al., 2019). Further, a qualitative content analysis of the hashtags associated with the Take-a-Knee movement showed that the hashtag "#BoycottNFL" was used by both those accusing the NFL of allegedly blacklisting Kaepernick, as well as those critical of the league for not disciplining players that knelt (Cosby, 2019). Also of note is the fact that the themes of these discussions sometimes devolve into reprimanding/endorsing the athletes and their actions and not the issues they were hoping to shed light upon (Schmidt et al., 2019), such as the debate surrounding Kaepernick's actions turning into an argument over what constitutes patriotism (Montez de Oca & Suh, 2019), as well interpretation of the first amendment to the constitution: it was either his right to protest how he saw fit, or the NFL was free to penalize him as they saw fit (Gift & Miner, 2017).

To this point, *how* people respond to political statements is somewhat known and echoes other political realms – acrimoniously and divisively – which researchers have analyzed for some of the more outspoken moments of the past few years. As for *why* people respond in the ways they do, not to mention whether these people are even fans of the players or the players' sport, there is much less literature.

Why Sports Fans Respond to Politics/Activism

Scholars have focused on power dynamics and sports, especially within the lens of critical race theory when trying to explain fan responses to political statements by players (Frederick et al., 2017, 2018; Gill Jr., 2016; Stratmoen et al., 2019; etc.). The premise of this idea is that fans generally represent the dominant ideology or hegemony of society in sports. For example, when a Black player speaks out, this challenges the dominant ideology (in this example, whiteness), which creates a kind of cognitive dissonance for fans with the opinion that injustice or systemic racism are not at issue. As a result of speaking out, the players make people uncomfortable, who then push back – calling out racism in sports makes the fan feel like they are being called out similarly. This can help explain why fans can say things like "stick to sports" and other common clichés (Frederick et al., 2017). Indeed, one of the comments analyzed in the Gill Jr. (2016) study provides evidence that some felt like the protest was an attack on whiteness: "Rams season ticket holders, most of whom are white, should demand these players be cut or refuse to renew their tickets (Gill Jr., 2016, p. 406). The concern with this sentiment is that it reinforces the idea that sports benefit whiteness by trying to reduce the importance of Black athletes' challenges, thus fortifying systemic racial issues. Similarly, sports themselves tend to support notions of nationalism, as they often reinforce dominant cultural ideologies (Schmidt et al., 2019). So, any action or statement perceived as being critical towards that or that is framed as unpatriotic – kneeling during the national anthem, for example – can feel like an attack, leaving some to feel the need to defend themselves (Frederick et al., 2018).

In addition to this notion of dominant cultural ideology, one of the appeals of being a fan of a sports team is the history associated with the organizations, which can foster "a sense of community that fans can tap into, strengthening the bonds and loyalty to a team and its traditions and the players themselves" (Osborne & Coombs, 2016, p. 112). And part of this rich history is also deeply entrenched in masculine ideologies (Stratmoen et al., 2019), which are reinforced through televised sports programming, found to strongly correlate with associations of traditional conceptions of masculine gender role norms (Scharrer & Blackburn, 2018; Scharrer & Warren, 2019). So, when something is perceived as anti-military or anti-traditionally masculine, people feel like their traditions are being encroached upon.

From a quantitative framework, not much is understood about fans' beliefs due to a dearth in research. One study that is an exception to this rule examined respondents' motivations behind speaking positively or negatively (word-of-mouth) in response to a Nike ad featuring Kaepernick with the slogan, "Believe in something. Even if it means sacrificing everything" (Kim et al., 2020, p. 1). Though the main analysis examined people's beliefs about the intentions of Nike in partnering with Kaepernick, the researchers did find that for those in the sample, being more liberal, female, more educated, and younger was associated with approving of the politicization of sports (Kim et al., 2020). It is worth noting that they only accounted for attitudes towards Nike, not Colin Kaepernick himself, and they did not measure football fandom.

Somewhat contradictory to the above demographics, Westhoff and Saint Louis (2019) found that gender and education did *not* influence boycotting behavior in response to the Take-a-Knee movement. Though, white respondents were more likely to say they would boycott than non-white respondents (Westhoff & Saint Louis, 2019). In that study, the more self-reported calls for boycott that respondents were exposed to – both liberal and conservative calls – the more respondents reported that they were boycotting the viewing of games and buying tickets. In other words, conservative calls for boycotting were effective for conservatives in the study, and liberal calls were effective for liberals, both with regard to viewing and attending games. However, liberal ideology *was* a significant predictor of the boycotting of *merchandise*, with conservatives less likely to boycott (Westhoff & Saint Louis, 2019). Taken together, it seems that who the NFL apparel is from – Nike or the NFL – can influence people's buying intentions when a brand is attached to a politically active player.

Another quantitative study examined how racial attitudes and adherence to masculine honor beliefs affected people's support for NFL players taking knees during the National Anthem (Stratmoen et al., 2019). In a longitudinal survey, the more strongly a respondent endorsed the Masculine Honor Beliefs Scale (Saucier et al., 2016) – measuring traditional beliefs about masculinity and honor – the more disrespectful and less appropriate they believed the protests to be, as well as more threatening to the reputation of the U.S. Likewise, the converse was true for those who tended to place blame on prejudice. In a second study, both of these predictors were moderated by race and behavior of the athlete, so the link between masculine honor beliefs and subsequent perceptions depended on the player's race and whether they were kneeling or standing (Stratmoen et al., 2019). Admittedly, they also did not control for fandom, which could weaken these relationships. Football is a physical sport. And, people that adhere to strong masculine honor ideologies may be more in line with retaliating physically (police aggression). Someone with low masculine honor beliefs may be less interested in a sport that rewards players for hitting as hard as possible.

However, sports can positively influence people outside of the actual competitions with regards to activism. Jang et al. (2019) looked at how various types of messages affected people's intentions to support former NBA player Dwyane Wade's charity by showing participants one of three videos: (1) Wade visiting a disabled child; (2) Wade pranking fans; or (3) Wade basketball highlights. Those participants that had low identification with Wade (i.e. non-fans) that watched the meaningful video had the highest support level. Interestingly, high identifying individuals (fans of Wade) did not differ across the three conditions (Jang et al., 2019). This suggests that for highly identified fans of Dwyane Wade, both on- and off-court videos equally increase their intent to support his charity, regardless of the videos' connection to the sport.

Despite some interesting results, these empirical studies outlined above that examine why people responded to the Take-a-Knee movement pointed solely to the role of the demographics of their respondents (Kim et al., 2020; Stratmoen et al., 2019). Yet, none accounted for fandom. Digital media and the internet, while allowing for more interaction and perceived closeness between players and fans, also allows for less direct conversation and more barriers of anonymity, allowing for "a more accurate societal barometer of fans' views on the relevance of race in sport" (Sanderson, 2010, p. 314). This could be creating a contrast of athletes trying to bring to light societal woes at the same time that fans feel more shielded to express themselves, sometimes politically incorrectly. So, more research is needed that examines how fan processes are affected as a result of their own reactions to these types of political statements and activism. In addition, much of the rhetoric in sports and mainstream media is concerned with how these protests and political statements are turning fans away. The research cannot effectively answer this question if it is not looking at fans particularly.

Untapped Areas of Potential Research

To help understand fan processes and responses to sports-based activism, one can turn to research examining other aspects of fan processes, motivations, behaviors, and emotions. For example, another reason for fans to feel threatened by political conversations within sports could be that they are generally watching because they expect positive emotional impact. From a uses and gratifications perspective, two of the motives of sports spectators are entertainment and relaxation (Raney, 2006). There are also strong correlations between the TV sports viewing motivation "to let loose" and the emotional and behavioral reactions one would expect a highly involved spectator to produce during a game (Gantz, 1981). So, sports viewing for many is a functional, purposeful way some let off steam and escape, as indicated by the factor of "preparing" for a sportscast in the study. Further, motivations are strongest for those most interested in sports. So, it is understandable that some people tuning in will be unwelcoming of political issues invading their relaxation and enjoyment time, especially when it was not planned. Plus, those more interested in sports are more likely to rely on TV to meet their gratifications rather than Twitter (Boehmer, 2016), where so much of these politically charged things begin. So, those more interested in sports might not be as privy to the typical social concerns and, at the same time, feel more encroached upon when those social concerns show up in their sports viewing content.

Another factor not yet considered is the role of fans' identities. Sports fans obviously identify with other sports fans, especially with others that root for the same teams/players as them. Yet, everyone has other identities to which they belong, be it feeling a part of a gender (Bussey & Bandura, 1999), political party (Becker, 2019), or racial group (Helms, 1990). So, sports fans may also identify with various groups that relate to the political statements or focus of activism of players. As a result, fans may feel that one of their alternative groups is being threatened, which can cause them to attempt to defend said group (Tajfel & Turner, 1979). Similarly, in discussing performative sport fandom, Osborne and Coombs (2016) suggest that female fans of the NFL must negotiate when and how they perform their fandom:

> Indeed women fans are caught in a catch-22 when it comes to performances. If they express extreme emotions, they run the risk of being labelled hysterical. If they do not, they run the risk of being seen as casual or bandwagon fans whose interest in football does not run deep enough.
>
> *Osborne & Coombs, 2016, p. 32*

This exact sentiment could be applied to fans with political identities. For fans of a team comprising some players with whom they disagree ideologically, if they still cheer for them, they may run the risk of being labelled as ideological hypocrites. If they refuse to cheer, they could run the risk of being seen as "casual or bandwagon fans whose interest in football does not run deep enough" (Osborne & Coombs, 2016, p. 32). The resulting question then is, does the coping with one identity threat lead to a different identity threat, leading to dissonance or imbalance? Unfortunately, that is beyond the scope of the current research.

Conclusion

Sports provide a quintessential window through which to analyze many conventional topics within social science disciplines. Issues like social capital, political empowerment, and corruption all emerge centrally in sports – and offer an ideal backdrop in which to probe these phenomena. Sports are flush with actors, institutions, and groups that mimic those found in familiar political spheres. Consequently, analyzing how these entities interact and respond to incentives can shed useful insight on politics writ large (Gift & Miner, 2017, p. 130). So, understanding how and why American sports fans respond to political statements could help shed light on how American politics in general are discussed, processed, and interpreted.

As seen in the cases above, race and inclusion are two of the more salient topics for American athletes. Actually, almost any study devoted to the topic of athletes and advocacy is about race. Athletes have a huge platform and have the potential to influence their fans, especially young fans, and the fans' beliefs, values and appraisals (Melnick & Jackson, 2002). In fact, because people give more leeway to people they admire, athletes may be "possibly the greatest contemporary messenger of opposing political views" (Galily, 2019, p. 4). It is for that reason that more research in all respects in needed to further develop the understanding of the relationship between sports fans, politics, and activism.

References

Andrews, M. (2020, July 21). NBA unveils Black Lives Matter on Orlando court. *ESPN.Com*. www.espn.com/nba/story/_/id/29510169/nba-unveils-black-lives-matter-orlando-court

Babiak, K., Mills, B., Tainsky, S., & Juravich, M. (2012). An investigation into professional athlete philanthropy: Why charity is part of the game. *Journal of Sport Management, 26*(2), 159–176. https://doi.org/10.1123/jsm.26.2.159

Becker, A. B. (2019). When comedy goes to extremes: The influence of ideology and social identity on source liking, credibility, and counterarguing. *Psychology of Popular Media Culture*. https://doi.org/10.1037/ppm0000265

Benigni, V. L., Porter, L. V., & Wood, C. (2014). The new game day: Fan engagement and the marriage of mediated and mobile. In A. C. Billings & M. Hardin (Eds.), *Routledge Handbook of Sport and New Media* (1st ed., pp. 225–236). Routledge. https://doi.org/10.4324/9780203114711.ch20

Billings, A. C., & Hardin, M. (2014). Defining ubiquity: Introduction to the Routledge Handbook of Sport and New Media. In A. C. Billings & M. Hardin (Eds.), *Routledge Handbook of Sport and New Media* (1st ed., pp. 1–3). Routledge. https://doi.org/10.4324/9780203114711.intro1

Boehmer, J. (2016). Does the game really change? How students consume mediated sports in the age of social media. *Communication and Sport, 4*(4), 460–483. https://doi.org/10.1177/2167479515595500

Bowman, N. D., & Cranmer, G. A. (2014). SocialMediaSport: The fan as a (mediated) participant in spectator sports. In A. C. Billings & M. Hardin (Eds.), *Routledge Handbook of Sport and New Media* (1st ed., pp. 213–224). Routledge. https://doi.org/10.4324/9780203114711.ch19

Bryant, J., & Holt, A. M. (2006). A historical overview of sports and media in the United States. In A. A. Raney & J. Bryant (Eds.), *Handbook of Sports and Media* (1st ed., pp. 21–43). Routledge. https://doi.org/10.4324/9780203873670.ch2

Burns, E. B. (2014). When the Saints went marching in: Social identity in the world champion New Orleans Saints football team and its impact on their host city. *Journal of Sport and Social Issues, 38*(2), 148–163. https://doi.org/10.1177/0193723513499920

Bussey, K., & Bandura, A. (1999). Social cognitive theory of gender development and differentiation. *Psychological Review, 106*(4), 676–713. https://doi.org/10.1037/0033-295X.106.4.676

Colleoni, E., Rozza, A., & Arvidsson, A. (2014). Echo chamber or public sphere? Predicting political orientation and measuring political homophily in Twitter using big data. *Journal of Communication, 64*(2), 317–332. https://doi.org/10.1111/jcom.12084

Coombs, D. S., & Cassilo, D. (2017). Athletes and/or activists: LeBron James and Black Lives Matter. *Journal of Sport and Social Issues, 41*(5), 425–444. https://doi.org/10.1177/0193723517719665

Cosby, N. B. (2019). How social media activists and their hashtags have encouraged and informed their followers on the Take-a-Knee movement. In S. D. Perry (Ed.), *Pro Football and the Proliferation of Protest: Anthem Posture in a Divider America* (1st ed., pp. 85–99). Lexington Books.

Edwards, H. (2016). The fourth wave: Black athlete protests in the second decade of the 21st century. *Invited Key Note at NASSS Annual Meeting*.

Filo, K., Lock, D., & Karg, A. (2015). Sport and social media research: A review. *Sport Management Review*, *18*(2), 166–181. https://doi.org/10.1016/j.smr.2014.11.001

Frederick, E. L., Pegoraro, A., & Sanderson, J. (2018). Divided and united: perceptions of athlete activism at the ESPYS. *Sport in Society*, *22*(4), 1–18. https://doi.org/10.1080/17430437.2018.1530220

Frederick, E. L., Sanderson, J., & Schlereth, N. (2017). Kick these kids off the team and take away their scholarships: Facebook and perceptions of athlete activism at the University of Missouri. *Journal of Issues in Intercollegiate Athletics*, *10*, 17–34. http://csri-jiia.org/wp-content/uploads/2017/03/RA_2017_02.pdf

Galily, Y. (2019). "Shut up and dribble!"? Athletes activism in the age of twittersphere: The case of LeBron James. *Technology in Society*, *58*, 1–4. https://doi.org/10.1016/j.techsoc.2019.01.002

Gantz, W. (1981). An exploration of viewing motives and behaviors associated with television sports. *Journal of Broadcasting*, *25*(3), 263–275. https://doi.org/10.1080/08838158109386450

Gantz, W., & Lewis, N. (2014). Fanship differences between traditional and newer media. In A. C. Billings & M. Hardin (Eds.), *Routledge Handbook of Sport and New Media* (1st ed., pp. 19–31). Routledge. https://doi.org/10.4324/9780203114711.ch2

Gift, T., & Miner, A. (2017). "Dropping the ball": The understudied nexus of sports and politics. *World Affairs*, *180*(1), 127–161. https://doi.org/10.1177/0043820017715569

Gill Jr., E. L. (2016). "Hands up, don't shoot" or shut up and play ball? Fan-generated media views of the Ferguson Five. *Journal of Human Behavior in the Social Environment*, *26*(3–4), 400–412. https://doi.org/10.1080/10911359.2016.1139990

Hambrick, M. E., Simmons, J. M., Greenhalgh, G. P., & Greenwell, T. C. (2010). Understanding professional athletes' use of Twitter: A content analysis of athlete tweets. *International Journal of Sport Communication*, *3*(4), 454–471. https://doi.org/10.1123/ijsc.3.4.454

Heere, B., & James, J. D. (2007). Sports teams and their communities: Examining the influence of external group identities on team identity. *Journal of Sport Management*, *21*(3), 319–337. https://doi.org/10.1123/jsm.21.3.319

Helms, J. E. (1990). *Contributions in Afro-American and African studies, No. 129. Black and White racial identity: Theory, research, and practice*. Greenwood Press.

Jang, W. (Eric), Kim, D., Lee, J. S., & Wann, D. L. (2019). The impact of hedonic and meaningful messages on sport consumers' responses to athlete foundations: A focus on fan identification level. *Communication & Sport*, 216747951983006. https://doi.org/10.1177/2167479519830063

Jordan, M. [@Jumpman23]. (2020, May 31). *Statement from Michael Jordan: [Image Attached] [Tweet]*. https://twitter.com/Jumpman23/status/1267195991964282881?s=20

Kim, J. K., Overton, H., Bhalla, N., & Li, J.-Y. (2020). Nike, Colin Kaepernick, and the politicization of sports: Examining perceived organizational motives and public responses. *Public Relations Review*, *46*(2), 1–10. https://doi.org/10.1016/j.pubrev.2019.101856

Meân, L. J. (2014). Sport websites, embedded discursive action, and the gendered reproduction of sport. In A. C. Billings & M. Hardin (Eds.), *Routledge Handbook of Sport and New Media* (1st ed., pp. 331–341). Routledge. https://doi.org/10.4324/9780203114711.ch29

Melnick, M. J., & Jackson, S. J. (2002). Globalization American-style and reference idol selection: The importance of athlete celebrity others among New Zealand youth. *International Review for the Sociology of Sport*, *37*(3–4), 429–448. https://doi.org/10.1177/1012690202037004027

Mitchell, F. R., Santarossa, S., & Woodruff, S. J. (2018). Athletes as advocates: Influencing eating-disorder beliefs and perceptions through social media. *International Journal of Sport Communication*, *11*(4), 433–446. https://doi.org/10.1123/ijsc.2018-0112

Montez de Oca, J., & Suh, S. C. (2019). Ethics of patriotism: NFL players' protests against police violence. *International Review for the Sociology of Sport*, 1–25. https://doi.org/10.1177/1012690218825210

Novick, J., & Steen, R. (2014). Texting and tweeting: How social media has changed news gathering. In A. C. Billings & M. Hardin (Eds.), *Routledge Handbook of Sport and New Media* (1st ed., pp. 119–129). Routledge. https://doi.org/10.4324/9780203114711.ch11

O'Neal, S. [SHAQ]. (2009, February 24). *I'm at the fashion sq mall, any 1 touches me gets 2 tickets, tag me and say yur twit u hv 20 min [Tweet]*. https://twitter.com/shaq/status/1245950406

Osborne, A. C., & Coombs, D. S. (2016). *Female Fans of the NFL* (1st ed.). Routledge. https://doi.org/10.4324/9781315767550

Parrott, S., Billings, A. C., Buzzelli, N., & Towery, N. (2019). "We all go through it": Media depictions of mental illness disclosures from star athletes DeMar DeRozan and Kevin Love. *Communication & Sport*, *xx*(x), 1–22. https://doi.org/10.1177/2167479519852605

Perry, S. D. (2019). Division and hermeneutical ignorance in America: Reasons to examine the Anthem kneeling controversy. In S. D. Perry (Ed.), *Pro Football and the Proliferation of Protest: Anthem Posture in a Divider America* (1st ed., pp. 1–13). Lexington Books.

Phua, J. J. (2010). Sports fans and media use: Influence on sports fan identification and collective self-esteem. *International Journal of Sport Communication, 3*(2), 190–206. https://doi.org/10.1123/ijsc.3.2.190

Phua, J. J. (2012). Use of social networking sites by sports fans: Implications for the creation and maintenance of social capital. *Journal of Sports Media, 7*(1), 109–132. https://doi.org/10.1353/jsm.2012.0006

Raney, A. A. (2006). Why we watch and enjoy mediated sports. In A. A. Raney & J. Bryant (Eds.), *Handbook of Sports and Media* (1st ed., pp. 313–329). Routledge. https://doi.org/10.4324/9780203873670.ch19

Rorke, T., & Copeland, A. (2018). Athletic disobedience: Providing a context for analysis of Colin Kaepernick's protest. *Fair Play, Revista de Filosofía, Ética y Derecho Del Deporte, 10*(84–107). www.raco.cat/index.php/FairPlay/article/view/327610/418146

Sanderson, J. (2010). Weighing in on the coaching decision: Discussing sports and race online. *Journal of Language and Social Psychology, 29*(3), 301–320. https://doi.org/10.1177/0261927X10368834

Sanderson, J., Frederick, E. L., & Stocz, M. (2016). When athlete activism clashes with group values: Social identity threat management via social media. *Mass Communication and Society, 19*(3), 301–322. https://doi.org/10.1080/15205436.2015.1128549

Sanderson, J., & Kassing, J. W. (2014). New media and the evolution of fan-athlete interaction. In A. C. Billings & M. Hardin (Eds.), *Routledge Handbook of Sport and New Media* (1st ed., pp. 247–258). Routledge. https://doi.org/10.4324/9780203114711.ch22

Saucier, D. A., Stanford, A. J., Miller, S. S., Martens, A. L., Miller, A. K., Jones, T. L., McManus, J. L., & Burns, M. D. (2016). Masculine honor beliefs: Measurement and correlates. *Personality and Individual Differences, 94*, 7–15. https://doi.org/10.1016/j.paid.2015.12.049

Scharrer, E., & Blackburn, G. (2018). Cultivating conceptions of masculinity: Television and perceptions of masculine gender role norms. *Mass Communication and Society, 21*(2), 149–177. https://doi.org/10.1080/15205436.2017.1406118

Scharrer, E., & Warren, S. (2019). *Adolescents' modern media use and beliefs about masculine gender roles and norms* [Paper Presentation]. AEJMC 2019 Conference, Toronto, Ontario, Canada.

Schmidt, S. H., Frederick, E. L., Pegoraro, A., & Spencer, T. C. (2019). An analysis of Colin Kaepernick, Megan Rapinoe, and the National Anthem protests. *Communication & Sport, 7*(5), 653–677. https://doi.org/10.1177/2167479518793625

Schmittel, A., & Sanderson, J. (2015). Talking about Trayvon in 140 characters: Exploring NFL players' tweets about the George Zimmerman verdict. *Journal of Sport and Social Issues, 39*(4), 332–345. https://doi.org/10.1177/0193723514557821

Seippel, Ø. (2018). Do sports matter to people? A cross-national multilevel study. *Sport in Society, 22*(3), 327–341. https://doi.org/10.1080/17430437.2018.1490263

Stratmoen, E., Lawless, T. J., & Saucier, D. A. (2019). Taking a knee: Perceptions of NFL player protests during the National Anthem. *Personality and Individual Differences, 137*, 204–213. https://doi.org/10.1016/j.paid.2018.09.009

Tajfel, H., & Turner, J. C. (1979). An integrative theory of intergroup conflict. In W. G. Austin & S. Worchel (Eds.), *The Social Psychology of Intergroup Relations* (1st ed., pp. 33–47). Brooks/Cole Publishing Company.

Vasilogambros, M. (2016, July). When athletes take political stands. *The Atlantic*. www.theatlantic.com/news/archive/2016/07/when-athletes-take-political-stands/490967/

Westhoff, M., & Saint Louis, J. (2019). Pigskins and protests: An examination of the NFL boycotts in response to the Take-a-Knee movement. In S. D. Perry (Ed.), *Pro Football and the Proliferation of Protest: Anthem Posture in a Divider America* (1st ed., pp. 225–240). Lexington Books.

Whannel, G. (1992). *Fields in vision: Television sport and cultural transformation*. Routledge.

Yan, G., Pegoraro, A., & Watanabe, N. M. (2017). Student-athletes' organization of activism at the University of Missouri: Resource mobilization on Twitter. *Journal of Sport Management, 32*(1), 24–37. https://doi.org/10.1123/jsm.2017-0031

Index

Note: Locators in **bold** refer to tables and those in *italics* to figures.

7 Line Army 255–256

accessibility: executive fandom 370–371; fantasy sport 295; netball as feminine sport space 39; social media 281; *see also* non-local fans
activism by athletes 102, 127–128, 388–398
admiration for athletes 116–123; achievement and value 118–119, 122–123; control 116–118; Tännsjö's reversal test 119–123; training 117–118
advertising: athletes' personal brand 239–240; executive fandom 366; fantasy sport 287, 296–297, 301; female fans 149–150; framing 96; non-local fans 253, 255; place and fandom 74–76; as revenue stream 62; women's sport 33, 316, 322
affective expression 25
African American athletes: activism by 127–128; assumptions about 14–15; framing in the media 99–100
age and fandom: intergenerational links 37, 40–41; lifelong involvement in sport 36–37, 154–157; participation research study 158–166; shifting patterns of viewership 155; theory-based explanation 155–157; *see also* lifelong involvement in sport
Agitos Foundation 185–186
agonistic conflict, sport as 10, 16–18
alcohol, drinking whilst watching games 379–381
anonymity, social media 278
appraisal theory 101
arousal 299
athlete activism 102, 127–128, 388–398
athletes of color: activism by 127–128; assumptions about 14–15; framing in the media 99–100; racist fans 125–126; research context 125
AthletesFirst 187
Atlanta Braves: civic identity 79–80; history of 44; new venue 73, 76–77
Atlético- MG 233

augmented reality (AR) 257, 268
autoethnography 86–87, 90–91, 207–212

backstage performances, social media 245, 246
Baharmast, Esse 342
Barcelona Fan Association (BFA) 359–360
beer drinking 379–381
behavior *see* fan behavior
belonging, sense of: female fans 36–37; fulfilling personal needs 22, 23, 24–25
betting 285–293; competitive fandom 285, 287–288, 291–292; conceptualizing 286–287; DFS players 288–289, 290–291, 293; in games 313–314; interface and betting products 289–293; season-long fantasy 288–289, 290–292, 293
BIRGing (Basking in Reflective Glory) 264
Black athletes: activism by 127–128; assumptions about 14–15; framing in the media 99–100
Black Lives Matter 125–126
bodies, and masculinity 15
Boston Red Stockings 44
Bourdieu, P. 330
Brazil, football supporter groups 225–235
broadcasting *see* mobile/streamed fandom; radio; television
broadcasting revenues 64, 66

cable TV 321
camaraderie 298
Canclini, Néstor Garcia 226, 228–229
Cascading Activation Model (CAM) 98
César, Benedito Tadeu 228
charangas 229–231
children: family role identity 138–139; Paralympic School Days (PSD) 186–187
China: authoritarian digital capitalism 357; transnational European football fandom 354, 357–363
citizen-fans 9, 366

401

Index

citizenship 79–80
civic identity 73–74; citizenship 79–80; entrepreneurial ecosystems in suburban and small cities 77–79; place and fandom 74–76; sprawl and suburbanization 77; stadium politics and local planning 76
Clarke, Stuart Roy 205–206, 212–221
club merchandise 64
Clubhouse 267–268
co-creation, social media 264–265
Cockroft, Hannah 185
CORFing (Cutting off Reflective Failure) 264
collaborative research 113–114
collectibles 268–269
commodification of sport: creating executive fandom 365–373; the media and the Nick Saban effect 328–338
communication: disabled athletes on social media 238–246; framing 95–96; social affordances 277; sport fulfilling societal needs 25–26; through media 240–241
communities: Fan-Based Internet Sports Communities (FBISCs) 392; Fan Controlled Football League (FCFL) 370–372; MyFootballClub 366–367, 372; non-local fans 250, 254–257; transnational European football fans 354–363
community identity 140–141
competitive fandom 285, 287–288, 291–292, 298
content framing 97
cooperative spirit 16–17
costs of fandom 61–63; elements of 63–69; in Europe 63–70, 66–67, **67**; non-local fans 251–252, 256
critical race theory 395
cultivation theory 172–173
cultural participation 368–370
culture: ethnographic methods 85–86; football supporter groups in Brazil 225–235; framing in the media 101; fulfilling personal needs 23–24; Māori and Pasifika fans 39–40; Paralympics and disability 183; socialization process 26

daily fantasy sport (DFS) 288–289, 290–291, 293, 296
data management, gaming 310–311
data privacy 266–267
democracy, and sport 10–11, 15–16
DFS *see* daily fantasy sport
digital engagement with sports 5; dark side 265–267, 269–270; future of 267–270; non-local fans 250–251, 256–257; privacy 266–267; reasons fans use digital media 262–263; research context 263–264; rise of 261; role of 264–265; studying fandom 109; theorizing 261–262; transnational European football fans 356–363; *see also* gaming; mobile/streamed fandom

direct broadcast satellite (DBS) 321, 322
disabilities: athletes on social media 238–246; language of 182–183; Para Sport Organizations 184–187; Paralympian fandom 180–188; "supercrip" label 182, 183, 187, 243–244
disciplinary approaches 2–3
displaced fans 252–253; *see also* non-local fans
distinctiveness, need for 22–23
DIY citizenship 307, 309
DraftKings 285, 287, 289–293

Elias, Norbert 88, 227
emotion: framing in the media 100–101; gaming 313; socioemotional selectivity theory (SST) 154, 156, 157, 164–166
employee identity 139
English Premier League (EPL) 196, 356
entrepreneurial ecosystems 77–79
escapism 299
ESPN (sports channel): age and fandom 154; fantasy sport 295, 299, 300–301; mediated fandom 321–322; SEC launch 328–329; sports fans vs. Olympic fans 168; women's sport 316, 318, 321
ethics 217–220
ethnicity: assumptions about 14–15; athlete activism 102, 127–128, 388–398; critical race theory 395; fan motives and behaviors 128; female fans 39–40, 41; framing in the media 99–100, 102; global context 128–129; and masculinity 15; research context 125; Take-a-Knee movement 394, 396
ethnographic methods 84–88; autoethnography 86–87, 90–91, 207–212; Chinese fandom of European football 357–363; definition 85; match-day experiences of Everton FC fans 88–89; rebounding 110–114; value of 87–88; women's sport 324
Everton FC 84, 88–89
executive fandom 365–373

Facebook: accessibility 281; disabled athletes 240; editability 277; network association 280; online performances of fandom 273, 277; searchability 280
FaceTime 280
family: female fans 36–37, 40, 147; gender-stereotypical roles 149–150; Māori and Pasifika cultures 40; performative role identities 137, 138–139
Fan-Based Internet Sports Communities (FBISCs) 392
fan behavior: gender differences 33; motives and race 128; as performance 108–109; racist fans 125–126
Fan Controlled Football League (FCFL) 370–372
fan democracy 227

Index

fandom: definition 2, 62–63; fulfilling personal needs 21–25; fulfilling societal needs 21, 25–27; overview of this volume 3–5; as performance 108–109; and place 74–76; research context 1, 27–28, 108; *see also* motivations for being a sports fan; participation in sport fandom
FanDuel 285, 287, 289–293
fantasy sport 295–296; competitive fandom 285, 287–288, 291–292; daily fantasy sport (DFS) 288–289, 290–291, 293, 296; emergence of 286–287; fandom 302–303; as industry 301–302; media offerings 300–301; motivation for play 296–299; non-local fans 256; online 286–287; participant consumption 299–300; season-long fantasy 288–289, 290–292, 293
Fantasy Sports Trade Association 302
feedback loops, social media 275–276
female fans: experiences of 32–33, 40–41; football supporter groups in Brazil 234–235; (in)authenticity 145–147, 148; mediated fandom 149–151; netball case study 32, 34–40; Olympic Games 170–172; perceptions of 145; performativity 140, 148–149; research gap 32, 152; stereotypes 145–146, 147
feminine fandom 38–39, 140, 150–151
fieldwork: ethnographic methods 84–91; positionality and proximity 107, 110, 112; rebounding as praxis 107, 110–114
FIFA series 310–311, 313
FIFA World Cups: in Qatar 381; video assistant refereeing 342–343, 345, 346, 348–349, 350
finances *see* costs of fandom; revenues
fitness apps 266–267
Florida Marlins 75
FNTSY Sports Network 301
food: beer drinking 379–381; fan experience 378–379; fan preferences 383–384; futures 384–385; relationship between fans and 377–378; in stadia options 381–383
football: commercialization and professionalization 61; commodification by the media 328–338; costs of fandom 62–69; cultural participation 368–370; definition 61; fandom as performance 108–109; revenue from 61–62, 69–70, **70**; sexual minorities and homophobia 192–201; supporter groups in Brazil 225–235; transnational European football fans 354–363; video assistant refereeing 342–351
Football Association (FA) 195–198, 200, 211
Football Manager 2019 306, 310–311
framing 95–104, 241–242
framing analysis 99, 102, 103–104
France, costs of fandom 67–68, 70–71

Galo Queer 234
gambling *see* betting

game attendance: costs of fandom 62, 65–66; falling attendances 377–378; food and drink 377–385; non-local fans 255–256
"game frame" 11–13
game metaphor, American politics 11–13
gaming: algorithms 311–313, 314; betting 285–293; competitive fandom 285, 287–288, 291–292, 298; data management 310–311; executive fandom 370; motivations for play 309–310; understanding sport videogames 305–314; women's sport 316–324; *see also* fantasy sport
Gantz, W. 156, 157, 297
gays *see* LGBTQ+ athletes; LGBTQ+ fans
GDP per capita **67**, 67–68, **69**
gender: difference in revenues between men's and women's sports 46–57; fandom behaviours 33; inequalities in digital media 265; misogynistic culture 146, 148; Olympic sports fans 170–172; performative role identities 140; sexualization in women's sport 321; sexualization of female fans 147, 150; Title IX 45–46, 52; *see also* female fans; women's sport
gender reversals 40–41
geographic identity 140–141; *see also* non-local fans
Gephi (social network analysis tool) 333
Germany, costs of fandom 67–68, 70–71
global context: Olympic sports fans 175–176; Paralympian fandom 180–182; racial make-up of fans 128–129
Goffman, Erving 99, 108–109, 239, 241
group framing 97

Halverson, E. 285, 287–291, 293
Halverson, R. 285, 287–291, 293
Hawk-Eye 346
health, relationship between fans and food/drink 377–385
hegemonic masculinity: beer drinking 380; performative role identities 140; photography 221; politics and sport 16–17; race 15
Hillsborough stadium, Sheffield, 1989 disaster 205–206, 209
historical context: media technology 240–241; men's and women's sports 45–46, 49–52
Hofstede, G. 23–24
homohysteria 193–194
homophobia 193–195, 198
hybridisation 228–229

identity *see* civic identity; sports fan identity
identity in society 27
identity-shift 275–276
IFAB (International Football Association Board) 342–343, 344, 345, 348, 350
IKEA effect 310

403

Index

inequalities: digital media 265; misogynistic culture 146, 148; racial assumptions 14–15; racism from fans 125–126, 266
integration, sport as means of 27
intergenerational links 37, 40–41; *see also* age and fandom
International Paralympic Committee (IPC) 180, 184, **184–185**, 186
internet media *see* digital engagement with sports; mobile/streamed fandom; social media
intersectionality 149
involvement *see* participation in sport fandom

James, LeBron 391
Jenkins, E. S. 308–309

Kaepernick, Colin 102, 127, 388, 394, 395
Kavanaugh, Brett 9, 13–16
Kazan, Russia 107
Kempf, Cheri 48–49, 56
kit sponsorships 62
knowledge of fans: competitive fandom 291–292; fantasy sport 295–296, 302; female fans 37–38, 146; gender reversals 40–41

language: Paralympics and disability 182–183; politics and sport 9, 10–15; sport fulfilling societal needs 25–26; "supercrip" label 182, 183, 187, 243–244
legal context: betting 287; Title IX 45, 52, 316
lesbians *see* LGBTQ+ athletes; LGBTQ+ fans
Lever, Janet 227–228
LGBT+ Fans Project 196–198, 200
LGBTQ+ athletes: inclusive attitudes 194–195; Rainbow Laces 199; rebounding as praxis 111
LGBTQ+ fans: British football 192–201; football supporter groups in Brazil 234–235; transnational European football fans 361–362
life, finding meaning in 24–25
lifelong involvement in sport: age and fandom 155–157; female fans 36–37; intergenerational links 37, 40–41; participation research study 158–166; sports fanship lifecycle 154
live TV *see* television
Liverpool FC: autoethnographic research 207, 211–212; ethnographic research 90–91
local identity 140–141
local planning: entrepreneurial ecosystems in suburban and small cities 77–79; sprawl and suburbanization 77; stadium politics 76
Los Angeles Angels 75
loyalty: across the lifespan 157; team identification 62–63; *see also* lifelong involvement in sport; participation in sport fandom
LPGA (Ladies Professional Golf Association) 317–318

Māori culture 39–40
Maradona, Diego 204–205
marketing: disabled athletes 239–240; executive fandom 366; fantasy sport 287, 296–297, 301; framing 96; non-local fans 253, 255; place and fandom 74–76; as revenue stream 62; women's sport 33, 316, 322
masculinity: beer drinking 380; and female fans 146, 148; hegemonic 15, 16–17, 221; homophobia 193–194; performative role identities 140; and race 15
Mason, L. 9–10, 12, 17
McLuhan, Marshall 308
meaning in life 24–25
media 5; answering questions about individual fans 99–103; commodification of sport 328–338; communication through 240–241; competition with social media 392–393; coverage of disabled athletes 242–245; coverage of sports fans 95; creating executive fandom 365–373; fantasy sport 300–301; female fandom 149–151; framing and framing analysis 97–99, 103–104; impact upon people 308–309; Olympic Games 169, 170, 173–176; women's sport 316–324; *see also* social media
media ecology theory 319
mental framing 97
merchandise: athlete activism 127, 396; costs of fandom 63, 64, 71, 252; fandom as performance 108–109; as revenue stream 62, 63, 66, 251–252; women's sport 322
metaphors, in American politics 11–13, 14–15
Miami Marlins 75
middle-zone communities (suburbanization) 77
migration, non-local fans 249, 250, 252–253
minimum wage **67**, 68, **69**
misogynistic culture 146, 148
MLB (Major League Baseball): augmented reality (AR) 268; Boston Red Stockings 44; place and fandom 74–76, 75; revenues 48, **50–51**, 55
MLS (Major League Soccer) 54, 55, 56, 369
mobile/streamed fandom: fantasy sport 301; non-local fans 251; Olympic sports fans 173–175; women's sport 317–324
motivations for being a sports fan: fantasy sport 296–299; fulfilling personal needs 21–25; fulfilling societal needs 21, 25–27; gaming 309–310; Olympic sports fans 169, 170–172; political conversations 397; racial make-up of fans 128; sex differences 171–172; social media 262–263
multichannel video program distributors (MVPDs) 321, 322
music, football supporter groups in Brazil 229–230
MyFootballClub 366–367, 372

Index

"narcosis" of the media 308
narrative inquiry 113–114
national identity: athlete activism 127; netball in New Zealand 35, 38; Olympic Games 170, 173; performative role identities 140–141
National League 44–45
National Paralympic Committee (NPC) 187
nationality, costs of fandom in Europe 63–70, 66–67, **67**
NBA (National Basketball Association): framing 96; players on social media 391, 394; racial make-up of fans 127; revenues **47**, 47–48, 49–51, **50–51**, 52, 53, **54**, **55**
NCAA (National Collegiate Athletic Association): broadcasting 317; revenue streams 96
netball, female fans case study 32, 34–40
network association 280
networked collectivisms 233
new supporting movements 232
New Zealand, netball 34–40
news framing 97–104, 241–242
NFL (National Football League): age and fandom 155; athlete activism 394–395, 396; place and fandom 74–76; racial make-up of fans 127; revenues 46–47, 49–51, **50–51**
NFL RedZone (N.D.) 301
NHL (National Hockey League): place and fandom 74–76; revenues 48, **50–51**
niche theory 319
non-fungible tokens (NFTs) 268–269
non-local fans 249–257; sense of community and social capital 254–257; transnational European football fans 354–363; types 252–254
NPF (National Pro Fastpitch) 46, 48–49, 56
NWHL (National Women's Hockey League) 318–319
NWSL (National Women's Soccer League) 46, 48, 56–57
NY Mets 255–256

offside, use of video assistant refereeing 346–347
Olympic sports fans: digital fandom 261; as distinctive demographic 168, 176–177; global involvement 175; mobile/streamed fandom 173–175; Paralympian fandom 180–188; sex differences 170–172; Social TV 176; vs. sports fans 168–169; TV consumption habits 170; watching men and women's sports 172–173
on-field review (OFR) 345
online fandom *see* digital engagement with sports; mobile/streamed fandom; social media
online performances of fandom 273–281
Optimal Distinctiveness Theory 22–23
over-the-air (OTA) 321
over-the-top (OTT) 321

Para Sport Fan Zone 184
Paralympian fandom 180–188; athletes on social media 240, 242–245; language of disability 182–183; Para Sport Organizations 184–187
Paralympic School Days (PSD) 186–187
parasocial relationships, via social media 273, 275, 281–283, 392
participation in sport fandom: with age 155–157; cultural participation 368–370; fanship lifecycle study 158–166; fantasy sport 297–298, 299–303; gaming 307–308; passion 37–38, 149–150, 160, **161**
participatory action research (PAR) 187
Pasifika culture 39–40
passion: fanship lifecycle study 160, **161**; female fans 37–38, 149–150
Peacock, Jonnie 184–185
penalty kicks, video assistant refereeing 342, 344–345, 348–349
performance of fandom: employee identity 139; family role identity 138–139; fandom as performance 108–109; female fans 148–149, 150–151; gender identity 140; geographic identity 140–141; online 273–281; political context 397; role identities 133, 135–141, **136**
personal identities 134; *see also* sports fan identity
personal needs, fandom fulfilling 21–25
personalization, social media 278
photography: 1989 Hillsborough stadium, Sheffield 205–206, 209; autoethnographic research 207–212; British football as captured by Stuart Clarke 205–206, 212–221; deception in photo of Diego Maradona 204–205; ethics 217–220; online self-presentation 274–275; purpose in sports 204
place: British football as captured by Stuart Clarke 219–220; cultural participation 368–369; entrepreneurial ecosystems in suburban and small cities 77–79; and fandom 74–76; geographic identity 140–141; in-person attendance 377; social capital 73; sprawl and suburbanization 77; stadium politics and local planning 76; *see also* non-local fans
planning *see* local planning
polarization, politics and sport 15–16
political context: athlete activism 102, 127–128, 388–398; authoritarian digital capitalism 357; Brett Kavanaugh hearings 9, 13–16; female fans 151; framing in the media 97–98, 100–101, 102–103; game metaphor 11–13; rise of sports and/in politics 388–390; social media 390–393; sport as agonistic contest 10, 16–18; sport's influence 9–11
politics of leisure 368–370
Portugal, costs of fandom 68
positionality in sporting fieldwork 107, 110, 112
postfeminist femininity 151

405

Index

power, in sporting fieldwork 107, 110
Pride games 111
privacy, online 266–267
Professional and Amateur Sports Protection Act 287
proximity in sporting fieldwork 107, 110
Purdy, Amy 185

Qatar, alcohol consumption 380–381
QQ 359–360
queer *see* LGBTQ+ athletes; LGBTQ+ fans

race: assumptions about 14–15; athlete activism 102, 127–128, 388–398; critical race theory 395; fan motives and behaviors 128; female fans 39–40, 41; framing in the media 99–100, 102; global context 128–129; and masculinity 15; research context 125; Take-a-Knee movement 394, 396
racist fans: as common 125–126; digital media 266
radio: emergence of technology 241, 393; fantasy sport 300–301; role of media in men's and women's sports 317, 318, 319, 322
Rainbow Laces 199
random reward mechanisms (RRMs) 313
Rapinoe, Megan 56, 394
rebounding 107, 110–114
Reds in Shanghai (RIS) 359–360
refereeing, and video assistance 342–351
reflexive methodologies 112
relational ethnography 110–112
replays *see* video assistant refereeing
research context: digital engagement with sports 263–264; disciplinary approaches 2–3; ethnographic methods 84–91; fandom 1, 27–28, 108; female fans 32; overview of this volume 3–5; positionality and proximity 107, 110, 112; race 125; "silo-ing" of sports 2
revenues: elements of 63–64, **64–65**; football 61–62, 69–70, **70**; framing in the media 96; franchise values 44, 51–57; maximization 70–71; men's sport 46–48, 49–56; Nick Saban effect 337; women's sport 48–49, 56–57
rhetoric 10–12
role identities 134–135, **136**, 137; *see also* sports fan identity
Royal Netherlands Football Association (KNVB) 344

Saban, Nick 328, 331–338, *337*
season-long fantasy 288–289, 290–292, 293
sedentary audiences 377–378, 382
self-dependency 305–306
self-esteem 298
self-presentation: disabled athletes 239–246; female fans 150–151; online selectivity 274–281, 282–283; social media 238, 239–240, 242–246; *see also* performance of fandom
self-reflection as a fan 307–308
serious leisure 63
sexuality: homophobia 193–195, 198; sexual minorities in football 192–201; transnational European football fans 361–362; *see also* LGBTQ+ athletes; LGBTQ+ fans
sexualization: "beer wenches" 380; female fans 147, 150; women's sport 321
Silver Ferns 35
Simmonds, Ellie 185
"Skinner box" 310
slow-motion *see* video assistant refereeing
Snyder, Brad 243
social affordances 276–277
social capital: non-local fans 254–257; Twitter Capture and Analysis Tool (TCAT) 333–334
social identification 133; *see also* sports fan identity
social identities 135, **136**, 137; age and fandom 156–157; fantasy sport 298; non-local fans 254–257
social justice: athlete activists 127–128; digital media 266; framing in the media 102
social media: accessibility 281; anonymity 278; asynchrony 279; Chinese fandom of European football 358–360; disabled athletes 239–240, 242–246; editability 277, 279; female fans 150–151; motives for using 262–263; network association 280; non-local fans 251; Olympic Games 261; online performances of fandom 273–281; Para Sport Fan Zone 184; parasocial relationships with players and teams 273, 275, 281–283, 392; persistence 277; personalization 278; platforms 267–268; searchability 280; social presence 280–281; sports/politics complex 390–393; value co-creation 264–265; visibility 278; *see also* digital engagement with sports
Social TV 176, 263
socialization process 26
socially valuable traits 122–123
societal needs, fandom fulfilling 21, 25–27
socioemotional selectivity theory (SST) 154, 156, 157, 164–166
Southeastern Conference (SEC) 328–338
Spain, costs of fandom 66, 71
spectatorship: attitudes to sexuality 192; definition 62; gender differences 171–172; transnational football fans 355–356, 358–359
Sport Commitment Model 297
Sport Fan Motivation Scale 128
Sport Spectator Identification Scale (SSIS) 87
sports, definition of 1
sports fan activity 4–5
sports fan identity: age 156–157; agonistic conflict 17; costs of 63–69; female fans 145; fulfilling personal needs 21–25; as multi-layered *134*,

134–135, 137; performative role identities 133, 135–141; political context 397; research context 108; social media 275–276; Sport Spectator Identification Scale (SSIS) 87
sports fans: definition 2; importance of 1; knowledge of 3–4; perspectives on 3, 4; research context 1
sports fanship lifecycle 154; age 155–157; participation research study 158–166; shifting patterns of viewership 155; *see also* lifelong involvement in sport
sports research *see* research context
standing Kop, Liverpool 207–208, *208*
stereotypes: female fans 145–146, 147, 149–150; framing in the media 97; gender and fandom behaviours 33; hegemonic masculinity 15, 16–17; Paralympics and disability 183
storytelling: ethnographic methods 86–87, 90–91; framing in the media 97, 101–102; Olympic sports fans 169; rebounding as praxis 113–114
Strava 266–267
streaming *see* mobile/streamed fandom
suburbs: entrepreneurial ecosystems 77–79; sprawl and suburbanization 77
"supercrip" label 182, 183, 187, 243–244

Take-a-Knee movement 394, 396; *see also* Kaepernick, Colin
Tännsjö's reversal test 119–123
Taylor, Ian 227–228
team identification: fulfilling personal needs 22, 24–25; loyalty 62–63; non-local fans 250, 251–254, 256–257; performative role identities 133, 137–138
technological affordances 276–277
technology 5; 20th century media developments 240–241; fantasy sport 295–296; future of 268–269; mobile/streamed Olympic fandom 173–175; non-local fans 250–251, 256–257; Social TV 176; transnational European football fans 354–363; video assistant refereeing 342–351; *see also* digital engagement with sports
television: age and fandom 155; Chinese fandom of European football 358; commodification of sport 328–329; digital engagement with sports 263; ESPN 300–301, 316; fanship lifecycle study 159–166; historical context 241; mobile/streamed fandom 173–175; non-local fans 251; Olympic Games 170, 173–176; Paralympics 180–182; parasocial relationships 281, 282; Social TV 176, 263; women's sport 317–324
tickets: costs of fandom 65–66; non-local fans 255–256; rebounding as praxis 110–111; *see also* game attendance
TikTok 267, 268

time commitment: fantasy sport 291; Olympic sports fans 169; *see also* lifelong involvement in sport; participation in sport fandom
Title IX 45, 52, 316
Toledo, L. H. d. 228, 230, 231
torcidas organizadas (TOs) 230–232, 234
torcidas uniformizadas 229–230
trading cards 268–269
training: admiration for athletes 117–118; refereeing 345, 346
transgender *see* LGBTQ+ athletes; LGBTQ+ fans
transnational fan experience 354–363; *see also* non-local fans
Truist Park-Battery Atlanta 74, 76, 78, 79–80
Turkey, costs of fandom 66–68
Twitter: commodification of sport 328, 332–338, *334*, *335*; disabled athletes 240; editability 279; fan opinion 329–330; live coverage of sporting events 263–264; motives for using 262; network association 280; parasocial relationships with players and teams 273, 281–283; searchability 280; women's sport 269
Twitter Capture and Analysis Tool (TCAT) 333–334

uncertainty reduction, fulfilling personal needs 23–24
United Kingdom: British football as captured by Stuart Clarke 205–206, 212–221; costs of fandom 66–68, 70–71; football supporter groups 226–227; sexual minorities in football 192–201
United States Women's National Team (USWNT) 322
urban sprawl 77

value co-creation 264–265
venues: entrepreneurial ecosystems in suburban and small cities 77–79; place and fandom 74–76; social capital 73; sprawl and suburbanization 77; stadium politics and local planning 76
Vercauteren, Frankie 205
video assistant refereeing (VAR) 342–351
videogames *see* gaming
vignettes, ethnographic methods 90–91
virtual reality (VR) 257, 268

WeChat 358, 359–360
Weibo 358, 359–360
Western Sydney Wanderers 87
White masculinity 15
WNBA (Women's National Basketball Association): digital media 269; female fans 33; rebounding 110, 111; revenues 48, 52, 56; streaming 318; Title IX 46
women as fans *see* female fans

Index

women's sport: demand for 45, 319–321, 323–324; digital engagement with 265, 269–270, 316–324; female fans of 33, 34–40; in games and media 316–324; Olympic Games 172–173; Paralympics 183; photography 221, *222*; revenues 48–49, 56–57; sexualization in 321; Title IX 45–46

World Cups: in Qatar 381; video assistant refereeing 342–343, 346, 348–349, 350

YouTube 322

Zanardi, Alex 184